THE HANDBOOK OF INTEREST RATE RISK MANAGEMENT

edited by

Jack Clark Francis
and
Avner Simon Wolf

Professional Publishing
Burr Ridge, Illinois
New York, New York

© JACK CLARK FRANCIS AND AVNER S. WOLF, 1994

All rights reserved. No part of this publication may be reproduced, stored in a retrieval system, or transmitted, in any form or by any means, electronic, mechanical, photocopying, recording, or otherwise, without the prior written permission of the publisher.

This publication is designed to provide accurate and authoritative information in regard to the subject matter covered. It is sold with the understanding that neither the author nor the publisher is engaged in rendering legal, accounting, or other professional service. If legal advice or other expert assistance is required, the services of a competent professional person should be sought.

From a Declaration of Principles jointly adopted by a Committee of the American Bar Association and a Committee of Publishers.

Project editor: Waivah Clement
Production manager: Irene H. Sotiroff
Art manager: Kim Meriwether
Compositor: Bi-Comp, Inc.
Typeface: 11/13 Times Roman
Printer: Arcata Graphics/Fairfield

Library of Congress Cataloging-in-Publication Data

The Handbook of interest rate risk management / edited by Jack Clark Francis and Avner Wolf.
    p.   cm.
   ISBN 1-55623-382-5
   1. Interest rate futures. I. Francis, Jack Clark. II. Wolf, Avner S., date.
   HG6024.5.H37   1994
   332.63'23—dc20   93–1267

Printed in the United States of America
1 2 3 4 5 6 7 8 9 AGF 9 8 7 6 5 4 3

Dedicated to my late parents Pamar and Avigdor Wolf, my wife Rachel, and my daughters Maya and Danna.

Avner S. Wolf

Dedicated to my son, Steven Douglas Francis.

Jack Clark Francis

FOREWORD

When we want a metaphor for something that starts small but grows rapidly to monumental proportions, we often think of Jack and the Beanstalk. The market for interest rate–dependent securities and specialized instruments for managing interest rate risk has certainly grown from a relatively limited market to a gigantic market in only a few years. However, the growth of this market is less like the magic beanstalk than the growth of an actual tree, the banyan. The banyan starts like a normal tree, with a trunk that soon sprouts branches. But as the tree gets bigger, the branches begin to put out shoots, which then take root themselves to become new trunks. This process of branching and then putting down new roots eventually leads, in the case of the banyan, to a mature "tree" that actually is more like an entire interconnected forest more than 500 feet in diameter.

Like the young banyan, the market for interest rate products until the 1970s was concentrated on a single trunk, consisting of a small number of standard sorts of bonds. But in rapid succession, we have witnessed both enormous growth and also enormous proliferation of instruments related to the basic bond market. Interest rate futures markets were established in the mid-1970s for short-term rates (Treasury bill futures), long-term rates (Treasury bond futures), and mortgages (GNMA futures). Meanwhile the "cash" bond market itself was developing new offshoots, including stripped (zero coupon) Treasury bonds, mortgage pass-throughs, and "junk" bonds. As these new products began to take root on their own, in many cases further proliferation occurred. "Simple" pass-throughs were soon joined by multitranche collateralized mortgage obligations (CMOs) and other complex mortgage-backed securities; traded interest rate futures begat options on futures, and so on.

Another major trunk took root in the 1980s, as major banks and other financial institutions began actively creating interest-contingent contracts and selling them over the counter. One of the most basic of these new instruments is the forward rate agreement, which simply fixes the interest rate for a loan to be issued at a later date. More complex, but wildly successful, are interest rate swaps. For U.S. banks alone, this subsidiary branch of the interest rate products tree had grown by the end of 1991 to the point where outstanding contracts had a nominal principal value of $1.5 trillion, and the growth rate shows little sign of slackening. In the last few years, innovation in interest rate derivative products has reached such a pitch that new and increasingly exotic instruments are being created almost daily. At times, one begins to feel that any interest rate instrument that can be conceived of is already available for sale somewhere.

This book serves an important need as a kind of practitioner's guidebook to the theory and the practice of the major interest rate products markets. It contains chapters on many diverse aspects of these instruments, each written by an expert in the field.

The first section presents the basics of interest rates. The theoretical and practical foundation upon which the entire interconnected structure rests is the term structure of interest rates on riskless bonds. Practically, this means the yield curve for U.S. Treasury securities, along with the related curves that are derived from Treasury yields, including yields and prices for zero coupon bonds and the structure of forward interest rates. But while these yield and price curves are conceptually easy to understand, actually fitting a smooth yield curve to a set of market prices for actual bonds with differing maturities and other characteristics presents some important empirical problems, such as how to deal with callability.

Changing yields and bond prices produce interest rate risk, and the interest rate derivative securities markets have developed largely from the search for effective ways to hedge, or more broadly, to *manage* this risk. Hedging is done in many ways: with traded contracts like futures and options; with over-the-counter contracts like forward rate agreements, swaps, caps, and floors;

with the options that are embedded in fixed-income securities, like the call feature; and, in some cases, with dynamic trading strategies based on option valuation theory that attempt to replicate the payoffs on such options synthetically. The most straightforward interest rate risk management tools are financial futures, consisting of standardized contracts trading in established and liquid markets with a high degree of financial integrity. Section Two describes both the financial futures instruments and markets, and also the major risk management uses for these contracts.

Successful risk management with interest-contingent securities requires attending both to the theoretical issues in structuring a hedge and also to the real-world issues of tax treatment, accounting principles, and legal questions. Generally speaking, these topics are arcane at best, yet extremely important. Indeed, insufficient understanding of accounting issues in recording the profits and losses in hedge transactions has produced many nasty surprises for unwary investors over the years. One of the most valuable features of this book is the large amount of material devoted to these practical issues. Each major section contains chapters relating to taxation, accounting, and other pragmatic topics.

Section Three covers interest rate options, which introduce a new dimension of flexibility in risk management. With options it becomes possible to achieve protection against losses without giving up profit potential in equal measure, as is normally necessary when hedging with futures. Options can also be used to structure a position that has an attractive payoff when the underlying asset's price does not move. Valuing interest-dependent options (as well as any option-like feature that may be embedded in the terms of a fixed-income instrument) requires an assumption about the behavior of the future path of interest rates. At this time, there are a number of competing interest rate models in existence, each leading to a different valuation model for interest rate options. One of the best-known and easiest models to manipulate is the one-factor approach developed by Black, Derman, and Toy, which is described in this section.

Section Four covers the most important over-the-counter interest rate derivative contract, the interest rate swap. This remarkable instrument has become one of the most important banking products in the last 10 years because it effectively allows managing the interest payment on a loan separately from the principal. Valuing swaps and relating the swap rates of differing maturities to one another rationally introduces a variety of theoretical and empirical issues.

A swap is like a bundle or "strip" of forward contracts with sequential expirations. It was natural to extend this idea to create bundles of interest rate options. That innovation gave rise to a great proliferation of new contracts, like caps, floors, collars, and swaptions. But despite their daunting complexity, like simple options, these new instruments open up new dimensions in sophisticated interest rate risk management.

Sections Five and Six of the book bring all of the earlier concepts together by looking at important interest rate risk management applications. Both conceptual questions of optimal hedge design and the choice of hedging vehicle, and also the practical issue of monitoring the hedge, are covered. Finally, in Section Seven, the book ends with an overview of where things stand today (or, more correctly, where things *stood* at the time the book was finished, bearing in mind that this area is constantly growing and developing) and where things are going in the future.

In total, this book offers a comprehensive and comprehensible map of the major trunks and branches of the burgeoning and interconnected forest of interest rate–dependent securities and risk management tools. No doubt as time goes on, new products and markets will continue being added to the field guide, but bankers and students, professors and practitioners will all find plenty here to serve as a base for further explorations.

Stephen Figlewski

PREFACE

The Handbook of Interest Rate Risk Management provides a current and comprehensive analysis of the field of fixed-income derivative securities. It is aimed mainly at those who need up-to-date information on emerging market structures, price modeling, and the risk management of fixed-income securities.

This book contains a great deal of practical information on interest rate structures, pricing mechanisms, models, trading, hedging strategies, taxes, law, accounting, and other aspects of interest rate risk management. We detail many aspects of the market that can be of use to a wide range of participants in the fixed-income markets. Finance professionals who are currently engaged in the fixed-income markets will find this book to be an excellent source of information and a reference book. Portfolio managers, traders, dealers, market makers, corporate treasurers, and other financial officers can use this reference in their daily trading activities.

Back-office managers and software professionals can use this handbook to program pricing formulas, monitor cash flows and profits and losses, mark accounts to the market, calculate financial and credit risks, and so on. This is also the ideal reference book for accountants, lawyers, and other professionals and academics who want to learn about the fixed-income market.

We include an analysis of the operating structure of the fixed-income market as well as the most advanced pricing models currently used by many investment banking and trading houses. Anyone interested in improving financial performance, finding a pricing formula for an exotic interest rate option, or monitoring risk in the most advanced way will find invaluable information.

The chapters are primarily written by professional market participants who make their living in the fixed-income markets and by academics, accountants, and lawyers who specialize in the area. All the chapters give a great deal of attention to practical aspects. We took the view that a good chapter is one that can be used by the reader. Thus, even some of the most sophisticated models have numerical examples that guide the reader who may not have previous experience with the model.

It was our goal that the book be organized and written in a way that is valuable to both the novice and the sophisticated professional. Reading the sections sequentially is not necessary. Each section is self-contained and separable from the others. Thus, if the reader is interested only in the interest rate swap market, for instance, he or she does not have to read the previous sections and need only read Section Four on interest rate swaps. Each section is divided into a number of chapters. Wherever possible, we included an introduction to the section where the structure and terminology are introduced.

This handbook is divided into seven sections. The first section is an introduction to interest rate risk management. It examines the term structure of the interest rate, the empirical estimation of the yield curve, and practical aspects of hedging. Important issues such as the interpretation of the yield curve, the information contained in the term structure of the interest rate, and under what market conditions one should hedge are discussed in this section.

The second section introduces financial futures. This section examines the structure of the financial futures markets, hedging, and the legal, tax, and accounting issues relevant to financial futures. A discussion on the forward markets enhances the understanding of the pricing aspects of some of the financial futures contracts.

Sections Three covers the listed interest rate options. As in the previous section, first the market structure is introduced; this is followed by a detailed analysis on the pricing of fixed-income options using a one-factor model. This model is increasingly used to price fixed-income options in many financial institutions.

We analyze interest rate swaps in Section Four, beginning with the structure of the swap market, which has an estimated notional amount of over $3 trillion. The section discusses the valuation of interest rate swaps, credit risk, and the swap yield curve. Due to the importance of pricing interest rate swaps, we include segments on the empirical estimation of the swap yield curve. A description of the accounting, tax, and some legal aspects of interest rate swaps concludes this section.

Due to the unique way over-the-counter (OTC) options are traded, we chose to devote a separate section to them. Section Five starts by introducing the history of OTC options and their characteristics. The focus of the section then turns to the application of OTC options. In order to complete the picture, we also cover the accounting, tax, and legal aspects of OTC options.

Managing financial risk is now inseparable from the trading of financial instruments. The importance of risk management was evident during the market crash of October 1987. As a result of this collapse, many market professionals are constantly on the watch whenever market volatility picks up. Section Six addresses asset and liability hedging as well as the practical design of fixed-income risk management. Special attention is given to monitoring hedges and examining their effectiveness.

The last section of the book looks at the future of the markets and common elements that seem to recur in interest rate derivatives. An end-of-book appendix contains valuable programs for the Hewlett-Packard 12-C hand-held calculator that will aid those who want to crunch a few numbers.

We are especially indebted to Susan Mangiero of Sacred Heart University; Sole Ohberg, assistant vice president, Kansallis-Osake-Pankki Bank; Professor Steven B. Lilien of Baruch College; and Ralph Rieves, executive editor, Irwin Professional Publishing. They provided inspiration and expert advice more than once.

Jack Clark Francis
Avner Wolf

ABOUT THE EDITORS

Jack Clark Francis received his bachelor's and MBA. degrees from Indiana University, served as a lieutenant in the U.S. Army, and then earned his Ph.D. from the University of Washington in Seattle. Francis was on the finance faculty of the Wharton School of Finance, University of Pennsylvania; served as a Federal Reserve Economist; and is now a professor of economics and finance at Bernard M. Baruch College in New York City. Dr. Francis has authored several editions of *Investments: Analysis and Management* and *Management of Investments*, published by McGraw-Hill; coauthored three editions of *Portfolio Analysis*, published by Prentice Hall; co-edited *Readings in Investments*, published by McGraw-Hill; coauthored *Schaum's Investments Outline*, published by the Schaum's Division of McGraw-Hill; and, co-edited *Interest Rate Risk Management*, published by the Irwin Professional Publishing division of Richard D. Irwin, Inc. Professor Francis has also had his research published in numerous academic journals.

Avner S. Wolf is a professor of finance and since 1992 has been the chairman of the department of economics and finance at Baruch College, City University of New York. He has published papers in academic and professional journals on derivative financial instruments, including options, futures, interest rate swaps and caps, floors, and collars, among others. He served on the editorial board of the *Journal of Futures Markets* from 1982 to 1992. Professor Wolf was the director of the doctoral program in finance at Baruch College and the coordinator of the weekly research finance seminar from 1988 to 1992. He has a wide practical experience as a consultant to financial institutions worldwide and conducted seminars for professionals on equity options, futures options, financial futures, and interest rate products throughout the world.

CONTRIBUTING AUTHORS

Peter A. Abken is a senior economist in the research department at the Federal Reserve Bank of Atlanta. He earned degrees in economics from Haverford College (B.A.) and Brown University (M.A. and Ph.D.). He joined the Federal Reserve Bank of Atlanta in September 1986 as an economist. He had previously worked as an associate economist at the Federal Reserve Bank of Richmond.

Robert Ariel obtained his B.A. from Dartmouth College and his M.A. from Oxford University. He received the Ph.D. in philosophy from the University of Minnesota and the Ph.D. in finance in 1989 from the Sloan School of the Massachusetts Institute of Technology. He has published articles in *The Journal of Finance*, *Journal of Financial Economics*, and the *American Association of Individual Investors Journal*. He is on the finance faculty of Baruch College, City University of New York.

Eileen Baecher received her B.A. in administrative sciences from Yale University and her MBA in finance from Columbia University. Then she worked as an options trader at Citibank for a few years before moving to the research department at Goldman, Sachs in New York City.

Harold Bierman, Jr., is the Nicholas H. Noyes Professor of Business Administration at Cornell University. Bierman formerly taught at Louisiana State University, the University of Michigan, the University of Chicago, and INSEAD in France. In 1990 he served as a senior academic fellow at the Financial Accounting Standards Board. He has written numerous books, including *The Capital Budgeting Decision* (with Seymour Smidt), *Financial Accounting, Managerial Accounting,* and *Financial Policy Decisions*, and more than a hundred journal articles. He received his Ph.D. from the University of Michigan.

xv

Fischer Black is a partner at Goldman, Sachs. He applies quantitative methods to fixed income and equity client portfolios, and designs new strategies that meet client needs. Before joining Goldman, Sachs (in 1984), he was professor of finance for 13 years at the University of Chicago's Graduate School of Business and at MIT's Sloan School of Management. Fischer developed (with Myron Scholes) the Black-Scholes option pricing formula.

Jane Sachar Brauer is currently a Vice President and Senior Fixed Income Strategist in New York Sales at Merrill Lynch. Prior to joining Merrill Lynch she was a Vice President and Manager of Marketing in Derivative Products at First Boston and later in Futures at Citicorp. Earlier in her career she served as an analyst in Financial Strategies at Goldman Sachs where she became a vice president. Jane received her Ph.D. in Applied Statistics from Stanford University.

Kosrow Dehnad is a vice president of Chase Securities Inc. in the derivatives origination and structuring group. Prior to joining Chase Securities in 1990, he was with AT&T Bell Laboratories, where he researched the mathematical foundation of quality control. He has been an adjunct professor at San Jose State University, Rutgers University, and most recently at the Department of Operations Research of Columbia University. He received a doctorate in applied statistics from Stanford University and a doctorate in pure mathematics from University of California at Berkeley, where he received his M.A. in mathematics and statistics. Dehnad received his bachelor of science in mathematics with first class honors from Victoria University of Manchester, England.

Emanuel Derman was born in South Africa. He obtained a Ph.D in theoretical particle physics from Columbia University, and taught and did research at the University of Pennsylvania, Oxford University, The Rockefeller University, the University of Colorado, Boulder, and AT&T Bell Laboratories in Murray Hill, N.J. He is currently the head of the quantitative strategies group in the equities division at Goldman, Sachs & Co.

Diane D. Fuller is a tax partner in KPMG Peat Marwick's financial services practice and the firm's national director of tax services for investment banking. She is a specialist in the taxation of financial instruments and the capital markets. She received a B.A. in English and psychology from Yale University and an M.S. in accounting from New York University.

D. Goldie-Morrison has worked in the banking industry since 1975. His first exposure to the derivatives markets was at Kleinwort Benson Limited (a leading UK merchant bank) where he executed his first currency swap in 1978. Following a spell as a vice president in Kleinwort Benson Chicago office, (1980–1984) he moved to Los Angeles to work in Kleinwort Benson Cross Financing Inc. (1984–1987), the specialist derivatives unit formed by Kleinwort Benson. This period at KBCF culminated in the position as managing director responsible for the UK subsidiary, KBCF Limited. In September 1987 he was recruited by Westpac Banking Corporation where he spent three years heading up the bank's global interest rate swap activity. In 1991 he was recruited to head up the National Westminster Bank PLC's global swap activity. In 1993 he took over responsibility for the equity derivatives and structured products businesses. He has been a director of the International Swap Dealers Association since 1979.

Laurie Goodman is a first vice president and fixed income strategist at Merrill Lynch & Co. She is responsible for assessing cross-sector relative value with emphasis on derivatives (futures, options, swaps) and mortgages. She is also responsible for special quantitative analytics projects and in-depth research reports. Prior to joining Merrill Lynch, she was a vice president and senior portfolio manager at Eastbridge Capital. She spent six years at Goldman, Sachs and Citicorp Investment Bank. She also spent four years as a senior economist at the Federal Reserve Bank of New York. Ms. Goodman received a B.A. in mathematics and a B.S. in economics from the University of Pennsylvania, and an M.A. and Ph.D. in economics from Stanford University. She has published over 90 articles in popular and professional journals.

Henry Green is a private consultant and a visiting professor at Imperial College of Science, Technology and Medicine, London, UK. Previously, Dr. Green has held executive and nonexecutive directorships in a number of investment and merchant banks.

Charles W. Haley is a professor of finance at the University of Washington. He received MBA and Ph.D. degrees in finance from Stanford University. An active teacher, researcher, and consultant in banking and finance, Professor Haley has designed three bank management simulations and has served as editor of the *Journal of Financial and Quantitative Analysis*. He is coauthor of *Theory of Financial Decisions* and *Introduction to Financial Management*, both published by McGraw-Hill.

Thomas S.Y. Ho received his Ph.D. in mathematics in 1978 from the University of Pennsylvania. He joined New York University's Stern School of Business and became a full professor in 1985. He has published articles extensively. As editor of the book, *Fixed Income Management: Issues and Solutions*, Tom Ho has compiled papers from many fixed income professionals. He founded the Global Advanced Technology Corporation in New York City in 1987.

Michael Hogan received a B.A. at the University of Virginia and Ph.D. in statistics from Stanford. Currently he is employed at Citicorp, in New York.

Joan C. Junkus attended the University of Illinois at Urbana-Champaign. After three years at Salomon Brothers, she returned to the University of Illinois where she received an MBA in 1980 and a Ph.D. in finance in 1983. She has taught in the graduate school of business at the University of California–Irvine and is presently an associate professor of finance at DePaul University in Chicago. She is the author of numerous articles on futures pricing and hedging and coauthor of the textbook *The Theory and Practice of Futures Markets*.

Ira G. Kawaller is vice president and director of the New York office for the Chicago Mercantile Exchange. After receiving a Ph.D. in economics from Purdue University, he served as an economist at the Federal Reserve Board in Washington. He subsequently worked for the AT&T Company and J. Aron Company Inc.

Joseph Langsam is a principal and research manager in the fixed income division of Morgan Stanley. He received a Ph.D. in urban studies and economics from M.I.T. and in mathematics from the University of Michigan. Prior to joining Morgan Stanley, he taught mathematics at Case Western Reserve University.

Mark R. Larson is a partner with Marshall & Associates (a financial engineering/consulting firm) where he is responsible for relationship management. Prior to his current position, he served as head of marketing and product development with MicroApplications, Inc.

Sang Bin Lee received his B.A. from Seoul National University, his M.A. in economics from Cornell University, and his Ph.D. in finance from New York University. He is an associate professor of management and technology at the Korea Advanced Institute of Science and Technology.

Anlong Li is a Vice President in the derivatives research group at Salomon Bros. in New York City. Before that he was in the swaps and financial product department at Lehman Brothers. Before joining Lehman he was a research fellow at the Federal Reserve Bank of Cleveland. He has published several papers in both operations research and finance journals. Li received his Ph.D. in operations research from Case Western Reserve University in 1992. He also holds M.S. and B.S. degrees in systems and industrial engineering from Huazhong University of Science and Technology in China.

George A. Mangiero is an assistant professor of finance and economics at Iona College in New Rochelle, New York. He has also taught at St. John's University in Jamaica, New York. He was formerly an electrical engineer with American Electric Power, where he worked in the area of system measurements. His graduate degrees include an M.S. in electrical engineering, Rensselaer Polytechnic Institute, an MBA in Finance, St. John's University, and an M. Phil. and Ph.D. in finance, New York University.

Susan M. Mangiero is an assistant professor of finance and economics at Sacred Heart University in Fairfield, Connecticut. She is a Chartered Financial Analyst and has written extensively on the subject of risk management. She was formerly an investment banker with several Wall Street banks. Her graduate degrees include a MBA in finance, New York University, and an M.A. in economics, George Washington University. She is a doctoral student in finance at the University of Connecticut.

Robert Mark is the partner in charge of Financial Risk Management Consulting at Coopers & Lybrand in New York City. Before that he was a managing director in the Asia, Europe, and capital markets (AECM) group of Chemical Bank and teaches as an adjunct professor at the Stern Graduate School of Business, New York University. He is also chairperson of the National Asset Liability Management Association. He earned his Ph.D. with a doctoral dissertation in options pricing from the New York University's Graduate School of Engineering and Science, where he graduated first in his class. He subsequently received an advanced professional certificate in accounting from New York University's Graduate School of Business. Prior to his current position, he was a senior officer at Marine Midland Bank/Hong Kong Shanghai Bank Group where he headed the technical analysis group within the capital markets Sector. Earlier, he was a director of systems profit center at American Express.

John F. Marshall is professor of finance at St. John's University, senior partner with Marshall & Associates (a financial engineering/consulting firm), executive director of the International Association of Financial Engineers, and the author of eight books in addition to numerous articles and book chapters.

Mehraj Mattoo obtained his B.A. in economics and mathematics from Kashmir University and an MBA and Ph.D. in financial economics from the University of London. He specializes in hedging and valuation of contingent debt securities. He is currently working in London as an associate director in the structured products group of NatWest Capital Markets.

Richard A. Miller is a partner in Katten Muchin & Zavis' financial services group and concentrates his practice in the specialized area of futures and derivatives law and regulation. His knowledge of the regulatory structure of the markets was put to special use when he was selected to serve on the Presidential Task Force on Market Mechanisms (known as the "Brady Commission"), which studied and reported to President Reagan on the causes of and solutions for the October 1987 stock market crash. In 1991 he was appointed to chair the Committee on Futures Regulation of the Association of the Bar of the City of New York. He is publisher and editor-in-chief of the *Futures International Law Letter*. A graduate of the State University of New York at Buffalo (B.A., cum laude, 1969), The Ohio State University (M.A. 1970), and New York University (J.D. 1973), he was an editor of the New York University Law Review.

David T. Novick is an associate in the law firm of Katten Muchin & Zavis, Chicago, Illinois. He graduated, summa cum laude, from Boston University with a bachelor of science degree in business administration and received his law degree in 1989 from the University of Illinois. He is a member of the corporate law department and is a member of the Chicago Bar Association Futures Regulatory Law Committee.

Thomas J. O'Brien is an associate professor of finance at the University of Connecticut. He holds an A.B. in economics from Davidson College, an MBA in finance from Wharton, and a Ph.D. in business administration in finance from the University of Florida. He has published research on a variety of financial topics. His textbook, *Introduction to Investments* (coauthored with Lewis Mandell) was published in 1992 by Macmillan.

Albert S. Pergam is a partner at Cleary, Gottlieb, Steen & Hamilton in New York City. His practice includes corporate and financial matters ranging from domestic securities offerings and investment funds to Eurobond issues and transnational corporate transactions. He began work at the firm in 1966 and became a partner in 1973. He was resident in the London office of Cleary, Gottlieb, Steen & Hamilton from 1980 to 1984. He received an LL.B. degree from Harvard Law School magna cum laude in 1964, studied as a Henry Fellow at St. John's College, Cambridge, in 1960–1961 and received his undergraduate degree from Yale College summa cum laude in 1960. He is a member of the bar of the State of New York and is admitted to practice before the United States Court of Appeals, Second Circuit. He has written numerous articles for the *International Financial Law Review* and serves as an editorial advisor of that publication.

Todd E. Petzel received his A.B., A.M., and Ph.D. in economics from the University of Chicago. He is the author of *Financial Futures and Options*, published by Quorum Books in 1989, and numerous articles. He served as the chief economist of the Coffee, Sugar & Cocoa Exchange in New York. From 1978 to 1982 he was on the faculty of Stanford University, and from 1976 to 1978 he taught at Macalester College. He is currently at the Chicago Mercantile Exchange, where he is the senior vice president in charge of the research division and chief economist.

Shaiy Pilpel received a B.S. in mathematics and a B.A. in philosophy from Tel-Aviv University, an M.S. in mathematics from the Hebrew University, a Ph.D. in statistics from University of California at Berkeley, and an MBA from Columbia University. He has worked as a research scientist at IBM's Yorktown Heights, New York facility, director of research at Tradelink in Chicago, and is a mortgage-backed securities portfolio manager for Steinhardt Partners in New York City.

Lawrence Pohlman joined BlackRock Financial Management in 1989 as a vice president. He was formerly an associate in the mortgage security research department at Goldman, Sachs & Co. He is a five-time graduate of Columbia University. He received a B.S. in nuclear engineering in 1977, a M.S. in operations research in 1980, an MBA in finance in 1980, an M.Phil., in finance in 1986, and a Ph.D. in finance in 1987.

Paul Potocki is a vice president in the derivative products group in the fixed income division of Lehman Brothers. He specializes in the pricing and hedging of exotic options on various interest rate indices. Previously he was the head of research at Indosuez Carr Futures, the financial futures subsidiary of Banc Indosuez. Before joining Indosuez Carr, he spent two years as an independent market maker on the Chicago Board of Trade. He recieved an MBA from the University of Chicago and a B.A. from the University of Notre Dame.

David R. Smith is a vice president in charge of risk management at AMBAC Capital Management, Greenwich, Connecticut. Prior to AMBAC, he was a director of asset liability management at New York Life Insurance Company. He has an MBA in finance from New York University Stern School of Business.

Kyu Hyun Son received his B.A. in economics from Korea University and his M.A. in management science from the Korea Advanced Institute of Science and Technology. He is currently a Ph.D. candidate in the department of management science at the Korea Advanced Institute of Science and Technology.

Leon Tatevossian is a vice president in the derivatives research group at Salomon Brothers Inc. His paper was written while he was a research associate in the fixed income division at Morgan Stanley & Co., where he worked from 1989 to 1992. Leon graduated from the Massachusetts Institute of Technology with an S.B. degree in mathematics and was a graduate student in mathematics at Brown University. Prior to moving to the finance industry, he was an instructor in the department of mathematics at Union College in Schenectady, N.Y.

William W. Toy is a graduate of the Massachusetts Institute of Technology where he received the S.B., S.M., E.E., and Ph.D. degrees. He worked for several years at Bell Laboratories/Bell Communications Research in Holmdel, N.J. He joined Goldman, Sachs in 1984 to work on options modeling for both equity and fixed income securities. He is currently a vice president in the equity derivatives department involved in structuring new products.

Julian Walmsley M.A., C.F.A. is current visiting research fellow, ISMA Centre for Securities Research, Reading University. He was formerly the chief investment officer of Mitsubishi Finance International plc, London, and before that senior investment officer, Oil Insurance Ltd, Bermuda. Prior to this he spent five years in the interest rate and currency swap market with NCNB and Barclays Bank in London in New York. He is the author of several books, including *The Foreign Exchange and Money Markets Handbook* (John Wiley, 1992), *Global Investing* (Macmillan, 1991), and *New Financial Instruments* (John Wiley, 1988).

Keith S. Weintraub has a B.S. in applied mathematics from the State University of New York at Stony Brook and a Ph.D. in statistics from the University of Pennsylvania. Currently he is head of derivative products research at Citicorp in New York.

J. Gregg Whittaker has a Ph.D. in economics from the University of Wisconsin. Gregg began his career as an economist for the Federal Reserve Bank. He then joined the Northern Trust Company in Chicago as a vice president in charge of fixed income derivatives. After building a successful swap and cap book, Gregg left Northern to join D.E. Shaw & Co. Recently, Gregg was recruited by S. G. Warburg as a senior vice president to build and run their structured products operation.

CONTENTS

SECTION 1   INTRODUCTION TO INTEREST RATE
RISK MANAGEMENT   1

CHAPTER 1   THE TREASURY YIELD CURVE AND ITS
INTERPRETATION   4

Introduction, 3 Drawing the Yield Curve, 4 Definition of Yield to Maturity for Coupon Bonds, 5 The Loss of Information in Considering only the Yield to Maturity of Bonds, 6 What Are These Forward Rates? 9 Methods for Determining the F from Treasury Bond Prices, 10 *The General Method for Determining F Rates*, 10 *A Simple Method for Determining F Rates*, 10 The Treasury Coupon Bond Yield Curve and the Yield Curve of One-Period Forward Rates, 11 Interpreting the Yield and Forward Rate Curves: Some Lessons, 13 *Lesson One*, 14 *Lesson Two*, 15 *Lesson Three*, 16 *Lesson Four*, 17 Conclusion, 18 Yield Curve for Treasury Coupon Bonds, 19 The Forward Interest Rate Curve, 20

CHAPTER 2   FACTORS INFLUENCING THE LEVEL OF INTEREST
RATES   26

Introduction, 26 *A Small Set of Forward Rates Determines All Bond Prices*, 26 *What Factors Determine the Level of Forward Rates?* 27 Influences on the Short Rate, 28 *The Mathematics of Inflation and Interest: Fisher's Law*, 28 *Will the Real Inflation Rate Please Stand Up!* 30 *What Determines What?*, 31 *Federal Reserve Policy: A Factor Influencing Short-Term Rates?* 34 Influences on the Long-Run Interest Rate, 36 *Traditional Theories of the Yield Curve*, 36 *Newer Theories of the Yield Curve*, 40 Summary, 41

CHAPTER 3   A CALL-ADJUSTED TERM STRUCTURE ESTIMATION
METHODOLOGY   46

Abstract, 46 Basics of the Spot Curve, 47 *A Simple Discount Function*, 47 *A Spot Curve for the Treasury Market*, 48 How to Incorporate the Callable Treasuries, 51 *The Noncall Approach*, 51 *The First Call Approach*, 51 *The Dummy Variable Approach*, 51 *The Option Pricing Approach*, 52 The Call-Adjusted Estimation Technique, 54 *An Iterative Procedure*, 54 *The Embedded Call Option Valuation*, 55, Empirical Results, 55 *Uniqueness and Existence of the Spot Curve*, 55 *The*

Significance of the Call Provision, 57 *The Diversity of the Call Provision,* 61 Summary and Concluding Remarks, 65 Appendix: Theoretical and Actual Spot Rate Curves, 66

CHAPTER 4 WHY HEDGE? 73

Introduction, 73 Impact of Interest Rate Changes on Asset Values, 73 *Determinants of Asset Values,* 73 *Interest Rate Sensitivity of Asset Values,* 75 *Coupon Effect,* 76 *Maturity Effect,* 78 Why Hedge? 80 Measures of Interest Rate Sensitivity, 82 *Duration as a Measure of Interest Rate Sensitivity,* 84 Appendix: a Generalized Duration Approach, 91

CHAPTER 5 HEDGING INTEREST RATE RISK: THE BASICS 95

Financial Risk, 95 Managing Risk, 96 *Insurance,* 97 *Asset/Liability Management,* 97 *Hedging,* 99 *Hedging Foundations,* 103 *Translating Market Risks to Firm-Specific Risks,* 104 *Quantifying Interest Rate Risk,* 106 *Developing Hedge Ratios,* 117 *Measuring Hedge Effectiveness,* 118 *Measuring Hedge Cost,* 120 *Determining the Hedge Horizon,* 122 *Selecting Hedge Instruments,* 123 Miscellaneous Considerations, 128

SECTION 2 FINANCIAL FUTURES 131

CHAPTER 6 INTRODUCTION TO THE FINANCIAL FUTURES MARKETS 133

Background, 134 Trading Uses, 135 *Eurodollar Swaps,* 136 *Synthetic Asset Allocation,* 139 *Inventory Hedging of Treasury Securities,* 141 Pricing, 142 Products, 146

CHAPTER 7 STRUCTURE OF THE FINANCIAL FUTURES MARKETS 159

Exchange Structure and Governance, 160 Mode of Trading, 162 Multilateral Offset and Clearing, 167 Financial Safeguards, 169 Futures Commission Merchants (FCMs), 176 Regulation, 179 Appendix: Major International Interest Rate Futures Exchanges, 181

CHAPTER 8 SHORT-TERM HEDGING APPLICATIONS USING FINANCIAL FUTURES 185

Hedging, 185 Financial and Cash-Settled Futures, 186 LIBOR (London Interbank Offered Rate), 189 Hedging Methodology, 191 *Determining the Direction of Hedging,* 192 *Choosing the Index,* 193 *Cash Flow,* 193 *Timing,* 194 *Scenario Analysis,* 198 Applicable Rate, 201 *Single Contract,* 201 *Multicontract,* 202 Rolling, 203 *Long-Term Exposure to Risk,* 205 Appendix A: The Tail Effect, 210 Appendix B: Eurodollar Futures Contract, 211 *Final Settlement Price,* 211 Appendix C: U.S. Treasury Bill Futures Contract, 212

CHAPTER 9 ACCOUNTING FOR FINANCIAL FUTURES AND FORWARD CONTRACTS 214

Futures and Forward Contracts, 214 Futures Contracts, 215 *FAS 80,* 216 Accounting for Forward Contracts, 217 *Accounting for a Forward Contract for a*

Financial Security, 217 Accounting for a Forward Contract for Foreign Currency: A *Premium*, 222 Accounting for a Forward Contract for Foreign Currency: A *Discount*, 223 *Separate Accounting*, 224 Conclusions, 225

CHAPTER 10 FORWARD RATE AGREEMENTS (FRA) 226

The FRA Market, 227 Availability and Pricing, 230 Applications, 232 FRAs versus Futures in Managing Interest Rate Risk, 234 *Liquidity*, 235 *Flexibility and Basis Risk*, 235 *Administration*, 235

CHAPTER 11 TASK ASPECTS OF FINANCIAL FUTURES 237

Straddles, 237 IRC Section 1256: Regulate Futures Contracts, 239 *Timing and Character Rules*, 240 IRC Section 1092: Taxation of Straddles, 241 *Offsetting Positions*, 242 *Rules Applied to Straddles*, 243 Avoiding Section 1256 and Section 1092 Rules, 244

SECTION III   LISTED INTEREST RATE OPTIONS   247

CHAPTER 12 INTRODUCTION TO OPTIONS APPLICATIONS 249

Eurodollar Time Deposits and Eurodollar Futures, 250 Foundations of Options, 251 How Option Traders Trade, 254 How Risk Managers Hedge, 258

CHAPTER 13 THE STRUCTURE OF MARKETS FOR INTEREST RATE OPTIONS 268

Introduction, 268 Introduction to Debt (Interest Rate) Options, 268 *Definition of an Option*, 268 *Option Prices*, 269 *Purchase of an Option*, 271 *Margin on an Option Position*, 272 *Exercise of an Option*, 272 Exchange-Traded Options, 274 *U.S. Markets*, 274 *Markets outside the United States*, 278 The Microstructure of Trading Systems, 282 *Physical Exchanges*, 282 *Electronic Markets*, 286 *Market Participants*, 289 *Credit Guarantees*, 289 Over-the-Counter Options, 293 *Market Participants*, 293 *OTC Market Microstructure*, 294 *Credit Arrangements*, 296 *Combinations of OTC Options*, 297 *Embedded Options*, 298 Conclusion, 299

CHAPTER 14 USING A ONE-FACTOR MODEL TO VALUE INTEREST RATE–SENSITIVE SECURITIES: WITH AN APPLICATION TO TREASURY BOND OPTIONS 302

The First Bond Option Valuation Models, 303 About this Chapter's Model, 303 Valuing Securities, 304 *Illustration of How to Get Today's Values from Future Values*, 305 *Finding Short Rates from the Term Structure*, 306 Valuing Options on Treasury Bonds, 310 *Coupon Bonds as Collections of Zeros*, 311 *Puts and Calls on Treasuries*, 312 *Option Hedge Ratios*, 314 *Reducing the Interval Size*, 316 Alternative Models, 317 *Computational Shortcuts*, 319

CHAPTER 15 TAX RAMIFICATIONS OF OPTIONS 321

Option Premiums, 321 Character of Income, 323 *Capital Assets*, 325 *Types of Market Participants*, 325 Hedging, 326

SECTION 4   INTEREST RATE SWAPS   331

CHAPTER 16   INTRODUCTION TO INTEREST RATE SWAPS   333

Types of Swaps, 334 Swap Characteristics, 335 Applications, 337 Execution of an Interest Rate Swap, 340 Interest Rate Swap Economics, 343 Swap Risks, 345

CHAPTER 17   EXISTING AND POTENTIAL CREDIT (OR DEFAULT) RISK IN SWAPS AND DERIVATIVE TRANSACTIONS   347

Introduction, 347 How and Why Do Exposures Occur? 348 Predicting Potential Mark-to-Market Value, 350 *Historic Observations*, 352 *Modeling*, 354 *Rule-of-Thumb Approach*, 357 *Summary of Market Price Expectations*, 358 Probability of Default, 359 *Bank Loan Pricing*, 359 *The Bond Markets*, 363 *Summary*, 365 What Happens when a Default Occurs? 367 Calculations, 369 *Limited Two-Way Payments*, 370 *Full Two-Way Payments*, 370 *Security*, 370 *Commercial Considerations*, 371 *Default History*, 372 *Default Survey*, 372 *The Regulatory Framework for Banks*, 373 Conclusion, 375

CHAPTER 18   A NO-ARBITRAGE TERM STRUCTURE MODEL AND THE VALUATION OF INTEREST RATE SWAPS   376

Introduction, 376 Interest Rate Swaps, 376 *Floating Short Rates*, 377 *Plain-Vanilla Interest Rate Swaps*, 378 *Delayed-Reset (In-Arrears) Swaps*, 379 Valuation of Plain-Vanilla Interest Rate Swaps, 380 No-Arbitrage Term Structure Models, 381 *Classes of Theoretical Term Structure Models*, 381 *Basic Characteristics of No-Arbitrage Term Structure Models*, 382 A Discrete-Time, Single-Factor Consol Rate Model, 383 *Short-Rate Movements*, 383 *The Consol Rate Movements and Consol Bond Values*, 385 *Relationship between Consol Rate and Short-Rate Movements*, 387 Example Application of the Model: The Valuation of a 3-Year Zero Coupon Bond by Dynamic Replication, 388 Valuation of Delayed-Reset Swaps, 393 Conclusion, 396

CHAPTER 19   THE INTEREST RATE SWAP TERM STRUCTURE   399

Introduction, 399 Short-Term Swaps, 401 Long-Term Swaps, 402 *Swap Spread Boundary Conditions*, 404 *Other Factors Affecting Long-Term Swap Spreads*, 406 Medium-Term Swaps, 408 Quantitative Swap Spread Trading, 408 *Step One: Term Structure Fitting*, 409 *Step Two: Forward Term Structure Estimation*, 410 *Step Three: Quantifying Risk and Return*, 413 Conclusion, 414 Appendix: Term Structure Fitting, 415

CHAPTER 20   TECHNIQUES FOR DERIVING A ZERO COUPON CURVE FOR PRICING INTEREST RATE SWAPS: A SIMPLIFIED APPROACH   417

Synopsis, 417 Introduction, 417 Definitions, 418 *Compounding Conversion Formulas*, 419 *Discount Factor*, 419 *Present Value*, 420 *Future Value*, 421 *Law of Exponents*, 421 Term Structure Estimation, 421 *Method I: Bootstrapping Using Linear Interpolation of Par Coupon Rates*, 422 *Method II: Bootstrapping Using Exponential Interpolation of Discount Factors*, 427 *Method III: Creating a Spot*

Curve from Eurodollar Futures, 432 Swap Pricing, 439 *Pricing a Four-Year Plain-Vanilla Swap*, 442 *Pricing a Forward Swap*, 443 *Pricing a Forward Amortizing Swap*, 445 *Solving for Unknowns*, 446 Conclusion, 447 Appendix: The MFE Group, Inc., SwapEngineer™ Computer Program, 448

CHAPTER 21 THE SWAP YIELD CURVE   452

Introduction, 452 What the Futures Curve Is Supposed to Be Telling Investors, 454 What the Futures Curve Is Really Telling Investors, 458 Getting Swap Rates from Discounting Rates, 460 *Cash-Settled Swaps*, 462 *An Example of a Cash-Settled Swap Settlement Computation*, 463 Information from the Swaps Curve, 464 Interpolation, 467

CHAPTER 22 ACCOUNTING IMPLICATIONS OF INTEREST RATE SWAPS   469

A Basic Interest Rate Swap, 471 External Reporting for a Counterparty, 473 Accounting for Termination, 476 Accounting for Principals, 477 The Timing of Swap Income, 478 The Risks of Matched Swaps, 479 *Trading Risk*, 480 *Clean Risk at Settlement*, 483 *Termination Loss*, 485 *Reset Risk*, 485 Statement of Financial Accounting Standards No. 105, 486 Materiality, 487 Accounting on a Cash Basis, 487 Accounting on a Market-to-Market Basis, 487 Hedge Accounting Issues, 491 Conclusions, 491

CHAPTER 23 SWAPS: A LEGAL PERSPECTIVE   495

Creation and Documentation of Swap Agreements, 495 *Enforceability Issues*, 496 *"Master" Agreements*, 499 *Standardization Efforts*, 501 *Authorization Issues*, 503 Termination, Damages, and Insolvency, 504 *Termination*, 504 *Measures of Damages*, 505 *Bankruptcy and Insolvency*, 508 The Netting Provisions of the Federal Deposit Insurance Corporation Improvement Act of 1991, 512 Regulatory Considerations, 512 *Bank Capital Adequacy Guidelines*, 512 *Securities Regulation*, 514 *Commodities Regulation*, 515 Secondary Market Issues, 516, Conclusion, 516 Appendix: ISDA Master Agreement and Schedule to the Master, 518

CHAPTER 24 TAXATION OF INTEREST RATE SWAPS   540

Periodic Payments, 542 *Example 1*, 543 *Example 2*, 544 Termination Payments, 544 *Example 3*, 545 Nonperiodic Payments, 546 *Example 4*, 546 Market Value Accounting, 548 Character, 548 Source, 549

SECTION 5   OVER-THE-COUNTER OPTIONS   551

CHAPTER 25 INTRODUCTION TO OVER-THE-COUNTER (OTC) OPTIONS   553

Interest Rate Caps, 554, Caps, Floors, and Collars in Terms of Call and Put Options, 555 Some Examples of Caps, Floors, and Collars, 560 Caps, Collars, and Floors in Practice, 565, The Over-the-Counter Market, 566 *End Users*, 568 Size of the Market, 570 Swaptions, 571 *Size of the Swaption Market*, 574 Equity Index Options, 574 Currency Options, 575 Exotic Options, 577

CHAPTER 26   CHARACTERISTICS OF OTC OPTIONS   580

Interest Rate Caps and Floors, 581 Pricing of Caps and Floors, 584 Some Applications, 587 *Caps with Varying Notional Amount*, 587 *Step-Up Caps*, 588 *Reducing Swap Rate*, 589 *Corridors*, 591 *Floors*, 591 *Lowering Cost of Fund*, 592 *Collars and Zero-Cost Collars*, 593 *Center Lock*, 595 Collars and Swaps, 596 Floortions, Spreadtions, and Yield Curve Options, 598 Swaptions, 599 Path-Dependent Options, 600 Down-and-Out and Up-and-in-Caps, 602 Trigger Options, 602 Summary and Concluding Remarks, 604

CHAPTER 27   APPLICATIONS OF OTC OPTIONS   606

Introduction, 606 Interest Rate Caps and Floors, 608 Hedging Interest Rate Risk Using Caps, 611 Selling Caps as Yield Enhancement, 612 Another Interest Rate Cap Example, 613 Buying Floors to Hedge Downside Risk, 614 Selling Floors to Reduce Financing Cost, 614 Interest Rate Collar, 615 Range Forwards, 616 Conclusions, 618

CHAPTER 28   ACCOUNTING FOR TRADED OPTIONS   619

The Premium, 620 *Market-to-Market*, 620 *Cost-Based Accounting*, 621 *Investor: Speculation*, 622 Intrinsic Value and Time Value, 623 *Investor Hedge*, 624 *Issuer: Speculation*, 626 *Issuer: Hedge*, 626 Recognition of Profit, 627 A Synthetic Future, 627 Buying Options to Hedge Stock Issue Commitments, 628 Options and Debt, 629 EITF Abstract: Issue No. 87–31, 631 Foreign Currency Options, 631 *Hedge Accounting: a Foreign Currency Option*, 632 *Hedging Risks with a Put*, 633 Conclusions, 634 Appendix: AICPA Issues Paper, *Accounting for Options* (March 6, 1986) 634

CHAPTER 29   THE LEGAL STRUCTURE OF OTC OPTIONS   642

Swaptions, 643 *Physical Delivery*, 643 *Cash Settlement*, 644 Caps, Floors, and Collars, 645 Commodity Trade Options, 646 Special Concerns, 647 *Unknown Size of the Market*, 647 *Illiquidity*, 649 Conclusion, 649

SECTION 6   ASSET-LIABILITY MANAGEMENT   651

CHAPTER 30   HEDGING AN ANTICIPATED DEBT OFFERING   653

Introduction, 653 Preliminary Considerations, 654 *Risk Identification*, 654 *Defining the Environment*, 655 *Balancing Hedge Objectives*, 656 *Hedge Design*, 658 Fixing a Rate, 660 *Full Rate Fix*, 661 *Fixing the Base Rate*, 662 *Fixing a Spread*, 673 Capping a Rate, 675 *Buying Put Options*, 675 *Caps and Collars*, 680 *Caputs*, 683 Summary, 684 Appendix A: Forward Sale of Coupon Bond, 685 Appendix B: Determining the Futures Hedge Ratio, 686

CHAPTER 31   FIXED-INCOME RISK MANAGEMENT: DESIGN AND
PRACTICE   689

Overview, 689 Defining Risk, 690 Valuation Models, 693 Measuring Risk, 694 Hedging, 702 *Current Risk Profile*, 703 *Modifying the Risk Profile*, 703 Hedging Instruments, 707 *On-the-Run Bonds*, 708 *Interest Rate Futures*, 709 *Interest Rate Options*, 710 *Swaps and Swaptions*, 712 Concluding Remarks and Summary, 713

CHAPTER 32   MANAGING A PORTFOLIO OF POSITIONS   717

Introduction, 717 Framework, 718 *Categories of Risk*, 719 *Risk Management Strategies*, 719 Objectives, 723 Volatility and Correlation, 727 *Time Series Data*, 727 *Statistical Methods*, 728 RMU of a Portfolio, 729 *Sample RMU Calculations for a Two-Instrument Portfolio*, 729 Hedging and Trading, 730 *RMU Hedging Approach*, 730 *Trading*, 732 RMU Applicability to Technical ALCO, 732 Conclusion, 734

SECTION 7   FUTURE OF THE MARKETS   737

CHAPTER 33   INNOVATIONS: BELLS AND WHISTLES   739

FRAs, SAFEs, and the FRA Clearinghouse, 739 *Forward Rate Agreement*, 740 *FRA Clearinghouse*, 741 *SAFEs*, 741 Swaptions, 742 Equity Swaps, 743 Warrant Issues, 745 New Directions, 745 New Financial Structures, 746

CHAPTER 34   THE ELEMENTS OF INTEREST RATE DERIVATIVES   749

Elementary Principles of Fixed-Income Derivatives, 750 *Exchange-Traded and OTC Derivatives Are Equivalent to Leveraged Cash Positions*, 750 *Outrights and Options Are Pieces of the Same Puzzle*, 752 *The Zero Coupon Yield Curve Is the Touchstone of Fixed-Income Cash and Derivative Markets*, 753 *Develop an Intuition about the Behavior of Option Prices and Sensitivities within a Portfolio of Options*, 756 *Measure Your Risks in Aggregate, Not Trade by Trade*, 758 Elementary Rules of Trading and Hedging, 759 *Transact in the Market that Offers You the Lowest Cost per Unit of Benefit*, 759 *Your Broker/Dealer Is a Resource*, 759 *You Must Be Able to Value What You Trade*, 760 *Consciously Choose the Risks You Are Prepared to Live with in Exchange for the Risks You Cannot Afford to Assume*, 760 *The More Customized the Derivative, the Less Liquid, and the More Expensive*, 761 *Know the Liquidity Associated with Your Name and That of Your Counterparty When Dealing in the OTC Market*, 761 *Avoid Self-Critical 20–20 Hindsight*, 762 Common Problems/Extra Costs, 762 *A Management Comfortable with Derivatives Is Rare*, 762 *You Have to Worry about Counterparty Defaults*, 764 *Do You Want to Pay for the Convenience of OTC Derivatives?* 765 *The Back-Office Processing of All Derivatives Will Make or Break You*, 766 *Your Regulatory Environment Dictates Which Derivatives Market to Use*, 767 *Accounting Treatment Will Define Success or Failure*, 767 *Using Derivatives' Tax Advantages Can be a Profitable Enterprise*, 768 Some Approaches to Usage, 769 *Banks Are Active in Both OTC and Exchange-Traded Markets*, 769 *Insurance Companies Are Becoming Increasingly Sophisticated*, 771 *Corporations Prefer the OTC Markets to the Exchange-Traded Markets*, 772 *Mutual Funds Have Been and Will Continue to Be More Active in Exchange-Traded Markets*, 773 *Pension Funds and Their Investment Advisors Are Moving beyond Exchange-Traded Derivatives into the OTC Market*, 774 Summary, 775

APPENDIX 777

HP-12C Program to Calculate the Risk (Standard Deviation) of a Three-Stock Portfolio, 777 HP-12C Program to Calculate Convexity for an Annual Coupon-Paying Bond (with Added Instructions to Calculate Modified Convexity), 779 HP-12C Program to Calculate Modified Duration for an Annual Coupon Paying Bond, 781 HP-12C Program to Calculate Duration for an Annual Coupon Paying Bond, 783 HP-12C Program to Calculate Duration for a Semiannual Coupon Paying bond, 785 HP-12C Program to Calculate Modified Duration for a Semiannual Coupon Paying Bond, 787 HP-12C Program to Calculate Convexity for a Semiannual Coupon Paying Bond (With Added Instructions to calculate Modified Convexity), 789 HP-12C Program to Calculate Horizon Yield for a Semiannual Coupon Paying Bond When Time to Horizon Is Less than Time to Maturity and Bond Yield to Maturity Has Changed, 791 HP-12C Program to Calculate European Call Price Using the Black-Scholes Option Pricing Formula, 793 HP-12C Program to Calculate European Call or European Put Price Using the Put-Call Parity Equation, 796 *To Calculate P^E when C^E is Known*, 800 HP-12C Program to Calculate Price Sensitivity Hedge Ratios, 801 HP-12C Program to Calculate Conversion Factors for T-Bonds Eligible for Delivery against T-Bond Futures Contracts, 803

INDEX 806

SECTION 1

INTRODUCTION TO INTEREST RATE RISK MANAGEMENT

CHAPTER 1

THE TREASURY YIELD CURVE AND ITS INTERPRETATION

Robert Ariel
Baruch College
City University of New York

INTRODUCTION

The time is long past when insurance companies and wealthy individuals bought long-term bonds and locked them away until maturity, and when bond departments at investment banks provided safe jobs for the dullard sons of wealthy families. The unprecedented interest rate volatility of the 1970s and 1980s has shown that it is neither prudent nor profitable to treat bonds as a passive holding or as the safe anchor of a portfolio.

Both the volatility of interest rates and the proliferation of new kinds of debt instruments have required the development of new tools for managing interest rate risk. The development of these tools in turn has been made possible by three interrelated advances in finance theory and finance practice.

First, financial instruments have been developed specifically for the purpose of managing interest rate risk. These instruments have become so important that when accident forced the Treasury bond futures markets to close in Chicago, trading volume in the primary government bond market dropped sharply. Later chapters in this volume describe some of these instruments.

Second, the development of these hedging instruments was in turn made possible by the invention of new financial theory leading to new financial technology. For example, managers wishing to hedge a specific risk need ways of quantifying that risk and of calculating the amount of the hedging instrument needed to manage that risk. These highly quantitative tasks employ the new financial technologies that have emerged since the 1970s. Later chapters in this volume also describe some of these advances in more detail.

Third, new ways of viewing traditional bond market information are required to permit concentrating on the most important factors in bond pricing. It is a profoundly erroneous truism that we should always examine all available information before making a decision. Indeed, science advances precisely by increasing the number of things that can be ignored in favor of a few truly important variables. While computers can store and produce unlimited quantities of information, it is still the manager's job to know which information is significant. The need for very selective attention has been exacerbated by the explosive growth in the number and variety of debt instruments.

This chapter describes a simple but powerful perspective for viewing bond market information derived from the prices of traded Treasury bonds. In a remarkable feat of simplification, this perspective reveals that behind the bewildering variety of bonds with different maturities, yields, prices, and so on, there are only a small number of fundamental variables that determine all the remaining bond features. The simpler perspective afforded by this underlying framework is useful for understanding, and equally importantly, to avoid misunderstanding, the message of the yield curve.

DRAWING THE YIELD CURVE

A yield curve of Treasury bonds is published daily in *The Wall Street Journal* and other financial publications. It is a widely available and widely quoted summary of the state of Treasury bond market yields.

The yield curve is obtained by plotting the yield to maturity (YTM) for Treasury securities on the vertical axis versus the time to maturity for those bonds on the horizontal axis.[1] The "yield curve" itself is plotted by drawing a smooth curve passing close to the YTM–versus–time to maturity points for many different bonds. Sometimes the simpler expedient is taken—choosing one benchmark bond for each of several key maturities, and then simply connecting the YTM–versus–time to maturity points for these benchmark bonds.

DEFINITION OF YIELD TO MATURITY FOR COUPON BONDS

The yield to maturity for coupon bonds is capable of several algebraically equivalent definitions.[2] A straightforward definition of *yield to maturity* is simply the bond's internal rate of return, that is, the single discount rate that equates the present value of the bond's payments (both coupons and balloon payments) to the actual market value of the bond. For example, the following hypothetical bond has an annual YTM calculated as follows:

Coupon bond 1: Market price of bond today: $980

Bond coupon to be paid 6 months and also 12 months from today: $40

Balloon (or terminal) payment of bond to be paid in 12 months: $1,000

$$\$980 = \frac{\$40}{(1 + Y/2)} + \frac{\$1,040}{(1 + Y/2)^2}$$

This formula equates the market price of the bond with the present value of the bond's payments for some particular discount rate Y. Whatever value of Y makes this equation hold true is the YTM for this bond.[3] The numerical solution gives $Y = 10.15\%$ (that is, 2×0.0575) as the annual YTM for this bond.

More generally, a coupon bond with a market price of P dollars paying T semiannual coupons of C dollars at semiannual intervals and a final balloon payment of B dollars will have an annual YTM of Y defined by.[4]

$$P = \frac{C}{(1 + Y/2)} + \frac{C}{(1 + Y/2)^2} + \cdots + \frac{C + B}{(1 + Y/2)^T}$$

For convenience and simplicity of exposition in the rest of this chapter, the basic unit of time—one period—will be taken to be six months and yields will be expressed as semiannual rates. Thus, discount rates will appear as Y rather than as $Y/2$.

THE LOSS OF INFORMATION IN CONSIDERING ONLY THE YIELD TO MATURITY OF BONDS

By a simple but very important change in perspective, a coupon bond can be viewed not as a single debt instrument but rather as a series of *separate* loans of different lengths. For example, coupon bond 1 in the last example can be viewed as composed of two separate loans, namely, one loan repaying $40 in six months and a second loan repaying $1,040 in one year. Given this perspective, it becomes reasonable to ask what the interest rate on each of these *separate* loans is.

This one bond does not provide sufficient information to answer this question, but fortunately there are additional bonds that can provide more information. Suppose that in addition to coupon bond 1 the following six-month Treasury bill is also trading:

Price: $9,708.73 per $10,000 face value

Hence, the interest rate during the six-month maturity of this bill is the rate F_1 such that $9,708.73 \times (1 + F_1) = \$10,000$, or $F_1 = 0.03$ or 3 percent for six months. Combining this information with the facts concerning the earlier bond yields:

$$\$980 = \frac{\$40}{(1 + 0.03)} + \frac{\$1,040}{(1 + 0.03) \times (1 + F_2)}$$

This equation explicitly uses an interest rate of 3 percent to discount the $40 coupon during the first 6 months, *and also to discount the $1,040 during the first 6 months* of the 12-month interval before it is received. During the second six months, *a different discount rate* of F_2 is the market-determined discount rate. This equation can be solved for F_2 to yield $F_2 = 7.28\%$. Examining only the single YTM rate for this bond obscures the fact that different interest rates apply to the first six months, $F_1 = 3$ percent, and to the second six months, $F_2 = 7.28$ percent.

The process just outlined, which combines information from two bonds (namely the six-month T-bill and the one-year coupon bond) to determine the separate discount rates appropriate for the first six months and for the second six months, can be generalized to more than two bonds and more than two periods. In general, any bond can be represented by an equation of the form:

$$P_k = \frac{C_k}{(1 + F_1)} + \frac{C_k}{(1 + F_1)(1 + F_2)} + \cdots$$
$$+ \frac{(C_k + B_k)}{(1 + F_1)(1 + F_2) \cdots (1 + F_T)} \quad (1\text{--}1)$$

where P_k is the market price of the kth bond, C_k and B_k are the coupon and balloon payments of the kth bond, and the F_t is the discount rates for the periods $t = 1, 2 \ldots T$. As this equation shows, the cash flow received, for example, at the end of the second period is discounted during the second period at a rate of F_2 and then discounted during the first period at a rate of F_1. More generally, each cash flow is discounted by *each* of the *different* discount rates that the market fixes as appropriate for each period until the cash flow is received.

A crucial point must be emphasized: While different Treasury bonds have different market prices, different coupon rates, and different times to maturity, the F_t, the discount rates applicable to different periods, *is the same for every Treasury bond*. There is only *one* discount rate for Period 1, and this rate discounts *every* cash flow paid by *every* bond that makes a payment at or after the end of Period 1. Likewise for F_2: Before any cash flow paid on or after Period 2 "becomes" a present value, it must run the gauntlet of both F_2 and F_1, being discounted by both these rates, and so on for distant rates beyond F_2. The F_t is a feature of the Treasury market *as a whole* and transcends any particular Treasury bond.

To see that the very same F_t must discount the cash flows from all bonds of the same risk, consider what would happen if there were different F_2s for different bonds. As a simple example, suppose there are two bonds both of which pay $100 at the end of Period 1 and $1,100 at the end of Period 2. Further suppose that for both bonds $F_1 = 10$ percent, but for one bond $F_2 = 8$ percent and for the other bond $F_2 = 12$ percent. Then the first bond will have a dollar price P of:

$$P = \$100/(1.1) + \$1,100/(1.1)(1.08) = \$1,016.84$$

while the second bond will have a price of:

$$P = \$100/(1.1) + \$1,100/(1.1)(1.12) = \$983.77$$

Faced with these bonds, an arbitrage opportunity (or "money machine") has been created and can be exploited by short-selling the high-priced bond and buying the low-priced one. Such a transaction generates an immediate profit of $1,016.84 − $983.77 = $33.07 per bond and does not expose the investor to any risk. The $100 cash flow from the long bond will exactly suffice to meet the coupon payment due on the short bond position, and likewise for final coupon and balloon payments. Such a series of transactions, which operates as a money machine (especially on the large scale that market makers could exploit), is so attractive that it *will* be exploited as long as it exists. But exploiting it requires selling the high-priced bond and buying the low-priced one; this buying and selling will push the prices into alignment, at which point the F_2 rate implicit in the two bonds will be identical. Putting the point the other way around, if the discount rate F_2 in the two bonds diverges at all, their price difference will create an arbitrage opportunity the exploitation of which will require buying and selling, which pushes the bond prices into "correct" pricing alignment, at which point the F_2 rates are equal across bonds.

While this example involves only two bonds, the underlying principle is completely general. Whenever one bond implicitly incorporates an F_t that differs from the prevailing F_t in all other equally risky bonds, an arbitrage opportunity will be created. Exploiting the opportunity will push the mispriced bond to its "correct" price, and force the F_t to be equal across bonds. We can also infer from this argument that the fact that the F_t are the same among all bonds is not merely a nice theoretical notion, but a real world fact, since it is grounded on the firm rock that if someone can risklessly make money, they will!

Further, since the F_t are the same in all bonds of the same risk, for example, Treasury bonds, and is a general feature of the Treasury market as a whole rather than of any particular bond, the F_t are the truly fundamental feature underlying the Treasury market: *Behind the dozens of Treasury issues outstanding, at any given time there exist a handful of* F_t *rates that determine the prices, the YTM, and the yield curve of Treasury bonds.* Examining these F_t will yield new insights into the yield curve.

WHAT ARE THESE FORWARD RATES?

These interest rates have been called F_t rates because they are technically forward interest rates. Forward contracts (or future contracts, which are very similar[5]) trade on many commodities and financial instruments. For example, the wheat grower and the wheat buyer agree today on the price at which the harvest will be sold and enter into a contract to sell the wheat "forward," which specifies the future time and price at which the wheat will be exchanged. In identical fashion, in the credit market a more abstract commodity, namely, "one-period *credit*," can be sold forward.

If one period is defined as six months, then consider an individual who desires a one-year loan. This individual could take out a one-period (six-month) loan today, and roll the loan over for another six months at the then-prevailing interest rate, or the individual could take out a one-year loan at a fixed interest rate. Economically, the one-year loan is equivalent to taking out a six-month loan today and, simultaneously, entering into a forward contract to "buy" sufficient one-period credit in six months' time to repay the original six-month loan with interest and have credit during the second six months. This way of thinking about a two-period loan is more than a mere conceptual exercise. If both the one-period (six-month) and two-period (one-year) interest rates are quoted as 3 percent for the first six months (simple interest not annualized) and 10.5 percent for the full year, then the interest charged by the one-year loan during the *second* six months (simple interest unannualized) is (1.105/1.03) = 1.0728 or 7.28 percent. This 7.28 percent is the very concrete forward interest rate imbedded in, and implicitly defined by, the quoted interest rates of the six-month and one-year loans.

In similar fashion, any long-term loan or bond whose interest rate (or coupon payments) is fixed can be viewed as a package that purchases the commodity of one-period credit at the prevailing "spot" interest rate for the first period, and, simultaneously, enters into multiple forward contracts to buy one-period credit for each successive period at a "price" (a *forward* interest rate) agreed on today. These successive one-period forward interest rates can be calculated from (and are imbedded in) the prices of traded bonds, and are as real as the commitment to make the cash flows specified in the loan or bond indenture. Stated differently, future rates are an invisible, but, nevertheless, totally concrete investment opportunity.

METHODS FOR DETERMINING THE F_t FROM TREASURY BOND PRICES

The General Method for Determining F_t Rates

Each day the market provides prices for a large number of traded Treasury bonds with known coupon rates and maturity dates. For each of these bonds, an equation of the form of Equation (1–1) can be written. Suppose one wants to determine the values of the first six F_t rates (i.e., $F_1, F_2, \cdots F_6$), where the F_t rates are the interest rates for period 1, $\cdots$ 6. (When dealing with bonds paying semiannual coupons, it is convenient to define a period as six months.) Then choose six bonds, including at least one that has a maturity in six periods, at least one in five periods, and so on, and write six equations like Equation (1–1). These six equations now contain six unknown F_t, and can be solved for these values of F_t. Solution by hand is algebraically cumbersome, but it is simple by computer. More significant is the conceptual point that all that is needed to find the first six F_t values are six bonds. Once the six F_t values are determined from these six bonds, the prices of all other bonds with maturities of six periods or less are precisely fixed. Behind the multiplicity of different bonds, there exists the simple structure dependent on these six F_t that determines all these bond prices once the six F_t rates are fixed.

A Simple Method for Determining F_t Rates

The existence of an active market in Treasury zero coupon bonds, or strips, greatly simplifies the task of determining the F_t rates by avoiding the need simultaneously to solve many complicated equations as described in the last section. To see this, consider a zero coupon bond due in one period, that is, a six-month Treasury bill. If the bill sells today for $9,708.23 per $10,000 face value, then

$$9{,}708.23 = \$10{,}000/(1 + F_1), \text{ or } F_1 = 0.03$$

Now consider a zero coupon bond due in two periods. If it sells for $9,290.06, then

$$\$9{,}290.06 = \$10{,}000/(1 + F_1)(1 + F_2)$$

or substituting $F_1 = 0.03$ permits solving for F_2 as $F_2 = 0.045$. Now consider a zero coupon bond due in three periods. If it sells for $8,848.25, then

$$\$8{,}848.25 = \$10{,}000/(1 + F_1)(1 + F_2)(1 + F_3).$$

F_1 and F_2 are already known, so this equation can be solved for F_3 to yield $F_3 = 0.05$. Continuing in this fashion it is possible to use strips to step one period at a time forward to determine the successive values of the F_t.

As a further simplification, note that the only difference between the price of the Period 2 Strip and the Period 3 Strip is that the latter has been discounted by an extra term of $(1 + F_3)$. Hence,

$$\$9{,}290.06/(1 + F_3) = \$8{,}848.25, \text{ or } \$9{,}290.06/\$8{,}848.25 = (1 + F_3)$$

The general principle here is that *the ratio of the prices of adjacent maturity zero coupon bonds gives the discount rate for the period between the maturity of the bonds.* That is,

$$\frac{\text{Price of a zero due in } t \text{ periods}}{\text{Price of a zero due in } t + 1 \text{ period}} = (1 + F_{t+1})$$

Clearly, it is now a trivial matter to calculate the F_t rates out as far as 30 years if one desires, since strips with maturities this long are actively traded.[6]

THE TREASURY COUPON BOND YIELD CURVE AND THE YIELD CURVE OF ONE-PERIOD FORWARD RATES

As noted above, the semiannual yield to maturity of a T period coupon bond is that *single* semiannual discount rate Y that equates the present value of the bond's payments with the bond's market price:

$$\text{Price} = \frac{C}{(1 + Y)} + \frac{C}{(1 + Y)^2} + \cdots + \frac{(C + D)}{(1 + Y)^T}$$

However, in light of the above discussion, the bond market in fact sets the price of this bond by discounting the cash flows, not at a single rate Y, but rather at different rates for different periods:

$$\text{Price} = \frac{C}{(1 + F_1)} + \frac{C}{(1 + F_1)(1 + F_2)} + \cdots$$
$$+ \frac{(C + D)}{(1 + F_1)(1 + F_2) \cdots (1 + F_T)}$$

Comparing these two equations it is evident that much information has been lost in concentrating on the single discount rate Y, rather than on the series of discount rates F_t, $t = 1, 2 \cdots T$, which are the economic determinants of the bond's value. Also evident is that the yield to maturity of the bond is a kind of "average" of the F_t discount rates; it is that single number that can be used in place of the many F_t discount rates to get the "right" price. Concentrating on a single Y instead of the many F_t affords a shortcut. However, the penalty for this convenience is not merely the loss of information (as all the separate F_t rates are merely summarized by Y), but a further loss (namely, a loss of universality) since the yield to maturity of a bond is a quantity *unique* to that particular bond, whereas the F_t values are universal discount rates that apply for the successive t periods for *all* Treasury bonds at a given instant in time.

The shape of the yield curve of coupon bonds mirrors the fact that the yield to maturity is a kind of average of the F_t prevailing over the bond's life. Yield curves tend to be smooth, as would be expected from the fact that YTMs tend to average changes in the F_t. However, by analogy with the *yield curve of coupon bonds*, it is possible to draw a *forward interest rate curve* that plots the forward rate F_t against time t. The forward rate curve can reveal features obscured by the usual yield curve.

For example, Figure 1–1 plots both the yield curve for coupon bonds and the forward interest rate curve for July 2, 1992. This particular day was chosen because the Fed had just lowered the discount rate by an unexpectedly large ½ percent, and the financial press was full of comment on the steepness of the yield curve. Indeed, Figure 1–1 does show that the yield curve rises from 3½ percent for T-bills to nearly 8 percent at 30 years. This is historically a very large rise. However, the forward interest rate curve

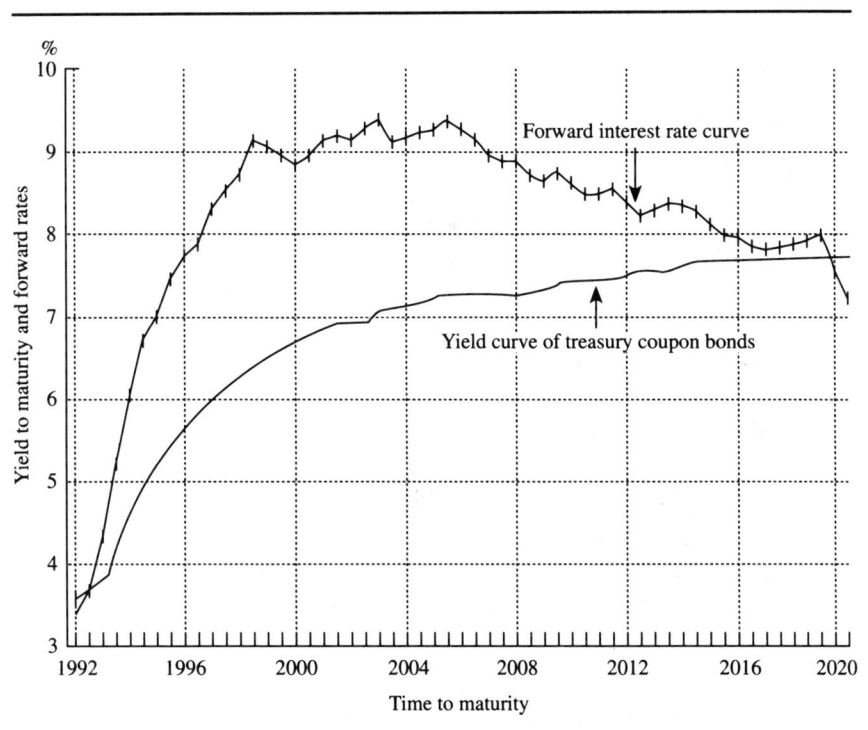

FIGURE 1-1
Yield Curve and Forward Rates for Treasury Coupon Bonds, July 2, 1992

tells an even more dramatic tale. In fact, interest rates were rising even more steeply than the yield curve revealed, rising to 9 percent within 6 years![7]

Clearly, examining the forward interest rate curve in addition to the yield curve of coupon bonds can help in interpreting the latter. The next section explores this point more fully.

INTERPRETING THE YIELD AND FORWARD RATE CURVES: SOME LESSONS

In comparing the forward rate curve and the yield curves, several features illustrated in Figures 1-1 and 1-2 deserve special mention. Figure 1-1, as noted above, depicts the actual yield and for-

FIGURE 1-2
Yield to Maturity of Bonds with Different Coupons and Maturities as Fixed by a Common Set of Forward Rates, July 2, 1992

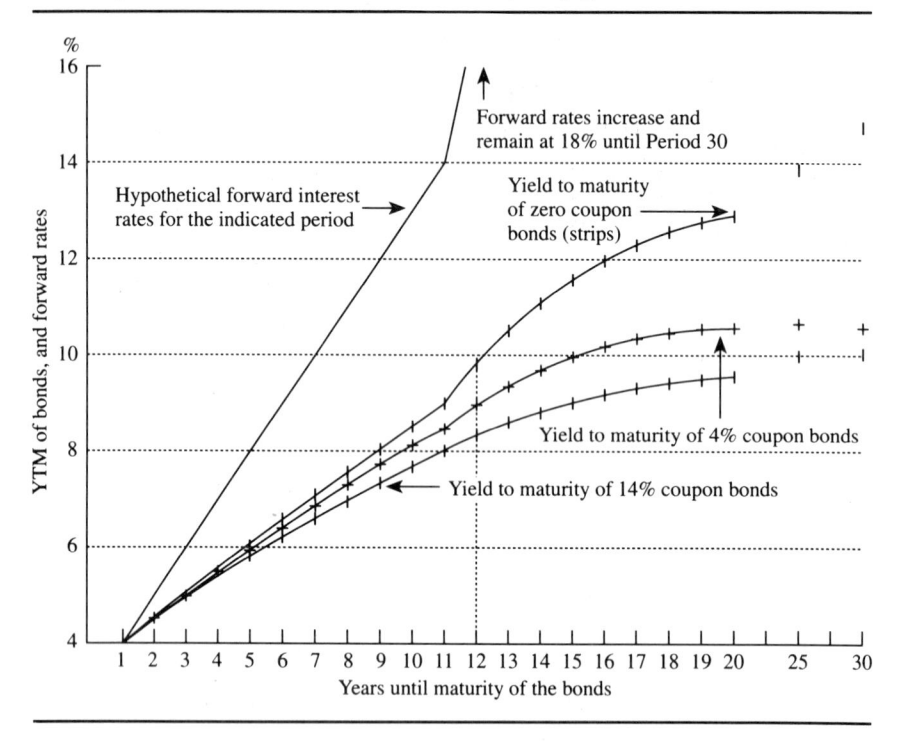

[Graph showing YTM of bonds and forward rates (%) on y-axis from 4 to 16, and Years until maturity of the bonds on x-axis from 1 to 30. Curves shown: Hypothetical forward interest rates for the indicated period (Forward rates increase and remain at 18% until Period 30), Yield to maturity of zero coupon bonds (strips), Yield to maturity of 4% coupon bonds, and Yield to maturity of 14% coupon bonds.]

ward rate curves for July 2, 1992. Figure 1–2 is an exhibit that depicts a hypothetical forward interest rate curve and the yield curves determined by these forward rates.

Lesson One

The discount rate appropriate to a future period is not the same as the yield to maturity of a bond maturing in that period. Many financial transactions explicitly or implicitly involve commitments to lend money at some future time for repayment at a yet more distant time. For example, a construction project may require the creditor to lend funds six years from the present for repayment in eight years when the project is completed and sold. What is the minimum rate the lender could charge? Assuming no risk of default, the Treasury market rate sets a lower bound on the interest rate. From Figure 1-1 the yield curve of Treasury coupon bonds gives yield to maturities for bonds due in six years (1998) to eight years (2000) as 6¼ percent to 6¾ percent. However, it is a profound mistake to conclude that rates in the 6 percent range are an appropriate rate for this loan. Figure 1-1 shows that the forward interest rates on Treasury bonds between 1998 and 2000 are around 9 percent, and a loan made in six years for repayment in eight years *is a forward loan*. Hence, the appropriate rate must be determined from the forward interest rate curve (at a rate around 9 percent), and *not* from the yield curve of coupon bonds (which gives a mistakenly low rate of 6 percent).

Lesson Two

The maximum (minimum) interest rate of the yield curve does not occur in the same period as the maximum (minimum) of the forward rates. Hence, the yield curve of Treasury coupon bonds cannot be directly "read" to infer current (or expectations of future) maximums in interest rates. In fact, the maximum (minimum) of forward interest rates occurs *in advance* of the maximum (minimum) of the yield curve. The YTM of coupon bonds, as a weighted average of forward rates between the present and the maturity date of the bond, obscures changes in the forward rates applicable to future years. Figure 1-1 shows that the forward interest rates rise rapidly between 1992 and 1998 from 3½ percent to 9 percent, but since the yield to maturities of coupon bonds combine the high 1995-98 forward rates with the low 1992-95 forward rates, these early, low rates act as an anchor, holding down the yield to maturity rates of the yield curve even as the forward rates soar. The maximum in forward rates occurs in a broad peak between 1998 to 2005. Beyond 2005, even though the forward rates gradually decline, the yield curve continues to rise! This is because the yield to maturity, as a weighted average, will continue to increase so long as the new forward rates entering the average are higher than the average itself (i.e., so long as the forward curve is above the yield to maturity curve). Thus, the forward rate maximum occurs far in advance of the yield curve maximum, and the yield curve continues to rise even though the forward rates are falling. Finally, in Figure 1-1 observe that during the last year, 2020, the forward curve does fall below the yield curve, and in fact the yield to maturity of Treasury coupon bonds does fall from 7.68 percent for the August 2019 bond to 7.66 percent for the August 2020 bond. (This very small decline is too small visually to observe on the yield curve.) Neither the rapid rise nor the gradual decline in forward rates could be inferred from visual inspection of the yield curve.

One practical consequence of the fact that the maximum (minimum) of the yield curve and the forward rate curve do not occur at the same time is to avoid the mistake of using the yield curve to infer market expectations of future short-term interest rates. It is common in the financial press and elsewhere to view a rising yield curve as indicating that the market "expects" short-term rates to rise in the future.[8] In fact, the market very directly tells us what short-term rate it is charging for loans in the year 2000: It is the one-period (six-month) forward rate for 2000, as determined from the forward rate curve. By trading bonds due after 2000, the market has already committed itself to a definite rate for loans that span the year 2000, and that rate is *not* the yield curve rate for 2000, but the forward rate for 2000.[9] Failure to make this distinction would lead believers in the expectations hypothesis of the yield curve to expect rising short rates as far as 2020 (Figure 1-1), whereas the forward rates actually decline after 2005.

Lesson Three

Large and important changes in the forward rates that occur many years in the future will produce small or invisible effects in the shape of the yield curve. As shown in Figure 1-1, the forward rate curve falls below the yield curve in 2019. But even the ¾ percent fall in forward rates from 2018 to 2020 produces no noticeable effect on the shape of the yield curve. This sluggishness of changes in yield to maturity in response to changes in forward rates is due to the fact that yield to maturity, as a weighted average of all the forward rates until the maturity of the bond, becomes progressively more sluggish as the number of items in the average increases. In economic terms, a bond's yield to maturity is that *single* discount rate that equates the bond's market price with the discounted value of *all* of its cash flows. But a sharp change in the forward rate for Year 30, for example, will have no effect on the present value of any cash flow paid prior to Year 30, and, therefore, only a small change on the bond's present value, and, hence, only a small change on the bond's yield to maturity. This is clearly illustrated in Figure 1-2, in which the hypothetical forward rates, after a smooth increase from 4 percent to 14 percent, suddenly jump to 18 percent between Year 11 and Year 12. Yet the yield curves implied by these forward rates for several types of bonds (i.e., zero coupon, low coupon, or high coupon bonds) hardly show any discernable effect from this sharp jump in forward rates. Moreover, even though the forward rates remain at 18 percent from Year 12 through Year 30, the yield to maturity for the coupon bonds scarcely exceeds 10 percent even after nearly *20 years* of 18 percent forward interest rates. Clearly the calculated yields to maturity of coupon bonds respond very sluggishly even to sharp and sustained changes in forward rates that occur more than a few periods in the future. Putting the point the other way around, an inspection of the yield curves for coupon bonds would not lead to the realization that a sharp increase in rates occurs in Year 12 and that rates remain high thereafter.

Lesson Four

If forward rates are rising (falling), then bonds with the same maturity date but different coupon rates will have different yields to maturity: This is called the *coupon effect* in calculating the yield to maturity. Figure 1-2 explicitly shows the three yield curves for bonds with three different coupon rates; these are the yield curves that are implied by the common forward rates that determine the prices and yields of all traded bonds. As the forward rates increase from 4 percent to 14 percent, bonds with the highest coupon rates respond most sluggishly to the rise. The intuitive reason is simple: High coupon bonds have their large, early cash flows "untouched" (not discounted) by the high, later forward rates, while strips, which pay no coupons, have the full value of the bond payment discounted by all the forward rates until the bond matures. In general, whenever the forward rate curve is rising (falling) sharply, then for any given maturity zero coupon bonds (strips) will have the highest (lowest) YTM, followed by low coupon bonds, with high coupon bonds having the lowest (highest) YTM. To give a concrete example, Figure 1–1 shows the forward rate curve rising sharply from 1992 to around 2000. Accordingly, we would expect bonds with different coupon rates but the same maturity to have different yields to maturity. This was indeed the case: On July 2, 1992, the yield to maturity of a zero coupon bond maturing in November 2001 was 7.38 percent, while the yield to maturity of a 7½ percent bond and of a 15¾ percent bond also due in November 2001 with the same maturity was 6.98 percent and 6.90 percent, respectively.[10] Naive investors, when choosing among bonds with the same maturity, sometimes mistakenly conclude that the bond with the highest yield to maturity is the best deal. In fact, as shown above, if the forward rate curve is rising (or falling) sharply, differences in yield to maturity are expected among bonds with different coupon rates even if they have the same maturity, and all such bonds are correctly priced; none is a bargain. As a humorous consequence of this point, a more sophisticated version of the same game could be played by bond mutual fund managers. If forward rates are rising sharply, a portfolio heavily weighted with high coupon bonds will have the highest current yield, but the lowest yield to maturity. On the other hand, a portfolio weighted towards low coupon bonds will have the lowest current yield, but the highest yield to maturity. Depending on which advertising pitch the fund manager wishes to make, either yield to maturity or current yield can be manipulated up or down by appropriate choice of coupon rate, even if the manager is tightly constrained to hold only Treasury securities of a limited range of maturities.

CONCLUSION

There is a discount rate, a forward interest rate, for each future period, and, collectively, this set of forward rates forms the framework that determines the familiar features of the Treasury bond market, such as the yield to maturity of bonds with different maturities and coupon rates. The forward interest rates are the market-determined price of credit for future periods, and frequently differ from rates derived from the yield curve. Failure to distinguish between the forward rate curve and the yield curve can lead to errors in interpreting the latter.

APPENDIX: CONSTRUCTING THE YIELD CURVE OF TREASURY COUPON BONDS AND THE FORWARD INTEREST RATE CURVE

Figure 1-1 depicts both the yield curve for Treasury coupon bonds and the forward interest rate curve for a particular date, July 2, 1992. The following describes how these curves can be drawn based on information available in *The Wall Street Journal*.

YIELD CURVE FOR TREASURY COUPON BONDS

The yield curve typically plots the yield to maturity versus the time to maturity for Treasury securities due anytime in the next 30 years. For maturities out to one year, it is convenient to use the yield on Treasury bills. Beyond one year, there are several common methods for drawing the yield curve.

The first method relies on a small number of recently issued (called *on the run* in the jargon) securities due in, say, 2, 5, 10, and 30 years (or whatever has recently been sold by the Treasury) and simply interpolates the curve between these points. This method has the advantage that recently issued securities are the most actively traded and, hence, their prices are the most current. Moreover, recently issued securities trade near par, and, hence, the fact (treated in the text) that bonds with different coupon rates will sell at different yields to maturity will not create a problem. The disadvantage of this method is the relatively few points involved in drawing the curve.

A second method seeks to use all outstanding Treasury issues (except for very low yield "flower bonds" and provides not a single smooth line, but rather a scatter of points within a band. The band's thickness is induced by different coupon rates on bonds of similar maturities, and also by call provisions on some bonds. A single smooth curve is then drawn through these points. (Until the 1980s, the Treasury Department simply used a "french curve" to draw by hand a best-fit line through the points and used this "yield curve" as the basis for calculating its constant maturity yield series. More recently, mathematical curve-fitting methods have supplanted these earlier methods.) This method has the advantage of using all available data, but it is cumbersome.

A third method takes features from the previous two by choosing annual or semiannual dates (corresponding to quarterly refunding months, e.g., February), and for each February choosing the coupon bond selling as close to par as possible. If no bond close to par trades, either a gap can be left or the yield on a nearby bond can be substituted. Finally, the seven years from 2007 and 2014 are problematic since the only traded bonds are callable, and the implicit option in these bonds influences their price and, hence, their yields. The expedient used in *The Wall Street Journal* for callable bonds is to calculate the yield to maturity if the bond is below par and the yield to first call if the bond is above par. However, this expedient implicitly assumes that an out-of-the-money option (i.e., the call feature) has no value, and this adjustment is therefore only a rough approximation. Rather than use such a rough approximation, this seven-year gap can be interpolated. The resulting curve thus seeks to take one (annual) or two (semiannual) points from each year and interpolates between points if the needed bonds do not trade.

THE FORWARD INTEREST RATE CURVE

While the yield to maturity of a bond is uniquely derived from that bond, (since it depends on the bond's coupon rate, and time to maturity, as well as the prevailing forward interest rates), the forward interest rates prevailing at any time are a feature of the Treasury market as a whole, and are rates to which all bonds respond.

The advent in the mid-1980s of an active market in Treasury zero coupon bonds, or strips, permits substantial simplification in calculating the forward interest rate curve. Previously, to calculate the 60 semiannual forward rates that span the Treasury market out to 30 years, one would have to use the characteristics of 60 different bonds to write 60 equations analogous to Equation (1–1) and then solve these 60 equations for the 60 unknown $F_1, F_2, \ldots F_{60}$.

The simple structure of strips permits a substantial simplification in the process. Per $100 of terminal value, the price today of a strip due in t periods and in $t + 1$ periods are, respectively:

$$P_t = \$100/(1 + F_1)(1 + F_2) \ldots (1 + F_{t-1})(1 + F_t)$$

and
$$P_{t+1} = \$100/(1 + F_1)(1 + F_2) \ldots (1 + F_{t-1})(1 + F_t)(1 + F_{t+1})$$
Hence, by simple algebraic cancellation of terms, one is left with:
$$P_t/P_{t+1} = (1 + F_{t+1})$$
Thus, the ratio of strip prices due one period apart gives the forward rate for that period. One period can be of arbitrary length, but it is convenient to choose semiannual or annual intervals as one period.

Using semiannual intervals, *The Wall Street Journal* for July 2, 1992, gives the following bid and ask prices for strips due in August and February. It is convenient to employ bonds issued in months corresponding to quarterly Treasury refundings. (Prices are customarily printed as 97:29, for example, to symbolize $97 + $29/32 per $100 face value. But in the following example, the fraction has been converted to decimal form.)

Maturity Date	Bid Price	Ask Price
Aug 1992	99.6875	99.6875
Feb 1993	97.9063	97.9375
Aug 1993	96.0000	96.0313
Feb 1994	93.4063	93.4375
Aug 1994	90.8125	90.8750

Taking the ratio of the ask prices for bonds due in successive semiannual periods gives semiannual forward rates:

(Aug 1992/Feb 1993) = (99.6875/97.9375) = 1.01787

(Feb 1993/Aug 1993) = (97.9375/96.0313) = 1.01984

(Aug 1993/Feb 1994) = (96.0313/93.4375) = 1.02776

(Feb 1994/Aug 1994) = (93.4375/90.8750) = 1.02820

Thus, the semiannual forward rate from August 1992 to February 1993 is 1.787 percent, which can be annualized either by doubling the value (a method that gives a value comparable with the usual convention of defining the yield of maturity for coupon bonds as twice the semiannual rate) to give 3.574 percent or by compounding 1.01787 for two periods (squaring this quantity) to give 1.0361, or a 3.61 percent annual discount rate.

In theory, this same method can be used to calculate forward rates as far into the future as strips mature (as of July 2, 1992, that was out to 2021), but as often happens, pure theory must be tempered with art to obtain uniformly reasonable results. At long maturities, the "granularity" of prices induced by bid-ask spreads becomes significant. At any time, the "true" price of the security lies at or between the bid and ask prices. Consider the following long-maturity prices (also as of July 2, 1992):

Maturity Date	Bid Price	Ask Price
Feb 2019	12.0938	12.1875
Aug 2019	11.6562	11.7500
Feb 2020	11.2188	11.3121
Aug 2020	10.6250	10.9063

For a short-maturity strips, with prices in the $90 range, the bid-ask spread, which typically amounts to $(2/32) = 6.25 cents, is virtually negligible. However, at long maturities, the bid-ask spread [which tends to be somewhat larger at $(3/32) = 9.4 cents] when compared with prices in the $10 range yields a bid-ask spread (3/32)/(2/32) × (90/10) = 14 times greater per dollar invested in long-maturity strips than in short-maturity strips. This can induce substantial inaccuracies in forward rate estimation. For example, using these prices:

(Bid Feb 2019)/(Bid Aug 2019) = (12.1875/11.7500) = 1.0372 or 3.72%

If the quoted bid price for the Feb 2019 strip were only $(1/32) lower, the calculated forward rate would be:

[12.1875 − (1/32)]/11.7500 = 1.0345 or 3.45%

This difference of almost 0.3 percent in the semiannual rate or 0.6 percent when annualized is very substantial. Moreover, since the bid-ask spread is $(3/32), the actual transaction price may differ from the recorded ask (or bid) by $(2/32) or more. Clearly, some method to minimize possible errors from this source must be found. Fortunately, there are two ready methods of correcting for these errors induced by bid-ask factors.

The first method starts with the observation that in taking the ratio of successive strip prices to obtain successive forward rates, the Feb 2019 price is used twice, once in the numerator and once in the denominator of a ratio. If this strip price is $(1/32) too low, the ratio (Feb 2019)/(Aug 2019) will be too low, but the previous period's forward rate (Aug 2018)/(Feb 2019) will be too high. Hence, a better estimate of the *true* forward rate for a given period can be obtained by averaging each period's calculated forward rate with the previous and subsequent calculated rate. For example, one averaging method might be to calculate the forward rate, F, for Feb 2019 to Aug 2019 by using bid prices as:

$(1 + F) = 0.25 \times$ (Aug 2018/Feb 2019) $+ 0.5 \times$ (Feb 2019/Aug 2019) $+ 0.25 \times$ (Aug 2019/Feb 2020).

This is the correction method employed in deriving the forward rate curve in Figure 1–1.

A second method for correcting bid-ask spread errors notes that in calculating forward rates using February–August semiannual periods, not all the information afforded by strip prices is being used. In particular, a similar calculation can be performed using May–November semiannual periods, to obtain forward rates for periods overlapping the original February–August periods. Finally, these two series can be averaged to obtain a forward rate curve in which the error has been reduced.

The two methods just described are not mutually exclusive, and so both can be used simultaneously to obtain good estimates of forward rates even for distant periods, despite the granularity of prices induced by bid-ask effects.

In addition, other chapters in this volume describe some sophisticated techniques for estimating the value of the imbedded call features in callable Treasury bonds. Once the value of the call feature is known, the observed market price can be corrected to obtain an estimate of the value of the "pure" bond (i.e., without the call feature). This "pure" bond price can then be used in the forward rate estimation process. In particular, for the period between 2007 and 2014, when all long bonds were issued with call features, the ability to estimate the value of the pure bond furnishes additional valuable data for estimating forward rates during this period.

NOTES

1. The generic term *bond* will be used to designate all Treasury debt instruments regardless of maturity. Thus, Treasury bills and notes are also *bonds*.
2. Unfortunately, one of the most popular definitions of *yield to maturity* is that rate that the bondholder would receive if all coupons were reinvested at the YTM rate when received. This reinvestment assumption is gravely unrealistic and has caused some to question whether YTM is a useful notion. However, an algebraically equiva-

lent definition of YTM is employed in this chapter that makes no reinvestment assumptions, and this definition may be more acceptable.
3. It is a convention that the *annual* YTM of a bond that pays semiannual interest is the solution to this equation in which the annual YTM is divided by 2 when discounting the semiannual payments. This convention was adopted because it results in a bond selling at par ($1,000) and making semiannual coupon payments of $40 having a YTM of 8 percent. For institutional reasons, it was desirable to have the quoted YTM of a bond be the YTM that the bond *would* yield *if* all coupons (in this case both $40 coupons) were received at the end of the year. In fact, the true economic yield of this bond is greater than 8 percent: If the annual discount rate is 8 percent, the semiannual discount rate is *not* 4 percent, but rather the square root of (1 + 0.08) = 1.0392 or 3.92 percent, because a 3.92 percent semiannual rate when compounded for the full year (i.e., multiplied by itself) yields 8 percent. In contrast, a 4 percent semiannual rate compounds to $(1.04)^2 = 1.0816$ or a 8.16 percent annual rate, and this is the true economic yield of this bond. The incremental 0.16 percent arises from the ability to invest the first $40 coupon for the second six months giving an extra $40 × 0.04 = $1.60 on a $1,000 bond selling at par, or an extra 0.16 percent.
4. Note that this equation implicity defines Y, the YTM for this bond, as whatever discount rate makes this equation hold true. This definition cannot be made more explicit because no equation exists of the form Y = so-and-so that permits the YTM of a bond to be calculated directly (although some approximate formulae exist). Rather, one must try different values for Y in the formula by trial and error until the correct value is found.
5. In the following discussion, forward contracts and future contracts will be used interchangeably; both are contracts entered into today that require the exchange of a commodity at a fixed price at a predetermined date in the future. As a practical matter, these types of contracts differ only in the timing of payments for the commodity.
6. Or at least it is simple in theory to determine the F_t rates out to 30 years. In practice, real-world data are not sufficiently "clean" (due, for example, to tax considerations, or bid-ask spreads) to permit such a simple approach. The appendix to this chapter describes how real-world prices drawn from the newspaper can be employed to determine the F_t in practice.
7. See J. C. Francis, *Investments: Analysis and Management*, 5th ed. (New York: McGraw-Hill, 1991), Appendix 12B, for a different nu-

merical example of how to compute the different, but simultaneous and equivalent, yield curves in terms of the yield to maturity, the spot rate, and the future rate.

8. Such statements reflect implicit acceptance of the so-called expectations hypothesis of the yield curve (i.e., that the shape of the yield curve is determined by expectations of future short-term rates). While the expectations hypothesis enjoys wide support, it should be noted that perhaps other factors are also at work in determining long-term rates (e.g., investors may demand a risk premium for lending long).

9. A caveat is appropriate here. The financial market commits itself today to a forward rate for the year 2000. Of course, the market can, and almost certainly will, change the price of short-term credit when 2000 arrives. Put differently, today's forward price for credit in 2000 can differ from the spot price for credit when 2000 arrives, much as the spot and forward prices for any commodity usually differ on the delivery day.

10. The comparison date of November 2001 was motivated by the simultaneous maturity in that month of a medium coupon and a high coupon bond. Both bonds are noncallable.

CHAPTER 2

FACTORS INFLUENCING THE LEVEL OF INTEREST RATES

Robert Ariel
Baruch College, City University of New York
Larry Pohlman
Vice President, BlackRock Financial Management

INTRODUCTION

A Small Set of Forward Rates Determines All Bond Prices

Chapter 1 describes how the entire term structure of interest rates and the prices of all (riskless noncallable) bonds are fixed by the set of one-period forward rates extending from the present onward. Once the, say, 60 six-month forward rates extending through the next 30 years are given, the price of every traded (riskless noncallable) bond is uniquely determined. Any deviation from the price determined by these forward rates provides an arbitrage opportunity, the exploitation of which will force the prices back into "correct" alignment. Actually, only slight deviations from "correct" pricing within the bounds of bid-ask spreads are possible. Except for bond traders, these slight deviations are economically unimportant and can be ignored. On the other hand, for traders who handle huge volumes with negligible transaction costs, these minute deviations from correct pricing constitute profit opportunities, and by exploiting these profit opportunities (i.e., selling the overpriced bonds and buying the underpriced ones), they force the prices back into correct alignment. This is an important fact to keep in mind: The pricing relationship between bonds is enforced by traders who seek to profit from deviations from these pricing relationships, and who, thereby, force the prices back into correct alignment. Put differently, these pricing relationships are not mere theoretical constructs, but are based on the undeniable fact that traders will make a profit if they can.

What Factors Determine the Level of Forward Rates?

In the last chapter, the values of the one-period forward rates were taken as given. In this chapter, some of the factors that the market uses in setting these rates will be explored.

As with all commodities, the prices of one-period credit, whether Period 1 credit (i.e., a loan from now until six months from now) or Period 20 credit (i.e., a loan from 10 years until 10 years and six months from now), is determined in the marketplace by supply and demand. Moreover, even for a commodity as "simple" as, say, copper, it is not possible to give a complete catalog of all factors influencing the supply and demand for the commodity, and their relative importance. How much more difficult, then, would it be to catalog all the factors influencing the supply and demand of that pivotal commodity named credit. Accordingly, only some of the most important factors influencing interest rates can be identified.

At the outset, a simplification will be made. Considered as pure theory, the mathematics of the forward rate model permits the successive forward rates $F_1, F_2, \cdots F_T$ to be independent of each other. Thus, F_1 could be 5 percent, $F_2 = 15\%$, $F_3 = 2\%$, and so on. Clearly, it is unrealistic to believe that the market sets successive rates in this sawtooth fashion. Hence, the simple model can be supplemented by the economic assumption that forward rates during successive periods change smoothly, that is, that the forward rate curve (such as those plotted in the previous chapter) is smooth rather than saw-toothed or with sharp spikes or dips. Indeed, econometric work shows that simply assuming that there are two independent interest rate "factors"—a "short factor" and a "long factor"—permits the simplification of treating successive F_i as a weighted combination of the two factors.[1] The forward rates thus derived capture a substantial amount of the different shapes that the yield curve can assume. Employing three factors, that is, short, intermediate, and long factor, permits the inverted U shape of forward rates such as is seen in Figure 1–1 in the previous chapter for July 2, 1992. Accordingly, for expositional purposes, the following treatment of influences on forward rates will be divided into two sections: The first describes influences on the short-term interest rates, and the second describes influences on the long-term or distant forward rates.

INFLUENCES ON THE SHORT RATE

Naturally, the supply of and demand for short-term credit determine the price. Some factors influencing credit availability, such as the business cycle, are too well known to need comment here. Instead, two controverted influences on short rates will be addressed, namely, *inflation* and *Federal Reserve Policy*.

The Mathematics of Inflation and Interest: Fisher's Law

Suppose that today you "lend" D dollars for *immediate repayment*, with the repayment made not in dollars but in quarters. Since repayment is immediate, there can be no inflation and you will demand to be repaid that number of quarters Q given by:

$$Q = D \times \frac{\text{(Purchasing power of dollars lent)}}{\text{(Purchasing power of quarters received)}} = D \times 4$$

That is, you will demand four quarters for every dollar lent.

Next, suppose that repayment of the loan is not today, but rather in one year. In addition, you demand a 5 percent increase in purchasing power to induce you to postpone immediate consumption, which is to say a 5 percent *real interest rate* (hereafter rr). Then you will demand to be repaid that number of quarters such that:

$$Q = D \times \frac{\text{(Purchasing power of dollars lent)}}{\text{(Purchasing power of quarters received)}} \times (1 + 0.05)$$
$$= D \times 4 \times (1.05)$$

Now, of course, loans are both made and repaid in units of dollars. *But* inflation changes the purchasing power of the dollars. If the purchasing power of dollars is measured by the consumer price index, then the inflation rate, *INF*, is defined as the ratio:

$$(1 + INF) = \frac{\text{(Consumer price index at end of period)}}{\text{(Consumer price index at beginning of period)}}$$

You will demand to be repaid the number of dollars you lent grossed up by a factor of $(1 + r)$ where r, the *nominal interest rate*, is defined by:

$$(1 + r) = (1 + INF) \times (1 + rr) \qquad (2-1)$$

The quantity r is what we normally think of as *the* interest rate on a loan; it is the "extra" that must be repaid over and above the amount borrowed, and is the number quoted by banks and in newspapers.

Equation (2–1) is called *Fisher's Law*,[2] and its derivation clearly shows that the nominal interest rate is the *multiplicative* product of the inflation rate and the real interest rate. From Equation (2–1) immediately follows:

$$r = INF + rr + INF \times rr \qquad (2-2)$$

During normal economic times, both the inflation rate and the real interest rate are only a few percent (e.g., 5% = 0.05), so the product $INF \times rr$ is negligible and can be ignored. It is because $INF \times rr$ is usually small that economic writers and newspapers sometimes state that "subtracting the inflation rate from the nominal interest rate gives the real interest rate." Strictly speaking, this statement is false and will be dangerously wrong in highly inflationary environments such as we have seen in recent years in countries of South America, Eastern Europe, and the former Soviet Union.[3]

Fisher's Law is not merely an academic exhibit, but rather an economic principle that can bite with savage viciousness during hard economic times. Consider: The nominal interest rate (r) can never fall below zero (i.e., dollar bills stuffed into the mattress, which earn a nominal rate of zero, dominate any loan with a negative nominal rate of return.) Now consider what happens if there is *deflation*, that is, falling prices—a negative inflation rate—such as occurred during the Depression in the United States. During the depression years from 1929 to 1933, the consumer price index fell by nearly 25 percent and the wholesale price index by 33 percent. During 1932 alone, prices (as measured by either index) fell by about 10 percent. The nominal interest rate (i.e., the yield on T-bills) was virtually zero at this time, but, of course, could not fall below zero.[4] So with the left-hand side of Equation (2–2) anchored at virtually zero, and with *INF* negative, the real rate in 1932 had to be a very high +10 percent to make Equation (2–2) hold, which is a very high real riskless rate of return even during good economic times. If this real interest rate is now treated as a *hurdle* rate that even riskless investments in plant and equipment must pass (and recognizing that risky projects require an added risk premium above this), it can readily be appreciated how even during good economic times investments in new plant and equipment can fail to meet this high hurdle rate. How much more difficult during the Depression! The innocuous symbols of Fisher's Law thus acted as a choke on new investment during that difficult time when new investment was most needed to stimulate the economy. This deadly consequence of Fisher's Law thus contributed to the severity of the Depression, and shows why true deflation (i.e., an actually falling price level) can be economically harmful.

Will the Real Inflation Rate Please Stand Up!

Of the three variables in Fisher's Law, the nominal interest rate can be determined with great precision—it is listed every day in the newspaper. The other variables, the inflation rate and the real interest rate, are more problematic. As a practical matter, the inflation rate is next estimated from government survey data, and the real rate is then taken to be whatever number it takes to make Fisher's equation hold.

However, the commonly used government survey numbers of "the" inflation rate, such as the *consumer price index* or the *GNP deflator,* may not accurately capture the *INF* variable in Fisher's Law. The reasons hinge on the fact that any survey that looks at the price change of some basket of goods from period to period should consider that in a market economy the price mechanism is used to *change* consumption patterns, and thus the composition of the basket of goods consumed.

Financial markets are very sophisticated and ignore any inflation that is not "core" inflation. For example, a drought in California's Imperial Valley may cause the price of vegetables to jump, and produce a corresponding blip in the price indexes. However, financial markets recognize this blip as temporary and ignore it. Perhaps more surprising, and as a great tribute to financial markets' sophistication, econometric studies show that financial markets are able to disentangle the effects of price increases caused by isolated economic events, even if large, from general price level changes.[5] For example, a price increase in a basic commodity such as oil will ripple through the economy, raising many prices. However, if consumers must spend more on petroleum products, they have less to spend on other goods and, hence, there need be no increase in the aggregate price level. As the above derivation of Fisher's Law shows, the core inflation variable *INF* in the law is the inflation that results from a change in the purchasing power of the dollar. The primary cause of this sort of change in the purchasing power of money is inflation resulting from excess money creation.

What Determines What?

Fisher's Law establishes a relationship between the nominal interest rate, the real interest rate, and the inflation rate. Moreover, immediately above it was noted that newspapers publish precise values for the nominal rate, and government surveys provide reasonably accurate values for inflation, but the real rate must be inferred from these other two. This statement concerns the ease of *knowing* the variables in Fisher's Law.

Now we pose a slightly different question. Fisher's Law decrees that given two of r, *INF*, and rr, the third is determined. We are exploring the factors influencing the short-term interest rate. Therefore we ask: In the real economy, which two variables *causally determine* the third? In particular, is the inflation rate a causal determinant of the nominal interest rate?[6]

In the special circumstance of the Depression, falling prices, together with the lower bound of zero for the nominal interest rate, causally determined a positive real rate. In "normal" times, however, it is not clear which two of the variables determine the third.

However, a reasonable model of the causal connections can be inferred if several facts are kept firmly in mind, and if the problem is broken into short-term and long-term aspects.

Short-Run Determination of r, INF, and rr

Fact One. Over the short term, the inflation rate (whether measured by the consumer price index, the GNP deflator, or some other "core" inflation measure) changes only slowly. Financial markets, of course, know this, and thus will assume that the inflation rate next quarter will be about the same as the inflation rate this quarter, with perhaps some slight adjustment (measured in tenths of a percent) for the market's assessment of the effects of the business cycle (and other factors).

Fact Two. Also over the short term, the interest rate on, for example, three-month T-bills can change substantially. The sharp spike in rates in 1980, when T-bill rates changed from 15 percent to 7 percent and then back to 15 percent all within 12 months, clearly shows that the market can change rates rapidly when it wants to.

Furthermore, it is reasonable to infer from the two preceding facts that over the short term exogenous economic factors fix the inflation rate and also the nominal rate, and these two then causally determine the real rate. Thus, over the short term, the real rate is a kind of residue. This conclusion is reinforced by the knowledge that sometimes, as in 1980–81, the nominal rate is *less* than the inflation rate, which means that buyers of T-bills were willingly accepting a real rate of return less than zero, that is, a loss of purchasing power. Why would investors buy T-bills in the full realization that purchasing power would be lost over the three-month life of the T-bill? First, investors do not expect such high inflation to persist indefinitely. Second, investors change their portfolio compositions only slowly; typically, investors simply roll over their bills or other short-term instruments. To put the point bluntly, if investors in the aggregate hold a certain (large) amount of short-term instruments and in the aggregate they want to sell, what could they buy instead? And to whom would they sell? Thus, over the short term, investors are neither inclined nor even *able* to change their aggregate holdings of short-term instruments, and tend to accept whatever real rate the market determines.[7]

Long-Run Determinants of r, INF, *and* rr

Over the long term, however, the situation is substantially different. Investors are naturally reluctant to accept a negative real rate of return on riskless assets forever. Moreover, over this longer term, investors *can* reduce their aggregate holdings of short-term instruments, for example, by simply not rolling over maturing T-bills. If enough investors do this, the required yield on T-bills will rise until the real rate is acceptable to buyers. Presumably, this minimally acceptable return is nonnegative. Can we quantify the real rate investors will demand over this longer term?

This question cannot be answered with only theory, but some empirical studies based on long-run returns from rolling over T-bills show that over the long run (since the end of World War I until the present) the real rate of return has averaged about zero. The often-quoted claim (in the financial press, for example) that the real riskless rate of return is about 3 percent is not supported by the evidence. While there have been periods of negative real returns (e.g., during some periods in the 70s and 80s) and also of positive real returns (e.g., the early 30s and so far in the 90s), these highs and lows average over the (recent) long run to about zero.[8]

The claim that over the long run the real rate is about zero can be made more intuitively plausible by recognizing that with their ready marketability and universal acceptance, T-bills are very money like. Even individual investors have access to interest-bearing checking accounts in banks and money market funds.[9] If money market instruments are the true "money" of our age, they can be expected to fulfill the traditional functions of money, namely, acting as a medium of exchange and, most relevant for our purposes, a "store of value."

The fact that the long-run real riskless rate of interest is about zero has a number of profound consequences for investment strategies, but these go beyond our immediate concerns.[10] For the moment, note that unlike the short-term case (where *INF* and *r* determine *rr*), over the longer term it is reasonable to suppose that investors insist that *r* rise to yield a nonnegative *rr*, which is to say that *INF* and *rr* influence *r*.[11]

Federal Reserve Policy: A Factor Influencing Short-Term Interest Rates?

The Federal Reserve is often described in newspapers and market commentaries as being all-powerful in setting the nation's interest rates. No doubt there is utility for writers and commentators to have an unobservable "they" to whose actions interest rate changes can be ascribed. In this section, we will try to describe a more realistic view of the Fed's power over interest rates.

The Fed's two principle *overt* tools for influencing credit markets are the *discount rate* and *open market operations*.[12] In addition, there is a *covert* tool, namely, Federal Reserve *"signals"* of its own assessment of the economy's direction.

The discount rate is the interest rate that the Fed charges banks to borrow overnight reserves (or fed funds); it is through offering these reserves to banks that the Fed functions as "the lender of last resorts." The Fed has absolute power to set this rate wherever it wants, but this power is usually without much "bite" for several reasons.

First, banks are reluctant to borrow from the Fed because borrowing is viewed as a sign of a weak bank balance sheet. Indeed, banks repay Fed borrowing as part of end-of-quarter window dressing so the borrowing will not appear on shareholder reports.[13]

Second, banks can also buy other banks' excess reserves in the fed funds market. If the fed funds rate is below the discount rate, banks have little incentive to borrow from the Fed. If the fed funds rate is above the discount rate, it profits banks to borrow from the Fed and lend these funds in the fed funds market, but the Fed discourages borrowing for such purposes. For these reasons, the Fed sets the discount rate close to the prevailing fed funds rate, since otherwise the discount rate would be completely ignored. In sum, therefore, the discount rate—the only interest rate over which the Fed has absolute control—is actually parasitic on the fed funds rate, and not really an independent policy tool.[14]

Third, total borrowing from the Fed, when not negligible, rarely exceeds several billion dollars. Several billion dollars of incremental credit is negligible compared to the several *trillion* dollars of outstanding short-term credit in the market. While the addition of borrowed reserves to the system may have several effects, considered purely as incremental credit added to the credit market, the effects of such borrowing are modest.

In contrast, *open market operations* is a more powerful but two-edged policy tool. Through the purchase of Treasury securities, the Fed can add reserves (as currency or fed funds) to the banking system. This increased supply of fed funds then lowers the fed funds rate. This lower fed funds rate then "spills over" into other short-term rates, lowering the rates on all short-term instruments.

However, in order to move and, more importantly, *hold* the fed funds rate at a level substantially different from the market-determined rate, the Federal Reserve must continuously pump out more and more new reserves. It is at this step that the other edge of the two-edged open market operations sword cuts, because these new reserves also function as monetary base, and (assuming cash holdings do not change) each dollar of new monetary base could result in the creation of up to 40 dollars of new money (M2).[15] The financial market, well aware that this new money can cause future inflation, adds an inflation premium to long bond rates. Thus the paradoxical result that, to *lower* and hold *short* rates at a level substantially below their "natural" rate, the Fed must abandon efforts to control the money supply, and must risk future inflation that in turn *raises current long* rates.[16] For these reasons, while the Fed may nudge the fed funds rate a few basis points or even a few tenths of a percent below its "natural" level, the Fed avoids trying to lower interest rates by the few percentage points needed to make a substantive difference to business borrowers.[17]

In sum, the *discount rate* follows the fed funds rate and is not an entirely independent policy variable. Meanwhile, the fed funds rate can be nudged by *open market operations* at most a few tenths of a percent away from its "natural" level, since changes of several percent would require injections of reserves sufficient to balloon the money supply beyond reasonable bounds. In sum, the *overt* Federal Reserve policy tools appear to have only limited power to influence short-term interest rates.

Why, then, is the Fed credited with absolute control over interest rates? The Fed has an additional, powerful, but *covert* policy tool, namely, its ability to "signal" the financial market.

Minutes of Fed policy meetings clearly show that sometimes the Fed takes specific actions at specific times with the goal of maximizing the action's visibility. Moreover, it could be argued, the Fed has access to information superior to any other single market participant. If the Fed nudges fed funds lower and takes the conspicuous step of cutting the discount rate, these actions clearly *signal* the financial markets that the Fed believes the economy is weak and in need of stimulus, *under which circumstances short rates will naturally be falling.* Little wonder that the bond market sees the Fed's action and reacts, regardless whether the Fed's action will *cause* the rate decline, or merely *signal* that a rate decline is already in progress.[18]

In sum, therefore, the power of the Federal Reserve to influence short-term rates is utilized sparingly. While the extent of its influence is sufficient to make its actions of direct importance to bond dealers and others on Wall Street, for other purposes (e.g., when interpreting the yield curve, or for the economy at large), the Fed is usually better viewed as a weather vane than a big wind.[19]

INFLUENCES ON THE LONG-RUN INTEREST RATE

As explained in the introduction to this chapter, much of the variation in the successive one-period forward rates from the present out to 30 years can be captured by a linear combination of a short factor and a long factor. The above section considered the impact of such influences on the short-term interest rate. This section describes some influences on the long factor. Because these two factors jointly explain much of the variation in the one-period forward rates (and these rates in turn determine the yield curve in the manner described in the last chapter), these influences on the long-term rate are commonly called "theories of the yield curve."

Traditional Theories of the Yield Curve

Economists have over the years advanced several plausible theories to explain the shape of the yield curve. These traditional theories have been supplemented in recent years by insights drawn from modern economic theory complete with its sophisticated mathematical technology. Immediately below, three traditional theories explaining the shape of the yield curve are described. More recent theories are then treated in the next section.

Traditional Theory 1: The Expectations Hypothesis

The forward price of a commodity will not usually equal the spot price when the forward contract comes due. For example, in March the forward price of wheat for September delivery may be $5 per bushel. But if a drought destroys the crop, then wheat's spot price in September may be $10. In March, though, when the September forward price was $5, did the market *expect* September spot wheat would sell for more or less than $5? Economists' opinions are divided on this question.[20]

However, for the commodity called *one-period credit,* the expectations hypothesis claims that the forward prices of this commodity for successive periods (that is, the forward interest rates for successive periods) are equal to their expected spot prices. For example, the expectations hypothesis holds that the forward interest rate for the year 2000 is presently 7 percent because the market expects that when January 2, 2000, arrives, the price of a one-year loan will be 7 percent. Now, of course, the market is not clairvoyant, so on January 2, 2000, the actual rate on a loan will likely be greater or less than 7 percent, but 7 percent is the market's best guess today.[21]

The expectations hypothesis sounds so attractive that sometimes the notion of a forward interest rate is (mistakenly) defined as "the interest rate the market expects" during future periods. However, as we will shortly see, there are other equally plausible factors in determining the long-term interest rates.

Traditional Theory 2: The Liquidity Premium Hypothesis

In its naive form, the liquidity premium hypothesis claims that given a choice between rolling over short-term debt for, say, 10 years, and buying a single 10-year bond, investors would prefer the former if the expected 10-year return is the same in the two cases. This is because investors value the liquidity that the short-term debt affords. Therefore, the argument continues, 10-year bonds must yield more than short-term debt in order to induce investors to purchase it. Put differently, long-term debt must yield an incremental return—a "liquidity premium"—to induce investors to purchase it. By obvious extension of the argument, the size of the liquidity premium must increase with maturity (i.e., a 20-year bond must be expected to yield more than rolling over two 10-year bonds, and so on). Therefore, the naive liquidity premium hypothesis makes an unambiguous prediction about the shape of the yield curve: It must slope up.

This version of the liquidity premium hypothesis is labeled *naive* because empirically the yield curve does *not* always slope up. However, a more sophisticated interpretation of the hypothesis claims that a liquidity premium is *one influence* among several in shaping the yield curve. In this more realistic but weaker form, the liquidity premium hypothesis merits attention since it does explain the empirical observation that the yield curve slopes up most of the time, and does accord with our intuition that investors require compensation for the price-fluctuation risk entailed by investing long term.

Traditional Theory 3: The Market Segmentation or Clientele Hypothesis

This theory starts from the premise that as soon as we draw a yield curve, we have committed the error of lumping apples and oranges together. This theory holds that there are distinct credit markets (in the plural) with different participants or clienteles and different prices for credit in each separate market. As a result of these differences, the market segmentation theory asserts that plotting the yields and times to maturity of the credit instruments in these different markets on the same graph is an oversimplification.

This theory assumes greater plausibility when it is realized that historically the long-term and short-term ends of the credit markets had very different origins, and only gradually "grew together." Short-term credit instruments had their origin in project-specific self-liquidating loans; thus, a merchant would take out a loan to finance a trading voyage and would repay the loan from the proceeds of the voyage. In sharp contrast, the long-term end of the credit market had its origin when kings, to raise money for wars, promised in return for a lump sum to make periodic payments usually with no definite maturity; sometimes these payments were annuities that ended with the death of the lender with no repayment of principal by the borrower.

Even as late as the early years of this century, short-term credit was used almost exclusively to finance inventory and trade; the notion of rolling over short-term paper indefinitely for "general business purposes" was unthinkable. Meanwhile, on the long end of the market, the bonds issued by governments and railroads were either of perpetual maturity (the famous British consols of the late 1800s—which are still outstanding) or of such long maturity that the present value of the repayment of principle was a negligible part of the bond's selling price (many U.S. railroads were financed with 100-year bonds).[22]

In more contemporary terms, there are some borrowers who want to lend short-term and others who want to borrow short term, and the price—the interest rate—at which short-term supply meets short-term demand determines the short-term interest rate. On the other hand, there are borrowers who want to borrow long term (e.g., utilities) in order to match the life of the bonds with the life of the asset financed by the bonds; at the same time, there are lenders who wish to lend long term (e.g., life insurance companies) so that the bonds will come due when the insurance claims must be paid. Again, where the supply of long-term credit meets the corresponding demand, the long-term interest rate is set, and likewise for intermediate maturities. Newspapers take the interest rates set in these *different* markets and plot them on the *same* graph and call the resulting chart a "yield curve." In brief, therefore, the market segmentation theory of the yield curve reduces to the claim that in seeking to explain the shape of the yield curve, we are asking the wrong question; we *should* seek to explain the interest rates in each of the separate markets.

Summary of the Three Traditional Yield Curve Theories
Taken by itself, none of the three traditional theories suffices to capture the rich variations in the yield curve. Evidence can be adduced in support of each theory, and it is perhaps best to take each theory not literally, but rather as a statement of one influence acting to shape the yield curve.

Newer Theories of the Yield Curve

The above three traditional theories of factors influencing the yield curve (the expectations, liquidity premium, and market segmentation hypotheses) have been supplemented (and may be supplanted) by theories with roots in academia developed over the last two decades. These new theories have in common the fundamental insight that the yield curve is not a static entity but rather that interest rates at all maturities are constantly changing. Rigorous analysis shows that interest rate movements at different maturities cannot be independent of each other.[23] Much as Black and Scholes showed that, by assuming a certain type of stock movement (i.e., a certain "stochastic process"), the relative movements of a stock and an option on that stock are linked, so likewise, assuming a certain type of movement in short interest rates, the relative movements of yields at different maturities are also linked. Cox, Ingersoll, and Ross explicitly develop a yield curve theory assuming one kind of interest rate movement.[24] Further theoretical developments in this field await better characterization of the interest rate movement process.

Simultaneous with these theoretical developments has been the explosive growth in new interest rate–sensitive instruments. Trading volume and open interest in the new interest rate futures and options have become so large that when the Chicago markets for these instruments were forced to close due to a temporary flooding accident in 1992, trading volume in the primary markets dropped significantly. The market in mortgage-backed securities has experienced the greatest innovation through the issuance of collateralized mortgage obligations (CMOs) and real estate mortgage investment conduits (REMICs), as well as a veritable zoo of related products. Common to all these new securities is that they contain embedded implicit or explicit interest rate *options,* and the valuation of these options also requires a model of the interest rate movement process.

At present, only incomplete theoretical frameworks are available for describing the term structure, and for pricing the embedded options in newer debt instruments. These incomplete models are given concrete and usable form by including a number of variable parameters whose values are estimated by fitting the models to give the correct (i.e., market-priced) valuations for a handful of actively traded benchmark bonds, in a process generally referred to as *calibrating* the model. Then the model can price other, less actively traded bonds relative to these benchmark bonds. In this way, incomplete but still useful theoretical models can be supplemented by observed data to yield results that neither along could achieve.

SUMMARY

This chapter has examined some of the fundamental determinants of the level of interest rates that underlie the multiplicity of debt securities. Factors influencing both the near and distant forward rates were treated separately. Finally, directions of future research were outlined.

NOTES

1. See M. J. Brennan and E. Schwartz, "Conditional Predictions of Bond Prices and Returns," *Journal of Finance* 35 (1980), pp. 133–55, and references therein.
2. The law was first enunciated in 1896 by Irving Fisher of Yale, a great economist during the early decades of this century. Regrettably for him, he is perhaps best remembered today as "that economist" who declared in September of 1929 that "stocks appear to have reached a permanently high plateau." His catastrophic misprediction, as shown by the stock market crash in October 1929, stands as an object lesson that economists should either never make public predictions or else make them both diversely and frequently.
3. There is an ambiguity in Fisher's Law because the inflation variable is sometimes taken to be the actual (ex post) inflation over the loan's life, and sometimes as the expected (ex ante) inflation over the loan's life. This latter interpretation is preferred today. See J. C. Francis, *Investments: Analysis and Management,* 5th ed. (New York: McGraw-Hill, 1991), Channel 12, for a discussion of this distinction.
4. During 1932 to 1936, T-bill yields ranged between 0.06 percent to 0.23 percent (i.e., from 6 to 23 basis points per year) and reached an

astonishing 0.0001 percent (one one-hundredth of a basis point) in 1938.
5. E. F. Fama and G. W. Schwert, "Inflation, Interest, and Relative Prices," *Journal of Business* 52 (1979), pp. 183–209.
6. The reader is warned that the relation between the inflation rate and the nominal interest rate is much controverted in economics. What follows is, therefore, one view of a moderate interpretation of the data. See Francis, *Investments,* for discussion and additional references.
7. This argument that the real rate is a "residue" draws on recent history for illustrative purposes. More detailed studies, some using more than 100 years of data, confirm the conclusion that in the short run the nominal rate does not follow the inflation rate closely. See R. J. Schiller and J. J. Siegel, "The Gibson Paradox and Historical Movements in Real Interest Rates," *Journal of Political Economy* 85 (1977), pp. 891–907.
8. See Ibbotson Associates, *Stocks, Bonds, Bills and Inflation: 1992 Yearbook* (Chicago, Ill., 1992), p. 29, Exhibit 9.
9. Indeed, the bulk of all currency appears to be used in the underground economy, so much so that the amount of outstanding currency that cannot be accounted for by the legitimate public is used to estimate the size of the underground economy. Another, growing use of U.S. currency is as a medium of exchange in countries experiencing high inflation, including, ironically, the countries of the former Soviet Union.
10. For example, since all interest is merely compensation for loss of purchasing power due to inflation, one cannot expect to withdraw from a pension plan that invests solely in T-bills any more purchasing power than one contributed over the years.
11. This claim can only be viewed as a reasonable surmise and not an empirically demonstrated fact for the simple reason that there are very few observations of the "recent long run"; in fact, almost by definition, only one observation. Modern central banking, with the widespread issuance and acceptance of fiat currency, is a phenomenon unique to this century. This profound structural change in the money mechanism has arguably made all previous monetary data irrelevant, so truly we do have only one "long-run" observation to examine.
12. The Federal Reserve can also influence the size of the money stock through changes in bank reserve requirements. But this monetary tool is too powerful for frequent use.
13. See L. Allen and A. Saunders, "Bank Window Dressing: Theories

and Evidence," *Journal of Banking and Finance* 16 (1992), pp. 585–623.
14. The exception that proves the rule arises when the Fed is aggressively tightening by draining reserves from the system, and, thereby, raising the market-determined fed funds rate. At such a time, the Fed may raise the discount rate sharply as a way of saying "and we mean it!"
15. As of this writing (1992), the ratio: (noncash components of M2) divided by (noncash component of monetary base) is roughly 40.
16. This last claim is a moderate version of the "rational expectations" position on monetary policy. However, the notion of the financial market knocking down the price of long-term bonds in response to a given Fed outpouring of reserves is too mechanistic. For one thing, this position fails to reckon with the claim of even the most ardent monetarists that money creation influences inflation and real output with a variable effect and variable lag. Still, even the popular press notes that fear of reigniting inflation "down the road" acts as a bar to extreme Fed vigor in pumping out reserves to fight economic downturns.
17. On the other hand, even a few basis point rate change can have powerful effects on the willingness of bond market makers to hold larger inventories. See the next footnote for more on this point.
18. In spreading the signal, the Fed is assisted by the most active private market participants in the bond market, namely, the market makers. These market makers finance their huge and highly leveraged bond inventories at the repo rate, which is closely tied to the fed funds rate. For these important (and vocal) market participants, even small Federal Reserve nudges to the fed funds rate can substantially change the profitability of these portfolios. Little surprise, therefore, that it pays these vocal market participants to seek assiduously to ascertain the Fed's intentions.
19. Although the Fed's power to create large changes in market interest rates may be limited, in one other policy action the Fed is not only a big wind, but a veritable hurricane. The Fed's extraordinarily powerful ability to create money has economic effects independent of the effects on interest rates. At the very least, this translates into the power to cause inflation, and, if the money stock is tied to economic output, to influence real activity as well.
20. For example, one venerable theory attributable to John Maynard Keynes holds that forward prices are higher than the expected spot prices since sellers demand a risk premium.
21. An alternate statement of the expectations hypothesis is that investors expect bonds of all maturities to yield the same total return over

the "next" period. This statement of the expectations hypothesis is virtually equivalent to the version in the text. Consider: When the next period is over, the same statement then applies to the "next" period again, and so on. The only way every bond can yield the same total return during each future period is if future spot rates equal present forward rates. Hence, the *expectation* that all bonds will yield the same total return during each future period is equivalent to claiming that forward rates equal *expected* future spot rates.

Recently, some subtle conceptual differences have been discerned between alternate statements of the expectations hypothesis, which had been thought identical. See John C. Cox, Jonathan E. Ingersoll, Jr., and Stephen A. Ross, "A Re-Examination of Traditional Hypotheses about the Term Structure of Interest Rates," *Journal of Finance* 36, no. 4 (September 1981), pp. 769–99. However, as a practical matter, differences between alternate statements of the expectations hypothesis are negligible. See J. H. Wood and N. L. Wood, *Financial Markets* (New York: Harcourt Brace Jovanovich, 1985), pp. 647–50.

22. Those who believe with Santayana that "those who do not learn from history are doomed to repeat its mistakes" are directed to the excellent *A History of Interest Rates*, 2nd ed., by Sidney Homer (New Brunswick, N.J.: Rutgers University Press, 1977); this volume is unique in having been written by the man who for many years was head of the bond department at Salomon Brothers. On the other hand, those who believe with Hegel that "we learn from history that we do not learn from history" may ignore this footnote.

23. For example, a "parallel yield curve shift" is forbidden, despite the fact that Macaulay's duration is the accurate bond risk measure only for this type of yield curve movement. (The following example employs the notions of duration and convexity, which are treated at length in later chapters.) Consider two portfolios: Portfolio 1 is a 50:50 mix of fed funds and 10-year zero coupon bonds (strips). Portfolio 2 is entirely invested in 5-year zero coupon bonds. Both portfolios have identical Macaulay's durations of five years, but Portfolio 1 has greater convexity. (Recall that for strips, duration is roughly equal to time to maturity, but convexity is roughly equal to the *square* of the time to maturity. Therefore, a portfolio that is half 10-year strips has more convexity than a portfolio that is all 5-year strips.) Therefore, Portfolio 1 will decline in value less following an upward parallel yield curve shift, and will increase in value more following a downward parallel yield curve shift than Portfolio 2. Now form a portfolio requiring zero investment by short-selling Portfolio 2 and using the

proceeds to buy Portfolio 1. The resulting portfolio requires no net investment, and has zero duration but positive convexity. Therefore, if the yield curve executes a parallel movement, whether up or down, this portfolio will increase in value; that is, this is an *arbitrage opportunity*—a guaranteed money maker. Since "there is no free lunch," the key assumption that the yield curve makes parallel movements is false.

This is one example of how only certain types of relative changes in yields at different maturities are allowed.

24. See Cox et al., "A Re-Examination of Traditional Hypotheses about the Term Structure of Interest Rates."

CHAPTER 3

A CALL-ADJUSTED TERM STRUCTURE ESTIMATION METHODOLOGY

Thomas S. Y. Ho
Founder, Global Advanced Technology Corporation
Sang-bin Lee
Korea Advanced Institute of Science and Technology
Kyu-hyun Son
Korea Advanced Institute of Science and Technology

ABSTRACT

The callable Treasury bonds could be incorporated into the estimation sample. One might argue that the present value of the option premium in each callable Treasury bond is small enough that some simple approximation (or even ignorance) of the option value would suffice for providing a useful estimation procedure of the discount function. Unfortunately, these errors in estimating the option values can generate significant errors in estimating the discount function. This chapter describes a call-adjusted term structure estimation methodology using an elaborate option pricing technique. By decomposing a callable security into its component parts—a noncallable bond and a call option on that bond—one can value the embedded options individually and thereby obtain estimates of the price of a comparable noncallable bond correctly.

BASICS OF THE SPOT CURVE

A Simple Discount Function

At any point in time, the market determines an implied discount function that represents the market consensus of the time value of money. In an effort to develop a methodology that will reveal the discount function at any point in time, one should try to estimate the discount function from the market prices.[1] The natural choice for these market prices is the entire range of Treasury issues.

The price of a Treasury bill with one-dollar par represents the present value of one dollar for the specified maturity. The bill prices plotted against the maturity can represent the time value of money up to a one-year maturity. This simple example of a discount function illustrates some of the complications involved in constructing a discount function for the whole Treasury market and motivates some of the applications of the discount function.

Given the bill prices, one can provide a theoretical price for a cash flow that can be replicated by holding a portfolio of Treasury bills. This portfolio of Treasury bills can be constructed in a straightforward manner. For each payment of cash flow, one just needs a Treasury bill with a maturity matching the payment date and a principal amount equaling the payment amount. A bond that has a cash flow that can be replicated by a portfolio of bills has the same value as the portfolio of bills, by the law of one price. This assumes that the bond has no default risk and the marketability level is similar to that of the bills.

In reality, Treasury bills do not mature each day, and, therefore, a portfolio of Treasury bills cannot replicate a cash flow with payments on any given day. For this reason, the bill prices must be interpolated so discount factors can be inferred for the days that do not have maturing bills. The underlying assumption here is that the discount function is smooth and the discount factors do not exhibit large changes.

The observed bill prices may not reflect the market time value of money exactly. For example, there may be different bid-ask spreads or the quotes may not be correctly reported, and the constructed discount function may incorporate these errors. A temporal imbalance in supply and demand may also result in the observed price not reflecting the equilibrium time value of money. How should one isolate these deviations from the equilibrium values that one wants to estimate? The best approach is to make an even stronger assumption about the bond market and the underlying time value of money. We will assume not only that the points between any two observations can be interpolated, but also that all equilibrium discount factors lie on a smooth curve and that any deviations of the observed bill price from this underlying curve can be treated as observation errors or deviations resulting from temporary supply and demand imbalances. Having made this assumption, we will seek a procedure to construct a smooth curve that best fits the observed bill prices.

A Spot Curve for the Treasury Market

The concept of the discount function for Treasury bills could be extended to the full spectrum of the term structure. The major difference between constructing a spot curve for the bills market and constructing one for the Treasury market is that the bills have no coupons. The Treasury bills without coupons are in fact, as we have argued, discount factors. However, the coupon issues' yields are internal rates of return from multiple cash flows. Therefore, the yield to maturity of a coupon issue is not the discount rate of any particular principal payment. To handle this problem, one needs to think of a coupon bond as a portfolio of zero coupon bonds. Each zero coupon bond has its own discount rate. To construct a spot curve is to determine the discount factors that can value this portfolio of zero coupon bonds so that (at least approximately) its present value equals the observed bond price. And this has to hold true for all bonds.

There is another difference between the bond market and the bills market. In the bond market, there are callable Treasury bonds. Some researchers delete these bonds from the estimation procedure. Since every outstanding Treasury security has some information about the term structure of interest rates, the term structure estimated with only noncallable Treasuries does not fully reflect all currently available information about the level and shape of the spot rate curve. Most noncallable Treasuries have maturities of less than 20 years, but a significant portion of callable bonds offer maturities of over 20 years. Because this represents a large segment of the spot curve, the change in the callable bond prices attributable to changes in the call option component has an important influence on the structure of the spot curve. If all callable Treasury bonds in the estimation sample were deleted, interpolating all the observations in such a broad range of years could result in substantial errors.

To illustrate this problem, we estimate the discount function using only noncallable bonds. Many mathematical formulations are available for specifying smooth curves. Such curves may be represented by polynomials, but most of the current research employs piecewise polynomial functions called *spline functions*. We estimate the discount function using a spline approximation.[2] For an estimation date (e.g., April 1983) when many callable bonds have longer maturities than the longest maturity among noncallable bonds, the resulting discount function estimated with only noncallable bonds is extrapolated to longer maturities in valuing the callables. However, we find that the extrapolated part of the estimated discount function slopes abnormally (too steeply upward). See Panel A of Figure 3–1.

On the other hand, when all the callable bonds have shorter maturities than the longest maturity among noncallables, one may avoid the hazardous extrapolation for pricing callables. Nevertheless, one may still face the problem of interpolations that are not fatal but still troublesome. Because the observations (noncallables) are too sparse for the maturity range (20 to 30 years) where nearly all the callables are outstanding, the intervening approximations are unreliable. Such a case is depicted in Panel B of Figure 3–1. The discount curve dips to negative values at the far end.

Several solutions are suggested to correct the anomalous portion of the approximation, such as the use of exponential splines (Vasicek and Fong 1982), the imposition of additional constraints upon the cubic spline approximation (Shea 1984), and an exponential prior restriction with regard to the degree of curvature allowed (Barrett 1988). However, these expedients do not directly attack the problem (paucity of data). Such a constraint specification is only ad hoc or excessively attached to the exponential shape of the discount curve, and reveals many serious defects. For a detailed discussion of the faults of exponential splines, see Shea (1985).

50 Section 1 Introduction to Interest Rate Risk Management

**FIGURE 3–1
Discount Curves Estimated Using Only Noncallable Bonds**

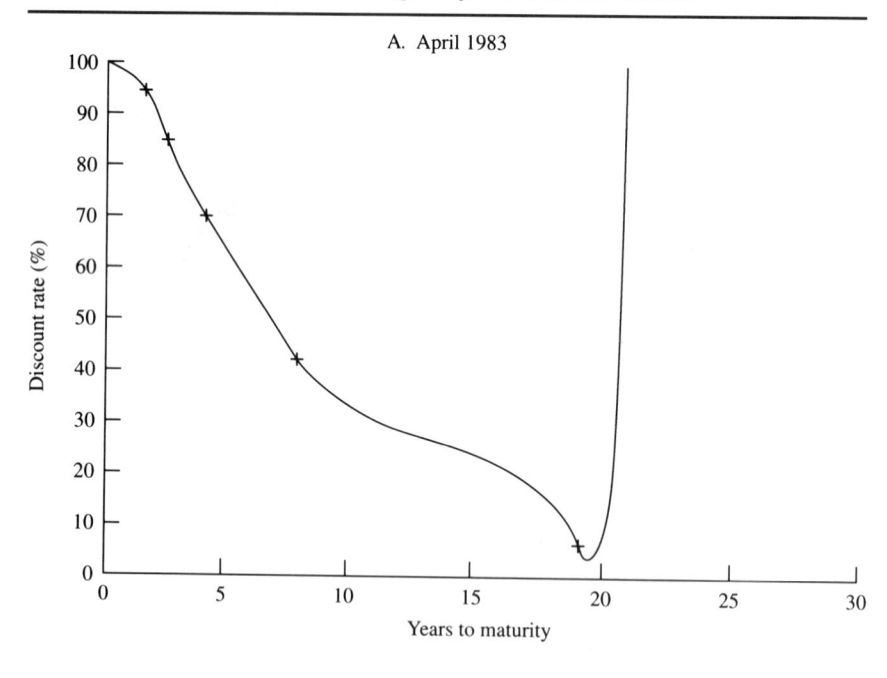

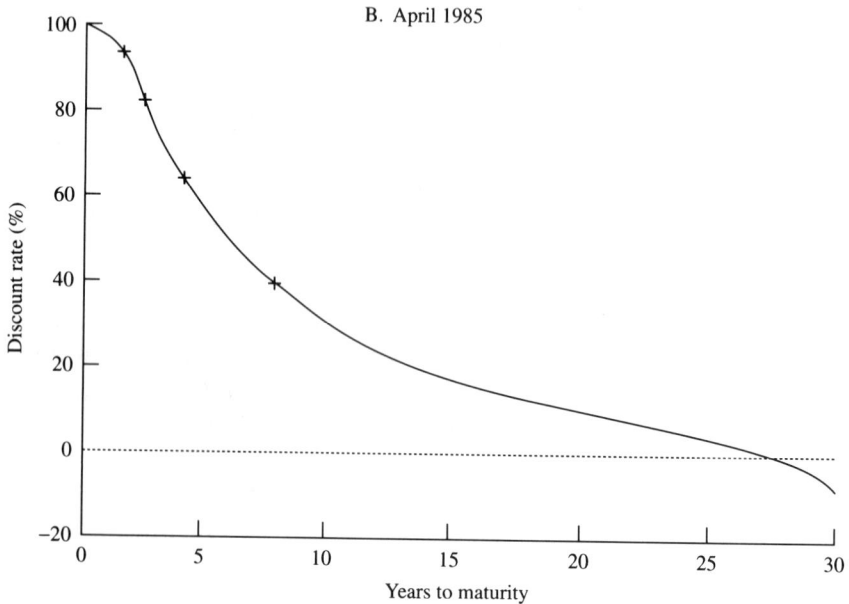

A. April 1983

B. April 1985

* Small +'s denote breakpoint locations in the cubic spline.

HOW TO INCORPORATE THE CALLABLE TREASURIES

The Noncall Approach

Several approaches can be taken to deal with these particular bonds. The simplest is to ignore the call feature and include all bonds as if they were all noncallables (hereafter this approach is called the *noncall approach*). This approach simply assumes that a callable bond will never be called for early redemption, and it will repay principal on its stated maturity date. This approach may be acceptable when almost all callables are traded below the par price. However, when many callables in the estimation sample are trading at a significant premium, the resulting pricing errors of the bonds selling at a premium can have a negative effect on the estimation procedures of the term structure because this approach does not consider the possibility of a call.

The First Call Approach

The second and most common approach to callable bonds is to assume that the bond will be redeemed at its first call date if it is priced at a premium, and that it will be redeemed at maturity if it is priced at par or at a discount (hereafter this approach is called the *first call approach*). In this case as well, the callable bonds are easily incorporated into the estimation procedure as in the noncall approach. However, the results are again questionable. An unreliable interpolation in the maturity range of more than 20 years may be unavoidable, since the maturity of a callable bond is replaced (shortened) by its first call date when the bond is priced at a premium.

The Dummy Variable Approach

The third way to incorporate callable bonds (the *dummy variable approach*) is to introduce a dummy variable for the call effect into the estimation model, for example, regression equation (15) in Vasicek and Fong (1982). This approach indiscriminately prices the callable bonds, regardless of the difference in their call features in the estimation sample. This approach may be acceptable if almost all embedded option values in the sample are similar. However, the call option values may be different for each callable bond because these bonds have different maturities and coupon rates. As a result, the callable bonds in the sample may contain embedded options that are in the money or out of the money.

The Option Pricing Approach

Finally, the most effective approach (the *option pricing approach*) is to use an option valuation model to approximate the value of the embedded option in each callable bond. In this case, we consider the bond as a portfolio composed of a straight bond (with the same stated maturity and coupon rate) and a short call option on this noncallable bond.

Once an option value is derived using a bond option valuation model, one can create an equivalent straight bond by adding the estimated option value to the observed callable Treasury price. By this procedure, all callable bonds are incorporated into the existing sample of noncallable securities. An estimation methodology can be applied to derive a discount function using this large sample.

For the estimation date when nearly all the callable bonds are trading at a significant discount to their principal values, as we have argued, the option pricing approach would produce essentially identical results as the noncall approach. This corresponds to the case where little likelihood exists that the call options in the estimation sample will be exercised.

When nearly all the bonds are trading at a significant premium over their principal values, interest rates are so low that there is little likelihood the options will *not* be exercised. In this case, the callable bonds are essentially equivalent to the noncallable bonds, redeemable at their first call date. However, the option pricing approach is not comparable to the first call approach. The first call approach shortens the stated maturities of the callable premium bonds, and essentially preserves the same shortcomings (extremely abnormal discount curves are produced for the maturity range where a paucity of noncallable bond data prevails) as the estimation procedures with only noncallable bonds. Figure 3–2 illustrates this case. However, the purpose of this chapter is to (accurately) add callable bonds to the set of noncallable bonds in

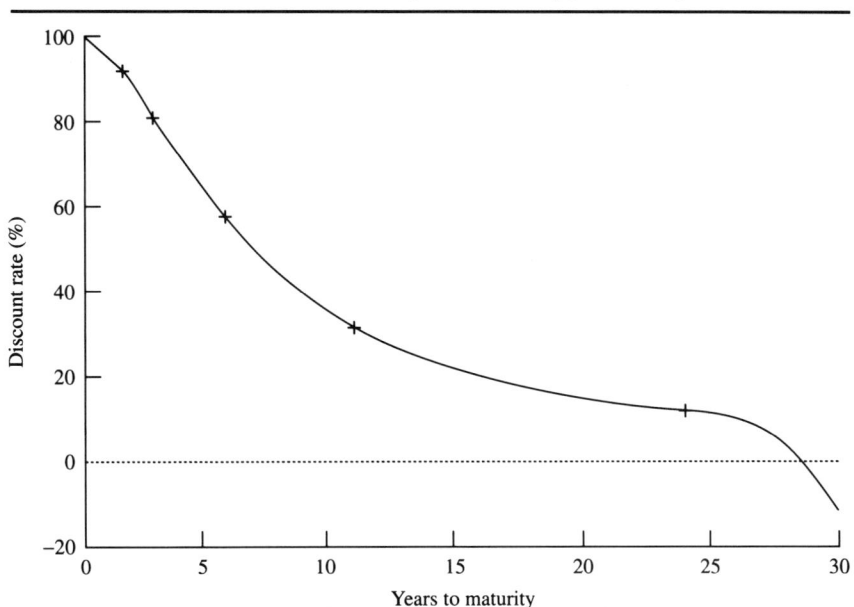

FIGURE 3-2
An Estimated Discount Curve Using First Call Approach, April 1983

* Small +'s denote breakpoint locations in the cubic spline.

the maturity range where noncallable bonds are sparse. The first call approach is certainly not helpful to our purpose and is therefore excluded from further analyses in this chapter.

Finally, when nearly all the bonds are priced at or near their principal values, one cannot be sure when the call options will be exercised. Hence, neither the noncall approach nor the first call approach can be applied. A similar argument can be applied when the discounts, the premiums, and the pars or near-pars are mixed without one type being dominant. Also, the dummy variable approach, which prices each embedded option without distinction, intrinsically gives rise to an erroneous estimation. Thus, analyzing a callable bond as a combination of a straight bond and a short call option leads to the discount function that best explains the prices of the observed callable Treasuries.

THE CALL-ADJUSTED ESTIMATION TECHNIQUE

An Iterative Procedure

Two main features exist for this four-step procedure. First, our bond option valuation model (mentioned in the following subsection) requires information on the specification of the underlying discount function. Second, the discount function can be estimated only after all the call options' values are known. This call-adjusted procedure treats the two problems as a simultaneous system; an interactive effect exists between the discount function and the call option value. An iterative process is used to take this interactive effect into consideration in estimating the discount function with all outstanding Treasuries.

Step 1: Determining the Initial Discount Function
For the first iteration, either the discount function or the call option value should be given as the initial value. Here, we adopt the discount function as the initial input between the two. Also, we temporarily assume that the call options have *no* value.

Step 2: Determining the Option Value
Having estimated the initial discount function, this discount function is now applied to the bond option valuation model in this chapter to price the call option embedded in each callable Treasury bond.

Step 3: Readjusting the Callable Treasury Bond Prices
Step 2 provides the first estimate of the call option value for each callable bond. Adding this option value to the observed callable Treasury price gives an estimate of the equivalent straight Treasury bond. Step 3 is to add the estimated option value to the observed callable Treasury prices and establish a new set of sample (straight) bond prices.

Step 4: The Looping Procedure
Now, with the new set of sample prices, we can repeat step 1 and determine a revised discount function with which to estimate the option prices. After using the revised option prices to adjust the

callable Treasury bond prices in step 3, we are again ready to repeat the estimation procedure in step 1.

The loop provides convergence to a solution, in the sense that values of the call option and of the discount function do not change with further iterations and simultaneously satisfy the pricing of both the straight bonds and the callable Treasury bonds after several iterations. The convergence criterion chosen is based on the root of the mean squared error (RMSE) of all Treasury bonds. If the difference between the RMSEs on two successive iterations is smaller than the prespecified value (10^{-5}), the iteration stops.

The Embedded Call Option Valuation

Previous literature has recognized that the embedded call option can be viewed as an interest rate–contingent claim. The simplest approach to the valuation of bond options, and probably the most widely used in practice, is the Black-Scholes model (1973). One obvious problem with the Black-Scholes model is its assumption that interest rates are constant while the bond price is stochastic. These two assumptions are clearly inconsistent, and they cause excessive pricing errors. Brennan and Schwartz (1979) not only model the interest rate–contingent claims, but also the bonds (the term structure) themselves. However, the current term structure is not used as an input to their model, but is rather derived from it. Their empirical estimation procedure first requires estimating the short- and long-rate volatilities using historical data. Errors introduced in this estimation would significantly affect the pricing model. To deal with these difficulties, the model used in this chapter is basically *Ho and Lee's (1988) bond provision pricing model* under interest rate uncertainty that is based on Ho and Lee's (1986) arbitrage-free interest rate movements (AR) model.

EMPIRICAL RESULTS

Uniqueness and Existence of the Spot Curve

The constructed spot curve is not unique. It seeks to achieve two objectives: to be smooth and at the same time to best explain the observed Treasury prices.

These two objectives are somewhat in conflict. First, a curve with many sharp turns that statistically fits and explains the observed bond prices very well will be most unlikely to reveal the underlying time value of money. This is not satisfactory because the purpose is to construct not a curve that fits the bond prices, but one that can reasonably represent the time value of money curve.

Second, the spot curve is not constructed to reflect what one thinks the spot curve should be, disregarding its ability to explain the observed bond prices. The construction recognizes the importance of the spot curve's ability to explain the observed prices and to behave reasonably well as a spot curve. Decisions about how smooth the curve should be and how well it should explain the observed bond prices are subjective, so the spot curve is not uniquely defined by the observed bond prices.

The issue more important to modeling is not the spot curve's uniqueness but its existence. The existence of a spot curve depends upon identifying a curve that satisfactorily fulfills these two criteria: (1) The curve can be used to interpret the time value of money, and (2) the curve can be used to accurately price the Treasury securities. If such a curve exists, and if one can construct another spot curve that is also a reasonable candidate, then probably the two curves cannot be very different. Therefore, on the practical level, it is not important to ensure the uniqueness of a spot curve for the Treasury market.

Perhaps the reason for the prevalent use of the spot curve is that researchers to date have shown that such a curve does exist, suggesting that the bond model is applicable to the Treasury market. Of course, a smooth curve can always be constructed as the *spot curve*, but it may be very unsatisfactory in explaining the observed bond prices. In such a case, one could argue that the bond model is not applicable and that the development of an underlying spot curve is doubted. We shall dwell on these empirical results in the following sections. The empirical results employ the monthly closing prices of all the Treasury securities, which are provided by the CRSP government bond tape. Flower bonds are not applicable to the theory that we have discussed, and are not included in our analysis.

TABLE 3-1
Summary Statistics of Mean Call Value Estimates for January 1983–December 1989 (par = 100)

Minimum	Maximum	Mean	Standard Deviation	Quartiles 1st	2nd	3rd
.0000	2.0848	.9100	.6619	.1774	.9059	1.4090

The Significance of the Call Provision

First of all, to investigate whether the embedded call option in the callable Treasury bond is negligible, one would like to examine the option premium. The *actual* option value is the actual difference between the prices of a callable and a straight (but otherwise identical) bond. However, comparable straight bonds do not always exist, so the next best alternative is to estimate the option value to be the difference between the actual price of the callable bond and the model price of an otherwise identical straight bond.

Table 3-1 presents the (actual) call value estimates from our bond option pricing model for each estimation time in our sample—namely, every month from January 1983 through December 1989. The mean of the estimated call values was 0.91 of one percent of the bond's face value (or principal) on average. Thus, the call provision on a Treasury bond seems negligible.

Then, to see whether a call provision is negligible *even* in the call-adjusted term structure estimation, the RMSEs in the three aforementioned models (except the first call approach) were computed for each (monthly) date during our sample period. Furthermore, to consider the callable bonds separately, we decompose the RMSE into two parts—one for the noncallables and the other for the callables. The results are summarized in Table 3-2. If a call provision has no value at all, the RMSE of the callable bonds in the noncall approach, which ignores the call feature, should not be significantly different from that of the callable bonds in the option pricing approach. If the value of a call provision has any information (i.e., some explanatory power), it would reduce the RMSEs.

TABLE 3–2
Summary Statistics of Estimation Error (RMSE) in Alternative Models for January 1983–December 1989 (par = 100)

					Standard		Quartiles	
Approach	Bond Type	Minimum	Maximum	Mean	Deviation	1st	2nd	3rd
Noncall	Noncallable	.3722	1.8481	.8888	.4173	.5538	.7827	1.0438
	Callable	.4499	3.3242	1.5437	.6705	1.0976	1.3538	1.8423
	Overall	.5387	1.7461	1.0269	.3757	.7287	.8298	1.2796
Dummy variable	Noncallable	.3733	1.8464	.8552	.3957	.5248	.7870	.9986
	Callable	.5118	4.7161	1.6666	1.0418	1.0522	1.3200	1.7201
	Overall	.5377	1.8351	1.0443	.4109	.7240	.8363	1.4038
Option pricing	Noncallable	.3156	1.8481	.8090	.4225	.4143	.7260	1.0299
	Callable	.3234	2.1525	1.0141	.5158	.6319	.8507	1.5010
	Overall	.3378	1.7484	.8529	.4049	.5067	.7995	1.0504

Table 3-3 presents the RMSE differences between the two models, the noncall approach and the option pricing approach. For the callable bonds, the RMSE difference between the two models (RMSE in the noncall approach minus RMSE in the option pricing approach) is 0.5297, on average, and the *t*-statistic is 6.95 for the null hypothesis that the mean difference is zero; RMSE in the option pricing approach is significantly different from (less than) the noncall approach. In addition, we implemented a simple sign test of the option pricing approach versus the noncall approach. The absolute pricing errors for the two models are compared, and the number of times that the option pricing approach's error is less than the noncall approach's error is counted. As can be inferred from Table 3-2 (the exact calculation results are not shown here), the option pricing approach significantly outperforms the noncall approach. Similar results are found for the noncallables and the overall Treasuries as well. This suggests that the call option model has some explanatory power for the behavior of a callable Treasury bond, and the value of a call provision on a Treasury is not negligible, at least for estimating the discount function. This result is as predicted in the previous sections of the chapter. The noncall approach may be acceptable for the estimation time when almost all callables are traded deeply below par price. But, when many callable bonds are trading at a significant premium, the noncall approach, which assumes that all callables will be redeemed at their maturities, surely gives rise to erroneous estimation.

A scatter diagram (Figure 3-3) clearly suggests how the callable premium bonds can affect the estimation result. The vertical

TABLE 3-3
Estimation Error (RMSE) Differences between Noncall Approach and Option Pricing Approach for January 1983-December 1989 (par = 100)

Bond Type	Mean Difference	Standard Deviation of Difference	t-Statistic
Noncallable	.0798	.1298	3.94*
Callable	.5297	.4879	6.95*
Overall	.1740	.1620	6.88*

* Significant at 1 percent.

FIGURE 3-3
Effect of Premium Callable Bonds

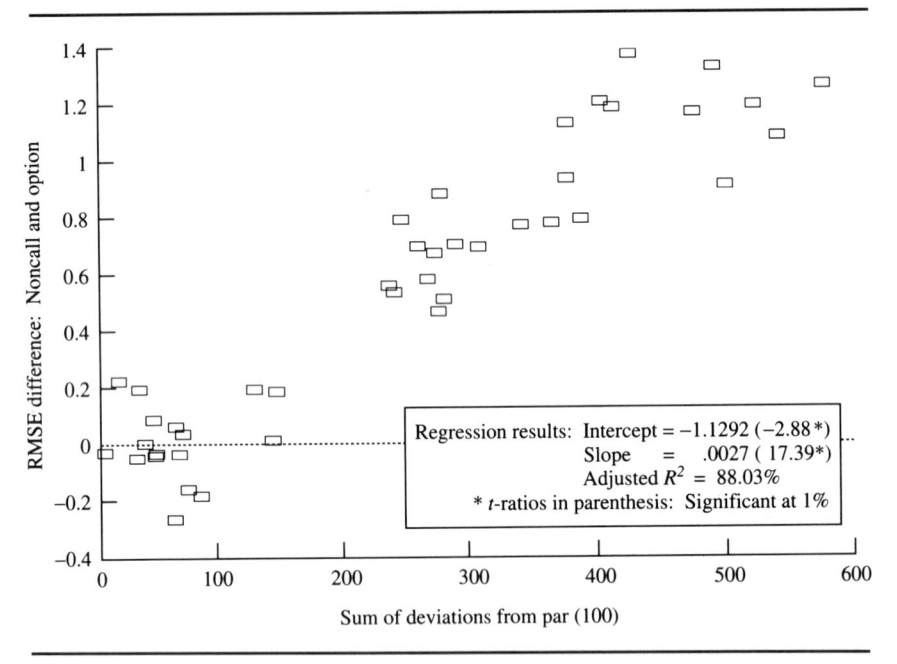

Regression results: Intercept = −1.1292 (−2.88*)
Slope = .0027 (17.39*)
Adjusted R^2 = 88.03%
* t-ratios in parenthesis: Significant at 1%

Y-axis: RMSE difference: Noncall and option
X-axis: Sum of deviations from par (100)

axis denotes the RMSE difference between the two models. The sum of deviations of prices for the callable bonds selling at a premium from par (100) is taken as the explanatory variable with a positive relationship with the RMSE spread expected. The strong positive association between these variables is apparent, and a regression result (also reported in Figure 3-3) proves this causality. The degree of the premium at which the callable bonds are selling can explain as much as 88 percent of the variation in the noncall–option pricing spread. The sign of the slope coefficient is positive, as expected, and also statistically significant at the 1 percent level, indicating that the greater the number of callable bonds trading at a significant premium at the estimation time, the greater the estimation errors in the noncall approach, which ignores the call possibility.

The Diversity of the Call Provision

In the dummy variable approach, one can simply approximate the embedded option value; it assumes that all call option values are the same without any distinction between different provisions for the particular estimation time. An examination of the estimation errors for the callable bonds in the dummy variable approach indicates whether the call values should be evaluated individually and consideration given to the value of the bond options.

Panel A of Table 3-4 presents the RMSE difference between the two models, the dummy variable approach and the option pricing approach. Based on this evidence, it is easy to reject the null hypothesis that the call option values can be approximated without considering the calls' values. Furthermore, in Panel B of Table 3-4, it does *not* appear that the dummy variable approach signifi-

TABLE 3-4
Examination of Estimation Error (RMSE) in Dummy Variable Approach for January 1983-December 1989 (par = 100)

A. Comparison with Option Pricing Approach: RMSE Difference between Dummy and Option

Bond Type	Mean Difference	Standard Deviation of Difference	t-Statistic
Noncallable	.0462	.0537	5.51*
Callable	.6526	.8216	5.09*
Overall	.1914	.2220	5.52*

* Significant at 1 percent.

B. Comparison with Noncall Approach: RMSE Difference between Dummy and Noncall

Bond Type	Mean Difference	Standard Deviation of Difference	t-Statistic
Noncallable	-.0336	.1283	-1.68
Callable	.1229	.4295	1.83
Overall	.0174	.1554	.72

FIGURE 3-4
Effect of Call Provisions

Regression results: Intercept = − .3656 (−2.66*)
Slope = .1064 (8.84*)
Adjusted R^2 = 65.32%
* t-ratios in parenthesis: Significant at 1%

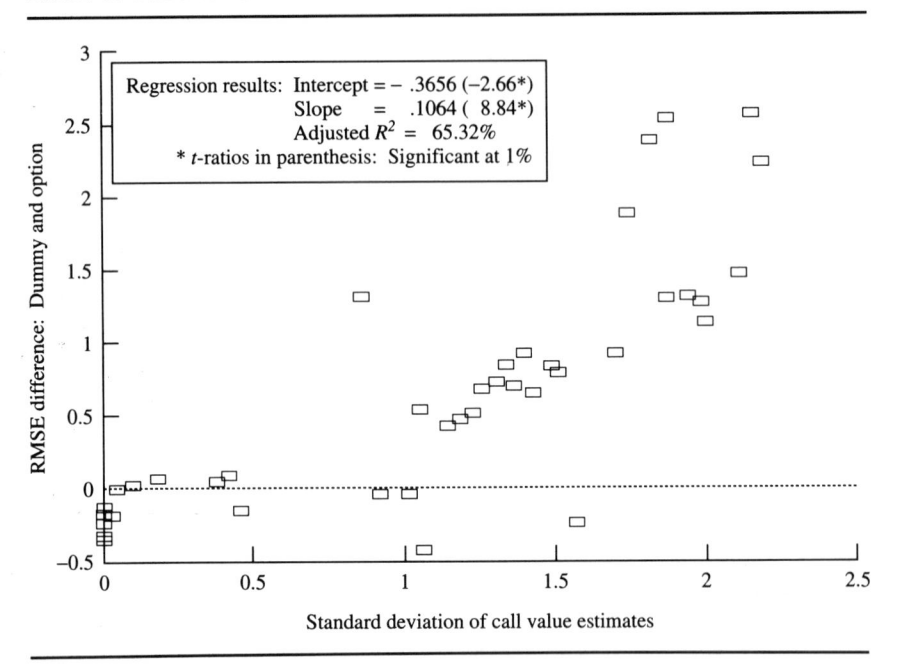

Y-axis: RMSE difference: Dummy and option
X-axis: Standard deviation of call value estimates

cantly improves the estimation procedure compared with the noncall approach. The call-adjusted estimation methodology, which indiscriminately prices each call feature in the estimation sample, results in almost the same discount function as the approach that ignores the call feature.

Figure 3-4 clearly illustrates that the embedded option should be evaluated individually. The abscissa of the scatter plot denotes the standard deviation of the call values *estimated* from our bond option pricing model in the option pricing approach. It can be concluded from Figure 3-4 that the inaccuracy of the dummy variable approach will grow larger as the call option provisions in the estimation sample become more dispersed.

Figure 3-5 presents a graphical comparison of the estimated spot rate curves under the alternative methods for the years of 1988 to 1989 every six months. In all the cases, as examined, the noncall and the dummy variable approaches produce very similar shapes,

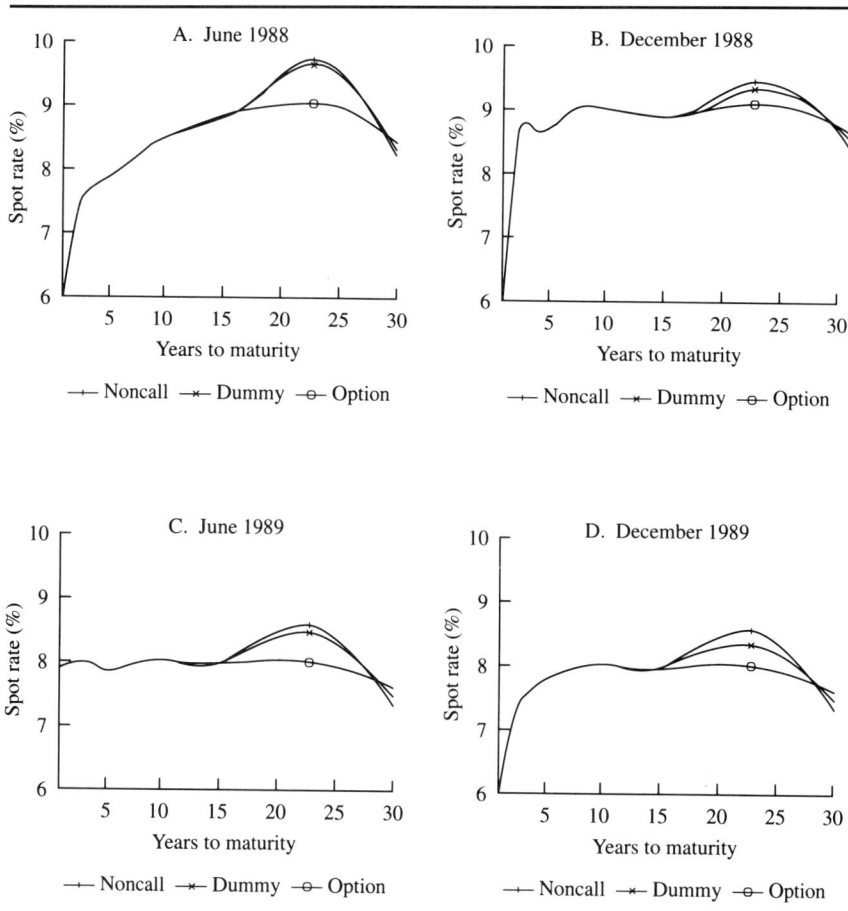

**FIGURE 3-5
Estimated Spot Rate Curves under the Alternative Methods**

A. June 1988

B. December 1988

C. June 1989

D. December 1989

—+— Noncall —*— Dummy —⊙— Option

while the option pricing approach produces quite different curves from the other two approaches. Specifically, the option pricing approach provides smoother and more stable curves for the maturity range (20 to 30 years) where a number of callable Treasuries are outstanding.[3]

It is interesting to compare our results with those derived from using the Black-Scholes model. Table 3–5 reports the summary statistics of the RMSEs for the option pricing approach with a

TABLE 3-5
Summary Statistics of Estimation Error (RMSE) for Option Pricing Approach Using Black-Scholes Model for January 1983–December 1989 (par = 100)

Bond Type	Minimum	Maximum	Mean	Standard Deviation	Quartiles 1st	2nd	3rd
Noncallable	.6081	2.5077	1.4809	.5943	.8830	1.3458	1.8464
Callable	1.2419	5.5942	3.2547	1.3771	1.9181	3.1332	4.5015
Overall	1.0915	2.9951	1.8744	.5743	1.2733	1.7788	2.2757

version of Black-Scholes applied to value the embedded call options. In comparison with the results provided in Table 3–2, the Black-Scholes model is significantly inferior to our model and does not outperform even the noncall and dummy variable approaches. As we have argued, an elaborate option pricing technique such as the Ho-Lee model should be employed for modeling the call-adjusted term structure. A simple approximation of the option value does not suffice to provide a useful estimation procedure.

Finally, to test the ability of the model to evaluate the embedded option value, one would like to compare the predicted difference between prices of a callable and a straight (but otherwise identical) bond with the actual difference between these two bonds. The results of regressing *actual* option values (as defined in

TABLE 3-6
Summary Statistics of Regression Results for January 1983–December 1989 (Alpha and Beta are the Coefficients from Regression of Actual Values on Predicted Values)

	Minimum	Maximum	Mean	Standard Deviation	Quartiles 1st	2nd	3rd
Alpha	−.89	1.64	.67	.76	−.04	1.05	1.24
Beta	1.49	7.85	2.48	1.34	1.74	2.07	2.25
Adjusted-R^2 (%)	53.91	97.29	88.63	8.87	84.04	92.26	93.70

the previous section) on predicted option values for each estimation date are presented in Table 3-6. Predicted option values were computed using the Ho-Lee bond option pricing model and model prices of the straight bonds were also computed using the same model. Every estimated slope coefficient is positive and statistically significant, but far from its theoretical value of unity. However, the model explains more than 80 percent of the variation in the option values for most estimation dates. These results indicate that our bond option pricing model provides a strong explanation of the variations in the option value of callable bonds.

SUMMARY AND CONCLUDING REMARKS

When estimating a yield curve empirically, the callable bonds must be incorporated into the sample. However, a callable bond has an embedded option, and, therefore, neither its maturity nor its cash flow stream is certain. As a result, this security cannot be treated as a portfolio of zero coupon bonds. In current research, this problem is typically simplified by treating the callable bond as a noncallable bond or introducing a dummy variable to account for the call effect. These approaches are seemingly acceptable because the callable Treasury bonds invariably have the same structure of calls five years prior to maturity at par. Moreover, the call option embedded in the callable Treasury bond does not expire for at least 10 years. One might argue that the present value of the option premium is small enough that some simple approximation (or even ignorance) of the option value would suffice for providing a useful estimation procedure of the discount function. Unfortunately, the errors in estimating the option values can generate significant errors in estimating the discount function. Even though separate pricing errors of the callable bonds seem negligible, the sum of the errors may *not* be insignificant. Furthermore, the callable bonds are an example of interest rate–contingent claims. Their embedded options and price behavior crucially depend not only on the current term structure, but also on its stochastic movements. To compensate for the problems posed by the outstanding callable Treasuries, one needs a *well-defined* bond option valuation model.

This chapter describes a call-adjusted term structure estimation methodology using an option pricing technique. By decomposing a callable security into its component parts—a noncallable bond and a call option on that bond—one can value the embedded options individually and simulate the price of a comparable noncallable bond correctly.

This procedure is consistent with two aspects of the Treasury market. First, it provides the discount function that best determines the prices of observed Treasury securities; and second, it obtains a discount function that explains callable Treasury prices.

APPENDIX: THEORETICAL AND ACTUAL SPOT RATE CURVES

In this appendix, we suggest some reasons why the theoretical spot rate curve differs (and maybe should differ) from the actual (stripped) yield curve, and describe the characteristics peculiar to the theoretical curve with references to the related literature. Especially, we also discuss the necessity of using the theoretical curve for professional traders to profit from the spreads between it and the actual yield curve.

I. *The theoretical spot rate curve that can be constructed from observed Treasury coupon bonds provides a natural basis for analyzing whether zeros are cheap or expensive relative to coupon Treasury bonds. Put another way,* hypothetical *spot obligations (defined as the hypothetical single payment claims bundled together in a coupon bond) provide an analytical bridge between bonds (from which they are derived) and zeros (which they resemble).*
   A. Since stripped Treasury securities are relatively new, there is some uncertainty as to how their yields should be compared to yields on coupon-bearing Treasuries. The proper comparison is not against coupon securities of equivalent maturity but against coupon securities of equivalent duration. For a coupon bond, the duration is less than the term to maturity; whereas for zero coupon securities, the duration is equal to term to maturity. An alternative, and better, device is constructing a zero coupon yield curve (a theoretical spot rate curve) implied by coupon Treasury securities so that yields on zeros can be compared to their coupon

Chapter 3 A Call-Adjusted Term Structure Estimation Methodology

Treasury security duration equivalents. For a detailed explanation, see Garbade (1984, 1–7).
B. Variations in zero yields away from the theoretical spot rate curve could *signal* trading or investment opportunities in the zeros or the equivalent coupons (Kochan and Mooney 1987, 303).
C. If we may assume that the theoretical spot rate curve is a reasonable proxy for the Treasury zero yield curve, we may address the question of how Treasury zeros should be valued in different interest rate environments. This should allow a portfolio manager to assess quickly the approximate yield level for zero coupon securities by estimating the theoretical spot rate curve (Klaffky 1987, 151).
D. It still makes sense to express the cheapness or dearness of zeros compared to bonds as a function of their spreads against spot yields, because the latter best reflects the value placed on single-payment Treasury obligations in the coupon market (Garbade 1984, 7).

II. *There are some reasons why the actual Treasury zero yield curve should differ from the theoretical spot rate curve.* In practice, actual bond yields have been remarkably close to what the theory suggests, given the many factors affecting both the Treasury bond and Treasury zero markets, and given the dramatic changes that occurred in the level of interest rates. Indeed, if one had been able to predict accurately the changes that have taken place in the Treasury yield curve since the introduction of Treasury zeros, one would be able to explain many of the changes that have occurred in the Treasury zero market. Nevertheless, the list below suggests some reasons why the yields of Treasury zeros differ (and perhaps should differ) from theoretical spot rates.
A. With coupon stripping, it is not possible to create long-maturity Treasury zeros without also creating short- and intermediate-maturity Treasury zeros. The activity in coupon stripping has repeatedly supplied more short- and intermediate-maturity Treasury zeros than investors have demanded, and this excess supply has led to an increase in the spread between these Treasury zeros and the corresponding theoretical spot rates.
B. Since zero coupon bonds are more volatile than Treasury bonds of equal maturity, short-term investors will generally attempt to purchase Treasury zeros when they expect interest rates to fall. Likewise, investors will generally sell volatile securities when they expect interest rates to rise. Reflecting this investor preference, Treasury zeros will tend to move less (in yield) than the

general market. In other words, when interest rates drop significantly (and investors begin to believe that there is more probability that rates will go up than down), the yield spread between Treasury zeros and theoretical spot rates will tend to increase. The yield spread change of 1986 is most probably the result of adverse investor expectations (Klaffky 1987, 174–76).

III. *Since 1989, the yields on stripped Treasury securities at quarterly intervals for terms out to 30 years have been published in* The Wall Street Journal *on a daily basis. The simplicity and apparent precision of measuring the term structure with these stripped security yields is attractive. However, the observed yields on zeros may be somewhat misleading.*

   A. The major potential problem is taxation. Stripped securities are treated as original-issue discount securities for tax purposes, and, thus, taxes must be paid on interest accrued under the constant or scientific yield method. If strips were held only by tax-exempt investors, then their yields would be true before-tax spot rates. However, this is not so if strips are not held exclusively by tax-exempt investors and the valuations of such investors affect stripped bond prices. A taxed investor would have to make intermediate tax payments on the accrued discount and these tax payments are like negative coupon receipts. In valuing these stripped bonds, the taxed investor would discount each cash flow to obtain the present value of the security and might apply different spot rates to each flow. The observed yields on the strips would then be yields for instruments with intermediate cash flows (McEnally & Jordan 1991, 1287).

   B. The yield curve that one observes consists of rates that have not been explicitly adjusted for taxes. The after-tax rate for a taxed investor is not simply the observed rate times 1 minus the tax rate (McEnally & Jordan 1991, 1287).

   C. The liquidity of the stripped Treasury market is not as great as that of the Treasury coupon market. Thus, the observed yields on stripped Treasury securities reflect a premium for liquidity (in the sense of marketability) (Fabozzi & Fabozzi 1991, 192).

IV. *It is the process of coupon stripping and rebundling that prevents the actual spot rate curve observed on zero coupon Treasuries from departing significantly from the theoretical spot rate curve. The stripping and rebundling are part of the arbitrage operations.*

   A. The regression approach that we employ for the estimation of the theoretical spot rates is implicitly based on a no-arbitrage condition in which a short position is the symmetric inverse image of a

long position. This assumption may be unreasonable in some conditions. To a certain degree, our approach always calculates an equilibrium, that is, break-even spot rate for each maturity, and arrives at a theoretical spot rate curve (Prisman 1990, 127–29).
B. If there is a disparity between zeros and coupons, arbitragers will enter the strips market and strip or rebundle. However, the observed stripping and rebundling do not always result in equilibrium spot rates. Only when there are active participants on both sides of this arbitrage will the Treasury zero yield curve resemble the theoretical spot rate curve more precisely. Moreover, if the market is always in equilibrium, there is no advantage to strip or rebundle and (with the exception of some incentives such as immunization) no bonds will be stripped or rebundled. Yet there was no stripping before July 1982 (the beginning year for stripping), and, thus, the immunizer's demand for long zeros cannot by itself explain stripping, although the immunization might add to the incentives to strip bonds under the post–July 1982 tax law. It was the 1982 tax law change that created an opportunity for financial institutions to profit from stripping Treasury securities (Klaffky 187, 175–76; Livingston & Gregory 1989, 3, 56).

V. Summary of Appendix
A. Our theoretical spot rate curve estimated from coupon-bearing bonds provides a benchmark for stripping and rebundling processes by comparing the theoretical curve to the actual stripped yield curve observed from the strips.
B. Since the strips are basically the derivative securities from the coupons, there is a certain degree of difference in the two markets.
C. The observed yields on strips cannot be simply adjusted for the taxation problem, because strips are treated as original-issue discount securities for tax purposes.
D. The yields on strips, actual spot rates, will be driven toward the theoretical (equilibrium) rates by stripping and rebundling, and, thus, it is natural that one make every effort to directly estimate the theoretical rates.

NOTES

1. Since 1989, prices and yields on Treasury strips at quarterly intervals for terms out to 30 years have been published in *The Wall Street Journal* on a daily basis. Therefore, the observed yield on stripped

Treasuries can justifiably be used to construct a spot rate curve. However, the object of our study is a theoretical spot curve, not the observable spot rate curve from the stripped Treasuries. The theoretical spot curve is not determined directly by the marketplace, but derived from the price structure of coupon-bearing bonds. The theoretical spot rate curve from the Treasury coupon bonds provides a natural benchmark for analyzing whether strips are cheap or expensive relative to bonds. In other words, *hypothetical* spot obligations, defined as the hypothetical single payment claims bundled together in a coupon bond, provide an analytical bridge between bonds (from which they are derived) and strips (which they resemble). Moreover, stripping and rebundling are part of the arbitrage operations based on the difference between the observed and theoretical spot rate curve. For detailed arguments, see the appendix to this chapter.
2. As a methodology for estimating the discount curve, McCulloch (1971, 1975) has proposed a polynomial spline approximation. Vasicek and Fong (1982) have recommended exponential splines as an alternative to polynomial splines. In a comparison of the two spline methodologies, Shea (1985) finds that estimation with exponential splines is no more convenient than estimation with polynomial splines and gives substantially identical estimates of the interest rate term structure as well, essentially because *polynomial splines are used after a change of variables*. Therefore, we use an ordinary spline technique, Litzenberger and Rolfo's (1984) cubic spline model, to approximate the present value function.
3. As for the spot and forward rate curves, a careful examination reveals that, in addition to the points of time presented in Figure 3–5 (though not shown here), our model also provides smoother and more stable curves than those provided by other models for most points of our sample period, 1983 to 1989.

REFERENCES

Barrett, W. Brian. "Term Structure Modeling for Pension Liability Discounting." *Financial Analysts Journal*, November/December 1988, pp. 63–67.

Black, Fischer, and Myron Scholes. "The Pricing of Options and Corporate Liabilities." *Journal of Political Economy*, May 1973, pp. 637–54.

Brennan, Michael J., and Eduardo S. Schwartz. "A Continuous Time Approach to the Pricing of Bonds." *Journal of Banking and Finance*, July 1979, pp. 135–55.

Fabozzi, F. J., and T. D. Fabozzi. "Treasury and Stripped Treasury Securities." In *The Handbook of Fixed Income Securities*. ed. F. J. Fabozzi and I. M. Pollack (Chicago: Probus Publishing, 1991).

Garbade, K. D. "Comparing Yields on Zeros to Yields on Treasury Bonds." In *Topics in Money and Securities Markets* (Bankers Trust Company, March 1984).

Ho, Thomas S. Y., and Sang-bin Lee. "Term Structure Movements and Pricing Interest Rate Contingent Claims." *Journal of Finance*, December 1986, pp. 1011–29.

———. "The Pricing of Corporate Bond Provisions under Interest Rate Risks." *Research in Finance*. ed. Andrew H. Chen (Greenwich, Conn.: JAI Press, 1988).

Klaffky, T. E. "Analysis of Treasury Zero-coupon Bonds." In *Advances in Bond Analysis and Portfolio Strategies*. ed. F. J. Fabozzi and T. D. Garlicki (Chicago: Probus Publishing, 1987).

Kochan, J. L., and M. Mooney. "Analysis of and Portfolio Strategies with Zero-coupon Treasuries." In *The Handbook of Treasury Securities: Trading and Portfolio Strategies*. ed. F. J. Fabozzi (Chicago: Probus Publishing, 1987).

Litzenberger, Robert H., and Jacques Rolfo. "An International Study of Tax Effects on Government Bonds." *Journal of Finance*, March 1984, pp. 1–22.

Livingston, M., and D. W. Gregory. "The Stripping of U.S. Treasury Securities." *Monograph Series in Finance and Economics* (New York University, 1989).

McCulloh, J. Huston. "Measuring the Term Structure of Interest Rates." *Journal of Business*, January 1971, pp. 19–31.

———. "The Tax-Adjusted Yield Curve." *Journal of Finance*, June 1975, pp. 811–30.

McEnally, R. W., and J. V. Jordan. "The Term Structure of Interest Rates." In *The Handbook of Fixed Income Securities*. ed. F. J. Fabozzi and I. M. Pollack (Chicago: Probus Publishing, 1991).

Prisman, E. Z. "A Unified Approach to Term Structure Estimation: A Methodology for Estimating the Term Structure in a Market with Frictions." *Journal of Financial and Quantitative Analysis*, March 1990, pp. 127–42.

Shea, Gary S. "Pitfalls in Smoothing Interest Rate Term Structure Data: Equilibrium Models and Spline Approximations." *Journal of Financial and Quantitative Analysis*, September 1984, pp. 253–69.

―――――. "Interest Rate Term Structure Estimation with Exponential Splines: A Note." *Journal of Finance*, March 1985, pp. 319–25.

Vasicek, Oldrich A., and H. Gifford Fong. "Term Structure Model Using Exponential Splines." *Journal of Finance*, May 1982, pp. 339–48.

CHAPTER 4

WHY HEDGE?

Mehraj Mattoo, Ph.D.
Associate Director, NatWest Capital Markets, London

INTRODUCTION

The 1950s and 1960s witnessed steadily accelerating worldwide inflation—slow at first but increasing rapidly from the mid-1960s. By the early 1970s, rising inflation assumed a high priority for the governments of the main industrialized countries. Since most of the governments found it difficult to curb spending, the main burden of inflation fighting fell on monetary policy. Governments aimed at controlling the quantity of money supply to fight inflation and worried less about its price—the interest rate. Interest rates, as a result, became extremely volatile. Figure 4-1 provides dramatic evidence of unprecedented volatility in interest rates since the early 1970s.

IMPACT OF INTEREST RATE CHANGES ON ASSET VALUES

Determinants of Asset Values

The price of a bond is equal to the present value of its future cash flows. For a coupon bond the price is given by[1]

$$P = \frac{C_1}{(1+Y)^1} + \frac{C_2}{(1+Y)^2} + \cdots + \frac{C_T + F}{(1+Y)^T}$$

FIGURE 4-1
Monthly Changes in 10-Year USD Yields

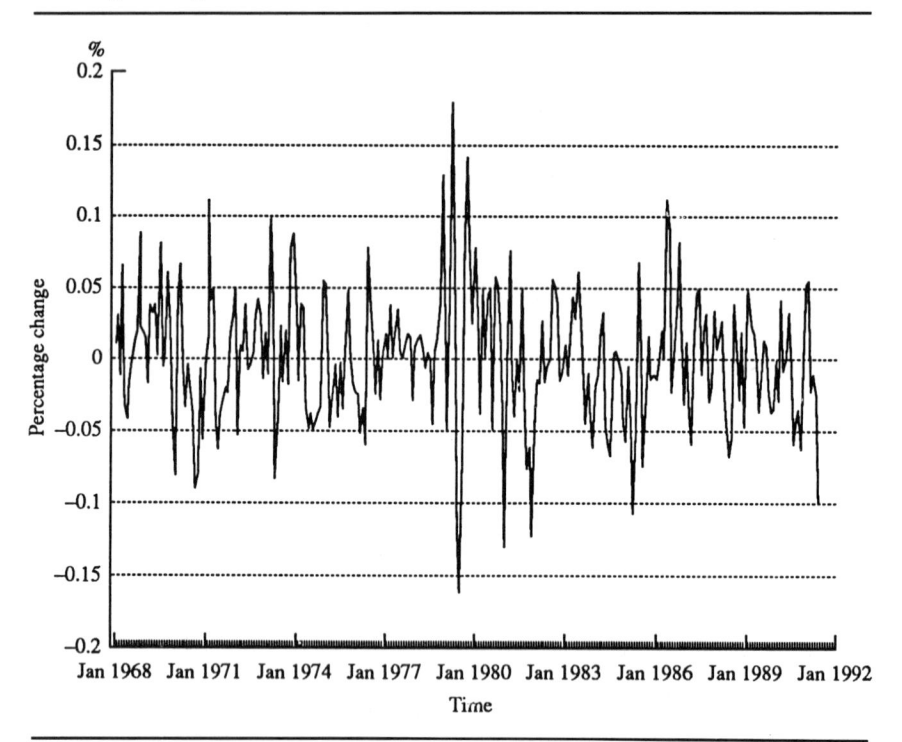

or

$$P = \sum_{t=1}^{T} \frac{C_t}{(1 + Y)^t} + \frac{F}{(1 + Y)^T} \qquad (4-1)$$

where

P = Price

C_t = Coupon at time t, $t = 1, 2, \cdots T$

Y = T-year yield to maturity

F = Face value of the bond

T = Time to maturity

From Equation (4-1) we observe that the price of a bond depends on four factors: coupon rate, face value, yield to maturity, and time to maturity. Of these four factors, the first two do not vary over the term of the bond. The latter two are, however, variables and cause changes in the value of a bond.

Interest Rate Sensitivity of Asset Values

Interest rates are the principal determinant of bond prices. When interest rates change, bond prices change too. However, some bond prices change more than others. The magnitude of the effect of a change in interest rates on a given bond price will depend on several attributes of the bond. In general, however, an increase in the level of yields will result in a fall in the price of a bond. A fall in the level of yields will, on the other hand, result in an increase in the price of a bond. This general price-yield relationship is obvious from Equation (4–1). Table 4–1 summarizes the effect of changes in the yield on a 10-year bond paying a 10 percent coupon.

This price-yield relationship is depicted in Figure 4–2. It is clear that the price of a bond is inversely related to its yield. Figure 4–2 is in fact the sensitivity chart for a bond. Thus, an investor who has a long position in a bond will gain from falling yields, while someone who has sold the bond short will gain from rising yields. The precise magnitude of a change in the price of a bond as a result of a given change in the yield to maturity will depend on its maturity and coupon rate.[2] Yield to maturity of a bond is, in itself, a complex average of forward interest rates implied by the prevailing yield curve or the term structure of interest rates.[3]

TABLE 4–1
Price-Yield Relationship

Rising Yields	Price	Falling Yields	Price
10.0%	100	10.0%	100
10.5%	96.99261	9.5%	103.1393
11.0%	94.11076	9.0%	106.4176
11.5%	91.34834	8.5%	109.8420
12.0%	88.69955	8.0%	113.4201
12.5%	86.15892	7.5%	117.1602
13.0%	83.72126	7.0%	121.0707
13.5%	81.38168	6.5%	125.1609
14.0%	79.13553	6.0%	129.4403

**FIGURE 4–2
Price-Yield Relationship**

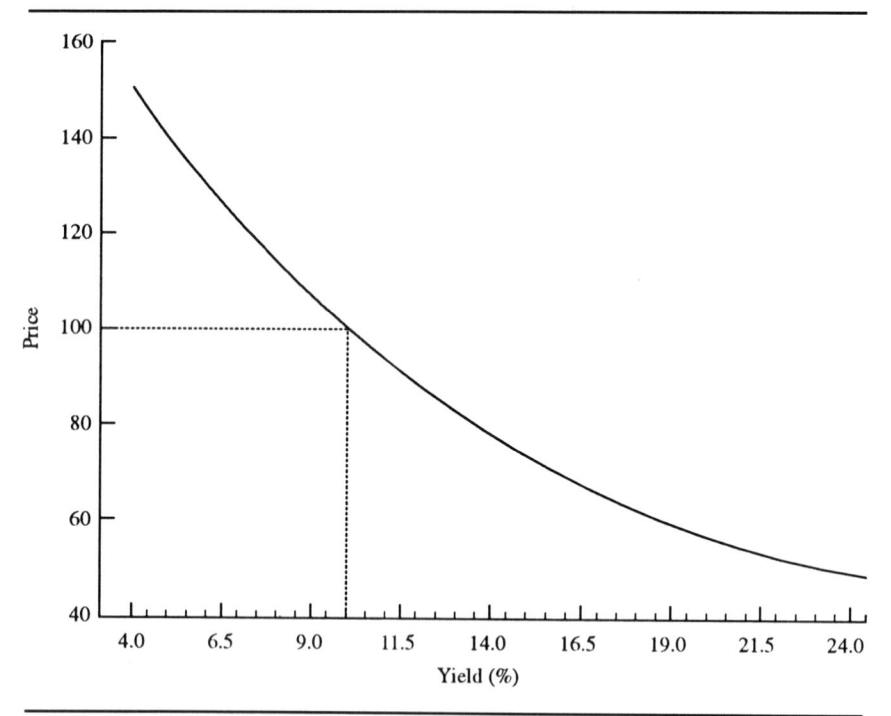

Coupon Effect

The coupon rate of a bond has a significant impact on the value of a bond. The effect of a given change in interest rates on the price of a bond depends on its coupon rate relative to its yield at the time of issuance. Thus, a bond that is issued with a coupon rate equal to the market yield will sell at par (par bond); a bond that is issued with a coupon rate that is higher than the market yield will sell at a premium (premium bond); and a bond that is issued with a coupon rate that is less than the market yield will sell at a discount (discount bond). In the extreme case, the latter category of bonds may carry no coupon (zero coupon bond). To assess the impact of changes in interest rates on these four types of bonds, consider the following example:

Example 1

	Type	Coupon	Maturity	Face Value
Bond 1	Premium	15%	10 years	100
Bond 2	Par	10%	10 years	100
Bond 3	Discount	5%	10 years	100
Bond 4	Zero	0%	10 years	100

Table 4–2 summarizes the effect of changes in the yield on the prices of these four bonds.

Figure 4–3 depicts the price-yield relationship for premium, par, discount, and zero coupon bonds. Panel A illustrates the price-yield relationship for a premium bond, and the curve is relatively flat. Panel B shows the same relationship for a par bond, and, in this case, the curve is relatively steeper than the premium bond's curve. Panel C depicts the price-yield relationship for a

TABLE 4–2
Price-Yield Relationship—Coupon Effect

	Price			
Yield	Bond 1	Bond 2	Bond 3	Bond 4
3.0%	202.3624	159.7114	117.0604	74.4093
4.0%	189.2198	148.6653	108.1108	67.5564
5.0%	177.2173	138.6086	100	61.3913
6.0%	166.2407	129.4403	92.63991	55.8391
7.0%	156.1886	121.0707	85.95283	50.8349
8.0%	146.9705	113.4201	79.86975	46.3193
9.0%	138.5059	106.4176	74.32936	42.2410
10.0%	130.7228	100	69.27716	38.5543
11.0%	123.5569	94.11076	64.66460	35.2184
12.0%	116.9506	88.69955	60.44843	32.1973
13.0%	110.8524	83.72126	56.59005	29.4588
14.0%	105.2161	79.13553	53.05495	26.9743
15.0%	100	74.90615	49.81231	24.7184
16.0%	95.16677	71.00063	46.83449	22.6683
17.0%	90.68279	67.38977	44.09675	20.8037
18.0%	86.51774	64.04730	41.57687	19.1064
19.0%	82.64426	60.94958	39.25491	17.5602
20.0%	79.03763	58.07527	37.11291	16.1505

FIGURE 4-3
Price-Yield Relationship—Coupon Effect

A. Premium bond

B. Par bond

C. Discount bond

D. Zero coupon bond

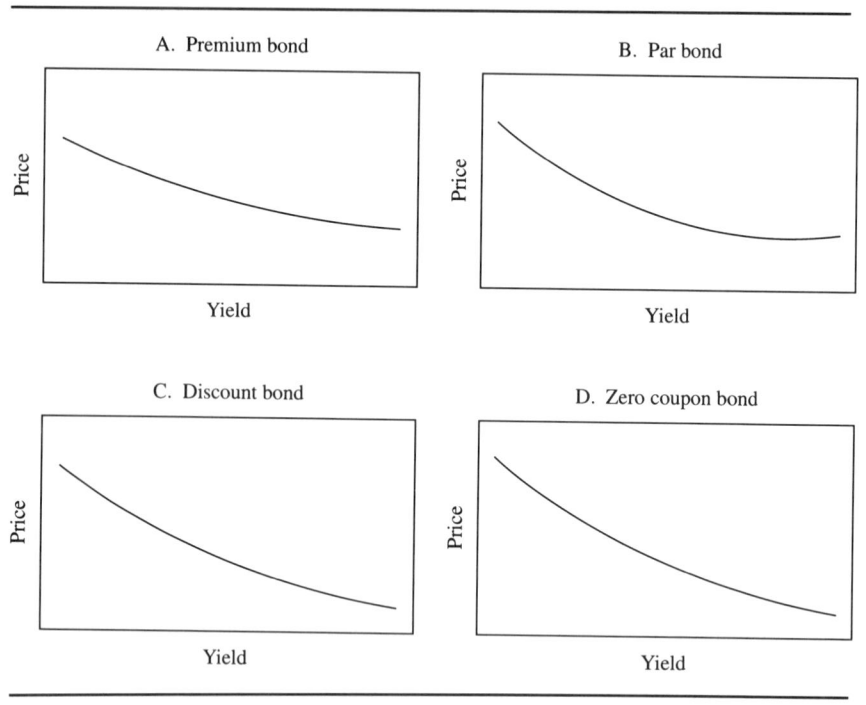

discount or low coupon bond. The curve in this case is steeper than that for a par bond. Panel D illustrates that the curve is steepest in the case of a zero coupon bond. Thus, for a given change in interest rates, the price change will be highest for a zero coupon bond followed by discount, par, and premium bonds. We can conclude, therefore, that zero coupon bonds have the highest interest rate sensitivity, whereas premium bonds are the least interest rate–sensitive bonds. Zero coupon bonds are, in other words, the most risky bonds.

Maturity Effect

It is well known that, all else being equal, for a given change in interest rates the price of a long-term bond changes more than the price of a short-term bond. To demonstrate this, consider two bonds each paying a coupon of 10 percent. The first bond has 10

TABLE 4–3
Price-Yield Relationship—Maturity Effect

Yield	2-Year Bond	10-Year Bond
4.0%	111.3165	148.6653
5.0%	109.2970	138.6086
6.0%	107.3335	129.4403
7.0%	105.4240	121.0707
8.0%	103.5665	113.4201
9.0%	101.7591	106.4176
10.0%	100	100
11.0%	98.28747	94.11076
12.0%	96.61989	88.69955
13.0%	94.99569	83.72126
14.0%	93.41335	79.13553
15.0%	91.87145	74.90615
16.0%	90.36860	71.00063
17.0%	88.90349	67.38977
18.0%	87.47486	64.04730
19.0%	86.08149	60.94958
20.0%	84.72222	58.07527

years to run while the second bond has only 2 years to run. Table 4–3 summarizes the effect of changes in the interest rates on the prices of these two bonds.[4]

The price-yield relationship for short- and long-term bonds is shown in Figure 4–4. Panel A depicts the interest rate sensitivity

FIGURE 4–4
Price-Yield Relationship—Maturity Effect

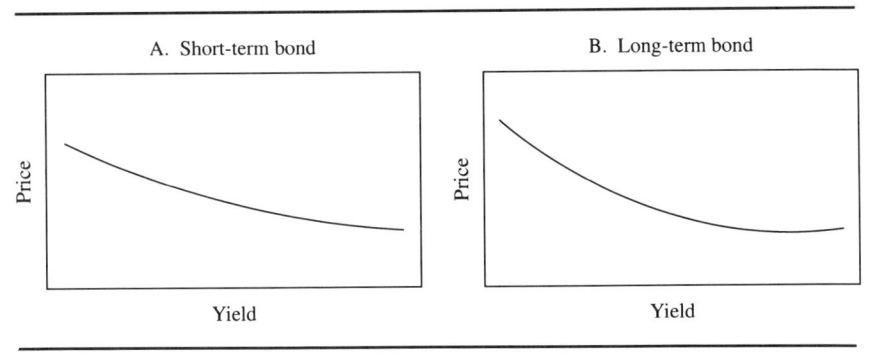

for a 2-year bond, whereas Panel B depicts the sensitivity for a 10-year bond. We observe that the rate of change for a long-term bond is higher than the rate of change for a short-term bond. We conclude, therefore, that long-term bonds carry greater interest rate risk than short-term bonds.

WHY HEDGE?

Figure 4–2 provides the basis for hedging a financial asset against changes in interest rates. It shows that the value of an asset changes as interest rates change. The magnitude of the change in the price of an asset, *ceteris paribus*, depends on the magnitude of the change in interest rates. If we consider the price-yield relationship for an asset as depicted in Figure 4–2 in conjunction with the historical changes in interest rates as depicted in Figure 4–1, the need to hedge against changes in interest rates is clearly demonstrated.

To show the effect of historical interest rate volatility on coupon-bearing bonds, consider the following bond:

Issue Date: August 1978
Maturity Date: August 1988
Issue Price: $100
Coupon: 8%

Figure 4–5 shows the changes in the market price of the above bond from value date to its maturity. It is obvious that given the level of interest rate volatility experienced over this period the price of the bond changed dramatically.

The motivation to hedge against unexpected changes in interest rates can, in general, arise for two distinct reasons: (1) The desire by investors in fixed-income securities to guarantee holding period returns; and (2) the need for portfolio managers to create dedicated bond portfolios to fulfill specific liabilities over time.

Coupon bonds or series of cash flows are characterized by complex holding period returns. For example, an investor wishing to invest for a period of five years in a coupon-bearing bond yielding 10 percent cannot be sure of the return over the entire holding period as changes in interest rates result in changes in reinvestment

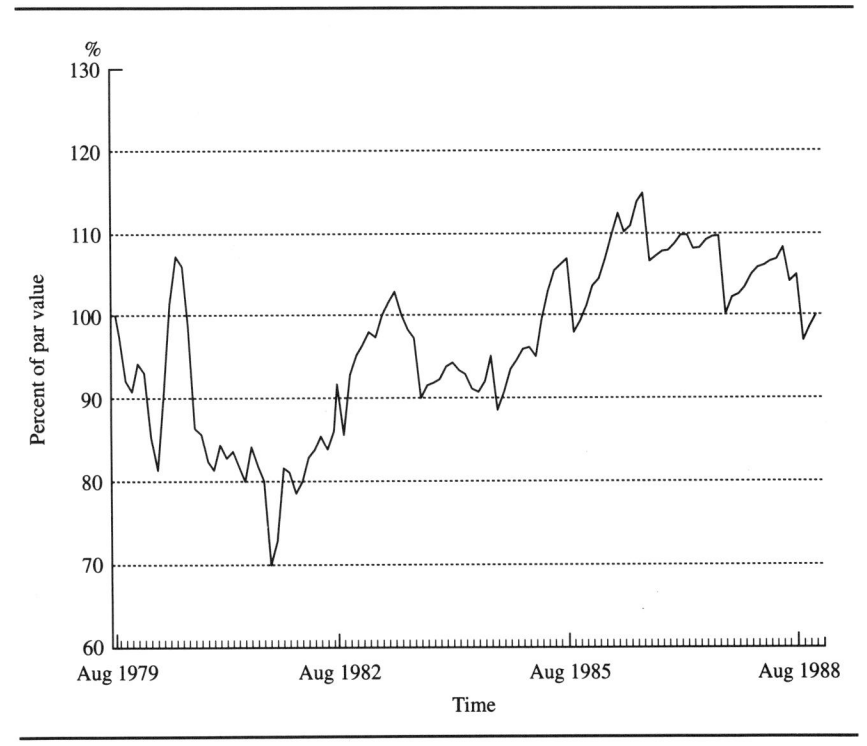

FIGURE 4–5
Historical Price Volatility of a 10-Year USD Bond

rates. The solution to the holding period return problem is to invest in a zero coupon bond. Figure 4–6 depicts the cash flow profiles of five-year zero coupon and coupon-bearing bonds. If the zero coupon bond is held to maturity, the investment return is hedged against all changes in interest rates over the investment horizon. Since there are no cash flows before maturity, a zero coupon bond is not subject to reinvestment risk. In other words, the promised yield, in this case, equals the realized yield.

Under a coupon-bearing bond, each coupon received is subject to reinvestment risk for the residual life of the bond. The realized yield, in this case, may not equal the promised yield. Since zero coupon bonds are still in relative short supply, investors have to use coupon bonds frequently. However, as will be shown in the

FIGURE 4–6
Zero Coupon versus Coupon Bond—Cash Flows

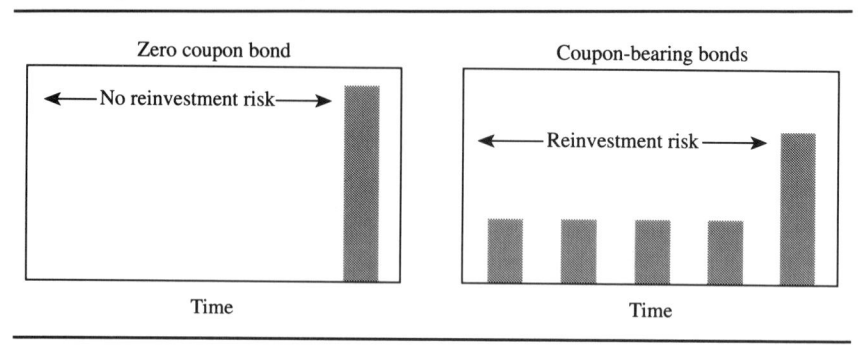

next section, investors wishing to hedge their holding period returns can use coupon bonds to mimic zero coupon bonds using techniques based on asset sensitivities.

The second motivation to hedge against unexpected changes in interest rates arises from bond portfolio managers' (and indeed banks' and thrifts') desire to create dedicated asset and liability portfolios. For pension funds and insurance companies, this requirement amounts to maintaining their solvency over time. Consider an insurance company with a known stream of nominal liabilities. The problem is to fund these liabilities such that they can be met regardless of subsequent interest rate changes. An obvious way to solve this problem is to purchase assets whose cash flows exactly match those of liabilities. This approach to cash flow dedication is very inflexible and is not always achievable. Even when cash flow dedication is possible, the cost of achieving it may be prohibitive. As shown in the next section, as in the case of a holding period return problem, the solution to this problem also depends on the sensitivity of asset and liability present values.

MEASURES OF INTEREST RATE SENSITIVITY

Whether it is the problem of hedging the holding period return of a bond or a dedication of assets and liability portfolios, interest rate sensitivity of asset and liability present values (or their market prices) plays a key role in the solution. To amplify this point, let us consider a liability with the price-yield relationship depicted in Panel A of Figure 4–7. Suppose we wish to hedge this liability with an asset such that the net position is equal to zero. Panels B, C, and D show the price-yield relationship for three different assets. At current interest rates, the market value of the asset is exactly equal to the market value of the liability. Therefore, the position holder is solvent in all the three cases, but only if yields do not change.

To show the effect of changes in interest rates, consider the asset shown in Panel B. At lower yields, the value of the asset is higher than the value of the liability. Therefore, the position holder would be solvent if interest rates were to fall over time. However, the position holder would be insolvent if interest rates were to rise, since the value of the liability would be greater than that of the asset. Panel C shows the case where the reverse holds true. Panel

FIGURE 4–7
Interest Rate Sensitivity of Assets and Liabilities

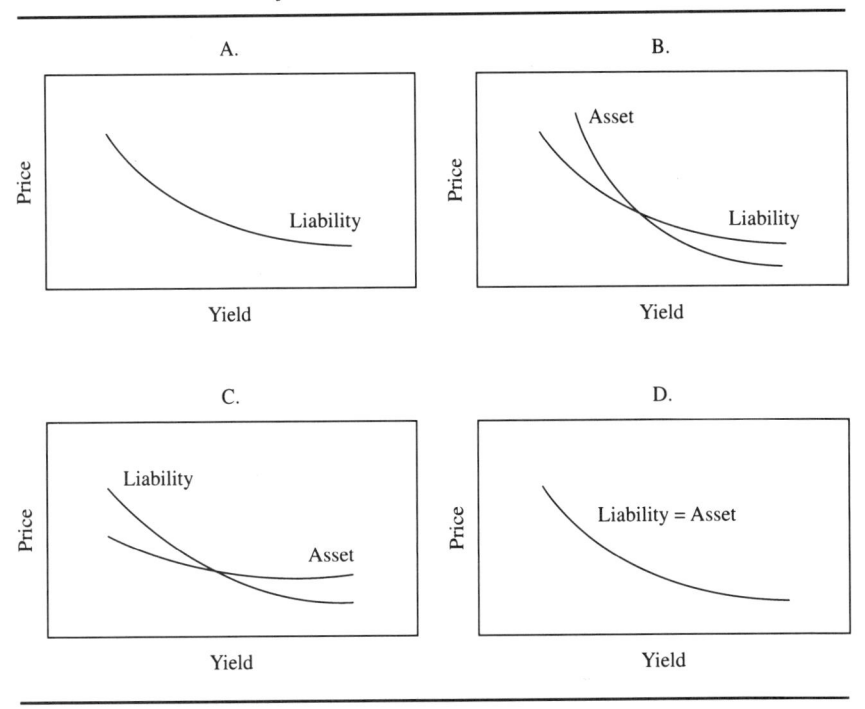

D depicts the case where the position holder will be solvent with respect to all changes in yields.

Figure 4–7 identifies the relevant parameter for hedging. It is the slope of the price-yield curve, in other words, the sensitivity of the price of an asset or a liability to changes in interest rates. For an asset with a coupon rate C and a maturity T, the slope is given by:

$$\Delta P = \frac{1}{1+Y} \left[\frac{f_1(C_1) + f_2(C_2)2 + \cdots + f_T(C_T + F)T}{P} \right] \quad (4-2)$$

where

f = Present value function for cash flow i, $i = 1, 2, \ldots T$
C = Coupon
F = Face value
Y = Yield to maturity
P = Market price of the bond

Equation (4–2) measures the percentage change in the price of the bond given a 1 percent change in the yield to maturity. The discerning reader would recognize that the term in the square brackets is the Macaulay duration. It is, however, not a coincidence, since Macaulay also was looking for a measure that could be used to "immunize" asset and liability portfolios.

Duration as a Measure of Interest Rate Sensitivity

Macaulay[5] defines the duration of a bond as:

$$D = \frac{1}{P} \left[\sum_{t=1}^{T} C_t t(1 + r_t)^{-t} \right] \quad (4-3)$$

where P is the price of a bond with maturity T, C_t is the cash flow at time t, and r_t is the t-period spot rate. Having rejected the idea that long rates are averages of expected future spot rates, he then went on to derive an alternative measure of duration using yield to maturity (Y) as a proxy for spot rates:

$$D = \frac{1}{P} \left[\sum_{t=1}^{T} C_t t(1 + Y)^{-t} \right] \quad (4-4)$$

For discrete period compounding, duration can be shown to be the elasticity of P with respect to Y. It can be interpreted as the weighted-average term to maturity of a stream of cash flows with the weights being the fraction of total value represented by each cash flow.

Most of the earlier applications used this simple measure of duration. However, the measure of duration given by equation (4–3) has the useful aggregation property that the duration of a portfolio of bonds is the weighted average of durations of individual bonds in the portfolio. Fisher and Weil[6], in their comprehensive study of immunization as an asset management strategy, championed the use of this measure of duration. The role of duration as a measure of price volatility or basis risk was first proposed by Hicks[7] and has been rediscovered by many researchers since. Formally, if we let P denote the price of a bond, then from Equation (4–4)

$$\frac{dP}{P} = -D \frac{dY}{1 + Y} \qquad (4\text{–}5)$$

Equation (4–5) implies that, for a given change in yields, the percentage change in a bond's price is proportional to its duration. This representation seems to justify the widespread practice in the bond market of using duration as a measure of volatility. Notice the similarity between Equation (4–5) and Equation (4–2). Equation (4–2) is the equation for modified duration.

From Equation (4–3) we can deduce an important property of duration. That is, for a zero coupon bond, all of the C_ts are zero except for the redemption amount; hence, the duration of a zero coupon bond must equal its maturity. Also, from Equation (4–5), it is clear that the higher the duration, the higher the price volatility of a bond. Thus, it is not surprising to note that zero coupon bonds are more volatile than coupon bonds of similar maturity.

Shortcomings of Duration as a Measure of Interest Rate Sensitivity

The usefulness of duration as a measure of interest rate risk is limited by three flaws. First, duration can be shown to provide a linear approximation to the true price-yield relationship of a bond (the problem of convexity). Second, durations of different bond portfolios can drift apart as time passes (the problem of duration drift). Third, the stochastic or probabilistic nature of future changes in interest rates renders duration models ineffective as they are usually based on a particular stochastic model of future changes in interest rates (the stochastic process risk).

Convexity. From Equation (4–1) for the price of a bond, it is clear that the price is not a linear function of yields. This can also be seen from Figure 4–2, which depicts the price-yield relationship for a bond. Now, Equation (4–5) is a model of changes in the price of a bond as a result of changes in yields. This model, based on the duration of the bond, approximates price changes as a linear function of yields.

Consider, for example, a five-year bond paying a 10 percent coupon annually. If the current yield (Y) is 10 percent, the price of this bond should be 100 and its modified duration will be 3.79 years. Equation (4–5) indicates that the value of this bond will change by 3.79 percent for a 1 percent change in yield. Thus, for a 1 percent fall and a 1 percent rise in yields, the new price of the bond should be 103.79 and 96.20, respectively. In fact, the actual price of the bond, should the yields fall by 1 percent, will be 103.89, and it will be 96.30 should the yields rise by 1 percent. The model, therefore, results in an error of 0.10 and 0.09 in the two cases, respectively.

Figure 4–8 depicts graphically the reason for these price discrepancies. The true price-yield relationship in this graph is curved, that is, convex. The price-yield relationship given by Equation (4–5) is, however, a straight line. Notice that for a large change in yields the discrepancy between the actual price and the predicted price grows significantly. Thus, duration-based hedging models hold only for small changes in yields.

Convexity is good for investors because given a yield change, the price of the more convex bond will fall more slowly and rise more quickly. From the point of view of hedging, however, convexity in fixed-income securities presents a major problem. In general, convexity of bonds with lower coupons, lower yields, and a longer maturity will be higher. These variables are also associated with increasing modified duration, and, hence, volatility.

Figure 4–9 depicts the price behavior of duration-hedged port-

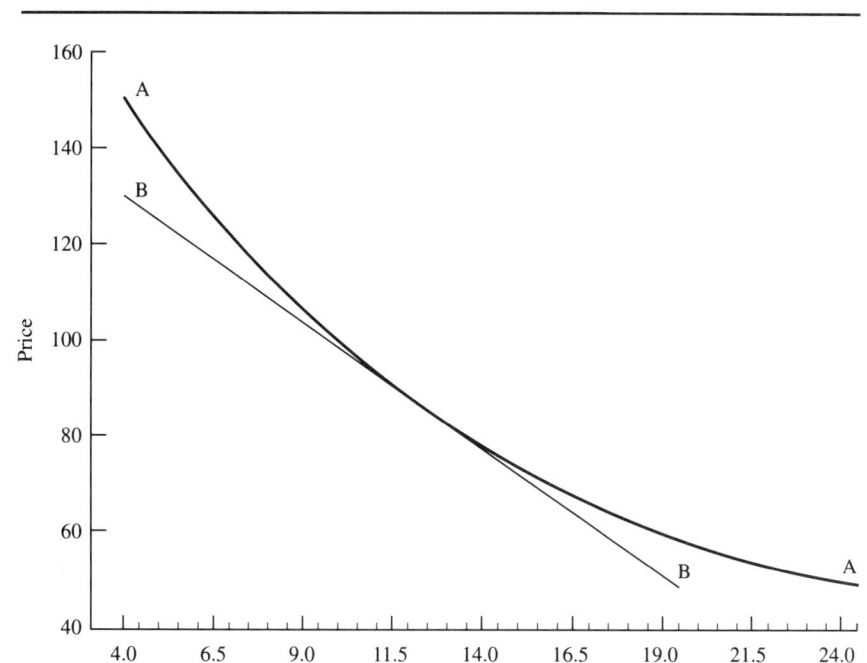

FIGURE 4-8
Duration Approximation of Price-Yield Relationship

folios with differing convexities. Notice that the duration-approximated price-yield relationship assumes that the rate of change in the price of a bond will be the same at all yield levels.

Duration Drift. A portfolio of assets and liabilities that is hedged using a duration-based model will not necessarily be hedged because the durations of coupon bonds do not age like zero coupon bonds. Thus, even if there were to be no change in interest rates, the two portfolios may diverge in value merely because of the passage of time. This phenomenon, referred to as *duration drift* is depicted in Figure 4-10.

Figure 4-10 shows that the duration of zero coupon bonds changes proportionate to their maturity. However, the duration of coupon-bearing bonds changes more slowly as the maturity of the

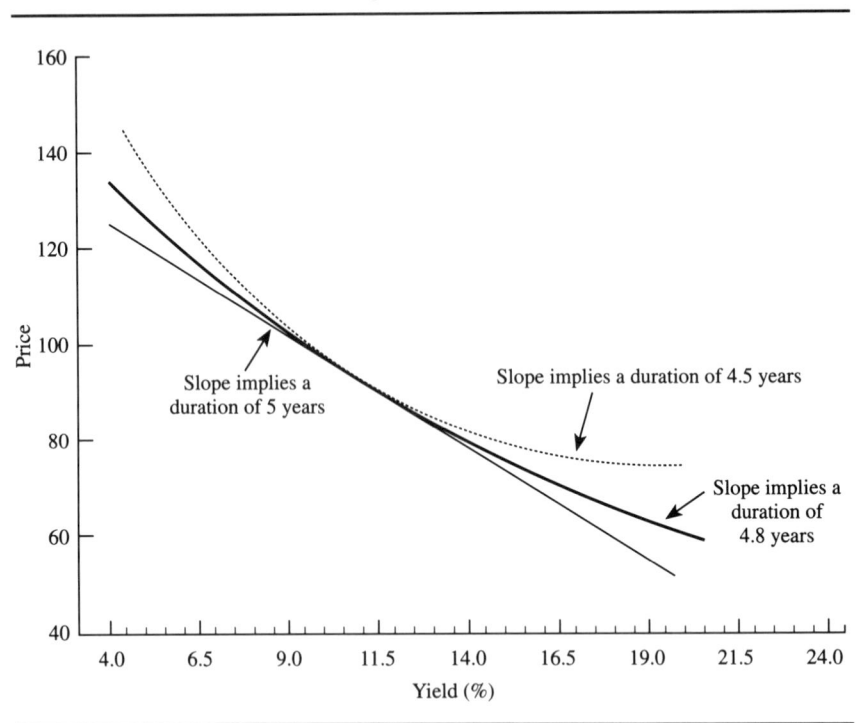

FIGURE 4–9
Price Behavior of Duration-Hedged Portfolios with Different Convexities

bonds shortens. Notice all coupon-bearing bonds have an upper limit to their durations as the maturity date becomes too distant. This limit is given by $\frac{(1+y)}{Y}$. The problem of duration drift requires that a hedged portfolio be rebalanced frequently.

Stochastic Process Risk. Macaulay duration is the simplest to compute and understand and, therefore, is the most popular and widely used measure of interest rate sensitivity. Its mathematical form, however, relies on two assumptions: (1) a flat yield curve and (2) changes in yields characterized by parallel shifts. Both these assumptions are empirically unrealistic. Efforts have, therefore, been made to refine the original measure of duration to incorporate more realistic assumptions about changes in interest rates. The

FIGURE 4–10
Duration Drift

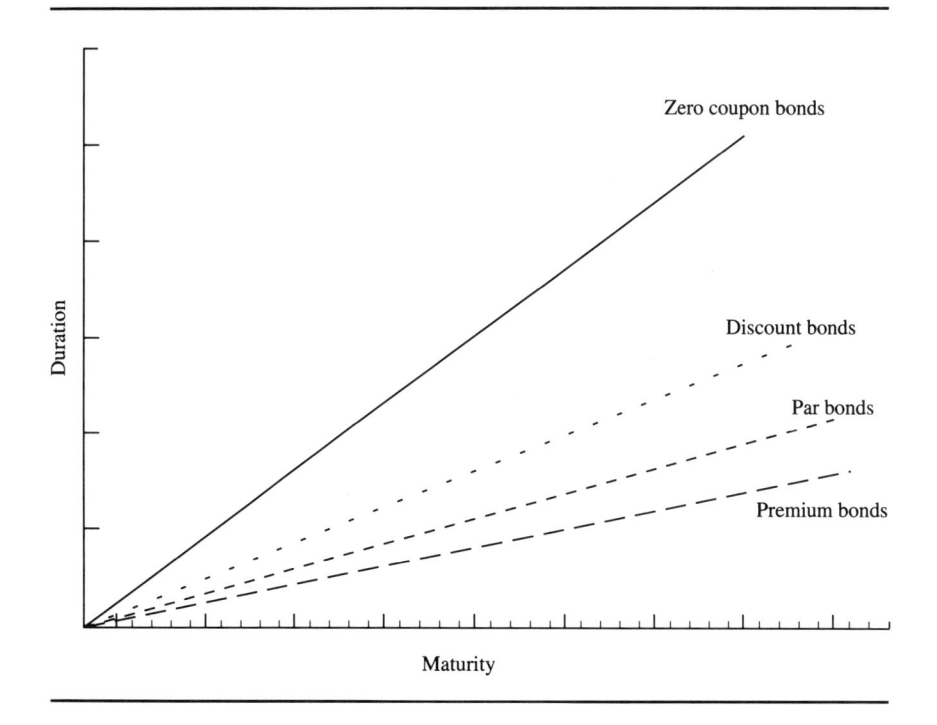

[Graph: Duration vs. Maturity showing four lines radiating from origin — Zero coupon bonds (steepest), Discount bonds, Par bonds, Premium bonds (shallowest)]

refined models assume that changes in the term structure of interest rates are governed by a particular stochastic process. However, to the extent that the actual stochastic process differs from the assumed process, errors in hedging can still arise even when using more sophisticated models. In fact, one recent study found that all stochastic duration measures are inferior to the simple measure of duration described above.[8] Figure 4–11 summarizes some of the alternative stochastic processes that have been proposed over the years.

Duration measures constructed on the assumption of a particular stochastic process will not provide effective hedging against interest rate risk arising from a different stochastic process. The success of a hedging strategy, therefore, depends on correctly identifying the stochastic process. Duration measures can then be constructed to correspond to the assumed process.

**FIGURE 4–11
Alternative Stochastic Processes**

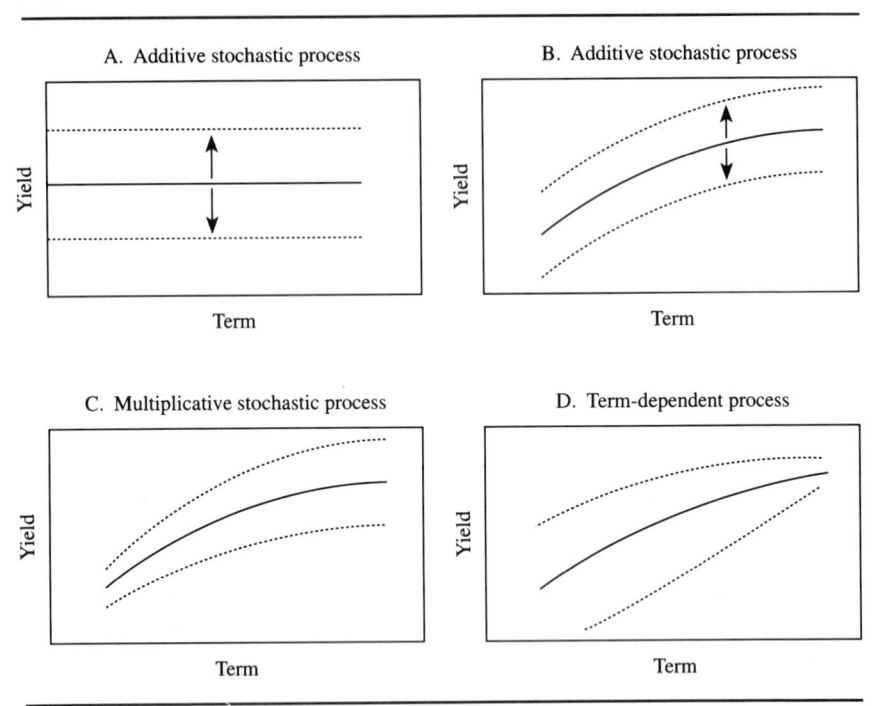

A. Additive stochastic process

B. Additive stochastic process

C. Multiplicative stochastic process

D. Term-dependent process

Concluding Remarks. All the problems arising from duration hedging have the same root cause—mismatched cash flows. The simple solution to these problems, therefore, is the same—minimization of the cash flow mismatch. Hedging strategies based on cash flow matching are generally not feasible. Even when it is possible to create a hedge on the basis of cash flow matching, the cost of doing so may be prohibitive. Optimization techniques from mathematical programming can, however, be used to achieve the desired trade-off between cash flow mismatch minimization and the cost of doing so. In general, it is possible to reduce the variability of price changes if the simple measure of duration is used in conjunction with a cash flow mismatch minimization model.[9]

Duration hedging provides a flexible way to hedge assets and liabilities. Rather than minimizing the mismatch in cash flows on each cash flow date, this approach positions the asset and liability cash flows to match on average. This averaging process results in errors arising from convexity, duration drift, and stochastic process risk. While it is possible to minimize the errors arising from convexity (see the appendix to this chapter), it is difficult to control duration drift (except by frequent rebalancing) and to control the stochastic process risk (except by identifying the true process governing changes in interest rates). This last issue has wider implications for pricing and hedging of financial securities and is dealt with in greater detail elsewhere in this book.

APPENDIX: A GENERALIZED DURATION APPROACH

Consider the following equation, described above as Equation (4–5):

$$\frac{dP}{P} = -D\frac{dY}{1+Y} \quad (4-6)$$

This price elasticity equation maps a straight line with duration as its slope. As shown earlier, the actual price-yield relationship is not linear but is curvilinear. Equation (4–6) is a good approximation of the percentage change in price given a small change in yields. As we have seen, the larger the change in yields, the greater the error arising from this approximation. One way of reducing this error is to expand the Taylor series for the percentage change in the bond price around the initial yield and add the higher-order terms. Thus:

$$\frac{dP}{P} = \frac{1}{P}\left(\frac{dp}{dR}\right)dY + \frac{1}{2!}\left(\frac{1}{P}\right)\frac{d^2P}{dR^2}dY^2 + \cdots + \frac{1}{t!}\left(\frac{1}{P}\right)\frac{d^tP}{dR^t}dY^t + \cdots$$

$$(4-7)$$

where

$R = 1 + Y$

Taking the derivative yields

$$\frac{dP}{P} = \frac{-\sum tC_t(1+Y)^{-t}}{P}\left[\frac{dY}{(1+Y)}\right]$$

$$+ \frac{\frac{1}{2}\sum t(t+1)C_t(1+Y)^{-t}}{P}\left[\frac{dY^2}{(1+Y)^2}\right] + \cdots$$

Substituting Macaulay duration yields

$$\frac{dP}{P} = -D\frac{dY}{1+Y} + \frac{1}{2}\left[D + \frac{\sum t^2(1+Y)^{-1}C_t}{P}\right]\frac{dY^2}{(1+Y)^2} + \cdots \quad (4-8)$$

Notice that duration is part of every term in Equation (4–8). However, with each subsequent term, it is combined with the progressively increasing information from higher-order terms. As the number of terms increases, the duration model provides a closer approximation of the actual price-yield relationship, therefore minimizing the errors associated with convexity.

NOTES

1. This formula is only correct if the bond is valued just after a coupon payment date or on the issue date. For valuation at any other time, the next coupon needs to be adjusted by the fraction of time remaining to its payment (i.e., accrued interest).
2. For the purposes of this chapter, we ignore the effect of credit quality, liquidity, and option features on the price of a bond.
3. For a discussion on the relationship between spot and forward rates, see Chapter 1.
4. To show the effect of interest rate changes on bond prices of differing maturities, we assume here that the yield curve is flat and changes are parallel in nature.
5. F. R. Macaulay, "Some Theoretical Problems Suggested by the Movements of Interest Rates, Bond Yields and Stock Prices in the U.S. since 1856" (New York: National Bureau of Economic Research, 1938).
6. Lawrence Fisher and Roman Weil, "Coping with the Risk of Interest Rate Fluctuations: Returns to Bondholders from Naive and Optimal Strategies," *Journal of Business* 44 (October 1971), pp. 408–31.
7. John R. Hicks, *Value and Capital* (Oxford: Clarendon Press, 1939).
8. N. Bulent Gultekin and Richard J. Rogalski, "Alternative Duration Specification and the Measurement of Basis Risk; Empirical Tests," *Journal of Business* 57, no. 2 (1984), pp. 241–64.
9. A goal programming approach is presented by M. Mattoo, "A Study of Interest Rate Swaps," Ph.D. dissertation, University of London, 1992.

REFERENCES

Bierwag, G. O. "Measures of Duration." *Economic Inquiry* 16 (October 1977), pp. 497–507.

———. "Immunization, Duration and the Term Structure of Interest Rates." *Journal of Financial and Quantitative Analysis* 12 (December 1977), pp. 725–42.

———. "Dynamic Portfolio Immunization Policies." *Journal of Banking and Finance* 3 (April 1979), pp. 23–41.

Bierwag, G. O., and Kaufman, G. "Bond Portfolio Strategy Simulations: A Critique." *Journal of Financial and Quantitative Analysis* 13 (September 1978), pp. 519–26.

Bierwag, G. O.; Kaufman, G.; Schweitzer, R.; and Toevs, A. "Risk and Return for Active and Passive Bond Portfolio Management: Theory and Evidence." *Journal of Portfolio Management* 8 (Spring 1981), pp. 27–36.

Bierwag, G. O.; Kaufman, G.; and Toevs, A. "Single Factor Duration Models in a General Equilibrium Framework." *Journal of Finance* 37 (May 1982), pp. 325–38.

Cooper, I. A. "Asset Values, Interest Rate Changes and Duration." *Journal of Financial and Quantitative Analysis* 12 (December 1977), pp. 701–24.

Cox, J. C.; Ingersoll, J. E.; and Ross, S. A. "A Theory of Term Structure of Interest Rates." Working paper, University of Chicago, 1978.

———. "Duration and the Measurement of Basis Risk." *Journal of Business* 52 (January 1979), pp. 51–62.

Fama, E., and MacBeth, J. "Risk, Return and Equilibrium: Empirical Tests." *Journal of Political Economy* (May/June 1973), pp. 607–36.

Fisher, L., and Weil, R. "Coping with the Risk of Interest Rate Fluctuations: Returns to Bondholders from Naive and Optimal Strategies." *Journal of Business* 44 (October 1971), pp. 408–31.

Hicks, J. R. *Value and Capital* (Oxford: Clarendon Press, 1939).

Hopewell, M., and Kaufman, G. "Bond Price Volatility and Term to Maturity: A Generalized Respecification." *American Economic Review* 63 (September 1973), pp. 749–53.

Ingersoll, J. "Is Immunization Feasible? Evidence from the CRSP Data." CRSP Working paper no. 58, University of Chicago, July 1981.

Ingersoll, J.; Skelton, J.; and Weil, R. "Duration Forty Years Later." *Journal of Financial and Quantitative Analysis* 13 (November 1978), pp. 627–50.

Khang, C. "Bond Immunization when Short-Term Rates Fluctuate More than Long-Term Rates." *Journal of Financial and Quantitative Analysis* 13 (November 1979), pp. 1085–90.

Lanstein, R., and Sharp, W. "Duration and Security Risk." *Journal of Financial and Quantitative Analysis* 13 (November 1978), pp. 653–68.

Leibowitz, M. "Bond Immunization: A Procedure for Realising Target Levels of Return" (New York: Salomon Brothers, October 10, 1979).

Leibowitz, M., and Weinberger, A. "Contingent Immunization: A Risk Control Procedure for Structured Active Management" (New York: Salomon Brothers, January 28, 1981).

Livingston, M., and Caks, J. "A 'Duration' Fallacy." *Journal of Finance* 32 (March 1977), pp. 185–87.

Macaulay, F. R. *Some Theoretical Problems Suggested by the Movements of Interest Rates, Bond Yields and Stock Prices in the U.S. since 1856* (New York: National Bureau of Economic Research, 1938).

Malkiel, B. "Expectations, Bond Prices and the Term Structure of Interest Rates." *Quarterly Journal of Economics*, no. 303 (May 1962), pp. 197–218.

Redington, F. M. "Review of the Principle of Life Office Valuations." *Journal of the Institute of Actuaries* 18 (1952), pp. 286–340.

Samuelson, P. A. "The Effects of Interest Rate Increases on the Banking System." *American Economic Review* 35 (March 1945), pp. 16–27.

Vasicek, O. "An Equilibrium Characterization of the Term Structure." *Journal of Financial Economics* 5 (November 1977), pp. 177–88.

Wallas, G. E. "Immunization." *Journal of the Institute of Actuaries* 15 (1960), pp. 345–57.

CHAPTER 5

HEDGING INTEREST RATE RISK: THE BASICS

John F. Marshall
St. John's University
Senior Partner with
Marshall & Associates

Mark R. Larson
Partner with Marshall & Associates

In this chapter, we are going to briefly explore the concept of interest rate risk, how this risk can be measured, how it can be managed, the instruments that are routinely used to manage interest rate risk, and various factors that a financial manager must consider in formulating a risk management program. Importantly, we cannot do much more in this one chapter than set the stage for the more focused and the more detailed discussions that follow in this book.

FINANCIAL RISK

A firm is exposed to many types of financial risk. In the final analysis, a perceived risk is real if and only if a manifestation of it has financial consequences for the firm. This in turn means that it makes the firm's profit (or other measure of performance) volatile.

Financial risks can be divided into *core business risks* and *strategic price risks*. The risks associated with such things as labor problems, changes in technology, and loss of key personnel are examples of core business risks. Changes in profit due to changes in input prices, output prices, and financial prices like interest rates and exchange rates are examples of strategic price risks. The focus of this chapter and, indeed, this book is on the management of strategic price risks and, more narrowly, on the management of one specific strategic price risk called interest rate risk.

Interest rate risk may be defined as the potential for unexpected change in the profits of the firm from an unexpected change in interest rates. Since a firm's market value is the discounted value of all of the firm's future profits, fluctuations in the firm's profits will be associated with volatility in the firm's market value (price of the stock).

A critical tenet of both financial theory and financial practice is that investors are risk averse. All other things being equal, the greater the risk, the lower the market value of the firm. It stands to reason then that risk management can add value for the firm's shareholders and this value will take the form of a higher market price for the firm's stock.

MANAGING RISK

There are three different, but related, ways to manage financial risks. The first is to purchase *insurance*. Insurance, however, is only viable for the management of certain types of financial risks. Such risks are said to be insurable. The second approach is *asset/liability management*. This involves the careful balancing of assets and liabilities so as to eliminate net value changes. (Asset/liability management is most often used in the management of interest rate risk and exchange rate risk.) The final approach, which can be used either by itself or in conjunction with one or both of the other two, is *hedging*. Hedging involves the taking of offsetting risk positions. Hedging is very similar to asset/liability management but, while asset/liability management, by definition, involves on–balance sheet positions, hedging usually involves off–balance sheet positions. This distinction between asset/liability management and hedging is important but often overlooked. In fact, many people consider asset/liability management strategies forms of hedging. For our purposes, it is worth maintaining the distinction.

Later, we will introduce some of the financial instruments used by risk managers to hedge price risks. The more important of these are swaps, futures, forwards, and options. Because hedging tools are often used to take up where asset/liability management leaves off, or as an alternative to asset/liability management, it is important to look at this activity as well. Insurance is of less importance to us, but we will say a few words about it in order to be clearer as to which risks are insurable and which are not. We will look at insurance, then asset/liability management, and, finally, hedging.

Insurance

An *insurable risk* is a risk to which many firms (or individuals) are exposed, for which manifestations of the risk are not highly correlated among those exposed, and for which the probability of a manifestation of the risk is known with a high degree of certainty. Insurable risks include such risks as death, loss from fire, loss from theft, liability, and medical expense. Consider the case of fire. Damage from fire results in financial loss, and the risk of fire is therefore a financial risk.

Insurance works because the insurer's risk, when spread across a large policy base, is a small fraction of the insured's risk. This is a natural consequence of diversification. The keys to the principle of insurance then are the independence of the individual exposures and the spreading of the risk across a large policy base.

Price risks are not insurable because individual manifestations of this risk are not independent of one another. Try to imagine, for example, an insurance company that sells "interest rate" policies that pay off for the policyholders if interest rates rise. If rates fall or do not rise, then the insurance company does not pay any policyholders. If rates do rise, then the insurance company pays every policyholder. In such a situation, insurance is meaningless because a serious manifestation of the risk would bankrupt the insurer, thereby rendering the insurance useless.

Asset/Liability Management

Asset/liability management is an effort to minimize exposure to price risk by holding the appropriate combination of assets and liabilities so as to meet the firm's objectives (such as achieving a stated earnings target) and simultaneously minimize the firm's risk.

The key to this form of risk management is holding the *right* combination of assets and liabilities.

Asset/liability management is most highly developed for managing interest rate risk. Indeed, few discussions of this approach to risk management are conducted in any other context. However, asset/liability management can be used and is often used in the management of exchange rate risk, commodity price risk, and stock price risk. Despite its applicability to other forms of price risk, we will limit our look at asset/liability management to the management of interest rate risk.

Asset/liability management strategies were first developed and implemented in the context of pension funds, so let's consider the subject in that context. Consider a pension fund that sells *guaranteed income contracts* or GICs. GICs guarantee a fixed stream of future income to their owners, that is, the policyholders, and constitute liabilities of the pension fund. The proceeds obtained from the sale of these policies are invested, by the fund, in financial assets that provide a return for the fund. Fluctuations in market interest rates, however, can and will cause the return on the firm's assets to deviate from the return promised to the fund's policyholders. For example, if rates decline, the fund might find itself investing future cash flows in assets that are yielding an insufficient return to meet the fund's obligations—as represented by the claims of the policyholders. An equivalent, but alternative, way to look at this problem is to consider the market value of the firm's assets and the market value of the firm's liabilities. While these values should initially be the same, they may not be equally sensitive to changes in interest rates. Thus, a fluctuation in rates may impact the value of the fund's assets more than the value of the fund's liabilities, or vice versa.

Ideally, asset/liability management should strive to match the timing and the amount of cash inflows from assets with the timing and the amount of the cash outflows on liabilities. An asset portfolio constructed to precisely match cash flows is called a *dedicated portfolio*. Unfortunately, it can be extremely difficult, if not impossible, to match cash flows precisely. Moreover, even when it can be done, it may be too expensive or may require the fund to pass up more attractive investment opportunities.

The solution is to forget about matching cash flows and to

concentrate instead on the value of the fund's assets and the value of the fund's liabilities and to make the value *difference* completely interest rate insensitive. The selection of assets so as to minimize the rate sensitivity of the difference between asset and liability values is called, in the context of asset/liability management, *portfolio immunization*. The concept of immunization and the strategy for implementing it were first developed by F. M. Redington in a paper published in 1952.[1]

Since the goal of immunization is to make the asset/liability value differential insensitive to interest rate fluctuations, the logical starting point for an immunization strategy is the measurement of interest rate sensitivity. We discuss several methods of measuring interest rate sensitivity shortly.

Hedging

Although closely related to asset/liability management and often used in conjunction with asset/liability management, hedging is a distinct activity. A *hedge* is a position that is taken as a *temporary substitute* for a later position in another asset (or liability) or to protect the value of an existing position in an asset (or liability) until the position can be liquidated. In keeping with accepted terminology, we will describe the position that the firm seeks to hedge, whether it be on the asset side of the balance sheet or on the liabilities side of the balance sheet, as the *cash position*.

Most hedging is done in derivative instruments. The instruments most often used for hedging are futures, forwards, options, and swaps. Futures, forwards, and swaps are off–balance sheet instruments. That is, they do not show up on either the assets side or on the liabilities side of the user's balance sheet. While most hedging is done in off–balance sheet instruments, it is important to note that a hedge can take the form of an on–balance sheet position. This is the case, for example, when swap dealers hedge their swap portfolios in Treasury bonds and bills. The key, in this case, is the *temporary* nature of the cash market hedge.

The easiest way to understand what hedging is all about is to visualize the activity graphically. We begin by constructing what are known as risk profiles. A risk profile depicts the firm's performance as a function of the price risk to which the firm is exposed.

FIGURE 5-1
A Firm's Risk Profile

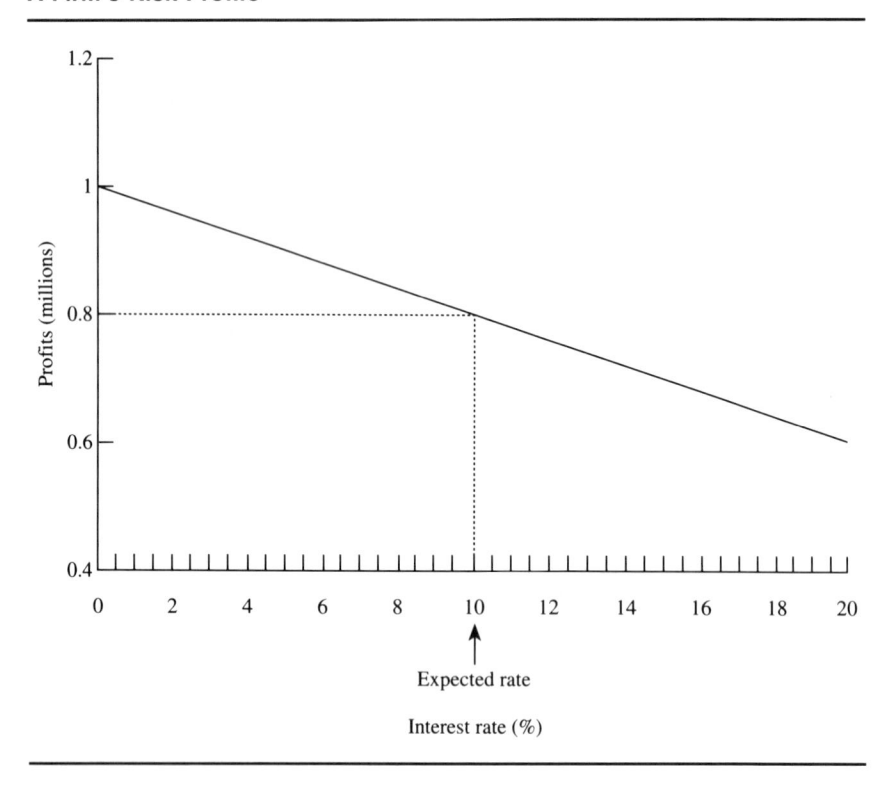

[Graph showing profits (millions) on y-axis from 0.4 to 1.2, and interest rate (%) on x-axis from 0 to 20. A downward-sloping line shows profits decreasing from about 1.0 at 0% interest rate to about 0.6 at 20% interest rate. An arrow at 10% indicates the "Expected rate," with dotted lines showing profits of 0.8 at that rate.]

The performance measure is most often the profit or loss that the firm will experience at various price levels. (In lieu of profit, we can use the firm's market value or share price as the measure of performance.) In our case, in which the relevant price is an interest rate, a risk profile will look like that in Figure 5-1.

In Figure 5-1, the expected value of the interest rate implies the profit level that the firm "expects" on its cash position, assuming no change in the firm's forecast. Of course, by definition, risk is a deviation from the expected. To hedge the risk depicted by the risk profile in Figure 5-1, we would take a position in another instrument that is interest rate sensitive, such as a futures contract. The position we take should have characteristics equal in magnitude to the existing price risk but simultaneously opposite in sign. We represent the outcomes of the hedge by what is called a *payoff*

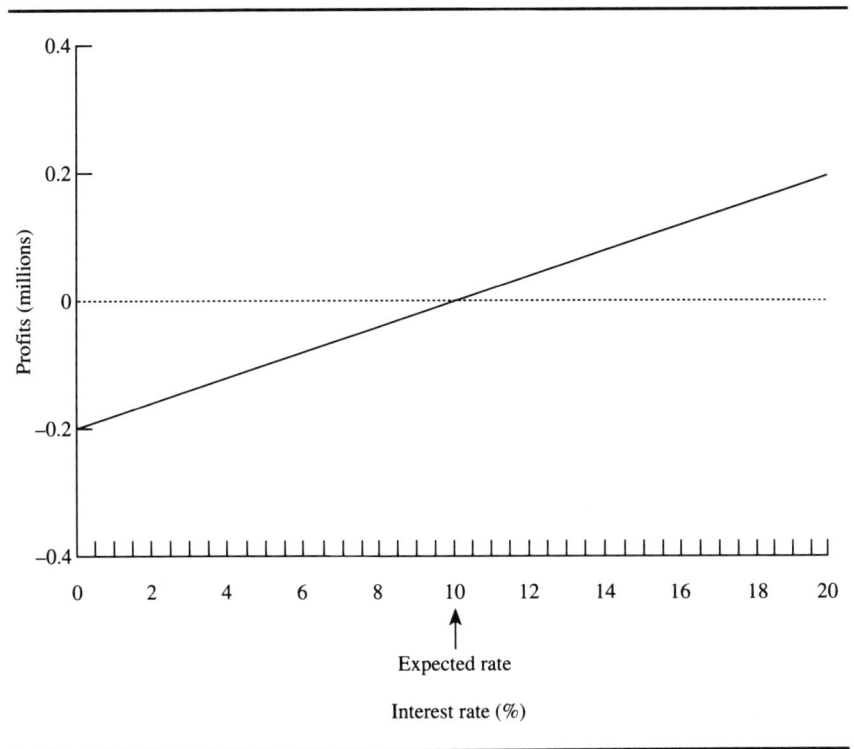

FIGURE 5-2
Hedge Payoff Profile for the Firm (futures hedge)

profile. A payoff profile for a costless hedge is depicted in Figure 5-2.

By combining the risk profile associated with the cash position in Figure 5-1 with the payoff profile of the hedge position in Figure 5-2, we can see how the hedge is intended to perform. This is depicted in Figure 5-3.

The rest of this chapter will concentrate on key considerations in the development of a hedge program. Note that, because asset/liability management and hedging share so much of their foundations and objectives, much of what is said in this chapter on hedging is equally applicable to asset/liability management. Before focusing on hedging, however, a few final comments on the source of interest rate risk are in order.

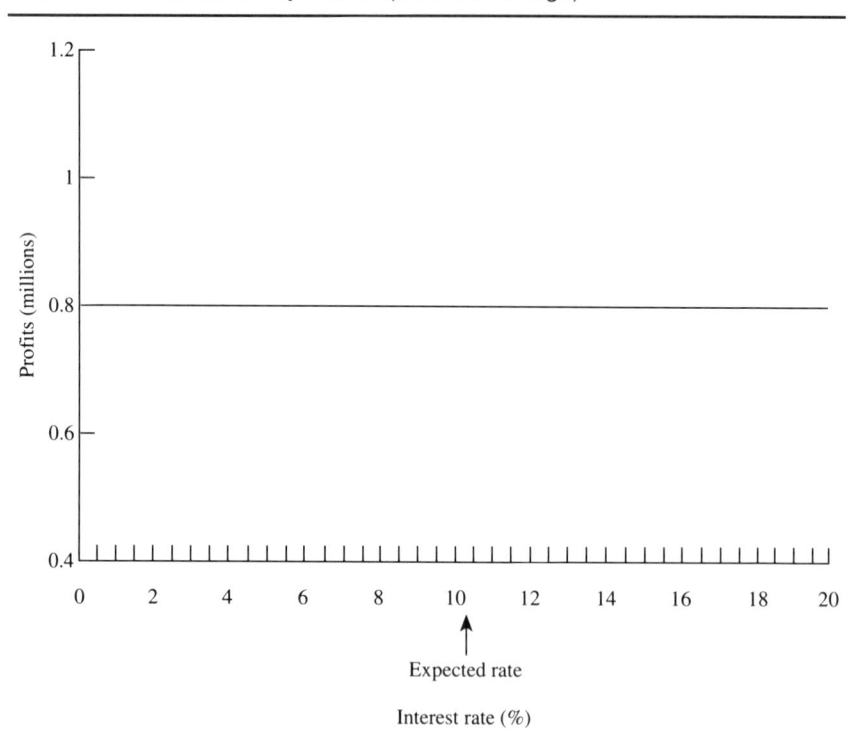

FIGURE 5-3
The Firm's Combined Exposures (cash and hedge)

[Graph: Profits (millions) vs Interest rate (%), horizontal line at 0.8, with arrow at 10 indicating "Expected rate"]

We have suggested that there is interest rate risk associated with assets and with liabilities that are interest rate sensitive in the sense that the market values will change as interest rate levels change. These balance sheet exposures represent transactions that have already been booked. There are at least two other sources of interest rate risk that we need to consider, and neither is identifiable from the balance sheet. These are anticipated transactions and sales revenue effects.

Anticipated transactions are transactions that are contemplated but have not yet been booked. Thus, they do not yet show up on the balance sheet. A decision, for example, to issue additional bonds to finance the firm would be an example of an anticipated transaction. There is typically a lag of several months between a decision to issue new debt and the actual offering to the public (due to a time-consuming SEC registration requirement). From the time the decision is made to issue the bonds to the time the bonds are offered to the public, interest rates can change considerably, and this can and will impact the cost of the issuance to the firm. Changes in the cost of the issuance have just as real an impact on the value of the firm as does a change in the value of a booked transaction.

Interest rate changes can also have an impact on sales revenue. For example, a rise in interest rates, all other things being equal, will generally result in a decline in automobile sales for an automobile manufacturer. A decline in sales revenue as a consequence of an increase in interest rates will, of course, mean less profit for the firm. Thus, the sales effect of interest rate fluctuations has a very real impact on the value of the firm. The upshot of these remarks is that when we are considering the hedging of interest rate risk, we need to consider the value changes of booked transactions, the value changes in anticipated transactions, and the sales consequences. All of these represent manifestations of interest rate risk.

HEDGING FOUNDATIONS

There are a number of critical factors that need to be considered in the design of a hedging program to manage interest rate risk. These are:

1. Translating market risk to firm-specific risk.
2. Quantifying interest rate risk.
3. Developing hedge ratios.
4. Measuring the effectiveness of a hedge.
5. Measuring the cost of a hedge.
6. Determining the hedge horizon.
7. Selecting the hedging instrument.

The remainder of this chapter will focus on these individual components of a hedging program.

Translating Market Risks to Firm-Specific Risks

Before delving directly into the measurement of interest rate risk, we need to recognize that, from the perspective of parties exposed to it, interest rate risk is a market risk. That is, the volatility of interest rates exists independently of whether or not any given firm is exposed to it. Since risk is defined as the potential for deviations from an expected outcome and an expected outcome is nothing more than the statistical "mean," it follows that the market value of this interest rate risk can be measured as variance of the interest rate or, alternatively, the square root of the variance, which is called the *standard deviation*. In Wall Street jargon, standard deviations are often called *volatilities*. In this chapter, we will use the accepted statistical terminology. Once we have such a measure, we can do such things as estimate confidence intervals and conduct hypothesis tests. We can also superimpose the risk profiles that we looked at in Figure 5–1 to translate the market risk to a firm-specific risk.

The approach just outlined requires that we make certain assumptions about the distribution of interest rates. The simplest assumption, but not likely an accurate one, is that future interest rates are normally distributed. There is overwhelming evidence that this is not the case, but we will make the assumption anyway just to illustrate the concepts and the steps involved.

Suppose that the firm's hedge horizon is one year and that the relevant interest rate currently stands at 10 percent. Suppose also that we have concluded that the current rate of 10 percent is also the best estimate of the rate one year forward. Thus, the relevant mean rate is 10 percent. Suppose now that the standard deviation of the relevant rate is 1 percent and that the one-year rate is approximately normally distributed.

Now, let's look at the familiar probability density function for a normal distribution having a mean of 10 percent and a standard deviation of 1 percent and let's simultaneously plot the 95 percent confidence interval. This is depicted in Figure 5–4. We can see that the lower bound for the confidence interval is 8.04 percent and the upper bound is 11.96 percent. Stated differently, if we could make this same forecast many times, each independent of the other, then, 95 percent of the time, we could expect that the market

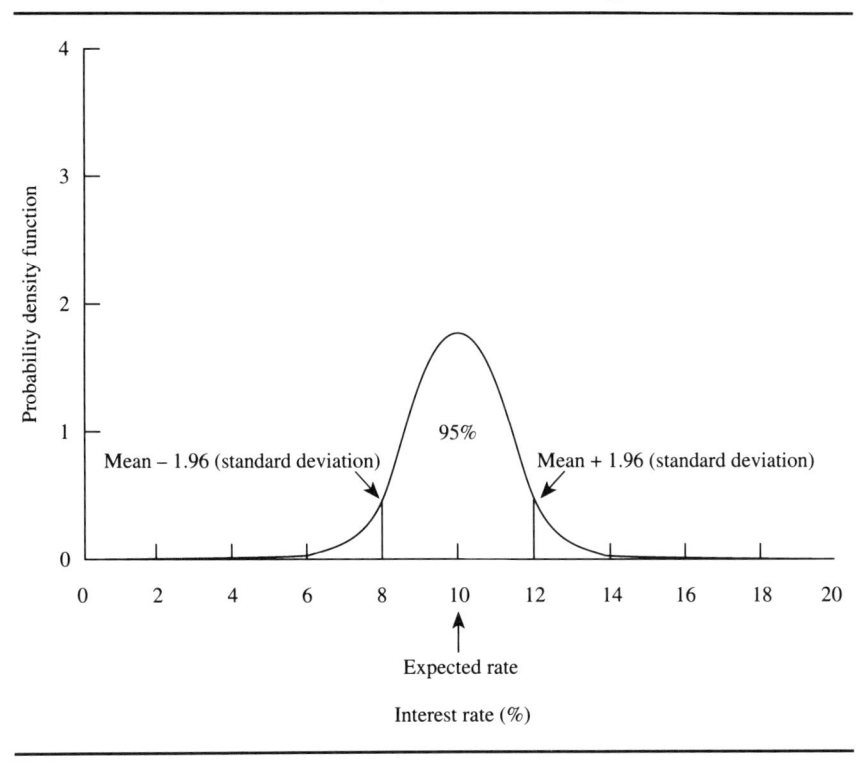

FIGURE 5–4
95 Percent Confidence Interval (interest rate volatility)

[Figure: Normal distribution curve centered at 10% (Expected rate) on the x-axis (Interest rate (%), 0 to 20), with y-axis Probability density function (0 to 4). 95% of area shaded between Mean − 1.96 (standard deviation) and Mean + 1.96 (standard deviation).]

interest will fall between 8.04 percent [i.e., 10% − (1.96)(1%)] and 11.96 percent [i.e., 10% + (1.96)(1%)].

Next, consider the risk profile in Figure 5–1. If we superimpose this risk profile on the probability density function, we can translate the market risk to a firm-specific risk. For example, we can see that the lower bound of the firm's profit is $0.7216 million and the upper bound is $0.8784 million at a 95 percent level of confidence. This is depicted in Figure 5–5.

One other observation is in order before proceeding. Notice that we have defined *risk* as *any deviation from the expected value.* Quite often, we wish to limit our definition of risk to negative deviations from the expected value. For example, in the case of the risk profile in Figure 5–5, we might want to protect ourselves from

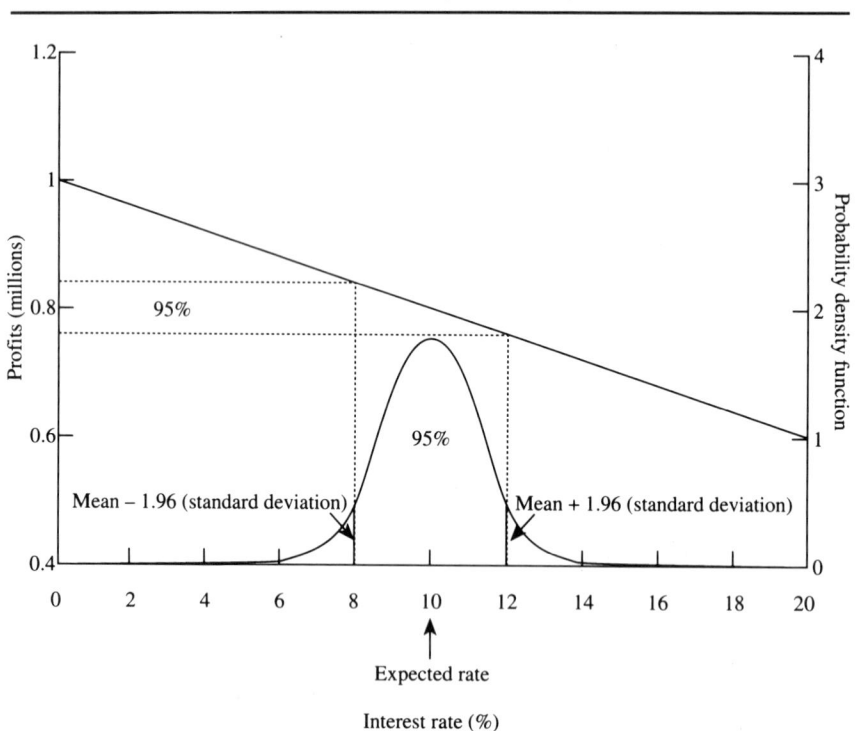

FIGURE 5-5
95 Percent Confidence Interval (firm-specific risk)

a rise in rates but preserve the opportunity to benefit from a decline in rates. When we wish to limit our definition of risk to negative deviations, we refer to the risk as *downside risk*.

Quantifying Interest Rate Risk

In order to manage interest rate risk, we must first be able to quantify it. A number of measures have been developed to accomplish this, but the most widely used are duration, the dollar value of a basis point, and the yield value of 1/32. We will briefly consider each of these measures. It will help to focus the discussion if we think in terms of the interest rate sensitivity of a debt instrument.

Duration and Convexity
It has been long known that maturity is a major determinant of the interest rate sensitivity of a debt instrument. This explains why yield curves were first constructed, and usually still are constructed, with respect to the term to maturity. However, it has also been long known that maturity is not the sole determinant of interest rate sensitivity. Other factors that contribute to interest rate sensitivity include the size of the coupon, the speed with which principal amortizes, the present yield, and the frequency of the coupon payments.

In 1938, Frederick Macaulay developed a measure of price sensitivity to yield changes that incorporates all the factors that influence price sensitivity.[2] This measure is known as *duration*. Assuming equal basis-point changes in yield (i.e., a parallel shift in the yield curve), two debt instruments that have identical durations will have identical interest rate sensitivities. Further, the ratio of two debt instruments' durations is an accurate measure of their relative price sensitivities to equivalent yield changes when such price sensitivity is stated on a percentage basis. Duration, which is measured in years and denoted here by *MD*, is often described as a *weighted-average time to maturity* of an instrument. The weights are the ratios of the present values of the future cash flows (including both interest and principal) to the current market price of the instrument. The current price of the instrument is, of course, the sum of the present value of all future cash flows associated with the instrument. One version of the duration formula is given by Equation (5–1).[3]

$$MD = \sum_{t}^{mT} w_t \times \frac{t}{m} \qquad (5\text{–}1)$$

where

$$w_t = \frac{C_t(1 + YTM/m)^{-t}}{\sum_{t} C_t(1 + YTM/m)^{-t}} \qquad t = 1, 2, 3, \ldots, mT$$

C_t = Cash flow during period t

YTM = Present yield to maturity on the instrument

m = The number of payment periods per year

T = The number of years covered by the cash flow stream

TABLE 5-1
Duration Calculation

t-Value	Cash Flow	Discounted Value of Cash Flow	Weight (w_t)	Time (t/m)	Product [$w_t \times (t/m)$]
1	$4.125	$ 3.961	0.0396	0.5	0.0198
2	4.125	3.805	0.0381	1.0	0.0381
3	4.125	3.654	0.0365	1.5	0.0548
4	104.125	88.580	0.8858	2.0	1.7716
Totals		$100.000	1.00000	MD =	1.8843

Let's consider the duration calculation for a simple bond. Consider a two-year bond having a coupon of 8.250 percent and an initial yield of 8.250 percent—so it is priced at par. The duration calculation for this semiannual bond, which reveals a duration of approximately 1.88 years, is shown in Table 5-1.

A different measure of interest rate risk, which is slightly more precise and which was published shortly after Macaulay's paper, was later shown to be closely related to duration and became known as modified duration. Modified duration, denoted here by *MMD*, is related to the Macaulay duration by Equation (5-2). All subsequent references to duration in this chapter are understood to mean modified duration.

$$MMD = \frac{MD}{(1 + y/m)} \quad (5\text{-}2)$$

Duration has a great many theoretical as well as practical applications. Consider one such application. Compare the duration of a 20-year conventional bond yielding 9.375 percent and carrying a semiannual coupon of 9.375 percent, so that it is also trading at par. The 20-year bond has a duration of 8.96 years. Now consider the duration of a 5-year bond yielding 8.75 percent and paying a semiannual coupon of 8.75 percent. The bond has a duration of 3.98 years. Notice that the 20-year bond has a duration that is approximately 2.25 times that of the 5-year bond. This means that the yield change necessary to cause a 1 percent decline in the market value of the 5-year bond will cause a 2.25 percent decline in the market value of the 20-year bond. Duration ratios, like the one we just used to compare the above two bonds, provide a measure of relative price sensitivities in terms of percentage changes in value. To convert these values to dollar terms, we must multiply the duration ratio by the ratio of the bonds' prices. Call this the *adjusted duration ratio (ADR)*. In the case of the example above, it is given by Equation (5–3).

$$ADR = \frac{MMD_{20\text{-yr}}}{MMD_{5\text{-yr}}} \times \frac{P_{20\text{-yr}}}{P_{5\text{-yr}}} \qquad (5\text{–}3)$$

Since both of these bonds were priced at par, the price ratio is 1.0. This will, of course, usually not be the case. Since it happens to be the case here, however, we can say that the yield change just sufficient to cause a $1 change in the value of the 5-year bond would cause a $2.25 change in the value of the 20-year bond. This suggests that durations can be used to obtain hedge ratios—a point to which we will return shortly.

A second important use of duration is in asset/liability management. As it happens, a portfolio duration is the weighted average of the individual components' durations. This implies that portfolio immunization can be accomplished by weighting the assets in the asset portfolio in such a fashion as to equate the asset portfolio duration with the liabilities portfolio duration. Indeed, this is the heart of all portfolio immunization strategies.

Let's consider a simple example and, as we say in the trade, run the numbers. Suppose that a pension fund sells a new policy that commits the fund to pay $100 each year for the next 15 years. The cash flows of the liability stream, together with their discounted values (using a 10 percent discount rate) and their contributions to duration (products), are depicted in Table 5–2. We see that the liability stream has a present value of $760.61 and a modified duration of 5.708.

The problem for the fund is how to invest the $760.61 proceeds from the sale of the policy to earn a return of at least 10 percent while assuring itself that the assets in which the fund invests will have a value at least equal to that of its liabilities at each and every point in time in the future. Suppose now that the fund has two instruments in which it can invest. The first is a 30-year Treasury bond paying a coupon of 12 percent and selling at par. The second is six-month T-bills yielding 8 percent (bond equivalent). The bond

TABLE 5-2
The Calculation of Modified Duration

Time	Cash Flow	Discounted Value of Cash Flow	Weight	Product
1	$100	$ 90.909	0.120	0.120
2	100	82.645	0.109	0.217
3	100	75.131	0.099	0.296
•	•	•	•	•
•	•	•	•	•
•	•	•	•	•
15	100	23.939	0.031	0.472
Total		$760.608	1.000	MD = 6.279
			MMD = 6.279 ÷ 1.1 =	5.708

has a modified duration of 8.080 years and the bill has a modified duration of 0.481.[4]

For the immunization strategy to be completely effective, the fluctuations in the value of the asset portfolio must precisely match the fluctuations in the value of the liability portfolio. This means weighting the bond and the bill in such a fashion as to produce an asset portfolio duration precisely equal to the duration of the liabilities. The weights must, of course, sum to 1.0. The model is given by Equations (5-4) and (5-5) where w_1 and w_2 are the weights on the bond (instrument 1) and the bills (instrument 2), respectively. MMD_1 and MMD_2 are the corresponding durations, and MMD_L denotes the overall duration of the liabilities.

$$w_1 MMD_1 + w_2 MMD_2 = MMD_L \qquad (5-4)$$
$$w_1 + w_2 = 1 \qquad (5-5)$$

Substituting the known duration values into Equation (5-4) and solving renders the appropriate weights. The solution is illustrated in Table 5-3.

The solution for w_1 implies that the solution for w_2 is 31.21 percent. Thus, we conclude that the pension fund should invest 68.79 percent of the proceeds it received from the sale of its policies in the 30-year bond and 31.21 percent in the six-month bill. This translates into a current investment of $523.23 in bonds and $237.38 in bills.

TABLE 5–3
The Determination of Immunization Portfolio Weights

$$w_1 8.080 + w_2 0.481 = 5.708$$

and

$$w_1 + w_2 = 1 \quad \text{implying that} \quad w_2 = 1 - w_1$$

substituting for w_2:

$$w_1 8.080 + (1 - w_1)0.481 = 5.708$$

finally, solving for w_1:

$$w_1 = 68.79\%$$

Now consider what happens if the yield curve moves upward by 10 basis points. This movement represents a parallel shift in the yield curve. The liabilities are now discounted at 10.1 percent instead of 10 percent, the bond is discounted at 12.1 percent instead of 12 percent, and the bill is discounted at 8.1 percent instead of 8 percent. The old values and the new values are depicted in Table 5–4.

Notice that the change in the value of the fund's assets (−$4.32), obtained by combining the value change in the bond and the value change in the bill, is precisely equal to the value change in the fund's liabilities. Thus, the immunization strategy has successfully protected the fund from a 10-basis-point change in asset and liability yields. In addition, this portfolio is "profitable" in the sense that the return on the assets exceeds the 10 percent cost of

TABLE 5–4
Performance of the Immunized Portfolio

	Pension Liabilities	Assets 30-Year Bond	Six-Month Bill	
Old value	$760.61	$523.23	$237.38	
New value	756.29	519.03	237.26	
Change in value	$ −4.32	−4.20 +	−0.12	= −$4.32

the liabilities. Had this not been the case, the fund would not have offered the policy for sale. The return on the fund's portfolio is computed as the weighted average of the return on the individual assets. In this case, the calculation is: (68.79% × .12) + (13.21% × .08) = 10.75%.

There are three problems with the immunization approach described above. First, the duration values are only reliable for short periods of time. That is, as time passes, the durations of the individual assets and the durations of the liabilities change, and these changes are not equal for all the instruments involved. Thus, a weighting scheme that works perfectly today will probably not work perfectly tomorrow. This is not to say that it will not work well tomorrow, only that it will not work as well as it does today; and, with each passing day, the weighting scheme becomes less reliable.

Second, it has long been known that, all other things being equal, the duration of an instrument will change as the instrument's yield changes. Until the 1980s, however, not much thought was given to these changes other than to point out that one needed to periodically recalculate durations and modify the hedge ratios or asset/liability mix accordingly. During the latter half of the 1980s, however, considerable interest developed in predicting changes in duration. The importance of this can be made clear by way of an example. Suppose that a corporate treasurer has developed an asset portfolio—using duration modeling—so as to match the asset portfolio duration to the liability portfolio duration. If yield rises, how do the two portfolio durations change? If the durations change by equal amounts, then the asset/liability mix is still correct. But, if the asset portfolio duration increases or decreases by more or less than the liability portfolio duration, then the asset/liability mix is no longer correct.

The key to understanding how durations change is the concept of *convexity*. If we plot the present value (PV) of an instrument against the instrument's yield, the negativity of the slope of this present value curve is the duration of the instrument. This is depicted in Figure 5–6. (The slope of the straight line drawn tangent to the PV curve is the slope of the PV curve at the point of tangency.)

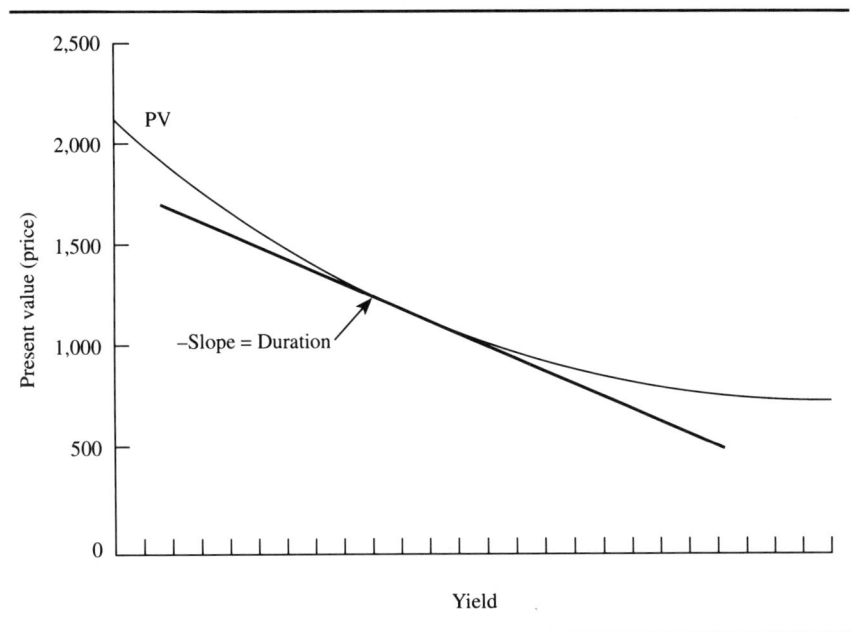

FIGURE 5-6
Duration, Convexity, and the Price-Yield Curve

[Graph showing Present value (price) on y-axis from 0 to 2,500 versus Yield on x-axis. A convex PV curve is shown along with a tangent line labeled "−Slope = Duration".]

We see that the PV curve is convex, meaning that the slope is continuously changing. Convexity measures the *rate of change* in the slope. The greater the rate of change, the more the duration changes as yield changes. Measuring convexity has become important for many risk management purposes. (Without examining the concept in detail, it should be intuitively clear that if the modified duration is the slope of the PV curve then modified duration can be measured as the first derivative of the PV curve with respect to yield. Similarly, convexity can be measured as the second derivative of the PV curve with respect to yield.)

The third problem with the simple duration-matching strategy described here concerns the assumption that all movements of the yield curve take the form of parallel shifts. This is simply not the case. Shorter-term rates are more volatile than longer-term rates; the rates on different types of instruments have different volatilities, even if they have the same maturities; and the same types of instruments with the same maturities may have different volatilities due to different degrees of default risk.

A very workable solution, however, is to adjust the size of the asset positions on the basis of the historic relationship between the yield changes on the assets and the yield changes on the liabilities. That is, if we assume that there is a proportionality to the yield change on an asset and the yield change on the liabilities, then we can measure this proportion using historic data. The statistical procedure used for this purpose is linear regression.

Let's illustrate this procedure using the pension fund example above. We begin by regressing the past changes in the yield on the 30-year bond against the past changes in the yield on the pension liabilities. The resultant regression coefficient is the required proportion. We call this coefficient the *yield beta*. The regression is given by Equation (5–6) in which Δy_1 denotes the yield change on the bond and Δy_L denotes the yield change on the liabilities, and β_1 denotes the yield beta that represents the proportionality factor for the bond.

$$\Delta y_1 = \beta_1 \Delta y_L + \alpha \qquad (5\text{–}6)$$

In the same fashion, we measure a yield beta for the six-month bill (relative to the pension liabilities). Once we know the bond and bill yield betas, we can "scale" the durations to account for non-parallel shifts in the yield curve. Denote these yield-scaled durations by SD. That is, $SD_1 = \beta_1 MMD_1$ and $SD_2 = \beta_2 MMD_2$. If we now substitute these yield-scaled durations for the modified durations in Table 5–3 and recalculate the weights, the problem of unequal yield changes is minimized.

There are more sophisticated immunization models, but none has been shown to be consistently superior to Redington's original model (with the adjustments we have noted) and so we do not go into these any further.[5] We should note that the risk profile for the pension fund (i.e., its value changes with respect to changes in interest rates, as illustrated in Figure 5–3) will be perfectly flat if the portfolio weighting was done correctly.

Dollar Value of a Basis Point
Closely related to duration as a measure of interest rate sensitivity is the dollar value of a basis point, denoted DV01 or DV.01 and

TABLE 6-5
Comparative DV01s

Maturity	Yield	Price	DV01
0.5	7.000	100.000	0.00483
1.0	7.750	100.000	0.00945
2.0	8.250	100.000	0.01809
5.0	8.750	100.000	0.03980
20.0	9.375	100.000	0.08953

read "dollar value of a zero one," and sometimes denoted DVBP. (The dollar value of a basis point is sometimes called the *price value of a basis point* and denoted PV01 or PVBP. It is also sometimes called the *present value of a basis point*.) An instrument's DV01 is the amount of value change per $100 of face value that will occur if yields change by one basis point. The DV01 values for five bonds, including the 2-year bond, the 5-year bond, and the 20-year bond discussed in the preceding sections, appear in Table 5-5.

The DV01s in Table 5-5 were obtained by calculating the price of the instruments at their actual yields, recalculating the prices at yields one basis point higher than their actual yields, and then taking the difference between the two prices. Consider for a moment the DV01 of the 5-year and the 20-year bonds. The 5-year bond has a DV01 of 0.03980 while the 20-year bond has a DV01 of 0.08953. The ratio of the DV01s provides a relative measure of the dollar-value changes that are associated with equivalent changes in yield. Thus, the 20-year bond is 2.25 times as price sensitive to yield changes as is the 5-year bond. This is exactly the same result we got from the duration calculation (after multiplying by the price ratio). We see then that DV01s and durations provide similar information and have many of the same applications. For the remainder of this discussion, we consider DV01 only.

Those involved in the management of interest rate risk often have positions in instruments of different maturities. A position in an actual instrument is called a *cash position*. Some of these cash positions may be long positions while others are short positions. Clearly, a short position in one debt instrument is a partial hedge for a long position in another debt instrument.

Unfortunately, knowledge of the instruments' DV01s is not sufficient, in and of itself, to effectively manage interest rate risk. The reason is simple. The DV01 measures the dollar value change that results from a single basis point change in yield. But, as we noted earlier, not all yield curve shifts are parallel and, hence, not all yields change by the same number of basis points.

To deal with this problem, risk managers typically convert all interest rate exposures to some "baseline" or "benchmark" equivalent. This is usually an instrument on which a futures contract is written. For example, the baseline instrument might be the 20-year Treasury bond or the 10-year Treasury note. Next, the historic yield changes for the cash instrument in which the firm has a position is regressed against the corresponding historic yield changes for the baseline instrument to get a yield beta. This is the same procedure described earlier.

Again, the yield beta measures the number of basis points the yield of the cash instrument is likely to change for each one-basis-point change in the yield of the baseline instrument.

To give an example, suppose that a bond trader has a long position in $2,000,000 (face value) 15-year bonds of Issuer Z. The bonds have a DV01 of 0.0792. The baseline 20-year Treasury bond has a DV01 of 0.0884. Finally, suppose that the yield beta (β_z) of the 15-year bonds of Issuer Z is 0.84. Then the DV01 hedging model can be used to determine the face value of the baseline instrument (denoted below by FV_b) that is *risk equivalent* to this long position. The DV01 model is given by Equation (5–7), in which FV_z denotes face value of the cash position in Issue Z. Face value is also called *par value*.

$$FV_b = FV_z \times \frac{DV01_z}{DV01_b} \times \beta_z$$

$$FV_b = \$2,000,000 \times \frac{0.0792}{0.0884} \times 0.84 \qquad (5-7)$$

$$= \$1,505,158$$

From this calculation, we see that the long position in $2,000,000 of Issuer Z's bonds is equivalent to a long position in $1,505,158 of baseline T-bonds.

Suppose that the firm also has a short position in $1,800,000 (face value) of 9-year notes of Issuer Y. Using the DV01 model, these notes are found to be equivalent to a short position in $1,066,500 of baseline Treasury bonds. By converting all positions to the same baseline equivalent, the risk manager can accurately assess the degree to which the firm's various exposures are offsetting. For example, the risk manager sums the baseline equivalent of the long position in Issue Z with the baseline equivalent of the partially offsetting short position in Issue Y to obtain a net exposure *equivalent* to a long position in $438,658 of the baseline security. Since a futures contract on the baseline security exists, the risk manager can hedge by taking a *short* position in the futures. In this case, each 20-year Treasury bond futures covers $100,000 of face value bonds. Thus, to fully hedge, the risk manager needs a short position in approximately 4.4 futures contracts.

Yield Value of 1/32

The yield value of 1/32 (YV32) is another method of measuring an instrument's interest rate sensitivity. The yield value of 1/32 is simply the number of basis points the instrument's yield must change in order for the instrument's price to change by 1/32 of a percentage point. It provides the same kind of information as a duration and a DV01, but, unlike duration and DV01, it is *inversely* related to volatility. That is, the greater an instrument's YV32, the less sensitive is the instrument's price to changes in yield.

A thirty-second of a percent is 0.03125 percent. Since the two-year bond in Table 5–5 had a DV01 of 0.01809, it must have a YV32 of 1.727 (this is calculated as 0.03125/0.01809). That is, the instrument's yield must change by 1.727 basis points for the instrument's price to change by 0.03125 percent. Similarly, the 20-year bond in Table 5–5 has a DV01 of 0.08953 and, hence, has a YV32 of 0.349 (i.e., 0.03125/0.08953). The relationship between the yield value of 1/32 and the dollar value of a basis point is given by Equation (5–8).

$$YV32 = \frac{0.03125}{DV01} \qquad (5-8)$$

Developing Hedge Ratios

Now that we have developed the tools to quantify interest rate risk and to compare interest rate sensitivities, we can focus more carefully on the notion of hedge ratios. The number of units of the hedging instrument necessary to fully hedge one unit of the cash position is called the *hedge ratio*. For example, if on average it takes two units of five-year T-note futures to offset the risk exposure from one unit of corporate debt, then the hedge ratio is 2:1. In the previous sections, we have seen that the proper measurement of interest rate risk is the key to developing hedge ratios. Using the tools we have already introduced and assuming that the yield beta is one (1), the hedge ratios, relative to some benchmark instrument, can be found using duration, using DV01, or using YV32.

1. Duration:

$$HR = \frac{MMD_{cash}}{MMD_{hedge}} \times \frac{P_{cash}}{P_{hedge}} \qquad (5-9)$$

2. DV01:

$$HR = \frac{DV01_{cash}}{DV01_{hedge}} \qquad (5-10)$$

3. YV32:

$$HR = \frac{YV32_{hedge}}{YV32_{cash}} \qquad (5-11)$$

In the event that the yield beta assumption of 1.0 is not appropriate, then the hedge ratio should be adjusted, no matter which of the three methods is used, to reflect the unequal yield changes between the cash instrument and the hedge instrument. For the remainder of our discussion, we assume that the correct hedge ratio is always used.

Measuring Hedge Effectiveness

No matter how careful we are at measuring the hedge ratio, there is still a very good chance that the hedge will not be perfect in the sense that it will not eliminate all of the interest rate risk. The reason for this is simple. Most hedges will involve a derivative instrument, such as a futures contract, that is written on some underlying instrument that is different from that which is the target of the hedge. This situation is described as *cross-hedging*. For example, a chief financial officer looking to hedge the interest rate risk associated with an offering lag (due to registration with the SEC) would, ideally, like to hedge in futures that are written on his or her corporation's bonds. But, alas, there are no corporate bond futures. There are, however, Treasury bond futures and these will, likely, be the hedging instrument of choice.

The problem, of course, is that yield changes in Treasury bond futures are not perfectly correlated with yield changes in the firm's bonds. The inclusion of a yield beta reflects the general relationship between the corporate bond yield changes and the Treasury bond yield changes, but it is not a precise measure of the relationship during subsequent periods—only a best estimate. Thus, there is residual risk. This residual risk, defined as the risk associated with the combined cash and futures position, is known as *basis risk*. Assuming that the hedge is at least partially effective in reducing interest rate risk, the basis risk will be lower than the interest rate risk associated with the cash position alone.

The effectiveness of a hedge is measured by the square of the degree of correlation (called the *coefficient of determination* and denoted below by R^2) between the value changes in the hedge position and the value changes in the cash position. The closer this coefficient is to 1.0, the more effective is the hedge. The precise relationship between basis risk and interest rate risk, when interest rate risk is measured as the variance of the interest rate, is given by Equation (5-12). Here, basis risk is also measured as a variance.

$$\text{Basis risk} = (1 - R^2) \times \text{Interest rate risk} \qquad (5\text{-}12)$$

For example, suppose R^2 is 0.87, then, the hedge will reduce the interest rate risk by 87 percent. Of course, 13 percent of the original risk will remain. This remaining part is the basis risk. For obvious reasons, the coefficient of determination is the most often used measure of hedge effectiveness.

Hedgers are often interested in the source of basis risk. By better understanding its source, one gains insights into how to construct better hedges. As already noted, basis risk exists because the value of the cash position and the value of the hedge position are not perfectly correlated. This is so because the demand and supply conditions in the cash market may evolve somewhat differently than the demand and supply conditions in the market for the hedging instrument. This suggests that if there are multiple hedge instruments available, it is worth the effort to consider the hedge effectiveness of each. This is done by gathering historic observations on the value of the cash position and the value of the hedge position (after employing the correct hedge ratio) and then estimating the R^2. This is repeated for each available hedge instrument. The R^2s are then compared to determine their comparative effectiveness.

Measuring Hedge Cost

While the effectiveness of a hedge is an important consideration in selecting a hedge instrument, it is not the only consideration. Another important consideration is the cost of the hedge. There is a great deal of literature on the subject of the cost of hedging. The consensus is that hedging is relatively cheap, particularly when futures contracts are the hedging instrument, but not free. There are two good reasons not to expect hedging to be costless. First, the risk that hedgers seek to shed when they take on a hedge must be borne by the counterparty to the hedge contract. If the counterparty is another hedger with a mirror-image exposure, then both hedgers enjoy some benefit and we would not expect either to have to compensate the other. But, more often, the counterparty to the contract is a speculator. The speculator is taking a position in order to earn a speculative profit. If speculation is privately costly to the speculator (that is, if resources are expended) and if speculators are risk averse, then we would expect speculators to require compensation for their risk-bearing services. To the extent that speculators are compensated for risk bearing, hedgers must bear the cost. The second reason for expecting hedging not to be costless is the presence of transaction costs. Every trade involves some transaction costs in the form of a commission, a bid-ask spread, or both.

Although hedging is not costless, not all hedges will be equally costly. It may be, due to inefficiencies in the market, that one type of hedge is less costly than another. Furthermore, the relative costs may change from one day to the next so that the cheaper hedge today might not be the cheaper hedge tomorrow. The prudent hedger compares the cost of alternative hedging strategies before committing to one.

FIGURE 5–7
Efficient and Inefficient Hedges

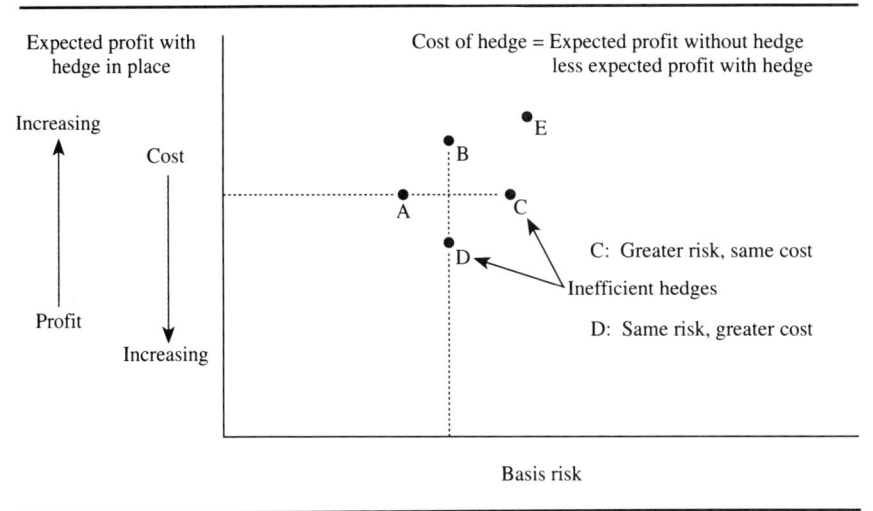

[Figure: A graph with vertical axis labeled "Expected profit with hedge in place" (Cost increasing upward, Profit increasing downward) and horizontal axis labeled "Basis risk". Top right label: "Cost of hedge = Expected profit without hedge less expected profit with hedge". Points A, B, C, D, E are plotted, with annotations "C: Greater risk, same cost", "Inefficient hedges", "D: Same risk, greater cost".]

The upshot of these remarks is that the hedger must consider both the effectiveness of the hedge and the cost of the hedge. Together, these factors determine the *efficiency of the hedge*. *Efficient hedges* are those that provide maximum risk reduction per unit of cost. Consider the five hedges depicted in Figure 5–7.

Notice that Hedge C is *inefficient* compared to Hedge A because Hedge C is less effective than Hedge A at the same cost. Notice also that Hedge D is inefficient compared to Hedge B because Hedge D is more costly than Hedge B while only equally effective. The efficient hedges then are Hedges A, B, and E.

The hedger who derives positive utility from reducing risk and negative utility from paying the cost must choose a hedge so as to balance these competing considerations. The hedge that maximizes the user's utility is then the *optimal hedge*. However, the optimal hedge for one hedger may not be optimal for another hedger. This is a reflection of the individual's own, very personal, utility function. The selection of a hedge must consider these differences.

There has been some confusion in recent literature concerning the meaning of the terms *effectiveness, efficiency,* and *optimality,* as these terms have been applied to hedging theory. The distinctions become exceedingly important when composite hedging is considered. A *composite hedge* is a hedge that involves more than one hedging instrument. Hedges involving individual hedging instruments are called *simple hedges*. The advantage of composite hedging is that such a hedge can reduce the basis risk otherwise associated with simple hedges. This is a simple application of portfolio theory to hedging. That is, if basis risks are unsystematic in nature, then diversification of the hedge can reduce overall basis risk.[6]

Determining the Hedge Horizon

Another important consideration in developing a hedge program is the length of the hedge horizon. There are two different dimensions to the hedge horizon issue. The first is the length of the horizon per se. The second involves the number of periods that must be spanned by the hedge. Consider the length of the horizon first.

By the length of the hedge horizon, we mean the length of time that the hedge will be needed. For example, in the case of the CFO planning the bond issue discussed earlier, the hedge horizon was three months in length. That is, it was expected that the hedge would be needed for three months. If Treasury bond futures were the hedge instrument of choice, then we would need bond futures having a delivery date at least three months forward. Shorter-term futures could be used, but then the hedge would need to be periodically "rolled over." Each rollover would involve additional transaction costs. On the other hand, if we hedge in a contract that is much more forward than that needed, it will tend to be less liquid and, again, involve greater transaction costs. Furthermore, the effectiveness of a hedge tends to decrease the greater the mismatch between the hedge horizon and the hedge instrument's maturity date. (The term *maturity date* is used here to include both delivery dates on futures and forwards and expiration dates on options.)

In many cases, we know precisely how long a hedge will be needed. In these cases, the specification of the length of the hedge horizon is easy. But, as in the CFO's case, the hedge horizon may be somewhat uncertain. The amount of time necessary to prepare an offering to the SEC's satisfaction, for example, can vary from about eight weeks to six months. Uncertain hedge horizons must be dealt with. The general rule of thumb is that it is better to err on the side of a hedge longer than that expected to be necessary, unless the greater transaction costs associated with an illiquid instrument dictate otherwise.

The question of liquidity is important. In the case of futures contracts, many are very liquid for near-term delivery dates but become progressively less liquid as we go further out. To make matters worse, many futures contracts are not even available for trading more than a few months out. In these cases, forward contracts, which trade over the counter in dealer markets, can be an excellent alternative. This is not to imply that forwards are only viable when futures are unavailable or illiquid. Quite the contrary. Forwards are often an excellent and sometimes, but not always, a superior alternative to futures for reasons we will discuss shortly.

The second dimension to the investment horizon involves the question of periodicity. For example, if the hedge involves the value of a single cash position to be liquidated or acquired on a single future date, then the hedge may be described as single period in nature. The length of the time span involved is irrelevant. Single-period hedges would most often make use of futures or forwards. However, many hedges can be viewed as multiperiod in nature. That is, the cash position involved will be liquidated (or acquired) over a number of successive periods. Hedging such positions can involve a sequence of futures or forwards maturing at different points in time. This is often referred to as a *strip*.

An important alternative to the futures or forward strip is a swap. *Swaps* may be viewed as multiperiod forward contracts. Whenever the cash position to be hedged involves multiple periods, with payments, liquidations, or acquisitions spaced out at well-defined intervals, the swap alternative might likely prove the superior hedge instrument.

Selecting Hedge Instruments

As already noted, most hedging takes place in instruments known as derivatives. *Derivative instruments* are instruments whose values are derived from that of other assets, called *underlying assets*. The most important types of derivative instruments are futures contracts, forward contracts, options contracts (including both single-period and multiperiod options), and swaps. Futures contracts and forward contracts are contracts for deferred delivery of the underlying asset. While forward contracts are tailored to meet the idiosyncratic needs of the end user and trade over the counter in dealer-type markets, futures contracts are highly standardized instruments that trade on futures exchanges in auction-type markets. Futures and forwards can be used to speculate on the direction of a price, hedge a price risk, and arbitrage between the cash and the derivative markets.

Futures contracts written on debt instruments or linked to specific interest rates are known as *interest rate futures*. There are futures on Treasury bonds, Treasury notes, Eurodollar deposits, Treasury bills, fed funds, foreign debt securities and foreign interest rates, and so on. Some of these interest rate futures are deliverable and others are cash settled. *Cash-settled futures* are futures that are settled by a final cash transaction based on the value of the underlying interest rate on the final settlement date. Forward contracts on interest rates are called *forward rate agreements* or *FRAs*. Forward rate agreements are always cash-settled contracts. The interest rate to which these contracts are tied is called the *reference rate*. Because forwards are tailored to meet the user's needs, they can employ any reference rate, including LIBOR, T-bill, fed funds, commercial paper, certificate of deposit, prime, and so on.

Swaps are relatively new derivative instruments making their first appearance in the early 1980s. In the 10 years that followed, the notional volume of these instruments grew so rapidly as to dwarf the growth of any other market in financial history. Yet, swaps cannot and would not exist in the absence of other financial markets, including the debt markets and the futures markets. There are many different types of swaps, but the focus of this discussion is on interest rate swaps. Swaps have spurred the growth of related instruments, including multiperiod options and forward rate agreements.

As simply put as possible, an *interest rate swap* is an agreement between two parties calling for the first party to pay a fixed rate of interest to the second party in exchange for the second party paying a floating rate of interest to the first party. The payments are based on some quantity of *notional principal*, which exists solely for the purpose of determining the size of the interest payments. Swaps are widely used to reduce financing costs and to hedge risks, but they have other uses as well.

Because swaps are multiperiod instruments, they are useful for hedging multiperiod interest rate risks. And, because they are tailored for the over-the-counter market, they can be written with very long maturities. The maturity of a swap is called its *tenor*. Swaps with tenors of 15 years or more are not uncommon. Over the tenor of the swap, the parties to it, called *counterparties*, will exchange interest payments many times.

The final type of instrument we will consider are interest rate options. The subject of options harks back to our earlier discussion of the difference between *risk* and *downside risk*. Recall that sometimes financial managers want to hedge the firm against unfavorable deviations from their expectations but wish to preserve the opportunity to benefit from favorable deviations from their expectations. This is where options come into the hedging program.

The simplest definition of an *option* is a right without an obligation. That is, the purchaser of an option has the right to do something but not the obligation to do it. In the case of deliverable single-period options, called *calls* and *puts*, the option holder has the right (for some period of time) to *buy* some number of units of the underlying asset (*call options*) or *sell* some number of units of the underlying asset (*put options*). These transactions would be made, if the option holder chose to exercise the option right, at the option's *strike price*.

A great many variants of the original call and put options have been introduced over the last 10 years. There are cash-settled options, which pay the holder upon the option's expiration the amount that it is in the money, or zero, whichever is greater; and there are multiperiod options that repeat the cash settlement process period after period for the tenor of the option. Such options are called *caps* and *floors*. There is also a plethora of exotic options that have been introduced, but these are beyond the scope of this short introduction.

The key to understanding options is to understand the payoff profile associated with holding the instrument. Consider the case again of the firm with the risk profile given in Figure 5–1. This is

**FIGURE 5–8
A Risk Profile**

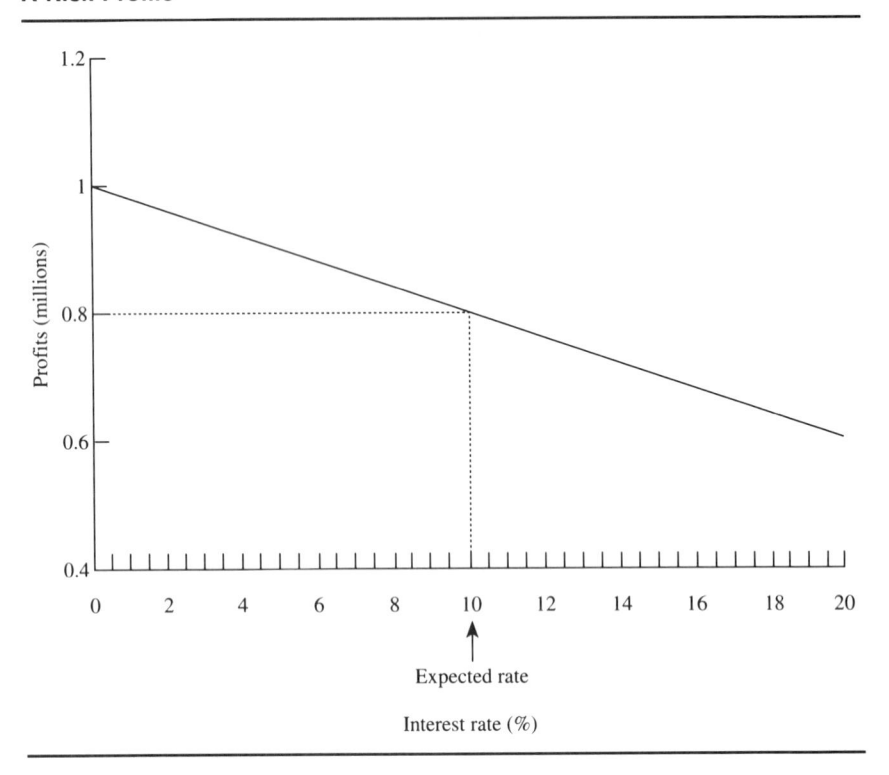

[Graph: Profits (millions) vs Interest rate (%). Downward sloping line from approximately 1.0 at 0% to about 0.62 at 20%. Dotted lines indicate that at the expected rate of 10%, profits are 0.8 million.]

depicted below as Figure 5–8. Also consider the payoff profile from holding a position in an option (the type of option involved is not important just now). This is depicted in Figure 5–9.

Now consider the combined outcome from holding both the cash position and the option. This is depicted in Figure 5–10.

Notice that the firm is protected from unfavorable changes in interest rates but will benefit from favorable changes in interest rates. Clearly, this is the attraction of options as a hedging tool. But don't be misled. There are no free lunches with options. The benefits afforded by options come at a price. The price takes the form of a premium that must be paid for the option up front, at the time the option is purchased.

Without getting too technical about it, there is one last point

FIGURE 5–9
Option Payoff Profile

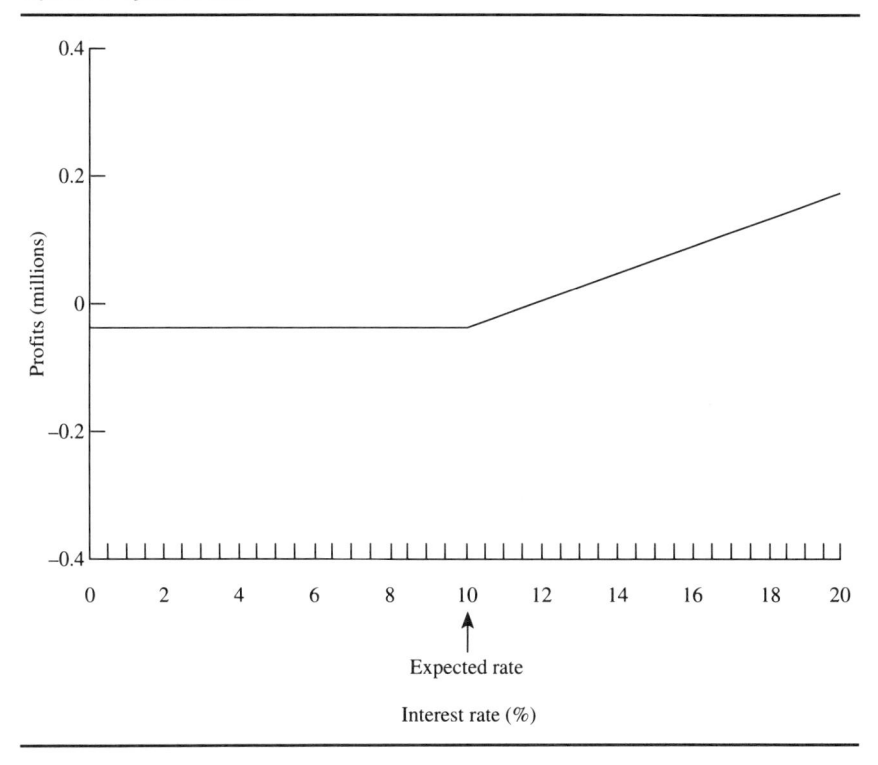

worth making on the subject of options. Options can be combined with other options and with other derivatives to engineer very interesting structures. Indeed, the right combination of option positions will replicate a futures contract. If a futures contract can be replicated with options, then the futures hedger should consider the comparative cost of hedging with a real futures contract and the cost of hedging with a *synthetic* futures contract (synthesized from options).

Critical to understanding derivative instruments are the cash flow diagrams and the payoff profiles associated with them. That is, there is a series of cash flows between the parties to derivative instruments and/or there is a payoff profile associated with a position in a derivative instrument. Understanding derivative instru-

FIGURE 5-10
Cash Position with Option Hedge

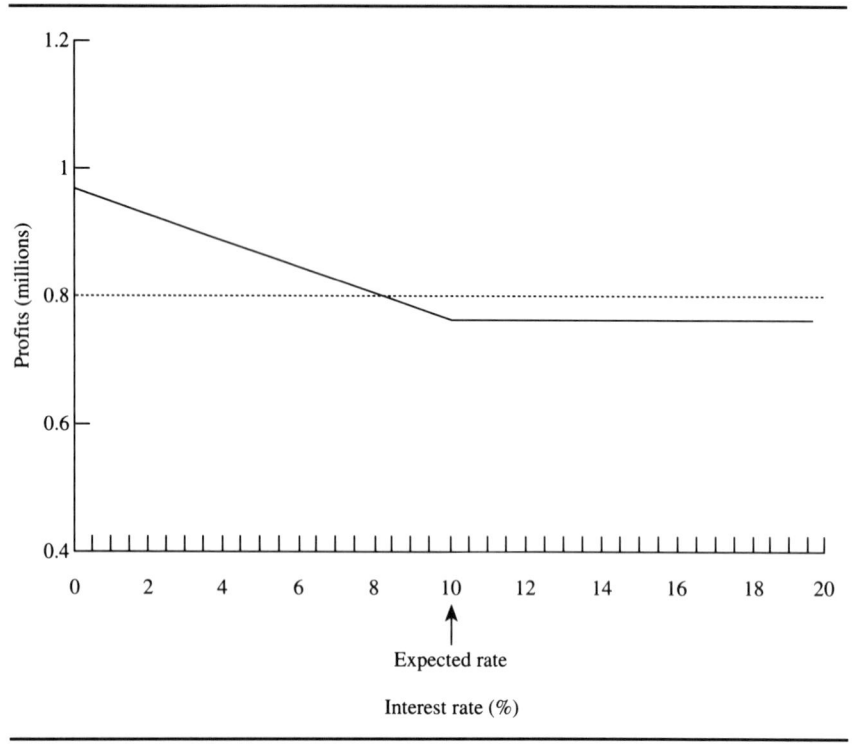

ments is largely a matter of understanding these cash flows and the payoff profiles. For these reasons, any discussion of derivative instruments will rely heavily on graphics to illustrate concepts.

MISCELLANEOUS CONSIDERATIONS

We argued that hedging is appropriate because both managers and shareholders are known to be risk averse. Thus, all other things being equal, less risk means a higher share price. However, hedging may have, and often does have, costs. To the extent that the costs of hedging offset the benefits of hedging, there is a trade-off that must be considered in making the hedging decision. Measuring this trade-off seems simple, but important considerations are often overlooked.

At first blush, it would seem that the easiest way to measure the costs of hedging is to estimate the expected profit to the firm in the absence of a hedge and the expected profit to the firm in the presence of a hedge. The difference would seem to be the cost of hedging. This, however, is a naive view. It overlooks (1) the effect of hedging on corporate taxes; (2) the credit effect from hedging; and (3) the economies of scale that can be enjoyed by firms that hedge, to name just three. Let's consider each of these in turn.

In a world of progressive corporate tax rates where tax rates rise as the corporation moves from one marginal tax bracket to another, total taxes paid over the long term will be greater for the firm with more volatile profits than for the firm with less volatile profits—even if the total profits earned over the full term are the same. Hedging, by reducing the volatility of profit, has favorable tax consequences for the firm and, therefore, enhances the firm's value.

A reduction in profit volatility reduces risk not just for shareholders but also for creditors of the firm. This suggests that creditors will view the hedged firm more favorably than the unhedged firm and the firm's borrowing costs will be lower. In addition, creditors will generally treat the hedged firm as having a greater debt capacity than the unhedged firm, all other things being equal. This reduction in borrowing costs and this greater capacity to carry debt can add to the bottom line.

The final consideration is the economies of scale that can be enjoyed by the hedged firm. Consider a simple example. Imagine an unhedged insurance company that, for each $1 of capital, can support $5 of policies. That is, the firm requires a $1 capital cushion against losses for each $5 of policies that the firm writes. These policies are the sources of the firm's profit. Suppose that, for each $1 of policies, the firm expects to earn $0.0075 after costs and taxes. Thus, the expected profit for this unhedged firm is $0.0375 per dollar of capital. Now, suppose that, with the hedge in place, the firm can carry $40 of policies for each $1 of capital with no greater overall risk. However, the cost of the hedge reduces the profit per dollar of policies to $0.0050. At first glance, we observe that the expected profit is reduced by $0.0025 per dollar of policies. This is a profit reduction *per dollar of policies* of 33.3 percent. However, when we recognize the greater number of policies that can be written, we realize that the *profit per dollar of capital* has risen to $0.20 from $0.0375—a gain of 430 percent. In addition, to the extent that fixed operating costs can now be spread across a larger policy base, the firm stands to benefit even further.

In sum, the gains to the firm from hedging can be enormous. To properly realize these gains requires a carefully structured hedge program that identifies the risks, quantifies the risks, properly develops hedge ratios, compares the effectiveness of different hedge instruments and strategies, weighs the costs of hedging against the benefits from hedging, and properly specifies the hedge horizon and the type of hedge instrument most appropriate for that hedge horizon.

NOTES

1. See F. M. Redington, "Review of the Principle of Life Office Valuations," *Journal of the Institute of Actuaries* 18 (1952), pp. 286–340.
2. See F. R. Macaulay, *Some Theoretical Problems Suggested by the Movement of Interest Rates, Bond Yields, and Stock Prices in the United States since 1856* (New York: Columbia University Press for the National Bureau of Economic Research, 1938).
3. Equation (5-1) is mathematically equivalent to the simpler duration formula given by Equation (4-3) in Chapter 4.
4. The modified durations and most of the other calculations in this chapter were performed using the inexpensive DOS-based analytical package *A-Pack: An Analytical Package for Business*, published by MicroApplications (telephone: 516-821-9355).
5. For a discussion of the empirical performance of the Redington model versus other, more sophisticated models, see S. M. Schaefer, "Immunization and Duration: A Review of Theory, Performance and Applications," In *Revolution in Corporate Finance*, ed. J. M. Stern and D. H. Chew (Oxford: Blackwell, 1986). See also N. Gultekin, N. Bulent, and R. J. Rogalski, "Alternative Duration Specification and the Measurement of Basis Risk: Empirical Tests," *Journal of Business* 57, no. 2 (1984), pp. 241–64.
6. The mathematics of composite hedging is described in Chapter 21 of J. F. Marshall and V. K. Bansal, *Financial Engineering: A Complete Guide to Financial Innovation* (New York: New York Institute of Finance, 1992).

SECTION 2

FINANCIAL FUTURES

CHAPTER 6

INTRODUCTION TO THE FINANCIAL FUTURES MARKETS

*Todd E. Petzel**
Senior Vice President and Chief Economist, Chicago Mercantile Exchange

Forward contracting for interest rate products and exposures is a practice that predates the establishment of formal interest rate futures by many years. The historical role of the government securities primary dealers of actively participating in the "when issued" market for Treasuries is perhaps the best example, though there are many others. When the first interest rate futures were introduced by the Chicago Board of Trade (CBOT) and the Chicago Mercantile Exchange (CME) in the mid-1970s, the range of forward transactions and *basis trades* (trades between futures contracts and particular cash instruments) grew markedly. The decade of the 1980s saw further evolution into cash-settled futures contracts, forward rate agreements, and swaps.

The distinction between exchange and off-exchange instruments is important in deciding how best to meet one's forward contracting needs. Off-exchange products can offer highly customized features to match precisely the risk environment at hand, but customization comes at a price. Exchange products are by their very nature highly standardized instruments, leaving the issue of basis risk to be resolved. They are, however, very low cost and provide extensive liquidity and credit guarantees not available with off-exchange transactions.

---

* The views in this chapter are those of the author and do not necessarily reflect those of the Chicago Mercantile Exchange.

This chapter begins with a brief history of the evolution of interest rate futures products in the United States, noting the explosive growth since October 1979, when the Federal Reserve Bank shifted its policy away from targeted interest rates. The types of users that spurred this growth are then outlined, demonstrating the variety of applications these contracts serve. The basic principles of pricing make up the next section of the chapter, providing a foundation for the more-detailed applications found later in the book. We discuss the array of futures products in the final section.

BACKGROUND

The concept of financial futures was first tested in 1972, when the CME created the International Monetary Market (IMM) division to trade foreign exchange futures. The early experience with exchange-traded products was positive, but hardly an unqualified success. The majority of the users that fueled the explosive growth in the 1980s had not yet tried this innovation. Risk had always been managed before using traditional cash market products. It would take a shift in environment and product line to establish financial futures in the premier position they occupy now.

In 1973 and 1974, inflation was running at a double-digit rate for the first time since World War II–era price controls were lifted. Interest rates were at postwar highs, and the yield curve was inverted. Banking regulations that set ceilings on interest rates caused a rush of funds out of banks, as savers tried to find positive real rates of interest on their investments. Money market mutual funds were invented to allow the public access to the interest rates available to institutions. In 1973–74, the glue holding together the relatively quiet times of the 1950s and 1960s began to age and crack. New tools were needed to face these challenges.

In October 1975, the CBOT began with its Government National Mortgage Association (GNMA) contract. The CME followed four months later with its 90-day Treasury bill futures. As in the agricultural markets that formed their heritage, the CBOT developed its interest rate product on "storable" mortgages, while the CME sought to trade the more "perishable" short-maturity T-bills. It is a division of product line that has held up for nearly 20 years. In subsequent years, important milestones were passed in the development of the T-bond futures at the CBOT (1977) and the world's first cash-settled futures, the CME's three-month Eurodollar Time Deposit (1981). These last two contracts have come to dominate their respective ends of the U.S. yield curve, far surpassing the original pioneering efforts.

Many other contracts have been tried both in the United States and abroad. Commercial paper, CDs, various maturity notes, municipal bonds, and other more esoteric ideas have all been used as a foundation for trading. Some have caught on, while many others have failed, including the original GNMA contract and several amended efforts. The bottom line has been that if a unique interest rate risk can be identified, and sufficient initial liquidity generated, a product can serve either a broad or narrow audience. Brief descriptions of the contract specifications for the currently popular interest rate futures worldwide are given in the appendix to this chapter. As with all contract specifications, the reader is urged to contact the respective exchanges in order to obtain the most-recent terms and relevant trading regulations.

For all the glamour and hype that surrounds the speculative aspects of trading futures, the reality in interest rate products is something quite different. The user list reads as a who's who among the international investment and commercial bank communities. The largest bond brokers/dealers all trade, as do many sophisticated pension and mutual funds. While there is always a measure of speculation in any investment decision, interest rate futures have succeeded around the world because they are an extremely cost-effective hedging tool.

TRADING USES

Three basic uses of futures will be described generally here:

1. Swapping floating for fixed interest rates using Eurodollar futures.

2. Synthetic asset allocation across the yield curve using futures.
3. Hedging the operation of a bond broker/dealer.

Many more specific applications will be discussed in subsequent chapters.

Eurodollar Swaps

Corporate treasurers have a wide variety of financing tools at their disposal that provide great flexibility in the management of long-term and short-term borrowing. In the decade of the 1980s, interest rate volatility generated tremendous growth in the bank swap market and the Eurodollar futures market. As an example, a corporate treasurer paying a floating-rate loan may be concerned that rates will soon increase. The treasurer may go to a bank and seek a similar maturity swap on which he pays a fixed rate and receives floating. The combination of the floating-rate debt and the swap produces a synthetic fixed-rate loan.

The same outcome can be achieved using Eurodollar futures. If the loan in the example were a $100 million two-year, LIBOR-based floating line, the treasurer could examine the rates implied by the Eurodollar futures spanning those eight quarters to arrive at a market-determined forecast of the interest rate expense. If this forecast met the needs of the firm, and if there was a concern that future interest rates would be higher than the Eurodollar prices implied, the interest expense could be "locked in" by selling a strip of Eurodollar futures short.

Constructing a strip of Eurodollars to hedge exposures spanning more than one quarter is a fairly mechanical proposition. Suppose the borrower has a loan commitment that is to begin in September, with interest floating at 150 basis points over LIBOR and changing quarterly. As the date of the loan approaches, the risk of such a position is from a sudden, unexpected rise in short-term rates.

To create a synthetic fixed-rate loan for the two years, the borrower would go short an appropriate number of September, December, March, and June Eurodollars futures contracts for each of the two years. Assume the following array of prices (and implied LIBOR) at the time of the hedge:

Month	Year	Price	Implied LIBOR	Basis	Expected Interest
September	1	96.54	3.46	1.50	4.96
December	1	96.19	3.81	1.50	5.31
March	1	96.09	3.91	1.50	5.41
June	1	95.75	4.25	1.50	5.75
September	2	95.35	4.65	1.50	6.15
December	2	94.77	5.23	1.50	6.73
March	2	94.57	5.43	1.50	6.93
June	2	94.22	5.78	1.50	7.28

If the June quarter each year has 92 actual days and the remaining quarters all have 91, the expected total payment (principal plus compound interest) at the end of any quarter is given by the formula:

$$\text{Payment}_n = \$100\text{m} \prod_{i=1}^{n}[1 + r_i(d_i/360)]$$

where:

r_i = Interest rate for the ith period
d_i = Actual number of days in that period

To find the appropriate hedge for each quarter, the borrower first takes the present value of the *change* in the payment above that results from a .01 change in interest rates during that quarter. The present value is then divided by $25, which is how much a Eurodollar futures contract changes when rates move .01, to find the optimal number of contracts. In the example above, for a hedge placed just prior to the initiation of the loan, the strip would work out to be 100, 100, 101, 100, 99, 99, and 100 of the contracts September 1 through June 2, respectively.

In general, because of the discounting, the number of contracts in the strip will decline as maturities extend. The slight undulating pattern is caused by the greater interest at risk in the 92-day June quarters.

Strip hedging is a dynamic process. Since it involves present values, the positions need to be evaluated as rates change and as time passes. Simpler, naive hedges can be employed, but they will not manage yield curve risks as precisely.

With such a strip in place, if market rates increase, Eurodollar prices will decrease, and profits from the futures will precisely offset the higher cash interest payments on the loan. Conversely, if rates should fall, any cash market advantage will be wiped away by losses in the futures. The net result is a synthetic fixed-rate loan.

How does one decide whether to use a swap or a strip of Eurodollars? There are several factors to consider, but the most important ones have to do with costs. When you ask a bank for a quote on a swap, they have already done the arithmetic of translating the strip of Eurodollars to a fixed rate. To this they will add whatever value they feel they can justify for the services of providing a customized swap.

The treasurer should also do these calculations in order to make informed decisions. If the timing of reset dates in the loan does not match the schedule of Eurodollar futures, then there will be *basis risk* from the Eurodollar strategy. If the original loan and swap are based on rates other than LIBOR, there is *quality basis risk*. The treasurer may decide this risk is manageable, or that it offers profit opportunities if the spreads move in expected ways. In this case, the futures position is preferred. If the risk is perceived to be great, then a swap might be better. The important point is that these decisions should be made on an informed basis using all of the market information available.

Shifting from a fixed-rate to a floating-rate borrowing environment when interest rates are expected to drop is done in a similar fashion. Here the borrower wants to reap the benefits of falling rates despite having already committed to a fixed-rate payment schedule. By going long a strip of Eurodollars, the treasurer will find that the profits from futures will subsidize the fixed-rate payments if rates decline, making them de facto floating. Of course, if rates rise, the synthetic floating loan will produce higher interest costs overall.

The tremendous growth in interest rate swaps and Eurodollar futures during the 1980s is, by and large, an example of complementary products making each better. Liquid Eurodollar futures allowed swap dealers to offer very competitive swap deals, because they could quickly lay off the rate risks given to them by their counterparties. As more business of this type flowed to the CME, tighter bid-ask spreads were available in more Eurodollar contract months, lowering the cost of hedging further. This cycle of ever more efficient futures and swaps continued unabated throughout the 1980s, and the experience in the early 1990s suggested that there is still tremendous growth potential.

For some market participants, there are regulatory and legal constraints to the free access to futures. For these individuals and firms, choice is restricted, and their competitive position must suffer. For everyone else, however, knowledge of both swaps and Eurodollar futures is essential to secure consistent, low-cost results in the management of short-term interest rate risk.

Synthetic Asset Allocation

Fixed-income fund managers are usually judged against an index that captures a certain part of the yield curve. Three-month Treasuries, the Merrill Lynch 1–3-Year Government Index, and the Lehman Brothers Government Corporate Bond Index are widely used benchmarks for short-, intermediate-, and long-term rates, respectively. Once a manager has a target firmly defined, it then becomes necessary to devise strategies to beat the target index. Frequently, these strategies involve shifting duration in an attempt to exploit rising or falling rates.

Once a base portfolio is established, executing duration shifts can be done either in the cash market or in futures. For instance, assume a manager targets the intermediate part of the yield curve, and suppose the benchmark index has an average maturity of two years. The manager has been tracking the index with a mix of short-term and intermediate-term Treasury instruments that also averages two years. A change in outlook would necessitate a shift in the portfolio.

Suppose the manager expects the Federal Reserve to ease credit, leading to a nearly parallel shift down in the Treasury yield curve. Being long securities, the manager is well positioned to profit from such an event. If the duration of the portfolio can be lengthened, however, there's a good chance of exceeding the benchmark if the expectation comes true.

The manager can act on this view by selling some short-term Treasuries and buying longer-term notes, or a futures strategy may be employed. By going long 5-year T-note futures of 6½–10-year T-note futures contracts in an amount equal to the T-bills that would have been sold in the cash market scenario, the manager has synthetically extended the duration of the portfolio. The cash T-bills themselves could be used for margining the position, and the savings in transactions costs from avoiding extra cash market trades can be significant.

Two points are worth noting in this example. First, there is no leverage involved in this transaction. The manager is simply creating synthetic five-year notes by combining the same quantity of T-bills and five-year T-note futures. The position is no more speculative than if the same shift had been performed in the cash market. The second point is that there is no free lunch either. While interest on the T-bills acting as margin is still being earned, the pricing of the futures contract is higher than that of a cash five-year note. If this were not true, longs against futures could receive all the benefits of ownership without having to finance the cash position. Arbitrageurs will see that this does not occur. The synthetic position will perform no better, or worse, on average than the underlying instrument apart from transaction costs.

If rates fall as expected, profits from the long futures position will augment the return, just like the longer-duration cash instruments would do. Of course, if rates rise unexpectedly, losses will decrease the return just as would happen with a longer-than-average-duration portfolio.

The opposite strategy of shorting futures against the cash instruments is employed when rates are expected to rise. Selling five-year T-note futures against similar cash notes produces the synthetic equivalent of cash T-bills, shortening the average duration of the portfolio. This activity is frequently described as *hedging* the portfolio, but this is much too limited a view of this activity. Reducing the duration of a portfolio using short futures is a parallel strategy to expanding it with long futures. Rather than call one approach *hedging* and the other not, it is more accurate to view both as the risk management tools that they are.

Inventory Hedging of Treasury Securities

The most classic hedging application in interest rate futures has a direct historical link to the foundation of commodity futures trading: inventory hedging. In the modern version, the government securities dealer is asked to quote a market for a particular bond, note, or bill, possibly in the when-issued market, and he most typically thinks in terms of the basis relative to the futures contracts that correspond most closely to the respective security.

To satisfy customers' particular needs, a dealer may maintain an inventory of various issues of securities, momentarily depleting the inventory if a customer buys, or adding to it if the customer sells. Since the cash Treasury securities market is both large and liquid, these inventories do not have to be huge, but they should be big enough to allow for short-term flexibility. The problem is market risk.

Since October 1979, the Federal Reserve has not tried to target specific interest rates explicitly. This has resulted in a greater reliance on market forces to shape the price of all Treasuries, and volatility at times has been quite severe. By shorting futures against the cash market inventory, this price risk is replaced by *basis risk*, which is much more manageable and tradable.

Hedging against the when-issued market poses the opposite problem. The customer seeks to secure a price for bonds, notes, or bills that will be auctioned shortly. The dealer guarantees a price, and, in doing so, exposes the firm to the risk that prices in the auction will be higher than anticipated, thereby eliminating the market-making profit. By going long T-bond, T-note, or T-bill futures, the position is hedged against that possible outcome.

The process is made more interesting by the pricing of the CBOT T-bond and T-note futures, a subject described more fully in the next section. The wide variety of coupons and maturities deliverable against the future makes it necessary to closely watch the basis relationships between the futures and any particular issue. Bond dealers actively trade the basis, selling cash instruments that are perceived to be expensive relative to the board and trying to acquire the relatively cheap bonds. Since the futures contract always tracks the price of the issue that is expected to be cheapest to deliver in the delivery month, and the cheapest to deliver can change depending on the rate environment, the opportunities and pitfalls are numerous.

PRICING

All forward interest rate contracts, whether traded on or off the exchange, are structured to provide either a cash instrument or the interest stream from a particular instrument, at some predefined point in the future. The degree of complexity can be quite high in a product like a forward swaption, but all forward transactions are made up of fairly basic building blocks. The pricing of these blocks comes from arbitrage relationships.

For the class of trades that calls for physical delivery of an instrument (e.g., a when-issued forward sale of two-year Treasury notes or a CBOT T-bond futures), the pricing is best seen by use of a simple example. Suppose a month from now you expect a receipt of $100 million, with which you want to buy six-month Treasury bills. There are at least two paths to this end that fix the price today. First, you could go to a government securities dealer and ask for a forward price on such an instrument. Alternatively, you could arrange to borrow one-month funds today, buy a T-bill with seven months to maturity, and then with the receipt of the funds a month from now, pay back the loan, leaving you with the desired position.

The second alternative may seem cumbersome, but it must be priced in order to evaluate the fairness of the pricing for the direct forward transaction. Fortunately, given the considerable skill and capital of the public securities dealer, and the highly competitive nature of the business, there are few instances of significant mispricing in the forward securities markets. To be sure, any services provided by the dealer in a forward cash sale will be paid for, and it is the customer's job to see if they are appropriately priced.

Pricing of delivered futures contracts is a bit more complicated because of the existence of multiple instruments that are deliverable at the seller's option. The 30-year CBOT T-bond contract is possibly the most analyzed futures contract in history because of the complicated nature of its delivery terms. Any bond that has at least 15 years before maturity, or before its earliest call date if it is callable, is potentially deliverable against the contract. Since this involves an extremely wide array of coupons and maturities, the CBOT invented a device known as a *conversion factor* to bring all of the bonds to a comparable footing.

The benchmark is a hypothetical 20-year 8 percent coupon instrument. All other deliverable bonds have a conversion factor that is approximately equal to the bond's price if it were to yield 8 percent. If the bond's coupon is greater than 8 percent, it is more valuable than a similar maturity 8 percent bond, so its conversion factor is greater than one. The opposite is true for bonds with coupons less than 8 percent. In general, the higher the coupon and the longer the maturity, the higher the conversion factor.

Conversion factors are important because they indicate what the invoice price will be for any given $100,000 face value delivery of bonds against the contract. One might think that the conversion factors bring all bonds into equality, but this is almost never true. The Treasury yield curve is never flat over the relevant range at 8 percent, and there are CBOT rounding conventions for time to maturity that cause at least modest differences across the deliverable bonds. Under normal market conditions, applying the standard conversion factors to the array of deliverable bonds produces one bond that is "cheapest to deliver." That is to say, it could be purchased in the cash market and delivered against the contract with less cost than any of the alternative bonds. The bond that is expected by the market to be cheapest to deliver during the delivery month will drive the pricing of the futures.

One of the most fascinating features of the T-bond futures contract is the variability of the cheapest-to-deliver bond as interest rates change. In a high interest rate environment, there will be one bond most likely to be deliverable, but a different bond could play that role as rates fall. Unfortunately, there is no simple rule of thumb that eliminates the need to calculate which bond is cheapest at any point in time, though every bond house can supply this information to its customers.

The bond pricing problem is made even more interesting by the variety of *delivery options* held by the short in the contract. In addition to having wide latitude in the choice of issue, there are major timing options as well. Bonds may be delivered on any business day of the delivery month, but trading stops eight days prior to the end of the month. If the yield curve is in a carry, that is, short rates are lower than long, it generally pays to delay deliveries to the last part of the month, but there may be other incentives for delay.

In the eight-day window after trading stops, the firm may own, and be prepared to deliver, the cheapest-to-deliver bond. By delaying deliveries, the short maintains the option that rates would shift in such a way that another bond could be bought and deliver, more cheaply. This option, and other more arcane delivery options, may not sound too significant, but in total influence the bond futures price. The "option-adjusted price" is an important concept that anyone seriously trading the bond basis relationships must understand.

The delivered T-note contracts at the CBOT are priced in a completely analogous way to the bond contract, but the range of deliverable instruments is smaller. There is more certainty in the choice of deliverable notes than there is in the bond contract, but by the same token, there is less chance to trade the basis aggressively. While the 6½–10-year and 5-year T-note futures contracts are significant trading instruments, the varied basis relationships for the T-bond futures has contributed greatly to this product being the most actively traded futures contract in the world.

Pricing the T-bill futures contract at the CME doesn't pose the same issues as the delivered bond and note futures. There is almost invariably only one bill meeting the delivery requirements (i.e., having 90, 91, or 92 days to maturity). The deliverable bill began life as a 52-week bill and was subsequently reopened as a 26-week and then a 13-week bill. There are no conversion factors to consider, and pricing is determined by the same arbitrage principles that were described in discussing cash versus forward sales. The T-bill futures contract at the CME is priced as an index by subtracting the annualized discount rate from 100 to determine the traded price. This convention makes the futures price behave like the price of a note or bond.

As previously mentioned, cash settlement of futures was pioneered by the CME in 1981 with the introduction of three-month Eurodollar futures. Cash settlement is a viable alternative to physical delivery if the latter is impossible, cumbersome, or subject to manipulation. In the case of Eurodollars, the underlying reference rate is for nontransferable London bank time deposits, so physical delivery is impossible.

The process of arriving at a final settlement price in Eurodollars involves an extensive survey process designed to minimize the chance of manipulation, which in turn works to provide an accurate final price. On the last trading day (typically the Monday before the third Wednesday of the delivery month), there are two surveys conducted at a random time in the final hour and a half of trading and at the halt of trading. The number of banks from which respondents are randomly drawn is large, and to further minimize the potential impact of spurious quotes, the exchange truncates each sample by eliminating the extreme quotes.

It is rare in the Eurodollar market that there is a significantly divergent view of the rate charged for borrowings by prime banks, but the extra precautions taken by the CME ensure that a single bank, or even a group of banks, cannot move the final settlement by their responses. In the case of Eurodollars, the process must be viewed as a success. In the early 1990s, it was routine for more than 100,000 contracts, representing more than $100 *billion* in normal value, to be cash settled in this manner. If the process were perceived to be weak or fraught with basis risk, users of the contract would trade out of their positions at known prices rather than wait for the cash-settled value.

PRODUCTS

The early history of trading interest rate futures was touched on briefly at the start of this chapter. The subsequent years have seen an expanding array of products designed to meet the demands for differentiation by maturity, quality, and national origin. While the process has had its ups and downs, interest rate futures typically form the core product group for any successful futures exchange being launched worldwide. Tokyo, London, Paris, and many more financial centers have been quick to copy the pioneering ways of the CME and the CBOT. Usually, if a new international exchange is going to succeed, interest rate futures will establish the franchise.

The appendix to this chapter contains the contract specifications for the world's most actively traded interest rate futures products. Most also have active options traded on the futures. While compiled from sources that are belived accurate at the time of publication, contract specifications can, and do, frequently change. It is highly recommended that before trading any of these instruments, the user contact her broker or the exchange for the most recent terms and conditions.

It is also an excellent idea to monitor the progress of the instrument one is interested in to ascertain the size of the order that is easily executed. Information on volume and open interest is readily available in daily business publications like *The Wall Street Journal* or the *Financial Times*. One's broker is also an excellent source of information on liquidity. While it is extremely unlikely that an order in the front months of Eurodollar or T-bond futures would ever face a liquidity constraint, orders in a newer, more-specialized contract might have to be managed more carefully to secure quality executions. It is the buyer's and seller's responsibility to be aware of any market impact their order might have and to act accordingly to achieve optimal results.

APPENDIX: INTERNATIONAL INTEREST RATE FUTURES CONTRACT SPECIFICATIONS

Three-Month Eurodollar Futures

Market	International Monetary Market Division of the Chicago Mercantile Exchange
Trading Hours	7:20 A.M. to 2:00 P.M. (Central time). Trading in expiring contracts closes at 9:30 A.M. (3:30 P.M. London time) on the last trading day. The market will close earlier on or preceding certain holidays.
Quote Basis	Eurodollar Time Deposits having a principal value of $1,000,000 with a three-month maturity
Contract Size	$1,000,000
Delivery Months	March, June, September, December, and spot month

Three-Month Eurodollar Futures (concluded)

Ticker Symbol	ED
Minimum Fluctuation	Prices quoted in terms of the IMM Three-Month Eurodollar Index, 100 minus the yield on an annual basis for a 360-day year. Minimum price fluctuations shall be in multiples of .01 (1 basis point) or $25.00 per contract.
Daily Price Limits	No limit
Position Limits	10,000 contracts net long or net short in all contract months combined
Termination of Futures Trading	Futures trading shall terminate on the second London bank business day immediately preceding the third Wednesday of the contract month.
Delivery Day	Last trading day
Delivery	Cash settlement

Three-Month U.S. Treasury Bill Futures

Market	International Monetary Market Division of the Chicago Mercantile Exchange
Trading Hours	7:20 A.M. to 2:00 P.M. (Central time). Trading in expiring contracts closes at 10:00 A.M. on the last trading day. The market will close earlier on or preceding certain holidays.
Quote Basis	Three month (13-week) U.S. Treasury bills having a face value at maturity of $1,000,000
Contract Size	$1,000,000
Delivery Months	March, June, September, and December
Ticker Symbol	TB
Minimum Fluctuation	Prices quoted in terms of the IMM Three-Month U.S. Treasury Bill Index.* Minimum price fluctuations shall be in multiples of .01 (1 basis point) or $25.00 per contract.
Daily Price Limits	No Limit
Position Limits	5,000 contracts net long or net short in all contract months combined, 2,500 contracts in the lead month

Three-Month U.S. Treasury Bill Futures (*concluded*)

	on or after the day three weeks prior to the first delivery, 750 contracts in the lead month on or after the day one week prior to the first delivery day
Termination of Futures Trading	Futures trading in the lead month shall terminate on the business day immediately preceding the first delivery day.
Delivery	Delivery shall be made on three successive business days. The first delivery day shall be the first day of the spot month on which a 13-week Treasury bill is issued and a one-year Treasury bill have 13 weeks remaining to maturity.

*The IMM Index is 100.00 minus the annualized T-bill discount note.

One-Month LIBOR Futures

Market	International Monetary Market Division of the Chicago Mercantile Exchange
Trading Hours	7:20 A.M. to 2:00 P.M. (Central time); Trading in expiring contracts closes at 9:30 A.M. (3:30 P.M. London time) on the last day of trading. The market will close earlier on or preceding certain holidays.
Quote Basis	The IMM One-Month LIBOR Rate Index: 100 minus the London Interbank Offered Rate for One-Month Eurodollar Time Deposits
Contract Size	$3,000,000
Delivery Months	All 12 calendar months
Ticker Symbol	EM
Minimum Fluctuation	.01 IMM One-Month LIBOR Index points or $25.00 per contract
Daily Price Limits	No Limit
Position Limits	5,000 contracts net long or net short in all contract months combined
Termination of Futures Trading	Two London bank business days prior to the third Wednesday of the contract month

One-Month LIBOR Futures (concluded)

Delivery	Delivery is by cash settlement. All open positions on the last day of trading will be marked to market based on the final settlement price of the IMM One-Month LIBOR Index. The clearinghouse will calculate the final settlement price based on a survey of primary market participants in the London interbank Eurodollar market.

Long-Term Municipal Bond Index Futures

Market	The Chicago Board of Trade
Trading Hours	7:20 A.M. to 2:00 P.M. (Central time). Trading in expiring contracts closes at 2:00 P.M. on the last trading day.
Quote Basis	Points ($1,000) and thirty-seconds of a point
Contract Size	$1,000 times the closing value of *The Bond Buyer*™ Municipal Bond Index.* A price of 90-00 reflects a contract size of $90,000.
Delivery Months	March, June, September, and December
Ticker Symbol	MB
Minimum Fluctuation	1/32 of a point, or $31.25 per contract
Daily Price Limits	3 points ($3,000/contract) above or below the previous day's settlement price (expandable to 4½ points)
Position Limits	5,000 contracts net long or net short in all contract months combined
Termination of Futures Trading	Seventh business day preceding the last business day of the delivery month
Delivery	Municipal Bond Index futures settle in cash on the last day of trading. Settlement price equals *The Bond Buyer*™ Municipal Bond Index value on that day.

*Copyright 1985, *The Bond Buyer*™ and the Board of Trade of the city of Chicago.

Five-Year U.S. Treasury Note Futures

Market	The Chicago Board of Trade
Trading Hours	7:20 A.M. to 2:00 P.M. (Central time), Monday through Friday; Evening trading hours are 5:00 P.M. to 8:30 P.M. (CST), Sunday through Thursday. Trading in expiring contracts closes at noon on the last trading day.
Quote Basis	Points ($1,000) and one half of 1/32 of a point
Contract Size	One U.S. Treasury note having a face value at maturity of $100,000 or a multiple thereof
Delivery Months	March, June, September, and December
Ticker Symbol	FV
Minimum Fluctuation	One half of 1/32 of a point ($15.625/contract) rounded up to the nearest cent/contract; par is on the basis of 100 points.
Daily Price Limits	3 points ($3,000/contract) above or below the previous day's settlement price (expandable to 4½ points); limits are lifted the second business day preceding the first day of the delivery month.
Position Limits	7,500 contracts net long or net short in all contract months combined
Termination of Futures Trading	Seventh business day preceding the last business day of the delivery month
Delivery Day	The last business day of the delivery month
Delivery Method	Federal Reserve book-entry wire-transfer system
Delivery	U.S. Treasury notes that have an original maturity of not more than five years and three months and remaining maturity of not less than four years and three months as of the first business day of the delivery month. The five-year Treasury notes issued after the last trading day of the contract month will not be eligible for delivery into that month's contract. The invoice price equals the futures settlement price times a conversion factor plus accrued interest. The conversion factor is the price of the delivered note ($1 par value) to yield 8 percent.

10-Year U.S. Treasury Note Futures

Market	The Chicago Board of Trade
Trading Hours	7:20 A.M. to 2:00 P.M. (Central time), Monday through Friday; Evening trading hours are 5:00 P.M. to 8:30 P.M. (CST), Sunday through Thursday. Trading in expiring contracts closes at noon on the last trading day.
Quote Basis	Points ($1,000) and one half of 1/32 of a point
Contract Size	One U.S. Treasury note having a face value at maturity of $100,000 or a multiple thereof
Delivery Months	March, June, September, and December
Ticker Symbol	TY
Minimum Fluctuation	1/32 of a point ($31.25/contract); par is on the basis of 100 points
Daily Price Limits	3 points ($3,000/contract) above or below the previous day's settlement price (expandable to 4½ points); limits are lifted the second business day preceding the first day of the delivery month.
Position Limits	7,500 contracts net long or net short in all contract months combined
Termination of Futures Trading	Seventh business day preceding the last business day of the delivery month
Delivery Day	The last business day of the delivery month
Delivery Method	Federal Reserve book-entry wire-transfer system
Delivery	U.S. Treasury notes maturing at least 6 ½ years, but not more than 10 years from the first business day of the delivery month. The invoice price equals the futures settlement price times a conversion factor plus accrued interest. The conversion factor is the price of the delivered note ($1 par value) to yield 8 percent.

U.S. Treasury Bond Futures

Market	The Chicago Board of Trade
Trading Hours	7:20 A.M. to 2:00 P.M. (Central time), Monday through Friday; Evening trading hours are 5:00 P.M. to 8:30 P.M.

U.S. Treasury Bond Futures (*concluded*)

	(CST), Sunday through Thursday. Trading in expiring contracts closes at noon on the last trading day.
Quote Basis	Points ($1,000) and one half of 1/32 of a point
Contract Size	One U.S. Treasury bond having a face value at maturity of $100,000 or a multiple thereof
Delivery Months	March, June, September, and December
Ticker Symbol	US
Minimum Fluctuation	1/32 of a point ($31.25/contract); par is on the basis of 100 points
Daily Price Limits	3 points ($3,000/contract) above or below the previous day's settlement price (expandable to 4½ points); limits are lifted the second business day preceding the first day of the delivery month.
Position Limits	10,000 contracts net long or net short in all contract months combined
Termination of Futures Trading	Seventh business day preceding the last business day of the delivery month
Delivery Day	The last business day of the delivery month
Delivery Method	Federal Reserve book-entry wire-transfer system
Delivery	U.S. Treasury Bonds that, if callable, are not callable for at least 15 years from the first day of the delivery month or, if not callable, have a maturity of at least 15 years from the first business day of the delivery month. The invoice price equals the futures settlement price times a conversion factor plus accrued interest. The conversion factor is the price of the delivered bond ($1 par value) to yield 8 percent.

Three-Month Eurodollar Futures

Market	The Singapore International Monetary Exchange (SIMEX)
Trading Hours	5:45 P.M. to 4:20 A.M. (Chicago time). Trading in expiring contracts closes at 9:05 P.M. (Chicago time) on the last trading day

Three-Month Eurodollar Futures (*concluded*)

Quote Basis	Eurodollar time deposits having a principle value of $1,000,000 with a three-month maturity. Quoted in terms of an Index, 100 minus yield.
Contract Size	US $1,000,000 per contract
Delivery Months	March, June, September, and December
Ticker Symbol	ED
Minimum Fluctuation	.01 (1 basis point) or $25.00 per contract
Daily Price Limits	No limit
Position Limits	3,000 contracts
Termination of Futures Trading	Second London business day immediately preceding the third Wednesday of the contract month
Delivery	The third Wednesday of the contract month

*Trading hours will be extended by 10 minutes, effective February 18, 1992.

Three-Month Euroyen Futures

Market	The Singapore International Monetary Exchange (SIMEX)
Trading Hours*	6:00 P.M. to 4:10 A.M. (Chicago time). Trading in expiring contracts closes at 8:00 P.M. on the last trading day
Quote Basis	Quoted in terms of an index, 100 minus yield.
Contract Size	100,000,000 yen per contract
Delivery Months	March, June, September, and December
Ticker Symbol	EY
Minimum Fluctuation	.01 (1 basis point) or 2,500 yen per contract
Daily Price Limits	No limit
Position Limits	3,000 contracts
Termination of Futures Trading	Second London business day immediately preceding the third Wednesday of the contract month
Delivery	Cash settlement on the third Wednesday of the contract month

* Trading hours will be extended by 35 minutes, effective February 18, 1992.

10-Year Japanese Government Bond Futures

Market	The Tokyo Stock Exchange (TSE)
Trading Hours	9:00 A.M. to 11:00 A.M.; 12:30 P.M. to 3:00 P.M. (Tokyo time)
Quote Basis	100 Points (JY 100) and 1/100th of a point
Contract Size	Standardized 6 percent, 10-year Japanese government bonds with a 100,000,000 yen face value
Delivery Months	March, June, September, and December
Ticker Symbol	6 7 03 00 01 6—Indicates futures contract 7—Indicates year (1992) 03—Indicates contract month (March) 01—Indicates 10-year JBG contract
Minimum Fluctuation	.01 (1 basis point) or a value of 10,000 yen per contract
Daily Price Limits	2 points above or below the previous day's closing price
Position Limits	Usually, the TSE does not impose any limitations on the number of positions that can be held by members. However, the TSE is entitled to limit the number of positions held when it finds abnormality in the market. (TSE rules do not stipulate any specific amount.)
Termination of Futures Trading	The ninth business day prior to each delivery date
Delivery Date	20th of each contract month
Delivery	Exchange-listed Japanese government bonds having a maturity of 7 years or more but less than 11 years

Three-Month PIBOR Futures

Market	The Marche a Terme International de France (MATIF)
Trading Hours	9:30 A.M. to 4:00 P.M. (Paris time)
Quote Basis	100 minus the implied rate of the contract (in percentage per annum)
Contract Size	5,000,000 French francs
Delivery Months	March, June, September, and December
Ticker Symbol	PIB
Minimum Fluctuation	.01 (1 basis point) or a value of 125 French francs

Three-Month PIBOR Futures (concluded)

Daily Price Limits	60 basis points above or below the previous day's settlement price
Position Limits	Position limits are a percentage of daily open interest at the close. Position limits on the lead-month contract cannot exceed 20 percent of that day's closing open interest, while position limits on the second-position contract cannot exceed 30 percent.
Termination of Futures Trading	The second business day before the 11th Thursday of each calendar quarter, not counting the 1st Thursday if it is the first day of the quarter
Delivery	This contract is cash settled. Any positions open upon contract expiration are automatically liquidated at the settlement price. The settlement price corresponds to 100 minus 3-month spot interest rate, rounded off to two decimals, established the day of expiration.

Note: PIBOR futures contract opening and closing dates are in the process of being modified. Proposed closing: the trading session two business days before the third Wednesday of the delivery month.

Long Gilt Futures

Market	The London International Financial Futures Exchange (LIFFE)
Trading Hours	9:00 A.M. to 4:15 P.M. (London time). Trading in expiring contracts closes at 11:00 A.M. on the last day of trading.
Quote Basis	Per 100 British pounds nominal
Contract Size	50,000 British pound nominal value notional gilt with 9 percent coupon
Delivery Months	March, June, September, and December
Ticker Symbol	G
Minimum Fluctuation	BP 1/32 per BP 100 nominal or a value of BP 15.625
Daily Price Limits	None
Position Limits	Positions are constantly monitored by the exchange and the London clearinghouse. However, there are "formal" position limits.
Termination of Futures Trading	Two business days prior to the last business day in the trading month

Long Gilt Futures (*concluded*)

Delivery Day	Any business day in delivery (at seller's choice)
Delivery	Delivery may be made of any gilt with 15–25 years to maturity, as listed by LIFFE. Stocks with an optional redemption date will be deliverable only if the earliest maturity is 15 years or more and the latest maturity is 25 years or less. Stocks must be delivered in multiples of BP 50,000 nominal. No variable rate, index-linked, convertible, or partly paid gilt may be delivered. Stocks are not deliverable within the period of three weeks and one day before or on the expiration day. Interest must be payable semiannually.

Three-Month Sterling Interest Rate Futures

Market	The London International Financial Futures Exchange (LIFFE)
Trading Hours	8:20 A.M. to 4:02 P.M. (London time). Trading in expiring contracts closes at 11:00 A.M. on the last trading day.
Quote Basis	100.00 minus rate of interest
Contract Size	500,000 British pounds
Delivery Months	March, June, September, and December
Ticker Symbol	L
Minimum Fluctuation	.01 (1 basis point) or a value of BP 12.50
Daily Price Limits	None
Position Limits	Positions are constantly monitored by the exchange and the London clearinghouse. However, there are "formal" position limits.
Termination of Futures Trading	Third Wednesday of the delivery month
Delivery Day	First business day after the last trading day
Delivery	Cash settlement based on the exchange delivery settlement price.
Delivery Settlement Price	Based on the interest rates for three-month sterling deposits being offered to prime banking names between 9:30 A.M. and 11:00 A.M. on the last trading day, stated by a random sample of 16 from a list designated banks. Having disregarded the three highest and the three lowest quotes, the settlement price will be 100 minus the average of the remaining 10 rates.

German Government Bond Futures

Market	The London International Financial Futures Exchange (LIFFE)
Trading Hours	8:10 A.M. to 4:00 P.M. (London time); trading in expiring contracts closes at 11:00 A.M. (Frankfurt time) on the last trading day.
Quote Basis	DM 100 nominal value
Contract Size	DM 250,000 nominal value notional German Government Bond with 6 percent coupon
Delivery Months	March, June, September, and December
Ticker Symbol	A
Minimum Fluctuation	DM 0.01 or a value of DM 25
Daily Price Limits	None
Position Limits	Positions are constantly monitored by the exchange and the London clearinghouse. However, there are no "formal" position limits.
Termination of Futures Trading	Three Frankfurt working days before delivery day
Delivery Day	Tenth calendar day of delivery month. If this day is not a working day in Frankfurt, then the delivery day shall be the next following Frankfurt working day.
Delivery	Delivery may be made of any Bundesnleihe with 8½–10 years remaining maturity as of the 10th calendar day of the delivery month on a free-of-reallowance basis, as listed by LIFFE. Delivery will take place through the Kassenverein system of the Federal Republic of Germany.
Delivery Settlement Price	The LIFFE market price at 11:00 A.M. Frankfurt time on the last trading day. The invoicing amount in respect to each deliverable Bund is to be calculated by the price factor system. A final list of deliverable Bunds and their price factors will be announced by the Exchange two weeks prior to the last trading day of the delivery month. Adjustment will be made for full coupon interest accruing as of the delivery day with no deduction for withholding tax.

Eurodollar Futures

Market	The London International Financial Futures Exchange (LIFFE)
Trading Hours	8:30 A.M. to 4:00 P.M. (London time)
Quote Basis	100 minus rate of interest
Contract Size	US $1,000,000
Delivery Months	March, June, September, and December
Ticker Symbol	E
Minimum Fluctuation	0.01 (1 basis point) with a value of US $25.00
Daily Price Limits	None
Position Limits	Positions are constantly monitored by the exchange and the London clearinghouse. However, there are no "formal" position limits.
Termination of Futures Trading	Two business days prior to the third Wednesday of the delivery month
Delivery Day	First business day after the last trading day
Delivery	Cash settlement based on the exchange delivery settlement price
Delivery Settlement Price	Based on the interest rates for three-month Eurodollar deposits being offered to prime banking names between 9:30 A.M. and 11:00 A.M. on the last trading day, stated by a random sample of 16 from a list of designated banks. Having disregarded the three highest and three lowest quoted, the settlement price will be 100.00 minus the average of the remaining 10 rates.

CHAPTER 7

STRUCTURE OF THE FINANCIAL FUTURES MARKETS

*Todd E. Petzel**
Senior Vice President and Chief Economist,
Chicago Mercantile Exchange

Financial futures and options are traded in the United States at exchanges designated as contract markets by the Commodity Futures Trading Commission (CFTC). These exchanges were once exclusively engaged in the trading of physical commodities, and, without exception in the United States, financial futures represent a diversification of product line instead of a brand new way of doing business. Newer exchanges in Europe, Asia, Latin America, and Australia have been formed since the financial futures revolution in the United States, and they frequently specialize in interest rate and stock index products.

A few years ago, there was one model of trading financial futures. Not-for-profit membership organizations traded via open outcry, just as they had done in previous decades for agricultural and industrial products. Recently, however, there have been innovations in both exchange structure and the methodology of trading.

In an exchange environment, there are many features of trading that are not present in over-the-counter transactions. These features are not without cost, but are designed to minimize the likelihood that futures trade is fraudulent or subject to financial

---

* The views in this chapter are those of the author and do not necessarily reflect those of the Chicago Mercantile Exchange.

default. There is no magic formula for providing effective markets, and competitors worldwide have worked hard to bring the most efficient organization and trading systems to bear upon the futures industry.

This chapter describes several features of exchanges that are important to fully understanding the environment in which interest rate futures contracts trade. The following sections describe exchange structure and governance, mode of trading, the importance of mutual offset and clearing, financial safeguards including performance bonds, dealing with a futures commission merchant (FCM), and regulation. The appendix to this chapter provides information on the major financial futures markets worldwide so that the interested reader may make direct contact to obtain more detailed information.

EXCHANGE STRUCTURE AND GOVERNANCE

Exchanges are typically structured as membership organizations with a fixed number of *seats*. Conveying both trading and voting rights, these seats are in many ways more comprehensive than shares in a publicly owned company. Any financially qualified individual may trade futures, but a seat is a precondition for *direct* futures trading. Usually seats change hands in organized auction markets, with the price varying according to the perceived advantages of belonging to that particular exchange. Seat values are often viewed as a barometer of an exchange's financial health.

There are several distinct groups of traders active in the futures markets at any given point in time: floor traders, FCMs, commercial traders, managed funds, and public customers. Only the floor traders must be members of the exchange. The others may find it advantageous to own memberships, but it is not necessary to initiate trades. A special group of members at any exchange are the *clearing members*. Ultimately, it is this group that stands behind every single trade from the time it is executed to the time it is offset or delivered.

While some foreign markets, through automation, have largely eliminated the role of the *floor trader*, this group remains a vital part of the trading scene on every U.S. exchange. These members serve different functions, some acting as brokers for customer orders and others trading for their own accounts. The *local traders* bring their own capital to the market, and, in trying to profit from short- and intermediate-term trades, provide liquidity to all market participants. The debate over the virtue of floor traders versus automation is not resolved, but it is still true that the two most active and liquid interest rate futures contracts in the world, T-bonds at the Chicago Board of Trade (CBOT) and Eurodollars at the Chicago Mercantile Exchange (CME), thrive in the open outcry environment.

Futures commission merchants (FCMs) provide the link between the customer and the floor. These firms typically provide a range of services covering order execution, research, and sometimes financing. An FCM does not have to be a clearing member of an exchange in order to have its customers trade there. If it is not a member, the FCM will open an account of its own at a clearing member, and its customer positions will be carried on an omnibus basis.

The *commercial users* of an exchange run the gamut of firms. Banks, swaps and bond broker/dealers, and the treasury departments of large corporations all actively participate in interest rate futures. The volume of trading can be massive, providing strong incentives for these firms to become members and clearing members themselves. A significant trend in the 1980s was the acquisition or start-up by commercial and investment banks of their own FCMs to minimize their brokerage commissions and to take advantage of the often significant discount on exchange fees for members.

Commercial traders use futures as temporary substitutes for cash market positions. The choice of cash or futures is a matter of price and transactions costs, with the trade occurring in the most favorable market. By trading futures, a firm may either reduce or enhance the risk of its overall position. Additional benefits of futures come from the convenience, credit protection, and cost effectiveness that these instruments provide.

Managed pools of funds are the fastest-growing segment of trading. Just as individuals discovered the advantages of mutual funds of stocks over individual shares, they have found that professional management and diversification through *futures funds* can offer superior opportunities. These funds are purely speculative, and use a wide variety of fundamental and technical trading systems. A relatively new phenomenon is the passive investment in long futures as a distinct asset class. The objective of this is to be long a diversified group of commodities, which are expected to vary negatively with inflation and the more traditional asset classes of stocks and bonds. All futures funds, whether actively or passively managed, provide an important source of trading capital that helps provide essential liquidity for hedgers.

The final class of traders is composed of public customers, who are attracted to futures because of the speculative purity of the instrument. By going long or short Eurodollar futures, one can express an opinion about short-term interest rates quickly, cheaply, and without tying up huge sums of capital. For the trader who is smaller than a commercial firm or bank, there are virtually no other viable alternatives.

Each of the major trading groups is represented in the *exchange governance* through the board of directors or the extensive network of committees most exchanges maintain. Such service is voluntary, but it is probably not the case that its motivation is charity. By serving on committees, members have a forum to promote their aims and those of their customers. It is also a useful way to keep an eye on competitors who are probably serving the exchange in a similar capacity.

All exchanges have professional, nonmember staffs to carry out operational, regulatory, legal, marketing, and research functions. It is the primary responsibility of these staffs to make the market as neutral and cost efficient as possible to both buyers and sellers. This is done by working with members and customers to identify areas of opportunity or concern, and then designing and implementing the resulting rule changes.

MODE OF TRADING

Competitive market makers operating in an open outcry environment have comprised the standard mode of trading in U.S. futures markets since the process began over 100 years ago. Unlike the specialist or designated market maker found at securities exchanges, no individual is given a special role or a preferred status on the trading floor. Individuals trade for their own accounts or act as brokers for customer orders, but these roles are flexible. With only a few exceptions, it is not possible to categorize the trading of an individual floor member ex ante.

The competitive nature of the system allows considerable flexibility in serving the varying demands of customers. There are natural forces working to create an equilibrium pit population, which can range from a small handful to many hundreds of individuals. As order flow grows, broker incomes rise, attracting new entries. *Locals*, who trade for their own accounts and thus provide liquidity for the customer order, also are attracted to increased order flow. The process works in reverse if business declines.

For large, diversified exchanges, the fixed number of seats poses few constraints on supporting active, growing contracts. The floor population for Eurodollars at the CME began as a small group of dedicated individuals laboring in the shadow of the then much larger T-bill futures market. It has since grown to more then 300 traders, drawn from seatholders who had previously worked in the livestock or currency areas.

Sometimes growth is constrained by the limited number of members available to serve new products or expanding markets. The solution to the problem has usually been to issue new seats. Like receiving a dividend, existing members can be provided with the new memberships (or sometimes fractions of seats that have to be combined through market transactions), which can be held or traded away. The net effect is an expansion of the member population without a loss of equity to the existing owners.

New memberships can have the same rights as the old, but, more typically, they carry restrictions covering the markets in which they may be used. This serves two purposes. First, the new individuals are forced to earn their livelihoods in fledgling markets, adding to the chance that the products will succeed. Second, by restricting access to the traditional markets, the extent of new competition faced by existing members is limited.

At the CME, there are three classes of membership. The full CME seat allows the owner access to all markets. The International Monetary Market (IMM) seat owner can trade anything except livestock futures. The Index and Option Market (IOM) seat only allows access to stock index futures and any option traded at the exchange. The creation of these divisions paralleled the expansion of the exchange into financial futures in 1972 (IMM) and into options and Standard & Poor's 500 futures in 1982 (IOM). However, anomalies in the historical relation sometimes appear; lumber futures are an IOM product, which is an artifact of efforts to attract additional traders to that pit. Seat divisions at other exchanges often have similar histories and patterns.

The membership seats trade in their own auction market. The differences in seat prices across divisions reflect the capitalized value of the additional rights contained therein. A full membership should never trade for less than a more restricted one, but if the relative advantage of the extra rights declines, the two seat values could converge. Seat prices are also affected by their scarcity, and exchanges walk a fine line in determining the appropriate total number. If there are too few seats, there will be a shortage of qualified traders to serve the market. Providing too many seats floods the market relative to the total demand for trading services. In this case, the marginal broker or trader cannot make a reasonable living, and nobody wants to enter the business. Seat prices in that environment fall toward zero. In itself, this is not bad, but the seat holders have little equity at risk. There are fewer incentives to develop the markets and the institution if it costs little for a member to cut and run.

The rules governing *open outcry trading* are remarkably simple. The first basic principle is that there should be only one best bid and one best offer in the pit at a time. If the market is 12 bid, offered at 14, a trader may not start bidding at 11, or offering at 15. Anyone may match the best bid or offer. If someone decides to bid 13, then all the previous bidders at 12 must either match the new best bid or stay quiet. The purpose of the rule is to ensure that any customer or trader will have clear access to the best prices at any time.

The second key rule is that a trader must trade with the first party you recognize who meets your bid or offer. This requirement is designed to provide fairness to all market participants. It has the side effect of generating shouts, jumps, waves, and all manner of devices employed by traders trying to be recognized in a busy pit, and many observers of open outcry trading never get past this first impression of chaos. The pit is a highly competitive and efficient way of discovering prices and shifting risks.

All exchanges have strict rules to protect customers from dishonest brokers and traders. Computerized reconstruction of trading helps identify possible violations, which are investigated by the exchange compliance staff. If sufficient evidence of wrongdoing is found, the case will be turned over to a disciplinary committee made up of members. Violators of the rules can be warned, fined, suspended, or expelled depending on the severity of the infraction.

The exchange community has the incentive to provide a fair and honest market. If an exchange has a reputation of allowing its members to abuse customers, those customers have every ability and incentive to seek trading services elsewhere. While the reputation of the exchange is important, it is absolutely necessary for each customer to monitor his or her broker's performance. Always buying at the highs or selling at the lows is a sign of implausibly bad luck, incompetence, or dishonesty on the part of the broker. If such a pattern or trading develops, it may be a sign to switch brokers.

Many modern observers say that open outcry trading could easily be replaced by computer screens listing bids and offers. Several such systems have been tried with mixed success. One of the earliest fully *automated trading systems* was Intex, which advertised itself as a more efficient alternative to trading gold in either New York or London. Liquidity never developed and the project was dropped. On the successful side of the ledger sheet are new exchanges in Europe like DTB (Germany) and SOFFEX (Switzerland). However, it is still the case that open outcry exchanges continue to compete and grow side by side with the more automated models.

Automated systems have several advantages, not the least of which is the reduction of errors caused by miscommunicated information. One trader in a pit may be buying two contracts, while a counterparty thinks the transaction is for 10. Careful hand signals and checking of trades minimize the risk of such errors, but they simply can't occur in a computerized system. A further advantage of some computer systems is strict price *and* time priority. The first individual to bid 12 for a contract has a secure spot in the computerized queue. The first order to sell at 12 will be matched to that order. In open outcry, on the other hand, it is the trader recognized that gets the fill, regardless of whether or not it was in the pit longest.

There are disadvantages to automation as well. In open outcry, a bid or offer is good only for the moment it is spoken. In one sense, every order is canceled if it is not filled immediately. Of course, the open outcry bid or offer may be repeated as long as necessary. On automated systems, orders stay active until they are filled or purposely canceled. While this makes great sense for resting orders, the market-making function of the traditional exchange local becomes more complicated. Placing a bid and offer in the system around the perceived market value in order to earn a "scalping" profit equal to the bid-ask spread runs the risk of having either side picked off when market conditions shift. The cancel order facility on automated systems tends to be quite quick, but it still requires a conscious step not needed in open outcry. The result may be that traders make markets in fewer instruments or widen their bid-ask spread to compensate for this free call option they are providing to traders looking at their bids and offers on the screen.

The CME and the CBOT have not ignored automation. By developing GLOBEX® in partnership with Reuters, these two exchanges have embarked on the most ambitious automated futures and options trading system yet. GLOBEX combines an order-matching trading system with an international network so that member traders in all the major market cities may one day have direct access to these products. Designed initially to operate between 6 P.M. and 6 A.M. Chicago time, GLOBEX is designed to complement the regular trading hours of the open outcry markets and to make CME and CBOT products available during the business hours of Asia and Europe.

Automation is also reaching into the trading pits. Computerized trading cards and order management systems are being developed to enhance order flow, reduce errors, and speed the trading and clearing process. As the volume of business continues to grow, these steps will keep the open outcry system fast, accurate, and cost efficient.

Whether one form of trading system will come to dominate the other remains to be seen. While vitally important to the men and women who trade both on and off the floor, the ultimate user will be well served in either case. It is clear that the existence of computerized trading will not immediately replace the very deep, liquid markets trading by open outcry. Whatever system prevails, and a blend is plausible, the user will be the winner because of the superior liquidity and cost efficiency provided.

MULTILATERAL OFFSET AND CLEARING

A common complaint heard from users of over-the-counter contracts is that while they usually get a good price establishing a position, the terms can become less favorable when they want to get out of the trade. This is not surprising because the counterparty is probably a bank or swap dealer with a book containing that position and others that, when combined, represent the exposure the firm desires. When the customer wants to get out of his position, adjustments need to be made that involve costs. But more importantly, there is the issue of market power. The customer is the party seeking to reverse. The counterparty is perfectly content with the status quo and will extract whatever price it can if it senses anxiety. After all, it knows the customer's current position, and it will certainly use that information to its advantage.

A vital difference between standardized, exchange-traded products and customized, over-the-counter instruments comes from *multilateral offset* and the role of the *clearinghouse*. If Mr. A goes long a June Eurodollar future by trading with Ms. B, he can offset that transaction by going short the same futures contract *with any counterparty*. This is a key advantage over a stand-alone bilateral contract; the competition across the pool of traders reduces the market power of any particular counterparty. Ms. B may try to exploit her knowledge of Mr. A's position, but will be limited in her ability to do so by the presence of other buyers in the market.

Multilateral offset works because of the role of the clearinghouse. Once Mr. A and Ms. B have made their trade, it is submitted for clearing and matched to confirm all the important details (contract, buying and selling clearing members, month, quantity, and price). Once the trade matches, it is figuratively broken in two.

The clearinghouse becomes the seller to Mr. A and the buyer to Ms. B. This process carries with it the financial guarantee of the trade, which will be discussed more fully below, but it also breaks any necessary link between the original long and short position.

In subsequent trades, if Mr. A goes short in a trade with Mr. C, the transaction will be treated as described above. The clearinghouse will now be the buyer to Mr. A's new sale. If Mr. A is simultaneously long and short with the clearinghouse, the positions offset and are removed from the books. In this simple example, Ms. B would remain short, and Mr. C would be long, with the clearinghouse in the middle.

The two concepts of *volume* and *open interest* can be described using the above example. Every time a contract is bought and sold, it is one lot of volume. Each contract must contain a long and a short side. *Open interest* is simply the number of contracts outstanding at any given point in time. After the first trade above, Mr. A held one lot of long open interest and Ms. B held one lot of short open interest. Open interest is reported by the exchanges daily and will reflect one side of the market, not the sum of the long and short positions. Note that when Mr. A went short with Mr. C, his long open interest was offset, but Mr. C acquired a unit of long open interest. Total open interest in the system was unchanged.

Volume can either create, reduce, or leave open interest unchanged. It is not unusual in the major interest rate futures markets to see several hundred thousand contracts traded in a day and have open interest shift up or down by only a few thousand. This is a reflection of active day trading by locals, many of whom do not like to take an exposure overnight, and by the activities of upstairs broker/dealers who trade around their books.

The facility of multilateral offset reduces the long-term costs of transactions by providing greater liquidity. Traders are always more willing to establish positions in a market where there will be a broad range of potential counterparties to the offsetting trades. Multilateral offset, along with the credit features of the system described below, are important characteristics uniquely possessed by standardized futures.

The system of multilateral offset in place at virtually all exchanges is in fact more complicated than the stylized example described above. The clearinghouse does interpose itself between buyer and seller, but there is another layer as well. The clearinghouse does not know the identity of Mr. A or Ms. B, but instead sees them as customer positions of Clearing Members Y and Z. The system works just as described above, but, for the financial safeguards that accompany the mutual offset system, this is a critical factor.

It should also be noted that Mr. A and Ms. B could both be customers of the same clearing member and the system would work identically. The clearing member may not keep offsetting customer positions on its own books only, and off the records of the clearinghouse. If a member did this, it would be a form of "bucketing" orders and neither customer would have the financial protection afforded legitimate positions carried at the exchange. It is strictly against U.S. regulations to bucket futures orders, but the practice is known to be tolerated in other countries. The customer must satisfy herself that her position is being handled appropriately. The final section of this chapter suggests steps that are available to the customer in this regard.

FINANCIAL SAFEGUARDS

In the previous section, the system of multilateral offset was described, and it was noted that the clearinghouse became the buyer to every seller and the seller to every buyer. From one perspective, this eases the costs of carrying an ever-growing chain of bilateral agreements, but it raises financial issues as well. When Mr. A trades with Ms. B, both may consider the other creditworthy, but what stands behind the clearinghouse?

For the major exchanges worldwide, the answer is the *collective clearing members* of the clearinghouse, and this is usually a most formidable array of institutions. At the CME and CBOT, there has never been a clearing member default on its obligations to perform on a futures or options contract. No customer has ever lost money due to the failure of a clearing member. That is not to say that no firm has ever gone out of business because of trading losses or other business failure, but it highlights the fact that there are extensive financial safeguards in place to cover the risks of such events.

At the heart of the system is the fact that it is the private capital of all the member firms that is the ultimate source of performance on a contract. There is no government-backed insurance scheme or any other external source of relief should a financial disaster occur. Since it is the collective wealth of the members on the line, there is the strongest possible incentive to make sound credit decisions privately and to implement rules to protect the system if every member's judgment isn't perfectly sound.

The process begins at the microlevel of the client–clearing member relationship. No individual, including an exchange member, is allowed to trade directly through the exchange. All trades must be transacted through, and guaranteed by, a clearing member. If a customer defaults on his obligation, the clearing member would liquidate the outstanding position, but the firm would still be responsible for any monies owed to the clearinghouse. The creditworthiness of customers is of paramount concern to each clearing member.

There is considerable competition across clearing members for customers, and one might imagine that firms would cut corners on creditworthiness in order to gain commission revenue. There are several checks on such behavior, but the most important one is the basic principle that the costs of bad decisions at the customer level are borne entirely by the clearing member guaranteeing that customer, at least until the firm is out of business. If Clearing Member Y chooses not to carry Mr. A. because of credit considerations, Clearing Member Z may come to the opposite business decision. In the final analysis, Mr. A will either be a good risk or not, but the consequences will fall entirely on Clearing Member Z.

While the link between the customer and the clearing member is an important one, it is the special set of obligations between clearing members and the clearinghouse of the exchange that sets futures contracts apart from over-the-counter instruments. The clearinghouse holds each clearing member accountable for every position it carries, and, in return, the clearinghouse is obliged to provide the net settlement from all transactions, since it is the counterparty to all longs and shorts.

The clearinghouse has many tools at its disposal in providing a system of great financial integrity: performance bonds, marking to market, segregation of customer funds, capital requirements, and both financial and market surveillance. Each of these is described below.

Performance bonds, also known more traditionally as *margins*, are good-faith deposits that must be made by holders on both long and short positions to guarantee performance. Unlike margins for the purchase of stock, there is absolutely no credit component to futures performance bonds. These funds are required promptly as a first step to ensure the customer's financial ability to withstand reasonable losses on the position.

There are two stages of performance bonds: initial and maintenance. Initial levels are the minimum deposits required to open either a long or short position. Maintenance performance bonds are set lower and form the minimum requirements to keep a position open. If losses in a position reduce an account to below maintenance levels, the customer must either deposit sufficient new funds to reestablish the *initial performance bond* level, or liquidate the position. Either step is designed to maximize the likelihood that the account owner is primarily risking her own capital and not that of the clearing member.

Performance bonds are set by the clearinghouse in anticipation of future volatility in the market. If the clearinghouse believes there is less than a one-in-twenty chance that Eurodollar futures could move by more than $500 in a trading session, it might set the maintenance level there and then scale up that number by some factor to arrive at an initial performance bond like $700. To arrive at these probabilities, the clearinghouse looks at distributions of historical price changes and current market conditions.

The exchange-set levels are the minimums that must be collected from customers. The clearing member is free to require more if there is any question about creditworthiness. It is not unusual for public speculative customers to be asked to open accounts with balances significantly larger than the exchange minimums required.

It is a major error in logic to calculate margin as a fraction of notional value to get a concept of the leverage available in a position. The $500 maintenance level for Eurodollar futures mentioned above is only .05 percent of the notional $1 million contract value. This does not translate to 2,000:1 leverage because the notional value is not the amount at risk. Instead, one should see that $500 represents 20 basis points of movement in the annualized interest rate, and that is a better reflection of the risk for both long and short. If the $500 represented a down payment on a $1 million deposit, which is the way stock margins work, the leverage argument would have some merit. However, the fundamental nature of futures margins is considerably different, leaving traditional analogies like these fatally flawed.

Clearinghouses can work in one of two ways: collecting performance bonds on either a net or a gross basis. In a *gross margining system*, each long and short position must deposit funds at the clearinghouse. In a net system, funds for all positions are collected by the clearing members, but only performance bonds on the net exposure are passed along to the clearinghouse.

As an example, suppose Clearing Member Z had in its customer account 800 long March Eurodollar futures and 1,000 short March Eurodollar futures. Under a gross margin system, funds for all 1,800 positions would be collected from the customers and passed on to the clearinghouse. If the system margined net, the same amount would be collected from customers, but margins for only 200 contracts would be passed on. The only difference between the systems is whether the bulk of the deposits reside at the clearinghouse or on the books of the clearing members.

There is an open debate as to which system is inherently more stable. For gross margining there is the virtue that with all the money at the clearinghouse there is immediate assurance that all of the participants have the necessary funds. Given this greater control, it is believed that the level of performance bonds can be set somewhat lower than in a net margining system. However, there is absolutely no empirical verification that margin levels vary across systems. In the final analysis, the two largest clearing systems at the CBOT and CME, one margining net, the other gross, have never had a clearing member default on its obligations.

Performance bonds can be deposited at the clearinghouse in cash, Treasury securities, or a restricted group of letters of credit. Liquidity of assets and stability of value are the prime characteristics needed for performance bond collateral. At the CME, late in 1991, performance bond collateral on deposit of all kinds was approximately $5 billion, and all of it was potentially available within one hour. There have been discussions on expanding the list of available performance bond assets, and if the standards of liquidity and security can be met, new assets will be allowed.

For the performance bonds posted by customers with their clearing members, a broader group of assets is allowed. However, if the assets carry price or liquidity risk, they are only allowed to be valued for performance bond purposes at some fraction of market value. These "haircuts" vary by type of asset, being quite large, for example, for cash equities and other risky assets. Traditionally, cash was required from customers, which formed a significant source of revenue to the clearing members earning interest on these deposits. Now, because of competition across clearing members, it is more likely to see the customer earn this income from performance bond deposits.

The method of calculating performance bond requirements used to be a back-of-the-envelope sum in the days when futures were the only contracts traded. Once options were introduced, the landscape changed considerably. Early performance bond systems for options relied on "strategies" to measure risk. Option spreads were less risky than outright options, and, hence, required less in terms of risk margin. Unfortunately, strategy-based systems break down quickly once you move beyond the simplest portfolios. Applying the rules on one combination of positions could give a different result than if a different application of the same rules was used, making it possible to "game" the system.

The next step on the evolutionary chain was "delta-based" performance bonds. In this format, each option is viewed as a fraction of a futures contract, with out-of-the-money options carrying a small weight and in-the-money options looking almost like futures. Being based on widely accepted option pricing theory, delta basing solved many of the problems of the strategy-based system, but created others.

The biggest flaw in delta-based margin performance bonds comes from the fact that nothing beyond delta—the instantaneous change in an option's price resulting from a small change in underlying futures price—is considered. Volatility, time delay, and the effect of shifting deltas are not part of a delta calculation, though they clearly affect the risk of any option portfolio. To solve these problems, a scenario-based performance bond system has evolved.

Developed by the CME in 1988, Standard Portfolio Analysis

of Risk (SPAN®) simulates what an option and futures portfolio would be worth under various combinations of rising and falling prices and volatilities. It attempts to identify the largest reasonable exposure, and then sets the minimum performance bond for the portfolio at that level. SPAN avoids the gaming problems of strategy-based performance bonds and closes the gaps of any delta-based system. By 1992, every U.S. futures exchange had adopted SPAN® as its performance bond system, and it was beginning to be applied internationally as well.

The security of futures and options positions is due in no small part to the careful setting of performance bonds, but another key ingredient is the cash-on-the-barrelhead philosophy that keeps exposures minimal. At least once a day, all futures and options positions are evaluated at current market prices. Losing positions are immediately identified, and the loss since the last marking called for. This variation payment is then turned immediately over to the side of the position holding the gain. Once this *marking to the market* has occurred, there are no outstanding debts in the system.

Payments of variation must be "same-day" funds to ensure the fulfillment on the losing party's obligation. In periods of extreme volatility, the clearinghouse may call for additional intraday variation payments as needed. Such variation payments at a major exchange like the CME usually exceed $100 million daily, and, at times of great volatility, have reached $2.5 billion.

No other settlement system is as stringent as the futures market's marking to the market. Interbank transactions, Treasury securities, and equity markets all have settlement features that require participants to assume some greater degree of credit exposure to the counterparties. This feature of futures clearing and settlement is widely recognized as a unique foundation for the financial safeguards of futures contracts.

Performance bonds and positions of customers are maintained at the clearing member in accounts segregated from those of the firm itself. This provision for segregation of customer funds helps protect customers in the event of insolvency of the clearing member. In such circumstances, the clearinghouse will attempt to transfer all segregated customer positions and funds to another clearing member, allowing those customers to continue participating in the market. Without segregated funds, the customer's fate would be tied to that of the house account of the failing firm, leading to delays and additional risk in extricating the position.

A further safeguard to the system comes from the capital required of the clearing members. Each exchange sets its own standards, at or above minimums set by the CFTC. The goal of the *capital requirements* is to see that firms participating in the market have capital commensurate with the size and riskiness of the business they are carrying. While many attempts have been made over the years to make the capital requirements more "risk based," these rationalization efforts have not been as successful as the steps taken in performance bond calculation described above.

In addition to a firm's capital and performance bond funds, many clearing organizations require security deposits that would be immediately available at a time of financial distress. It is also the case for clearing members that are owned by larger entities that the parent must guarantee the proprietary trading of the clearing member.

Just because performance bonds have been set, variation payments distributed, customer funds segregated, and firm capital set aside, the exchange cannot just sit back and expect the system to be self-maintaining. Auditors monitor the system for continuing compliance with the financial rules and market surveillance personnel watch the composition of the market in order to identify potentially risky situations. The goal of financial and market surveillance is to discover problems while they are still manageable.

While there has never been a clearing member default at the CME or the CBOT, many steps are in place if such an event would occur. The procedure is well known to staff and all member firms so that each knows its role and obligations.

If a default occurred in the proprietary account of a clearing member, the following steps would be taken by the clearinghouse:

- Attempt to transfer customer-segregated positions to other clearing members.
- Assume and possibly liquidate the proprietary positions.
- Apply the house margins and any security deposits to the failed obligation.
- Attach any assets like membership seats to apply to the debt.
- Invoke the parent guarantee.

It is important to note that customer positions and funds under control of the clearinghouse may not be used to cover the obligations arising from a default in the house account. Should a loss occur in the customer account, the clearing member has the obligation to cover the loss of its customer. If the loss was so large that the clearing member could not cover it, resulting in a default, the same steps described above would be taken except that only noninvolved customer positions would be transferred and the parent firm guarantee would not apply. Note that it is still the case that house positions and assets would be used to offset the customer's loss since the firm had guaranteed the customer.

While the customer funds are segregated from the proprietary accounts of the clearing members, there is no further segregation across customers. If a default is of customer origin, the clearinghouse has the right to apply all customer performance bonds toward the loss. This means that while traders of other clearing members are protected against such defaults, customers do have some exposure if another customer causes a default at their firm.

If all the above steps still fail to satisfy the obligation, the exchange would apply its own surplus funds and the security deposits posted by all clearing members. Beyond that, the exchange would look to its other clearing members to make up the loss. The extent to which exchanges may make claims upon its members varies widely. Some exchanges, like the CME, have "good to the last drop" rules that eventually provide access to the firms' total capital. In late 1991, the CME's ultimate backing from margins, memberships, security deposits, surplus funds, and firm capital exceeded $22 billion. Other exchanges may have different rules and, hence, different ultimate funding. The major exchanges worldwide are all quite well backed, but it is the obligation of every customer to make a careful evaluation of the risks before entering into any market.

FUTURES COMMISSION MERCHANTS (FCMs)

Futures commission merchants are the link between the public customer and the exchange. In serving that function, the FCM takes on the roles of gatekeeper, accountant, and position guarantor. Since the FCM has full responsibility for the activities of its customers, it must exercise considerable caution in establishing and monitoring its accounts.

An FCM will typically screen its customers according to their net liquid assets and income, hoping to minimize losses from customers lacking the ability to cover losses that may arise. Opening an account with an FCM is similar to opening a stock market account, but since the nature of the products is different, there are more detailed and extensive risk disclosure documents to be read and signed by the customer. In addition to the appropriate documents, an FCM may require a substantial initial deposit of funds to open an account.

Today, virtually every element of the customer-FCM relationship is open to negotiation. Contract commissions, size of minimum balances, and the interest earned on those funds are all open terms. But the customer must maintain an appropriate perspective in these matters. Someone expecting to trade only a handful of contracts each month should not expect to receive the same business terms given to a commercial hedger or commodity trading advisor who trades many times each day.

There is a wide range of futures brokers offering different services for different customers, and the fees vary accordingly. At one end of the spectrum are the full service firms that provide considerable quantities of research and trading advice to their customers. At the opposite extreme are the firms that provide the most basic execution services. But no matter what the level of services provided, the FCM always guarantees the customer performance, and this element alone deserves compensation.

An investor at an FCM should think of himself as a party to a contract, rather than simply a customer. As such, there are several things the investor should expect from the FCM. First and foremost, one should be able to receive complete and accurate information about any futures or options product contemplated. Contract specifications, key transaction dates, and the risks that a trade could face should all be easily and clearly available. The investor should also be able to receive a complete description of the costs of trading, which may include commissions, "loads," maintenance or service charges, redemption fees, and penalties.

The customer must decide what level of *trading control* to give to the FCM. Many customers give no latitude to the broker, allowing only the execution of trades explicitly authorized by the customer. Others give their brokers wide discretion in the initial creation of trades and their ultimate offset. The more discretion that is allowed, the more confidence the customer must have in the broker. The risks of having an account traded for the benefit of generating commission income for the broker rather than for profits by the customer cannot be dismissed. All responsible FCMs have programs in place to supervise such activity by their employees, but the history of trading in all investments shows vivid examples of trading practices that should be watched for and avoided.

The customer of an FCM who allows any discretion in the trading of her account does not give up any of the rights described above. In particular, the customer should have complete access to the trading records, account status, and fees and commissions paid. If any of this information is not available on a prompt basis, inquiries should be made at whatever level is necessary to get the situation remedied.

The customer-FCM relationship is also colored by the fact that in the event of a default by the customer of an FCM, the funds of all the other customers at that firm are exposed to some risk. As stated in the previous section, if such an event were to occur, attempts would be made to isolate and transfer the nondefaulting customer positions. There is however, the possibility that the funds in the aggregate customer-segregated account would be called upon to meet the default. For this reason, customers should investigate potential FCMs in a fashion similar to the way that the customers are screened. Information on the finances of an FCM, including capital on hand to support the positions carried, should be freely available to potential customers.

As a rule, all clearing members of an exchange meet financial standards set by the exchange on an ongoing basis. But there are many worthy FCMs that do not maintain clearing status at each exchange. Information is available from every FCM that can be compared across firms, and the customer should be able to satisfy himself that he is dealing with a reputable, financially secure institution.

REGULATION

Regulation of futures markets starts at the exchanges and extends to the federal government's independent agency, the Commodity Futures Trading Commission (CFTC), and the National Futures Association (NFA), a private, independent self-regulatory organization set up by the Congress. Each body plays an important role in protecting the financial and trading integrity of the futures markets.

The financial oversight of the market is primarily the responsibility of the exchange and clearinghouse, and this was discussed at length above. The other regulatory functions served by the exchange are in the area of enforcing the trading rules. The open outcry system has several rules to protect customers and to ensure open and competitive trading. An example is the *trading ahead rule*, which prohibits a broker from trading for her own account while holding an executable customer order. Other rules operate on a more macrolevel and are designed to prevent attempts at market manipulations. The exchanges understand that these markets are completely voluntary, and it is simply sound business practice to police the markets so that customers have confidence in the institution.

Federal regulation of the futures markets dates back to 1922 when the Grain Futures Act was passed. The initial federal efforts were focused on alleged manipulation issues, but, in fact, the "manipulation" that brought on congressional action in the early 1920s was the inevitable drop in grain prices that occurred after a post–World War Europe began to get its agricultural sector back on track.

For more than 50 years, federal oversight was confined to futures on domestic agricultural products, and, consequently, the Grain Futures Administration and its successor, the Commodity Exchange Authority, were divisions of the U.S. Department of Agriculture. Tropical commodities and metals had no federal oversight at this time. By the 1970s, however, rapid change was underway in the development of futures products and in the relationships between securities and futures markets. In 1974, Congress passed the Commodity Exchange Act creating the first independent agency for the oversight of futures trading.

The CFTC's structure is built on the exchange's own self-regulatory activities where possible. Instead of looking at trading records on a regular basis to identify infractions, the CFTC performs "rule reviews," which are audits of an exchange's procedures to ascertain whether rules are being enforced. The CFTC does its own surveillance of markets to detect signs of manipulation, but throughout its history, it has tried to work with the exchanges in this area so that the commission would not have to exercise its own powers. In the majority of cases, it has been successful in letting market forces and the exchanges work out stressful situations, but there have been a few extraordinary instances where the commission has actively involved itself.

The CFTC is also charged with enforcing *trade practice rules* that are set out in the Commodity Exchange Act and its regulations. These rules are designed to apply to all market participants, whether they are exchange members or not. Since the disciplinary reach of an exchange is limited to its members, the CFTC must provide coverage for the rest of the community. It has on several occasions successfully prosecuted nonmember firms for inappropriate sales practices, but it has also built part of its enforcement record by prosecuting members who had already been sanctioned by an exchange.

The National Futures Association (NFA) was created in the early 1980s by Congress to license and regulate individuals and firms that participate in soliciting public orders for the futures industry. Congress realized that many of these individuals were not exchange members, to whom private rules would apply, and that it would probably be a poor use of the CFTC's limited resources to serve in an extensive registration capacity. The NFA was created along lines similar to the National Association of Securities Dealers (NASD) for securities brokers, and provides considerable services to the trading public, brokers, and commodity trading advisors and pool operators.

Every broker soliciting business for futures must be a member of the NFA. If a customer has any questions about the disciplinary record of an individual or a firm, she may call the NFA's Disciplinary Information Access Line (DIAL) at 1-800-676-4NFA for a report. This clearinghouse for disciplinary data contains information concerning actions taken by the futures regulatory bodies and 13 exchanges. If information about a broker is not available through DIAL, this could be a signal that the broker does not have all the appropriate registrations in place. DIAL is an important resource to the investing public to minimize the chance of dealing with an unscrupulous broker or firm.

Regulation of futures markets is performed at many levels, but the most-effective regulation still begins with knowledgeable customers who demand quality performance from their brokers. Investors can take great comfort in the layers of oversight that exist, but there is no regulation that will compensate a customer against losses stemming from his own lack of knowledge or diligence. The broad success of interest rate futures and options is as much a testament to the skills and knowledge of the customers as it is a positive statement about the regulatory oversight provided by the exchanges, the CFTC, and the NFA.

APPENDIX: MAJOR INTERNATIONAL INTEREST RATE FUTURES EXCHANGES

Exchange	Chicago Mercantile Exchange	
Address	30 South Wacker Drive Chicago, Illinois 60606	
Telephone Number	(312) 930–1000	
Fax Number	(312) 930–3439	
Date Founded	December 1, 1919	
Members	CME memberships	625
	IMM memberships	812
	IOM memberships	1,287
	Total	2,724
Major Futures and Options Products Traded	Eurodollars S&P 500 Deutschemark Japanese yen Swiss francs	

182 Section 2 Financial Futures

Exchange	Chicago Board of Trade	
Address	141 West Jackson Blvd. Chicago, Illinois 60604	
Telephone Number	(312) 435–3500	
Fax Number	(312) 435–7170	
Date Founded	April 1848	
Members	Full seat	1,402
	AM	752
	GIM	229
	COM	643
	IDEM	635
	Total	3,661
Major Futures and Options Products Traded	U.S. Treasury bonds Corn Soybeans Treasury notes—10 year Treasury notes—5 year	

Exchange	The London International Financial Futures Exchange (LIFFE)	
Address	Royal Exchange London EC3V 3PJ	
Telephone Number	44-071–623–0444	
Fax Number	44-071–588–3624	
Other Offices	New York	
Date Founded	September 1982	
Members	Futures member	160
	Associate futures members	3
	Options members	114
	Associate options members	7
	Total	284
Major Futures and Options Products Traded	German government bonds 3-month pound Long gilt Euromark Financial Times Index	

Exchange	The Marche a Terme International de France (MATIF)	
Address	176 Rue Montmartre 75002 Paris	
Telephone Number Fax Number	33-1-40-28-8282 33-1-40-28-8001	
Date Founded	February 1986	
Members	General clearing members	10
	Individual clearing members	73
	Negotiating brokers	12
	Independent floor traders	53
	Agricultural members	17
	Total	165
Major Futures and Options Products Traded	Notional bond CAC 40 Index 3-month PIBOR ECU bond Sugar	

Exchange	The Singapore International Exchange (SIMEX)	
Address	1 Raffles Place 07-00 OUB Centre Singapore 0104	
Telephone Number Fax Number	65-535-7382 65-535-7282	
Date Founded	September 1984	
Members	Corporate clearing members	37
	Corporate nonclearing members	36
	Commercial associate members	12
	Individual nonclearing members	465
	Total	550
Major Futures and Options Products Traded	Eurodollar Nikkei 225 Index Euroyen High sulfur oil Deutschemark	

Section 2 Financial Futures

Exchange	The Tokyo International Financial Futures Exchange (TIFFE)	
Address	2-2 Otemachi 2-chome Chiyoda-ku Tokyo 100 Japan	
Telephone Number	81-3-3275-2111	
Fax Number	81-3-3275-4840	
Date Founded	June 30, 1989	
Members	Clearing members	108
	General members	153
	Total	261
Major Futures and Options Products Traded	Euroyen Eurodollar Japanese yen U.S. dollar/Japanese yen	

Exchange	The Tokyo Stock Exchange (TSE)	
Address	2-1 Nihombashi-Kabuto cho Chiyoda-ku Tokyo 103 Japan	
Telephone Number	81-3-3666-0141	
Fax Number	81-3-3663-0625	
Date Founded	May 15, 1878	
Members	Japanese member companies	99
	Foreign member companies	25
	Saitori members*	1
	Total	125
Major Futures and Options Products Traded	Euroyen Eurodollar Japanese yen U.S. dollar/Japanese yen	

* Saitori members specialize in matching orders placed by all other members.

CHAPTER 8

SHORT-TERM HEDGING APPLICATIONS USING FINANCIAL FUTURES

Shaiy Pilpel, Ph.D.
Steinhardt Partners, New York City

HEDGING

Webster's dictionary defines *risk* as: "Possibility of loss or injury." In the financial world, where physical injury is (at least theoretically) counted out, risk is the possibility of loss. Modern portfolio theory links financial risk with reward. The greater the risk, the greater the expected reward. People's appetites for risk vary as do the risk levels they are ready to assume. Regardless, a common goal is to optimize the risk-reward function, that is, to minimize the risk associated with an expected reward level.

Given this definition of *risk*, it is common to equate risk with uncertainty or with the unknown. The more a scenario is predictable or can be forecasted, the less random it is; the smaller the potential for loss, ergo—the less the risk.

Hedging is the act of protecting oneself by eliminating or minimizing the uncertainties, thereby minimizing the risk. Hedging does not prevent undesired situations, nor can it predict the future. When possible, it allows the mitigation of the impact of future situations, be they happy or sad.

This is a crucial point about hedging. If structured correctly, hedging can minimize only the uncertainties of the combined position, hedge included. Hedging does not minimize the uncertainties of the future. If a company hedges the interest rate at which it borrows, it does not predict the future interest rate. By hedging, it has, however, fixed an ex ante target rate, thereby minimizing the variance between that rate and the ex post rate (combined with the hedge) that the company will experience.

Uncertainty cannot be totally eliminated. Hedging may be impossible, or it may eliminate only a part of the risk. It works only under certain assumptions and, therefore, is effective only in a set of given scenarios. All financial bets are off, for example, if the United States experiences an atomic holocaust, and it is obvious that in this type of scenario hedging loses its function.

This chapter deals with hedging interest rate uncertainties using financial futures. These financial instruments are traded on many securities exchanges around the globe. Financial contracts are structured to meet the specific needs and regulations of most countries. The structure of futures contracts combined with the liquidity and credit quality provided by the exchanges make them the first choice of any hedging program.

FINANCIAL AND CASH-SETTLED FUTURES

Futures contracts are the exchange-traded version of the common forward contracts. Forward contracts are two-sided agreements to deliver some goods at a specified time in the future for a predetermined price. Traditionally, these contracts referred to physical commodities: wheat, corn, rice, gold, copper, and so on.

A thorough examination of the structure of forward contracts revealed that there was no reason to limit the set of "future-traded entities" to physical commodities. This insight led to the creation of two new types of futures contracts: financial futures and cash-settled futures.

Financial futures are futures contracts on financial instruments, for example, government bonds. The delivery mechanism is similar to that of other commodities. Instead of delivering 5,000 bushels of wheat or 1,000 troy ounces of gold, delivery requires the transfer of $100,000 face value of a prespecified government bond per contract.

The set of deliverables, terms of payments, and the delivery mechanism are specified in the same way as they are for physical commodities. The detailed nature of financial contracts may be more complex. The set of deliverables may include more than one bond, or it could allow different delivery dates. In essence, however, these contracts follow the same pattern as physical goods' contracts.

The key feature of a classical forward contract is that one side delivers some goods at some agreed time in the future at a predetermined price regardless of the then-current market price. The other side pays the agreed price, again, regardless of the then-prevailing market price. The net effect is that one side gains or loses the price differential between the spot market price and the contract's price. Cash-settled futures are structured to capture this net differential.

The following example clarifies this point by comparing an old-fashioned forward contract on wheat to a hypothetical cash-settled contract.

Example 1
Contract 1 (Delivery version):
- A will pay B $5.25 per bushel for 5,000 bushels of wheat.
- B will deliver 5,000 bushels of wheat for $5.25 per bushel.

Contract 2 (Cash-settlement version):
- A will pay B 5,000 times the difference between $5.25 and the market's price for a bushel of wheat. If this difference is negative, A will receive that amount from B.

Both contracts are in effect equivalent. Under both contracts, A is guaranteed 5,000 bushels of wheat at $5.25 per bushel and B is guaranteed that price for the wheat. While this is clear for Contract 1, observe what happens under Contract 2 if at expiration date the market price for wheat is $5.30 or $5.10.

	Market Price of $5.30			Market Price of $5.10		
	Buy/Sell	Get/Pay	Net	Buy/Sell	Get/Pay	Net
A	($26,500)	$250	($26,250)	($25,500)	($750)	($26,250)
B	26,500	(250)	26,250	25,500	750	26,250

In both cases, A eventually pays $26,250 for 5,000 bushels, which is $5.25 per bushel. Likewise, in both cases, B receives a net payment of $5.25 per bushel.

In light of this equivalence, market participants may choose between either type of contract, delivery or cash settled. From a practical point of view, cash-settled contracts are more desirable than physical delivery contracts. Hedgers using delivery contracts must offset their position by buying or selling prior to expiration if they want to avoid delivery. Cash-settled contracts, on the other hand, do not require the delivery of goods at their expiration, thus forming a more efficient hedging tool. These contracts also enable the hedging of "related items" that have no traded contracts, but are priced according to the prices of their raw materials. For example, an electrical utility company that purchases copper wires (not copper) can hedge against changes in the price of the wires by buying copper contracts. Since the utility company does not need the copper, it has to sell the future contracts before they expire; otherwise, it might find itself with unwanted copper. A cash-settled copper contract eliminates the double procedure. (It is assumed that the wire manufacturer prices its products according to the prevailing cost of copper.)

Cash-settled contracts cannot always replace delivery contracts. Some technical and fundamental prerequisites are necessary in order to establish cash-settled contracts. The most important demand is *convergence*: The contract value at expiration should be equal to the index that it represents. Thus, the settlement index should be uniquely defined and resistant to manipulation (among other things). The most well known stock market index, the Dow Jones Industrial Average, is a good example of an index that can be used as a basis for a future contract. (It is interesting to note that the Dow Jones company prohibits the use of their index in futures contracts.) Other indexes, including Standard & Poor's 500, as well as other major foreign stocks indexes, also fill these requirements. Futures contracts based on these indexes are traded in exchanges all over the world.

Delivery contracts carry an inherent distinction between buyers and sellers, between those who produce and deliver the goods and those who pay for them. Since the price of goods is effectively determined in a forward contract, a price increase in the market benefits the payer who can fetch higher prices if the goods are sold.

Symmetrically, the producer gains from a price decrease. The terminology used follows the stock market's definitions: The producer is *short* while the payer is *long*. This distinction between those who gain from a price increase and those who lose from a price increase is used in defining buy versus sell positions in cash-settled contracts. The buyer of a contract (a long position) gains from an increase of the contract's price. The seller of a contract (a short position) gains from a decrease in the contract's price.

LIBOR (LONDON INTERBANK OFFERED RATE)

There is no single number that can hold the title *the interest rate*. Even a secure borrower such as the U.S. government pays different yields for bonds of different maturities. Plotting the corresponding yields as a function of time to maturity generates the yield curve.

There is a clear distinction between long- and short-term interest rates. While the long-term rates are determined by a conglomeration of economic indicators, the short-term rates are influenced mostly by supply and demand. Short-term rates are basically the current cost of credit.

Banks and other financing institutions prefer to tie their borrowing or lending rates to the prevailing short-term rates. Even long-term bank commitments carry variable rates tied to some benchmark. These rates differ for different borrowers, mainly based on their credit quality. They are not usually quoted in absolute terms, but as a spread to some yardstick. For example, Company A can borrow money at prime plus 1 percent, while Company B has to pay prime plus 1.5 percent.

The Federal Reserve has some control over the cost of money via its fed funds rates. Yet these rates do not mirror all of the market's forces. An improved measure for estimating the cost of money is the short-term Treasury bill yield. This yield better reflects the market's prevailing rate, but it fails to capture the total economic environment.

The main problem with the aforementioned rates is that they do not reflect the rates that a "real" borrower has to pay. During periods of economic instability, for instance, investors or even banks prefer to keep their money in the safe hands of the government rather than to deposit it in banks or to lend it directly to factories, thus creating a discrepancy between this yield and the market's cost of funds. In other words, the spread between the market's rate and the government's short-term rate varies.

Eurodollar rates were found to be a better index for reflecting the cost of short-term borrowing. Eurodollars are bank deposit liabilities, denominated in U.S. dollars, not subject to U.S. banking regulations. The term *Eurodollar* dates from an earlier period when the market was located primarily in Europe. Banks in the Eurodollar market compete with each other to attract dollar-denominated funds. Since this market is almost free of regulation, banks can operate on narrower margins or spreads between borrowing and lending rates than can banks in the United States. Moreover, since they pay higher rates than U.S. banks, they have to lend their funds and cannot deposit them in short-term U.S. government securities.

The most commonly used benchmark for short-term financing cost is an interest rate called the *London Interbank Offered Rate (LIBOR)*. This is the rate on U.S. dollar loans that is charged by the major banks in London among themselves. Different borrowing horizons carry different rates. The one-month LIBOR differs from the three-month LIBOR, which differs from the one-year LIBOR. The same holds for different currencies: The rate for the dollar differs from the rate for the Japanese yen, which, in turn, differs from the rate for the Swiss franc, and so on.

LIBOR is common in financing agreements even in the non-Eurodollar markets. Banks may charge a company three-month LIBOR + 2 percent, which means that each quarter the interest on the outstanding amount borrowed by the company will be 2 percent over the prevailing LIBOR rate. Banks pay LIBOR-related interest on short-term deposits.

As much as the use of futures floating rates is convenient, it is, as its name implies, presently undetermined. Financial managers may prefer, from time to time, to know or to be able to determine their cost of financing for the foreseeable future. They may not like this cost, but they need an accurate forecast of it to price products or plan the financial structure of the company. Moreover, they may wish to lock in a certain financing rate for the future. We shall deal with this hedging process later in this chapter.

The International Monetary Market, a division of the Chicago Mercantile Exchange (CME), in order to accommodate hedging, introduced two "short-term" futures contracts:

- Three-month Treasury bill contract: This contract was introduced in 1976. Its deliverables are three-month U.S. government T-bills.
- Three-month Eurodollar time deposit: This contract was introduced in 1981 and is cash settled. This Eurodollar future settles at an average LIBOR rate at a specific date. The final value is determined through a complex procedure designed to eliminate market manipulation by banks and traders.

The exact specifications of these contracts appear in appendixes B and C at the end of the chapter.

To mimic the behavior of other bond market instruments that increase in price when interest rates decrease, the LIBOR futures contract is quoted as "100 less the LIBOR rate." Both Eurodollar and T-bill contracts are quoted without the decimal point. For example, if the market settles at a three-month LIBOR rate of 5.29 percent, the contract's settlement price will be 94.71 percent (equal to 100 − 5.29%) quoted as 9471.

It is important to keep in mind the time span covered by the Eurodollar futures contract. The rate that is sampled and determined (see Appendix A for the specific procedure) covers three months' borrowing starting at the sampling date, that is, expiration date. Therefore, a futures contract expiring on March 15 settles at the rate of a hypothetical three-month loan taken on March 15 with principal and interest paid on June 15.

New contracts based on one-month Eurodollar time deposits, or on other currencies' time deposits, were introduced through the years. We shall deal, however, with the two aforementioned contracts since the structure of the others is basically the same, using different settlement yardsticks.

HEDGING METHODOLOGY

Any hedging program should follow these basic steps:

1. Determining the direction of hedging

2. Choosing the index
3. Cash flow analysis
4. Timing
5. Scenario analysis

Determining the Direction of Hedging

First and foremost in any hedging program is to hedge correctly—to determine whether it is appropriate to buy or to sell futures. It may seem redundant to mention this point, but there are documented examples of companies that have lost all their quarterly profits due to inverse hedges. Such an error, instead of eliminating the risk, doubles it!

Since the price of a futures contract is diametrically opposite to the interest rate level, a long position in Eurodollar or T-bill futures means that the holder benefits from a *decrease* in the interest rate. Symmetrically, a short position benefits from an *increase* in the interest rate.

The interest rate exposure of a fully hedged position is zero. Therefore, to establish a hedge, the futures contracts' risk profile should be the inverse to that of the hedged instrument. If the instrument "loses" from an interest rate increase, the hedge should "gain" from that increase and vice versa. Financing (i.e., borrowing) becomes more expensive following an increase in the interest rate. Therefore, in order to hedge borrowing, a short futures position should be established. Using the same argument in reverse shows that to hedge lending a long futures position should be established.

To sum up:

To lock in a finance rate (borrowing)—sell futures.

To lock in an investment rate (lending)—buy futures.

When hedging is carried out using a delivery contract, one must remember to unwind one's position before the contracts expire and delivery takes place.

Choosing the Index

The specific choice of the hedging tool should reflect the risk exposure. If the exposure is to the Eurodollar rate (e.g., LIBOR-based borrowing), then hedging should be carried out using Eurodollar futures. If the exposure is tied to the T-bill rate, then the hedging program should reflect that.

A perfect hedge is practically impossible. There will always be mismatching between the time specified by the futures contract and the borrowing or investing dates. The actual borrowing may be longer or shorter than the futures' specification. Sometimes, hedging with one instrument or even a collection of instruments is not enough to eliminate all risks. Nevertheless, even an imperfect hedge that eliminates a major portion of the risks is superior to no hedge at all. The residual risk that cannot be hedged is called *basis risk*. An effective, well-structured, hedging program minimizes the basis risk.

Cash Flow

There are a variety of methods with which one can determine the number of contracts needed to hedge a given position. Some of them use rules of thumb while others use the most sophisticated mathematical models. The difference between competing methods is mostly in their ability to handle different responses of the hedged instrument to interest rate changes. Some methods need constant monitoring while others involve less frequent inspections.

The methodology described here uses cash flow analysis. This methodology has two major advantages:

- The hedger, after all, needs to offset cash flow uncertainties.
- It is easy to understand the structure of the hedged position and verify its effectiveness by testing it under various "stress scenarios."

Other methods are, in essence, cash flow analyses in disguise. They use parameters calculated from cash flow instead of the cash flow itself.

The hedger starts with the unhedged cash flow scenario as a

base case. Assuming an interest rate shift, a modified cash flow stream is calculated. The difference between these two cash flow streams is the *risk cash flow* that needs to be eliminated. This way, the hedger observes the position's exposure at each specific time as well as its cumulative change in value.

The price change of each Eurodollar or T-bill futures contract is the change in the cost of borrowing $1,000,000 for three months. Therefore, as a hedging instrument, each contract generates $25 per basis point [$1,000,000 × (3/12)/10,000]. Thus, if, for a given position, a rate change of 10 basis points exposes the cash flow to $750 risk, three contracts are needed to offset that exposure.

The method of looking at the cash flow differential measures, implicitly, the interest rate risk exposure of the position. Intuitively, the exposure of a six-month paper to interest rate shift is twice that of a three-month paper. One year's investment exposure is four times that of a three-month Treasury bill. These factors are treated automatically with the cash flow method.

Cash flow analysis methodology is most accurate where the relationship between cost or benefit to interest rates is linear. It is applicable to funding, revolving credit, commercial paper issuance, floating-rate instruments, and so on.

Not all interest rate–sensitive instruments bear such a direct relationship between changes in interest rate and the value of the instrument. Compounding, for example, introduces quadratic and higher-order effects since reinvestment of proceeds includes interest on interest. Yet, if the compounding term is relatively short, that nonlinear effect is negligible. Therefore, the cash flow analysis methodology is adequate in hedging short-term bonds. The more complex issue of hedging options and the like requires "dynamic" hedging and is outside the scope of this chapter.

Timing

Cash flow analysis includes careful monitoring of time and money. In the static case, where the yield curve is unchanged, this serves as a tool to set up the initial hedges. During the scenario analysis phase, shifts in the yield curve are introduced. The analysis follows the various cash flows and their effect on the position.

The key element in a successful hedging program is that all risks are covered at all times. To ensure that, a time table listing all the exposures and their relevant dates should be constructed and carefully reviewed to eliminate time gaps or cash flow mismatching.

The table is constructed in two stages: First the exposure is determined, and then the futures are added. The exposure column lists all dates where changes are made in the risk level, either when the size parameters are changed or when rates are determined. This allows the hedger to calculate the risk exposure to interest rate changes at any time. The futures column lists all applicable expiration dates, as well as dates on which a position change takes place (buy, sell, roll).

Example 2

Starting January 1, a company plans to borrow $50,000,000 for six months and increase it to $100,000,000 for the next six months. The company has a credit agreement with a bank to borrow these sums paying interest quarterly at a rate of 1 percent over the three-month LIBOR. Rates are determined at the beginning of each quarter.

Date	Action	Exposure

Jan. 1	Borrow $50 million
	Determine January interest
		$50 million for Apr.–July quarter
		  Risk: $1,250 per basis point (BP)
		$100 million for July–Sep. quarter
		  Risk: $2,500 per BP
		$100 million for Sep.–Dec. quarter
		  Risk: $2,500 per BP
		Total risk: $6,250 per BP

Apr. 1	Borrow $100 million
	Reset April interest
		$100 million for July–Sep. quarter
		  Risk: $2,500 per BP
		$100 million for Sep.–Dec. quarter
		  Risk: $2,500 per BP
		Total risk: $5,000 per BP

July 1	Borrow $100 million Reset July interest	$100 million for Sep.–Dec. quarter Risk: $2,500 per BP Total risk: $5,000 per BP
Oct. 1	Reset October interest	No more interest rate uncertainties
Dec. 31	Pay loan	

Sometimes, it is advantageous to use a less detailed table, where only total exposure is specified. This depends on the general hedging scheme to be used. Two common hedging methods applicable to these alternative presentations, strip or stack, will be defined later.

In this specific example, the total exposure table is:

Date	Action	Exposure
Jan. 1	Borrow $50 million Determine interest	$250 million for 1 quarter Risk: $6,250 per BP
Apr. 1	Reset interest	$200 million for 1 quarter Risk: $5,500 per BP
Jul. 1	Borrow $100 million Reset interest	$100 million for 1 quarter Risk: $2,500 per BP
Oct. 1	Reset interest	No more interest rate uncertainties
Dec. 31	Pay loan	

The previous example implicitly assumes that the company has cash available to pay the interest. If the company borrows that money (from another source or, indirectly, by increasing its credit line), this should be reflected in the table. This point is illuminated even more in the case of financing investment positions in which the available cash is used either to decrease borrowing or is reinvested, yielding the compound return. The position's risk decreases or increases depending on the specific use of cash. If the position's cash flows are uncertain, this creates a secondary risk effect that should be continuously monitored.[1]

Example 3

An investor is offered, in the secondary market, $50MM face value of an "old" bond of Company XYZ. The trade parameters are:

Coupon: 9.625 percent paying semiannually
Settlement: 4/1/92
Maturity: 3/31/93
Price: 102

The investor arranged term financing of up to $45MM until September 31, 1992, at a rate of 4.625 percent (paid at the end of the term). Thereafter, the rate is reset at the beginning of each quarter to LIBOR plus 25 basis points. If the investor plans to use September's coupon to reduce the loan, the interest rate exposure for the October–December period is reduced by the coupon received less financing charges. Financing charges should be added to the January–March period's exposure. On March 20, 1992, the September 1992 Eurodollar futures contract settled at 9467 and the December contract settled at 9385. Assume the investor can lock in the implied LIBOR rate for the two quarters.

Table 8–1 summarizes the cash flow and the investment's expected returns.

The rates on October 1 and January 1 are not determined at the time the bond is purchased. October's borrowing amount is

TABLE 8–1
Cash Flow and Expected Return

Date			Rate
4/1/92	Buy bond: Principal	$51,000,000	
	Accrued	1,315	
	Borrow	45,000,000	4.625%
	Investment	6,001,315	
9/30/92	Coupon	2,406,250	
	Interest payment	1,052,188	
10/1/92	Borrow	43,645,938	5.330%
1/1/93	Interest payment	594,506	
	Borrow	44,240,444	6.150%
3/31/93	Coupon	2,406,250	
	Bond principal	50,000,000	
	Loan principal	44,240,444	
	Interest payment	672,639	
	Net to investor	7,493,167	
	Return on investment		24.86%*

* Note the discrepancy between the implied one-year LIBOR, which is 5.27 percent, and the hefty 24.86 percent return on this specific trade. This is because the investment in XYZ bonds carries some risk. The investor's excess return results from excess risk. The market estimates that there is a fair chance the company would default on its obligations. Such a default risk is unhedgeable; therefore, it yields a risk premium.

known in advance, so the risk exposure is determined in advance. The implied future rate is a good estimate of January's borrowing amount and therefore useful for calculating the interest rate exposure on January 1.

Scenario Analysis

Futures contracts are dynamic in contrast to the static quality of forward contracts. Scenario analysis is an important mechanism that enables the hedger to combine all listed procedures and verify the accuracy of both the static and dynamic aspects of the hedging program. The specific structure of futures contracts, namely mark to market, calls for cash transfers following changes in the interest rate. This may create a residual exposure that may not be observed unless a scenario including a change in the interest rate is assumed and the effective margin change is calculated. Running different scenario procedures enables the hedger to detect other nonlinear components hidden in the portfolio's behavior. We shall explore this point further when dealing with the tail risk.

The following example illustrates the items discussed above:

Example 4
A company's chief financial officer (CFO) intends to borrow $100 million for two months starting June 20. The company has a revolving credit agreement with a bank under which it can borrow such a sum at a rate of the three-month LIBOR plus 125 basis points.

On April 1, the CFO feels that the LIBOR rate may increase and she decides to lock in the current rate. June Eurodollar futures trade at 9465; the resulting implied Eurodollar rate is 5.35 percent.

1. Since the hedge's goal is to control the financing exposure, the CFO should *sell* Eurodollar futures.

2. The optimal contract to use is the June Eurodollar futures contract. Some basis risk still remains: The rate of the June contract is determined on a date other than June 20, and it is based on a three-month borrowing period and not two. This is still the best the CFO can achieve using the available futures contracts.

3. The company's interest rate exposure to a one-basis-point yield shift is:

$$\$100,000,000 \times (2/12)/10,000 = \$1,667.7$$

Since, for each futures contract, one basis point equals $25, the CFO should short $1,667.7/$25 = 66.7, rounded to 67 June Eurodollar contracts.

4. Assume that the CFO's fears are correct and LIBOR rises by 70 basis points the next day. If the CFO shorts the 67 Eurodollar contracts, the margin account will pick up $117,250 (67 × $25 × 70). That money should be invested until August 20 when she will pay back the loan at the higher interest.

This tail investment should be hedged as well by *buying* June Eurodollar futures contracts. The following formula approximates the number of contracts needed to hedge the tail:

Tail = Number of contracts × Implied interest rate
× (Days to end of term/360)

A detailed discussion of the tail and explanation for the above formula appear in Appendix A at the end of the chapter.

The following points should be kept in mind when using the tail:

- The tail hedges the hedge. It is, therefore, positioned against the futures' position.
- The number of days to the end of term changes with time, causing the tail to decrease proportionately.

In this specific example, the number of contracts in the tail is 1.4 [67 × 5.35% × (141/360)].

To summarize: In order to establish the hedge, the CFO should short only 65 (66.7 − 1.4) June Eurodollar contracts.

Observe, now, how this hedging scheme works under two scenarios:

Scenario 1: On April 2 the interest rate climbs by 70 basis points (to 6.05 percent).

Scenario 2: On May 1 the interest rate declines by 120 basis points (to 4.15 percent).

		Scenario 1	Scenario 2
4/1	Sell 65 futures at 9465		
4/2		Futures at 9395 Receive $113,750 and invest at 6.05%	
5/1			Futures at 9585 Pay $195,000 and borrow at 4.15%
6/15	Futures expire		
6/20	Borrow $100MM at	6.05%	4.15%
8/20	Pay loan + interest Interest on margin Finance cost Effective rate	$101,008,333 $2,676 $891,907 5.351%	$100,691,667 ($2,495) $889,862 5.335%

The example above shows that the difference in rates is less than two basis points, even under these two extremely divergent scenarios.

Was the hedging tactic just described sufficient? Had all interest rate risks been eliminated? Critical auditing of the previous table as well as of the timing chart reveals that there are five days on which no hedge exists. That happens between June 15, when the June futures contracts expire, and the borrowing date, June 20. If during that period interest rates shift, no protection is in place. To eliminate that risk, the CFO should sell 66 June Eurodollar futures contracts when the March contracts expire. The June contracts should be bought back immediately after the loan rate is determined. Timing is essential; at no time should the company have double exposure, that is, neither short both March and June futures nor have the loan rate fixed while still maintaining a position in the June futures.

Underlying this "new" hedge is the assumption that a rate change will affect both March's and June's rates equally. The residual risk, namely, that the change in March's rate differs from the change in June's rate, cannot be eliminated. However, it is minor compared to assuming all the rate change risks. A method of changing the contracts' months without increasing the risk, called *rolling*, will be described later.

It is important to follow the exact dates at which money changes hands. If, for example, interest is deducted when the loan is taken, this would affect the number of days in the tail calculation (decreased by 61). More importantly, it would change the interest rate exposure, which would be approximately $1,652 per basis point, needing exactly 66 contracts to be sold.[2]

APPLICABLE RATE

Locking in futures rates allows the hedger to calculate the weighted cost of funds throughout the hedging period, namely, the applicable rate. This is the rate that the market forecasts for that period if there is no rate change risk. The following paragraphs are devoted to calculating that rate.

Single Contract

Let

R = Spot rate for the hedged period (e.g., two-month spot rate if one tries to hedge two-month borrowing)

F = Percentage price of the futures contract used for hedging (at the date hedging takes place)

Rm = Three-month spot Eurodollar rate (Assume this contract is used for hedging.)

Rf = Rate implied by the futures contract

From the contract's definition, $Rf = 100 - F$, which is the "anticipated" three-month LIBOR when the futures contract expires. The hedger, however, may target a different rate, for example, the two-month rate.

If the yield curve experiences a parallel shift, all rates are changed by the same quantity; therefore, the difference between any two rates remains unchanged. Thus, $R - Rm$ remains constant following any parallel shift. Hedging locks in this spread relative to Rf; that is:

$$Rf + (R - Rm)$$

Rearranging the variables, hedging locks in the following rate:
$$R + (Rf - Rm)$$
If the hedged position is the three-month LIBOR, we have:
$$R = Rm$$
Therefore, the applicable rate is:
$$Rm + (Rf - Rm) = Rf$$
which is the implied future rate.

In the previous example, the three-month LIBOR was used even though the time period was two months, because we assumed these were the credit terms. Therefore, the applicable rate was the implied future rate.

Multicontract

Assume the situation calls for using a sequence of successive contracts having different implied rates. Calculating a single applicable rate is done in two steps: The first is to calculate the applicable rate for each term. The second step uses the compounding formula to generate a single rate.

If the terms are of lengths $T_1, T_2, \ldots, T_n$ with corresponding linear applicable rates $R_1, R_2, \ldots, R_n$, then:

$$[1 + R(T_1 + T_2 + \cdots + T_n)]^{(T_1+T_2+\cdots+T_n)}$$
$$= (1 + R_1 T_1)(1 + R_2 T_2) \cdots (1 + R_n T_n)$$

Thus,

$$R = \{[(1 + R_1 T_1) \times (1 + R_2 T_2) \cdots (1 + R_n T_n)]^{\frac{1}{(T_1+T_2+\cdots+T_n)}} - 1\}$$
$$\times \frac{1}{(T_1 + T_2 + \cdots + T_n)}$$

Note: This assumes borrowing equal amounts at each term. If these sums differ, they should be weighed accordingly.

It should be mentioned again that the prices of futures contracts are market driven and the hedgers have to accept them as given. One may have a different opinion than that of the market (as embedded in the price) and decide not to hedge, or even take a speculative position. This is fine, as long as one knows that no rate has been locked in and risk has not been eliminated.

Example 5

In January, a company approved a capital expense plan under which a new production facility will be constructed. To budget this project, the company needs an estimated $50,000,000 for a one-year period starting July. The CFO plans to float a one-year commercial paper paying interest semiannually. The investment bankers estimate that the rate the company will have to pay is the six-month LIBOR plus 1.25 percent.

Spot three-month LIBOR is 4.3125%.

Spot six-month LIBOR is 4.4375%.

June three-month Eurodollar contract is quoted at 9535 (implied rate − 4.65%).

December three-month Eurodollar contract is quoted at 9426 (implied rate − 5.74%).

The applicable term rates are, therefore:

July–December: 1.25 + 4.4375 + (4.65 − 4.3125) = 6.025%

January–June: 1.25 + 4.4375 + (5.74 − 4.3125) = 7.115%

The applicable annual rate is:

$(1 + 6.065\%/2) \times (1 + 7.115/2) - 1 = 6.6772\%$

ROLLING

Futures contracts contain an inherent time dimension. They cease to exist after their expiration date; therefore, they provide protection only until that date. Rolling is a common technique under which a futures' position can be maintained indefinitely.

Calendar spread is defined as concurrently having a futures position in one expiration month and a reverse position in another expiration month, such as long the June contract and short the September one. Since a spread position is a synthetic position, there is no natural meaning to buying or selling a spread. The convention is to name the spread position after the position in the earliest month. Thus, a long position in the March–June spread means long the March futures and short the June futures.

Calendar spreads are quoted on the exchange floors as a single instrument.[3] This gives the hedger two alternatives with which to build a spread position:

1. Legging. Buy one contract and sell the other as two independent transactions. There is no guarantee that the spread between the two prices will be what is hoped for.
2. Trading the spread. Since the spread is quoted, one can buy or sell it as a single instrument. The floor traders are those who take the risk of legging into the spread.

Rolling a futures position is performed by taking an offsetting position in the calendar spread. If the original position was to long a contract, rolling takes place by selling the spread. If that position was to short a contract, then the roll takes place by buying the spread. The outcome of such a roll is, in essence, the same position, only this time in the next expiration future.

Note that this procedure depends only on the generic characteristics of the futures' contract and not on the specifics of the contract. In other words, it is the same procedure whether the underlying commodity for the contract is government bonds, Eurodollar deposits, gold bullion, or soy beans.

Example 6
Rolling from a March position to a June position, a hedger has:

> Initial position: Short 100 March futures.
> Roll: Long 100 March–June spreads.

The roll can be broken into:

> Long 100 March futures.
> Short 100 June futures.

The short and long March positions cancel out. Therefore:

> Final position: Short 100 June futures.

Thus, the position is shifted three months forward.

Had the original position been long 100 March contracts, the roll would have consisted of selling the spread as opposed to buying it. Thus, *in a roll, the spread position is opposite to the original.*

Long-Term Exposure to Risk

Rolling enables hedgers to create complex hedging structures that span a long period of time and involve more than one contract. Even the simple case of Example 4 shows that the CFO could face the risk of being exposed for five days, due to mismatch between expiration and loan structure dates. In reality, most occurrences are even more complex and involve long-term exposure: long-term revolvers, financing commitments, adjustable-rate mortgages, and so on.

There are two classical methods to deal with a long-term hedging problem:

Strip consists of a series of successive futures contracts that match expected cash flows. The number of each specific contracts used matches the rate exposure contributed to that time frame.

Stack consists of building a position on the front futures contract, or the contract that matches the first cash flow, and then rolling it successively to the next contract.

To clarify the use of these abstract definitions, observe how these different tactics are applied to the following set of examples.

Example 7

On December 15, a company borrows $100,000,000 for one year. Interest is paid quarterly at a rate of 1.25 percent over the three-month LIBOR. In such cases, the rate is determined at the beginning of the quarter and paid at the end. The first quarter's interest is, therefore, set on December 15 and presents no uncertainties, so there is no need to hedge it. The position's interest rate exposure on December 15 is, therefore, the rate exposure for nine months, or $7,500 per basis point [$100,000,000 × (9/12) × (1/10,000)].

To do a strip hedge, break the risk exposure into successive terms:

1. March–June: $2,500 per one-basis-point shift.
2. June–September: $2,500 per one-basis-point shift.
3. September–December: $2,500 per one-basis-point shift.

Hedging each part separately, the hedge position consists of:

Short 100 March Eurodollar contracts.
Short 100 June Eurodollar contracts.
Short 100 September Eurodollar contracts.

(Tail hedging is now applied independently to each contract.)

To do a stack hedge, hedge the total exposure using the first contract, the March Eurodollar futures contract. Afterwards, roll the remaining position into the following contract, and so on. The mechanism is, therefore:

Short 300 March Eurodollar contracts.

When the March contracts expire, or shortly before that, roll 200 of the March contracts into June contracts. The remaining 100 March contracts are allowed to expire.

When the June contracts expire, or shortly before that, roll 100 of the June contracts into September contracts. The remaining 100 June contracts are allowed to expire.

(Again, the tail is calculated and applied; however, this time only to the prevailing contract.)

Example 8

Suppose the loan in Example 7 was taken on January 1 and reset on April 1, and so on. Since the Eurodollar futures contracts expire, approximately, on the 15th, the position could be at risk for two weeks. This case is treated as in Example 4; only this time it applies to the specific strategy.

The strip hedge starts the same way. However, in order to cover the two-week differential, the 100 March Eurodollar contracts that were previously allowed to expire are first rolled into the June contracts. These 100 June contracts are bought back on April 1, when the loan interest is reset.

To clarify the procedure, observe the position on three different dates:

January 1: Short 100 March Eurodollar contracts.
Short 100 June Eurodollar contracts.
Short 100 September Eurodollar contracts.

March 20: Short 200 June Eurodollar contracts (100 + 100!).
Short 100 September Eurodollar contracts.

April 2: Short 100 June Eurodollar contracts (post reset).
Short 100 September Eurodollar contracts.

The stack hedge is also implemented in phases:

January 1: Short 300 March Eurodollar contracts.

March 15: Roll 300 March Eurodollar contracts into June.
Net position is short 300 June contracts.

April 1: Buy 100 June Eurodollar contracts.
Net position is short 200 June contracts.

June 15: Roll 200 June Eurodollar contracts into September.
Net position is short 200 June contracts.

Example 9

Using the dates of Example 8, suppose that for the June–September period the CFO planned to increase borrowing to $150,000,000 instead of the $100,000,000.

For a strip hedge, the only difference between this position and the previous one is that the June–September amount at risk is $150,000,000. Hence, the exposure changes to $3,750 per basis point [$150,000,000 × (3/12)/10,000]. Thus, 150 June Eurodollar contracts are needed.

For a stack hedge, adding the pieces shows that when hedging begins, the risk exposure of the total borrowing is $8,750 per basis point ($2,500 for the March–June period, $3,750 for the June–September period, and $2,500 for the September–December period). Therefore, the CFO should sell 350 March Eurodollar contracts. The new risk exposure is calculated before any roll or expiration. Therefore, on March 15, since the exposure is still unchanged, the 350 March contracts are rolled into June contracts. On April 1, 100 contracts should be bought back, and on June 15 the remaining 150 June contracts should be rolled into September contracts. On July 1, however, 150 (not 100) contracts that represent the risk exposure for that period should be bought back.

Stack versus Strip

Choosing either to stack or to strip is more a matter of taste, preference, and convenience than a scientific weighing of the pros and cons of each method. Here are some of the features of each technique.

The advantages of a stack hedge are:

- Use of the front months' contracts. This means greater availability of contracts, liquidity, and minimal bid-ask spread.
- Simplicity. The position contains at each time only one contract. It is easy, therefore, to calculate the tail and to keep track of the dates and quantities of rolls or changes in the position.

The advantages of a strip hedge are:

- Better tracking of the exposure. If different time periods have different exposures, the total exposure may be hard to calculate.
- Protection against changes in the shape of the yield curve. The short-term yield curve may experience a nonparallel yield shift. If rates at different maturities shift differently, the strip hedge method captures this change while stacking leaves some residual exposure. This is by far the most important advantage of stripping, and, if practical, it is the recommended method. The liquidity of today's Eurodollar futures markets allows easy stripping to almost two years.

Brokers prefer the stack method since it involves almost twice the number of transactions. This, however, does not come at the expense of the user, since the extra commissions' cost is offset by a tighter bid-ask spread than exists in the front months.

Combination

Exchange-traded futures contracts can be viewed as a set of generic building blocks with which one can construct a hedging structure. If one assumes that all yield curve shifts are parallel, hedges can be tailored to suit almost any need. The parallel shift assumption is the rationale for hedging time periods that lack "perfect matching" to futures contracts. This assumption is acceptable if the term differential is small. Sometimes a needed contract may exist but may not be available when the hedge is set up. A combination of contracts of different natures (liquid and illiquid) allows the hedger to overcome this problem and to minimize the risk associated with nonparallel rate shifts.

Example 10
Suppose an investor owns a LIBOR-based bond paying monthly. This is a common structure in collateralized mortgage obligation (CMO) tranches. In January, he believes that LIBOR has bottomed down and wishes to lock in the market's rate for the next two years. (Assume the bond's principal is untouched during that period.) Note that he does not lock in the current one-month LIBOR for the rest of the term, but the forward rate as implied by the market.

Optimally, the investor should purchase a strip of one-month LIBOR contracts. The number of each month's contracts depends on the size of his bond. Unfortunately, one-month LIBOR contracts span only six months and the back months are illiquid.

A practical solution is to combine early-expiration one-month contracts with a strip of three-month contracts. With time, the three-month contracts are sequentially replaced by one-month contracts as they become available.

In this specific case, assume the investment is $10,000,000. The investor begins by setting up the following position:

Short 3 January one-month Eurodollar contracts.
Short 3 February one-month Eurodollar contracts.
Short 10 March three-month Eurodollar contracts.
Short 10 June three-month Eurodollar contracts.
Short 10 September three-month Eurodollar contracts.
Short 10 December three-month Eurodollar contracts.
Short 10 March three-month Eurodollar contracts.
Short 10 June three-month Eurodollar contracts.
Short 10 September three-month Eurodollar contracts.

The last strip is of the following-year contracts.

During (the first) March, when the one-month contracts become more liquid, the investor replaces his short position in the March three-month contracts by executing the following:

Short 3 March one-month Eurodollar contracts.
Short 3 April one-month Eurodollar contracts.
Short 3 May one-month Eurodollar contracts.

(He must remember to buy back March's three-month contracts.)

The same process is repeated in June, September, and so on. This way, the relationship between the three one-month applicable rates and the three-month overlapping rate is maintained.

APPENDIXES TO CHAPTER 8

APPENDIX A: THE TAIL EFFECT

Exchange-traded futures contracts differ from classical forward contracts in that they are marked to market daily. This introduces a dynamic aspect of cash flow that is missing from forward contracts. This "tail" effect is secondary; yet it may still be in the order of some percentage points.

Mathematically speaking, a perfect hedge should reflect the market's volatility by hedging the embedded option. To put it in a nonmathematical context, the hedge, that is, the futures' position, needs to be hedged as well. The same risk management procedure should, therefore, be applied to this hedging.

Assume the following scenario:

The hedge consists of K long Eurodollar contracts.

The hedged position terminates in D days.

Funds can be either invested or borrowed for that period at the prevailing rate R.

A shift of one basis point in the rate adds (or subtracts) $25 \times K$ dollars to the margin account.[4] As mentioned before, a basis point is worth $25 for each contract. Investing this amount for the remaining D days generates $25 \times K \times R \times (D/360)$ extra dollars. The number of Eurodollar contracts needed to hedge this surplus cash flow is $K \times R \times (D/360)$.

Therefore, to hedge K contracts, the tail consists of

$$-K \times R \times (D/360)$$

contracts. The minus sign indicates that the tail's direction is the reverse of the hedging futures position. In other words, hedging with the tail results in less contracts than without it.

The reinvestment rate R is unknown. Using the implied rate from the futures' value serves as a reasonable approximation to R. The number of remaining days, D, decreases with time (at a rate of one day per each elapsing calendar day). Therefore, the tail level should be checked periodically and modified when needed.

Note the importance of scenario analysis to discover the dynamic aspect of the hedge. Without it, the volatility, that is, the option effect, can be wrongly assumed to be zero.

APPENDIX B: EURODOLLAR FUTURES CONTRACT

Each Eurodollar futures contract shall be for a Eurodollar time deposit having a principal value of \$1,000,000 with a three-month maturity (or $3/12$ of one year). Therefore, if the rate changes by one basis point (1/10,000 of 1 percent), it amounts to $\$1,000,000 \times .0001 \times (3/12) = \$25$ per contract.

We quote here the procedure that determines the final settlement price for the Eurodollar futures contract. It shows that this is indeed a robust estimator that reflects real market rates and is very hard to manipulate.

Final Settlement Price

The final settlement price shall be determined by the clearinghouse as follows. On the last day of trading, the clearinghouse shall determine the London Interbank Offered Rate (LIBOR) for three-month Eurodollar time deposit funds both at the time of termination of trading and at a randomly selected time within the last 90 minutes of trading. The final settlement price shall be 100 minus the arithmetic mean rounded to the nearest 1/100th of a percentage point, of the LIBOR at these two times.

To determine the LIBOR at either time, the clearinghouse shall select at random 12 reference banks from a list of no less than 20 participating banks that are major banks in the London Eurodollar market. Each reference bank shall quote to the clearinghouse its perception of the rate at which the three-month Eurodollar time deposit funds are currently offered by the market to prime banks. These rates must be confirmed in writing by telex before they are accepted as official; only after confirmation will they be used to determine the final settlement price. The two highest and two lowest quotes shall be eliminated. The arithmetic mean of the remaining eight quotes shall be the LIBOR at that time. If for any reason there is difficulty in obtaining a quote within a reasonable time from one of the banks in the sample, that bank shall be dropped from the sample, and another shall be randomly selected to replace it.

APPENDIX C: U.S. TREASURY BILL FUTURES CONTRACT

A delivery unit shall be composed of a U.S. Treasury bill(s) maturing 90 days from the first delivery day with a face value of $1,000,000 at maturity.

At the seller's option, a delivery unit may be composed of U.S. Treasury bills bearing maturities of 91 or 92 days from the first delivery day. All bills in a delivery unit must bear uniform maturity dates. Payment shall be made in accordance with the provisions of rule 3203.F., reflecting the maturity date of the U.S. Treasury bill(s) actually delivered.

The following formula shall be used to calculate the value of the delivery unit:

$$\text{Dollar value} = \$1,000,000 - D \times TY \times \$1,000,000/360$$

where

D = Days from issue date to maturity date

TY = T-bill yield

For the purpose of this formula, the T-bill yield shall be the difference between the IMM Index at settlement on the last day of trading and 100.00 multiplied by 0.01. [For example, a settlement price of 95.00 would create a T-bill yield of $(100.00 - 95.00) \times 0.01 = .0500$.]

NOTES

1. Therefore, if it is practical to list all the coupons and their corresponding reinvestment parameters, the cash flow method does not introduce any error, even to multiyear bonds.
2. Under the modified terms, the approximated interest is $891,667 = \$100,000,000 \times 5.35\% \times (2/16)$. Therefore, the company is expected to borrow only $99,108,333, which gives a $1,652 exposure per basis point.

3. Even though the spread is quoted as a single instrument, once traded, the clearing corporation treats it as two transactions. The prices at which the specific contracts were traded is irrelevant since the marking-to-market procedure offsets the differential and sets it to the end-of-day level.
4. This occurs since margins are updated every night through the marking-to-market process.

CHAPTER 9

ACCOUNTING FOR FINANCIAL FUTURES AND FORWARD CONTRACTS

Harold Bierman, Jr.
Cornell University

The Financial Accounting Standards Board (FASB) defines the accounting for financial futures in Financial Accounting Standards No. 80 (FAS 80), *Accounting for Futures Contracts*. This standard deals only with the accounting for futures. This is interesting since the November 14, 1980, exposure draft was titled *Disclosure of Interest Rate Futures Contracts and Forward and Standby Contracts*. As of this date, the accounting for forward contracts has not been specifically defined by the FASB, but the FASB is studying the issues. The 1980 draft required extensive disclosure of gains and losses as well as market values for futures. We cannot conclude with confidence that the accounting for futures also applies to forwards.

FUTURES AND FORWARD CONTRACTS

A futures or forward contract is a contract to buy (or sell) at a fixed date, a specific amount of a given security, currency, or commodity. The exchange price is fixed at Time 0, and the value of the contract changes through time. The two types of contracts differ in very significant ways:

Chapter 9 Accounting for Financial Futures and Forward Contracts **215**

Futures Contract	*Forward Contract*
Standardized	Nonstandard
Limited maturity dates	Any date
Made with market	Made with a second party
Marked to Market:	Not Marked to Market:
Payment is made daily	Payment is made at maturity
Margin is required	No margin is required

FUTURES CONTRACTS

The costs to the buyer of a futures contract are:

1. Cost of interest on the margin (the margin may be cash or Treasuries). This cost may be zero if the interest on the Treasuries accrues to the owner.
2. Trading commissions.
3. Dividends or interest lost on the security being purchased via the futures.

The security is marked to market daily, meaning that the purchaser must pay or receive funds from the broker on a daily basis as the market price changes.

Assume a buyer of a futures wants to establish a price of $300 now for a product that can only be bought in the future. First, we will assume the security pays zero dividends and there is a zero margin requirement. The purchased futures give the right to buy at $300. The price of the product goes to $290 before maturity.

Transaction		Cash Flow
Buy futures with an obligation to buy at	$300	No cash outlay with the purchase of the futures
The price of the product goes to	290	
	$ 10	Cash paid by buyer of the futures
Seller of futures receives	$ 10	

The buyer can now buy the product in the market at $290, but since the buyer of the futures has already lost $10 on the futures, the total cost of the product is $300. This was the price set by the futures. A comparable situation takes place if the price of the product goes up to $310 (the buyer of the futures gains $10).

FAS 80

This statement requires that futures contracts be marked to market for accounting purposes (matching the economics of the transaction, which also requires a marking to market). This requirement is a simple well-defined rule.

The complexity arises because a futures used to hedge does not have to be marked to market. The hedge criteria for futures specified by FAS 80 capture the essence of the hedge accounting issues for a wide range of securities.

FAS 80 (paragraph 4) requires a consideration of whether the hedge *reduces enterprise risk* (rather than reducing the risk of a transaction). Secondly, it requires that the futures transaction *be designated* by management as a hedge. Thus with two identical transactions, the accounting may differ depending on whether or not there is a designation as a hedge.

If the futures contract qualifies as a hedge, then changes in the market value of the futures contract affect the carrying amount of the hedged item rather than affecting income (paragraph 6).

The hedged item *may be an anticipated transaction* if two conditions are satisfied (paragraph 9). The characteristics and terms of the anticipated transaction must be identified, and it must be probable that the transaction will occur.

The statement requires that the results of a futures contract designated as a hedge be assessed using a correlation test. A high correlation is required. The profession has not come to an agreement as to how this test should be implemented (e.g., how high a correlation is required).

It is very likely that the rules of FAS 80 will either be extended by analogy to other securities, or that the FASB will revise the recommendations of FAS 80 when it specifies the accounting for the other securities involved in hedging.

In the next sections, the accounting for forward contracts will be considered. The fact that the FASB has not issued a definitive statement on the accounting for forward contracts should be kept in mind.

ACCOUNTING FOR FORWARD CONTRACTS

We will consider the accounting for two types of forward contracts, a forward contract for financial securities and a forward contract for foreign exchange. The objective is to evaluate the use of separate accounting. FAS 80 dealing with futures contracts discourages the use of separate accounting except in unusual circumstances (paragraph 6). The following discussion applies to futures contracts as well as to forwards with relatively minor changes. One complexity that we omit for simplicity of discussion is that the change in value of the futures contract is in practice equal to the change in value of the "cheapest-to-deliver security." This is relevant for T-bonds, and T-note contracts. The nominal security for a T-bond or a T-note always has an 8 percent interest rate. The futures for an 8 percent bond is converted to a cheapest-to-deliver bond by a conversion factor (found in conversion tables).

Accounting for a Forward Contract for a Financial Security

A financial forward contract obligates the owner of the forward to buy a given amount of a well-defined financial security at a given price on a given day. Thus, the buyer has an obligation (to pay the forward price) and an asset (the value of the security to be purchased). On maturity, there will be a net receipt or disbursement of cash.

Assume a zero coupon security with a maturity value in two years of $1,000,000 has a spot price of $849,618. A forward to buy at the end of Year 1 a security paying $1,000,000 at Time 2 at a cost of $909,091 reflects a 10 percent market interest rate for the second year.

Assume at Time 0 a firm owes $1,000,000 payable at Time 2 ($849,618 market value at Time 0) and expects to receive $909,091 at Time 1. The firm could speculate on the available return that could be earned on a one-year security at Time 1 or it can buy the forward described above. The spot and forward prices are tied together by the following relationship:

$$F = S(1 + r) = \$849,618(1.07) = \$909,091$$

where F is the forward contract price, S is the spot (current) price, and r is the investors' cost of money for the first year.

Assume the firm buys the above forward with a Time 1 contract price of $909,091. If everything occurs as forecasted and one-year securities can be purchased to yield 10 percent, at Time 1, the forward will have zero value and the firm will invest the $909,091 received at Time 1 to earn 10 percent. Note that with these facts there is zero gain or loss on the forward. An investor who paid $849,618 for the security at Time 0 would earn 7 percent and would have a security worth $909,091 at Time 1. An investor who, at Time 0, bought a forward with a contract price of $909,091 for the security could invest $849,618 to earn 7 percent for one year and would have $849,618(1.07) = $909,091 at Time 1. This is enough to pay the contract price of $909,091 for the security maturing in one year for a value of $1,000,000. Immediate buying of the $1,000,000 security at a cost of $849,618 and the buying of the forward and investing in a one-year 7 percent security result in identical outcomes.

Now, assume the actual one-period rate at Time 1 is 20 percent rather than 10 percent and the one-year security at Time 1 sells for $^{$1,000,000}/_{1.20}$ = $833,333. There is a loss of $75,758 on the forward, but the amount at Time 1 needed to pay the debt maturing at Time 2 is now only $833,333, a saving of $75,758 (comparing $833,333 to $909,091). With these facts, we see that the forward has been an effective hedge. The value changes are equal and opposite in sign for the two values.

One logical entry by the buyer of the forward to record the initiation of the contract is:

```
Forward Receivable. . . . . . . . . . . . . . .   849,618
Forward Premium  . . . . . . . . . . . . . . .    59,473
    Forward Payable . . . . . . . . . . . . .              909,091
```

The receivable is set equal to the current value of the security to be acquired. The liability is set equal to the amount that will be paid for the security in one year in accordance with the forward contract. The difference in the two amounts is by convention defined to be a premium if the forward price exceeds the spot price.

A second reasonable entry for the forward contract is to record only the forward premium and the net liability:

```
Forward Premium. . . . . . . . . . . . . . . .    59,473
    Forward Payable . . . . . . . . . . . . .               59,473
```

A third possibility is to record nothing except memo entries that are separate from the formal accounting system. This is consistent with the fact that initially the forward contract has zero value. There is not an explicit asset or an explicit liability. Recording no entries is consistent with the accounting if a futures is purchased rather than a forward.

If after one year the spot price is $909,091, then no entry is made at Time 0 and no entry is made at the maturity of the forward.

If the spot price at Time 1 differs from $909,091, the forward will have a gain or loss. For example, if the spot price at Time 1 is $900,000, there is a loss of $9,091, and with cash settlement the following entry would be made:

Loss on Forward 9,091
    Cash 9,091

If the spot rate for the security at Time 1 is $950,000, there is a $40,909 gain on the forward and with cash settlement the following entry would be appropriate:

Cash 40,909
    Gain on Forward 40,909

Accounting for the Premium

If the accounting period ends before the forward matures, should the premium account be amortized? Should an expense account be debited when the premium is credited?

If there is no change in the interest rates that were used by the market to value the security and the forward at Time 0, there would be no need to write off the premium account. Only if interest rates were to change and the forward contracts were marked to market would there be a gain or loss. With no change in interest rates, the premium write-off should not affect income and the forward will have no gain or loss.

The above arguments would apply equally to futures contracts. With no change in interest rates, there would be a daily debit to the receivable and a credit to premium as the spot value of the security increased, but there would be no gain or loss (income would not be affected). There would have to be a change in interest rates for the futures to have a gain or loss. There are four alterna-

tive methods of accounting for a premium (and four comparable methods for a discount) associated with a forward contract:
1. The write-off can be deferred until the forward matures.
2. The premium can be amortized over the life of the contract and the asset associated with the forward debited.
3. The premium can be amortized over the life of the contract and an expense account debited.
4. The premium can be amortized over the life of the contract and the liability associated with the forward debited.

There is no reason to assume a decrease in the liability, so (4) is not acceptable. There is no reason to assume an expense is created through time, so (3) is not acceptable unless the forward is marked to market. An expense might occur if the actual events are different from those forecasted, but it might not occur. Both alternatives (1) and (2) are feasible alternatives. If the forward is marked to market, then there would be a credit to premium and the debit entry would be split between a debit to an asset and, if there is a change in interest rates, to an expense, with the possibility of a net gain occurring rather than an expense.

Forwards Paying Interest

Now assume the forward contract is for a security that pays either interest or dividends of D. We have:

$$F = S(1 + r) - D$$

where F is the forward contract price, S is the spot price today, and r is the market rate of interest. Assume a two-year $1,000,000 interest-bearing bond selling at face value is paying 12 percent interest per year. The market has a 10 percent cost of money for the first year and a 14.286 percent cost for the second year. The forward contract price would be:

$$F = \$1,000,000(1.10) - \$120,000 = \$980,000$$

If the price of the bond at Time 1 is actually $980,000 (reflecting a one-period rate of 14.286 percent), the investor buying the bond for $1,000,000 at Time 0 will have a $120,000 gain of interest and a $20,000 capital loss.

At Time 0 the journal entry could be:

Contract Receivable.	1,000,000	
Discount		20,000
Contract Payable		980,000

An alternative is to make no entry at Time 0 (this is consistent with the accounting for futures).

At Time 1 the above entry or its equivalent is reversed, and if the price of the bond is $1,000,000, the $20,000 gain on the forward is recorded:

Cash	20,000	
Gain on Forward		20,000

Is there an expectation at Time 0 of having a $20,000 gain at Time 1 on the forward? The expected gain on the forward is zero, and there is no reason (ex ante) to assume that the $20,000 discount shown above will translate into a gain.

If the bond price is $1,000,000 at Time 0 and the money cost (say 15 percent) for the first year exceeds the 12 percent dividend rate, then at the initiation of the forward we have:

$$F = \$1,000,000(1.15) - \$120,000 = \$1,030,000$$

At Time 0 the journal entry could be (one alternative is to record no entry):

Contract Receivable	1,000,000	
Premium	30,000	
Contract Payable		1,030,000

At Time 1, after the interest payment, if the security only has a value of $1,000,000, the investor loses $30,000 on the forward. The loss arises because the $1,000,000 security is only earning 12 percent interest and for the first time period the money costs 15 percent. For an investor to buy the $1,000,000 security when it pays 12 percent interest and money costs 15 percent, there has to be the expectation of a price increase. If the security price is expected to increase from $1,000,000 to $1,030,000, then it is not obvious that the premium should be amortized to an expense account.

Accounting for a Forward Contract for Foreign Currency: A Premium

A forward contract creates an implicit asset and a liability. There is no gain or loss on initiating the contract. The liability is defined to be the forward contract price. The asset is the current spot price. The difference between the two amounts is defined to be a discount or premium.

For example, assume for a foreign exchange forward:

$S = \$.80$ = Spot rate for one yen

$r = .10$ = Domestic (U.S.) interest rate

$i = .04$ = Foreign interest rate

$F = \$.84615$ = Forward rate (consistent with no arbitrage profits) for one yen in one time period

$FCA = 130 \text{ yen}$ = Foreign currency amount

The firm wants 130 yen in one time period. Note that unlike the domestic situation there are two relevant interest rates and two relevant exchange rates.

Assume a forward contract to acquire in one period 130 yen at a contract cost of $.84615 per yen. The forward contract's liability to be paid in one period is 130(.84615) = $110 in terms of U.S. dollars. Using the spot rate, the dollar value of 130 yen today is 130(.80) = $104. Since F is larger than S, the difference between $110 and $104 is defined to be a premium. The accounting entry in dollars at contract initiation could be:

Contract Receivable (foreign currency)	104	
Premium	6	
Contract Payable		110

There are other possible accounting entries, including making no entry at all for the forward contract. "No entry" is consistent with the accounting for futures. The $110 amount of contact payable is not due to be payable until one period passes. The "premium" results because of the difference in interest rates in the domestic (10 percent) and the foreign (4 percent) markets. More exactly $F = S[(1 + r)/(1 + i)]$.

If the spot rate at Time 1 is $.84615 (equal to the value of F), the buyer of the forward to buy yen will have zero gain or loss. If the buyer of the forward needs 130 yen, he will pay $110 for the 130 yen, and the forward has zero gain or loss.

The spot price can increase (or decrease) through time without affecting the value of the forward or resulting in a gain or loss. However, the forward's value will be affected by a change in the spot price that was not implicitly forecasted by the values of r and i.

Accounting for a Forward Contract for Foreign Currency: A Discount

Now assume the following facts:

$S = \$1.44$ = Spot rate for one yen

$r = .10$ = Domestic (U.S.) interest rate

$i = .20$ = Foreign interest rate

$FCA = 83.333$ = Yen foreign currency amount

The firm wants 83.333 yen in one time period. Assume that $F = \$1.32$.

$$F = S\left(\frac{1+r}{1+i}\right) = \$1.44\left(\frac{1.10}{1.20}\right) = \$1.32$$

One alternative is for the firm to buy a forward contract to buy 83.33 yen at a price of $1.32 or a total cost of $110. Investing $100 domestically the company will have $110 after one period. This will buy $^{\$110}/_{1.32} = 83.33$ yen. The forward contract effectively guarantees the $1.32 exchange rate for 83.333 yen. For example, if the actual exchange rate at Time 1 is $1.50, the firm can only buy $^{110}/_{1.50} = 73.33$ yen but the firm makes a gain of 83.33 (1.50 − $1.32) = \$15$ or $^{15}/_{1.50} = 10$ yen on the forward. In total, the firm again has 83.33 yen.

The journal entry at the initiation of the contract could be:

Contract Receivable (83.33 × 1.44) 120		
Contract Payable.		110
Discount.		10

An alternative is to make no entry at Time 0, consistent with the accounting for futures.

If the forecasted change in the exchange rate from $1.44 to $1.32 actually occurs, there is no gain or loss on the forward.

Separate Accounting

Separate accounting involves the premium or discount of a forward (or futures) contract and its write-off over the life of the contract. The write-off may or may not affect income depending on conditions specified by Financial Accounting Standards Nos. 52 and 80.

FAS 80 dealing with futures discourages the use of "separate accounting" except in unusual circumstances:

> A change in the market value of a futures contract that qualifies as a hedge of an existing asset or liability shall be recognized as an adjustment of the carrying amount of the hedged item. A change in the market value of a futures contract that is a hedge of a firm commitment shall be included in the measurement of the transaction that satisfies the commitment. An enterprise may recognize the premium or discount on a hedge contract in income over the life of the contract if the commodity or financial instrument being hedged is deliverable under the terms of the futures contract, and if it is probable that both the hedged item and the futures contract will be retained to the delivery date specified in the contract. The premium or discount is computed at the inception of the hedge by reference to the contracted futures price and the fair value of the hedged item. (paragraph 6)

FAS 52 requires the premium or discount on a nonspeculative forward contract be accounted for separately from the changes in value:

> A gain or loss (whether or not deferred) on a forward contract, except a forward contract of the type discussed in paragraph 19, shall be computed by multiplying the foreign currency amount of the forward contract by the difference between the spot rate at the balance sheet date of inception of the forward contract (or the spot rate last used to measure a gain or loss on that contract for an earlier period). The discount or premium on a forward contract (that is, the foreign currency amount of the contract multiplied by the difference between the contracted forward rate and the spot rate at the date of

inception of the contract) shall be accounted for separately from the gain or loss on the contract and shall be included in determining net income over the life of the forward contract. However, if a gain or loss is deferred under paragraph 21, the forward contract's discount or premium that relates to the commitment period may be included in the measurement of the basis of the related foreign currency transaction when recorded. If a gain or loss is accounted for as a hedge of a net investment under paragraph 20, the forward contract's discount or premium may be included with translation adjustments in the separate component of equity. (paragraph 18)

FAS 52 precludes the use of separate accounting for a speculative forward contract. However, when forwards are used as hedges, separate accounting must be used. The write-off of the premium or discount of a hedge must be accounted for separately, and the write-offs will affect net income over the life of the forward contract.

With an anticipatory hedge, the write-off *may* be included in the measurement of the basis. With a hedge of a net investment (currency transactions), the write-off may be included with translation adjustments. Thus, management has an option with those two types of transactions whether or not income is affected immediately by the use of separate accounting.

CONCLUSIONS

The accounting for the discount or premium associated with forward contracts requires an analysis of the underlying economic events. We cannot conclude, without reference to market values, what should be the appropriate disposition of the discount or premium. One solution (not yet approved by the FASB) is to use market values or fair values. The accounting for forwards is not yet well-defined by the FASB, but fair value accounting is likely.

The accounting for futures not being used to hedge is to use market values (specified by FAS 80). If futures are being used to hedge, then the hedge accounting rules apply (deferral of gains and losses).

CHAPTER 10

FORWARD RATE AGREEMENTS (FRAs)

Charles W. Haley
University of Washington

Until the mid-1980s, major international banks routinely entered into contracts to borrow or lend a given currency for a specified period at a time in the future for a fixed interest rate. For example, a bank might agree to take a three-month $10 million deposit one month from the date of the agreement and promise to pay 11 percent per year. This type of contract is called a *forward forward*.[1] If the market rate of interest on such deposits is less than 11 percent on the delivery date, the depositor/investor has a good deal. If the interest rate is greater than 11 percent, the bank has a good deal. Note that by entering into this contract the bank has fixed its cost of raising $10 million one month in the future and the investor has fixed the return on its investment. Note also that the investor has made a promise to come up with $10 million next month and the bank has made a promise to accept that amount at the 11 percent rate.

Suppose that there exists a publicly available market interest rate for three-month deposits. Instead of going through the business of exchanging $10 million in one month's time, both parties simply agree to exchange any interest differential between depositing $10 million for three months at 11 percent and depositing the same amount of money at the market rate for three months. If the market rate is lower than 11 percent, the bank will pay the differences. If the market rate is greater than 11 percent, the investor will pay. If the market rate is exactly 11 percent, no one pays. This second type of contract is called a *forward rate agreement* (FRA), pronounced "frah" or "FRA." Note that, unlike the forward forward, an FRA is settled in a cash amount reflecting only the differential in interest rates and either party might be responsible for making the payment. This is similar to the practice in Euro futures. A forward forward, which can (and normally does) involve delivery of the asset in exchange for cash, is similar to the practice in T-bill and CD futures where the contract must be reversed to avoid delivery.

THE FRA MARKET[2]

FRAs are essentially an over-the-counter form of financial futures and, as we discuss later, are a substitute for financial futures in interest rate risk management. They originated in 1981 in private transactions among a few large banks, but significant activity began in 1984 in the London Eurodollar market. At first, FRAs were used primarily by banks in the management of their interest rate risk exposures and were confined pretty much to U.S. dollars and British pounds sterling. They have now become available in virtually any convertible currency including the ECU, Portugese escudo, Saudi riyal, South African rand, and Mexican peso. As of July 1992, Japanese yen FRAs are confined to the offshore markets due to rulings by Japan's Ministry of Finance that they constitute "gambling" under Japan's penal code. There is continuous pressure by the banks to eliminate this restriction because it prevents them from offering a full range of financial services in Tokyo.

Nonfinancial corporations are significant users of FRAs; they enter into the contracts with their banks. There is an active broker market for the contracts with two-way quotes in the more active currencies—both a bid and an offer price are quoted. The largest volume of business is still done in London, with New York in second place, but the market is really worldwide. There is significant activity in all major European financial centers, Hong Kong, Bahrain, and Sydney. Japanese banks offer FRAs in yen and other currencies through their foreign branches and off-shore subsidiaries. Actual figures on the volume of business are very difficult to obtain due to the private nature of the transactions; however, there is general agreement that the notional amount of outstanding contracts is large (hundreds of billions of dollars) and growing.

As a customized credit product, the terms and conditions on an FRA can vary according to the institution offering the contract and the requirements of the customer. However, there is a standard set of terms and conditions in the market that were originally established by the British Bankers' Association—FRABBA terms. (FRABBA is pronounced "frah-bah.") First, the contract is quite specific that neither party to it has any commitment to lend or borrow the notional principal amount of the contract. Second, failure to pay any required cash settlements becomes the equivalent of failure to perform on the conditions of a loan agreement.

The amount of any settlement required is calculated according to a formula specified in the contract. The formula is based on the logic of the forward forward. That is, first calculate the amount of interest that would be gained or lost on a deposit at a contract rate different from the market rate in effect on the settlement date. However, since interest on a deposit is not paid until the maturity of the deposit, an adjustment for the timing of the interest payment must be made. This is done by discounting the amount of interest gained or lost back to the settlement date at the market rate. Prior to 1985, this discounting was not normally done.

The original statement by the British Bankers' Association (BBA) was:[3]

> Whenever two parties enter into a F.R.A. the Buyer will agree to pay to the Seller on the Settlement Date (if the Contract Rate exceeds the BBA Interest Settlement Rate), and the Seller will agree to pay to the Buyer on the Settlement Date (if the BBA Interest Settlement Rate exceeds the Contract Rate) an amount calculated in accordance with the following formula:
>
> (a) when L is higher than R
>
> $$\frac{(L - R) \times D \times A}{(B \times 100) + (L \times D)}$$
>
> or (b) when R is higher than L
>
> $$\frac{(R - L) \times D \times A}{(B \times 100) + (L \times D)}$$

where

L = BBA Interest Settlement Rate (expressed as a number and not a percentage, e.g., 10.11625 and not 10.11625%)

R = Contract Rate (expressed as a number and not a percentage)

D = Days in Contract Period

A = Contract Amount

B = 360 except where the Contract Currency is Pounds Sterling (or any other currency where the contract rate is calculated on 365 days according to market custom) when $'B' = 365$

The BBA Interest Settlement Rate is LIBOR (London Interbank Offer Rate) for the contract currency and time period as determined by the BBA from a sample of bank quotes each day. The formulas above apply only to contract periods less than or equal to one year. The BBA also provided formulas for contract periods in excess of one year; however, such contracts are very uncommon. (See note 4 at the end of this chapter.)

As an example, suppose that the contract rate (R) is 11.0 percent, the settlement rate (L) is 11.4 percent, the contract period (D) is 91 days, and the contract amount is $10 million. Using the 360-day convention and (a) above, since L is greater than R, we get the amount owed to the seller (cash settlement) as:

$$\text{Cash settlement} = \frac{(11.4 - 11.0) \times 91 \times \$10,000,000}{(360 \times 100) + 11.4 \times 91}$$
$$= \frac{\$36,400,000}{37,037.4}$$
$$= \$982.79$$

We could obtain the same result by first calculating the interest differential that would be received on a $10,000,000 deposit for 91 days, then discounting back 91 days. The interest differential is:

$$\text{Interest differential} = \frac{(L - R)}{100} \times \frac{D}{B} \times A$$
$$= \frac{(11.4 - 11.0)}{100} \times \frac{91}{360} \times \$10,000,000$$
$$= \$1,011.11$$

This amount of interest needs to be discounted back to the settlement date using the market interest rate. The discount factor is:

$$\text{Discount factor} = 1/(1 + D/B \times L/100)$$
$$= 1/(1 + 91/360 \times 11.4/100)$$
$$= 0.97199$$

The cash settlement is then the interest differential times the discount factor:

$$\text{Cash settlement} = \$1,011.11 \times 0.97199$$
$$= \$982.79$$

We get the same answer as the BBA formula because the formula is derived algebraically from the expressions for the interest differential and the discount factors above.

In this transaction, the buyer can be thought of as a bank receiving (buying) funds and the seller is the party investing (selling) funds. Since the market rate is higher than the contract rate, the seller owes the buyer the difference in interest. Corresponding to this analogy, in the FRA market one buys and sells rather than bids and offers. If you buy the rate, you are borrowing at that rate and hope that rates will rise. If you sell the rate, you are lending at that rate and hope that rates will fall. Note that this terminology is the reverse of that for a futures contract; that is, when you "buy" a futures contract, you hope that rates will fall. This is due to the pricing of futures contracts as (100 − Interest rate). When you "buy" a futures contract, you are "selling" the interest rate.

AVAILABILITY AND PRICING

FRAs tend to be offered with settlement dates of less than one year and with contract periods corresponding to the standard periods for Euro market rate quotes—3 months, 6 months, 9 months, and 12 months. Three-month contract periods are by far the most common because this corresponds to Euro market futures contracts. Contracts with notional amounts of $1 billion or more can be done in dollars and sterling with these terms. However, longer settlement dates, out as far as 48 months, are readily available for the major currencies, especially dollars and sterling, although with smaller contract amounts. Nonstandard ("broken date") contract periods are also available but are almost exclusively confined to periods less than 12 months.[4] However, at a high enough price, one can find almost anything in this market.

The terminology of the market reflects the evolution of FRAs from forward forwards. A 2 versus 5 has a settlement date two months in the future and a three-month contract period. The five in this example corresponds to the maturity date of a three-month notional deposit made two months from now. Similarly a 6 versus 18 has a settlement date 6 months from now and a 12-month contract period, which is equivalent to a 12-month notional deposit made 6 months from now and maturity 18 months from now.

Contract prices are driven by the futures market in the relevant currency, where such markets exist, and by the cash (securities) market where they don't. For example Eurodollar futures contracts on the IMM are available out to four years based on the three-month LIBOR. The "buy" rate for dollar FRAs with three-month contract periods and settlement dates of four years or less will be priced directly from the futures prices if the settlement date matches the futures contract date. For example, if you obtained a quote for an IMM FRA (same date as an IMM Eurodollar futures contract) of 96.00, implying a yield of 4.00 percent, you would likely receive a quote of 4 − 3.95. Thus, you could buy a contract from the party making the quote at 4.00 percent and sell a contract at 3.95 percent. If the FRA settlement date does not match the futures contract date, the buy rate will be a linear interpolation between the rates of the two futures contracts bracketing the FRA settlement date. The "sell" rate on the FRA will then be four to five basis points less than the "buy" rate. Since the interest rate risk in an FRA can be hedged by an equivalent futures contract, liquidity in the FRA market is greatest for FRA contracts that match those available in the futures market.

Where a futures market does not exist, as in the less liquid currencies or for longer maturities than available in the futures market, FRA pricing is done off the implied forward rates taken from the term structure of interest rates in the cash market for the currency in question. The spreads between buy and sell rates are greater than four basis points in these FRAs because it is more difficult/risky/expensive to arbitrage in the cash market, especially in less liquid currencies, than it is in the futures markets.

APPLICATIONS

FRAs can be used to manage or hedge interest rate risk in the same situations as described for financial futures in Chapter 6. They can be used to eliminate the interest risk for a bank in funding relatively long-term fixed-rate loans with short-term or variable-rate deposits. They can be used by a corporate borrower to convert a variable-rate loan to a fixed-rate loan. They can be used by a corporate treasurer to increase the yield on a portfolio of money market securities while maintaining liquidity. To illustrate the mechanics, let's look at a moderately complex example of a corporate borrower. (We are assuming familarity with the simpler examples presented in earlier chapters.)

Aden Corporation has an outstanding loan of $20 million that calls for semiannual principal and interest payments. The principal payment due each period is $5 million. The interest rate is six-month LIBOR plus 1.0 percent where the rate is set at the beginning of each six-month period. Interest payments at the end of each six-month period are based on the outstanding balance and interest rate at the beginning of the period. Aden's treasurer would like to fix the interest cost of this loan over its remaining term. The first step is to determine what contracts will be needed.

The next scheduled payment is three months away; the interest due at this time is fixed at this point so there is no need to hedge it. The schedule for principal (and interest) payments and the remaining balances are as follows:

Month	Principal Payment	Remaining Balance
3	$5 million	$15 million
9	5 million	10 million
15	5 million	5 million
21	5 million	–0–

Aden is therefore faced with an unknown interest expense on $15 million for 6 months starting 3 months from now, on $10 million for 6 months starting 9 months from now, and on $5 million from 6 months starting 15 months from now. The interest cost can be fixed using FRAs by buying $15 million 3s-9s, $10 million 9s-15s, and $5 million 15s-21s. As a simple rule to remember, you fix the cost of borrowing by buying FRAs and fix the return on investing by selling FRAs.

The next step is to find out what the interest cost will be. The treasurer obtains rate quotes from Aden's bank of account and another large bank that has been seeking Aden's business. The quotes are essentially the same, so only one set is shown below:

$15 million 3 versus 9	8.22
10 million 9 versus 15	8.48
5 million 15 versus 21	8.80

Aden borrows at six-month LIBOR plus 1 percent. If the treasurer decides to lock in using these contracts, Aden's borrowing costs will be 1 percentage point higher than the quoted rates—9.22 percent on $15 million, 9.48 percent on $10 million, and 9.80 percent on $5 million over the relevant time periods. This is so regardless of what happens to LIBOR over the next 15 months. Aden will have eliminated its interest rate risk by buying these FRAs.

To see exactly how the numbers work out, suppose that six-month LIBOR in three month's time is 8.72 percent. Since the market rate exceeds the contract rate, the seller would owe Aden [using formula (a) shown earlier]:

$$\text{Cash settlement} = \frac{(8.72 - 8.22) \times 182 \times \$15 \text{ million}}{(360 \times 100) + (8.72 \times 182)}$$
$$= \$36,315.70$$

Suppose that this sum is invested for six months at LIBOR, 8.72 percent. Aden would receive $37,916.67 at the end of six months. In the meantime, Aden will accrue interest on the $15 million loan outstanding at 9.72 percent (LIBOR + 1%). The interest owed at the end of six months will be $737,100. (We are assuming that the loan is also based on a 360-day convention and are using 182 days for the six-month period.) The net cost of the loan will, therefore, be the interest paid less the proceeds from the invested cash settlement, or $699,183.33. This amounts to an annual rate of interest on the $15,000,000 of 9.22 percent, calculated as

$$9.22\% = (\$699{,}183.33/\$15{,}000{,}000) \times (360/182) \times 100$$

which is what we said it would be. Note that variations in interest calculations might make minor changes from the numbers we have assumed here, but the fundamental hedge is perfect.

FRAs VERSUS FUTURES IN MANAGING INTEREST RATE RISK

Given that the interest rate risk being managed is the same (both the FRA settlement rate and the financial futures contract refer to the same cash market asset, e.g., LIBOR and the Eurodollar futures contract), what difference would it make whether one used an FRA or the appropriate number of futures contracts? The answer is that it depends on the situation. Each type of contract has its advantages and disadvantages. We can summarize these as follows:

Credit Risk

Futures contracts have little or no credit risk, as they are effectively backed by the margins required and the exchange on which they are traded. FRAs are agreements between two parties either of which may not be able to fulfill its contract. However, the credit risk is considered to be relatively small in that the only amount involved is the cash settlement. An indication of the lack of perceived credit risk is that different prices are not being charged to customers with different credit ratings; that is, there is a general lack of tiered prices in the FRA market. Nevertheless, small, risky firms with generally poor access to the financial markets may find it difficult to enter into FRAs. For such firms, the futures market would be a better (or the only available) choice.

Liquidity

The ability to reverse one's position in a hedge requires a liquid market and is essential for futures contracts to avoid delivery of the underlying asset. Futures markets are generally much more liquid than FRA markets, and, as a result, futures positions can be reversed faster and at a lower cost. A firm with fixed obligations is unlikely to want or need to reverse its position; therefore, FRAs would be preferable. If the firm is subject to a changing situation, futures will be preferable.

Flexibility and Basis Risk

Futures contracts are relatively inflexible, as they come in fixed minimum amounts and are limited in the time periods that they are available. This is a potential source of basis risk arising from mismatched delivery dates or inappropriate contract amounts relative to the cash position being hedged. FRAs can be tailored to the exact requirements of a company eliminating this source of risk. Note the trade-off here between liquidity and basis risk. Futures offer better liquidity due to their standardized contracts at a cost of some basis risk.

Administration

Futures contracts are marked to market and settled daily. The position requires constant attention, as cash may be accumulating in the account or cash must be paid in to maintain the required margin. FRAs require only a single cash payment (receipt) at the settlement date.

The net result is that large companies with good credit ratings can avoid the costs of daily margin calls and obtain exact hedges of known commitments using FRAs. It appears that more hedging transactions involve FRAs than futures when either one would be suitable. FRAs are simpler, easier to explain to nonfinancial managers and directors, and more convenient to use. The major price paid for this convenience is less liquidity.

NOTES

1. An "ordinary" forward contract is an agreement to exchange one currency for another at a future date at a fixed exchange rate. In a forward forward, there is only one currency involved; the exchange involves the time value of money for that currency. Forward forwards and forward rate agreements deal with interest rates in a given currency, not exchange rates relative to another currency.
2. John Fry of Devon Systems provided significant assistance on the current (July 1992) state of the FRA market and its history.
3. British Bankers' Association, *Forward Rate Agreements ("FRABBA" Terms)*, August 1985, p. 8, London, England.
4. Note that as the contract period and contract amount increase, the potential for large cash settlements also increases. Thus the credit risk in a long contract period is higher than that for a short contract period for the same contract amount. To take an extreme example, a 2 percentage point difference between a market settlement rate of 10 percent and the contract rate on a five-year contract period results in a required cash settlement equal to 8.93 percent of the contract amount. This would mean a cash settlement of $8.93 million on a $100 million contract. The same interest differential with a one-year contract period results in a cash settlement for only 2.2 percent of the contract amount or $2.2 million on a $100 million contract. The credit risk issue is discussed later.

REFERENCES

Ross, Derek. "Interest Rate Management: Put to the Test." *Accountancy,* December 1991, pp. 109–11.

Smith, Clifford W., Jr.; Charles W. Smithson; and D. Sykes Wilford. *Managing Financial Risk* (New York: Harper & Row, 1990).

Stignum, Marcia. *The Money Market.* 3rd ed. (Homewood, Ill.: Dow Jones-Irwin, 1990).

CHAPTER 11

TAX ASPECTS OF FINANCIAL FUTURES

Diane D. Fuller*
KPMG Peat Marwick's Financial Services Practice

If you were to pick up a tax textbook on derivative products, you would not typically find chapters titled "Futures," "Listed Options," or "OTC Options." Instead, you would see titles such as "Section 1256," "Straddles," and "Dealers, Traders, and Investors." Although the fact that a financial instrument is exchange traded may affect its tax implications, in many cases, the same general tax principles apply to a range of derivatives. As a consequence, between a chapter on futures and a chapter on options, I have attempted to cover many of these general principles without unnecessary repetition. Thus, this chapter will discuss Section 1256 contracts, straddles, and related rules, while Chapter 15 on options will focus more on the character of income issues.

STRADDLES

Contemplation of the taxation of futures contracts leads almost naturally to a consideration of two key interrelated Internal Revenue Code (IRC) sections: IRC Section 1092, which deals with

---

*The author gratefully acknowledges the assistance of James Hunt, Patrick Murphy, Richard Solway, and Richard Turnure of KPMG Peat Marwick in preparing this chapter.

straddles, and IRC Section 1256, which governs the treatment of "Section 1256 contracts," since regulated futures contracts were the first instruments covered by both of these rules. These rules were introduced as part of the 1981 Economic Recovery Tax Act (ERTA) in an effort to put an end to certain "tax shelter" type transactions taxpayers were employing both to defer income and to change the character of that income from ordinary income and short-term capital gain into long-term capital gain. These are complex rules that attempt to address both the timing and character aspects of the transactions.

In a typical pre-ERTA transaction, a taxpayer might in August sell silver futures contracts short for July delivery while simultaneously purchasing a like amount of silver futures contracts for March delivery. By December, changes in market rates might have led to an unrealized loss in the long position offset by an unrealized gain in the short position. The taxpayer would then sell the long position to realize the loss and immediately purchase silver futures for May delivery to rebalance his holdings. In February of the following year, the remaining positions would be sold or closed out. In the first year, the taxpayer would report a short-term capital loss that might offset a short-term capital gain from other transactions, and in the second year, the taxpayer would report a long-term capital gain. In this way, the taxpayer sought to accomplish both a deferral of income and an advantageous change in character through a series of transactions that, in all likelihood, resulted in the aggregate in a pretax loss after commissions.

In Revised Rule 77-185, the Internal Revenue Service concluded that neither the short-term capital loss in Year 1 nor the overall out-of-pocket losses should be allowed as a deduction in connection with transactions of this type since the taxpayer had no reasonable expectation of deriving an economic profit. This ruling was the subject of much controversy, and the Internal Revenue Service was forced to litigate many such "straddle" transactions. As a consequence, Congress decided to take action and provide specific rules within the Internal Revenue Code addressing the treatment of these transactions. The following reasons cited in the legislative history for taking such action are common, if not always consistently used, rationales for provisions affecting financial instruments:

1. The use of tax straddles has received substantial public attention.
2. The revenue loss could grow substantially because of the low transaction cost and significant leverage available in many commodity futures transactions.
3. The widespread tax sheltering activity could cause substantial disruption in the commodity markets.
4. Taxpayers currently confront unnecessary uncertainty in the area of futures and forward contracts. Greater simplicity in the rules governing such transactions and greater certainty about the results of common transactions are essential.

At least the final concern with uncertainty and simplicity is one that remains much in the news to this day.

IRC SECTION 1256: REGULATED FUTURES CONTRACTS

Let's look first at IRC Section 1256, since this is the section that took part of its justification from the mechanics of the futures markets. This section provides timing and character rules for certain defined classes of derivative products. As originally enacted, it covered only regulated futures contracts; however, subsequent legislation has extended it so that it now covers the following four types of transactions:

1. *Regulated futures contracts.* These include contracts that are traded on a qualified board or exchange and with respect to which the amount required to be deposited and the amount that may be withdrawn depend on a system of marking to market. A qualified board or exchange includes a national securities exchange that is registered with the Securities and Exchange Commission, a domestic board of trade designated as a contract market by the Commodities Futures Trading Commission, or any other exchange, board of trade, or other market designated by the secretary of the Treasury. The International Futures Exchange (Ber-

muda), Ltd., and the Mercantile Division of the Montreal Exchange have been designated as qualified boards or exchanges.
2. *Foreign currency contracts.* This category covers forward contracts on certain foreign currencies that are traded in the interbank market. The covered currencies include the Australian dollar, the British pound, the Canadian dollar, the ECU (European currency unit), the French franc, the German deutschemark, the Japanese yen, and the Swiss franc.
3. *Nonequity options.* Any listed option that is not an equity option is a nonequity option for purposes of IRC Section 1256.
4. *Dealer equity options.* Listed equity options purchased or granted by an options dealer in the normal course of its business of dealing in options are included.

Timing and Character Rules

Once a contract has been determined to be a Section 1256 contract, it becomes subject to both a timing rule and a character rule. Exceptions to the general rules will be covered later. Under the timing rule, known as the *mark-to-market rule,* each Section 1256 contract held by the taxpayer at the close of the taxable year is treated as sold for its fair market value on the last business day of the taxable year and any resulting gain or loss is recognized.

When this rule was introduced, it represented something of a departure from normal tax rules. In general, the tax code requires recognition of gains and losses on a closed transaction basis; that is, gain or loss is typically recognized when the underlying asset is sold or otherwise disposed of. Prior to the enactment of IRC Section 1256 as part of ERTA, mark-to-market accounting was only permitted in very limited circumstances, such as for inventories of securities dealers. The expanded use of mark-to-market accounting in a number of areas, including foreign currency transactions and derivatives, continues to be explored as a potential means of reducing the distortions between the economic substance and the tax treatment under current tax law. For example, legislation before Congress as this chapter is being written would require securities dealers to use mark-to-market accounting for their inventories and certain other broadly defined types of securities. The mechanics of the futures markets provided Congress with a rationale for extending mark-to-market rules to futures contracts, since the taxpayer might be viewed as constructively disposing of the futures as a result of the exchanges' daily mark-to-market and deposit and withdrawal rules. However, such an analysis is difficult to extend to the other types of financial instruments that were added to IRC Section 1256 by later legislation.

Under the character rule, gain or loss with respect to a Section 1256 contract is generally treated as 40 percent short-term capital gain or loss and 60 percent long-term capital gain or loss. It should be noted that the preferential tax rates for net long-term capital gains that were in effect when this section was enacted were eliminated as part of the Tax Reform Act of 1986, although a limited capital gain benefit has since been reintroduced for individuals.

IRC SECTION 1092: TAXATION OF STRADDLES

Because IRC Section 1256 is closely tied to the straddle provisions under IRC Section 1092 as mentioned above, it may be appropriate to describe those rules at this time. First, it is necessary to explain what constitutes a straddle for tax purposes. A *straddle* is made up of offsetting positions with respect to personal property. To understand this definition, one must understand what constitutes personal property for this purpose and when positions are considered to be offsetting. Personal property means any personal property of a type that is actively traded. No definition of *actively traded personal property* is included in IRC Section 1092. However, in connection with the issuance in 1991 of proposed regulations concerning notional principal contracts, the Treasury Department released a proposed regulation under IRC Section 1092 defining the term as including any personal property for which there is an established financial market. Established financial markets include national securities exchanges registered under the Securities and Exchange Act of 1934, exchanges exempted from registration because of limited volume, domestic boards of trade designated as contract markets by the Commodities Futures Trading Commission, foreign securities exchanges or boards of trade subject to analogous regulatory requirements in their home jurisdictions, interbank markets, and interdealer markets. Clearly, this is a much broader definition than that of a qualified board or exchange used for IRC Section 1256 purposes.

Offsetting Positions

Similarly, the concept of *offsetting positions* in a straddle is much broader than those given in other parts of the Internal Revenue Code for qualifying hedging transactions. Positions are offsetting if there is a substantial diminution of the taxpayer's risk of loss from holding any position with respect to personal property by reason of his holding one or more other positions with respect to personal property (whether or not of the same kind). There is no guidance currently available as to how much of a reduction in risk will be deemed to be a substantial diminution. IRC Section 1092 does state that there is a rebuttable presumption that two or more positions are offsetting if:

1. The positions are in the same personal property (whether established in such property or a contract for such property).
2. The positions are in the same personal property, even though such property may be in a substantially altered form.
3. The positions are in debt instruments of a similar maturity.
4. The positions are sold or marketed as offsetting positions (whether or not such positions are called a *straddle, spread, butterfly,* or similar name).
5. The aggregate margin requirement for such positions is lower than the sum of the margin requirements for each such position (if held separately).

Noteworthy is the lack of any requirement that the taxpayer intend for the transactions to be offsetting or that the taxpayer identify the transactions as part of a straddle, requirements that are generally present for a taxpayer to avail herself of various hedging rules. This contrast underlines the status of the straddle rule as a weapon in the hands of the Internal Revenue Service, whereas the hedging provisions are generally taxpayer safe harbors. Despite the potentially broad reach of the straddle rules, they do not seem to have been applied frequently in connection with tax examinations up to this time.

Rules Applied to Straddles

Transactions that are considered to be straddles become subject to a loss-deferral rule, modified wash-sale and short-sale rules, and capitalization-of-straddle-interest and carrying-charges rules. Under the *loss-deferral rule,* a loss from the closing of one position of a straddle is only recognized to the extent that it exceeds any unrecognized gains on the other positions. Thus, in the example of the silver futures straddle described above, the loss from the sale of the long position in the first year could not be recognized since there was an unrealized gain on the short position. Any loss that is not recognized is carried over to the next year where it may once again have to be compared against unrecognized gains on offsetting positions.

The loss-deferral rule is extended by means of the *modified wash-sale rule.* Under the regular wash-sale rules of IRC Section 1091, a loss may not be recognized on the sale or disposition of stock or securities if the taxpayer acquires, or enters into a contract or option to acquire, substantially identical stock or securities within a period beginning 30 days before the date of disposition and ending 30 days after that date. The tax basis of the substantially identical stock or securities is adjusted by the amount of the unrecognized loss. IRC Section 1092(b) directed the Treasury Department to draft regulations that would apply the principles of the wash-sale rules to straddles. Under the modified wash-sale rules, losses are deferred to the extent that there are unrecognized gains with respect to:

1. Successor positions.
2. Offsetting positions to the loss position.
3. Offsetting positions to any successor position.

The following example from the regulations illustrates the application of the modified wash-sale rules:

On November 1, 1985, A enters into offsetting long and short positions. On November 8, 1985, A establishes a second short position (successor position) that is offsetting with respect to the long position. On November 10, 1985, there is $20 of unrealized gain in the long position and A disposes of one of the short positions at a $20 loss. At year end, there is $18 of unrecognized gain in the offsetting long position and $18 of unrecognized gain in the successor short position. Under these circumstances, the entire loss will be disallowed because there is more than $20 of unrecognized gain in both the successor short position and the offsetting long position.

The modified short-sale rule seeks to prevent taxpayers from converting short-term capital gain to long-term capital gain and long-term capital loss to short-term capital loss. The rule accomplishes this by suspending the holding periods of positions in a straddle and characterizing a loss as a long-term capital loss if, at the time the straddle was established, an offsetting position had been held for the long-term holding period.

The last of the straddle rules is found in IRC Section 263(g) and requires the taxpayer to capitalize interest and carrying charges that are allocable to personal property that is part of a straddle that does not consist solely of Section 1256 contracts.

AVOIDING SECTION 1256 AND SECTION 1092 RULES

Some or all of the straddle and Section 1256 rules may be avoided or modified under one of several elections available to taxpayers. The most significant is possibly the IRC Section 1256(e) hedging exception. A transaction that qualifies under IRC Section 1256(e) is exempted entirely from IRC Section 1092 and IRC Section 1256. The requirements to qualify as a hedging transaction under IRC Section 1256(e) are described in Chapter 15 on options. There are also special rules for identified straddles, qualified covered calls, married puts, stock positions, straddles made up exclusively of IRC Section 1256 contracts, identified mixed straddles, and mixed straddle accounts.

Among the most useful of these special rules are those concerning mixed straddles. A *mixed straddle* is a straddle in which at least one but not all of the positions consists of Section 1256 contracts. As a result of the special timing and character rules included in IRC Section 1256, a mixed straddle involves an increased risk that there will be a mismatch in either the timing or character of offsetting gains and losses. Thus, one position may be subject to the mark-to-market rules while another position is on a closed transaction basis. Similarly, one position may be subject to 60/40 long-term/short-term capital treatment while another position is all short term. Based on the legislative history, mixed straddle–type rules might also be applied to straddles where one position is capital while another is ordinary.

The mixed straddle account election may be the most commonly used of the mixed straddle rules, particularly for taxpayers whose high volume of transactions makes straddle-by-straddle identification impractical. A taxpayer may elect to establish one or more mixed straddle accounts. The election is an annual election and is made by attaching Form 6781 together with a statement describing the activities in the mixed straddle account to the taxpayer's income tax return for the immediately preceding year (if filed by the original due date) or to a request for an automatic extension of time to file that return.

If the mixed straddle account election is made, gains and losses in all positions in the account are determined and offset on a daily basis. Positions not closed at the end of the day are treated as if they had been sold for their fair market value at the close of each business day. Gains and losses from Section 1256 contracts and non-Section 1256 positions are netted separately. The daily net Section 1256 contract gain or loss is offset against the daily net non-Section 1256 gain or loss from the same mixed straddle account. If the daily account net gain or loss is attributable to Section 1256 contracts, then it receives 60/40 long-term/short-term capital gain or loss treatment. If the net gain or loss is attributable to non-Section 1256 positions, then it receives short-term or long-term capital gain or loss treatment based on the holding period of the position on the date the mixed straddle is created. Appropriate adjustments are made to the previously recognized gains and losses when the positions in the mixed straddle account are actually disposed of. At the end of the year, the daily gains and losses are combined to determine annual gains and losses. Under further limitations, no more than 50 percent of any net gain can be treated as long-term capital gain and no more than 40 percent of any net loss can be treated as short term capital loss. Since all of the positions in the mixed straddle account are marked to market, there is no timing mismatch, and the daily netting of Section 1256 contract gains and losses with the gains and losses from the non-Section 1256 positions mitigates any character mismatch.

SECTION 3

LISTED INTEREST RATE OPTIONS

CHAPTER 12

INTRODUCTION TO OPTIONS APPLICATIONS

Ira G. Kawaller
Vice President–Director, Chicago Mercantile Exchange, New York Office

Although options have long been negotiated in business and financial dealings—probably for centuries—they became formally institutionalized in 1972 with the advent of the Chicago Board Options Exchange. For the first time, options on equity issues were listed as an independent, tradable financial instrument. Since then, options markets have expanded to include a host of other "underlying instruments," including fixed-income securities, currencies, and futures contracts of all sorts. For the most part, options are options, regardless of what the instrument underlying the options happens to be.

In essence, options use falls into one or the other of two categories: trading and hedging. In the first case, those with no existing price exposure or risk will initiate an options position in the hopes of profiting from correctly anticipating a price adjustment. In the second case, the options are used as an overlay to an existing market sensitivity, such that if an adverse price move develops, the option position will generate an offsetting gain. This chapter first provides a foundation with a discussion of basic options characteristics and nomenclature and then examines each of the alternative uses more closely. It does so in the context of options on Eurodollar futures and interest rate risk management issues. Given this orientation, a brief discussion of the Eurodollar time deposit market and Eurodollar futures will serve as a prelude to the discussion on options.

EURODOLLAR TIME DEPOSITS AND EURODOLLAR FUTURES

The Eurodollar time deposit market is simply a market for dollar-denominated bank deposits held outside the continental shores of the United States. Actively quoted markets are made for cash deposits with maturities of overnight, seven days, one, two, three, six, and nine months, and one year. Interest accrues on these deposits on the basis of an "actual days" divided by 360 convention. For example, the interest on a $1 million deposit with a maturity of 90 days and a rate of 10 percent would be $1 million × 10 percent × 90/360 = $25,000. London is a major center for trading these deposits, and a daily quotation is disseminated from there: the London Interbank Offered Rate (LIBOR). This is the offered side of the Eurodollar deposit market, quoted at 11:00 A.M. London time.

The Eurodollar futures contract sets offered rates on three-month Eurodollar time deposits, commencing on a specific forthcoming date—the third Wednesday of March, June, September, or December, depending on the contract expiration month. Operationally, futures prices are derived by subtracting an interest rate (in percentage points, carried to two decimal places) from 100. Therefore, as interest rates rise, futures prices fall, and vice versa. Every basis-point move in the futures price (yield) translates to a cash adjustment of $25. This amount corresponds to the value of a basis-point change in yield on a $1 million Eurodollar deposit with a 90-day maturity. In general, movements in the Eurodollar futures market will be closely correlated to yield movements in the underlying Eurodollar time deposit market, though changes will not be precisely equal over any given period of time.

As long as one maintains the futures position—either long (expecting that the market will rise in price, decline in yield) or short (expecting that the market will decline in price, rise in yield)—the participant will be obligated to mark the contract to market and make cash settlements for any changes in value, daily. This obligation can be terminated at any time by simply trading out of the position (i.e., making the opposite transaction). Upon expiration of the contract, any participant still maintaining contracts will have a final mark-to-market adjustment, with the final settlement price based on an average derived from a survey of London bankers who report their perception of the cash market three-month LIBOR at the time of the survey.

FOUNDATIONS OF OPTIONS

Options come in two types: calls and puts. Calls are the right to buy something at a fixed price. Puts are the right to sell at a fixed price designated as the *strike* or *exercise* price. Both calls and puts have a limited period for which they are in effect; and the stipulation of this expiration period and the strike price define each particular instrument. For example, an 89.00-strike June call on a Eurodollar futures contract gives the buyer of this option the right to purchase a June Eurodollar futures contract at a price of 89.00. This right terminates in June, coincidentally with the expiration of the June futures.[1] It should be clear that the right will go unexercised if the June futures can be purchased in the open market for less than 89.00. In this case, this option is called *out of the money*. If the market for June futures is trading at a price greater than 89.00, the 89.00-strike call option would be called *in the money*. And finally, when the futures price equals the strike price, the option is called *at the money*.

When options are in the money, the difference between the strike price and the underlying's market price is called *intrinsic value*. As long as some time remains before the option expires, the option price, or premium, will likely exceed this intrinsic value, with this excess being referred to as *time value*. Importantly, the time value of an option is sensitive not only to the time remaining before expiration, but also to the markets' perception of volatility that is likely to be reflected in the underlying instrument's price during the remaining life of the option. With time remaining, a view that markets will exhibit greater (lesser) volatility will inflate (depress) time value, all other considerations remaining equal.

Often, market participants will speak of the *implied volatility* of an option. This term refers to the measure of volatility that would be used as an input in an option model,[2] such that the theoretical price of an option generated by the model under this assumed volatility equals the option's prevailing market price.

When holding options to expiration, a call will make money only if the underlying instrument rises above the strike price plus the price paid for the option; and a put will make money only if the underlying security falls below the strike, less the price paid for the option. In any case, however, the maximum at risk for either the call buyer or put buyer is the price originally paid for the option. At expiration, options on Eurodollar futures are cash settled. That is, both long and short option positions will be offset (or liquidated) at their intrinsic value.

Option buyers pay for their options at the time of purchase. No further cash flow adjustments are required until either the option is exercised or sold. The option seller, on the other hand, receives the price of the option upon its sale. With exchange-traded options, however, the seller must post a margin deposit with the appropriate exchange (via a broker). This margin amount typically will exceed the price of the option. Moreover, if the option appreciates in value, additional margin will likely be required. Conversely, if an option declines in price, the short option position may be permitted to reduce the value of the posted margin.

In general, call option prices move directly with the price of the underlying instrument and put option prices move inversely with the price of the underlying. The relative price movement of the option as compared to the underlying depends upon the relationship between the underlying price and the exercise price of the option. When an option is deep in the money, the option will move almost one for one with the underlying price. In this case, we say that the *delta* approaches unity (+1 for calls, −1 for puts).[3] For the case when options are deep out of the money, the relative move of the option with the underlying price (or the *delta*) approaches zero. For at-the-money options, the *delta* is about .5. Importantly, *deltas* also will vary with the time to maturity, as well as with price fluctuations.

Aside from being sensitive to changes in the price of the underlying instrument, *deltas* are also sensitive to time. That is, even if the underlying instrument's price change is stable, *deltas* will change over time. For in-the-money options, the passage of time will increase the absolute value of the delta; and for out-of-the-money options, the passage of time will decrease the absolute value of the *delta, ceteras paribus.*

These sensitivities are shown graphically in Figure 12–1. The zero on the horizontal scale reflects the at-the-money option. Increasing values to the right reflect movement into the money; decreasing values to the left of center reflect movement out of the money. The general S shape of the graph becomes increasingly steep as time passes, and this S is most extreme at expiration, showing a discrete movement from 0 for any out-of-the-money options to 100 percent for in-the-money options.

The exercise of an option results in the enactment of the right conferred by the option. For example, exercising an option on a futures contract results in the establishment of a futures position. If the buyer of a call option exercises that option, he then will hold a long futures position, initiated at the exercise price. A seller of that

FIGURE 12–1
Option Deltas (percent)

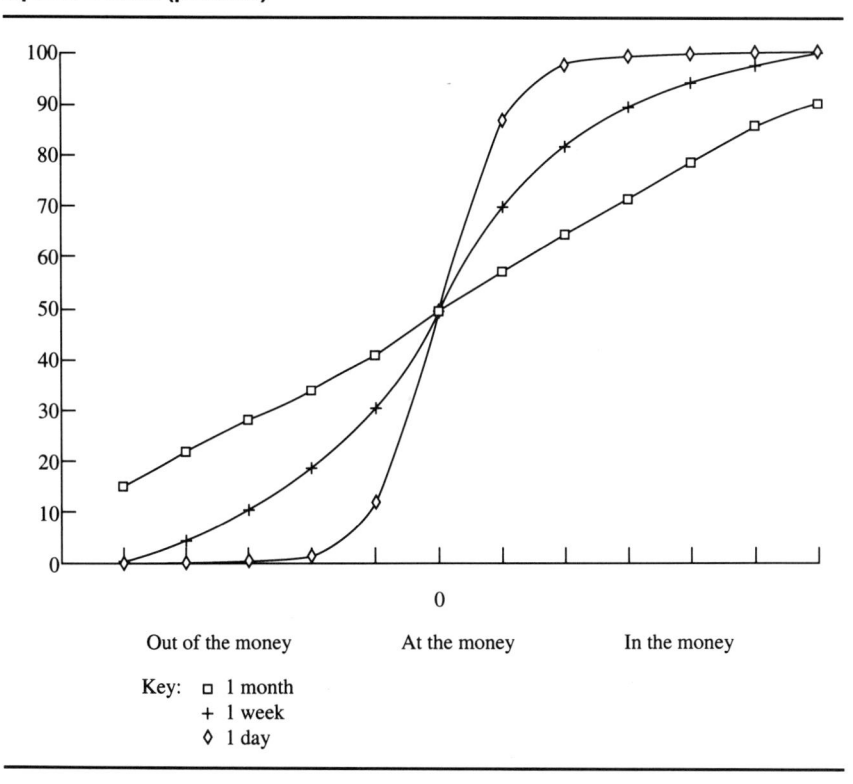

Key: □ 1 month
+ 1 week
◊ 1 day

call will be assigned a short futures position, also entered at the strike price. Conversely, the buyer of a put position will establish a short futures position at the strike price upon exercise, while a seller of the put will be assigned a long futures position at the exercise price.

HOW OPTION TRADERS TRADE

Although option trading may be motivated by an expected price move of the underlying instrument, perhaps the majority of professional option traders who buy and sell exchange-traded options originate positions because of relative value considerations. In essence, this approach requires the identification of "mispriced" options. Put in a slightly different way, these traders try to identify options with implied volatilities that differ from some expected or forecasted value. An expected rise in implied volatility justifies the purchase of the option (henceforth called the *original option position*) while an expected decline justifies a sale. In the former case, the option would be considered underpriced or cheap; and in the latter case, it would be overpriced or expensive. In both cases, the initiation of an option trade, all by itself, creates an exposure not only to a change in implied volatility but also to a change in the price of the underlying instrument. For trades motivated by the volatility consideration alone, this latter price sensitivity is undesirable. It can be mitigated to a large degree, however, by the imposing a delta-neutral hedge.

The remainder of this section explains (1) how to construct a delta-neutral position, (2) how such a position must be monitored and adjusted over time, and (3) what factors could influence the outcome of the trade and foster unexpected results. Treatment of the concept of *gamma* neutrality follows.

For expository purposes, the delta-neutral hedging process is initially illustrated with futures contracts used as the hedge vehicle.[4] Assume a trader sells 60 calls on Eurodollar futures with a delta of 50 percent on each call. The delta of the portfolio as a whole, then, is simple −60 calls[5] multiplied by .5, or a total of −30. Put another way, the futures equivalent of this portfolio is 30 short futures. Therefore, the appropriate offset requires buying 30 Eurodollar futures. While correct at the outset, this particular hedge ratio may need to be adjusted if and when the delta of the original option changes.

For instance, as the underlying futures price rises (as interest rates fall), the call options will move deeper in the money, and thus the delta of the portfolio will rise in absolute value as well. As a consequence, if the original hedge is not altered, the change in the value of the futures position will be insufficient to cover the loss of the original option position. Thus, to hedge appropriately, one would need to adjust the long futures position—a process often referred to as *dynamic hedging*—by purchasing additional Eurodollar futures as the underlying futures price increases. Unfortunately, if such adjustments were made and the market subsequently reversed itself, the reversal would foster losses on the "extra" hedge position.

In the case of declining futures prices (with rising interest rates), the call options would move deeper out of the money, and, therefore, the delta of the portfolio would decrease in absolute value. As a result, a correct hedge would require a reduction in the size of the long futures position (i.e., the sale of some of the Eurodollar futures initially purchased). Otherwise, losses on the futures position would outpace the profits generated by the short options. As before, a reversal would again foster losses on the adjustment portion of the futures hedge.

Whether the starting position is short calls, as above, or short puts, this conclusion would still apply. That is, in both cases, failure to adjust the hedge when called for would result in losses if a sustained market move were to develop. Moreover, losses would also accrue if adjustments were initiated but market prices ultimately returned to (or near) their original levels.

Coupled with these less than sanguine prospects is the fact that the maintenance of a delta-neutral hedge is not costless. Costs derive from buying at offered prices and selling at bid prices for all hedge transactions, paying commissions, and outright tracking error because the hedge results fail to match the desired changes in the option prices. On the positive side, the possible saving grace is that in stable markets, these costs will be minimal (hopefully near zero); and as long as the stability persists, the time value of the short options will likely decay, working to the benefit of the short option position taker.

Next, turn to the delta-neutral hedge that starts with a long option position, dictated by the presence of an underpriced option. Whether long calls or long puts, failure to adjust the delta-neutral hedge when significant price trends arise would prove to be beneficial. As an example, consider an original option position of long calls hedged by short futures. Rising futures prices would foster losses on the short futures hedge and incrementally larger gains on the calls, because of the rising delta. With declining futures prices, gains on the futures would outpace losses on the options, due to the declining delta. In other words, with no change in the hedge ratio, as underlying prices trend either up or down, the gradual change in the options' delta will cause greater gains from one side of the combination position (i.e., the futures or the options) than losses on the other. Perhaps equally attractive, if an adjustment is made to the hedge ratio following a price change (up or down) and a subsequent reversal occurs, this adjustment will involve buying futures low and selling high, or vice versa. Thus, each such reversal will generate incremental trading gains.

These seeming potential benefits, however, may not be overriding. First, the prospect of stable markets again exists; and with the long option starting point, stability means loss of time value. Secondly, even if the adjustments to the hedge do generate trading profits, these gains may not be sufficient to offset the transaction costs associated with the adjustment activity.

From the above discussion, it should be clear that both transaction costs and prospects for tracking error would be reduced if the hedge instrument's delta automatically adjusted along with the initial option's delta. This ideal is approached when implementing a *gamma*-neutral hedge.

The *gamma* of an option measures the sensitivity of the delta to a change in the price of the underlying instrument. The gamma is positive for long option positions (both puts and calls) and negative for short option positions, because higher (lower) futures prices force call deltas to become more (less) positive and put deltas to become less (more) negative. Moreover, the magnitude of the effect of a given price change on delta is greatest for at-the-money options and gets smaller, approaching zero, as the options move deeper and deeper in or out of the money.

Consider the situation of the option trader interested in minimizing the need for adjustments to her delta hedge imposed on a portfolio of option positions. The solution to this problem starts with the calculation of the deltas and gammas of the portfolio in question. Like the delta of the portfolio, the gamma of the portfolio is found by adding up the component gammas. The portfolio's gamma would then be neutralized by overlaying a hedge position with an equal and opposite gamma.[6] And finally, the last step would be to use futures (for which the gamma is zero) to delta neutralize any remaining delta on the gamma-neutral position.

It appears that the delta-neutralized short options position will benefit from stable markets and suffer with greater volatility; and the reverse is true for the delta-neutralized long option position. Transactions costs, however, are adverse to both starting points. Depending on the criteria used for making hedge adjustments, these costs may or may not be directly related to volatility.

Realizing the potential for a delta-neutral trade to perform imperfectly, traders would likely initiate trades only if the mispricing conditions were sufficiently generous to grant a high probability of success. Put another way, at some sufficiently high price (i.e., implied volatility), it makes sense to sell options on a delta-neutral basis; and at another sufficiently low price, it makes sense to be long options, delta neutral. If done properly, some mismatching would likely still arise over time, as gammas, like deltas, are also somewhat variable. Compared to a futures-only delta-neutral hedge, however, a gamma- and delta-neutral hedge can be expected to offer a second stage of risk protection.

At the same time, because a gamma-neutral hedge requires selling options against an original long option position (or buying options against an original short option position), establishing gamma neutrality will tend to mitigate both the pros and cons of imposing a futures-only delta-neutral hedge. That is, the uncertainty (opportunity as well as risk) associated with the adjustment process will be reduced, as will be the importance of the time value considerations if a gamma- and delta-neutral hedge is put in place, rather than only a delta-neutral hedge.

The object of employing a delta-neutral hedge is to capture the value of the perceived mispricing of some original option. Such a trade has its risks, however, so some threshold of mispricing must be surpassed to justify undertaking the position. The more conservative the trader, the more extreme these thresholds of mispricing would have to be; and, presumably, the more infrequently they would occur. Nonetheless, the professional option trader will make these judgments on an ongoing basis and trade when the conditions warrant.

HOW RISK MANAGERS HEDGE

In contrast to the options trader, the hedger has a different time horizon and, as a result, a different approach to using options. The remainder of the chapter demonstrates this approach by examining the case of an institution exposed to short-term interest rate risk. Options on the Eurodollar futures would likely be the instrument of choice for managing this exposure.

Irrespective of the fact that the risk in question may not relate specifically to three-month Eurodollar rates, per se, the number of contracts used for both the futures hedges and static option hedges generally should be determined as follows: Calculate the value of the basis point on the instrument to be hedged and divide by the value of the basis point on the futures contract, or $25. For example, consider the interest rate exposure of a $5 million three-month (90-day) U.S. domestic bank deposit. The value of a basis point would be $125, from $5 million $\times$ .0001 $\times$ 90/360 = $125. Thus, the correct hedge ratio would be 125 $\div$ 25 = 5 contracts.[7] In contrast, if the deposit had a six-month maturity with the same face value, the value of the basis point would be $250, and the appropriate hedge ratio would be 10 contracts. If concerned about rising rates, the hedger should sell the contracts or go "short"; if worried about falling rates, he should buy or go "long."

Before assessing the possible outcomes, two assumptions are made: First, the hedge is implemented with the correct number of contracts; and second, the hedge is maintained until the rate on the exposure is set, when no further interest rate risk remains. The effective rate realized inclusive of hedge results (Re) would then turn out to be the rate associated with the futures price when the hedge is implemented ($Rf1$), adjusted by the spread between the spot rate of the exposure (Rs) and the rate implied by the final futures price ($Rf2$) when the rate setting occurs and the hedge is liquidated. Algebraically,

$$Re = Rf1 + (Rs - Rf2) \qquad (12-1)$$

The accompanying example shown in Figure 12–2 assumes (1) the hedge ratio is calculated using the above-described value-of-a-basis-point methodology, and (2) the hedge is initiated at a futures price of 92.00, reflecting a rate of 8.00 percent. The figure demonstrates outcomes that would result with rising rates (top) and declining rates (bottom). In both cases, three scenarios are shown: Column 1 shows outcomes where deposits are issued at the same

FIGURE 12–2
Futures Hedge Example

Objective:	Lock up a funding rate on $15 million 60-day deposits
Hedge ratio:	Basis-point value = $15 million × .0001 × (60/360) = $250 Hedge ratio = $250/$25 = 10 futures (short)
Initial futures price:	92.00 (8.00%)

Outcomes with Rising Rates

Liquidation futures price	88.00	88.00	88.00
Rate paid on deposits	12.00%	11.75%	12.25%
	$Rs - Rf2 = 0$	$Rs - Rf2 = -25$	$Rs - Rf2 = 25$
Interest paid to depositors	$300,000	$293,750	$306,250
Profit (loss) on hedge	$100,000	$100,000	$100,000
Net interest	$200,000	$193,750	$206,250
Effective interest rate	8.00%	7.75%	8.25%

Outcomes with Rising Rates

Liquidation futures price	95.00	95.00	95.00
Rate paid on deposits	5.00%	4.75%	5.25%
	$Rs - Rf2 = 0$	$Rs - Rf2 = -25$	$Rs - Rf2 = 25$
Interest paid to depositors	$125,000	$118,750	$131,250
Profit (loss) on hedge	($75,000)	($75,000)	($75,000)
Net interest	$200,000	$193,750	$206,250
Effective interest rate	8.00%	7.75%	8.25%

rate as the rate associated with the futures price upon liquidation (i.e., $Rs - Rf2 = 0$); column 2 shows outcomes where deposits are issued at 25 basis points below the liquidation futures rate ($Rs - Rf2 = -25\%$); and column 3 shows results when deposits are issued at 25 basis points above the futures rate ($Rs - Rf2 = 25\%$). This display demonstrates the validity of Equation (12–1), above, whether interest rate rise or fall or whether the difference in rates at hedge liquidation is due to (1) the spread between spot LIBOR and the spot exposure rate or (2) a nonzero basis of the futures contract.

Besides selling futures, a manager facing the risk of higher interest rates might also consider buying put options or selling call options. Both option strategies would make money if interest rates do, in fact, rise. The two would have different outcomes, however, depending upon the magnitude of the interest rate change. Buying puts allows hedge profits to be generated from rising interest rates; but with rates declining, the loss on the hedge is limited to the price of the options. Put buying may be seen as analogous to purchasing insurance with a deductible clause. A claim can be filed if interest rates rise, and the insurance policy will pay off. Conversely, if interest rates stay the same or fall, the put buyer simply lives with the fact that she paid for insurance but does not file a claim.

Alternatively, suppose the hedger sells calls to protect against rising interest rates. If rates do move higher, the call will lose value. It can then be bought back cheaper, fostering a gain. Thus, with rising rates, the call seller gets to keep some—and perhaps all—of the initial selling price of the options, but no more. If interest rates decline, on the other hand, the option price will rise; and the call seller will be forced to buy back her option position at a higher price and therefore at a loss. Put another way, by choosing this method of coverage, the manager only achieves hedge profits for a limited interest rate increase; but she is completely exposed to an unlimited loss on her hedge if rates unexpectedly decline.

For those who suffer under declining interest rates, all the above solutions are reversed. That is, the choice now becomes buying futures contracts, buying call options, or selling put options. The characteristics are analogous: Futures lock in an effective interest rate[8] and thereby eliminate both risk and opportunity;

option buying (calls) offers unbounded hedge profit potential and limited risk; and selling options (puts) offers limited profit potential and unbounded risk.

Whether protecting against rising or falling rates, if the hedge is removed simultaneously with the options' expiration, hedge positions will be offset or liquidated at prices equaling the options' intrinsic value (i.e., the difference between the futures price and the strike price, if beneficial). In contrast, if termination of the options' position were to occur prior to the contracts' expiration, the liquidation price would be greater than the intrinsic value, the difference being equal to the options' time value. The long option hedger thus benefits by being able to liquidate (sell) her hedge before expiration, while the short option hedger is adversely affected—assuming a given price of the underlying futures.

Returning to the problem posed in Figure 12-2, now consider the use of a long put position as a hedge vehicle to protect against the risk of rising deposit rates. Using the same hedge ratio as that calculated for the futures hedge (i.e., 10 contracts), and continuing the assumption that the hedge is maintained until the options expire, put profits will offset higher interest rates—as long as futures prices decline below the strike price of the option.

Figure 12-3 shows results from employing a long 92-put hedge, where the puts are initially purchased at a price of .50. It reflects the assumptions that (1) the options are liquidated with no remaining time value and (2) futures and spot prices (rates) are equal at the time the interest rate is set on the exposure. Figure 12-4 graphs the outcomes associated with the short 92-call hedge, sold at a price of .50, again under those same assumptions. These figures reveal the fact that long put options offer the same prospective outcomes as do "interest rate caps" or "ceilings," while the calls offer the same results as "interest rate floors."

Relaxation of the two underlying assumptions will alter the effective interest rate realized: For a given spot market interest rate, a nonzero basis condition when option positions are liquidated may or may not influence liquidation option prices, depending upon whether or not the intrinsic value of the option is affected. With respect to the time-value issue, as noted above, greater time value at hedge termination necessarily benefits long option hedges

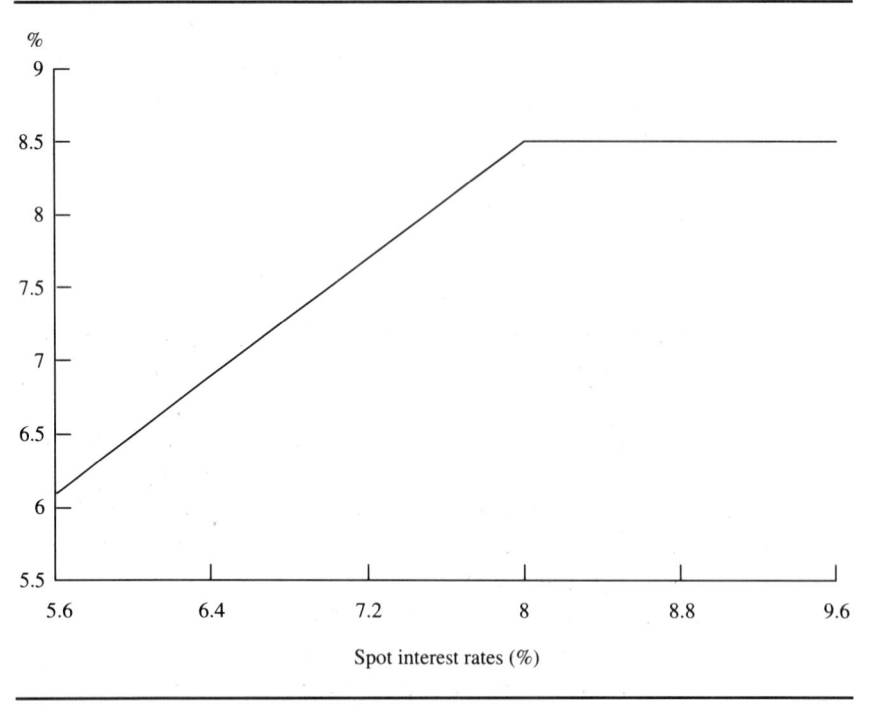

FIGURE 12-3
Effective Interest Rates—Exposure plus Long 92.00 Puts

(i.e., lowers effective interest costs or increases effective returns) and adversely affects short option hedges (i.e., raises interest costs; lowers returns).

At the time a hedge is initiated, it is not clear whether the best results will be generated by using futures contracts, buying options (calls to protect for declining interest rates or puts to protect for rising interest rates), or selling options (the opposite of the long option choices). In fact, depending on how the underlying interest rate changes, any one of the three choices could be the best. The manager's decision should depend on (1) the certainty that the manager attaches to the associated interest rate forecast and (2) the comfort level associated with the potential outcomes of the respective choices. The manager with great confidence in his forecast and an expectation of a sizable adverse interest rate move would be

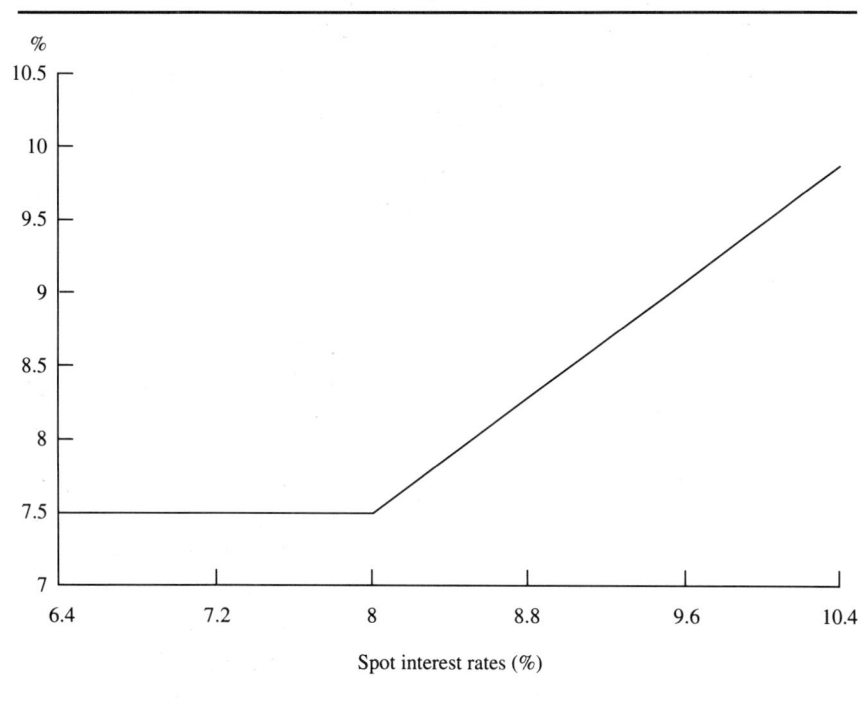

FIGURE 12–4
Effective Interest Rates—Exposure plus Short 92.00 Calls

best served by a futures contract. Alternatively, if one expects a large move but has less confidence in the forecast, the long options would likely be preferred. And finally, the short option choice would be best when a relatively small adverse rate move is anticipated, but still some cushion of safety is desired.

From the perspective of a hedger, the choices and trade-offs can be stated in the following way: Hedging with futures insulates the hedger from the effects of subsequent interest rate moves—either adverse or beneficial. Buying options is analogous to purchasing insurance for one-way protection. And finally, selling options offers a fixed, maximum amount of protection (regardless of the magnitude of an adverse interest rate change) and the prospect of forgoing the positive effects of a beneficial market move.

With these basic alternatives understood, the hedge manager

can now consider a myriad of alternative strategies that can be developed by combining option positions. Among the more commonly constructed option combination hedges are collars (also referred to as *fences, range-forwards,* and *cylinders*) and vertical spreads. Both are examples of hedges that are designed to offer some degree of protection at a cheaper price than the outright long option hedge.

A *collar* is nothing more than the purchase of a put (or series of puts) and the sale of a call (or series of calls) to protect against rising interest rates; and the opposite trades to protect against falling rates.[9] In effect, the collar imposes both a floor and a ceiling. Thus, the strike prices of the put (i.e., the ceiling) would always be lower than the strike prices of the call (i.e., the floor). Both of the relevant options would have the same expiration date, and the number of contracts to buy (and sell) would be determined from the value-of-the-basis-point method used for sizing the futures hedge.

While a collar appears to foster the security of a worst-case outcome for a cheaper dollar outlay than would be the case for the basic long option hedge, part of the cost of this protection is hidden in the form of an opportunity cost. That is, the short option component of the collar removes the prospect of an unbounded benefit that would otherwise accrue because of a beneficial interest rate move. Thus, the collar leaves the effective interest rate constrained somewhere within best-case/worst-case boundaries.

The *vertical spread hedge* has the opposite outcome. Within a range of spot interest rates dictated by the strike prices of the component options, the effective rate realized with this hedge is fixed—like the outcome of a futures contract. At both higher and lower interest rates than those specified by the above-mentioned range, the hedger is exposed to the effects of further interest rate changes.

Vertical spreads are constructed with the purchase of some original option—puts to protect against rising rates, calls to protect against falling rates—with a coincident sale of a cheaper option of the same type. As before, the options should have the same expiration date; and the number of options bought and sold should be found by the value of a basis-point method. Figures 12–5 and 12–6 show the outcome potentials realized by imposing collar and verti-

FIGURE 12–5
Effective Interest Rates (percent)—Exposure plus Collar: Long 92.50 Put and Short 93.00 Call

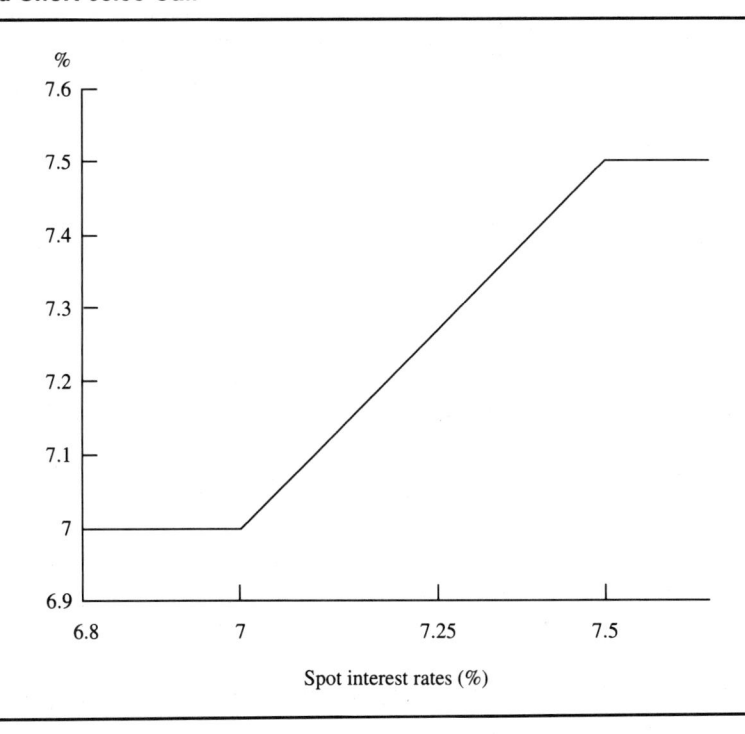

cal spread hedges, respectively, for a hypothetical hedger concerned about the risk of rising interest rates.[10]

It becomes the manager's responsibility to understand the risks and opportunities associated with the alternative hedge choices available—whether the futures hedge, long options, short options, or some combination of any of the above. No single choice will be right for all situations or all managers. Instead, a business judgment is required, reflecting (1) the inescapable trade-off between price and protection, and (2) the tolerance for uncertainty of outcome, which, to a greater or lesser extent, is inherent in virtually all hedging strategies.

FIGURE 12–6
Effective Interest Rates (percent)—Exposure plus Vertical spread: Long 92.75 Put and Short 92.25 Put

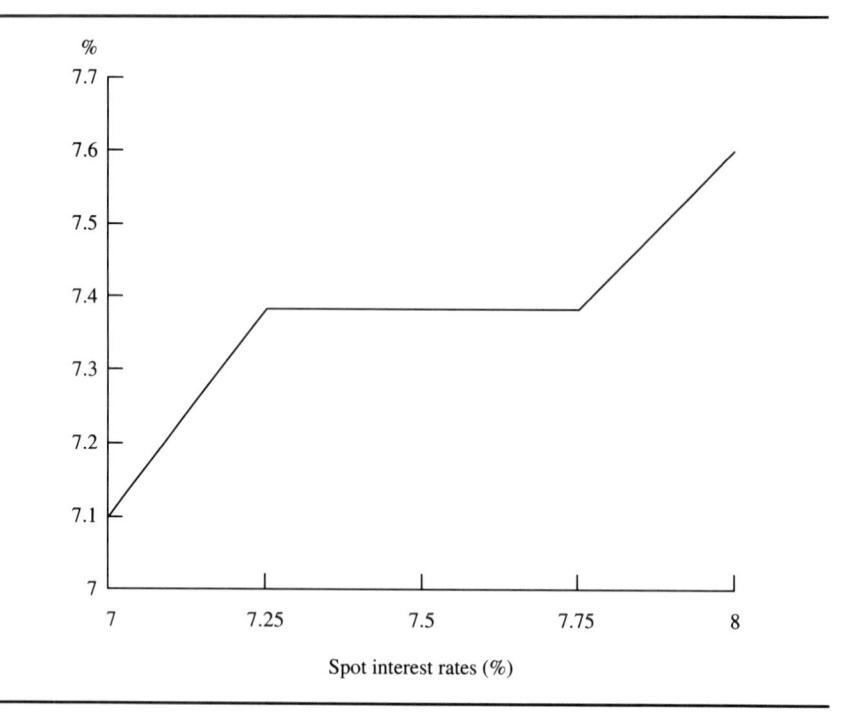

NOTES

1. Not all options expire coincidentally with their underlying futures. For instance, the option on Deutschemark futures expires two Fridays before the third Wednesday of the option expiration month, while the underlying futures contract expires two business days before the third Wednesday.
2. Volatility is expressed as an annualized standard deviation of rates of change of the underlying price.
3. Some models report *deltas* in percentages, rather than in decimal notation (e.g., 50 percent, rather than 0.5).
4. In fact, one may construct delta-neutral positions using spot markets, futures, or other options. When constructed with other options, how-

ever, one would certainly try to avoid the sale of options deemed to be underpriced or the purchase of options deemed to be overpriced.
5. A negative sign is required due to the *sale* of these options.
6. This offset can be arranged by any number of option combinations, so the astute hedger would want to be sensitive to relative-value considerations and commission charges that would apply to the various possible hedge constructs.
7. This approach ignores the issue of present value versus futures value. See Ira G. Kawaller, "Hedging with Futures Contracts: Going the Extra Mile," *Journal of Cash Management*, June 1986. This article discusses a technique called *tailing*, which can be used to remedy this concern.
8. Characterizing futures as "locking in" an effective rate may somewhat overstate these instruments' capabilities, in that some minor degree of uncertainty may remain due to basis risk. The issue relates to the prospective uncertainty as to the magnitude of $(R_s - R_{f2})$ in Equation (12–1).
9. Generally, the proceeds from the second options' sales are less than or equal to the cost of the long options.
10. These figures reflect different option prices than those used in the prior examples.

CHAPTER 13

THE STRUCTURE OF MARKETS FOR INTEREST RATE OPTIONS

Joan Junkus
DePaul University, Chicago

INTRODUCTION

Exchange-traded options on interest rate assets include both options on futures contracts and options on specific debt assets (actuals). Options on interest rate futures have been listed in the United States since 1982 and are also increasingly available on non-U.S. exchanges. Some non-U.S. exchanges list options on physical interest rate assets as well. In addition, there is also a large and well-developed U.S. over-the-counter market in options on actuals. This chapter describes the kinds of options currently available and then discusses the structural aspects of the various options markets, including market organization and participation, option exercise, and the operation of credit guarantees.

INTRODUCTION TO DEBT (INTEREST RATE) OPTIONS

Definition of an Option

A *put* option gives the owner the right to sell an underlying asset at a fixed price, the exercise or strike price, for a defined period of time. An option on a physical asset (for instance, a three-month 95 put option on a $100,000 face value U.S. Treasury bond with an 8 percent coupon and maturity of 2014) conveys the right to sell and deliver this specific Treasury bond and receive payment of 95 percent of par value, or $95,000, any time within three months. The put seller, or *writer* of the option, is obliged to buy the Treasury bond if the option is exercised and must pay $95,000 for it no matter what the true value, or price, of the bond is at the time of exercise. A put option on a *futures* contract, on the other hand, gives the owner the right to a short futures position at a futures price equal to the exercise price, and obliges the put seller to take the corresponding long futures position at that futures price if exercised.

A *call* option, on the other hand, conveys the right to *buy* the underlying asset for a defined period of time. For instance, a March call option on the five-year Treasury note futures contract, with exercise price of 100, listed on the Chicago Board of Trade (CBOT) gives the owner the right to a long futures position in the CBOT's $100,000 face value, five-year T-note contract at any time until March for a futures price of 100, or $100,000. The call writer is required to take the corresponding short futures position at a futures price of 100.

Most options listed in the United States are *American* options, which give the holder the right to exercise at any time before maturity. A *European* option, on the other hand, allows exercise only at maturity of the option. Despite the names, there is nothing essentially "national" about when exercise takes place, and both American and European options are listed in the United States.

Option Prices

To illustrate the purchase of an option and its exercise, assume that you are interested in purchasing one of the call options on Treasury bond futures listed at the Chicago Board of Trade. A range of options with different exercise prices and maturities is available. A typical set of option price (or *premium*) quotations is shown in Table 13–1.

The September options series has as its underlying asset the $100,000 face value, 8 percent coupon, 15 years to maturity or call Treasury bond futures listed at the CBOT for delivery in September. Prices for the underlying futures contract are quoted in terms

TABLE 13–1
Trade Prices for the CBOT Treasury Bond Futures Option

	Prices at Maturity Dates			
	Calls		Puts	
Exercise Prices	September	December	September	December
96	4-04	3-30	0-46	1-36
98	2-45	2-13	1-06	2-31
100	1-12	1-26	2-24	3-44
102	0-37	0-54	3-49	5-08

Prices are expressed as percentage of par ($100,000) and 64ths.

of percentage of par. Thus, the September 96 call represents the right to a long September T-bond futures position at a futures price of 96, or $96,000. The price or premium of the option is 4 4/64 of $100,000 par value, or $4,171.875. The seller of this option would receive the price, or premium, of $4,171.875, and would then be obliged to go short in T-bond futures at $96,000 if the option is exercised. A call option with a higher exercise price, giving the owner the right to purchase the same futures contract at a less attractive price, say, 98 or $98,000, would be correspondingly cheaper, costing only 2 45/64, or $2,703.125.

Call options are also available for the December T-bond futures contract, maturing three months later, at exercise prices of 96 through 102. Note that there are two distinct assets underlying the September and December options, a T-bond futures with a September delivery and another T-bond futures with a December delivery date.

The put option series, or the right to a short futures position in these contracts, is also depicted in Table 13–1. For instance, the right to a short position in the September T-bond futures at a futures price of 98 would cost 1 6/64, or $1,093.75. The put seller in this case would receive $1,093.75 and be obliged to take the corresponding long September T-bond futures position at a futures price of 98. As you can see from the table, put options representing the right to sell at a better, or higher, exercise price are correspondingly more expensive.

The price of the option depends on five factors:[1] the exercise price, the current futures price, the time to maturity of the option, the volatility of the underlying futures price, and the current short-term interest rate. Assume the current futures price on the September T-bond futures contract is 99 20/32, or $99,625. The September 98 call option price of $2,703.125 has two components. The *intrinsic value*, the value of the option if exercised, or the difference between the futures price of 99 20/32, and the exercise price of 98, is here $1,625. The other component is a *time value* of $1,078.125.

Purchase of an Option

When you call your broker for a quote on the September option, he will generally furnish you with bid and ask quotes. With the last transaction price on the September call of 2 45/64, assume the bid quote is 2 44/64 (the broker is willing to buy the call from you at 2 44/64) and the ask quote is 2 46/64 (the broker is willing to sell you the call for 2 46/64). The broker earns the bid-ask spread by buying at the lower price and selling at the higher, and the spread thus represents part of the transaction costs for the contract. In competitive markets like the T-bond futures option, the spread is generally very small, usually two ticks, or 2/64, as it is here. If you accept the price quote of 2 46/64, your broker will phone your order to buy the option to the floor of the CBOT, where it will be carried or hand-signaled over to a broker in the T-bond option pit. The broker will offer to buy one option at market price and must do the trade with the first person in the pit to respond. Once the trade is executed, a confirmation will be carried back to the phone clerk and you will receive notification of your purchase of the September 98 call at 2 46/64.

The total cost of the option will also include commission costs. A "round-trip" commission on the T-bond futures option is relatively low, around $30, so the final price of the option would be $2,718.75 plus $30, or $2,748.75. Because of the short-term nature of the security purchased, the round-trip commission includes the initial purchase and also the final offset, sale, or exercise of the option.

Margin on an Option Position

A purchaser of an option must pay the option price plus commission. The seller of the option, however, does not receive the full price paid. Because of the risky nature of the seller's obligation—the obligation to go short at a futures price of 98 no matter what the current market futures price is—the seller of an option must generally post margin with her broker. *Margin* on an option is a good-faith deposit to guarantee performance. The minimum size of the margin is determined by the exchange and generally reflects the possible losses on the option if exercised immediately as well as some forecast of possible losses based on recent price volatility. In addition, the margining system may also calculate margin levels based on other, related positions that the seller might have in the market. For instance, the call seller may also have a long futures position in the T-bond contract. In this case, exercise against the option seller would oblige him to take a short futures position, which would then offset his already established long position. By writing a *covered call* such as this, his losses are limited to the difference between his known purchase price of the long futures and the known exercise price on the offsetting short futures position. He thus has less risk than an option seller without a corresponding futures position, and the margin requested would probably be less for this writer.

The margin is given to the option seller's broker, who in turn deposits it with the exchange clearinghouse. The *clearinghouse* of the exchange is a group of exchange members whose function is to guarantee the financial integrity of the exchange. They do this by, among other things, guaranteeing the performance of each individual exchange contract, setting margin levels, collecting margin, and monitoring the possible losses throughout the life of the option.

Exercise of an Option

As the call owner, you have the right to exercise, or go long, in the underlying futures contract until September. However, an option owner will rarely choose to exercise before expiration. The reason for this is that upon exercise the option owner will receive only the intrinsic value of the option, or the difference between the market futures price and the exercise price, and will lose any time value remaining. It is always more profitable to sell the option to another investor, and in this way receive both the intrinsic value and also any time value remaining in the option price.

At *expiration,* the call option owner should exercise the option if the futures price is greater than the exercise price. (Many exchanges will automatically exercise the option for the owner if it has intrinsic value.) Note that the exercise value may not be large enough to offset the original option premium plus commisions. For instance, to break even on the September 98 call, the futures price must be at least $98,000 plus $2,718.75 plus $30, or $100,748.75. However, any intrinsic value will be a positive cash flow to the option owner, and will serve to offset at least some of the purchase price and commission costs.

Most options exchanges handle exercise in the same way, through a clearinghouse structure that assigns positions and controls the fund transfers involved. The following discussion of exercise primarily reflects the practice of the Chicago Board of Trade.

To *exercise* the September T-bond 98 call option, the option owner must give notice to the exchange's clearinghouse. Overnight, the clearinghouse will assign the corresponding short futures position to one of the writers in the pool of option sellers. At the CBOT, assignment of the exercise is random. On other exchanges, assignment is based on the first-in, first-out principle: The clearing member with the oldest written position will be exercised first. Before the beginning of trading on the next business day, the clearinghouse will establish for the option owner a long futures position in the September T-bond futures at a futures price of 98 and a short futures position for the writer of the option at a futures price of 98. Margin on both of the futures positions is then required, and the positions will be marked to market at the current settlement price of the futures. When marked to market, then, the option owner will receive the intrinsic value of the option, the difference between the exercise price and the current settlement price of the futures. After exercise, the futures position is indistinguishable from any other and operates under CBOT regulations for T-bond futures contracts.

As stated above, exercise at expiration can be automatic. Besides the CBOT's contracts, at the Chicago Mercantile Exchange (CME) T-bill contracts will be automatically exercised if they are sufficiently in the money. However, there is no automatic exercise with the CME Eurodollar option contract.

Unlike stock options, where the underlying asset has an infinite life, options on futures involve an underlying asset that matures at a date very close in time to the maturity of the option itself. For some options, such as the CBOT's mortgage-backed option, the last trading day is the same as the futures delivery day. For these options, exercising at maturity involves a cash settlement on the intrinsic value of the option rather than establishment of a futures position. For other options, the last trading day is a week or two before the futures delivery date. For instance, the last trading day for a March option on the CBOT T-bond futures would be on a Friday in the last week or two of February. Exercise would then give the option owner a futures position for approximately two weeks. In any case, for most options, trading ceases on a Friday, but the option holder has until Saturday morning to exercise.

EXCHANGE-TRADED OPTIONS

U.S. Markets

Table 13-2 lists the most actively traded interest rate options in the United States. While trading activity is concentrated in options on futures at the two Chicago futures exchanges (the CBOT and the CME), other U.S. exchanges such as the American Stock Exchange, the Chicago Board Options Exchange (CBOE), the New York Cotton Exchange (NYCE), and the Philadelphia Board of Trade have at one time listed various interest rate options contracts. These exchanges retain the possibility of relisting these contracts at a later time.

Trading in options on interest rate assets in the United States grew out of the very successful trading in stock options at the CBOE and trading on futures at the CBOT and the CME. The first options on interest rate futures were listed in 1982 as part of a pilot program in trading options on nonstock assets. Initially, each fu-

TABLE 13-2
U.S. Futures Options, Average Month-End Volumes, 1989–1990

		Volume	
Exchange	Futures Option	Calls	Puts
CME	$1,000,000 90-day Eurodollar deposit	189,281	170,970
	$1,000,000 90-day U.S. Treasury bill	945	501
	$3,000,000 30-day LIBOR	n.a.	n.a.
CBOT	$100,000 8% (notional) 15-year maturity Treasury bond	333,701	291,584
	$100,000 8% 7- to 10-year maturity Treasury note	27,392	23,137
	$100,000 8% 5-year maturity Treasury note	3,352	2,810
	$100,000 8% notional Muni Bond Index	7,939	7,934
	$100,000 variable coupon mortgage-backed bond	1,304	1,826
NYCE	$100,000 8% 5-year maturity Treasury note	n.a.	n.a.

n.a. = Not available.

Source: Commodities Futures Trading Commission, Annual Report, 1990.

tures exchange was given permission by the regulatory authority for futures exchanges, the Commodities Futures Trading Commission (CFTC), to list two options on futures contracts. After these were successful, the number permitted to each exchange was gradually increased. Now a futures exchange can apply to the CFTC for permission to list an option on any of its futures contracts.

Options on specific debt assets (actuals) were first listed in 1985 but have proven less popular than options on futures. The Philadelphia Stock Exchange, through its subsidiary the Philadelphia Board of Trade, was the first exchange to list an option on an actual, a $1,000,000 90-day Eurodollar deposit. This option has since been delisted. The American Stock Exchange offered options at one time on physical U.S. Treasury notes and bills. In 1992, the CBOE delisted its option series on specific long-term $100,000 U.S. Treasury bond issues. Currently, no options on actual interest rate assets are traded in the United States.

Several explanations have been offered for the greater *popularity of options on futures*. The availability of information has played a part. Since price information on individual cash assets is not as widely or as frequently disseminated as futures prices, the pricing of options on actuals can involve more uncertainty. In addition, trading of the cash asset is usually separated physically from trading in the option. Executing trades that involve both contracts, for arbitrage or hedging purposes, is thus more difficult than it is with futures, where trading usually takes place in adjoining trading pits. Also, since delivery on an actual contract specifies one particular bond issue or cash asset, there can be a potential for a market squeeze. This is not a problem with futures options, where the supply of futures is virtually unlimited. Moreover, the cash asset underlying the option and futures is usually defined as one of a number of specific assets. Finally, exercise of an option on an actual asset involves payment of the full exercise price—the price of the cash asset—plus accrued interest. As discussed above, exercise of a futures option involves a proportionately smaller margin payment, and so the exercise of the futures option can be accomplished more easily than exercise of an option on a physical asset.

To list an option on a cash asset, an exchange must apply to the Securities and Exchange Commission (SEC). The SEC, through an agreement with the CFTC, has regulatory authority over any option contract on a cash asset.

Chicago Mercantile Exchange Contracts

The CME and CBOT offer options on their most liquid interest rate futures contracts.

The CME's contracts—options on 90-day Treasury bills and Eurodollar deposits and on a 30-day LIBOR—involve the *short-term end of the yield curve*. For instance, exercise of the Treasury bill option gives the owner a futures position at the CME based on a $1,000,000 face value Treasury bill with 91 or 92 days to maturity as of the delivery date of the futures contract. Similarly, the Eurodollar contract gives the owner a futures position based on a $1,000,000 face value Eurodollar deposit with 90 days to maturity as of the maturity date of the futures contract.

Price quotes for these options contracts are based on the system used for the underlying futures contracts. Quotes are based on an annual yield on the 90-day security, and are expressed in terms of an index level of 100 less the annual yield. A futures price of 95 denotes a (100 − 95) 5 percent yield quote on the 90-day security. The actual dollar value of the quote would be based on the $1,000,000 face value less the 5 percent interest discount: $1,000,000 less (.05 × $1,000,000 × 90/360), or $987,500. Similarly, an options price is quoted in terms of this index point system. For instance, an option on a March T-bill 95 call may have a price of 1.25 index points, or 125 basis points on a yield basis. The dollar value of the option quote is based on a $25 value for each basis point on the underlying $1,000,000 face value Treasury bill (one basis point, or .0001 × $1,000,000 × 90/360 = $25). The dollar value of 1.25 index points would then be 125 × $25 per basis point, or $3,125.00. Option maturities correspond to the maturity date of the underlying futures contracts and are on a quarterly March, June, September, December cycle.

The LIBOR options contract specifies delivery of a futures based on a $3,000,000 face value, 30-day interest rate asset. Because the underlying asset has a shorter, 30-day maturity, the LIBOR options maturities are monthly rather than quarterly.

Exercise prices and subsequent increments are fixed and determined by the exchange based on the underlying futures settlement price. On the first day of trading in a new contract month, exercise prices are fixed at specified intervals above and below the current settlement price in the futures contract. As the futures price moves, new exercise prices are added in 25-basis-point increments. For instance, if the current Eurodollar futures price settles at 95.80 (representing an annualized yield on the $1,000,000 Eurodollar deposit of 100 − 95.80, or 4.20%), option strike prices will be fixed at 95.55, 95.80, and 96.05.

Chicago Board of Trade Contracts
The CBOT lists options on *long-term interest rate futures,* including futures on a $100,000 face value U.S. Treasury bond with at least 15 years to maturity or call and on Treasury notes with 10, 5, and 2 years to maturity. Like the underlying futures and cash assets, strike prices are expressed in percentage of par (or face value) and also in 32nds. A futures price of 98-15 means a dollar price of 98 15/32 of $100,000, or $98,468.75. The strike prices are set at

different intervals for the three contracts: at two-point intervals from the settlement price for the T-bond futures option (e.g., for a futures price of 99, exercise prices of 95, 97, 99, 101, and 103), at one-point intervals for the 10-year Treasury notes, and at ½-point intervals for the 5-year notes. Options maturities are on the quarterly March, June, September, December cycle, but there is also a contract maturity in the front month of the current quarter. For instance, for the first quarter of the year, a January maturity option would be listed as well as the March, June, September options maturities.

In addition to the options on various Treasury securities, the CBOT offers options on futures on other long-term interest rate assets including the *Muni Bond Index futures* and the mortgage-backed bond futures. The Muni Bond Index futures contract is based on a basket of 40 recently issued municipal bonds, with inclusion in the index based on such bond characteristics as the size of the issue, callability, and lack of special features. The option on this index futures thus relates to the current-issue volatility in the municipal market. The Muni futures contract is structured to resemble the other CBOT long-term futures, with an underlying $100,000 face value, 8 percent coupon standard, and a quarterly March, June, September, December maturity cycle.

The *mortgage-backed* futures is based on the most recently issued cash GNMA bond. The options and futures contracts are constructed to track the volatility of a newly packaged GNMA pool of mortgages. In contrast to the notional 8 percent coupon standard underlying the Treasury futures, in this contract a new notional coupon is listed on the futures as new cash GNMA coupon levels change. Because the current cash coupon is sampled and reset on a monthly basis, the maturity cycle for both the futures and options contracts is four consecutive months.

The CBOT suspended trading in an option and futures based on a long-term Japanese government bond in 1992 because of insufficient trading volume.

Markets outside the United States

Table 13-3 summarizes the exchange-traded interest rate options listed on non-U.S. exchanges.

Unlike exchanges in the United States, many foreign ex-

TABLE 13-3
Options on Non-U.S. Exchanges

Country	Exchange	Option
Australia	Sydney Futures Exchange (SFE)	A$ 500,000 90-day bank-accepted bills (OF) A$ 100,000 12% coupon 3-year Commonwealth Treasury bond (OF) A$ 100,000 12% coupon 10-year Commonwealth Treasury bond (OF) A$ 100,000 12% coupon 5-year semi-government (government agency) bond (OF) A$ 100,000 12% coupon 10-year semi-government bond (OF)
Canada	Montreal Exchange	C$ 25,000 10-year government of Canada bonds (O) C$ 250,000 90-day Canadian T-bill (O)
	Toronto Stock Exchange (TSE)	C$ 100,000 10-year government of Canada bond (O)
Denmark	Copenhagen Stock Exchange & Guarantee Fund for Danish Options and Futures (FUTOP)	DKK 1 million 9% coupon Danish government bonds (various maturities) (OF) DKK 1 million 9% 2006 annuity mortgage credit bonds (O)
France	Marche a Terme International de France (MATIF)	FF 500,000 10% coupon 10-year government bond (OF) FF 5 million 90-day PIBOR (Paris Interbank Offered Rate) (OF) Italian bond (OF) DM 1 million 90-day EuroDM
Germany	Deutsche Terminboerse (DTB)	DM 250,000 6% coupon 8.5–10-year notional government bond (O)
Japan	Tokyo International Financial Futures Exchange (TIFFE)	90-day Euroyen deposit (OF)
	Tokyo Stock Exchange (TSE)	JY 100 million 6% coupon 10-year government bond (OF)
Netherlands	European Options Exchange (EOE)	NG 10,000 Dutch government bonds (O) FTA Bullet Bond Index (O)
New Zealand	New Zealand Futures and Options Exchange (NZFOE)	3-year government bond (OF) 5-year government bond (OF) 10-year government bond (OF) 90-day bank-accepted bills (OF)
Singapore	Singapore Monetary Exchange (SIMEX)	US$ 1 million 90-day Eurodollar deposit (OF) JY 100 million 90-day Euroyen deposit (OF)
Spain	Mercado de Opciones Financieras Espanol (MEFF)	Pta 10 million 3-year notional government bond (O)

TABLE 13-3 (*concluded*)

Country	Exchange	Option
		5-year notional government bond (O) Pta 10 million 90-day MIBOR (Madrid Interbank Offered Rate) (O)
Sweden	OM Stockholm	SEK 1 million 11% coupon 7-year government notional bond (O)
United Kingdom	London International Financial Futures Exchange (LIFFE)	BP 50,000 9% coupon long (15–25-year) gilt (OF) DM 1 million 90-day EuroDM deposit (OF) US$ 1 million 90-day Eurodollar deposit (OF) BP 500,000 90-day Eurosterling deposit (OF) US$ 100,000 U.S. 8% coupon 15-year maturity Treasure bond (OF) DM 250,000 6% coupon 8.5–10-year maturity German government bond (OF)

O = Options; F = Futures

changes list *options on actuals,* usually government bonds, rather than on futures. These options on actuals reflect the origin of many non-U.S. options markets as an arm of an established stock exchange where cash government bonds are also traded. For instance, the European Options Exchange (EOE) in the Netherlands was organized by the Amsterdam Stock Exchange where Dutch government bonds are listed. All of the EOE's listed options are on cash securities rather than on futures. Currently, there are separate options series on nine individual Dutch (government) bonds ranging from a 7 percent coupon of 1993 to a 7.5 percent coupon of 1999. Similarly, the Montreal Exchange, the Danish exchange (the Copenhagen Stock Exchange and Guarantee Fund for Danish Options and Futures, or FUTOP), and the German options exchange (the Deutsche Terminboerse, or DTB) list options on specific government bonds.

At a minimum, most foreign futures exchanges list contracts based on a national stock index, on a long-term government bond, and on a short-term interest rate asset. This is true, for instance, for the Spanish exchange (the Mercado de Opciones Financieras

Espanol, or MEFF) and the French exchange (the Marche a Terme International de France, or MATIF). Commonly, futures contracts are listed first, and options on the futures are added if futures volume is sufficient to support them. Depending on the size of the underlying cash government bond market, the yield curve will be "filled in" by intermediate maturities. An example of this is the Sydney Futures Exchange, where options on 90-day bill futures and long-term government bond futures have been joined by options on 3- and 5-year bond futures.

Some exchanges also list *options* (and/or futures) *on nonnational or foreign securities*. The London International Financial Futures Exchange (LIFFE) in particular is attempting to develop a truly international market, with options and futures on U.S., German, and Italian government bonds. Given the increasingly automated nature of derivatives trading, physical location of the exchange is no longer as important as trading hours, liquidity, and institutional characteristics like taxation and regulation. A similar development is taking place in the Far East, where the Singapore Monetary Exchange (SIMEX) offers options contracts on both a Japanese Euroyen deposit and a U.S. Eurodollar deposit.

Because of the listing of options on foreign securities on many exchanges, *24-hour trading* in some derivatives is possible. With the CME, SIMEX, and LIFFE offering identical contracts in the 90-day U.S. Eurodollar deposit contract, it is possible to trade this derivative in the United States, Far East, and European time zones. Further, SIMEX has a clearing arrangement with the Chicago Mercantile Exchange so that any Eurodollar position entered on one exchange can be offset on the other. Similar three-exchange trading was possible at one time in U.S. Treasury bonds (at the Sydney Futures Exchange, the Chicago Board of Trade, and the London International Financial Futures Exchange) and Japanese government bonds (at the Tokyo Stock Exchange, the CBOT, and LIFFE). However, trading volume in at least one of the time zones was never large, and the Sydney Futures Exchange has since suspended trading on the U.S. bond, and, as mentioned, the CBOT has delisted the Japanese government bond contract.

One other development is worth noting. The European Community (EC), as part of the general unification process, has mandated the establishment of *common policies* on the taxation, clearing, and regulation of trading on all member-country exchanges. Implementation of these common policies should be completed near the due date of January 1, 1993, so that all EC options contracts will trade under a common regulatory structure. Further, as part of the longer-term monetary and political union process, the European Community has proposed the development of an EC-wide system for price dissemination and eventual centralized trading of all European exchange products, the Price Information Project Europe (PIPE) system. The first stage in the process involves a joint network for the collection and dissemination of trade price information at the separate exchanges. As of this writing, the United Kingdom, the Netherlands, Germany, and France are participants in this stage. After successful implementation of the first stage, it is expected that the system will be extended to include order routing and trading functions so that eventually there will be a common market for derivatives in the European time zone.

THE MICROSTRUCTURE OF TRADING SYSTEMS

The organization of the options exchanges and the mechanics of trading are as varied as the exchanges themselves. Table 13–4 lists the market organization, volume, and commission structure of the exchanges on which debt options are traded.

Physical Exchanges

Pure Open Outcry Markets
In the United States, interest rate options are traded on futures exchanges in an open outcry, continuous auction market. Overseas, the open outcry system is also employed in London at the LIFFE, in Paris at the MATIF, in Sydney at the SFE, and in Singapore at the SIMEX. In this system, orders are transmitted to the floor of the exchange where they are taken by runner or hand-signaled over to the specific options pit. The order is offered in open outcry to all participants in the pit, and the trade must be done with the first person to respond.

Under the open outcry system, there are no specifically designated market makers (i.e., specialists or individuals who must stand ready to supply a bid and offer price). Instead, locals in the

Chapter 13 The Structure of Markets for Interest Rate Options   283

TABLE 13-4
Exchanges Offering Debt Options

Exchange	Cash/ Futures	Date of Opening*	Market Organization†	Monthly Trading Volume‡	Commissions/ Fees§
CBOT (United States)	F	1848	O	2,196,982	N
CME (United States)	F	1919	O	1,049,095	N
DTB (Germany)	F	1988	E	46,417	DM 2–14
FUTOP (Denmark)	C/F	1988	E	10,060	DK 50 + .005%
EOE (Netherlands)	C	1978	O	5,364	N
LIFFE (United Kingdom)	F	1982	O/E	260,564	N
MATIF (France)	F	1962	O/E	612,932	FF10–100 + VAT
Montreal (Canada)	C/F‖	1874	O	1,955	C$ 50/transaction
MEFF (Spain)	C	1989	E	11,955	
NZFOE (part of SFE)	F	1985	E	3,157	$NZ 2.10
OM (Sweden)	C	1985	E	52,000	N
SFE (Australia)	F	1960	O/E	74,819	Based on volume
TIFFE (Japan)	F	1989	E	29,000	JY 150
TSE (Japan)	C	1988	E	169,128	
TSE (Canada)	C	1852	O/E	–0–	C$ 50

*Date of incorporation of exchange or of electronic trading.
†O = Open outcry; E = Electronic; O/E = Day trading with open outcry with night trading with electronic; for TSE, trading is routed to brokers or the electronic system.
‡Volume figure for total trading in debt options at that exchange as of February or March 1992.
§N = Negotiable.
‖Proposed.

Source: *Futures and Options World*, March 1992.

pit, individuals who trade for their own account, supply liquidity. For instance, one group of locals, called *scalpers,* specialize in making offers for the option at a *tick* (minimum price fluctuation) higher than the current market and bids at a tick below. This readiness to trade incrementally away from the current market price supplies brokers who have customer orders to fill with an opportunity to fill an order quickly with the minimum loss in price.

Since there is no specialist or group of market makers assigned to the contract as there is in U.S. stock trading, there is no individual with the responsibility to ensure an "orderly market." Thus, prices are free to move in response to supply and demand. To control price volatility, the exchanges generally establish price limits for most contracts, specifying the maximum price change from the settlement price of the day before.

Note also that without a specialist or market maker, any orders at a price away from the market, such as a limit order, are not held in a central order book nor displayed to other market participants. Instead, all orders away from the market price are the responsibility of the individual broker.

The open outcry system requires that every order must be offered to the market for execution. However, because of the high volume of order flow in some pits, various changes to the order flow are under discussion in the United States. For large volume block trades, it has been proposed that *cross-trading* be allowed. Under cross-trading, the transaction is prearranged upstairs or off-exchange, at market prices, as is done for block trades on the New York Stock Exchange. The issue of cross-trading is controversial, however, since the pit system does not have a specialist to monitor the trading, and transparency is important for customer protection. Cross-trading is currently allowed with restrictions on the SFE, SIMEX, and MATIF. Additionally, the Tokyo Stock Exchange, which is an electronic, order-driven exchange, allows cross-trading in its index futures.

Until recently, *dual trading* was permitted at the Chicago exchanges, and it is still practiced on the Sydney Futures Exchange. Under the dual trading system, a broker is allowed to fill orders for customers *and* to trade for his own account as long as customer orders are given priority. With dual trading, there is no physical separation of the broker function from that of the market maker, a system which is similar to the operation of the over-the-counter market in stocks in the United States. Supporters of dual trading argue that it increases liquidity by allowing brokers to participate in the market even when there are no customer orders to fill. Because of the potential for conflict of interest, however, the Chicago Merchantile Exchange has temporarily banned dual trading and a permanent ban is under discussion.

Because trading in the contract is not assigned to one or more market makers, the exchanges have implemented procedures to regulate the *order flow* and ensure *fair pricing*. To ensure an audit trail, for instance, a customer order is time-stamped as it arrives on the floor and hen the broker receives it in the pit. After execution, a confirmation of the trade is sent back to the phone clerks and a second copy of the trade is time-stamped and submitted to the exchange at timed intervals: in 15-minute batches at the Chicago exchanges and in 1-minute batches at the Sydney Futures Exchange. In the near future, hand-held electronic trading decks will be introduced at the Chicago exchanges that will provide instantaneous on-line reporting and monitoring of trades. The Sydney exchange is experimenting with a similar, voice-operated input device.

Several exchange employees monitor the activity in the pit. Currently at the U.S. exchanges, floor reporters transmit information to the electronic information services such as Reuters on any trade that is executed at a price different from the last price in that contract. (Because of the volume of activity involved, continuous reporting of all trades and prices, as is done for the stock exchange, is impractical.) Floor monitors enforce rules and arbitrate disputes on the trading floor as they arise.

Open Outcry/Specialist Markets
Other options exchanges, such as the Toronto Stock Exchange and the Dutch EOE, are based on the organization of the Chicago Board Options Exchange. The CBOE trading system combines the open outcry process of the futures exchange discussed previously with aspects of the stock specialist system of the NYSE.

As at U.S. futures exchanges, brokers and locals participate in a general open outcry auction in designated areas. In addition, however, there is also an *order book official,* an employee of the exchange, who performs several specialist functions. Like a NYSE stock specialist, the order book official handles orders away from the market and can execute trades in order to facilitate the flow of orders in the option. Thus, there is a designated participant with some responsibility for price volatility. While preserving some of the market control of the specialist, the CBOE system differs from the NYSE in that there is no possibility of monopoly trading profits for the order book official as there is for the NYSE specialist. Unlike the NYSE specialist system, the order book official discloses to the pit the best limit orders awaiting execution. This is generally more information than is available in either the NYSE or the pure open outcry pit system. Another difference is that the order book official cannot trade for her own account as the NYSE specialist can. In this system, market makers are allowed to dual trade but dual trading is more restricted than under the pure open outcry system. Like dual trading in futures, any market maker can also take on the broker function, but he can do this only on days separate from those in which he acts as a market maker.

In most markets, commissions and fees are negotiable and quite small. In the United States, an options commission is on the order of $30 per round trip (both buy and sell, or exercise). Usually there is a floor fee levied by the exchange to compensate for exchange services and the clearinghouse. In addition, any transaction will also involve clearing fees paid to the clearing member. These fees are incorporated into the bid-ask spread and in brokers' commissions.

Electronic Markets

Since 1985, when the French market, the MATIF, was organized as an open outcry market, all new derivative markets have been organized as electronic exchanges rather than as physical floors. Thus, the German exchange (the Deutsche Terminboerse, or DTB), the Belgian exchange (the Belgian Futures and Options Exchange, or BELFOX), and the Swedish exchange (the Stockholm Options Market, or SOM) are screen-based trading systems and have never had a centralized, physical market organization. Additionally, the Danish exchange (the Copenhagen Stock Exchange and Guarantee Fund for Danish Options and Futures, or FUTOP) converted from a physical, open outcry trading system to a fully electronic screen-based system.

There are basically two methods to organize an electronic trading system: an order-driven, continuous auction market, and a price-driven (or quote-driven) dealer market. An *order-driven* market attempts to duplicate the operation of the traditional auction markets like the NYSE and CBOT. Most electronic exchanges are organized in this way. In this system, the flow of incoming customer orders drives the market. Bid and ask prices and the size of the desired trade are collected by the system, as in the physical auction process, and the best bid (highest) and offer (lowest) price—in some systems with the size of order—are displayed for market participants. Most systems prioritize orders in a time and then price sequence. Orders matching these prices are automatically executed. On most systems, the computer will also operate a limit order book, retaining bid and ask quotes away from the current market as well as other special orders such as "good til canceled" for eventual execution. In some systems, this information is available to all market participants, permitting a degree of transparency not currently available in the United States.

One of the disadvantages of an electronic, purely order-driven exchange is the retention of priced limit orders. Such orders, when eventually executed, can create sudden liquidity problems if they are of large size compared to current volume of trading. In addition, it is generally more difficult in an electronic system to respond flexibly to changes in market volatility. On many exchanges, such as Sweden's SOM and Spain's MEFF, large orders are handled separately from the electronic system through a telephone-based marketplace. Block order officials handle these trades physically, but the price of execution is reported to the electronic system for dissemination to the public.

The alternative to an order-driven system is a *dealer* market. In this type of market, dealers supply competing bid and ask quotes for a designated size of the trade. This is the system used in the United States by the over-the-counter stock market, the National Association of Securities Dealers Automated Quote System (NASDAQ). In Europe, the Swiss Options and Financial Futures Exchange (SOFFEX) has developed software that is now used by the German exchange (DTB). Besides furnishing bid and ask quotes, designated market makers also ensure an orderly market in the options contract by trading for their own accounts if price conditions warrant. One advantage of the dealer market is that it involves telephone communication to execute trades. Because of this, there is a greater flow of information between market participants than in an order-driven market. Also, a larger range of trading options can generally be accomplished under this type of organization.

Some exchanges, notably London (LIFFE), Sydney (SFE), and Paris (MATIF), have taken a middle route and combine open outcry trading with electronic trading after hours. For instance, the SFE offers an after-hours system called SYCOM (Sydney Computerized Market), and the LIFFE uses an automated pit trading (APT) system. The CME and CBOT have recently introduced an electronic system called GLOBEX.

Most *after-hours systems* attempt to replicate the operation of the open outcry pit system available at the exchange during the day trading session. Usually, various screen windows are presented to the user. One window allows the entry of options orders, including combinations, that are released to the system for eventual execution. On the SYCOM, another window allows trading on a real-time basis by matching existing bid and offer quotes. A trader can store a "deck" of conditional orders to be released to the market as conditions change. Both the APT and SYCOM systems also support a preopening period to determine an opening price for the session. Although the SYCOM system has real-time capabilities, trades on the overnight system are cleared with the next day's contracts. GLOBEX, on the other hand, will use real-time clearing.

On GLOBEX, there will also be a "working" option that allows for incremental submission of large orders, an alternative to the telephone block system in place on current electronic systems. In addition, there will be a "dealing" option in which a trader can make a market, as a dealer does, by adjusting the spread or moving the bid-ask prices up or down together.

The London exchange's APT system comes closest to a real-time open outcry system: Trades are made as they are in the pit, and there is no automatic order-matching capability.

Market Participants

In the United States, *membership* and the right to trade are limited. All seats must be purchased by individuals, either locals who trade for their own accounts or employees who act as agents for a broker or dealer. Most of the volume of customer orders in U.S. debt options involve institutions: banks, government dealers, and portfolio managers such as pension funds and insurance companies.

Outside the United States, the exchanges are in most cases dominated by the primary financial institutions of the country, and on many exchanges individuals are not permitted to own seats. For instance, Germany's exchange is owned and dominated by the 17 largest German banks. France's MATIF membership includes stockbrokers, banks, and other credit institutions. Only recently has the MATIF allowed individuals to buy a seat on the exchange and trade as a local.

The number of seats, or of equity owners, in an exchange varies considerably. The CME has approximately 2,700 members, while the Tokyo futures exchange (the Tokyo International Financial Futures Exchange, or TIFFE) has 216. By contrast, Sweden's options market has over 2,000 shareholders, and the shares of the exchange can themselves be traded on the Stockholm Stock Exchange. Market participants, on the other hand, are the major Swedish banks and brokerage firms. In addition, unlike in the United States, private (nonfinancial) companies are also permitted to act as market makers for the options.

On many exchanges, partial memberships are available at a reduced price that allow the holder to trade in only a limited number of exchange contracts. In addition, on most exchanges seats can be leased for a fee that reflects the current cost of funds and the current volume of trading on the exchange.

Credit Guarantees

Every options and futures exchange uses a *clearinghouse* structure to act as a credit guarantor. The clearinghouse *guarantees* both the buyer and seller of the option. In the event of a default by either party, the clearinghouse stands ready to perform, acting therefore as a seller to every buyer and a buyer to every seller. In this way, individual market participants do not have to be concerned with the creditworthiness or capitalization of their counterparty.

The clearinghouse usually has as its members a subset of the exchange's members, generally the largest and best capitalized firms, who then become the exchange's clearing members. All exchange trades must take place through a clearing member; if a broker is not a clearinghouse member, then she must establish a clearing relationship with a firm that is.

Besides the guarantee of performance, the clearinghouse has several other functions. The clearinghouse usually oversees the matching of trade specifics, trade reconciliation, and the swift resolution of *out-trades*. Most exchanges require a two-sided match; that is, both the buyer and seller submit the particulars of the trade and any mismatch of the information becomes an out-trade to be reconciled before next day's trading. Some exchanges, notably the SFE, require only the seller to submit information; the buyer is asked to confirm the information afterwards.

The clearinghouse generally controls option exercise, as discussed above, receiving notice of exercise and assigning the corresponding position to one of its clearing members.

The clearinghouse also calculates minimum margin funds required for a position, collects and safeguards the funds, and manages the flow of margin funds as position values change. In addition, the clearinghouse will generally hold a guarantee fund that is available to compensate clearing members for any contract default.

Margin takes the form of a good-faith deposit of funds with the clearinghouse, and its function is to ensure performance of the contract's terms. The size and form of the margin required usually reflects the risk involved in the position. In addition, most margin systems involve a marking-to-market function, a periodic change in value of the margin account to reflect changing values or risk on the contract position. Minimum margin amounts are set by the clearinghouse, but brokers can add to this basic required amount depending on their perception of the customer.

Because the owner of an option will choose to exercise only if it is economically profitable, most option buyers have fixed their maximum loss as the option price, and merely pay the price of the option when they purchase. The option seller, on the other hand, who is *obliged* to take the corresponding opposite position, usually must post a margin based on the possible loss on the position.

At its most stringent, margin may require the deposit of the underlying asset itself. For instance, in the case of a written call, the margin required could be the physical security or the short futures position itself. On many exchanges, the initial option margin is set at some percentage, generally between zero and 10 percent, of the underlying asset value.

For a futures option, the *initial margin* generally takes the form of a deposit of an interest-bearing asset; thus, margin does not involve loss of interest on the deposited funds. Because an option on a physical asset can involve a possibility of nonperformance due to scarcity of the underlying asset, options on actuals usually require initial margin in cash. There are exceptions, however: On the German exchange (DTB), initial margin on its options on actuals can be cash, collateral, or a guarantee by a third-party bank.

The *maintenance margin*—the minimum value that must remain in the margin account through time—is calculated on the basis of the possible loss on the options position. This is usually based on either the option value, or premium, or the intrinsic value of the option, the amount of loss to the option writer if the option is exercised. For instance, the Dutch exchange (EOE) requires not only the option premium as a margin deposit but also a fixed percentage, set by the exchange periodically, of the option's intrinsic value.

In the United States and on the London LIFFE, the initial margin and *changes in the margin* are calculated according to a set of possible scenarios involving the option seller's total position. Under this system, the margin reflects not only the risk of the option position but also the risk of positions in assets that change in value along with the option position. For instance, the writer of a covered call (in which the writer owns the underlying asset she is obliged to sell) will have much less risk than the writer of a naked call (in which the writer does not own the asset), and the initial margin on this portfolio would be set at a correspondingly smaller amount. In addition, any further loss due to changes in the option's value—and thus any change in the margin as it is marked to market—will also be less for the covered writer since a change in the option value will always be less than the offsetting change in the underlying asset.

Generally, the margining system constructs a matrix of outcomes on the option's value in combination with any asset or other option position held by the trader that is related to it. This matrix calculates the possible loss related to (1) changes in the volatility of the underlying asset; (2) changes in the underlying asset price; and (3) the possibility of an extreme move of the underlying asset. For instance, the SPAN (Standard Portfolio Analysis of Risk) system at the Chicago exchanges calculates an array of 16 possible outcomes based on a range of increases or decreases in volatility, futures price changes between zero and (currently) 100 percent, and "extreme" futures price changes. The parameters of the model, including the range of volatility estimates, futures price changes, and the modeling of extreme price movements, are combined in an options pricing model to calculate a set of possible value losses on the writer's combined position. The worst-case scenario—the largest loss—determines the minimum margin level for the portfolio.

Systems like SPAN have the advantage of recognizing and including additional positions besides the option that may impact the writer's total risk. In addition, the ranges on all of the parameters can be adjusted quickly by the exchange and clearinghouse to reflect changes in current market conditions. Ranges on the futures price, for instance, are calculated on the basis of a probability distribution of recent futures prices. The French exchange (MATIF) and the Spanish exchange (MEFF) use a similar worst-case scenario matrix of their own modeling that is similar to the SPAN system.

On electronic exchanges, the clearing and margin calculations are done continuously in real time, as the trades are executed. Open outcry pit trading generally involves periodic margin calculation depending on the volatility of prices and volume of trading. The CBOT, for instance, matches trades in approximately one-hour increments through the trading day, and normally calculates margin requirements and makes margin calls at set times during the day as well.

Most U.S. exchanges reserve the right to make margin calls on their clearing members throughout the trading day as market conditions warrant. Generally, if a margin account falls below the maintenance margin level, a variation margin call will result. A margin call requires that same-day funds be deposited with the clearinghouse before trading commences in that contract the next trading day. During periods of extreme market volatility, intraday margin calls may require deposit of funds within 60 minutes of the call request. Failure to comply will result in a formal default, and the defaulting member's open positions will be closed or offset as soon as possible. As mentioned above, if and when a default occurs, the clearinghouse will have guarantee funds available to compensate the defaulting firm's counterparties.

OVER-THE-COUNTER OPTIONS

In addition to exchange-traded options, there is a large and growing market in the United States and overseas in over-the-counter (OTC) options on specific interest rate assets such as fixed-income securities, bond portfolios, and loans. The U.S. OTC interest rate options market is modeled after the larger, more active OTC market in currency options. OTC debt options were developed to hedge the specific interest rate positions of large financial institutions such as pension funds and insurance companies. These institutions are the major clients of investment banks and major government securities dealers who are the largest traders in the OTC market. The majority of trading in the OTC market is in U.S. dollars, but there are smaller OTC options markets on foreign currency securities in, for instance, France, Denmark, and Norway. U.S. regulations prohibit off-exchange trading in options on futures, and so all U.S. OTC options are on actuals.

Market Participants

Since the market is off-exchange, and lightly regulated, little verifiable information is publicly available on the size of the market, the securities involved, or the activity or positions of the major participants. Occasionally, some indication of the size of individual positions is revealed when, as in 1989, a major bank reported a sizable loss—in this case, $33 million—on an OTC options position. One unofficial estimate of the size of the market puts the average daily trading volume at over $1 billion. Individual OTC options trades are generally of a larger size than trades in exchange-listed options, on the order of $1,000,000 lots.

Because options pricing is so strongly dependent on knowledge of the underlying asset price, trading in OTC options is generally dominated by dealers in the underlying cash market. Although an OTC option can be structured on any interest rate asset that a client wishes to protect, U.S. Treasury, mortgage-backed, and LIBOR-related securities are the primary underlying securities in the U.S. OTC options market. The *major market makers* in the option market are thus the commercial banks, investment bankers, and government dealers who maintain active positions in these underlying securities. Currently, it is estimated that there are 25 to 30 large institutions who regularly make markets in OTC options, and most of these institutions are primary government dealers.

OTC options are usually structured according to the specific needs of the *client,* who is generally an institutional investor. Thus, each feature of the option—the underlying asset, maturity, delivery, and contract size—are specific to the option and individually negotiated. Since each option tends to involve unique features, the possibility of a secondary market in these options is limited. To offset an OTC option, the buyer of an option must usually deal with his original counterparty. Secondary trading is also limited because most OTC options are not readily assignable, that is, the original counterparty must agree to a transfer of the position to another. Recently, the OTC market has seen some standardization of options characteristics in response to the success of exchange-traded interest rate options. Some dealers now standardize their OTC option contract terms to relate more closely to exchange-traded options contracts. This standardization may permit more secondary trading and offset of OTC options in the future.

OTC Market Microstructure

The organization of the market is similar to that of the government securities on which it is largely based. In contrast to the open outcry system used for options listed on the exchanges, dealers in OTC options will maintain bid and offer prices for a variety of options with a range of maturity dates and exercise prices. Most commonly, the underlying security issues are Treasury issues on the run (the most recently auctioned long-term Treasury bonds) and occasionally selected off-the-run securities. Thus, the OTC dealer system operates much like the automated NASD system for stocks. Like the physical or cash Treasury market, OTC option dealers have available to them brokers who will show price information by phone or Telerate on basic options maturities of one and two weeks and one month. Although a commercial bank, Security Pacific, received permission from the Federal Reserve to operate a computerized trading system for OTC Treasury bond options, the system does not appear to be popular with OTC dealers.

Since the OTC market is generally not as liquid as the exchanges, *bid-ask spreads* are usually twice as large as that in the futures options market, and can be between $2/32$ and $4/32$ depending on the maturity and volatility of the underlying asset.

The *prices* of OTC options generally reflect equilibrium values. First of all, options prices must conform to the put-call parity or arbitrage will be possible between OTC dealers. Also, an OTC dealer can hedge any of her written OTC option positions with the cash asset or (less exactly) with an exchange-traded option. This makes the risk premium in OTC options positions relatively low. Finally, an OTC option dealer will generally have a superior flow of information on cash asset prices because of his participation in the cash market, and on competing option bid and ask quotes, lowering price uncertainty.

Option *maturity* can be as little as one day or as long as several years. Some options activity respond to specific supply and demand situations in the cash market. For instance, short-term (one-day) options are sometimes traded around Treasury auctions or the announcement of particular economic news like the money supply or unemployment figures. Most of the options volume, however, responds to the particular long-term needs of portfolio managers, and the average maturity of OTC options tends to be longer than exchange-listed options. Also, since they are used for long-term hedging purposes, OTC options are generally European, particularly those that are long dated (greater than three-year maturities). OTC options, however, can be American if the client desires it.

Because OTC options may be long dated and written on illiquid underlying assets, the purchase price can be substantial. Various strategies have been employed to *minimize the expenditure* necessary to acquire the option's protection. Some OTC premiums are structured in installments: The buyer pays a percentage of the price up front and agrees to a series of paydowns over a fixed time period. For many participants in bid situations, in which it is likely that the underlying asset may not be acquired, the client can buy an option on the option, with a correspondingly smaller premium. If the bid is successful, the client can exercise the option on the option and acquire the protection on the underlying asset.

Another popular strategy to minimize the cost of protection is to construct a *range-forward* or *cylinder* position, in which the option buyer pays for the option by writing a related option with a different exercise price. For instance, the client can buy a put on a bond portfolio—locking in a floor value on the portfolio—and pay for this put by writing a call on the portfolio with a higher exercise price. This establishes a range of values on the underlying asset. If the value of the portfolio falls below the exercise price of the put option, the put option will gain in intrinsic value and offset the losses on the cash portfolio position. On the other hand, if the portfolio value increases beyond the exercise price of the call option, the put protection is not needed but the call option will have intrinsic value. Since the portfolio owner wrote or sold the call option, she will be required to pay the intrinsic value on the call, thus limiting the gain on the portfolio position. Thus, the long put position provides a floor value on the asset, but the written call with the higher exercise price establishes a maximum ceiling value because it obliges the client to sell the portfolio (or pay the intrinsic value of the option) at the higher exercise price.

Credit Arrangements

Because there is no clearinghouse on the OTC market, the credit guarantee structure is different from that of an exchange. The rule is, as with dealing in the cash market, "know your customer." Since many of the options positions are crafted as part of an ongoing dealer-client relationship, information on credit standing is generally readily available to the options dealer. If not, some sort of credit verification will generally be required, particularly for a written position.

Each participant is responsible for making his own arrangements to guarantee financial integrity, and credit problems are addressed in a variety of ways. Generally, because of the limited liability of the position, an options purchase will not require margin but only payment of the price of the option. For the writer, margin or collateral is required as soon as a transaction has been completed, and the dealer can also stipulate a provision for additional capital if market conditions change. Because of the additional liquidity risk, dealers may be reluctant to allow their customers to write options.

While the calculation of specific margin levels is up to the individual dealer, most *margining systems* will involve calculations on volatility ranges and possible future price moves similar to the margining systems discussed above for the futures exchanges. For internal use, a dealer will generally gauge her own credit risk on her total open options positions book in the same way. A dealer calculates the possible losses on various asset classes in her total book and on her total position under various scenarios of adverse price moves and volatility changes. Of course, there is more uncertainty in estimating the probability distribution of price changes and of volatilities if the assets are thinly traded or if they are new and have little trading history.

As mentioned above, several foreign countries, particularly Denmark and Norway, have small and relatively illiquid OTC markets for options on government bonds. In addition, Norway has a small OTC market in options on mortgage bonds. France's OTC option market is perhaps the most developed. There is routine OTC trading of options on certain long-term and medium-term government bonds (actuals) as well as official off-exchange, or after-hours, trading of the exchange-listed (MATIF) futures options. The MATIF uses the volume of OTC trading in a particular asset as an indication of investor interest, and when OTC volume is sufficiently high, will usually develop an option for exchange listing.

Combinations of OTC Options

Options packages have been developed in the OTC market that combine simple one-maturity options. It is common for large institutions and broker/dealers to structure a *series* of agreements on interest rate levels in successive periods—interest rate caps and floors—for banks and primary lenders who in turn include these options in loan agreements with their commercial loan clients. A *cap* (*floor*) is a portfolio of European calls (puts) that protect the owner from the added interest expense arising when a floating rate, usually LIBOR, is above (below) a specified level, or cap (floor) rate. The combined position essentially gives the owner the right to receive a cash flow at periodic intervals equal to any excess of the current rate over (or under, in the case of a floor) the specified rate.

Cap positions can be combined to minimize the cost of multi-period protection, much like the range forward strategies discussed previously. For instance, a *corridor* is a long position in a cap combined with a sale of a cap at a higher rate. Similarly, a *collar* is a long cap position at one rate paid for with the premium obtained from selling a floor at a higher rate.

Embedded Options

Another area in the OTC options market involves options that are packaged with other securities. Generally, these options cannot be traded separately. One example is the *swaption*, a swap agreement that includes the right to terminate early if rates move beyond a fixed range.

Another example of a nontradable option is the *embedded option bond*, which links the payoff of principal or interest to specified value levels of a given index. This gives the investor an options position on the index through ownership of the bond. For instance, one embedded option bond based on the Nikkei index pays a higher than market coupon rate initially, but links a diminishing repayment of principal to lower levels of the stock index. In this way, the bond buyer can purchase the payoff pattern equivalent of a written put—premium income immediately and a value depreciation if the stock index declines—without trading in physical Japanese options. Many of these options positions, as with the Japanese embedded bond above, are attractive because of the restrictions placed on the trading of derivative securities in many national markets. With such restrictions on trading, or on participants in national markets, it may only be possible to obtain a desired option position through purchase of the embedded option bond. The advantage for the bond issuer then is that the coupon expense will be reduced because the bond buyer is willing to accept a lower price for an attractive but rare option position.

CONCLUSION

Options contracts are available on futures and on physical assets for a variety of interest rate assets. U.S. exchanges currently list only options on futures, and the market microstructure reflects the open outcry system developed on U.S. futures exchanges. Traders in the auction process act as competing market makers, and exchange procedures limit price volatility and promote market transparency. Options are available along a wide spectrum of interest rate assets, from 30-day LIBOR assets through U.S. Treasury bond futures with 15 years to maturity.

Overseas, the markets list options on both futures and actuals. A wide variety of market organizations are used, reflecting the development of options markets from both futures exchanges and cash markets. Many non-U.S. exchanges combine an open outcry system with a limited specialist role. Other exchanges have been organized as electronic exchanges, and trading is either dealer-driven or order-driven. Generally, the options listed on non-U.S. exchanges relate to the cash government bond market in each country.

The OTC market in the United States permits institutions to structure positions that reflect their individual portfolio characteristics. The trading organization of the OTC market derives from the underlying cash government bond market. The OTC market has the maximum amount of flexibility in terms of options structure, payment mechanisms, and risk-return trade-off.

NOTE

1. For a good introduction to options pricing, see Chapter 22 of J. C. Francis, *Investments* (New York: McGraw-Hill, 1991); and R. Kolb, *Options, An Introduction* (Miami, Fla.: Kolb Publishing, 1992).

REFERENCES

Anderson, Torbenjuul. *Currency and Interest-Rate Hedging* (New York: Prentice Hall, 1987).

Bass, Arthur. "Differences Between Exchange-Traded and Over-the-Counter Options." *Intermarket,* July 1988, pp. 61–62.

Chicago Board of Trade. *Japanese Government Bond Futures and Options Delivery and Reference Handbook* (Chicago, 19xx).

―――. *Morgage-Backed Futures and Options: An Introduction* (Chicago, 19xx).

―――. *Options on U.S. Treasury Futures Contracts* (Chicago, 19xx).

Chicago Mercantile Exchange. *Globex* (Chicago, 19xx).

―――. *One-Month LIBOR Futures and Options* (Chicago, 19xx).

―――. *SPAN: A Risk-based Margining System* (Chicago, 19xx).

European Bond Commission. *European Options and Futures Markets* (Chicago: Probus Publishing, 1991).

Figlewski, Stephen, and William Silber. "Introduction: Options and Options Markets." In *Financial Options.* ed. Stephen Figlewski, William L. Silber, and Martin G. Subrahmanyam (Homewood, Ill.: Business One Irwin, 1990).

Francis, J. C. *Investments* (New York: McGraw-Hill, 1991).

Futures Magazine. *1992 Reference Guide to Futures/Options Markets.*

Geist, Charles R. *A Guide to the Financial Markets* (New York: St. Martin's Press, 1982).

Goodman, Laurie S. "Introduction to Debt Options." In *Winning the Interest Rate Game.* ed. Frank Fabozzi (Chicago: Probus Publishing, 1985).

Ho, Thomas, and Allen Abrahamson. "Options on Interest Sensitive Securities." In *Financial Options.* ed. Stephen Figlewski, William L. Silber, and Martin G. Subrahmanyam (Homewood, Ill.: Business One Irwin, 1990).

Honeygold, Derek. *International Financial Markets* (New York: Nichols Publishing, 1989).

Kolb, Robert W. *Options: An Introduction* (Miami, Fla.: Kolb Publishing, 1991).

London International Financial Futures Exchange. *U.S. T Bond and Eurodollar Futures and Options* (London, 19xx).

The 1991 *Handbook of World Stock and Commodity Exchanges* (Cambridge, Mass.: Basil Blackwell, 1991).

Pitts, Mark, and Frank Fabozzi. *Interest Rate Futures and Options* (Chicago: Probus Publishing, 1990).

Rawls, S. Waite, and Charles W. Smithson. "The Evolution of Risk Management Products." In *The Handbook of Currency and Interest Rate Risk Management.* eds. Robert J. Schwartz, and Clifford W. Smith, Jr. (New York: New York Institute of Finance, 1990).

Rutz, Roger D. "Clearance, Payment, and Settlement Systems in the Futures, Options, and Stock Markets." *Review of Research in Futures Markets* 3 (1988), pp. 346–70.

Silber, William. "Market Making in Options: Principles and Implications." In *Financial Options.* ed. Stephen Figlewski, William L. Silber, and Martin G. Subrahmanyam (Homewood, Ill.: Business One Irwin, 1990).

Stapleton, Richard C., and Martin G. Subrahmanyam. "Interest Rate Caps and Floors." In *Financial Options.* ed. Stephen Figlewski, William L. Silber, and Martin G. Subrahmanyam (Homewood, Ill.: Business One Irwin, 1990).

Stoll, Hans. "Trading On and Off Exchanges." *Institutional Investor*, November 1991, pp. 11–13.

Sydney Futures Exchange. *Sydney Computerized Futures Market.*

Wolf, Avner. "Fundamentals of Commodity Options on Futures." *Journal of Futures Markets* 2 (1982), pp. 391–408.

Wong, M. Anthony. *Trading and Investing in Bond Options* (New York: John Wiley & Sons, 1991).

CHAPTER 14

USING A ONE-FACTOR MODEL TO VALUE INTEREST RATE–SENSITIVE SECURITIES: WITH AN APPLICATION TO TREASURY BOND OPTIONS

Fischer Black
Goldman, Sachs & Co.
Emanuel Derman
Goldman, Sachs & Co.
William Toy
Goldman, Sachs & Co.
Jack C. Francis
Bernard M. Baruch College, New York City

In 1973, Black and Scholes published a closed-form option valuation model that is now widely used for equity options.[1] Shortly thereafter, Black published another continuous time model for valuing options on futures contracts that has been used successfully.[2] Although these option valuation models are seminal, they are not widely used to value interest rate options for two reasons. First, both models are built on the assumption that the volatility of the underlying asset is constant throughout the life of the option. Since the volatility of a bond's price declines to zero as its term approaches maturity, this assumption undermines the usefulness of the Black-Scholes and the Black models for valuing options on bonds. Second, both models also assume that interest rates are constant. This assumption is not appropriate for interest rate–sensitive securities. As a result, newer models have been developed to assess the value of options on interest rate–sensitive instruments.

THE FIRST BOND OPTION VALUATION MODELS

In 1979, Rendleman and Bartter developed the first binomial bond option valuation model.[3] Their model is based on a term structure of interest rates composed of a risk-free rate that grows at a constant rate. Later in 1979, Cox, Ross, and Rubinstein published a binomial option valuation model that starts with a lattice of possible outcomes that can be evaluated to determine the value an option.[4] The Cox-Ross-Rubinstein model can be used to value options on stocks, bonds, and other assets. In 1986, Ho and Lee developed a model that included an entire term structure of interest rates. All interest rates have volatilities that are equal in the Ho and Lee model.[5]

ABOUT THIS CHAPTER'S MODEL

This chapter describes a more recent model that can be used to estimate the value of zero coupon bonds, coupon-paying bonds, options on bonds, interest rate caps, and callable coupon bonds. Its use can also be extended to mortgages with prepayments that are a function of market interest rates, options on mortgages, and other interest rate–sensitive securities.[6] In explaining how it works, we begin by showing how to value a default-free zero coupon bond. Then, a coupon-paying Treasury bond is valued. Finally, we value an option on a Treasury bond. It is left as an exercise for the reader to adapt the model to value other interest rate–sensitive securities.

The model presented here has three key features.

1. Its fundamental variable is the short rate—the annualized one-period interest rate. The short rate is the one factor of the model; its changes drive all security values.

2. The model takes as inputs an array of long rates (yields on zero coupon Treasury bonds) for various maturities and an array of yield volatilities for the same bonds. We call the first array the *yield curve* and the second the *volatility curve*. Together these curves form the *term structure*.

3. The model produces an array of means and an array of volatilities for the future short rate to match the inputs.[7] All the security values that the model suggests are consistent with whatever term structure of interest rates is input. As we move out the term structure, the future volatility changes in a rational manner, and the future mean reversion changes accordingly.

We examine how the model works in an idealized world in which changes in all bond yields are perfectly correlated; expected returns on all securities over one period are equal; short rates at any time are lognormally distributed; and there are no taxes or trading costs.

Mathematically speaking, the changes in interest rates are assumed to be locally lognormal. This means that infinitesimally small changes in r, denoted dr, during the next infinitesimally small increment of time, dt, are proportional to r. More formally, we assume the following return-generating function:

$$dr = u(t)rdt + \sigma(t)rdZ$$

The term $u(t)$ represents the expected growth rate, σ denotes the standard deviation of percentage changes in the short rate r that drives the model, and dZ describes a normal distribution of random percentage changes in the short rate over the time period represented by dt. The proportionality of dr to r guarantees that the short rate can never become negative if its starts out positive.[8]

VALUING SECURITIES

Suppose we own an interest rate–sensitive security worth S dollars today. We assume that its value can move up to S_u or down to S_d with equal probability over the next time period. Figure 14–1 shows the possible changes in S for a one-year time step, starting from a state where the short rate is r.

The expected value of S one year from now is $\frac{1}{2}(S_u + S_d)$. The expected return is $[(\frac{1}{2})(S_u + S_d)]/S$. Because we assume that securities are priced as if all expected returns were equal, and because we can lend money at r, we deduce:

$$S = \frac{\frac{1}{2}S_u + \frac{1}{2}S_d}{1 + r} \qquad (14\text{--}1)$$

where r is today's short rate.

**FIGURE 14-1
A One-Step Tree**

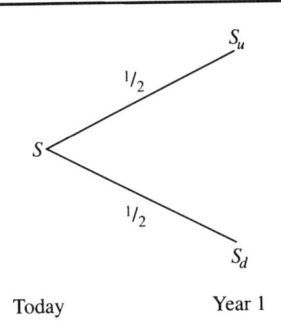

```
                        S_u
                 1/2  /
              S <
                 1/2  \
                        S_d

            Today      Year 1
```

Illustration of How to Get Today's Values from Future Values

We can use the *one-step tree* to relate today's value to the values one step ahead. Similarly, we can derive values one step in the future from values two steps in the future. In this way, we can relate today's values to values two steps away.

Figure 14-2 shows two-step trees for interest rates and dollar values. The short rate starts out at 10 percent. We expect it to rise to 11 percent or drop to 9 percent with equal probability.

The second tree shows values for a two-year, zero coupon Treasury bond that are derived from the rates in the first tree. In two years, the zero's value will be $100. Its value one year from now may be $91.74 ($100 discounted by 9 percent) or $90.09 ($100 discounted by 11 percent). The expected value one year from now is the average of $90.09 and $91.74, or $90.92. Essentially, we use Equation (14-1) to find today's value by discounting this average by 10 percent to give $82.65.

The numerical examples above will not be used in the rest of this chapter. They are merely illustrative. We can value a zero coupon bond of any maturity in this way, provided our tree of future short rates goes out far enough. We simply start with the security's face value at maturity and find the value at each earlier node by discounting future values using the valuation formula and the short rate at that node. Eventually, we work back to the root of the tree and find today's value.

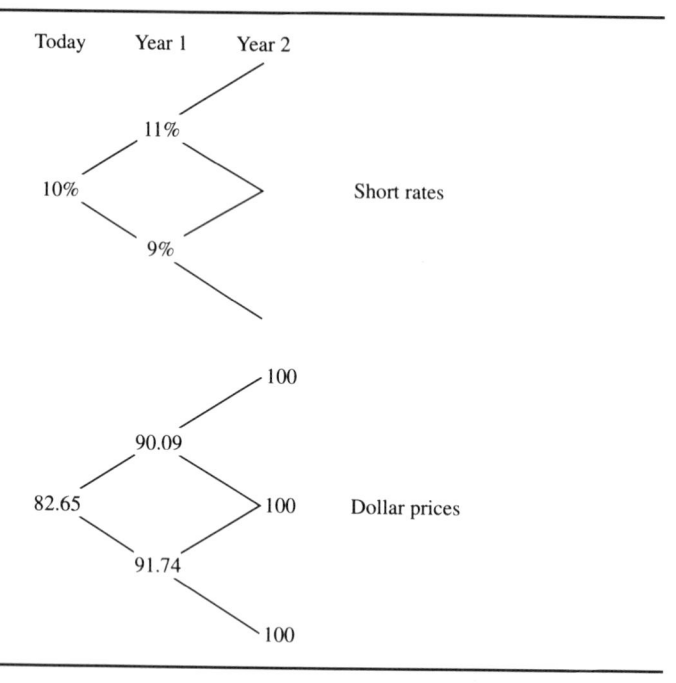

FIGURE 14-2
Two-Step Trees of Short Rates and Prices

```
         Today      Year 1       Year 2
                             
                        11%
              10%                         Short rates
                        9%


                                  100
                       90.09
              82.65              100      Dollar prices
                       91.74
                                  100
```

Finding Short Rates from the Term Structure

The term structure of interest rates is quoted in yields, rather than dollar values. Today's annual yield of the N-year zero in terms of the security's value, S, is found by solving Equation (14–2) for y.

$$S = \frac{\$100}{(1+y)^N} \quad (14\text{–}2)$$

Similarly, the yields y_u and y_d one year from now correspond to the values S_u and S_d, as shown in Equations (14–3a) and (14–3b).

$$S_u = \frac{\$100}{(1+y_u)^{N-1}} \quad (14\text{–}3a)$$

$$S_d = \frac{\$100}{(1+y_d)^{N-1}} \quad (14\text{–}3b)$$

TABLE 14-1
A Sample Term Structure

Maturity (years)	Yield (%)	Yield Volatility (%)
1	10%	20%
2	11%	19%
3	12%	18%
4	12.5%	17%
5	13%	16%

We want to find the short rates that assure that the model's terms structure matches today's market term structure. Table 14-1 gives the assumed market term structure that will be used throughout the remainder of this chapter.

The value of a zero coupon bond today is the expected value one period in the future discounted to today and using the short rate. The short rate, r, is assumed to be 10 percent. Using the tree of values in Figure 14-3, we see that $S_u = S_d = \$100$, and $S = \$90.91$ by using Equation (14-1).

$$\$90.91 = \frac{(\frac{1}{2})\$100 + (\frac{1}{2})\$100}{1.1} = \frac{\$100}{1 + r}$$

Short Rates One Period in the Future

We can now find the short rates one year from now by looking at the yield and volatility for a two-year zero using the term structure of Table 14-1.

FIGURE 14-3
Finding the Initial Short Rate Using a One-Year Zero

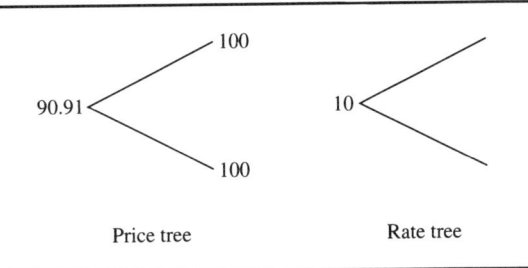

Price tree: 90.91 → 100, 100
Rate tree: 10

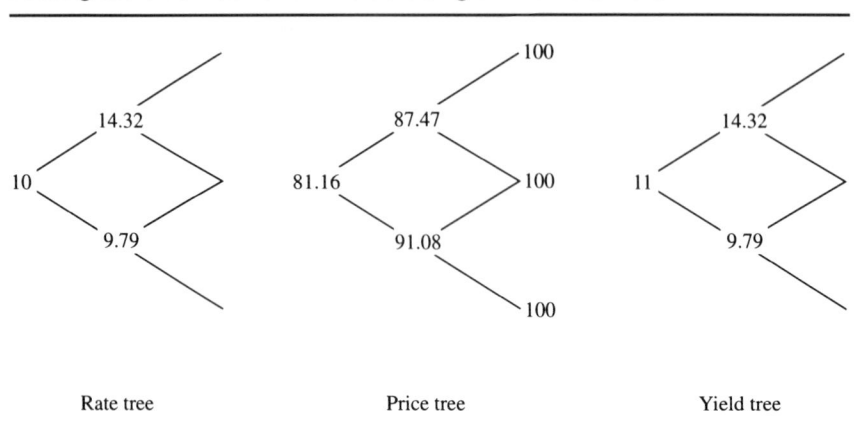

FIGURE 14-4
Finding the One-Year Short Rates Using a Two-Year Zero

```
       14.32              87.47              14.32
                  100                               
10        >    81.16  >  100      11       >
       9.79              91.08              9.79
                          100
```

Rate tree   Price tree   Yield tree

Look at the two-year short-rate tree in Figure 14-4. Let's call the unknown future short rates r_u and r_d. We want these rates to be such that the yields and volatility of the two-year zero match the yields and volatility in Table 14-1.

We know today's short rate is 10 percent. Suppose we guess that $r_u = 14.32$ percent and $r_d = 9.79$ percent.

Now look at the value and yield trees in Figure 14-4. A two-year zero has a value of $100 at all nodes at the end of the second period, no matter what short rate prevails. Using the valuation formula—Equation (14-1)—we can find the one-year values by discounting the expected two-year value by r_u and r_d. This discounting results in values of $87.47 and $91.08. Using Equation (14-3), we find that yields of 14.32 and 9.79 percent correspond to these values. These are shown on the yield tree in Figure 14-4.

Now that we have the two-year values and yields one year out, we can use the valuation formula to get today's value and yield for the two-year zero. Today's value is obtained with Equation (14-1) by discounting the expected one-year-out value by today's short rate of $r = 10$ percent.

$$\frac{\frac{1}{2}(\$87.47) + \frac{1}{2}(\$91.08)}{1.10} = \$81.16$$

We can get today's yield for the two-year zero, y_2, by using Equation (14–2) with today's value as S. As the yield tree in Figure 14–4 shows, y_2 is 11 percent.

The volatility (or standard deviation) of these two-year yields is defined as the natural logarithm of the ratio of the one-year yields.[9]

$$\sigma_2 = \frac{\ln \frac{14.32}{9.79}}{2} = 19\%$$

With the one-year short rates we have chosen, the two-year zero's yield and yield volatility match those in the term structure of Table 14–1. This means that our guesses for r_u and r_d were right. Had they been wrong, we could have found the correct ones by trial and error.

So an initial short rate of 10 percent followed by equally probable one-year short rates of 14.32 and 9.79 percent guarantees that our model matches the first two years of the term structure.

More-Distant Short Rates

We found today's single short rate by matching the one-year yield. We found the two one-year short rates by matching the two-year yield and volatility. Now we find the short rates two years out.

We already know the short rate out to one year. Figure 14–5 shows the short rates out to two years. The three unknown short rates at the end of the second year are r_{uu}, r_{ud}, and r_{dd}.

FIGURE 14–5
Finding the Two-Year Short Rates

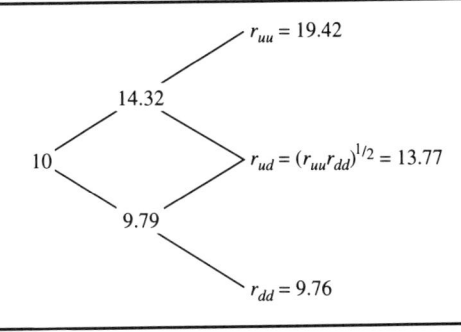

```
                    r_uu = 19.42
              14.32
        10          r_ud = (r_uu r_dd)^{1/2} = 13.77
              9.79
                    r_dd = 9.76
```

The values for these three short rates should let our model match the yield and yield volatility of a three-year zero. We must therefore match two quantities by guessing three short rates. This contrasts with finding the one-year short rates, where we had to match two quantities with two short rates. As a rule, matching two quantities with two short rates produces only one unique set of values for the short rates. Matching two quantities with three short rates is not unique; many sets of three short rates produce the correct yield and volatility.

Remember, however, that our model assumes that the short rate is lognormal with a volatility (of the log of the short rate) that depends only on time. One year in the future, when the short rate is 14.32 percent, the volatility is $(\frac{1}{2})\ln(r_{uu}/r_{ud})$; when the short rate is 9.79 percent, the volatility is $(\frac{1}{2})\ln(r_{ud}/r_{dd})$. Because these volatilities must be the same, we know that $r_{uu}/r_{ud} = r_{ud}/r_{dd}$, or $r_{ud}^2 = r_{uu}r_{dd}$.

So we don't really make three independent guesses for the rates; the middle one, r_{ud}, can be found from the other two. This means we have to match only two short rates, r_{uu} and r_{dd}, with two quantities, the three-year yield and volatility in the model. This typically has a unique solution.

In this case, Figure 14–5 shows that values for r_{uu}, r_{dd}, and r_{ud} of 19.42, 9.76, and 13.77 percent, respectively, produce a three-year yield of 12 percent and volatility of 18 percent, as Table 14–1 calls for.

We now know the short rates for one and two years in the future. Using a similar process, we can find the short rates on tree nodes farther in the future. Figure 14–6 displays the full tree of short rates at one-year intervals that matches the term structure of Table 14–1.

VALUING OPTIONS ON TREASURY BONDS

Given the term structure of Table 14–1 and the resulting tree of short rates shown in Figure 14–6, we can use the model to value an option on a bond.

FIGURE 14-6
Short Rates that Match the Term Structure of Table 14-1

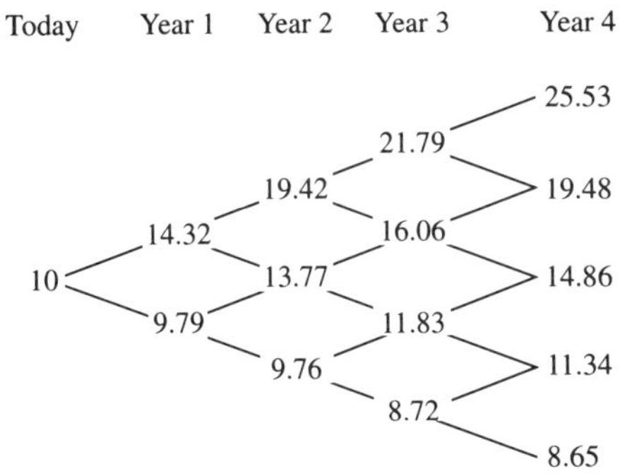

```
       Today    Year 1   Year 2   Year 3    Year 4
                                          ╱ 25.53
                                  21.79 ╱
                           19.42 ╱      ╲ 19.48
                   14.32 ╱      ╲ 16.06 ╱
             10    ╱    ╲ 13.77 ╱      ╲ 14.86
                   ╲ 9.79 ╱    ╲ 11.83 ╱
                         ╲ 9.76 ╱     ╲ 11.34
                               ╲ 8.72 ╱
                                     ╲ 8.65
```

Coupon Bonds as Collections of Zeros

Before we can value Treasury bond options, we need to find the future values of a Treasury bond at various nodes on the tree. Consider a Treasury with a 10 percent coupon, a face value of $100, and three years left to maturity. For convenience, consider this 10 percent Treasury as a portfolio of three zero coupon bonds—a one-year zero with a $10 face value; a two-year zero with a $10 face value; and a three-year zero with a $110 face value.

This portfolio has exactly the same annual payoffs as the 10 percent Treasury with three years to maturity, so the portfolio and the Treasury should have the same value. The tree in Figure 14-6 was built to value all zeros according to today's yield curve; hence, we can use it to value the three zeros in the portfolio above.

Panel E of Figure 14-7 shows the value of the 10 percent Treasury bond as the sum of the present values of the zeros—$95.51. The tree in Panel (F) gives the values of three-year Treasury bonds obtained after subtracting $10 of accrued interest on each coupon date.

FIGURE 14–7
Three-Year Treasury Values Obtained by Valuing an Equivalent Portfolio of Zeros

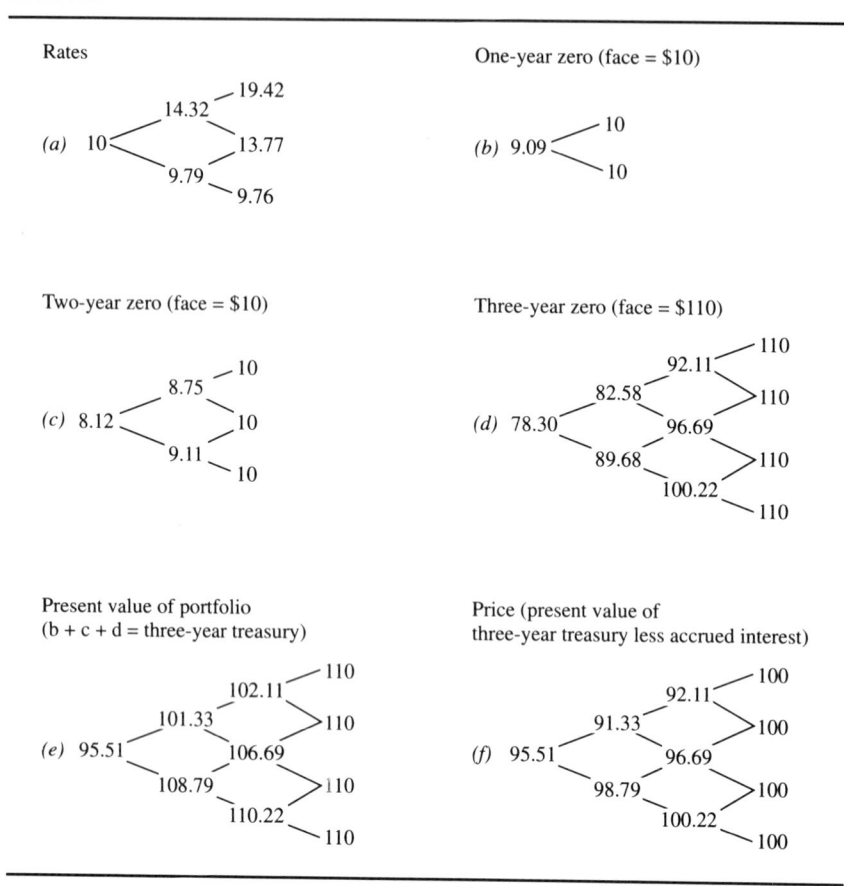

Rates

(a) 10 → 14.32 → 19.42
14.32 → 13.77
10 → 9.79 → 13.77
9.79 → 9.76

One-year zero (face = $10)

(b) 9.09 → 10
9.09 → 10

Two-year zero (face = $10)

(c) 8.12 → 8.75 → 10
8.75 → 10
8.12 → 9.11 → 10
9.11 → 10

Three-year zero (face = $110)

(d) 78.30 → 82.58 → 92.11 → 110
92.11 → 110
82.58 → 96.69 → 110
78.30 → 89.68 → 96.69 → 110
89.68 → 100.22 → 110
100.22 → 110

Present value of portfolio
(b + c + d = three-year treasury)

(e) 95.51 → 101.33 → 102.11 → 110
102.11 → 110
101.33 → 106.69 → 110
95.51 → 108.79 → 106.69 → 110
108.79 → 110.22 → 110
110.22 → 110

Price (present value of
three-year treasury less accrued interest)

(f) 95.51 → 91.33 → 92.11 → 100
92.11 → 100
91.33 → 96.69 → 100
95.51 → 98.79 → 96.69 → 100
98.79 → 100.22 → 100
100.22 → 100

Puts and Calls on Treasuries

We found that a three-year, 10 percent Treasury bond had a value of $95.51. The security is below par because it has a 10 percent coupon, and today's yield curve is above 10 percent.

We want to value options on this security—a two-year European call and a two-year European put, both with exercise prices of $95. From Panel (e) of Figure 14–7, we see that in two years the three-year Treasury bond may have three different values—

$110.22, $106.69, or $102.11. The corresponding values without accrued interest are $100.22, $96.69, and $92.11.

At expiration, the $95 call is in the money if the bond is worth either $100.22 or $96.69. The call's value will be the difference between the bond's value and the option's exercise price. The $95 call will be worth $5.22 if the bond is trading at $100.22 at expiration, and $1.69 if the bond is trading at $96.69. The call is out of the money, and therefore worth zero, if the bond is trading at $92.11 at expiration. Figure 14–8 shows the short-rate tree over two years, as well as possible call values at expiration of the option in two years.

At expiration, the put is in the money if the bond is worth $92.11 (without accrued interest). The put's value will be the difference between $92.11 and the $95 exercise (or strike) price, or $2.89. The put is worthless if the bond is worth one of the two higher values, $100.22 or $96.69. The lower panel of Figure 14–8 gives the put values.

Knowing the call values at expiration, we can find the possible

FIGURE 14–8
Two-Year Options on a Three-Year Treasury

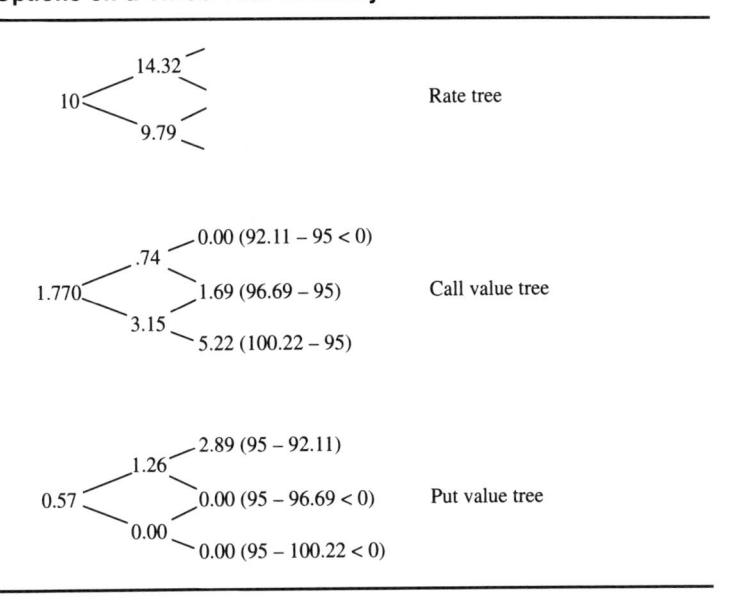

```
           14.32
       /
   10
       \
           9.79
```
Rate tree

```
                   0.00 (92.11 − 95 < 0)
            .74
   1.770            1.69 (96.69 − 95)
            3.15
                   5.22 (100.22 − 95)
```
Call value tree

```
                   2.89 (95 − 92.11)
            1.26
   0.57             0.00 (95 − 96.69 < 0)
            0.00
                   0.00 (95 − 100.22 < 0)
```
Put value tree

values of the call one year before expiration by using the valuation formula, Equation (14-1). If the short rate is 14.32 percent one year from today, the call's value one year before expiration will be 74 cents.

$$\frac{\frac{1}{2}(0.00) + \frac{1}{2}(\$1.69)}{1.1432} = \$0.74$$

If the short rate is 9.79 percent one year from today, the call's value will be $3.15.

$$\frac{\frac{1}{2}(\$1.69) + \frac{1}{2}(\$5.22)}{1.0979} = \$3.15$$

Given the call values one year out, we can find the value of the call today when the short rate is 10 percent:

$$\frac{\frac{1}{2}(\$0.74) + \frac{1}{2}(\$3.15)}{1.1} = \$1.77$$

Put values are derived in a similar manner. Figure 14-8 shows the full trees of call and put values.

We have found the values of European-style options at any node by determining their discounted expected values one step in the future. American-style options can be valued with little extra effort. Because an American option may be exercised at any time, its value at any node is the greater of its value if held or its value if exercised. We obtain its value if held by using the valuation formula to get any node's value in terms of values one step in the future. If exercised, the value of the option is the difference between the bond value at the node and the strike price.

Option Hedge Ratios

When market interest rates change, so do the market values of bonds and bond options. Bond option investors are naturally interested in how much option values change in response to changes in the value of the underlying bond. We measure this relation by a hedge ratio. The hedge ratio is frequently called *delta*.

Figure 14-9 shows one-step trees for a Treasury, a call, and a put. For a call worth C dollars on a Treasury with a value of T dollars, the hedge ratio is:

FIGURE 14-9
Hedge Ratios for a Call and a Put on a Treasury

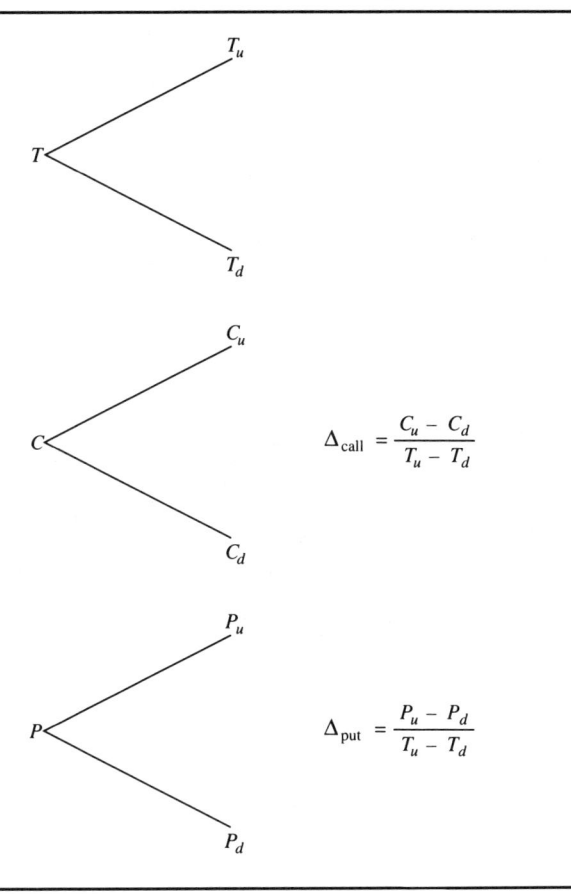

$$\Delta_{call} = \frac{C_u - C_d}{T_u - T_d}$$

$$\Delta_{put} = \frac{P_u - P_d}{T_u - T_d}$$

$$\Delta \text{ call} = \frac{C_u - C_d}{T_u - T_d} \quad (14\text{--}4)$$

where C_u and C_d are the values of the call one period from today in the tree corresponding to possible short rates r_u and r_d. An analogous formula holds for the premium on a put, represented by P, on a Treasury; we simply replace C with P in Equation (14-4).

For the two-year put and call on the three-year Treasury considered above, we start by finding the differences between possible values one year from today. Given the Treasury values shown in Figure 14–7 and the option values from Figure 14–8, we have:

$$T_u - T_d = \$91.33 - \$98.79 = -\$7.46$$
$$C_u - C_d = \$0.74 - \$3.15 = -\$2.41$$
$$P_u - P_d = \$1.26$$

Using Equation (14–4), we can now derive the following hedge ratios:

$$\Delta \text{ call} = \frac{C_u - C_d}{T_u - T_d} = \frac{-\$2.41}{-\$7.46} = 0.32 \qquad (14\text{–}5)$$

$$\Delta \text{ put} = \frac{P_u - P_d}{T_u - T_d} = \frac{\$1.26}{-\$7.46} = -0.17 \qquad (14\text{–}6)$$

These hedge ratios give us the sensitivity of the option to changes in the underlying Treasury value by describing the change in the option's value per dollar change in the Treasury's value. They therefore tell us how to hedge the Treasury with the option, and vice versa. The call hedge ratio is positive because the call premium increases when the value of the Treasury bond increases. In contrast, the hedge ratio is negative because put premiums decrease when the values of Treasury bonds increase.

Reducing the Interval Size

In the examples above, the short-rate tree had one-year steps, Treasuries paid annual coupons, and options could only be exercised once a year. This simplified presentation is too coarse to produce accurate values.

To get accurate solutions for option values, we need a tree with more finely spaced steps between today and the option's expiration. Ideally, we would like a tree with one-day steps and a 30-year horizon, so that coupon payments and option exercise dates would always fall exactly on a node. We would also like to have many steps to expiration, even for options on the verge of expiring.

If the time intervals between the nodes in the lattice of values are decreased to almost zero, the number of time periods must be increased accordingly. One of the advantages of using this model is that it can be modified to value different kinds of assets and accommodate different outcomes. However, if too many small time periods are analyzed, the model can become computationally infeasible.

For example, our computer doesn't have enough memory to build a 30-year tree with daily steps. And even if it did, it would take us hours to value a security. Instead, we can build a sequence of short-rate trees, each with the same number of steps but compressed into shorter and shorter horizons. Thus, each tree has finer spacing than the one before it. For example, we might use today's term structure to build short-rate trees that extend over 30 years, 15 years, 7 ½ years, and so on. In this way, no matter when the option expires, we will always have one tree with enough steps to value the option accurately.

To value an option on any Treasury security, we use two trees—a coarse one with enough steps to value the Treasury bond accurately from its maturity back to today, and a fine one with enough steps to value the option accurately from its expiration until today. We find the Treasury values on the coarse tree by using the model's valuation formula from maturity to today. Then we interpolate these Treasury values and insert them into the fine tree, which may often have as many as 60 periods. Maturity, expiration, and coupon dates that fall between nodes are carefully interpolated to the nearest node in time. In this way, the option can be accurately valued.

Interpolating across trees gives us accurate, yet rapid, results. Once model values have been found to match the term structure, we can value options in a few seconds.

ALTERNATIVE MODELS

We considered more complex models that use more than one factor to describe shifts in the yield curve. Increasing the number of factors improves the model results. But a multifactor model is much harder to think about and work with than a single-factor model. It also takes much more computer time. We therefore think it pays to work with different single-factor models before going to a multifactor model.

Along these lines, we examined the effects on our model of letting forward mean reversion and forward short-rate volatility vary independently. (They are tied together in the current model only by the geometry of a tree with equal time spacing throughout.) We found that varying forward mean reversion and varying forward short-rate volatility give very different results. We can change one or the other alone, or a mixture of both, when endeavoring to match a specific term structure.

Hull and White (HW) proposed a model that incorporates not only the time-varying volatility of our model, but also permits the future volatility of the short-term rate to be set independently of the model's other parameters. They analyze two versions of their model.[10] The HW model that assumes rates are normally distributed can lead to negative rates. The second HW version overcomes the problem with negative rates, but is not as analytically tractable as their first model. The HW models are trinomial instead of binomial. Trinomial models require more computations than binomial models, and research suggests that they yield no better solutions than the simpler binomial models.[11]

Black and Karasinski (BK) developed a one-factor model that is driven by lognormally distributed short rates that are mean reverting.[12] Negative interest rates and interest rates of zero do not occur in the BK model. The BK model is a generalized version of the binomial Black-Derman-Toy model presented in this chapter. The BK model can match the yield and volatility curves explained above (plus the "cap curve") by using the target rate (or drift) as a function of time, local volatility as a function of time, and mean reversion as a function of time. BK used their model to analyze one plausible version of the HW model. The yield curves generated by the BK model, like those generated by the HW model, turn downward at long maturities and eventually approach zero. By allowing the time spacing to vary, the BK model generates these yield curves using a binomial model with 50-50 probabilities, like the model described in this chapter. In contrast, the HW model uses a complicated trinomial tree that requires considerable human intervention to operate.

Computational Shortcuts

Applications-oriented researchers have developed computational algorithms that are more efficient than the procedures originally suggested by Black-Derman-Toy. Professor Tian has developed a method for "pruning the tree" (to eliminate negative interest rates and unrealistically high interest rates that might arise in the lattice, for example) that reduces the number of computations without decreasing the accuracy of the solved value.[13] Dr. Anlong Li has extended Tian's work and developed a binomial model that converges to the Cox-Ingersol-Ross model.[14] Farshid Jamshidian has shown how to use forward induction to expedite the computations.[15]

NOTES

1. Fischer Black and Myron Scholes, "The Pricing of Options and Corporate Liabilities," *Journal of Political Economy,* May–June 1973, pp. 637–54.
2. Fischer Black, "The Pricing of Commodity Contracts," *Journal of Financial Economics* 3 (1976), pp. 167–79.
3. Richard J. Rendleman, Jr., and Brit J. Bartter, "Two-State Option Pricing," *Journal of Finance* 34 (December 1979), pp. 1093–110.
4. John C. Cox, Stephen A. Ross, and Mark Rubinstein, "Option Pricing: A Simplified Approach," *Journal of Financial Economics* 7 (September 1979), pp. 229–63.
5. Thomas S. Y. Ho and Sang-Bin Lee, "Term Structure Movements and Pricing Interest Rate Contingent Claims," *Journal of Finance* 41 (1986), pp. 1011–29.
6. The model was developed by Fischer Black, Emanuel Derman, and William Toy, "A One-Factor Model of Interest Rates and Its Application to Treasury Bond Options," *Financial Analysts Journal,* January–February 1990, pp. 33–39.
7. The values generated by the model align with one another in such a way that the model cannot be used to generate arbitrage profits.
8. A model similar to this, but with σ proportional to $r^{-0.5}$, has been solved by John C. Cox, J. E. Ingersoll, and S. A. Ross, "A Theory of

The Term Structure of Interest Rates," *Econometric* 54 (1985), pp. 385–407.
9. The variance of two lognormally distributed turns is defined as:

$$\text{Var}[\ln(r)] = (\tfrac{1}{2}) \sum_{t=1}^{2} [\ln(r_t) - E\{\ln(r)\}]^2$$

If the logarithms of the two returns are ln(14.32%) = 2.661 and ln(9.79%) = 2.281, then the expected value of the logarithms is [(2.661 + 2.281)/2] = 2.471, and the variance is .0361.

$$\text{Var}[\ln(r)] = (\tfrac{1}{2})\{[2.661 - 2.471]^2 + [2.281 - 2.471]^2\} = .0361$$

The square root of the variance is the standard deviation of .19. Since $[\ln(r_1/r_2)] = [\ln(r_1) - \ln(r_2)]$, the same standard deviation can be obtained with the following computationally efficient formula:

$$\sigma = [\ln(r_1/r_2)]/2 = [\ln(14.32/9.79)]/2 = .19 = 19\%$$

10. John Hull and Alan White, "Pricing Interest Rate Derivative Securities," *Review of Financial Studies* 3, no. 4 (1990), pp. 573–92. More recently, see John Hull and Alan White, "One Factor Interest-Rate Models and the Valuation of Interest-Rate Derivative Securities," *Journal of Financial and Quantitative Analysis*, June 1993.
11. Yisong Tian, "A Simplified Binomial Approach to the Pricing of Interest Rate Contingent Claims," *Journal of Financial Engineering*, 1, no. 1 (June 1992), pp. 14–37.
12. Fischer Black and Piotr Karasinski, "Bond and Option Pricing when Short Rates Are Lognormal," *Financial Analysts Journal* 7, no. 4 (July–August 1991), pp. 52–59.
13. Yisong Tian, "A Simplified Binomial Approach to the Pricing Of Interest Rate Contingent Claims," *Journal of Financial Engineering* 1, no. 1 (June 1992), pp. 14–37.
14. Anlong Li, "Three Essays on Contingent Claim Pricing," Ph.D. dissertation, Department of Finance, Weatherhead School of Management, Case Western Reserve University, Cleveland, Ohio, May 1992.
15. Farshid Jamshidian, "Forward Induction and Construction of Yield Curve Diffusion Models," *The Journal of Fixed Income*, June 1991, pp. 62–74.

CHAPTER 15

TAX RAMIFICATIONS OF OPTIONS

Diane D. Fuller*
KPMG Peat Marwick's Financial Services Practice

Many of the relevant tax rules cover a variety of interest rate derivatives. Given this fact, I have attempted to divide the key issues between this chapter on options and the chapter on futures (Chapter 11). Both chapters should be read in order to have a sense of the overall picture. This chapter will focus on two areas: first, specific rules concerning the timing of option income and loss including the treatment of option premiums and, second, general principles affecting the character of income as capital or ordinary.

OPTION PREMIUMS

The chapter on futures discusses in detail IRC Section 1256, which greatly changed the treatment of regulated futures contracts and most listed options. But what rules applied prior to the enactment of this section and continue to apply to options that fall outside the purview of IRC Section 1256? Not surprisingly, these rules follow basic tax principles in requiring closed transaction reporting and,

---

*The author gratefully acknowledges the assistance of James Hunt, Patrick Murphy, Richard Solway, and Richard Turnure of KPMG Peat Marwick in preparing this chapter.

in most cases, capital treatment. Please keep in mind that the following discussion of options does not apply to options covered by IRC Section 1256, that is, listed nonequity options and listed dealer equity options other than those that qualify for the IRC Section 1256(e) hedging exception described below. Such options will generally be subject to mark-to-market accounting, and any gains and losses will typically be treated as 60 percent long-term capital gain or loss and 40 percent short-term capital gain or loss.

When people talk about the rules for the timing of income and loss with respect to an option, they usually talk about a "wait-and-see" approach. Under this approach, there is no recognition of income or loss on the receipt or payment of an option premium, but, rather, the holder or writer of the option must wait and see what happens with the option. Typically, the option will either be exercised, will lapse without exercise, or will be disposed of either through a sale, assignment, or a closing transaction. The implications of the wait-and-see approach with respect to the timing of income and deduction can be summarized by the following table:

Treatment of Option Premium

	Long (Holder)	Short (Writer)
Call		
Exercise	Added to the tax basis of the property acquired	Added to the amount realized on the sale of the underlying property
Lapse	Loss on the date of lapse	Income on the date of lapse
Disposition	Included in the tax basis of the option in determining the gain or loss on disposition	Gain or loss is measured by the difference between the premium received and the amounts paid to close the short position
Put		
Exercise	Subtracted from the strike price to determine the amount realized on the sale	Reduces the tax basis of the property acquired
Lapse	Loss on the date of lapse except for stock options subject to the married put rules	Income on the date of lapse

	Long (Holder)	Short (Writer)
Disposition	Included in the tax basis of the option in determining the gain or loss on the disposition	Gain or loss is measured by the difference between the premium received and the amounts paid to close the short option position

A general summary of the tax treatment of options can be found in Revenue Ruling 78-182, 1978-1 C.B. 265. Commissions and fees paid by a seller of an option reduce the premium received. Similar expenses paid by a purchaser of an option are added to the premium paid. The timing rules described above may be affected by the straddle or the wash-sale provisions, which are discussed in the chapter on futures. Interestingly, the wash-sale rules did not initially apply to options. In *Gantner v. Commr.*, 91 T.C. 713 (1988), later proceeding *Gantner v. Comm'r*, 92 T.C. 192 (1989, aff'd, 905 F.2d.), the taxpayer purchased and sold exchange-traded call options on stock through a broker. On December 3, 1980, the taxpayer sold and bought 100 identical stock options. The taxpayer reported a loss on the sale transaction by using the cost of his earlier purchase of 100 identical stock options as his basis. The Internal Revenue Service denied the deduction, asserting that the sale and purchase were a wash sale and that the taxpayer must defer the loss until he sold his remaining options in January 1981. The Tax Court, however, held that stock options were not "stock or securities" within the meaning of the wash-sale rules and that the loss should be allowed. Congress quickly remedied the problem by amending IRC Section 1091(a) to state that the term *stock and securities* would include contracts or options to acquire or sell stock or securities.

CHARACTER OF INCOME

Disputes and uncertainty concerning the character of income and loss as capital or ordinary are among the most contentious and significant tax issues affecting a variety of financial products at the current time. This is, to some degree, surprising since the Tax Reform Act of 1986 eliminated the preferential tax rate for long-term capital gains, although a limited benefit for noncorporate taxpayers has been reintroduced and there has been talk of extending such benefits as a means of stimulating the economy and encouraging savings and investment. On the other hand, perhaps it isn't so surprising since the current state of the law places the Internal Revenue Service in almost a no-lose position as it seeks to characterize losses as capital losses. For, even though the benefits of capital gains have been largely eliminated, the superstructure of capital characterization remains in place together with the limitations on the deductibility of capital losses. Thus, capital losses may generally only be deducted to the extent the taxpayer has capital gains, although individual taxpayers are permitted to deduct up to $3,000 annually in net capital losses.

In acknowledgement of the fact that this is, at least nominally, a chapter on options, let's look first at any provisions dealing specifically with the character of option income or loss. For holders of options, IRC Section 1234(a)(1) states that:

> Gain or loss attributable to the sale or exchange of, or loss attributable to the failure to exercise, an option to buy or sell property shall be considered gain or loss from the sale or exchange of property which has the same character as the property to which the option relates has in the hands of the taxpayer (or would have in the hands of the taxpayer if acquired by him).

For grantors of options with respect to stock, securities, or commodities, IRC Section 1234 (b) provides that:

> Gain or loss on any closing transaction with respect to, and gain on the lapse of, an option in property shall be treated as a gain or loss from the sale or exchange of a capital asset held not more than one year.

Prior to the enactment of the IRC Section 1234(b), grantors recognized ordinary income or loss on the lapse of an option. (See, for example, Revised Rule 58-234, 1958-1 C.B. 279.) Under IRC Section 1234(c)(2), the provisions of IRC Section 1234(a) and IRC Section 1234(b) are extended to cash settlement options.

While the short-term capital gain or loss characterization for the grantor of an option is clear in the language of IRC Section 1234(b) itself, the rules for holders under IRC Section 1234(a) require further investigation into the character of the property underlying the option. How, then, is the character of property as capital or ordinary determined?

Capital Assets

Capital gains and losses result from sales or exchanges of capital assets. Under IRC Section 1221, the term *capital asset* is defined by exception rather than by inclusion. Thus, the property held by a taxpayer is considered to be a capital asset unless it falls within one of the following excluded categories:

1. Stock in trade, inventory, or other property held by a taxpayer primarily for sale to customers in the ordinary course of trade or business.
2. Depreciable property or real property used by a taxpayer in trade or business.
3. Certain copyrights; literary, musical, or artistic compositions; letters or memoranda; or similar property.
4. Accounts or notes receivable acquired in the ordinary course of trade or business for services rendered or from the sale of inventory.
5. Certain publications of the U.S. government.

Types of Market Participants

The next step in determining character is to decide how the taxpayer is using the financial product. The five categories of market participants described most frequently are investors, traders, dealers, hedgers, and brokers. *Investors* generally seek to profit from changes in the market prices of their investments. *Traders* are professional investors that trade more frequently than investors but for the same purpose. *Dealers* are merchants of financial products who buy and sell to customers in the ordinary course of their business. Dealers often profit from a markup or other dealer concession (for example, bid-ask spreads), although they are also affected by market fluctuations when dealing with markets as volatile as the securities markets. *Hedgers* acquire financial products to protect themselves against price, interest rate, foreign exchange, or other risks with respect to assets or liabilities they hold or anticipated future transactions. *Brokers* act as agents for their customers and receive commissions and fees. The way in which the nature of a taxpayer's activities will affect the characterization of gain and loss can be seen if you consider how the tax law defines capital assets.

In connection with stocks, securities, and other financial instruments, it is clearly the first capital asset exception for inventory and stock in trade that is the most significant. Property held by a dealer for sale to customers, that is, inventory, is not a capital asset, and any gains and losses from the sale of inventory will be ordinary. If a taxpayer holds an option on property with respect to which he is a dealer, then under IRC Section 1234(a) gain or loss from the sale or lapse of the option will be ordinary. Investors and traders do not hold securities for sale to customers and would not fall under the inventory exception. Thus, gain or loss on the sale or lapse of an option would result in capital gain or loss to an investor or trader.

It is important to distinguish between a dealer in options as opposed to a dealer in the property subject to the option. Although option market makers and specialists were historically viewed as dealers eligible for ordinary income and loss treatment, market makers and specialists in listed options have been treated as traders for tax purposes since 1984 and receive capital gains and losses.

HEDGING

The term *hedging* is used in several different way for tax purposes, all of which vary at least to some extent from the accounting concept of hedging. For example, under the foreign currency regulations, there are integrated hedging transaction rules that would permit the combination of a debt instrument with its hedge to create a synthetic instrument with different terms. For example, a floating-rate deutschemark-denominated loan might be combined with a floating-for-fixed, U.S. dollars for deutschemarks, currency swap to create a fixed-rate U.S. dollar loan. In general, the tax definitions of hedging transactions are narrower than the accounting definitions. Some accounting or economic hedges would be treated as straddles rather than hedges for tax purposes and would be subject to the straddle rules of IRC Section 1092, which are described in Chapter 11. The balance of this section will look at the current controversy concerning ordinary income and loss treatment for hedging transactions.

Ordinary income and loss treatment of hedging transactions has been the center of controversy since the decision of the Supreme Court in *Arkansas Best*, 485 U.S. 212 (1988). Although this case has created tremendous uncertainty with respect to the treatment of financial hedging transactions, the facts of the case have nothing to do with hedging. *Arkansas Best* involved a diversified holding company that had purchased stock in a failing bank. When the majority of the bank stock was sold at a loss, the company sought to treat the loss as ordinary, arguing its purchases of the bank stock had been motivated by a business purpose, that is, a desire to protect its business reputation that would have suffered from the failure of the bank, rather than an intent to make an investment. A series of cases and rulings had grown into a "*Corn Products* doctrine" under which virtually any asset acquired or held for a business, rather than an investment, purpose might be treated as a noncapital asset. In concluding that the bank stock losses incurred by Arkansas Best were capital losses, the Supreme Court rejected such a broad interpretation of the earlier Supreme Court decision in *Corn Products Refining Co.*, 350 U.S. 46 (1955).

Corn Products is of particular significance with respect to the tax treatment of hedging since it actually involved hedging transactions in which the taxpayer, a manufacturer of corn products, acquired corn futures as part of its corn buying program and as an economical way of obtaining an adequate supply of raw corn. When the taxpayer attempted to treat gains realized from the futures contracts as capital gains, the Supreme Court concluded that the gains were ordinary on the basis that the futures transactions were an integral part of the taxpayer's business designed to protect its manufacturing operations against a price increase and to assure an adequate future supply of corn. Before discussing the way in which the Court narrowed its interpretation of the *Corn Products* case in *Arkansas Best* and the arguments used in the current Tax Court case involving the Federal National Mortgage Association, which is described below, it might be interesting to look at the following statements from the *Corn Products* decision:

1. Congress intended that profits and losses arising from the everyday operation of a business be considered as ordinary income or loss rather than capital gain or loss.
2. The definition of capital asset must be narrowly applied and its exclusions interpreted broadly.
3. It (the Treasury Department in General Counsel Memorandum 17322) held that hedging transactions were essentially to be regarded as insurance rather than a dealing in capital assets and that gains and losses therefrom were ordinary business gains and losses.

Notwithstanding this broad and multifaceted support for ordinary treatment of hedging gains and losses in the original opinion for the *Corn Products* case, the Supreme Court took a much more restrictive approach in *Arkansas Best* where the Court concluded that "*Corn Products* is properly interpreted as standing for the narrow proposition that hedging transactions that are an integral part of a business' inventory-purchase system fall with the inventory exclusion of IRC Section 1221."

The first major post–*Arkansas Best* case dealing with financial hedging transactions is *Federal National Mortgage Association* (FNMA), 100 T.C., No. 36 (June 17, 1993). FNMA purchased residential mortgages from mortgage originators and held the mortgages to maturity as part of its portfolio. The mortgage purchases were funded with the proceeds of debt regularly issued by FNMA to the public. FNMA used options, futures, and short sales of Treasury securities to hedge its interest rate risk with respect to commitments to acquire mortgages and anticipated debt issuances. The Internal Revenue Service argued losses incurred on the hedging transactions should be capital losses based on the narrow interpretation of the *Corn Products* doctrine expressed by the Supreme Court in the *Arkansas Best* case. FNMA used a variety of arguments including business insurance, substitution for interest income and expense, and treatment of the mortgages as accounts receivables acquired in the ordinary course of business for services rendered in seeking ordinary loss treatment. In deciding the case in favor of FNMA, the court adopted the last of these arguments by concluding that FNMA's mortgage portfolio qualified as accounts for services rendered (one of the capital exceptions) and that gains and losses from futures, options, and short positions entered into to hedge this portfolio should be treated as ordinary gains and losses in accordance with the *Corn Products* and *Arkansas Best* decisions. Significantly, the *FNMA* decision extends ordinary treatment to transactions hedging debt that was issued to fund the mortgage portfolio.

One aspect of the tax law that is directly affected by the uncertain treatment of hedging transactions is the hedging exception of IRC Section 1256(e). If a transaction qualifies as a hedging transaction under the section, it is exempted from the mark-to-market and character rules of IRC Section 1256 and from the loss-deferral and other straddle rules of IRC Section 1092. Under IRC Section 1256(e), a transaction qualifies as a hedging transaction if:

1. The transaction is entered into in the normal course of the taxpayer's trade or business:
    a. To reduce risk of price change or currency fluctuations with respect to property that is held or to be held by the taxpayer, or
    b. To reduce risk of interest rate or price changes or currency fluctuations with respect to borrowings made or to be made, or obligations incurred or to be incurred, by the taxpayer.
2. The gain or loss on such transactions is treated as ordinary income or loss.
3. Before the close of the day on which such transaction was entered into, the taxpayer clearly identifies such transaction as being a hedging transaction.

This definition of hedging transaction is clearly based on the broader pre–*Arkansas Best* interpretation of the *Corn Products* doctrine. However, the Internal Revenue Service currently takes the position, based on *Arkansas Best,* that a hedge of a liability cannot qualify for ordinary treatment. As a result, 1(*b*) above would be meaningless since such a transaction could never satisfy requirement 2. Internal Revenue Service agents have also attempted in a number of instances to whipsaw taxpayers by treating hedging losses as capital and hedging gains as ordinary.

SECTION 4

INTEREST RATE SWAPS

CHAPTER 16

INTRODUCTION TO INTEREST RATE SWAPS

Susan M. Mangiero
Sacred Heart University, Fairfield, Connecticut

Since its inception in the early 1980s, the interest rate swap market has mushroomed to $5 trillion.[1] Cost reduction, yield enhancement, structural flexibility, and speed of execution have all contributed to the growing popularity of this risk management tool.

An *interest rate swap* is a legal arrangement between two counterparties to exchange specified payments. The typical swap mandates the fixed-rate payor[2] to make a fixed payment every year. A second counterparty, the floating-rate payor, makes several payments each year. The amount of each floating-rate payment is based on a variable rate base that has been mutually agreed upon by both counterparties. For example, the floating-rate payments could be based on the three-month LIBOR (London Interbank Offer Rate).

Because an interest rate swap involves no principal payment, the face value of the swap is referred to as the *notional amount*. All cash payments exchanged between the two counterparties are based on this dollar size. Figure 16–1 illustrates the payment flow for a typical interest rate swap.

This type of swap is usually referred to as a *coupon swap*. The secondary swaps market for this type of swap is highly developed. Although swaps can be structured in many different ways to accommodate counterparty needs, pricing for all swaps is based on the current market price for a fixed–LIBOR coupon swap with a specified maturity.

FIGURE 16–1
Typical Swap Configuration

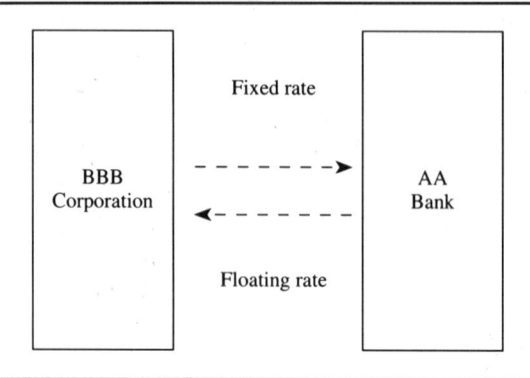

```
           Fixed rate
┌─────────┐ ------>  ┌─────┐
│   BBB   │          │ AA  │
│Corporation│ <------  │Bank │
└─────────┘          └─────┘
          Floating rate
```

TYPES OF SWAPS

There are a wide variety of interest rate swaps. The exchange of prespecified payments is a common denominator. What varies among transactions are the types of payments to be exchanged. Essentially, a customized swap combines a coupon swap with some type of embedded option. Brief definitions of some of the more common types of swaps follow.

An *extendable swap* provides the fixed-rate payor with the option to lengthen the term of the swap. Should interest rates rise during the term of the original swap, the fixed-rate payor would find it cheaper to extend its term to maturity rather than enter into a new swap.

A *forward swap* is a swap that starts on a specified future date. In anticipation of rising swap costs, a company might choose to lock in the rate today for any project that needs to be funded later on.

A *swap option,* sometimes called a *swaption,* grants the buyer the right, but not the obligation, to be a future fixed-rate payor. The rate or spread over a specified U.S. Treasury note yield is set today. This feature was popularized several years ago because of the uncertainty of completion associated with a tender bid. In exchange for the up-front fee, a company can lock in a funding rate in the event that the acquisition is made. If the transaction is not completed, the option buyer can walk away without any obligation to complete the swap.

A *callable swap* includes an embedded option to terminate an existing swap, without penalty, before the contractual maturity date. A callable swap is an ideal way for the fixed-rate payor to reduce its costs should rates fall.

A *puttable swap* allows the floating-rate payor to terminate a swap, without penalty, before its contractual maturity date. Should interest rates rise, the swap is put back to the fixed-rate payor. The floating-rate payor can then initiate a new swap whereby it receives a higher fixed rate.

Both counterparties to a *basis swap* are designated as floating-rate payors. Each party exchanges payments based on a defined variable-rate benchmark. For example, one counterparty might make swap payments pegged to the three-month LIBOR. The remaining counterparty might make swap payments tied to the Federal Reserve Commercial Paper Index. Financial institutions are natural counterparties to basis swaps because of their reliance on short-term funds.

A swap with a *delayed rate set* feature allows the fixed-rate payor to wait before locking in a fixed swap rate. This feature is attractive when rates are expected to decline in the near future. Unlike a forward swap, which locks in a rate today, both the fixed rate and the cash flows are deferred to the future with a delayed rate set swap.

Although swap types vary, all swaps share some common features. See Table 16-1 for a list of selected features.

SWAP CHARACTERISTICS

Each interest rate swap transaction is described in a legal contract between the two counterparties. No detail is too small. Any misunderstanding regarding a structural term can be costly. The International Swap Dealers Association (ISDA) has published a book of definitions and terms to aid in standardizing swap contracts. Listed below are some of the important elements of a swap contract.

TABLE 16-1
Important Features of Swaps

Off-blance sheet transaction
No principal exchange
Separate from funding or related investment
Credit risk limited to a fraction of notional principal amount
Flexible cash flow structure
Liquid secondary market
Standardized documentation
Maturity range from 1 year to 10 years
Transaction size from $5 million to $1 billion
Rapid execution
No margin requirements
Can be used with new or old assets or liabilities
Can provide asset or liability structure otherwise unavailable
Can reduce net funding cost
Can extend or shorten asset or liability maturity
Reduces interest rate risk
Can be used for anticipatory hedges
Can alter tax or accounting gains or losses
Can enhance return on investments

1. *Notional principal amount (NPA):* The size of the swap. The NPA is used as the basis for calculating swap payments.
2. *Interest rate swap date:* The date upon which the accruals of the fixed- and floating-rate amounts commence. This is not necessarily the same as the transaction date.
3. *Maturity date:* The expiry date of the contractual agreement.
4. *Floating-rate payor:* The counterparty responsible for making payments based on the floating-rate definition.
5. *Floating-rate definition:* Includes the benchmark plus any premium above the benchmark value that will determine the floating rate.
6. *Floating-rate payment intervals:* The period used to calculate the cash flow payable by the floating-rate payor. Payments are usually made in arrears.
7. *Floating-rate reset frequency:* Could be semiannually, quarterly, monthly, weekly, or daily.

8. *Fixed-rate payor:* The counterparty responsible for making payments based on the fixed rate agreed upon by both counterparties when the swap agreement is established.
9. *Fixed-rate payments:* The fixed swap rate is typically determined by taking the yield of a specified U.S. Treasury note at the time of the swap closing and adding an agreed-upon number of basis points (bps).
10. *Calendar assumption:* The fixed-rate payment amounts are normally computed on a "bond equivalent basis." The floating-rate payment amounts are normally computed on a "money market equivalent basis" using a 360-day year. See the section on swap economics for more detail.
11. *Fixed-rate payment period:* Fixed-rate payments are usually made in arrears on a semiannual or annual basis. The payment dates are based on the contract maturity date. For example, if a swap matures on March 12, 19xx, the semiannual fixed-rate payments would be made on every September 12 and March 12 until the swap matures. Allowances are made in the event those dates fall on holidays or weekends when the banks are closed.
12. *Settlement basis:* Net or gross. If the settlement basis is *net*, the counterparty owing the higher dollar amount pays the difference between what is owed and what is to be received.
13. *Documentation:* Most swaps today use the swap document form suggested by either the ISDA or the British Bankers Association (BBAIRS). Frequent swappers employ a master swap document.
14. *Governing law:* Specifies which country's legal code will be used to settle disputes or enforce the contract.

APPLICATIONS

Each counterparty has a different motivation to enter a swap. Historically, counterparties have entered into a swap in order to change the nature of their liabilities. Consider two counterparties. Big Corporation is A-rated and raises funds by issuing commercial paper. Every month, Big Corporation reissues commercial paper for another 30 days. In anticipation of rising rates, Big Corporation would like to lock in a fixed liability cost for five years. It can either issue a medium-term note for a cost equal to the 8.25 percent coupon, February 1997 Treasury note yield plus 90 basis points, assumed to be 8.66 percent per year, or pay a fixed swap rate.

Big Bank is rated AA and is interested in locking in a source of funds pegged to the six-month LIBOR in order to match-fund a

TABLE 16–2
Counterparty Costs Associated with the Swap

Annual Cost to Big Corporation

Short-term funding	30-day commercial paper
Receipt from swap	6-month LIBOR
Average LIBOR–CP spread	30 basis points
Swap obligation	8.71%
Net cost of funds	8.41% per year
Annual savings due to swap	.25% or 25 basis points

Annual Cost to Big Bank

Five-year certificate of deposit	8.56% per year
Receipt from swap	8.71% per year
Swap obligation	6-month LIBOR
Net cost of funds	6-month LIBOR – 15 basis points
Annual savings due to swap	.15% or 15 basis points

Benefits Produced by Swap

1. Big Corporation obtains a lower fixed-rate liability than otherwise available in the medium-term note market.
2. Big Corporation maintains its borrowing capacity by not issuing the medium-term note.
3. Big Corporation maintains transaction confidentiality.
4. Big Bank obtains a lower cost of variable-rate borrowing than otherwise available in the LIBOR market.
5. Big Bank eliminates an asset-liability mismatch by funding a variable-rate five-year loan with variable-rate term funds.
6. Big Corporation may find that the swap contract contains less restrictive covenants than those associated with a public debt issuance.

The split of swap benefits between counterparties will vary according to market conditions.

FIGURE 16–2
Liability-Driven Swap

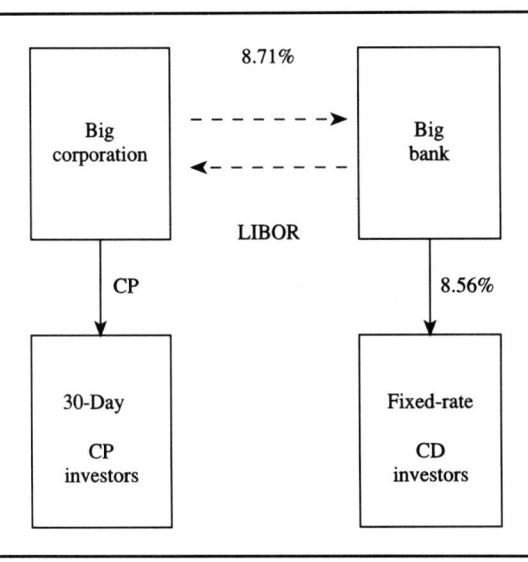

```
                    8.71%
      ┌──────────┐ ------> ┌──────────┐
      │   Big    │         │   Big    │
      │corporation│        │   bank   │
      │          │ <------ │          │
      └──────────┘  LIBOR  └──────────┘
           │                    │
           │ CP                 │ 8.56%
           ▼                    ▼
      ┌──────────┐         ┌──────────┐
      │  30-Day  │         │Fixed-rate│
      │    CP    │         │    CD    │
      │ investors│         │ investors│
      └──────────┘         └──────────┘
```

variable-rate five-year term loan. Big Bank can borrow in the interbank market at the prevailing six-month LIBOR and roll over this short-term funding twice a year for five years. Alternatively, Big Bank can issue a five-year certificate of deposit and swap this fixed liability for a six-month LIBOR obligation. Its current five-year fixed-rate cost of funds is 80 basis points above the 8.25 percent coupon, February 1997 U.S. Treasury note, assumed to be 8.56 percent per year.

By using a swap, Big Corporation saves 25 basis points per year. Big Bank saves 15 basis points per year. Table 16–2 breaks down the counterparties' costs associated with the swap. Figure 16–2 illustrates the mechanics of the swap. Assume that the average six-month LIBOR–commercial paper spread is 30 basis points and that the yield on the 8.25 percent, February 1997 U.S. Treasury note is 7.76 percent per year.

Recently, swaps have been used to enhance investment returns. Consider two counterparties. Smart Investor is a AAA-rated insurance company that raises funds by issuing five-year guaranteed investment contracts and then invests the proceeds in five-year fixed-income securities. Its current investment goal is to earn the 8.25 percent coupon, February 1997 U.S. Treasury note yield plus 80 basis points, assumed to be 8.56 percent per year. Smart Investor's current cost for five-year funds is 8.46 percent per year. Foreign Bank is a AA-rated non-U.S. bank. It is currently raising short-term funds at a rate equal to the six-month LIBOR minus 25 basis points. However, anticipating interest rates to rise, Foreign Bank would like to lock in a five-year rate to match-fund a five-year loan just made. Its prevailing cost of fixed-rate funds is 8.66 percent per year, a 90-basis-point premium above the 8.25 percent coupon, February 1997 U.S. Treasury note yield. A second need is to sell part of its investment portfolio—a $25 million floating-rate note (FRN) issued by an A-rated U.S. regional bank. The FRN pays interest every six months at a rate equal to the prevailing six-month LIBOR plus 15 basis points. The market price for this FRN is 99.50 percent of par value, which is unchanged from the original purchase price.

Smart Investor can buy a five-year, A-rated note with the target return. Alternatively, Smart Investor can buy the FRN from Foreign Bank and concurrently enter into an interest rate swap with Foreign Bank. By using a swap, Smart Investor increases its annual investment income by 40 basis points per year. Foreign Bank reduces its funding costs by 20 basis points per year. Table 16–3 highlights the counterparties' swap flows. Figure 16–3 illustrates the mechanics of the swap.

EXECUTION OF AN INTEREST RATE SWAP

Once a company or bank makes a decision to complete a swap, the actual transaction time is brief. This section traces the execution of a swap from start to finish.

> 9:30 A.M. The assistant treasurer of Any Corporation phones the swap trader at Some Bank and asks for a four-year swap quote. The swap trader quotes a two-way bid of 90 to 100 basis points above the 8.25 percent coupon, February 1997 U.S. Treasury note yield, subject to swap credit line availability.

TABLE 16-3
Counterparties' Swap Flows

Annual Return to Smart Investor

Receipt from swap	8.71% per year
Swap obligation	6-month LIBOR
FRN return	6-month LIBOR + 15 basis points
Gain from buying FRN at discount	10 basis points per year
Net return	8.96% per year

The difference between the FRN market price of 99.50 and par is 50 basis points. Over a five-year period, this represents a 10-basis-point-per-year gain, on average. Compared to its investment target of 8.56 percent per year, Smart Investor has increased its income by 40 basis points since the combined swap and FRN investment produce an annual rate of 8.96 percent per year.

Annual Cost to Foreign Bank

Receipt from swap	6-month LIBOR
Swap obligation	8.71% per year
Funding cost	LIBOR−25 basis points
Net cost of funds	8.46% per year

To fund its fixed-rate loan, Foreign Bank could raise term funds at a cost of 8.66 percent per year by issuing a certificate of deposit. By accessing a fixed-rate liability via the swap, its annual cost is reduced by 20 basis points to 8.46 percent.

Benefits Produced by Swap

1. Smart Investor increases its annual investment income by roughly 5 percent (.40%/8.56%).
2. Smart Investor augments its pool of acceptable investments.
3. Foreign Bank reduces its funding costs.
4. Foreign Bank preserves its term debt borrowing capacity.
5. Foreign Bank accomplishes its investment objective to sell its FRN.
6. Foreign Bank reduces its interest rate risk.

Ordinarily, Smart Investor would face one risk only, namely the default risk associated with the purchase of a fixed-income security. By entering into a swap, Smart Investor is faced with the additional risk that the fixed-rate payor could default, thereby leaving Smart Investor exposed to the effect that changing interest rates have on both the swap and the FRN. Clearly, the enhanced return of the combination swap-FRN must be large enough to offset the assumption of this incremental risk.

10:00 A.M. The assistant treasurer phones the swap trader at Some Bank and asks for a firm swap quote whereby Any Corporation will be the fixed-rate payor.

FIGURE 16–3
Asset-Driven Swap

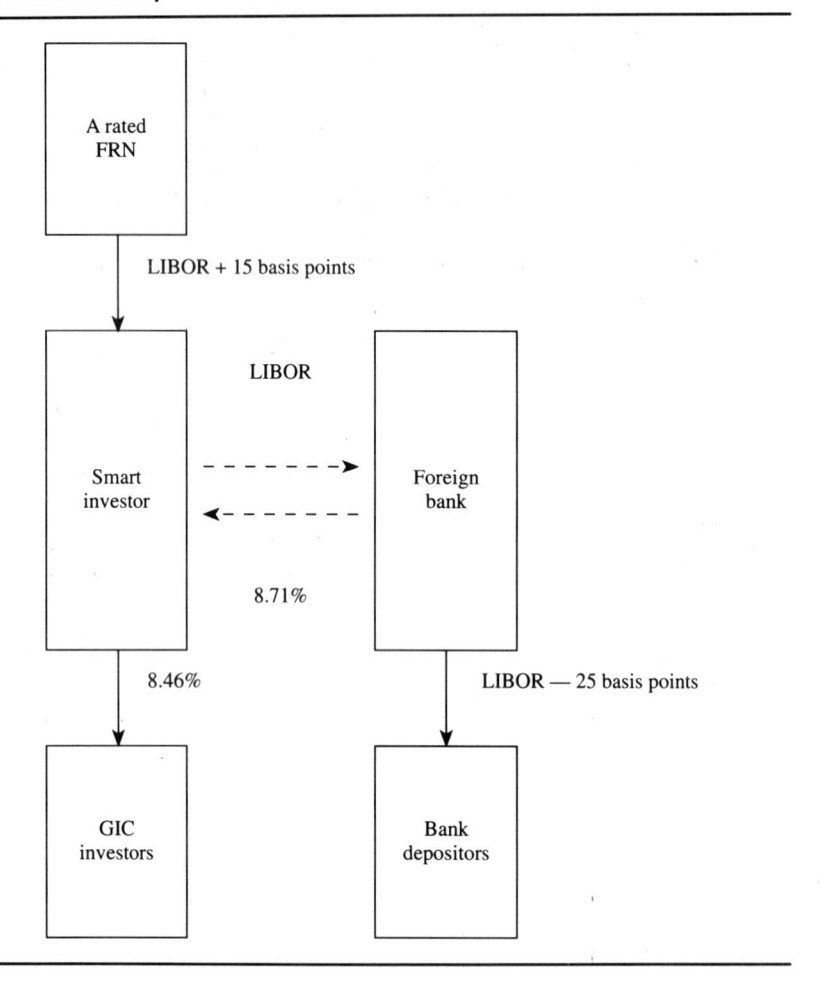

```
        ┌──────────┐
        │  A rated │
        │   FRN    │
        └────┬─────┘
             │ LIBOR + 15 basis points
             ▼
        ┌──────────┐       LIBOR      ┌──────────┐
        │          │ - - - - - - - -▶ │          │
        │  Smart   │                  │ Foreign  │
        │ investor │ ◀- - - - - - - - │   bank   │
        │          │      8.71%       │          │
        └────┬─────┘                  └─────┬────┘
             │ 8.46%            LIBOR — 25 basis points
             ▼                              ▼
        ┌──────────┐                  ┌──────────┐
        │   GIC    │                  │   Bank   │
        │ investors│                  │depositors│
        └──────────┘                  └──────────┘
```

10:01 A.M. All terms except for the absolute fixed rate are mutually agreed upon to include the following:
  1. Some Bank will pay six-month LIBOR as defined by ISDA.
  2. Any Corporation will pay a fixed rate equal to 100 basis points plus the 8.25 percent coupon, February 1997 U.S. Treasury note yield at the time the swap is completed.
  3. Settlement dates will include every February 22 and August 22 until February 1997.
  4. Payment of interest will take place in arrears.

5. Payments will be made on a net (not gross) basis.
6. An initial LIBOR of 8 percent per annum is specified.
7. Notional principal amount is equal to $25 million.
8. U.S. law will be the governing law.

10:10 A.M. The assistant treasurer is put on hold while the swap trader phones Some Bank's bond trader for the exact price and yield of the 8.25 percent coupon, February 1997 U.S. Treasury note. This yield is used to fix the swap rate. The swap trader immediately gives the assistant treasurer a swap fixed rate of 8.76 percent, 100 basis points plus a note yield of 7.76 percent. The assistant treasurer agrees to this swap rate.

10:11 A.M. The swap trader puts the assistant treasurer on hold once more while instructing Some Bank's bond traders to sell the 8.25 percent coupon, February 1997 U.S. Treasury notes as a hedge against the bank's swap obligation.[3] The swap trader then tells the assistant treasurer to expect a summary telex confirming all verbally agreed upon details.

In this example, the swap transaction takes 11 minutes. Assuming that documentation and credit availability have been preapproved by both counterparties, completion of a swap can take as little as five minutes.

INTEREST RATE SWAP ECONOMICS

Understanding the economics of a swap is critical. Quotation conventions vary. Day counts and frequency of interest rate settlement can impact the effective cost of a swap.

1. *Quotation conventions:* Some debt instruments are quoted on a discount basis, meaning that interest is paid as the difference between a discounted price and par. Other debt instruments pay interest on a coupon basis. To make the conversion from a discount rate to a simple interest in-arrears quotation, the following formula can be used:

$$\text{Simple interest rate} = \frac{365 \times \text{Discount rate}}{360 - (\text{Discount rate} \times DTM)}[4]$$

where *DTM* refers to the number of days from settlement to maturity.

2. *Day count:* Most interest rates are quoted on an annualized basis. However, the calendar year can be defined several different ways. The floating-rate swap interest is computed on the basis of the notional principal amount (NPA) as follows:

NPA × Relevant discount swap rate
× (Period weight equal to the number of actual days in a specified period as a percentage of 360 days)

The fixed-rate swap interest paid on the basis of a premium added to a U.S. Treasury note yield is computed as the NPA × Swap rate × (Period weight equal to the number of actual days in a specified period as a percentage of 365 days). Any fixed swap rate quoted on a discount basis should be converted to a bond equivalent basis.[5] This conversion is easily made by multiplying the annual discount rate quotation by 365/360. For example, a 9.86 percent discount quote equates to a 10 percent bond equivalent basis rate, 9.86% × (365/360) = 10.00%. It is illusory to think that the fixed-rate payor is paying a lower effective rate when the quoted rate is provided on a discount basis.

3. *Frequency of interest payments:* Swap rates are quoted on an annualized basis. However, payment of interest may occur on a monthly, quarterly, semiannual, or annual basis. The frequency of interest payments can affect their true value. It is easy to convert an annual nominal rate to an annual effective rate by using the formula,

$$r^* = (1 + r/t)^t - 1$$

where:

r^* = Effective annual swap rate paid

r = Nominal annual swap rate

t = Number of times interest is paid per year

For example, an annual rate of 12 percent with payment made once per year is equivalent to an annual rate of 11.66 percent with payments made twice per year.[6] The fixed-rate payor must be wary in assessing quoted annual swap rates. If payment of interest occurs more than once per year, the effective swap rate is higher than the quoted or nominal rate.

SWAP RISKS

There are two primary types of risk associated with swaps, counterparty default risk and opportunity risk. *Counterparty risk* is defined as the probability that a swap counterparty will no longer be able to fulfill its contractual obligations. As interest rates change, a counterparty default could result in increased costs for the counterparty who remains. Many swap trading banks use Monte Carlo simulation techniques to measure possible default risk. Myriad studies have been undertaken to accurately assess counterparty risk. While the methods may differ, most researchers conclude that default risk is much less than the face value of the swap.[7] The default risk is a function of the expected future swap fixed-rate–floating-rate differential.

Opportunity risk is difficult to quantify ex ante. Many companies engage in break-even studies that try to measure when the cost of entering a swap would be unattractive relative to direct funding or investment alternatives. Suppose that a company locks in a fixed swap rate today at 10 percent per year and rates unexpectedly fall shortly thereafter. Because the company is obligated to perform under the swap contract, the fixed-rate payor has forgone the opportunity to directly finance its assets with relatively lower rates. Any company seeking to hedge must determine, a priori, the tolerance for how changing economic conditions can affect future financial health.

In conclusion, swaps are a versatile asset-liability management tool. Increased globalization in the financial markets continues to make this product more accessible to companies and financial institutions at competitive costs.

NOTES

1. "Swap Fever: Big Money, Big Risks," *Business Week,* June 1, 1991, pp 102–6.
2. The terms fixed-rate payor and floating-rate payor are defined in the ISDA (International Swap Dealers Association) code of terms and definitions.

346 Section 4 Interest Rate Swaps

3. The amount of U.S. Treasury notes sold short depends on the hedge ratio used. This ratio is a function of the basis risk between swap prices and U.S. Treasury note prices. The chief swap trader usually determines the hedge ratio, which changes over time as market conditions change.
4. Marcia Stigum, *Money Market Calculations: Yields, Break-Evens, and Arbitrage* (Homewood, Ill.: Dow-Jones Irwin, 1981), p. 32.
5. The price of a U.S. Treasury note or bond is equal to the sum of the present value of all future expected payments, (CF_t). Each cash flow represents the dollar payment to the bondholder for a specified six-month period starting with $t = 1$ to $t = n$. The total amount of six-month periods is represented by n.

$$\text{Bond price} = \text{Sum of } [CF_t/(1 + ytm)^t]$$

The yield to maturity, *ytm*, is the semiannual rate used to determine the present value of each dollar cash flow. Usually, this discount rate is doubled to annualize the yield to maturity. When a bond's price is computed this way, the yield to maturity is referred to as the *bond equivalent yield*. An underlying assumption is that all dollar interest payments are reinvested at the *ytm* rate. For more information, see *Bond Markets, Analysis, and Strategies* by Frank J. and T. Dessa Fabozzi (New York: Prentice Hall, 1989), pp. 85–90, 202.

6. Consider a $25 million swap with a fixed rate of 12 percent. Annual interest is $3 million or $25 million × .12. If that same size swap had a fixed rate of 11.66 percent with interest payments made twice a year, total interest is computed as follows:

```
      .1166 × 183/365 × $25 million    = $1,461,493.15
+ $1,461,493.15 × (.1166 × 182/365) =     $84,971.61
    + .1166 × 182/365 × $25 million   = $1,453,506.85
                           Total    $2,999,971.61 or approximately
                                              $3 million
```

7. Several articles discuss how to measure swap counterparty default risk. See "Survey Shows Losses Are Low in Swap Market" by Lisabeth Weiner, *American Banker* 53, no. 2 (July 20, 1988). Also see "Modeling Credit Exposure on Swaps" by Mark Muffett in *Conference on Bank Structure and Competition* (Federal Reserve Bank of Chicago, 1987); and "The Default Risk of Swaps" by Ian A. Cooper and Antonio S. Mello, *The Journal of Finance,* June 1991.

CHAPTER 17

EXISTING AND POTENTIAL CREDIT (OR DEFAULT) RISK IN SWAPS AND DERIVATIVE TRANSACTIONS

Duncan Goldie-Morrison
National Westminster Bank PLC

INTRODUCTION

Since the financial derivatives market began in the early 80s, the growth rate, size, and diversity of activity have astonished the financial community. The absolute size of the market (U.S. $4,000 billion in notional contracts) has attracted considerable attention from users, financial intermediaries, and, recently, regulators. The graph in Figure 17-1 illustrates the growth profile of the market since the reporting commenced in 1987.

The market has obviously grown to its current level because it provides a valuable tool to risk managers around the globe. Prior to the development of swaps and other derivatives contracts, it was expensive, time consuming, and balance sheet intensive for post facto risk reprofiling to be conducted by corporations and investment managers. The private nature of the market had enabled large positions to be managed without the market being aware of such activity. This discretion has considerable benefits and has obviously been a contributing factor to the growth. However, the bilateral and customized nature of the market has, embedded in it, fundamental variations from other hedging markets; that is, as contracts are between two parties, the nonperformance of a counter-

FIGURE 17–1
Reported Swap Market Size

```
                                                                          ■
                                                                       ♦

                                                                  ■
                                                              ♦

                                                         ■
                                                 ■       ♦         ●
                                         ■      ♦            ●
                                       ♦               ●                △
                                           ●                      △
                                ●                △
                  △      △
```

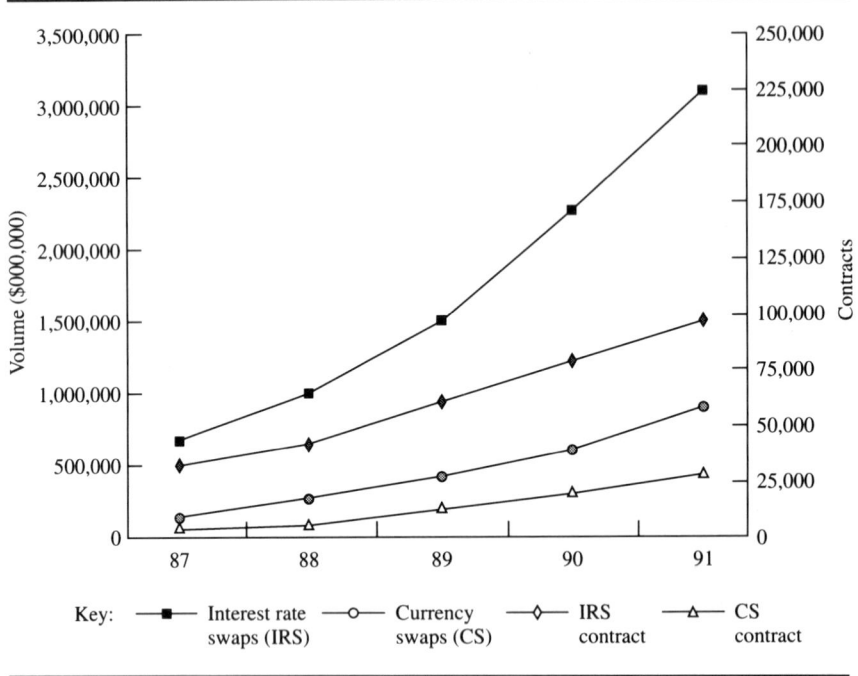

Key: ■ Interest rate swaps (IRS) ○ Currency swaps (CS) ♦ IRS contract △ CS contract

party may lead to loss of expected income and the "disappearance of a hedge." This bilateral exposure, firstly, its probability of occurrence and, secondly, the resulting loss, is the key issue covered in this chapter.

HOW AND WHY DO EXPOSURES OCCUR?

Using market terminology, swaps contracts move *in* and *out of the money* as market prices and rates move. A contract is in the money when the failure of a counterparty to perform on the contract would result in a present value loss, as illustrated in Fig. 17–2.

In Figure 17–2, we see that from Party A's perspective, if Party B defaults and as a result fails to pay the floating rate, Party A would be required to pay a fixed rate of 8 percent, 2 percent above the original contract rate of 6 percent to replace the cash flow from the floating rate. This additional cost of 2 percent per annum, or present value loss of 2 percent per annum discounted at the prevailing market rates for the remaining term of the contract, implied that the original contract had a market value to Party A. Therefore, the contract was in the money.

Contracts remain at the money for very limited periods. Markets are very rarely completely stable. There are a considerable number of reasons for contracts to move away from the money. These would include:

1. Foreign exchange rate movements' effects on currency swaps.
2. The mere passage of time when yield curves are not flat.
3. Change in market volatilities on option contracts.
4. Frequency of payments differing on either side of a swap (e.g., pay quarterly, receive annually).
5. Movement in interest rates over the life of a transaction.

In the 11 years since 1982, global economies have gone through numerous interest rate and currency cycles. In this time period, interest and exchange rates have varied significantly, as displayed in Table 17-1. It is these very market movements that

FIGURE 17-2
Standard Swap Contract

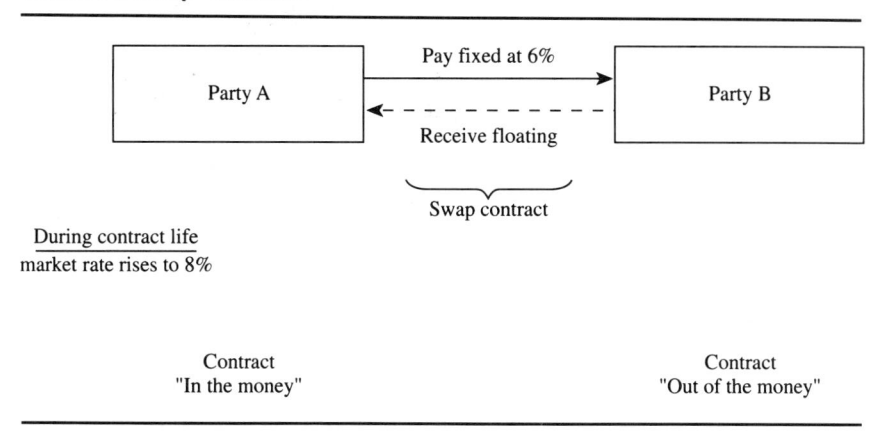

Party A — Pay fixed at 6% → Party B
Party A ← Receive floating — Party B

Swap contract

During contract life
market rate rises to 8%

Contract "In the money" — Contract "Out of the money"

TABLE 17–1
11-Year Price Movement in Market Instruments

Market	Maximum	Minimum
U.S. $ interest rates (6-month LIBOR)	17%	3 3/16%
£ interest rates (6-month LIBOR)	15 7/8%	6 5/8%
U.S. $/deutschemark	3.4538	1.391
U.S. $/yen	227.4634	119.35
$/£	2.004	1.0525

are both the reason for hedging by counterparties and the cause of exposures. As rates move in a direction that suggests that the hedge was appropriate, then an exposure on the counterparty comes into being. In fact, the movement of a hedge contract into the money is, from an end user's perspective, confirmation that the hedge was timely and appropriate. As a result, it is a rule that any contract on the books that has a positive mark-to-market value (that is, the present value of all future receipts exceeds the present value of all future payments) results in an exposure on the counterparty.

These exposures are a normal characteristic of the market and only become of concern when the size of the exposures becomes considerable or the quality of the counterparty (that is, the confidence that the counterparty will perform on its obligations) is in doubt. It is, therefore, key to have a view on both the size of the potential exposure and the relative quality of the counterparty.

PREDICTING POTENTIAL MARK-TO-MARKET VALUE

The value of a hedge contract is expected to change over its life. The extent and pace of this movement are dependent on the underlying variables in the original contract. If the contract is a straightforward single-currency basis trade (6-month LIBOR against three-month LIBOR), then the exposure will be relatively small, predictable, and of short duration. If, on the other hand, the contact is of a long maturity, composed of numerous variables with a zero covariance, and the receipt is structured as a zero coupon–

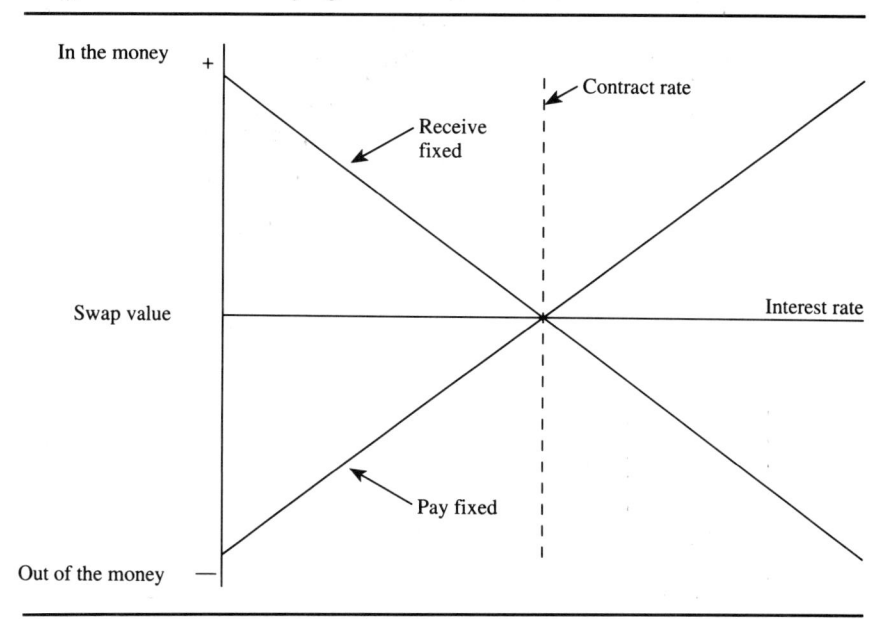

FIGURE 17–3
Swap Valuations in Varying Rate Environments

style payment at maturity, the potential exposure may be very considerable (potentially even greater than the original notional amount of the contract).

The straightforward graphical display in Figure 17–3 illustrates the type of exposures created by interest rate swap values as rates move. Figure 17–3 concerns a swap where one receives the contract rate. The swap value moves to a positive mark-to-market in-the-money value if interest rates fall below the contract rate and vice versa if they rise.

The same analogy would apply to any other forms of derivative contracts be they currency swaps, currency options, interest rate options, or something else. The key issue is to determine the extent of the potential exposure over the life of the contract. Therefore, in the example above, provided we have a relatively high degree of confidence over the maximum potential rate movement over the life of the contract, we have a relatively accurate ability of determining the value of the contract and, therefore, the amount that it may move into the money.

TABLE 17-2
Price of Standard Contract as Replacement Rate Varies

		\multicolumn{5}{c}{Original Term to Maturity}
		5 Year	4 Year	3 Year	2 Year	1 Year	0 Year
Deviation in rate	3.0	−11.09	−9.31	−7.33	−5.14	−2.70	0.00
	−2.5	−9.36	−7.84	−6.16	−4.31	2.26	0.00
	−2.0	−7.57	6.34	−4.97	−3.47	−1.82	0.00
	−1.5	−5.76	4.81	−3.76	−2.62	−1.37	0.00
	−1.0	−3.89	−3.24	−2.53	−1.76	−0.92	0.00
	−0.5	−1.97	−1.64	−1.28	−0.89	−0.46	0.00
	0.00	0.00	0.00	0.00	0.00	0.00	0.00
	0.5	2.02	1.67	1.30	0.90	0.47	0.00
	1.0	4.10	3.39	2.62	1.81	0.93	0.00
	1.5	6.23	5.14	3.97	2.73	1.41	0.00
	2.0	8.42	6.93	5.35	3.67	1.89	0.00
	2.5	10.68	8.76	6.74	4.62	2.37	0.00
	3.0	12.99	10.64	8.17	5.58	2.86	0.00

Table 17-2 above displays the change in contract value in percentage terms when rates deviate from the contract rate against various years to maturity. In this example, we have calculated the contract value change in an interest rate swap from the perspective of the recipient of the fixed payment. It can be seen that the value of the contract increases the longer the term to maturity and the further market rates move away from the contract rate. As a result, the potential value of the contract may be determined relatively simply using very straightforward present value techniques, provided that the expected prevailing rate may be modeled. This aspect is the one detail of this process that leaves the most to be interpreted. How do we do this?

Historic Observations

By using market rate observations, it is possible to build a database for potential rate movements. In this way, we can develop a pattern of expected rate movements. If such a system is to be effective, it needs to be able to be updated and must take into account the prevailing interest rate environment and yield curve shape, together with an ability to absorb any structural changes in the markets. As a consequence, this approach, if it is to be all encompassing, will be very cumbersome and potentially unusable. Therefore, a practical but not a perfect solution is to develop a generic table that indicates potential rate movements regardless of prevailing interest rates and whether the contract is an asset or liability (see Table 17–3).

A brief explanation of Table 17–3 follows:

1. The horizontal axis is the original life of the contract.
2. The vertical axis is the remaining life of the contract.

Therefore:

1. A 10-year original maturity contract with 5 years remaining life has a replacement interest rate that may be 460 basis points away from the original contract rate.
2. A 7-year original maturity contract with 2 years remaining has a potential replacement interest rate that may be 608 basis points away from the original contract rate.

The shortcoming of this approach has been outlined previously and should be obvious to the reader. This historical analysis may be refined to minimize some of these problems, but there are more effective ways of achieving this objective.

TABLE 17–3
Historic Observation Method of Estimating Movement from Current Rates (in Basis Points)

Remaining years in maturity	1	2	3	4	5	6	7	8	9	10
10										159
9									161	171
8								165	194	224
7							170	206	244	284
6						175	218	263	310	360
5					190	238	289	343	400	460
4				210	263	319	378	441	508	578
3			245	301	361	425	493	565	641	721
2		270	329	392	459	531	608	689	774	864
1	300	360	425	495	570	650	735	825	920	1020

Original Term to Maturity

Modeling

We are all aware that interest rates tend to move in a random or stochastic fashion. The ability to model the exact movement in the term structure of interest rates or other variables is the last key to determining the potential market value of a contract. There are two approaches to modeling the term structure of interest rates that are widely available.

   1. *The equilibrium approach.* This method was pioneered by Cox, Ingersoll, and Ross.[1] The approach starts with a description of the underlying economy and assumptions about the stochastic evolution of one or more exogenous factors or state variables in the economy. Assumptions are also made about the preferences of a representative investor. Within this framework, general equilibrium considerations are used to endogenously derive the interest rate.

   2. *The arbitrage approach.* This modeling method, on the other hand, starts from assumptions about the stochastic evolution of one or more interest rates, and derives the prices of all interest rate–contingent claims by imposing the condition that there are no arbitrage opportunities in the economy. This approach was pioneered by Vasicek[2] and Brennan and Schwartz.[3] A significant variation of this approach was developed by Ho and Lee[4] and Heath, Jarrow, and Morton.[5] Whereas the Ho and Lee approach looks at the initial yield curve and considers movements in this curve consistent with the no-arbitrage condition, Heath, Jarrow, and Morton look at movements in forward rates consistent with no arbitrage.

   The equilibrium approach has several advantages over the arbitrage approach. For example, both the term structure and its dynamics are endogenously determined in the former approach. Furthermore, the functional forms of the factor risk premiums (market price of risk) are also obtained as part of the equilibrium. In contrast, the arbitrage approach is silent as to the form of the factor risk premiums. Moreover, the arbitrary choice of the functional form can lead to internal inconsistencies or arbitrage opportunities. The arbitrage approach, however, has the significant advantage of being simple to implement.

In summary, there has been considerable academic research into the modeling of the term structure of interest rates. The reader may wish to delve deeper into this topic. Sources with an intentionally greater analytical content can be reviewed to provide this information.

Testing the Models

There are a multitude of potential models that may be created to forecast future yield curves. A complete chapter could be developed to outline the various approaches, from the simple to considerably more complex mathematical solutions.

Suffice it to say that we may build a model with various modifications that gives a logical, understandable, and defensible set of potential yield curves and absolute rate distributions over a given time frame. This would use some form of lognormal distribution, agreed volatilities at various spot or forward rates, and some form of reflecting barriers or mean-reverting process to prevent rates tending to the absurd in long-maturity transactions (below zero and above some predetermined level).

In summary, the modeling of market rates and prices is a key and fundamental component in determining the potential market value of a contract. To complete this process, it is necessary to determine what level of "comfort" the reader wishes to acquire from this process. Market values of any particular contract may be determined but to this there needs to be added a controlling probability factor. The distribution of potential market values will be similar in appearance to Figure 17–4. This figure depicts a lognormal distribution usually applied to interest rates.

A contract that is out of the money has no risk. Therefore, if the probabilities are symmetrical, then half of the potential distribution results in no loss. The aspect of subjectivity that requires addressing is: At what level does the reader wish to place "the line of confidence"? In Figure 17–5, various probability limits are set down so that the reader may appreciate the necessity for a subjective decision about the level of comfort.

The decision as to what proportion of probable outcomes needs to be catered for in developing such a potential exposure

FIGURE 17-4
Probability Distribution of Potential Interest Rates

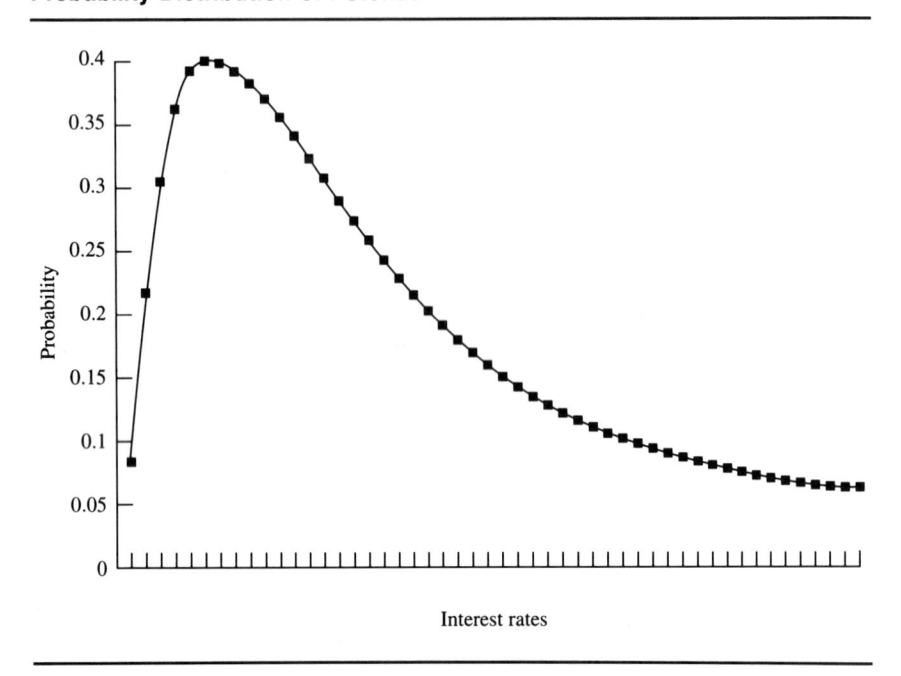

FIGURE 17-5
Normal Probability Curve with Suggested Probability Bands

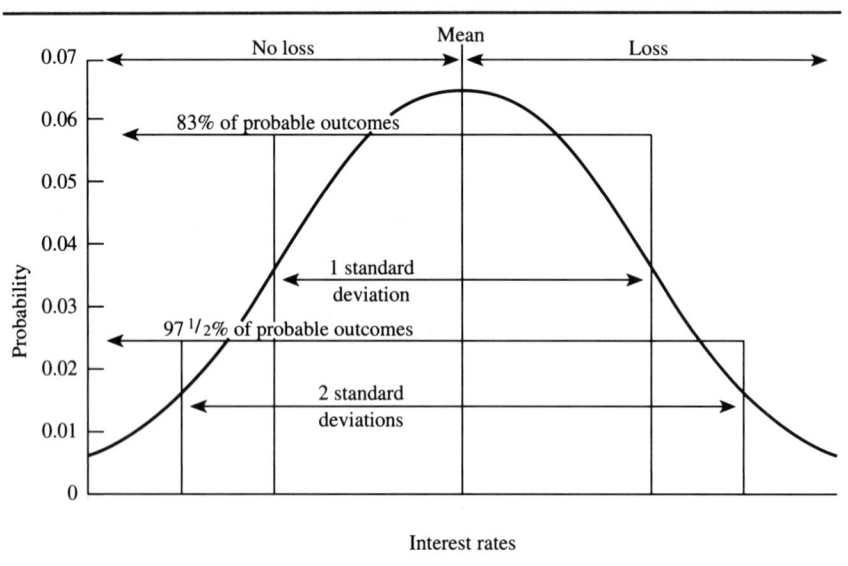

model has significant business implications. In Figure 17–5, if it is decided that one standard deviation is sufficient, 83 percent of potential outcomes are covered. This would create a credit limit usage figure that could be breached significantly in certain circumstances. To avoid such risk of frequent breeches, it may be appropriate to use two standard deviations. This will cover 97½ percent of potential outcomes, a considerably more conservative position. This approach would, on the other hand, apply a potentially higher credit limit usage number and thereby reduce availability for other transactions when the probability of using all credit limits is low.

It is therefore at this point that a business decision needs to be taken to decide the appropriate level of comfort. There is no correct answer; the level and type of activity together with the type of organizations with which one deals need to be considered.

In summary, determining the potential future market rates is not a particularly complex issue. Considerable academic work has been conducted by a number of organizations and individuals to enable the modeling of interest rates and other market variables. The issue that must be determined is: What is the desired level of comfort and how much can this process be simplified to allow for practical implementation?

Rule-of-Thumb Approach

In the early days of the market, various organizations used relatively straightforward guidelines for plain-vanilla transactions. For interest rate swaps, the guideline was 3 percent of the notional value per year of the original maturity of the transaction. For example, a U.S. $100 million five-year swap has a risk amount of U.S. $15 million. U.S. $100 million × 3% × 5 years = U.S. $15 million. Currency swaps used the following guideline: 20 percent of the notional amount for maturities up to three years and then 5 percent additional per year of final maturity up to a maximum of 50 percent, as illustrated in Figure 17–6.

The fact that market rates may be picked, historically, to show that such guidelines would be insufficient to cover exposures in certain circumstances does not detract completely from the use of

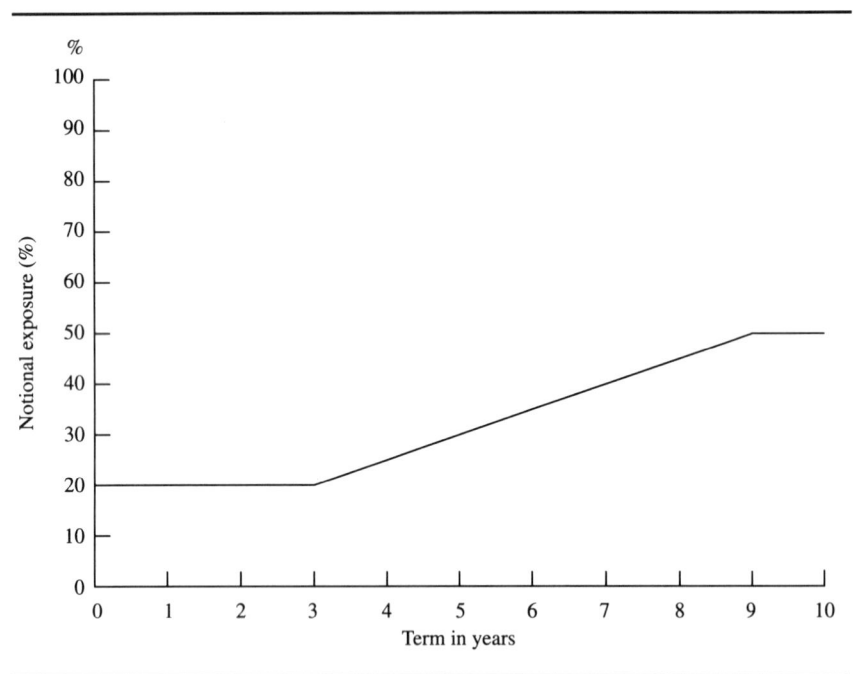

FIGURE 17-6
Rule of Thumb for Cross-Currency Exposure Table

a relatively straightforward set of assumptions, provided the level of activity is relatively minimal and the quality of the counterparties with whom one is transacting is undoubted (this is a very key issue). Such an approach should not be ruled out.

Summary of Market Price Expectations

This section of the chapter has outlined a number of ways of assessing the expected market values of contracts over their life. The simplest and obviously least sophisticated approach is the rule-of-thumb approach that is not structure or prevailing rate sensitive. Developments progressed to a level where historic observations were obtained and statistical profiles were generated on expected rate movements. A further sophistication is the simulation modeling of interest rates and, therefore, a method by which, using computers, expected interest rate curves may generate potential exposure values for transactions over their lives.

The methods outlined above may be refined and further defined indefinitely. Closed-form models may be created, but the differential mathematics become complex. It is my belief that diminishing returns set in relatively rapidly and that the methods, particularly using some of the techniques that have been outlined in this chapter, are totally sufficient for the purposes for which they are intended. Greater research and development is possible but this would have greater application in pricing and portfolio management models than in determining potential credit exposures.

PROBABILITY OF DEFAULT

Now that we have elected to use a particular approach in determining the potential worst-case mark-to-market value of a contract over its life, we need to determine the probability of the counterparty defaulting during the term of the contract. This area of analysis is considerably more subjective and open to greater degrees of error than the previous component. Analysis of default probability is one of the lesser developed disciplines. Next, a number of approaches are discussed and their merits analyzed.

Bank Loan Pricing

Pricing in the market for syndicated bank credits, multiple option facilities, and note issuance facilities is in the public domain. Therefore, by looking at the relative credit quality, expected return on capital for bank stocks, the capital structure of banks, Bank for International Settlements (BIS) capital adequacy guidelines, and the credit quality of borrowers, it is possible to determine the implied premium demanded by the market to absorb the credit risk.

Required Return on Equity
The following formula suggests how to determine an appropriate equity risk premium:

$$ERP = (R_1 + D_1 + I_1) - (R_2 + I_1)$$

where

ERP = Equity risk premium

R_1 = Market return on equity

D_1 = Long-term dividend growth rate

I_1 = Long-term inflation expectations

R_2 = Risk-free return (yield on index-linked risk-free securities)

Therefore:

$$ERP = R_1 + D_1 - R_2$$

If we substitute the values of:

$$R_1 = 5.15\%$$
$$D_1 = 1.9\%$$
$$R_2 = 4.32\%$$
$$ERP = 5.15 + 1.9 - 4.32$$
$$ERP = 2.73\%$$

In the United Kingdom, bank stock currently trades at a discount to the market of 40 percent; therefore, the required return on bank stock is 2.73 × 1.40 = 3.82%.

The Capital Structure of Banks

The loan portfolio of banks is supported by various forms of capital: equity, preferred stock, and subordinated debt. The BIS controls the relative amounts of each category of capital. From this may be determined the weighted return required on capital of a normally structured financial institution. A generic acceptable capital structure would look as follows:

Capital Type	Proportion (%)	Yield over Risk-Free Return	Sum (%)
Common stock	40%	4%	1.6%
Preferred stock	15%	2.5%	0.375%
Subordinated debt	45%	1.0%	0.45%
	100%		2.425%

This gives a weighted-average yield over the risk-free return of 2.43 percent after all costs. From this may be determined the minimum spread required on assets in a bank's balance sheet using the following simple equation:

$$R_3 = [(RFR + ERP) - RFR] \times LR$$

where

R_3 = Required spread over cost of funds net of administration costs, and so on

ERP = Equity risk premium

LR = Leverage ratio

RFR = Risk-free return

As a bank may earn the risk-free return on its free capital, banking assets need to generate only the equity risk premium.

Solving the equation using a leverage ratio of 8.5 percent results in a required spread of about 21 basis points on a 100 percent weighted asset. The 8.5 percent leverage ratio is used since this is the arbitrary figure determined by the BIS, together with the Organisation of Economic Cooperation and Development (OECD) central banks, to be the key ratio for banks under their jurisdiction.

$$R_3 = 2.43 \times .085$$
$$R_3 = .206125, \text{ approximately 21 basis points}$$

This required spread is then used in a comparison of actual spreads achieved in the banking market so that the premium over the minimum spread may be determined. An excess over that amount defined above to produce an adequate return on capital must either be classified as extraordinary profit or that amount determined to cover potential default.

$$POD = \frac{R_4}{CW} - R_3$$

where

POD = Probability of default

R_3 = Required return over cost of funds net of administration costs, and so on

R_4 = Actual return on asset

CW = Counterparty BIS weighting[6]

Using this analysis and publicly available data on syndicated credits completed over the last year, it is possible to determine the probabilities of default and, more importantly, the relative probabilities between various types of borrowers. Table 17–4 displays the credit quality, term, and relative probabilities of default of a wide range of publicly reported syndicated credits. At first glance, Table 17–4 suggests either that the theoretical pricing of loan facilities by banks is suspect or that the analytical approach adopted has faults. As the table shows, there are occasions when the probability of default is less than zero. The numbers or the assumptions used to determine the probabilities must, therefore, be at fault. The results of this analysis are less than satisfactory. It can be seen that

TABLE 17–4
Probability of Defaults Determined from Syndicated Credit Facilities (percent)

Term (years)	AAA	AA	A	BBB
1	−0.0025	−0.0021	0.0004	
1		−0.0001	−0.0021	
1		−0.0002	−0.0005	
1		0.0037	0.0025	
2				0.0010
3	0.0032	−0.0002	0.0066	0.0010
3		−0.0021	−0.0002	0.0027
3			0.0022	
3			−0.0007	
3			0.0005	
3			−0.0013	
3			−0.0011	
4		0.0021	0.0010	
4			0.0058	
4			−0.0012	
5	−0.0025	−0.0025	−0.0010	0.0024
5	−0.0026	−0.0005	0.0022	0.0035
5		−0.0004	−0.0002	0.0035
5		−0.0011	−0.0012	0.0148
5			−0.0006	0.0017
6			−0.0002	0.0030
6			−0.0003	
7			0.0015	

the output appears to be influenced by the following list of exogenous events:

1. The supply of appropriate quality assets.
2. Balance sheet constraints or hunger for assets.
3. Relative cost of borrowing of various organizations.
4. Relationship value. (The ability to balance the rewards received on an individual piece of business against the overall return across all forms of business with a particular customer.)
5. The relative efficiency of the lending organization and its cost of originating and administrating loans.
6. The fact that certain regulators and bank management don't adhere to capital guidelines at all times.

Despite the lack of confidence over Table 17–4, it is apparent that lesser-quality credits do pay more for funding. This can only be an appreciation by the lenders of greater potential default risk. As a consequence, we do not disregard these findings but use them in conjunction with other analyses.

The Bond Markets

Issuance in the public bond markets, both internationally and within domestic markets, is open to public analysis. In addition, the quality of information is deemed to be sound. Since the expansion in the array of issuers tapping the markets during the 80s and the reasonably wide default experience, it is possible to create a picture of historic default probabilities for various quality issuers, terms of issuance, and debt rankings (senior/subordinated debt). Considerable research has been conducted by the rating agencies and academics. A summary of the findings is outlined below:

1. The longer the term of the issuance, the greater the probability of default.
2. The lower the ranking of the debt, the higher the probability of default.
3. The lower the credit quality of the issuer, the higher the probability of default.

364 Section 4 Interest Rate Swaps

In Figure 17–7, the different probabilities of default are graphed by credit quality and term of original obligation. It may be seen that:

1. AAA credits have a very low probability of default (zero for 1-year obligations rising to .09 percent for 10-year obligations).
2. CCC credits have a very high probability of default even for 1-year claims (8 percent), but the gradient of the default line is relatively flat, rising to approximately 9 percent for 10-year obligations.

FIGURE 17–7
Probabilities of Default of Various Quality Credits (basis points)

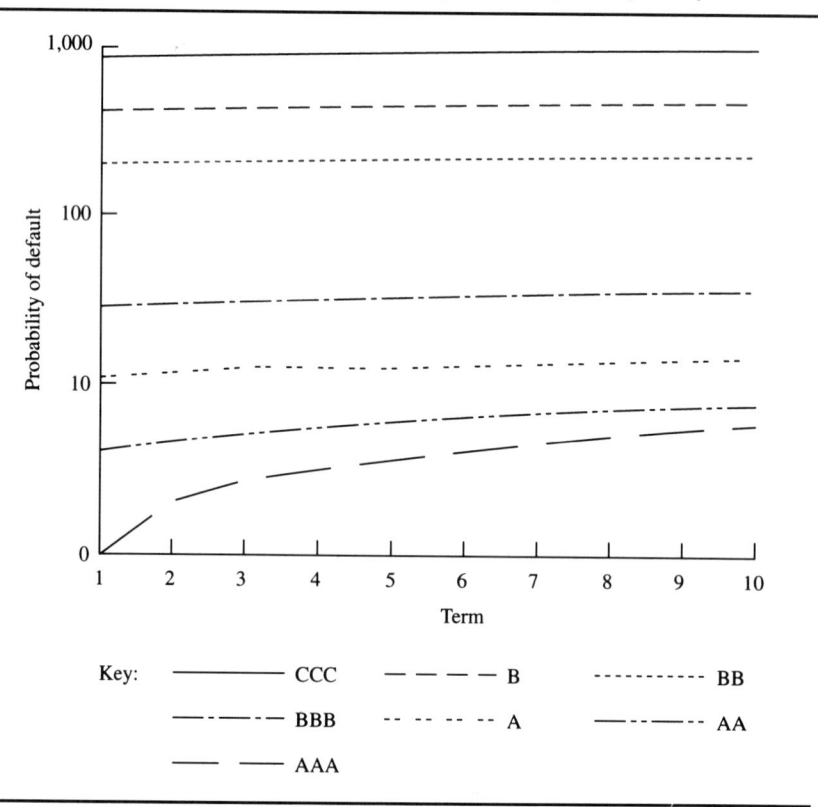

Key:	——— CCC	— — — B	·········· BB
	—·—·— BBB	— ·· — ·· A	—··—·· AA
	—— —— AAA		

The results of this analysis are perfectly logical in principle, but there may be some questions over the exact values being generated. Nevertheless, it is believed that these results present a more logical guide to the probability of default of various qualities and maturities of issuers and issuing structures than the previous approach. There are again exogenous factors that may suggest these results should not be taken as gospel.

1. The period of default analysis is limited to the 1980s.
2. The experience has principally taken place in the United States and has had a large influence exerted on it by the defaults of excessively leveraged companies created during the buyout binge in the mid-80s. The steady conversion of equity to debt that occurred in this period has abated considerably, and, therefore, the analysis today may be different.
3. The fact or potential for government intervention in various economies, particularly with respect to bank crises, is not awarded its complete premium.
4. The effect of rescheduling and recoveries is not as well known. For example, if a defaulting party repays its complete obligations, then, despite the fact that a default occurred, no actual loss was incurred.
5. The bond market analysis works for generic-rated entities, but it is not possible to divide the risks by industry, segment, or geography.
6. The default probability may be influenced by the same factors that cause exposures on swaps contracts. Therefore, it is possible to either have compensating or exacerbating positions.

Summary

Assessing the probability of default of a counterparty is less than accurate despite the sophisticated research that has taken place in producing the findings. There are, in fact, a number of other methods that may be used to hone further the results, but it is my belief

TABLE 17-5
The Required Return on Interest Rate Swap to Cover the Probability of Default Only (Basis Points per Annum)

Maturity (years)	AAA	AA	A	BBB	BB
1	0.0	0.0	0.0	0.05	0.25
2	0.0	0.0	0.05	0.15	0.9
3	0.0	0.05	0.1	0.35	1.85
4	0.05	0.1	0.2	0.55	3.1
5	0.1	0.15	0.35	0.9	4.6
6	0.15	0.25	0.5	1.25	6.25
7	0.25	0.4	0.65	1.65	7.55
8	0.4	0.5	0.8	2.1	9.8
9	0.5	0.65	1	2.55	11.6
10	0.6	0.8	1.25	6.1	13.4
11	0.75	0.95	1.45	3.55	15.15
12	0.9	1.15	1.65	4.05	16.85
13	1.05	1.35	1.9	2.3	18.55
14	1.25	1.5	2.15	5.15	20.2
15	1.45	1.75	2.35	5.65	21.8
16	1.6	1.95	2.6	19.7	23.35
17	1.8	2.15	2.9	6.8	24.9
18	2.05	2.35	3.15	7.4	26.4
19	2.25	2.55	3.4	7.95	27.85
20	2.45	2.85	3.65	8.55	29.20

that these new and advanced methods will not change the results radically.

We now have some idea of both the expected cost of default (ECOD) discussed in the previous section of this chapter and the probability of such default occurring. In this way, we may determine the effect on a participant in the derivatives markets in terms of weighted probable loss over the life of a portfolio and, therefore, the appropriate levels of reserves.

Table 17–5 illustrates summary "insurance premia" in basis points per annum to create a reserve sufficient to cover expected credit losses over the life of the substantial portfolio of mature interest rate derivatives contracts (principally, interest rate swaps in a wide range of currencies).

The values displayed in Table 17–5 are interesting, but how should they be used?

1. For end users, the key must be the ultimate performance of the counterparty, not necessarily the aggressiveness of the price. Therefore, the table may be used as a set of guidelines as to the minimum expected price differences required to compensate for different maturities and credit qualities of counterparties.

2. For market makers, Table 17–5 sets down the minimum reserve levels necessary to cover counterparty default. It is assumed that there is no such thing as a credit risk–free portfolio of derivative contracts unless all trades are with the domestic government in the domestic currency. As a result, despite the fact that counterparties are of prime quality, there is a probability that a default will occur over time. This probability is exceedingly small with very high quality credits and particularly if the term of the contracts is short. Nevertheless, the risk is still there. As a result, it is prudent and sensible to create a "reserve" to cover anticipated credit losses on a portfolio. The figures in Table 17–5 suggest the type of level of reserve that are appropriate. It may be seen that an AAA entity has a negligible reserve when the term is short whereas BB entities, due to the higher probability of default, require a considerably greater reserve as maturities lengthen.

WHAT HAPPENS WHEN A DEFAULT OCCURS?

The mechanics and reality of handling a default do not always mirror each other. The mechanics are reasonably straightforward and are governed by the document containing the terms and provisions of the contract. We do not offer a detailed analysis of the International Swap Dealers Association (ISDA) document. However, it may nevertheless be appropriate to summarize the ISDA's default mechanism, which is designed to be simple yet complete. Swap transactions have, for the past five years, been transacted almost exclusively on the basis of the ISDA's document published in 1987. This document has been superseded by ISDA's 1992 Agreement, which modifies the earlier version, attempts to rectify various shortcomings, and reflects market practice as it stands today. The following discussion incorporates, where relevant, the 1992 modifications.

In the first place, it is important to realize that the occurrence

of any one of the following events will constitute an event of default under the provisions of Clause (5a) of the ISDA document:
1. Failure to make any payments due under the ISDA agreement.
2. Breach of the ISDA agreement.
3. Credit support default.
4. Default under any specified transaction.
5. Cross default.
6. Bankruptcy.
7. Merger without assumption.

It is not necessary to explore the various events in any detail; it is sufficient to appreciate that they constitute a series of individually separate ways to default under the ISDA agreement and that by far the most discussed—and, perhaps, the most important—is bankruptcy.

If an event of default does occur, the nondefaulting party has the right, but is not under any obligation, to give up to 20 days' notice specifying that a particular date will be an early termination date. However, in regard to bankruptcy under the 1987 version of the ISDA document, an early termination date will automatically occur. Under the terms of the ISDA 1992 Agreement, the parties have the option of specifying in a "schedule" that "automatic termination" will apply, in which case upon bankruptcy an early termination date will occur.

Upon early termination, certain calculations will need to be made. In order to understand the mechanism, the following terms must be understood: market quotation, settlement amount, and unpaid amounts.

Probably the most complicated definition contained within the ISDA document is that of *market quotation*. The following list attempts to set out the basic principles:
1. Market quotation is always looked at with respect to a particular party.
2. The ISDA spells out which party is to obtain any market quotation(s):
    a. Where an event of default has occurred, any market quotation(s) will be obtained by the nondefaulting party.
    b. Where a termination event has occurred, any market

quotation(s) will be obtained by one or both parties (depending upon whether or not both are affected parties).
3. Each market quotation relates to a specific swap transaction between the parties.
4. Market quotations provide a figure representing the amount to be paid to or by a third party in order that it will enter into a swap transaction on identical financial terms beginning on the first day of the current rollover period.
5. The market quotation is derived from figures provided by individual banks known as reference market makers. If more than three quotations are obtained, the highest and lowest are discarded; the market quotation is defined as the average of the remaining quotations.
6. The figure will be positive if the party obtaining the market quotation will have to pay a third party to enter into a replacement swap (i.e., the swap is in the money).
7. The figure will be negative if the party obtaining the market quotation will receive payment from a third party for entering into a replacement swap (i.e., the swap is out of the money).

Having obtained market quotations for each live transaction in a portfolio, the sum of those market quotations (whether negative or positive) is defined as the *settlement amount*. If that figure is positive, the portfolio is in the money to the nondefaulting party. If it is negative, the portfolio is out of the money to the nondefaulting party.

Unpaid amounts are defined essentially as amounts that remain unpaid to each party and that were due as at the end of the last rollover period.

Calculations

In the event of early termination, the settlement amount is added to the unpaid amounts of the nondefaulting party. The unpaid amounts of the defaulting party are then deducted to obtain a final figure that will be positive or negative. A positive figure indicates that the nondefaulting party [*not* the swap(s)] is out of the money. A negative figure indicates that the defaulting party [*not* the swap(s)] is out of the money.

Limited Two-Way Payments

Some parties opt for termination on the basis of *limited two-way payments* (renamed *first method and market quotation* in the ISDA 1992 Agreement). This has the following effects. If the final figure is positive, the nondefaulting party's out-of-the-money position must be made good. However, if the final figure is negative, the defaulting party's out-of-the-money position will not be made good. The defaulting party simply walks away from the counterparty.

Although there are various cases to be made for this approach, the perceived unfairness of permitting the nondefaulting party to benefit from an undeserved windfall has led several swap participants to opt instead for *full two-way payments*.

Full Two-Way Payments

Termination using full two-way payments (renamed *second method and market quotation* in the ISDA 1992 Agreement) has the following effect. If the final figure is positive, the nondefaulting party's out-of-the-money position must be made good. He or she will therefore be paid the figure by the defaulting party. Conversely, if the final figure is negative, the defaulting party's out-of-the-money position must be made good. He or she will therefore be paid the figure by the nondefaulting party. Essentially, where the parties opt for full two-way payments termination, the position of the parties regarding settlement payment in an event of default situation will mirror the mutual obligations imposed when a termination event occurs.

Security

It is generally unusual for swap parties to be specifically secured with respect to their swap transactions, and, under the ISDA language, neither party takes security over the assets of the other. This can be a cause for serious concern during cash crises or periods of administration. However, large financial institutions—particularly banks—will also provide a swap counterparty with routine banking services for which the counterparty may have deposited cash, securities, or other assets.

In the event of nonpayment, by liquidation or winding up of the defaulting party, the holder of such securities will normally be permitted to set off any amounts due with respect to a terminated swap transaction against the realizable value of his or her share of those securities. If the debt is still not satisfied after setoff, the party will become a general creditor for the remaining amount.

Where a party is wholly unsecured, he or she becomes an unsecured creditor for the full amount owed.

Commercial Considerations

If net, the swap portfolio is in the money to the nondefaulting party—and going deeper into the money—and the nondefaulting party may consider holding off from calling default and designating an early termination date (since the value of the portfolio will crystallize on the basis of the yield curve's values at the early termination date). However, to play the market in this way during a default situation can seriously damage your swaps portfolio. First, the market may move against you quickly and unexpectedly. Second, if you are considering calling default, others are probably doing the same; there is little point in delaying the establishment of your claim. Third, a liquidator may claim that any profit made as a result of delaying a default call constitutes a preference (where the defaulting party cooperates in the delay) and may seek to reclaim it. Fourth, you risk facing the argument that you have waived the default, particularly if it is one of the "lesser events." Fifth, it is not particularly good manners; your counterparty should know where he or she stands.

As a general rule then, if you intend unequivocally to call default, you should do so as soon as possible and designate an early termination date. You should simultaneously hedge your position on the early termination date or you will be exposed. The speed at which the value of a transaction may move further against the nondefaulting party may be very rapid and, therefore, immediate action is the best course of action.

Although it is essential to be aware of what is going on at termination, it is important to speak to an experienced swaps lawyer. A lot of money may be lost very quickly if correct procedures are not followed. We have seen a bank take a large hit because it did not follow the ISDA's notation procedure exactly.

As stated previously, the reality of terminating a contract and eliminating the implied risk involves considerably more complex issues than those outlined above. There is insufficient space to deal in detail with other factors such as extra-swap relationships and political pressures.

Default History

Despite the absolute size of the market and its phenomenal growth over the last 10 years, as outlined in the opening of this chapter, there has been a very limited number of defaults. This information is very subjective and patchy as reporting of losses on bilateral market contracts is not well defined or publicly available. Nevertheless, it is public knowledge that one dealer defaulted (Drexel Burnham Lambert), but the extent of losses, if, in fact, there were any losses, is not publicly known.

It is believed that the users of the financial derivatives markets are of the highest quality; therefore, default and loss experience is expected to be low. This view has been endorsed by the BIS when it recommended that swaps receive a maximum counterparty weighting of 50 percent.

The one major exception to this loss experience is the multi-lateral rescinding of contracts by the U.K. local authorities in 1988–89. This declaration by a number of local authorities that the contracts were void caused significant losses to the banking community. This event should not be classified as a credit loss but more a legal loss. The courts held that the local authorities were not empowered to enter into hedging contracts and, therefore, declared all hedging contracts *ultra vires* (outside the powers of). This issue has opened up a whole debate on the enforceability of hedging contracts with unincorporated entities. The contents of these legal problems are outside the scope of this chapter.

Default Survey

A recent release from the ISDA stated that in a recent survey of a representative group of major dealers (representing 70 percent of market activity) loss experience totaled U.S. $358.36 million or 0.0115 percent of the contract notionals outstanding at the time.

U.K. local authorities accounted for almost 50 percent of this loss and, therefore, actual credit losses were in the order of U.S. $175 million or 0.0056 percent of notional contracts outstanding.

A conclusion that may be drawn from these results is that swap users have historically been of the highest quality and that, although the default analysis is necessary, the actual experience of loss across the whole industry has been very low.

The Regulatory Framework for Banks

Until 1987, the regulation of financial institutions and, in particular, banks was conducted by the national regulators. There was no single system or level playing field. In July 1988, the BIS issued a paper entitled "International Convergence of Capital Measurement and Capital Standards." This document was intended to be used by national regulators as guidelines for the capital structure and capital allocation against risk assets of banks within OECD countries. The guidelines for derivatives contracts and, in particular, swaps are listed below.

There are two approaches:

1. *The original exposure method.* Participants in the market who are not very active are able to use a charge against capital determined using an agreed percentage of the original notional amount. This method is called the *original exposure method* as a deemed capital exposure and risk asset position is assumed throughout the life of the contract, regardless of its market value.

2. *Current market value (replacement value approach).* The regulators anticipated and now require more market makers and market participants to apply the following method to determine the size of risk assets held within the derivatives books and, therefore, the amount of "capital" required to support these risk asset positions.
    a. For contracts up to one year, determine the size of risk assets by using mark-to-market value.
    b. For interest rate contracts over one year, use mark-to-market value plus 0.5 percent of the notional amount.
    c. For currency swaps, use mark-to-market value plus 5 percent of the notional amount.

These asset positions as defined by the guidelines above need to be adjusted by the counterparty weightings to convert them to risk-adjusted assets. Counterparty weightings are defined by local regulators and their interpretation of the BIS paper. A simple interpretation of this, which is not accurate in all places, is the application of a 20 percent weighting for regulated financial institutions (banks) and a maximum of 50 percent for corporations and nonbank entities. Government and quasi-government entities are treated differently depending on jurisdiction, but vary between zero and 50 percent. From this we may determine the risk-adjusted assets.

Example 1
A U.S. $100 million interest rate swap has a value of $10 million with a corporation.

$$\text{Risk-adjusted assets} = [\$10 \text{ million} \times (100 \times 0.5)] \times 0.5$$
$$= \$5.25 \text{ million}$$

Example 2
A U.S. $100 million five-year swap has a value of (−$10 million) with the bank.

$$\text{Risk-adjusted assets} = 100 \times 0.5\% \times 20\%$$
$$= \$100,000$$

The regulatory framework devised by the BIS in conjunction with key national regulators (the Federal Reserve, The Bundesbank, the Bank of England, and so on) is continually being reviewed. In addition, particularly in Europe, other international regulators have input. The EEC is codifying capital guidelines within its sphere of authority to cover banks and securities houses. These guidelines are expected to cover not only capital and credit aspects but also market risk and large exposures. The BIS currently has initiatives under way that are researching the concept of netting and its effect on capital. This topic is of considerable interest to the derivatives businesses because considerably more regulatory capital is required to support a gross position than a net position (in which long and short positions provide offsets to each other).

CONCLUSION

This chapter should have provided the reader with a feeling, if not a view, on the reasons that counterparty risks are inherent in financial derivatives transactions, their quantifications, and the probabilities of risks occurring. There is no substitute for working through various examples to gain an understanding of the practical applications of the concepts contained here.

NOTES

1. J. C. Cox, J. E. Ingersoll, and S. A. Ross, "A Theory of the Term Structure of Interest Rates," *Econometrica* 53 (1985), pp. 385–407; J. C. Cox, J. E. Ingersoll, and S. A. Ross, "A General Equilibrium Framework for Asset Pricing," *Econometrica* 53 (1985); and J. C. Cox, J. E. Ingersoll, and S. A. Ross, "A Reexamination of the Term Structure of Interest Rates," *Journal of Finance* 52 (1981).
2. O. A. Vasicek, "An Equilibrium Characterization of the Term Structure," *Journal of Financial Economics* 5 (1977), pp. 177–88.
3. M. J. Brennan and E. S. Schwartz, "A Continuous Time Approach to Pricing of Bonds," *Journal of Banking and Finance* 3 (July 1979), pp. 133–55.
4. T. S. Y. Ho and S. B. Lee, "Term Structure Movements and Pricing Interest Rate Contingent Claims," *Journal of Finance* 41 (1986), pp. 1011–29.
5. David Heath, Robert Jarrow, and Andrew Morton, "Bond Pricing and the Term Structure of Interest Rates: A Discrete Time Approximation," *Journal of Financial and Quantitative Analysis* 25, no. 4 (1990), pp. 419–40.
6. Counterparty weightings are arbitrary BIS-defined weightings applied to various asset classes in banks. They are principally designed to adjust the amount of capital required to support specific assets. The leverage ratio of 8.5 percent is adjusted by the counterparty weighting when determining the amount of capital required to support that asset. Loans to regulated financial institutions are weighted 20 percent whereas loans to corporations attract a 100 percent weighting; swap contracts attract a maximum weighting of 50 percent regardless of counterparty.

CHAPTER 18

A NO-ARBITRAGE TERM STRUCTURE MODEL AND THE VALUATION OF INTEREST RATE SWAPS

Thomas O'Brien
University of Connecticut

INTRODUCTION

The primary objective of this chapter is to explain the details of a no-arbitrage model of the term structure of interest rates. The second objective is to demonstrate the valuation of default-free interest rate swaps and to apply the term structure model to a particular kind of swap. Default (credit) risk is ignored, although it is a significant issue, in order to focus on interest rate risk.

The chapter first explains the distinction between two basic varieties of interest rate swaps, (1) plain-vanilla, or generic, swaps, and (2) delayed-reset, or in-arrears, swaps. The valuation of plain-vanilla swaps is relatively easy and does not require a theoretical term structure model. All that is necessary is the observed yield curve. The valuation of delayed-reset swaps is not as easy, however, and, in order to find the value of a delayed-reset swap, a theoretical term structure model must be used.

INTEREST RATE SWAPS

Interest rate swaps have a set maturity and a contractual fixed interest rate. Swap cash flows are based on the difference between a floating, or short, interest rate and the fixed, contractual rate of the swap.

Floating Short Rates

A hypothetical lattice of potential short rates is shown in Figure 18–1. The short rates in Figure 18–1 may be viewed as possible LIBOR spot rates (with default risk assumed away). For convenience, these rates are assumed to be one-year rates; correspondingly, swap cash flow settlement is assumed to take place annually, even though semiannual settlements are standard in practice. The current one-year LIBOR spot rate is observable and is assumed to be 6 percent.

The *short rate* is defined to be the rate on a default-free, single-period bill. Over a single period, this rate is what finance theorists have referred to as the (nominal) *risk-free rate*. Even though the short rate is assumed to be stochastic and state-dependent, the short rate for a given single period is always known at the beginning of its period.

FIGURE 18–1
Hypothetical Short-Rate Movements

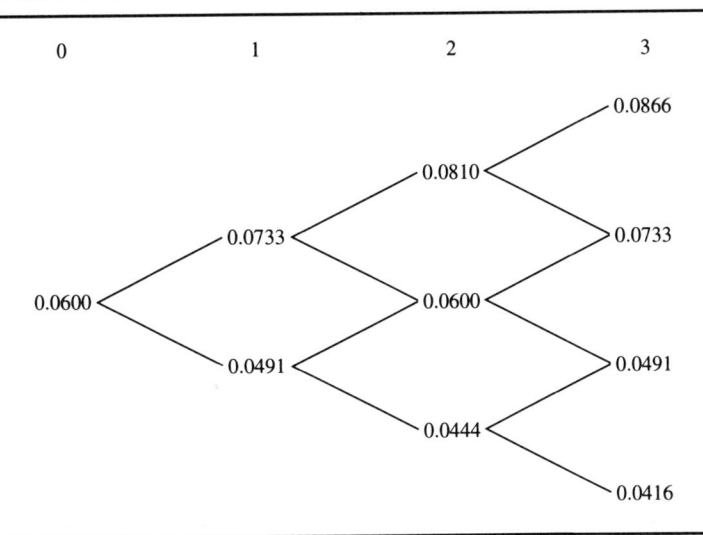

```
      0           1          2          3
                                     0.0866
                            0.0810
                  0.0733              0.0733
      0.0600                0.0600
                  0.0491              0.0491
                            0.0444
                                     0.0416
```

If the short rate at Time t is 7 percent, for example, this means that a bill with a face value of 100 at Time $t + 1$ has a Time t value of $100/1.07 = 93.46$.

Plain-Vanilla Interest Rate Swaps

The basic idea behind a plain-vanilla swap is that the Time $t + 1$ cash flow to the long swap position is found by multiplying the notional principal by the difference between the Time t floating (short) rate and the swap's contractual fixed rate.

For example, consider a three-year plain-vanilla swap with a fixed rate of 7 percent. For a notional principal of 100, the Time 1 swap cash flow is $100(0.06 - 0.07) = -1.00$, since the Time 0 short rate is 6 percent. Since the swap cash flow is defined from the perspective of the receipts by the long position, a swap cash flow of -1.00 means that the long position must pay 1.00 to the short position. If the Time 1 up state (the top-most rate) occurs and, thus, if the Time 1 short rate is 0.0733, the Time 2 cash flow is $100(0.0733 - 0.07) = 0.33$; if the Time 1 short rate is 0.0491, the Time 2 cash flow is -2.09, and so forth.

Figure 18–2 shows all of the potential cash flows for the three-year plain-vanilla interest rate swap, given the possible short rates hypothesized in Figure 18–1.

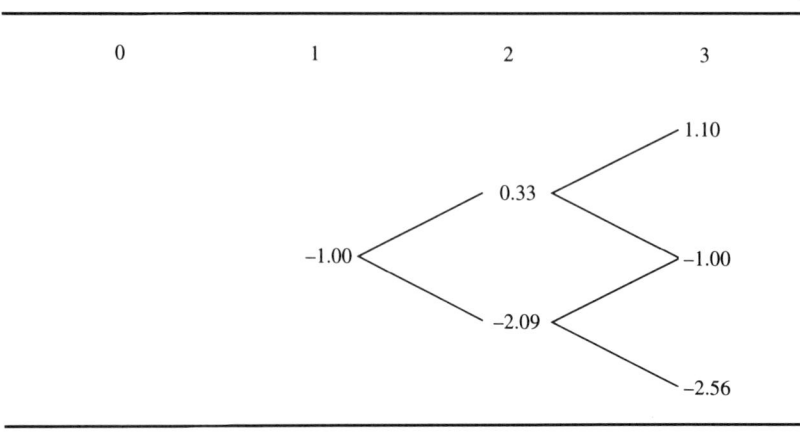

FIGURE 18–2
Cash Flows of a Three-Year 7 Percent Plain-Vanilla Interest Rate Swap

```
     0          1          2          3

                                      1.10
                         0.33
              -1.00                  -1.00
                        -2.09
                                     -2.56
```

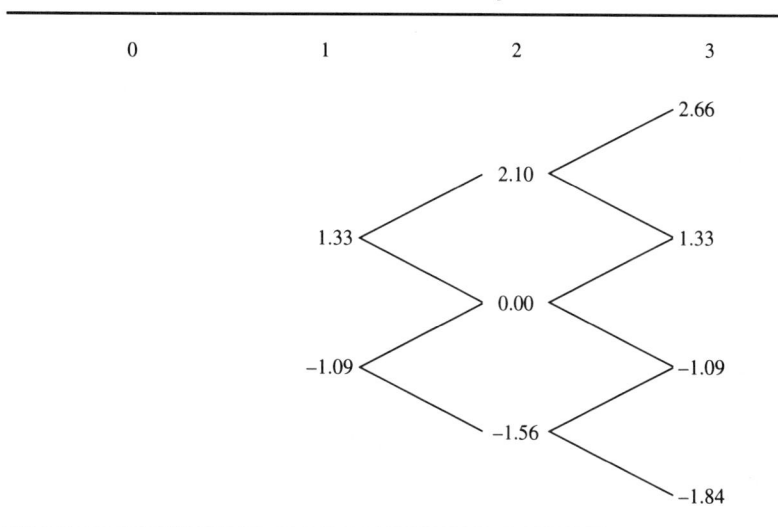

FIGURE 18-3
Cash Flows of a Three-Year 6 Percent Delayed-Reset Interest Rate Swap

```
       0            1            2            3
                                           2.66
                               2.10
                  1.33                     1.33
                               0.00
                 -1.09                    -1.09
                              -1.56
                                          -1.84
```

Delayed-Reset (In-Arrears) Swaps

A delayed-reset swap is similar to a plain-vanilla swap, but the difference is that the cash flow at Time t is determined by the short rate observed at Time t rather than the short rate at Time $t - 1$. (See Smith, Smithson, and Wilford 1990.)

For example, consider a delayed-reset swap with a fixed rate of 6 percent and notional principal of 100. At Time 1, if the up state occurs, the swap's long position will receive $100(0.0733 - 0.06) = 1.33$ from the short position. If the down state occurs at Time 1, the swap's long position receives $100(0.0491 - 0.06) = -1.09$, which means that the long position must pay 1.09 to the short position.

All of the cash flows of a 6 percent delayed-reset swap, given the floating-rate movements of Figure 18-1, are shown in Figure 18-3.

An "at-market" swap originates at a fixed rate that results in a Time 0 value of zero for the swap and thus no Time 0 cash flow in either direction. If the fixed rate of a swap is "off market," there will be some Time 0 value to the swap.

Valuation of Plain-Vanilla Interest Rate Swaps

The guiding principle in the valuation of a plain-vanilla swap is the notion that the swap may be viewed as a combination of a floating-rate note and a fixed coupon bond.

A floating-rate note is an instrument whose Time $t + 1$ interest payment is always determined by the Time t short rate. Thus, given our example, a floating-rate note would pay 6 percent interest at Time 1. At Time 2, the floating-rate note would pay either 7.33 percent or 4.91 percent interest, depending on which state of nature occurs at Time 1.

Thus a floating-rate note has the characteristic that each period's cash flow is determined by the same rate at which it should be discounted. Therefore, the floating-rate note should always have a value of par.

Since the par values of a floating-rate note and a fixed coupon bond wash at maturity, a long position in a plain-vanilla swap is equivalent to a long position in a floating-rate note and a short position in a fixed coupon bond, with the coupon rate equal to the swap's fixed interest rate.

Thus, since the value of a floating-rate note is always par, valuing a plain-vanilla swap is essentially a matter of valuing a fixed coupon bond, which can be easily accomplished using the currently observed discount yield curve. To demonstrate, consider an example valuation of a three-year, seven percent coupon bond, assuming the following observed discount yield curve:

Time to Maturity	Yield to Maturity
1 year	6%
2 years	6.2%
3 years	6.4%

The value of the 7 percent coupon bond (for par of 100) is $7/1.06 + 7/1.062^2 + 107/1.064^3 = 101.64$.

The value of the plain-vanilla swap, from the long position perspective, is the value of the floating-rate note (par) minus the value of the 7 percent coupon bond, since the long swap position is equivalent to a long position in the floating-rate note and a short position in the coupon bond. Thus the Time 0 value of the swap is

100 − 101.64 = −1.64. The interpretation of this negative value is that the short position must pay 1.64 to the long position to originate this swap at Time 0.

Thus the valuation of a plain-vanilla swap is a relatively easy matter. The valuation can be accomplished by observing the current discount yield curve and does not require a theoretical model of the term structure.

A delayed-reset swap is not as straightforward to value, however. A delayed-reset swap cannot be viewed as a portfolio of a floating-rate note, with a constant value of par, and a fixed coupon bond. In a delayed-reset swap, the floating-rate component may be viewed as a note that pays Time t interest at a rate determined by the realization of the short rate at Time t. Thus, this note pays interest at a rate that is uncertain at the time prior to the payment. Thus the cash flow is *not* generated and discounted at the same rate, and the floating-rate note component does not maintain a constant par value. This feature is what calls for the application of a theoretical term structure pricing model.

NO-ARBITRAGE TERM STRUCTURE MODELS

Classes of Theoretical Term Structure Models

There exist a number of theoretical no-arbitrage term structure models. Existing models fall into one of three classes, according to how much of the currently observed yield curve is used as an input to the model.

One class of models makes assumptions about (1) the current short rate, (2) the stochastic process of the short rate, and (3) the market price of interest rate risk function. The object is then to use this information to derive the theoretical yield curve and its stochastic movements. Some well-known models in this class are Vasicek (1977); Cox, Ingersoll, and Ross (1985); and Rendleman and Bartter (1980).

A second class of models uses the entire currently observed yield curve as an input, makes assumptions about volatility and the market price of interest rate risk functions, and derives stochastic processes for all rates consistent with this information and no-arbitrage conditions. Two well-known examples in this class are Ho and Lee (1986) and Black, Derman, and Toy (1990).

The first class of models is, in principle, useful in trying to specify what the theoretical yield curve should look like. The second class of models is useful in the valuation of interest-sensitive derivative securities, relative to the currently observed actual yield curve.

A third class of models consists of hybrids of the first two. For example, the Brennan-Schwartz (1982) model assumes (1) the current short rate, (2) a stochastic process for the short rate, (3) the current consol rate, and (4) a stochastic process for the consol rate. Thus the Brennan-Schwartz model specifies more information about the currently observed and future yield curves than the first class, but not the entire term structure. The third class of models appears useful in identifying potential arbitrage strategies between bonds of various maturities along the yield curve, given that the parameter inputs for the model are correct.

Basic Characteristics of No-Arbitrage Term Structure Models

Term structure models of any of the above classes may differ in three basic characteristics. The first is trading horizon, that is, discrete versus continuous. The majority of models employ continuous trading, but a few are in discrete time. The easiest setting to understand is the discrete-time binomial (two-state) framework employed by Rendleman and Bartter (1981) and Ho and Lee (1986).

The second characteristic is the number of general economic factors influencing the yield curve's shape. The Brennan-Schwartz model, for example, is a two-factor model, but the simplest and most popular models are single-factor models, like Vasicek (1977), Rendleman and Bartter (1980), Black, Derman, and Toy (1990), and the single-factor versions of Cox, Ingersoll, and Ross (1985), and Ho and Lee (1986). Single-factor models can be made quite rich by allowing the market price of interest rate risk to vary with the level of the short rate.

The third characteristic is the stochastic process assumed for the short rate. Following Cox, Ingersoll, and Ross, processes with mean-reverting characteristics, with rates never falling below zero, are the most popular.

A DISCRETE-TIME, SINGLE-FACTOR CONSOL RATE MODEL

Following Brennan and Schwartz, the model here employs stochastic movements of the consol rate, or yield on a perpetual, coupon-paying, default-free bond, as an input, along with the assumed stochastic process for the short rate. This feature places the model here into the third class of term structure models outlined above.

The popular assumption of a single-factor model is also made. Thus the model is something of a single-factor special case of the Brennan-Schwartz two-factor model (except that different stochastic processes are employed).

The single-factor assumption implies that yields on debt instruments of all maturities are perfectly correlated over the shortest holding period. This feature permits the use of the consol bond as an underlying "pricing bond," implicitly accounting for the market price of interest rate risk function, as well as for the stochastic process probabilities. The use of the consol as a pricing bond results in a method for finding preference-free, no-arbitrage values for the rest of the yield curve and interest-sensitive derivatives. This concept was originally employed by Vasicek (1977).

Unlike Vasicek, however, we employ a discrete-time, binomial framework in order to convey the intuition of the model. In that sense, the model is similar in spirit to the no-arbitrage stock option model of Cox, Ross, and Rubinstein (1979).

Short-Rate Movements

One is free to construct one's own two-state lattices of potential short-rate and consol rate movements, within the limits of reasonable economic judgment. Figure 18–1 shows the particular three-period short-rate movements to be employed in the exposition here. The method used to construct Figure 18–1 is explained after a discussion of some of the process characteristics and features.

No probabilities of up-state and down-state movements are specified in Figure 18–1. The reason for this feature, as will be made clear later, is due to the use of the consol as an underlying pricing bond. The situation is similar to the use of underlying stock movements, without probabilities, in the Cox-Ross-Rubinstein (1979) binomial stock option valuation model.

The short-rate movements in Figure 18-1 possess the property that the dispersion of the N-year possible rates grows less than proportionately to N. In other words, and for example, the dispersion of the possible rates two years from now is less than twice the dispersion of possible rates one year from now. This characteristic is intuitively appealing and is consistent with the notion of negative correlation and mean reversion.

The movements in Figure 18-1 also possess the feature that volatility, for a given level of interest rates, does not depend on calendar time. For example, for a given horizon, the future volatility from the 6 percent node at Time 0 is the same as the future volatility from the 6 percent node at Time 2 and any future times. Volatility does depend on the rate level, with volatility decreasing as rates diverge from the central tendency. Thus, volatility may change over time as rates change, but volatility does not change due to the mere passage of time.

Of course, if one forecasts that basic economic uncertainty is going to change in the future for fundamental reasons, then one may purposely input a process for rates for which volatility does change with calendar time. In the absence of such a forecast, there appears to be no economic reason for the volatility of interest rates to be different at one point in time than at any other point in time, given the same interest rate levels.[1]

Finally, the movements in Figure 18-1 are characterized by the standard feature of path independence, meaning that an up movement followed by a down movement results in the same state as a down movement followed by an up movement. Some call this a *lattice that recombines*.

As pointed out above, the choice of interest rate process is up to the user. No particular process is necessary to apply the no-arbitrage concept. The method used to generate the interest rates, in both Figure 18-1 (for short rates) and Figure 18-4 (for consol rates) is mechanical and has no fundamental economic basis. However, the method results in a more intuitive volatility of interest rates than the equally mechanical alternative of assuming constant volatility that does not depend on interest rates, as in Rendleman and Bartter (1980), for example.

The interest rate movements are generated by the following procedure:

1. For the path of maximum up-state rates, or "upper envelope" of the lattice, the rate at any Time t is equal to the rate at Time $t - 1 \times \exp(v/t^b)$, where v is the volatility for Period 1, and b is a parameter that dictates how the N-period volatility grows as N increases, as is discussed further below.

2. For the path of minimum down-state rates, or "lower envelope" of the lattice, the rate for any Time t is equal to the rate at Time $t - 1$ divided by $\exp(v/t^b)$.

3. For all other points in the interior of the lattice, the rate at Time t is set equal to what it was at that lattice level (i.e., at the same net difference between the number of up-state and down-state moves) at prior times.

The b parameter can be interpreted as follows: The greater that b is, the more narrow the dispersion of possible future rates for a given N-period horizon and a given basic Period 1 volatility parameter (v). Thus, given v, the b parameter dictates how the outer envelope of rates "tapers" in the future.

Figure 18–1 is constructed assuming that $v = 0.20$ and $b = 1$. For example, the Time 3 high rate of 0.0866 is found by $0.081[\exp(0.20/3^1)]$. As indicated, other types of stochastic process movements can be used without changing the basic idea. The particular movements in Figure 18–1 should be viewed as an example.

The Consol Rate Movements and Consol Bond Values

The consol rate movements are assumed to be of the same form as the short-rate movements. Casual observation about the real-world volatility of short rates, versus the volatility of yields on long-term bonds, tells us that the volatility parameter for the consol rate should be lower than that for the short rate. The assumed consol rates used in the chapter's numerical examples are given in Figure 18–4 ($v = 0.15$ and $b = 1$). The observed Time 0 consol rate is assumed to be 8 percent.[2]

For our purposes, it will be useful to transform the consol rate process into the corresponding process for the values of a representative consol bond. The choice of coupon rate for the represen-

386 Section 4 Interest Rate Swaps

FIGURE 18–4
Assumed Consol Rate Movements

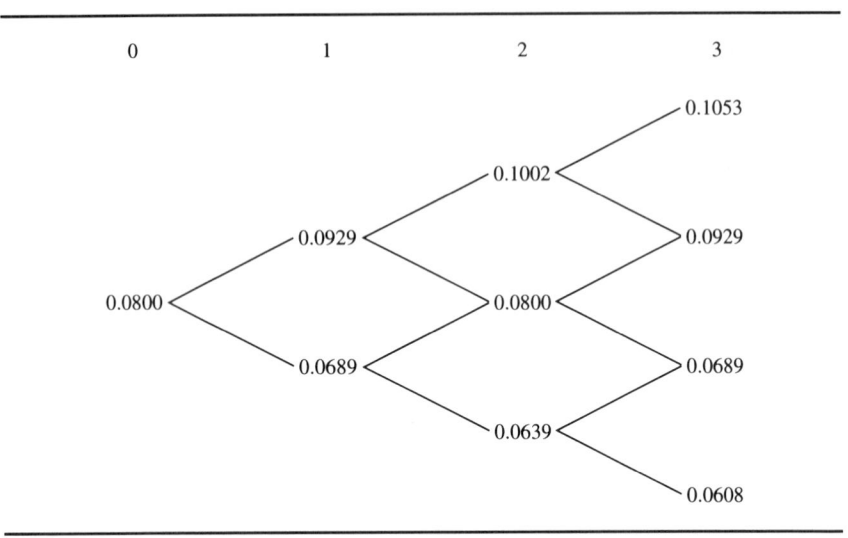

```
       0          1          2          3
                                      0.1053
                             0.1002
                    0.0929           0.0929
       0.0800               0.0800
                    0.0689           0.0689
                             0.0639
                                      0.0608
```

FIGURE 18–5
Ex-Coupon Values for the 8 Percent Coupon Consol Bond

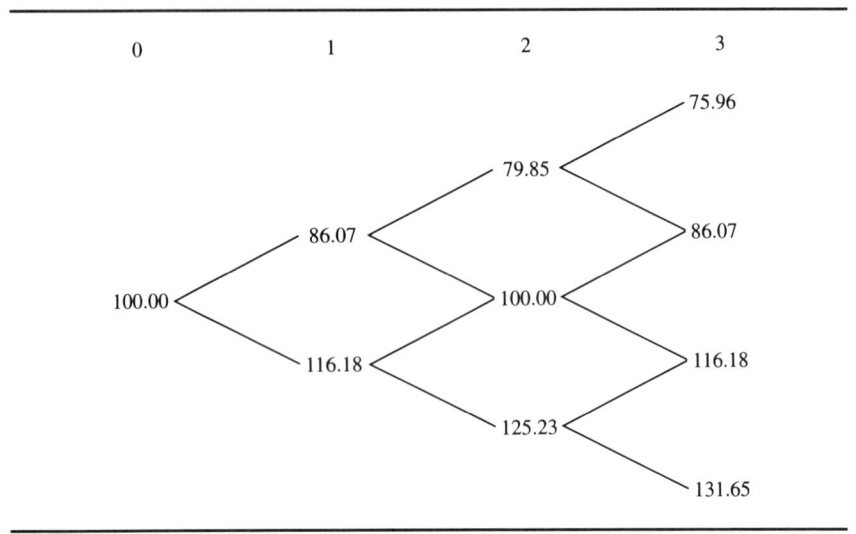

```
       0          1          2          3
                                      75.96
                             79.85
                    86.07            86.07
       100.00              100.00
                   116.18           116.18
                            125.23
                                     131.65
```

tative consol bond is arbitrary, as the valuation results of the term structure model below do not depend on this choice.

Figure 18–5 shows the ex-coupon values of an 8 percent coupon consol bond, with par value of 100, found by dividing the coupon of 8 by the corresponding consol rate. (The actual rates were used, rather than the rounded ones shown in Figure 18–4.)

It is the simple reciprocal relationship between the consol rate and its value, by virtue of the consol bond's infinite maturity, that makes the model here work. Given the hypothesized potential consol rate movements, the potential values for the consol bond can be established by "working forward" in time from Time 0, without using a theory of the term structure. No finite-maturity bond will work as an underlying pricing bond, since its lattice of potential values must be found by "working backward" from a par value at maturity; the only way to accomplish this task would be to already have the term structure model that one is trying to establish.

Relationship between Consol Rate and Short-Rate Movements

As pointed out previously, in any single-factor term structure model, the movements of all interest rates along the term structure are perfectly correlated over any single holding period. This is a result and an implication of the general nature of any single-factor term structure model.

Thus, by assuming a single-factor model of the term structure, we are assuming that whenever the short rate moves up (down), the consol rate also moves up (down), and vice versa. This is an important assumption that allows us to tie elements on the consol lattice with corresponding elements on the short-rate lattice. It is important to realize that this correspondence is not a special assumption that is being made here; it is a general implication of all single-factor term structure models, including those referenced earlier.

By assuming the volatility of the consol rate to be lower than that of the short rate, the perfect short-term correspondence between movements in the short rate and the consol rate results in spreads between the consol rate and the short rate that increase as rates fall and decrease as rates rise, even going negative at very high rates. These features are congruent with intuition and with the observation of changes in these spreads through the business cycle (see Fama 1986).

Let us summarize to this point and plan where we are going. First, we take two observed yield curve endpoints, the short rate and the consol rate. Second, we make assumptions about the future stochastic movements of these two rates. Third, we assume a single-factor model, allowing us to link the single-period movements of the two rates. Next, we will use this information to establish no-arbitrage values of all other default-free interest rate securities.

EXAMPLE APPLICATION OF THE MODEL: THE VALUATION OF A THREE-YEAR ZERO COUPON BOND BY DYNAMIC REPLICATION

Zero coupon bonds, or zeros, are pure discount instruments. The vast, global market for Eurocurrency loans and deposits is essentially a market of zeros. The yield curve for zeros is called the *discount yield curve*. Since coupon bonds can be viewed as portfolios of zeros, the discount yield curve is the most fundamental information about the term structure of interest rates for a given currency. For consistency, this chapter will refer to any pure discount instruments as *zero coupon bonds* (or *bills,* in the case of single-period zeros).

Given the fundamental role of the discount yield curve, the valuation of zeros is a principal task for a term structure theory of either the first or third class of models outlined previously. Figure 18–6 shows an example lattice of no-arbitrage values that will result for a three-year zero coupon bond that has a face value of 100, given the short-rate movements in Figure 18–1 and the consol rate movements in Figure 18–4. This section describes how the values for this lattice are determined.

Of course, a bond that is a three-year bond at Time 0 is a two-year bond at Time 1, and a one-year bond (or bill) at Time 2. However, to avoid confusion, we will refer to the Time 1, Time 2, and Time 3 values for a three-year bond, when we really mean the Time 1, Time 2, and Time 3 values of a bond that was a three-year bond at Time 0.

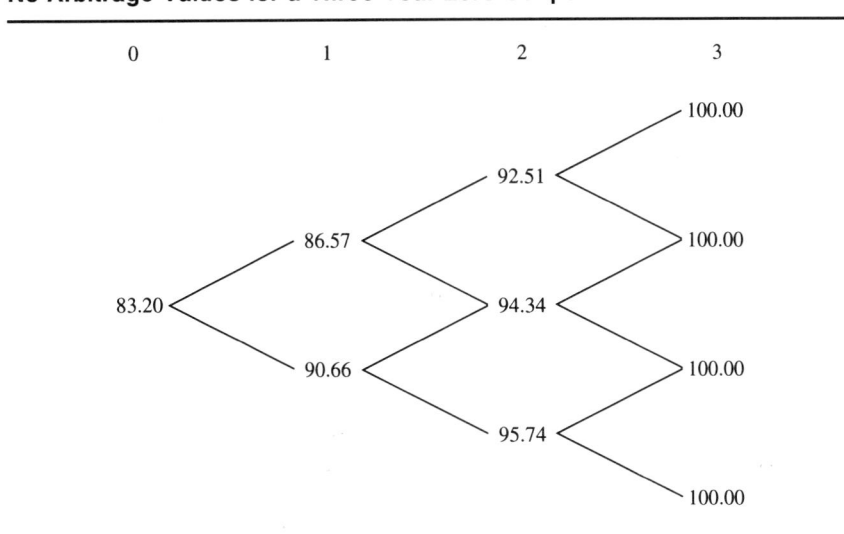

FIGURE 18-6
No-Arbitrage Values for a Three-Year Zero Coupon Bond

```
     0          1          2          3
                                     100.00
                         92.51
                86.57              100.00
     83.20               94.34
                90.66              100.00
                         95.74
                                   100.00
```

Values for the three-year zero coupon bond in Figure 18–6 are found by working backward from the Time 3 maturity value of 100 in the following fashion.

First, compute the Time 2 bond values using the Time 2 short rates and the notion that at Time 2, the bond is a one-year instrument, whose price must be either $100/1.0810 = 92.51$, $100/1.06 = 94.34$, or $100/1.0444 = 95.74$, depending on which Time 2 state of nature obtains.

To work further backward, the consol bond values (Figure 18–5) are employed with the short rates (Figure 18–1) in a "dynamic replication" of the zero coupon bond values. For those familiar with this idea from binomial stock option theory, the consol values play the same role that stock values play in binomial stock option valuation; the main other difference is that here the risk-free rate is stochastic. For those who are not confident with the dynamic replication concept, it is explained next in detail.

It may help to diagram what we know at this point about the future values of the three-year zero coupon bond. We know the given Time 3 face values and the Time 2 values calculated above, but not the Time 1 values or the Time 0 value, the latter being what

FIGURE 18-7
Partial Solution of No-Arbitrage Values for a Three-Year Zero

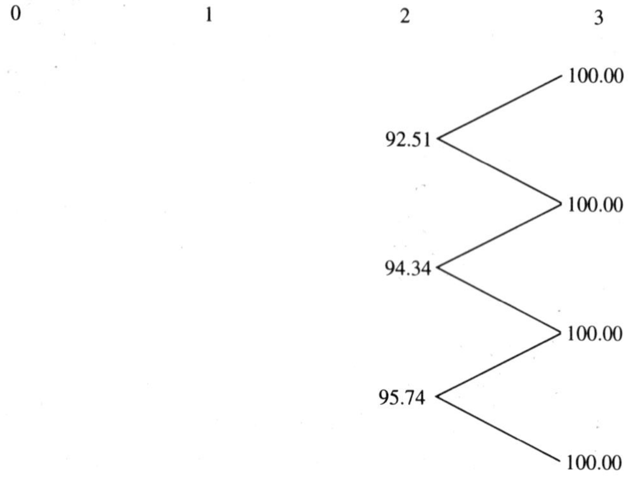

```
        0           1           2           3

                                          100.00
                                92.51 <
                                          100.00
                    94.34 <
                                          100.00
                                95.74 <
                                          100.00
```

we ultimately wish to find. Figure 18-7 represents what we know at this point.

The idea behind dynamic replication is to work backwards through the lattice, focusing on one "building block" of the binomial lattice at a time, where a building block consists of two states at the end of a period and the corresponding beginning-of-period state.

For example, we will start with the building block consisting of Time 2's two topmost states and Time 1's up state. We know already that the possible Time 2 values for the three-year zero are 92.51 and 94.34 (Figure 18-7). We also know (from Figure 18-5) that the corresponding possible Time 2 consol bond values are 79.85 and 100.00. We do not know yet what the Time 1 value of the three-year zero coupon bond is, but we know that the Time 1 consol value in the up state is 86.07 (Figure 18-5) and that the single-period risk-free bill rate at the Time 1 up state is 0.0733 (Figure 18-1).

With this building block information, we will establish the Time 1 up-state value of the three-year zero coupon bond via a no-arbitrage replication. We first find the combination of the (8 percent coupon) consol bond and the short-term (single-period) bill that replicates the payoffs of the three-year zero coupon bond at Time 2, if following the Time 1 up state.

Thus, we find m and B, such that

$$m(79.85 + 8.00) + B = 92.51$$

and

$$m(100.00 + 8.00) + B = 94.34$$

The solution is $m = 0.0909$ and $B = 84.52$, indicating that a Time 1 position of 0.0909 units of the 8 percent consol and 84.52 of face value of the single-period bill maturing at Time 2 will replicate the Time 2 action of the three-year zero, for this particular building block. Thus, the total capital necessary to create a "synthetic" three-year zero in the Time 1 up state is 0.0909 times the Time 1 price of the consol bond (86.07) plus the discounted value of the 84.52 bill, using the relevant Time 1 short rate of 0.0733. This total capital outlay is $0.0909(86.07) + {}^{84.52}\!/_{1.0733} = 86.57$. This is the three-year zero coupon bond's theoretical value as of the Time 1 up state.

The rest of the lattice in Figure 18–7 is determined by continuing to work backward in the same fashion. The final Time 0 answer is 83.20. Readers familiar with how this solution is ultimately obtained may skip to the next section, as the rest of this section provides the details for someone wishing to see the solution worked out completely. Note: There are rounding discrepancies in the exposition.

Next we move onto the building block emanating from the Time 1 down state. For this building block we know the Time 2 values of the three-year zero are 94.34 and 95.74 (Figure 18–7) and the Time 2 values of the consol bond are 100.00 and 125.23 (Figure 18–5). We wish to find m and B, such that

$$m(100.00 + 8.00) + B = 94.34$$

and

$$m(125.23 + 8.00) + B = 95.74$$

The solution is $m = 0.0557$ and $B = 88.33$. Since the consol value in the Time 1 down state is 116.18 and the short rate is 4.91 percent, the total capital necessary to create a synthetic three-year zero in the Time 1 down state is $0.0557(116.18) + 88.33/1.0491 = 90.66$. Thus 90.66 is the value of the three-year zero in the Time 1 down state.

Finally, for Time 0, we use the Time 1 zero coupon bond value results (86.57 and 90.66), the Time 1 consol values (86.07 and 116.18), the Time 0 consol value (100.00), and the Time 0 short rate (6 percent). We now wish to find m and B, such that

$$m(86.07 + 8.00) + B = 98.57$$

and

$$m(116.18 + 8.00) + B = 90.66$$

The solution is $m = 0.1356$ and $B = 73.81$. Thus, the total capital necessary to create a synthetic three-year zero at Time 0 is $0.1356(100.00) + 73.81/1.06 = 83.20$. Thus, the final answer is that the Time 0 value of the three-year zero coupon bond is 83.20.

After completing the valuation process by working backward, it is useful to stand back and interpret the results from a forward-looking point of view. The analysis essentially implies that if we begin with 83.20 allocated to a specific portfolio of the consol bond and a short-term bill, and then reallocate to a new combination of consols and bills in a specific, self-financing way each period, we can replicate the ultimate Time 3 payoffs on a three-year zero coupon bond. Since the dynamically adjusted strategy with consols and bills replicates the three-year zero, the three-year zero should have a Time 0 value that is consistent with the capital necessary to originate the replicating strategy at Time 0.

If the computed Time 0 value of 83.20 [corresponding to a yield to maturity of $(100/83.20)^{1/3} - 1 = 0.0632 = 6.32\%$] does not reconcile with the observed price of an actual three-year zero, then the actual zero is incorrectly priced, given the assumed short-rate and consol rate movements. In principle, a dynamic arbitrage strategy can be employed to capture the misvaluation.

For example, if the Time 0 yield on the actual three-year zero were lower than 6.32 percent (and thus if the actual price is greater than 83.20), one could short the actual three-year zero and arbitrage by dynamically constructing an equivalent, offsetting synthetic for the cheaper price of 83.20. If the actual three-year zero's Time 0 yield to maturity is over 6.32 percent (i.e., if the actual price is lower than 83.20), then one should buy the actual and arbitrage by "selling" the synthetic three-year zero (shorting the combination of consols and bills) at the higher price of 83.20.

Values and yields to maturity for all zero coupon bonds with maturities less than or equal to the horizon are found in a similar manner, resulting in the construction of a theoretical discount yield curve consistent with the assumed stochastic movements for the short rate and the consol rate and with no-arbitrage conditions.

VALUATION OF DELAYED-RESET SWAPS

As explained previously, the valuation of a delayed-reset swap cannot be accomplished in as straightforward a manner as with a plain-vanilla swap. However, a valuation can be made using term structure pricing theory.

The idea is the same as was employed above to find the value of the zero coupon bond, using no-arbitrage principles, the short rates (Figure 18–1), the consol values (Figure 18–5), and the dynamic replication method.

In this case, however, there are intermediate cash flows to blend into the process. Thus the horizon cash flows are first used to find the "ex–cash flow" value of the swap as of the previous period; to this value is added that period's swap cash flow at that state, and the total is the "cum–cash flow" value of the swap. The cum–cash flow value is then used as that period's swap value for purposes of working back to the previous period.

For example, consider the valuation of the 6 percent delayed-reset swap (cash flows in Figure 18–3). The details of the swap valuation are layed out in full below, but the solution swap values are first shown in Figure 18–8.

The Time 0 value of 1.64 means that the 6 percent delayed-reset swap is an off-market swap. Because of the relatively low fixed rate of 6 percent, the buyer of the swap would have to pay 1.63 to the seller at Time 0.

The values in Figure 18–8 are found as follows. First consider how the 4.27 figure in the first state at Time 2 is found.

The Time 3 cash flows of 2.66 and 1.33 have a Time 2 value of 2.17; this value is found by first solving the following two equations

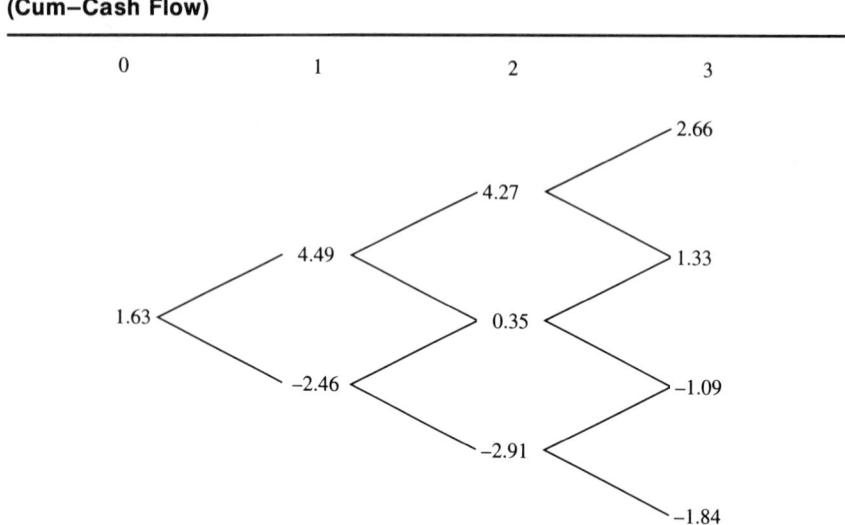

FIGURE 18-8
Values for the Three-Year 6 Percent Delayed-Reset Swap
(Cum-Cash Flow)

```
       0         1         2         3
                                    2.66
                            4.27
                   4.49              1.33
        1.63                0.35
                   -2.46             -1.09
                            -2.91
                                    -1.84
```

for m (the number of units of the 8 percent consol bond) and B (the face value of bills), that replicate the Time 3 swap cash flow:

$$m(75.96 + 8.00) + B = 2.66$$
$$m(86.07 + 8.00) + B = 1.33$$

The solution of $m = -0.1314$ and $B = 13.69$ indicates that the replicating portfolio requires shorting consols and going long bills.

Next, note that the cost of the replicating position at the Time 2 up state is $-0.1314(79.85) + 13.69/1.0810 = 2.17$. This value is added to the Time 2 swap cash flow of 2.10, for a total value of 4.27 for the swap at the Time 2 up state.

From this point, the same procedure is repeated for the remaining steps at Time 2, and then similar steps are taken for Time 1 and then Time 0. For the full details, continue to read on through the rest of the section.

Next, consider how the 0.35 figure in the second state at Time 2 is found. The Time 3 cash flows of 1.33 and -1.09 have a Time 2 value of 0.35; this value is found by first solving the following two equations for m (the number of units of the 8 percent consol bond) and *B* (the face value of bills) that replicate the Time 3 swap cash flow:

$$m(86.07 + 8.00) + B = 1.33$$
$$m(116.18 + 8.00) + B = -1.09$$

The solution is $m = -0.0802$ and $B = 8.88$. The cost of the replicating position at the Time 2 up state is $-0.0802(100.00) + 8.88/_{1.06} = 0.35$. Since the Time 2 swap cash flow is 0.00, the total value of the swap position at the Time 2 middle state is 0.35.

For the last state at Time 2, the Time 3 cash flows of -1.09 and -1.84 have a Time 2 value of -1.35; this value is found by first solving the following two equations for *m* (the number of units of the 8 percent consol bond) and *B* (the face value of bills) that replicate the Time 3 swap cash flow:

$$m(116.18 + 8.00) + B = -1.09$$
$$m(131.65 + 8.00) + B = -1.84$$

The solution is $m = -0.0487$ and $B = 4.97$. The cost of the replicating position at the Time 2 up state is $-0.0487(125.23) + 4.97/_{1.0444} = -1.35$. Since the Time 2 swap cash flow is -1.56, the total value of the swap position at the Time 2 down state is $-1.35 - 1.56 = -2.91$.

For the up state at Time 1, the Time 2 values of 4.27 and 0.35 have a Time 1 value of 3.16; this value is found by first solving the following two equations for *m* (the number of units of the 8 percent consol bond) and *B* (the face value of bills) that replicate the Time 2 swap value:

$$m(79.85 + 8.00) + B = 4.27$$
$$m(100.00 + 8.00) + B = 0.35$$

The solution is $m = -0.1946$ and $B = 21.36$. The cost of the replicating position at the Time 2 up state is $-0.1946(86.07) + 21.36/_{1.0733} = 3.16$. Since the swap cash flow at Time 1 is 1.33, the total value of the swap position at the Time 1 up state is $3.16 + 1.33 = 4.49$.

For the down state at Time 1, the Time 2 values of 0.35 and -2.91 have a Time 1 value of -1.37; this value is found by first solving the following two equations for *m* (the number of units of the 8 percent consol bond) and B (the face value of bills) that replicate the Time 2 swap value:

$$m(100.00 + 8.00) + B = 0.35$$
$$m(125.23 + 8.00) + B = -2.91$$

The solution is $m = -0.1290$ and $B = 14.28$. The cost of the replicating position at the Time 2 down state is $-0.1290(116.18) + 14.28/1.0491 = -1.37$. Since the swap cash flow at Time 1 is -1.09, the total value of the swap position at the Time 1 down state is $-1.37 - 1.09 = -2.46$.

Finally, for Time 0, the Time 1 values of 4.49 and -2.46 have a Time 0 value of 1.63; this value is found by first solving the following two equations for m (the number of units of the 8 percent consol bond) and B (the face value of bills) that replicate the Time 1 swap value:

$$m(86.07 + 8.00) + B = 4.49$$
$$m(116.18 + 8.00) + B = -2.46$$

The solution is $m = -0.2308$ and $B = 26.20$. The cost of the replicating position at the Time 2 up state is $-0.2308(100.00) + 26.20/1.06 = 1.63$.

CONCLUSION

This chapter presented a preference-free version of no-arbitrage term structure theory, via a single-factor consol rate model, applying Vasicek's (1977) insight in a two-state (binomial) setting.

Interest rate swap valuation was also covered. The no-arbitrage valuation of plain-vanilla swaps, and the reason that the valuation does not require a term structure theory, was explained. The consol rate term structure model was applied to the valuation of delayed-reset swaps.

NOTES

1. The Black-Derman-Toy model can imply rate volatility that differs based upon calendar time. This implication may be reasonable if the observed term structure, which is an input to the Black-Derman-Toy

model, reveals information about the market's expectations of changes in fundamental economic uncertainty.
2. For a long-enough time horizon, the processes assumed here can encounter some consistency problems in distant periods, if the short rate becomes higher than the maximum return on the consol bond, in violation of no-arbitrage conditions. Nelson and Ramaswamy (1990) discuss means to handle this problem. The problem does not arise in the three-period (interpreted as three-year) numerical example of the chapter.

It may be necessary, for consistency, to impose a drift on the short rate, given the observed consol rate and the assumed consol rate process, or make the short-rate volatility depend on the consol rate. This is an agenda item for future theoretical research. This chapter still conveys the basic elements of the valuation of other interest rate–sensitive securities, given the short-rate and consol rate processes.

REFERENCES

Black, F.; E. Derman; and W. Toy. "A One-Factor Model of Interest Rates and Its Application to Treasury Bond Options." *Financial Analysts Journal*, January–February 1990, pp. 33–39.

Brennan, M., and E. Schwartz. "An Equilibrium Model of Bond Pricing and a Test of Market Efficiency." *Journal of Financial and Quantitative Analysis*, September 1982, pp. 301–29.

Cox, J.; J. Ingersoll; and S. Ross. "A Reexamination of Traditional Hypotheses about the Term Structure of Interest Rates." *Journal of Finance*, September 1981, pp. 769–99.

———. "A Theory of the Term Structure of Interest Rates." *Econometrica*, March 1985, pp. 385–407.

Cox, J.; S. Ross; and M. Rubinstein. "Option Pricing: A Simplified Approach." *Journal of Financial Economics*. September 1979, pp. 229–63.

Fama, E. "Term Premiums and Default Premiums in Money Markets." *Journal of Financial Economics*, September 1986, pp. 175–98.

Ho, T., and S. Lee. "Term Structure Movements and Pricing Interest Rate Contingent Claims." *Journal of Finance*, December 1986, pp. 1011–29.

Nelson, D., and K. Ramaswamy. "Simple Binomial Processes as Diffusion Approximations in Financial Models." *Review of Financial Studies* 3, no. 3 (1990), pp. 393–430.

Rendleman, R., and B. Bartter. "The Pricing of Options on Debt Securities." *Journal of Financial and Quantitative Analysis,* March 1980, pp. 11–24.

Smith, C.; C. Smithson; and S. Wilford. *Managing Financial Risk.* New York: Harper & Row, 1990.

Vasicek, O. "An Equilibrium Characterization of the Term Structure." *Journal of Financial Economics,* November 1977, pp. 177–88.

CHAPTER 19

THE INTEREST RATE SWAP TERM STRUCTURE

J. Gregg Whittaker
Senior Vice President and Manager of Structured Products
S. G. Warburg & Co. Inc.

INTRODUCTION

The term structure is the relationship that exists between yield and time to maturity. The stochastic processes that underlie this dynamic relationship, however, are not easily explained. But the study of term structure in general is an ongoing discipline that, to date, has produced literally volumes of financial literature on the subject. There are three principal theories used to describe the term structure of interest rates. They are the liquidity premium theory, the segmentation theory, and the expectations theory.[1]

The liquidity premium theory asserts that investors are willing to pay a price premium for the liquidity offered by shorter-term securities relative to longer-term securities. Given this and the inverse relationship between bond prices and yields, short-term yields tend to be lower than long-term yields, resulting in what is commonly referred to as a *normal* or upward-sloping yield curve.

The segmentation theory claims that the yield curve is composed of a series of somewhat independent maturity segments. Certain classes of investors are interested only in certain segments of the market. Consequently, the yields within a given maturity segment are relatively independent of other yields and are determined primarily by the supply and demand conditions specific to that particular maturity segment.

The expectations theory asserts that long-term yields are simply an average of the short-term yields that investors expect to prevail over time. Therefore, current long-term yields will be lower than current short-term yields, resulting in an "inverted" yield curve, only if investors expect short-term rates to fall over time. Conversely, a normal yield curve is the result of investors expecting short-term rates to rise over time.

The term structure of dollar swap rates, however, is complicated by the fact that swap rates themselves are composed of two parts, the underlying Treasury yield and the swap spread.

Swap spread = Swap rate − Treasury yield

Swap rates are subject, then, to factors that affect both interest rates in general and *swap spreads* in particular. For the purposes of this discussion, we will take as given the underlying risk-free term structure, leaving it to the interested reader to read Chapters 12 and 13 in a textbook like *Investments: Analysis and Management* by Francis[2] to learn more about this relationship. Here, we will focus our attention on the relationship between swap spreads and time to maturity—the swap spread term structure or swap yield curve.

Furthermore, swap spreads vary according to the variable-rate index used in the swap. The three most common indexes used are LIBOR, Treasury bill, and AA Composite commercial paper rate, with LIBOR being the dominant index. As such, this chapter will assume throughout that the LIBOR is the variable index used. However, the discussion will be general in that it will be applicable to T-bill and commercial paper swaps as well.

The discussion of swap spreads is best divided into three parts: short-, medium-, and long-term swap spreads. *Short-term swap spreads* are those with maturities of three years or less. *Medium-term swap spreads* are those with maturities greater than three years but less than or equal to five years. And, finally, *long-term swap spreads* are those with maturities greater than five years.

SHORT-TERM SWAPS

Short-term swap spreads are determined almost solely by the Eurodollar futures market. As a matter of fact, the swap market to three years is not even quoted in terms of spreads, as are all longer-dated swaps, but rather as an absolute rate closely determined by the rate implied by the Eurodollar futures "strip." For example, the two-year swap market may be quoted as 4.25/4.30. This means that the dealer will pay an annual money market rate of 4.25 percent on a two-year swap and receive 4.30 percent. Note that a swap is simply a series of forward rate agreements where a variable interest flow is exchanged for a fixed interest flow, or vice versa. The same effect can be achieved via Eurodollar futures contracts. For example, say that you had an obligation to pay the three-month LIBOR on $10 million each quarter for the next three years. If you chose to lock in a fixed rate, you could enter into a three-year, $10 million swap in which each quarter you receive LIBOR and pay a fixed rate equal to the three-year Treasury yield plus the swap spread. Alternatively, you could sell short a series (or strip) of Eurodollar futures contracts. Specifically, given that each Eurodollar futures contract represents $1 million, you could sell approximately 10 of each of the front 11 contracts (this may be adjusted for differences in timing between payment dates and contract expirations, the time value of money, and margin or "tail" considerations).

Given that a swap, therefore, can be synthetically created with a strip of Eurodollar futures contracts, the swap rate and "strip rate" must be about the same (differences may result from daily futures mark-to-market and margin requirements as well as the aforementioned timing differences that introduce a basis risk between the two instruments). The strip rate is calculated as follows:[3]

Strip rate = $(\{[1 + r(d/360)] \times [1 + f_i(t_i/360)]\}^{1/n} - 1) \times 360/365$

where

r = Cash LIBOR to expiration of nearby futures contract

d = Number of days to expiration of nearby futures contract

f_i = Futures rate implied by contract i

t_i = Number of days from futures contact i expiration to next contract expiration or strip maturity, whichever comes first

n = Maturity of strip in years

Given the Eurodollar futures prices, therefore, we can determine the strip rate, which, in turn, determines the corresponding swap rate. For example, assume that the nearby and next two deferred Eurodollar futures prices are, respectively, 9500, 9450, and 9400. These prices imply interest rates of 5 percent, 5.5 percent, and 6 percent, again respectively. Further assume that these contracts expire in 91, 182, and 273 days and that the 91-day cash LIBOR is 4.5 percent. The one-year strip rate is then calculated as follows:

$$\begin{aligned}\text{1-year rate} = &(\{[1 + 0.045(91/360)] \times [1 + 0.05(91/360)] \\ &\times [1 + 0.055(91/360)] \times [1 + 0.06(91/360)]\} - 1) \\ &\times 360/365 \\ = &\ 5.34\%\end{aligned}$$

This 5.34 percent rate, then, comprises one point on the swap yield curve.

There is such liquidity and efficiency in these markets that the Eurodollar futures strip and swap rates are virtually never more than a few basis points apart. Wider discrepancies would certainly imply an arbitrage opportunity.

LONG-TERM SWAPS

Long-term swap spreads, with maturities in excess of five years, are affected primarily by rates in the traditional corporate financing markets.[4] For instance, a Eurobond issuance in conjunction with a swap is now seen as an alternative to borrowing in the variable-rate markets for higher-rated entities. As such, the fixed rate and, therefore, the swap spread is affected by the traditional variable rate market. By viewing the swap market as an alternative to the more traditional corporate financing markets, we can establish upper and lower bounds on swap rates and, given the Treasury yield, therefore, swap spreads. A brief explanation of comparative advantage as it pertains to swaps will help us illustrate this point.

The law of "comparative advantage" is an important motivation behind the use of dollar interest rate swaps. In 1817, David Ricardo established the principle that mutually beneficial trade can always take place between two countries (or investors) whose pre-trade cost and price structures differ. In this case, assume the investors are a highly rated sovereign or financial institution (End User AA) and a lower-rated corporation (End User A). End User AA can raise five-year funds in the debt markets at a fixed rate of 8 percent or a variable rate of LIBOR minus 25 basis points. End User A can raise five-year funds in the debt markets at a fixed rate of 9 percent or a variable rate of LIBOR plus 25 basis points. Obviously, End User AA has an absolute advantage in raising both fixed- and variable-rate debt over End User A. However, the absolute advantage in the fixed-rate market is 100 basis points compared to only 50 basis points in the variable-rate market. This implies that End User AA has a comparative advantage in raising fixed-rate funds, but End User A has a comparative advantage in raising variable-rate funds. Therefore, if End User AA desires variable-rate liabilities while End User A desires fixed-rate liabilities, it is profitable to both for them to enter into a trade or swap. In other words, both benefit if End User AA borrows funds in the fixed-rate market, End-User A borrows funds in the variable-rate market, and both enter in a swap and exchange interest rate obligations.

The table below illustrates how a swap can enable investors to exploit their positions by borrowing in markets in which a comparative advantage exists, and swapping obligations with others who have a comparative advantage in the market in which they have an interest.

		End User AA	
Alternative 1	Borrow in variable-rate market		LIBOR − 25bp*
Alternative 2	Borrow in fixed-rate market	8.0%	
	Enter swap to receive fixed and pay variable interest payments	(8.5%)	LIBOR
	Net variable rate with swap		LIBOR − 50 bp
Benefit to end user of swapping			25 bp

End User A

Alternative 1	Borrow in fixed-rate market		9.0%
Alternative 2	Borrow in variable-rate market	LIBOR + 25bp	
	Enter swap to receive variable	(LIBOR)	
	and pay fixed interest payments	8.5%	
	Net fixed rate with swap		8.75%
Benefit to end user of swapping			25 bp

*bp represents basis points.

As stated above, End User AA can borrow in the variable-rate market at LIBOR − 25 basis points. If, however, End User AA borrows in the fixed-rate market and then enters into a swap to pay a variable rate of LIBOR and receive a fixed payment at 8.5 percent, the net variable funding cost will be reduced by 25 basis points to LIBOR − 50 bp. Conversely, End User A can borrow in the fixed-rate market at 9 percent. However, End-User A could also borrow in the variable-rate market and enter into the swap agreement defined above with End User AA and reduce the fixed-rate funding cost by 25 basis points to 8.75 percent. Therefore, in this instance, the swap does not rob Peter to pay Paul, but rather allows both end users to exploit their comparative advantages to their mutual benefit.

Swap Spread Boundary Conditions

We are now in a position to develop the boundary conditions on swap spreads alluded to previously. Referring to the table above, and assuming perfect capital markets, end user AA would be willing to receive a fixed rate on the swap as low as 8.25 percent. At any rate below this, End User AA would be better off borrowing in the variable-rate market directly and bypassing swaps altogether. Conversely, End User A would be willing to pay a fixed rate on the swap of up to 8.75 percent. Again, at any rate above this, End User A would be better off borrowing in the fixed-rate market directly. Therefore, given the corresponding Treasury yield of 8 percent, the boundary conditions on the swap spread are from 25 to 75 basis points. This exercise can be done at all appropriate maturities, thereby establishing boundary conditions for the entire long-term swap spread term structure. The only caveat is that capital markets are not perfect.[5]

While these boundary conditions are rather robust, a variety of capital market inefficiencies could cause swap spreads to deviate outside the established intervals. For instance, savings and loan companies are regulated as to the kind of assets and liabilities that they may book on their balance sheets. Typically, an S&L balance sheet will exhibit long-duration assets (mortgages) and short-duration liabilities (passbook savings accounts and CDs). By law, they cannot freely enter the long-term fixed-rate debt markets to directly match the durations of the assets and liabilities. Since long-term fixed-rate debt is not an option, therefore, S&Ls are not necessarily bound by the upside condition on swap spreads. Upon entering into a swap agreement to pay fixed and receive variable interest payments, they may be willing to pay a higher swap spread than is indicated by the boundary conditions, which assume perfect capital markets.

Another inefficiency in the way the market allocates resources stems from the accounting practices for the long-term portfolios of commercial banks. If a commercial bank purchases a Treasury security for the purpose of holding until maturity, said bank is not required to mark the security to market. Rather, the security is held at book value and merely accretes or depreciates to par over its life. If, subsequently, the bank should desire to sell the security before maturity, it would be forced then to recognize any profit or loss from the sale. As such, the bank may be reluctant to sell if recognition of the profit or loss could have adverse effects on its financial statements or adverse tax consequences. Let us consider the following example.

Suppose Bank X buys a five-year Treasury security that it holds at book value. Subsequently, Bank X desires to lengthen the duration of its assets in anticipation of falling interest rates. However, rates have risen substantially since the security was purchased, and their position is, therefore, significantly underwater. Unwilling to recognize such a loss, selling the security is not a viable option. Instead, Bank X enters into a swap in which it pays variable and receives fixed interest payments. Again, because of the existing capital market imperfections, Bank X may be willing to receive a lower fixed rate than is indicated by the lower boundary condition on swap spreads.

Other Factors Affecting Long-Term Swap Spreads

Even given the above-mentioned and other capital market inefficiencies, long-term swap spreads still mirror the shape of the corporate spread curve. As such, all of the factors that affect the U.S. corporate market affect the U.S. dollar swap market. For example, as investors become more sensitive to credit risk, both corporate and swap spreads tend to rise. Intuitively, as the risk of counterparty default rises, compensation for providing long-term fixed-rate financing rises relative to the risk-free rate. Therefore, corporate spreads will rise. Since borrowing in the variable markets and paying fixed on a swap is an alternative to issuing long-term fixed-rate corporate debt, swap spreads will rise as well. And since uncertainty grows the farther out into the future one goes, 10-year swap spreads would tend to rise by more than, say, 7-year swap spreads in this instance.

Interest rate volatility also affects long-term swap spreads. Volatility and uncertainty go hand in hand. As such, a fall in volatility leads to a fall in uncertainty and, for the reasons discussed above, swap spreads tend to fall. Furthermore, given an absence of other long-term risk management tools, swaps are the primary tool used to hedge long-dated interest rate risk. It is no wonder, than, that interest rate swaps were born in the early 80s as interest rate volatility was at previously unprecedented levels. And viewing swap spreads as a risk premium, it follows that swap spreads tend to vary directly with interest rate volatility.

The supply and demand of fixed-rate payers, possibly motivated by anticipated changes in the level or shape of the yield curve, is another contributing factor. Historically, as indicated by the empirical data, swap spreads have moved inversely with Treasury yields. As yields rise, from an asset swap perspective, more and more investors choose to lock in a fixed return by receiving fixed, which tends to reduce swap spreads. Conversely, pressure to increase swap spreads often results from a decline in Treasury yields. Moreover, as stated earlier, many of the new fixed-rate Eurobond issues are combined with an interest rate swap to create attractive variable-rate financing. Consequently, if a $1 billion, seven-year Eurobond issue comes to market, it may very well be that the issuer will also seek to receive fixed on a $1 billion, seven-year swap. A single swap of that size could tend to reduce swap spreads for the same reason that a bumper crop could tend to reduce wheat prices.

Foreign exchange concerns can even affect swap spreads. The customer base for U.S. corporate debt is worldwide. Therefore, concerns about the value of the dollar can affect demand for U.S. assets and, therefore, swap spreads. For example, let us assume that an easy Federal Reserve monetary policy sparks inflationary fears for the dollar. A relatively high rate of U.S. dollar inflation implies a devaluation of the dollar relative to other currencies. As such, U.S. assets, which pay in dollars, become less attractive. To induce foreign investors to purchase U.S. corporate debt, then, the yields would have to rise commensurately. To the extent that this was not offset by a corresponding rise in government yields, both corporate and swap spreads would rise as a result of this concern over the value of the dollar.

Finally, hedging costs faced by swap dealers are in important determinant of swap spreads. At the inception of the swap market, dealers acted as brokers, bringing two counterparties together with equal but opposite needs, and running a "matched" book. Today, however, swap dealers abound who are willing and able to make markets in a variety of swap structures without the need to immediately find another counterparty to enter into an offsetting swap. As a result, hedging of swap positions is required. Typically, long-dated swaps are hedged in the Treasury bond market.

For example, say a dealer enters into a swap transaction with a customer in which the dealer pays fixed and receives variable-rate payments. Consequently, the dealer is at risk to falling interest rates. If rates subsequently fall, the dealer will receive lower and lower variable-rate payments while locked into paying an above-market fixed rate. In other works, this swap has the same market price characteristics as being short a fixed-rate bond and long a floating-rate note. This is referred to as a *short swap position.* To hedge, therefore, the dealer can purchase, go long, a Treasury security of comparable maturity, financed in the repurchase agreement (repo) market. Assuming stable swap spreads, such a hedge is robust indeed. However, there exists a cost of carry in this hedge resulting from the difference in the LIBOR swap payment received and the repo payment made. (Note, a cost of carry resulting from the difference in the Treasury coupon received and the fixed-rate swap payment also exists. However, this difference is by definition the result of the swap spread, not the cause of it.) Therefore, as repo rates rise relative to LIBOR, the hedge becomes more expensive to carry. Dealers will then be more aggressive in finding an offsetting swap by being willing to accept a lower fixed rate. It follows, then, that dealers become less aggressive as repo rates fall relative to LIBOR, thereby reducing the cost of carry. Consequently, swap spreads tend to vary directly with the LIBOR less repo rate spread.

MEDIUM-TERM SWAPS

Medium-term swap spreads, with maturities greater than three years and less than or equal to five years, are affected by a combination of the factors that influence both short- and long-term swap spreads. For example, the Eurodollar futures trip actually extends out to four years, and some dealers will extrapolate out to five, thereby pricing swaps out to five years based on the implied strip rate. However, beyond three years. Eurodollar futures contracts become very illiquid, and pricing based on such contracts is tenuous. Furthermore, using existing contracts to extrapolate to five years exposes the user to yield curve risk as well. Just recently, the Chicago Board of Trade (CBOT) introduced a three- and a five-year swap contract. If these new contracts are successful, pricing swaps out to five years based on futures prices will become the norm. Today, however, the CBOT swap contracts are still in their infancy and have as yet not become predominant factors in the swap market.

QUANTITATIVE SWAP SPREAD TRADING

Taking positions on swap spreads is a virtual necessity of making markets in medium- to long-dated swaps. As stated previously, a long-dated and, sometimes, medium-dated short swap, where the dealer pays fixed- and receives variable-rate payments, is hedged by purchasing a Treasury security. Then, any changes in the swap's mark-to-market position resulting from a change in the underlying government yield will be offset by the Treasury hedge. However, if swap spreads change, the swap value can change while the Treasury value remains stable. Suppose swap spreads fall and Treasury yields do not move. There would be no change in the hedge value, therefore, to offset the resulting swap mark-to-market loss. In other words, an implicit swap spread trade is inherent in the traditional means of hedging swaps. While there is evidence that swap spreads are correlated to the spread between Treasury bill and Eurodollar futures prices (the TED spread), most dealers believe the relationship to be too volatile to use this spread in the hedging of swaps.

Furthermore, taking overt positions in swap spreads is every bit as integral a part of the swap traders' business as is taking positions in Treasury securities for bond traders. A substantial amount of the swap book profit and loss for most dealers is attributable to the swap spread positions explicitly taken by the traders. Consequently, whether due to implicit or explicit positioning, swap spread movements can have a dramatic impact on the bottom line of the swap dealer. As such, an ability to analyze these movements in a quantitative, analytical way can prove crucial to the swap participant's success.

I use a three-step approach to quantify the risk and return of a swap spread position. First, I smooth the Treasury and swap yield curves by fitting the data to an exponential spline. Second, I generate a distribution of forward Treasury and swap yield curves. Given the forward Treasury yields and swap rates, the forward swap spreads are easily calculated as the difference in the two. Third, I calculate return vectors and a covariance matrix for the various swap spread positions, which enables me to estimate their expected risks and returns. These three steps are explained below.

Step One: Term Structure Fitting

The exponential spline methodology proposed by Vasicek and Fong (1982) to model term structure has desirable asymptotic properties for long maturities, is flexible enough to fit a myriad of term structure shapes, and is sufficiently robust to produce stable forward rates. Further adjustments can be made to account for tax effects and call features on U.S. Treasury bonds. (See the appendix to this chapter for further details.)

Step Two: Forward Term Structure Estimation

The fitted swap rates can now be used as the starting point for developing an arbitrage-free distribution of forward swap rates. This is done via the methodology proposed by Black, Derman, and Toy (1990) and discussed in Chapter 12. This methodology generates results consistent with the empirical data, uses actual swap rate level and volatility data, incorporates mean reversion of short-term rates, and satisfies the put-call parity relation. While it is a one-factor model based on the short-term rate, the flexibility to use varying volatility estimates for different maturities results in a robust distribution of forward term structures. In other words, when the overall level of the forward curve is high, the curve itself will tend to be inverted. And when the overall level of rates is low, the curve tends to be normal, thereby consistent with intuition and the empirical data.

The core assumption is that short-term rates (r) are distributed lognormally and can be specified by a mean $u(r, t)$ and a standard deviation $s(t)$ (note that s is invariant with respect to r, but not t). We start by ostensibly guessing a mean and standard deviation for r at all futures times out to, say, 20 years. The guesses are then continually adjusted until the model's term structure (both swap rate levels and volatilities) matches the known, current term structure. With the valuation formula, to be discussed later, these expected future short rates can be used to find the value and rate of a zero coupon swap of any maturity out to 20 years. This rate will simply be the rate of that zero coupon bond on today's smoothed term structure, since future short rates were adjusted to guarantee this. We can then fairly price a standard swap and estimate its volatility by duplicating it with a portfolio of zeros that mature on the swap payment dates and at the swap maturity. We then apply the valuation and sensitivity formulas to the portfolio.

The model creates binomial trees of short-term forward rates, values, and swap rates that are consistent with the current term structure, including both rates and volatilities. In general, if over the next year, a zero coupon swap value can only move up to S_u or down to S_d with probability ½, out estimate of the value today (S) is:

$$S = (0.5S_u + 0.5S_d)/(1 + r)$$

where r is today's short rate. This valuation formula is then used for every point in the future on the expanded binomial tree out to 20 years. The objective is to develop the short-term rate tree, and the implied value and swap rate trees, that are consistent with the current term structure.

The assumption of a lognormal distribution allows us to find unique points on the binomial trees. In the above valuation formula, we have two unknowns and one equation. Another equation is required to find unique solutions. Given that short rates are distributed lognormally, the distribution of swap rates is approximately lognormal too. Therefore, the swap rate volatility is calculated as:

$$s_y = \ln(y_u/y_d)/2$$

where y_u and y_d are the swap rates implied by S_u and S_d respectively. Specifically each value, S_u and S_d, implies a certain swap rate defined by:

$$S_{u,d} = 100/(1 + y_{u,d}/2)^{2n}$$

where n is the number of years to maturity of the zero valued as $S_{u,d}$ and assuming semiannual swap payments. Therefore, the choice of S_u and S_d implies a y_u and y_d. Only one value of S_u and one value of S_d ensure that the model is consistent with both the current value and volatility figures.

The following example, adapted from Black, Derman, and Toy (1990), serves to illustrate the process. Let us assume that the one-year semiannual swap rate is given to be 10 percent, with a volatility of 20 percent, while the two-year swap rate and volatility are 11 percent and 19 percent, respectively. Further assume that the discrete periods in our binomial tree correspond to one year (i.e., the short-term rates are one-year rates). Since the one-year semiannual swap rate is 10 percent, we can show that the current short-term or one-year rate must be 10.25 percent. To see this, note the current value of a one-year zero swap is $90.70 = 100/(1 + .10/2)^2$. From our valuation formula above, we know that:

$$S = (0.5S_u + 0.5S_d)/(1 + r)$$
$$90.70 = [0.5(100) + 0.5(100)]/(1 + r)$$
$$r = 10.25\%$$

We can now find the expected short rates one year from now given the two-year swap rate and volatility plus the one-year short-term rate. We known that the current value of a two-year zero swap is $80.72 = 100/(1 + .11/2)^4$. Let us initially guess that the unknown short rates one year forward, r_u and r_d, are 14.81 percent and 10.02 percent, respectively. Let us use the valuation formula to check our guesses.

$$S_u = (0.5S_{u,u} + 0.5S_{u,d})/(1 + r_u)$$
$$S_u = [0.5(100) + 0.5(100)]/(1 + 0.1481)$$
$$S_u = 87.10$$

Similarly,

$$S_d = [0.5(100) + 0.5(100)]/(1 + 0.1002)$$
$$S_d = 90.89$$

Calculating the current two-year zero swap value implied by this binomial tree:

$$S = [0.5(87.10) + 0.5(90.89)]/(1 + 0.1025)$$
$$S = 80.72$$

Therefore, the short-term rate tree we have developed is indeed consistent with the current swap rates. However, we must still determine if it is consistent with the current volatility figures. Given one-year zero swap values one year forward, we can calculate the one-year zero swap rates one year forward:

$$87.10 = 100/(1 + y_u/2)^2$$
$$y_u = 14.30\%$$

Similarly,

$$y_d = 9.78\%$$

From our volatility equation defined above:

$$s_y = \ln(y_u/y_d)/2$$
$$s_y = \ln(14.30/9.78)/2$$
$$s_y = 19.00\%$$

The short-term rate tree now has been shown to be consistent with the entire term structure out to two years.

The procedure is iteratively continued until an arbitrage-free binomial tree of short-term rates is fully developed. The end result is a distribution of arbitrage-free swap term structures that are consistent with the current term structure. This allows us to take the third and final step in our process of quantifying the risks and returns of various swap spread positions.

Step Three: Quantifying Risk and Return

The distribution of forward term structures enables us to estimate the expected risks and returns by calculating the return vectors and a covariance matrix for the various swap spread positions.

Clearly, given the known cost of carry and a swap rate in the future, we can easily calculate the total return on a swap. The cost of carry is simply the difference between the amount received and the amount paid on the swap. If you are paying fixed, you know with certainty the amount paid on each payment date over the life of the swap. The amount received is variable, but can be estimated over the life of the swap since the model generates an entire term structure distribution for all points in time out to 20 years. Since the term structure includes 3-month, 6-month, and 12-month rates, we can calculate a mean and variance for the floating rate. Therefore, we can calculate a mean and variance for the cost of carry for any given swap spread position.

The market price movements can be estimated as well. Note that a swap is valued as a bond and a floating-rate note. Paying fixed on a swap is tantamount to selling a bond and buying a floating-rate note. Therefore, the value of such a swap is simply the value of a floating-rate note less the value of a bond. And given the appropriate swap rate and short-term rate, we can value the bond and floating-rate note and, therefore, value the swap and determine the overall mark-to-market changes. Given an entire distribution of such valuations, we can then estimate the mean and variance. Combining this with the cost-of-carry estimates, we can calculate the overall mean and variance, thereby quantifying the risk and return of any single swap spread position.

While beyond the scope of this discussion, one more step

would allow us to create an optimal portfolio of swap spread positions. The analysis above relates to a single position. However, by applying portfolio theory and generating an entire covariance matrix covering the spectrum of swap spread positions, we can analyze an entire portfolio of trades. By choosing an appropriate objective function, we can then construct an optimal portfolio. The function should, at a minimum satisfy the following conditions:

1. Increase in return.
2. Decrease in risk.
3. Imply convex indifferences curves with respect to risk and return.

One such objective function is:

$$U = u - ks^2$$

where

u = Mean portfolio return

s^2 = Variance of portfolio return

k = Risk aversion parameter

That portfolio of swap spread positions that maximizes the objective function is then defined to be the optimal portfolio.

CONCLUSION

The dollar interest rate swap term structure is made up of the underlying Treasury yield curve, which we take as given here, and the swap spreads. Short-term swap spreads are determined almost solely by the Eurodollar futures market. Long-term swap spreads are affected primarily by rates in the corporate financing markets, as well as interest rate volatility, the supply and demand of fixed-rate payers, foreign exchange rates, and, finally, hedging cost. Medium-term swaps spreads are affected by a combination of the factors that influence both short- and long-term swap spreads.

A quantitative swap trading model can be developed using a three-step process. First, smooth or fit the existing term structure, using exponential spline methodology. Then, using the fitted yield curve as a base, generate a distribution of forward, arbitrage-free swap yield curves. Finally, use modern portfolio theory to estimate the expected risks and returns of various portfolios by calculating the implied return vectors and a covariance matrix. Then, we can identify the portfolio that maximizes some reasonable objective function.

APPENDIX: TERM STRUCTURE FITTING

The Vasicek and Fong (1982) model postulates that bond (swap) prices are linearly described by, among other things, a discount function of exponential shape, $D(t) \cong e^{-rt}$. However, splines are ill suited to fit an exponential-type curve. One possible alternative is to work with the logarithm of the discount function, $\log D(t)$. However, the overall model would then be nonlinear in t, necessitating the use of complex nonlinear estimation techniques. The solution is to transform the argument of the function $D(t)$, namely t, as opposed to transforming the function itself. The result being that the function is now linear in some arbitrary parameter, x.

$$t = -1/a \times \log(1 - x)$$

where a is some constant. This gives us:

$$D(t) = D[-1/a \times \log(1 - x)]$$

where is approximately linear in x. Let us define the discount function above with a transformed argument as $G(x)$. Given that $D(t)$ is approximately exponential,

$$D(t) \cong e^{-rt}$$

where

$$0 <= t > \text{infinity}$$

The function $G(x)$ is approximately a power function,

$$G(x) \cong (1 - x)^{r/a}$$

where

$$0 <= x <= 1$$

We now estimate the function $G(x)$, which can be very well fitted by cubic splines, while preserving the linearity of the overall model. Furthermore, it can be shown that a represents the limiting value of the forward rates.

NOTES

1. Jack Clark Francis, *Investments: Analysis and Management*, 5th ed. (New York: McGraw-Hill, 1991), pp. 339–47 and Appendix 12B.
2. Ibid.
3. Lawrence Grannan and Walid Khouri, "Strips—Arbitraging the Eurodollar Cash and Futures Markets," *Intermarket*, August 1988, pp. 15–17.
4. Ellen Evans and Gioia M. Parente, "What Drives Interest Rate Swap Spreads," in *Interest Rate Swaps*, ed. Carl R. Beidleman (Homewood, Ill.: Richard D. Irwin, 1991).
5. Those who contend that markets are perfectly efficient believe that the comparative advantages hypothesized for End Users AA and A above could never actually arise. As a result, the efficient markets theorists propose other economic arguments to rationalize the existence of swaps. For a review of efficient markets theory, see Chapter 18 of Jack Clark Francis, *Investments: Analysis and Management*, 5th ed. (New York: McGraw-Hill, 1991).

REFERENCES

Black, Fischer; Emanuel Derman; and William Toy. "A One-Factor Model of Interest Rates and Its Application to Treasury Bond Options." *Financial Analysts Journal*, January–February 1990, pp. 33–39.

Evans, Ellen, and Gioia M. Parente Bales, "What Drives Interest Rate Swap Spreads." In *Interest Rate Swaps*. ed. Carl R. Beidleman. Homewood, Ill.: Business One Irwin, 1991.

Francis, Jack Clark. *Investments: Analysis and Management*. 5th ed. New York: McGraw-Hill, 1991, pp. 339–47 and Appendix 12B.

Grannan, Lawrence, and Walid Khouri. "Strips—Arbitraging the Eurodollar Cash and Futures Markets." *Intermarket*, August 1988, pp. 15–17.

Vasicek, Oldrich A., and H. Gifford Fong. "Term Structure Modeling Using Exponential Splines." *The Journal of Finance* 37 (May 1982), pp. 339–48.

CHAPTER 20

TECHNIQUES FOR DERIVING A ZERO COUPON CURVE FOR PRICING INTEREST RATE SWAPS: A SIMPLIFIED APPROACH

David R. Smith
AMBAC Capital Management

SYNOPSIS

This chapter discusses three approaches for creating a zero coupon curve for pricing interest rate swaps. Two recursive (bootstrap style) methods using swap rates are presented as well as a method using Eurodollar futures. These term structure estimation methods are illustrated using the convenient properties of continuous compounding. A technique for deriving a "curved" term structure is presented using exponential interpolation of discount factors. Actual swap pricing examples are provided.

INTRODUCTION

Swap pricing methods that value only the fixed side of an interest rate swap and assume that the future floating-rate side is reset to par are limited in the variety of swaps that can be priced. The bond equivalent method[1] requires a number of adjustments for variations from the standard plain-vanilla swap. In contrast, the zero coupon curve approach can be used to price a wide range of swaps with unusual structures using the same fundamental approach. This approach involves projecting the cash flows on each side of the swap and then present valuing them using a discount factor for each cash flow. The difference in present value of the two sides of the swap would be the net present value or the price of the swap. This approach is commonly used for managing a swap book (portfolio) because of the ease of consolidating all of the swap cash flows into an aggregated book. This approach can price a wide variety of swaps such as forward swaps, amortizing swaps, basis swaps, roller coaster swaps, swaps with reset frequencies greater than the payment frequency with compounding, and swaps with weekend and holiday reset and payment avoidance.

The first component of this approach—the projection of cash flows—is fairly straightforward calculations of interest, although considerable attention must be given to swap conventions such as the day count methods and weekend and holiday calendars. The second component of this approach involves the derivation of discount factors for every date of the cash flows. The term structure estimation technique and interpolation method used for deriving these discount factors for any date has a large impact on the price of the swap.

In a previous article,[2] I discussed using the bootstrap method for pricing swaps using zero coupon rates. This article presented the bootstrap method using semiannually compounded spot rates with linear interpolation of half-yearly (e.g., 1.5-, 2.5-year) par coupon swap rates. This chapter expands and extends this discussion. It presents the bootstrap recursive approach in terms of continuous compounding, avoiding the more cumbersome algorithms of noncontinuous compounding. It also discusses the exponential interpolation of discount factors and Eurodollar futures curve pricing. The recursive (bootstrap) method is a simple method for deriving spot rates and has been shown to outperform other more advanced techniques under simulation testing.[3]

DEFINITIONS

To facilitate the presentation, the following basic fixed-income terms and equations must be defined:

i = Annually compounded interest rate
m = Compounding periods per year

where if $m = 2$, then i^m denotes the semiannually compounded interest rate.

t = Number of years from the valuation date (exactly specified as .5, 1.0, 1.5, etc., in the bootstrap method—in other words, as 30/360 day-basis years)
v_t = Discount factor at Time t
FV_t = Future value at Time t
δ_t = Continuously compounded spot rate at Time t

Compounding Conversion Formulas

For conversion to annual compounding:

$$i = \left(1 + \frac{i^m}{m}\right)^m - 1 \qquad (20\text{-}1)$$

$$i = (e^\delta - 1) \qquad (20\text{-}1a)$$

For conversion to other compounding rates:

$$i^m = m[(1 + i)^{1/m} - 1] \qquad (20\text{-}1b)$$

$$i^m = m[e^{\delta/m} - 1] \qquad (20\text{-}1c)$$

Continuous compounding:

$$\delta = \left(1 + \frac{i}{m}\right)^m \qquad (20\text{-}2)$$

for $m \to \infty$, as m approaches infinity.

δ is defined as the continuously compounded rate:

$$\delta_t = \frac{\ln(FV)}{t} \qquad (20\text{-}2a)$$

$$\delta_t = \frac{\ln\left(\frac{1}{v}\right)}{t} \qquad (20\text{-}2b)$$

Discount Factor:

$$v_t = \frac{1}{e^{\delta t}} \qquad (20\text{-}3)$$

Given a continuously compounded spot rate and the number of years t, a discount factor can be calculated as follows:

$$v_t = e^{-\delta t} \tag{20-3a}$$

A restatement of Equation (20-3) is:

$$v_t = \frac{1}{FV_t} \tag{20-3b}$$

The discount factor has an inverse relationship with the future value:

$$1 = FV_t \times v_t \tag{20-3c}$$

A money market discount factor is defined as:

$$\frac{1}{1 + \text{Rate} \times \frac{\text{days}}{360}} = v_t \tag{20-3d}$$

Money market rates (such as LIBOR with less than one year to maturity) are already spot rates, and one can directly derive discount factors. Using Equation (20-2b), a continuous compounding spot rate (δ_t) can be calculated (but Time t is defined as the number of years on a 30/360 basis, which is neither Number of days/360, nor Number of days/365). The esoteric issue of how many years exactly is a date from another date does not come up if one uses money market discount factors directly. The money market rate represents an exact return on investment of future value that is best used to derive discount factors rather than a theoretically derived discount factor from δ and t because of the counting of the number of years problem.

Present Value

The present value of a cash flow can be derived using the following combinations:

$$PV_0 = \text{Cash flow}_t \times e^{-\delta t} \tag{20-3e}$$

$$PV_0 = \text{Cash flow}_t \times v_t \tag{20-3f}$$

$$PV_0 = \frac{\text{Cash flow}_t}{FV_t} \tag{20-3g}$$

Future Value

Future value is defined as the growth value of a $1 investment invested at Time 0 up to the horizon time.

$$FV_t = \frac{1}{v_t} \quad (20\text{-}4)$$

Future value is the value of a $1 investment invested at the spot rate at Time 0 at Time t in the future. FV_t is inversely related to v_t.

$$FV_t = e^{\delta t} \quad (20\text{-}4a)$$

Given only δ and t, continuous compounding will provide FV.

A money market future value would be:

$$\left[1 + \left(\text{Rate} \times \frac{\text{Number of days}}{360}\right)\right] = FV \quad (20\text{-}4b)$$

The above is a direct calculation of FV using money market rates, which are spot rates.

Law of Exponents

$$a^r a^s = a^{r+s} \quad (20\text{-}5)$$

$$\frac{a^r}{a^s} = a^{r-s} \quad (20\text{-}5a)$$

TERM STRUCTURE ESTIMATION

Given the fundamental equations, definitions, and the market rates in Table 20-1, we will delineate three methods for deriving discount factors with illustrated examples.

Table 20-1 shows market rates as of 12/31/91 at 1:00 P.M. It shows the semiannually compound Treasury rates, the swap spreads, cash LIBOR out to one year, and the Eurodollar futures prices. The Treasury rates plus the swap spreads equals the absolute swap rates. Cash LIBOR is an annually compounded actual/360 day-basis rate. The Eurodollar futures rates are actual/360 rates for three-month LIBOR beginning on the futures expiration date. Eurodollar futures rates are equal to the Eurodollar futures price subtracted from 100.

TABLE 20-1
Market Rates

Year	Treasury Yield	Swap Spread	Swap Rate	LIBOR Tenor	Cash LIBOR	Eurodollar Strip	Eurodollar Futures Price
0.5	3.9920			O/N:	4.0000%	03/16/92	95.95
1	4.0820			1 month	4.3125%	06/15/92	95.86
2	4.7590	0.165	4.924	2 months	4.2500%	09/14/92	95.64
3	5.0500	0.505	5.555	3 months	4.2500%	12/14/92	95.16
4	5.4910	0.530	6.021	4 months	4.2500%	03/15/93	94.91
5	5.9310	0.480	6.411	5 months	4.1875%	06/14/93	94.45
7	6.3450	0.490	6.835	06/30/92	4.1875%	09/13/93	94.02
10	6.7010	0.505	7.206	12/31/92	4.3125%	12/13/93	93.49
30	7.4030	0.705	8.108			03/14/94	93.41
						06/13/94	93.16
						09/19/94	92.95
						12/19/94	92.61
						03/13/95	92.61
						06/19/95	92.47
						09/18/95	92.33
						12/18/95	92.14

Method I: Bootstrapping Using Linear Interpolation of Par Coupon Rates

The first method for deriving discount factors is a plain-vanilla bootstrapping method with semiannual cash flows. Linear interpolation of par coupon rates is used for midyear points.

Par Yields

The absolute swap rates shown in Table 20–1 represent swap yields or internal rates of return for a fixed-rate investment with semiannual cash flows. A two-year yield ($y_{2.0}$) is a rate that would apply in the following formula:

$$1 = \frac{c_{2.0}}{\left(1 + \frac{y}{2}\right)^1} + \frac{c_{2.0}}{\left(1 + \frac{y}{2}\right)^2} + \frac{c_{2.0}}{\left(1 + \frac{y}{2}\right)^3} + \frac{1 + c_{2.0}}{\left(1 + \frac{y}{2}\right)^4} \quad (20\text{--}6)$$

where c_t is the semiannual cash flow, which is one half the yield. Define c_t as the semiannual cash flow that would apply from a par yield at Time t. y_t is defined as the par yield at Time t.

$$c_{2.0} = \frac{y_{2.0}}{2}$$

The swap rates are yield rates and are also called *par swap rates* because they are average discounting rates that generate a par price of 1.

Spot Rates

Zero coupon spot rates are rates that apply discretely to each cash flow as follows:

$$1 = \frac{c_{2.0}}{\left(1 + \frac{s_{.5}}{2}\right)^1} + \frac{c_{2.0}}{\left(1 + \frac{s_{1.0}}{2}\right)^2} + \frac{c_{2.0}}{\left(1 + \frac{s_{1.5}}{2}\right)^3} + \frac{1 + c_{2.0}}{\left(1 + \frac{s_{2.0}}{2}\right)^4} \quad (20\text{–}6a)$$

where

$s_{.5}$ = Six-month semiannual spot rate
$s_{1.0}$ = One-year semiannual spot rate
$s_{1.5}$ = 1.5-year semiannual spot rate
$s_{2.0}$ = Two-year semiannual spot rate

These spot rates can be derived by iteration, that is, by solving for each one successively beginning with the one-year rate, then finding the 1.5-year rate, then the two-year rate, and so on.[4]

Since we know that

$$\left(1 + \frac{s_t}{2}\right)^{t \times 2}$$

is the same as v_t, now we have the basic formula:

$$c_{2.0} \times v_{.5} + c_{2.0} \times v_{1.0} + c_{2.0} \times v_{1.5} + (1 + c_{2.0}) \times v_{2.0} = 1 \quad (20\text{–}6b)$$

An iterative procedure could be formulated to derive directly the discount factors freeing up the mathematics from semiannual compounding spot rates.

A generalized bootstrapping equation can be written as follows:

$$c_T \times \sum_{t=.5}^{T-.5} v_t + (1 + c_T)v_T = 1 \quad (20\text{–}6c)$$

where $t \in D$ and $D = \{t = .5, 1, 1.5, \ldots, T - .5, T\}$.

In essence, the sum of all of the previous period semiannual discount factors times the cash flows plus the final coupon plus principal times the final discount factor (v_t) equals 1, where

$$c_t = \frac{y_t}{2}$$

and c_t = Swap par yield at Time t divided by 2 or the semiannual cash flow. Equation (20–6c) can be rearranged as follows:

$$v_T = \frac{1 - c_T \times \sum_{t=.5}^{T-.5} v_t}{1 + c_T} \qquad (20\text{–}6d)$$

Table 20–2 shows an example of the plain-vanilla bootstrapping technique with semiannual cash flows using the linear interpolation of the midyear point swap coupon rates, given the market rates provided in Table 20–1.

The bootstrapping begins at the 1.5-year point because discount factors can be derived directly from the cash LIBOR out to 1.0 year [see Equation (20–3d)].[5] A "hypothetical" semiannual par coupon rate can be calculated from these money market rates using a variation on Equation (20–6c):

TABLE 20–2
Linear Curve with Plain-Vanilla Four-Year Swap

	0.5(182)	1.0(366)	1.5(548.5)	2.0(731)	2.5(913.5)	3.0(1,096)
						Year (Days)
					Bootstrap with Linear	
Coupon yield	0.0000	0.0000	4.630118	4.9240	5.239500	5.5550
Coupon	0.00000	0.00000	0.02315	0.02462	0.02620	0.02778
Semiannual spot rate	0.000000%	0.000000%	4.637780%	4.941208%	5.271295%	5.606200%
Discount factor	0.9792687	0.9579978	0.9335392	0.9069907	0.8780290	0.8471547
Future value	1.0211701	1.0438438	1.0711923	1.1025472	1.1389145	1.1804219
Annual spot rate	4.278845%	4.384375%	4.691552%	5.002247%	5.340761%	5.684773%
Continuous compounded spot rate	4.189833%	4.290981%	4.584824%	4.881157%	5.203026%	5.529064%
6-month forward	4.392130%	5.172511%	5.770153%	6.490501%	7.159257%	7.225116%
Hypothetical coupon	4.234028	4.336235	4.630118	4.924000	5.239500	5.555000
						Pricing with
Fixed side	3.010500	3.010500	3.010500	3.010500	3.010500	3.010500
Float side	2.117014	2.220356	2.619989	2.927098	3.298483	3.6444468
Net cash flow present values	0.874963	0.756956	0.364557	0.075645	−0.252858	−0.537069
Sum of present values	0.874963	1.631919	1.996477	2.072121	1.819264	1.282194

Chapter 20 Deriving a Zero Coupon Curve for Pricing Interest Rate Swaps   425

$$y_T = \left[\frac{1 - v_T}{\sum_{t=.5}^{T} v_t}\right] \times 2 \qquad (20\text{--}6e)$$

Equation (20–6e) generates a bond equivalent "hypothetical" coupon rate at Year 1.0 of 4.336235 percent as in Table 20–2. Linear interpolation between this rate and the two-year par swap rate yields 4.630118 percent, the 1.5-year coupon yield. The calculation of Equation (20–6d) using the known variable $v_{.5}$ and $v_{1.0}$ with a coupon of .02315 (.04630118/2) yields .9335392, the 1.5-year discount factor.

Equation (20–6d) is repeated at the two-year point using $c = .02462$ and the now known variables, namely, $v_{.5}$, $v_{1.0}$, $v_{1.5}$. The 2.5-, 3.5-, 4.5-, 5.5-, 6.0-, and 6.5-year par yields are linearly interpolated between the observed par swap coupon yields given in Table 20–1. The future value (FV_t) in Table 20–2 can be calculated from Equation (20–4), the continuous compounded spot rate from Equation (20–2a) or (20–2b), and the annual spot rate from Equation (20–1a).

3.5(1,278.5)	4.0(1,461)	4.5(1,643.5)	5.0(1,826)	5.5(2,008.5)	6.0(2,191)	6.5(2,373.5)	7.0(2,556)
Interpolation of Coupon							
5.788000	6.0210	6.216000	6.4110	6.5170	6.6230	6.7290	6.8350
0.02894	0.03011	0.03108	0.03206	0.03259	0.03312	0.03365	0.03418
5.855435%	6.109201%	6.323923%	6.543106%	6.659039%	6.777994%	6.899938%	7.024912%
0.8170970	0.7860695	0.7556552	0.7247578	0.6974796	0.6703601	0.6434358	0.6167418
1.2238449	1.2721522	1.3233549	1.3797712	1.4337337	1.4917356	1.5541565	1.6214240
5.941151%	6.202507%	6.423903%	6.650137%	6.769896%	6.892847%	7.018961%	7.148286%
5.771357%	6.017753%	6.226002%	6.438354%	6.550582%	6.665672%	6.783584%	6.904354%
7.742524%	7.891994%	8.349523%	7.672866%	7.931652%	8.198534%	8.474360%	7.908106%
5.788000	6.021000	6.216000	6.411000	6.517000	6.623000	6.729000	6.835000
Linear Curve							
3.010500	3.010500						
3.678604	3.947172						
−0.545905	−0.736289						
0.736289	−0.000000						

Forward Rates

Future value ($FV_t = e^{\delta t}$) is defined in Equation (20–4a). Then the forward rate is defined as an interim rate that begins in the future and ends at some more distant horizon point. One would be indifferent between investing at a short-term rate and then at the forward rate or simply investing in a long-term rate that ends at the same point. For example, if the 1-year future value is equal to:

$$FV_{1.0} = e^{\delta_{1.0} \times 1}$$

and the 1.5-year future value is equal to:

$$FV_{1.5} = e^{\delta_{1.5} \times 1.5}$$

then the 1 year forward continuous compounding forward rate for a term of .5 year ($\delta_{1f.5}$) would be derived from the formula:

$$e^{\delta_{1.0} \times 1} \times e^{\delta_{1f.5} \times .5} = e^{\delta_{1.5} \times 1.5}$$

The forwards are defined using the notation 1f.5, where 1 indicates 1 year forward, and .5 indicates a term of .5 years, maturing in 1.5 years.

The 1f.5 rate in Table 20–2 is 5.172511 percent. The forward rate calculation is generalized as:

$$e^{\delta_{pt} \times pt} \times e^{\delta_{ptf(t-pt)} \times (t-pt)} = e^{\delta_t \times t} \qquad (20–7)$$

Rearranging (20–7) gives:

$$\delta_{ptf(t-pt)} = \frac{\ln\left[\dfrac{e^{\delta t}}{e^{\delta pt}}\right]}{(t - pt)} \qquad (20–7a)$$

where

t = End of the time period in years, the final maturity

pt = (Previous time) beginning time in years of the forward rate

pt is the start of the forward period and t is the end of the forward period.

Following from the second law of exponents given in Equation (20–5a), we obtain:

$$\delta_{ptf(t-pt)} = \frac{\delta_t{}^t - \delta_{pt}{}^{pt}}{(t - pt)} \qquad (20–7b)$$

Periodic forwards can also be directly calculated from the discount factors such that:

$$ptf(t - pt) = \frac{v_{pt}}{v_t} - 1 \qquad (20\text{--}7c)$$

A periodic forward means that it is not an annualized rate. We will return to the topic of forward rates in the discussion concerning projecting the floating-rate swap cash flow.

Method II: Bootstrapping Using Exponential Interpolation of Discount Factors

Method I arbitrarily imposes a linear shape to the yield curve, which can cause problems in the pricing of swaps, if one believes the spot curve should have some curvature. For example, the Method I approach might overprice a swap that receives fixed and matures in 18 months by arbitrarily creating a low 18-month spot rate. And likewise, Method I would result in a fairly low forward rate between 1 year and 1.5 years due to the low 1.5-year spot rate. What would happen if Method I was used to price an 18 × 12 forward rate agreement (FRA)?[6]

In order to create a "curved" term structure, one can assume, as in Method II, that the discount factors are exponentially interpolated and follow a shape that is implied by the forward rates between two points. Suppose that, while doing the bootstrap iteration, we make a guess at the 2-year discount factor and at the same time exponentially interpolate the 1.5-year discount factor from the 1-year discount factor and the 2-year discount factor. Then continue guessing until a price of 1 for the bond is achieved. A bootstrap method with exponential smoothing is structured as follows.

The Interpolation of Discount Factors
Define d as the target date in years or the date for which one wishes to interpolate a discount factor. Define pt as the previous time of an available discount factor in years or the last available semiannual coupon payment date. Define t as the number of years until the next date available with a discount factor or the next available payment date. Define p as the fractional distance of d or the targeted date for interpolation between pt and t in years.

TABLE 20-3
Exponential Curve with Plain-Vanilla Four-Year Swap

	0.5(182)	1.0(366)	1.5(548.5)	2.0(731)	2.5(913.5)	3.0(1,096)
				Year (Days)		
			Exponential Interpolation of Half-Year Discount			
Coupon				4.92%		5.56%
Discount factor	0.9792687	0.9579978	0.9321624	0.9070237	0.8766168	0.8472292
Continuous compounded spot rate	4.189833%	4.290981%	4.683216%	4.879333%	5.267413%	5.526134%
Hypothetical semiannual coupon	4.234028%	4.336235%	4.728300%	4.924000%	5.303304%	5.555000%
6-month forward	4.392130%	5.467685%	5.467685%	6.819735%	6.819735%	7.479054%
Future value	1.0211701	1.0438438	1.0727745	1.102507	1.1407493	1.1803181
						Pricing with
Fixed side	3.010500	3.010500	3.010500	3.010500	3.010500	3.010500
Float side	2.117014	2.220356	2.771555	2.771555	3.468670	3.468670
Cash flow present value	0.874963	0.756956	0.222736	0.216729	-0.401640	-0.388175
Sum of present values	0.874963	1.6319193	1.8546552	2.0713843	1.6697447	1.2815696

$$p = \frac{d - pt}{t - pt} \qquad (20\text{--}8)$$

Exponential interpolation of discount factors gives us:

$$v_d = v_{pt}^{(1-p)} \times v_t^p \qquad (20\text{--}8a)$$

For example, if $d = 1.5$, $t = 2$, $pt = 1$, $v_t = v_{2.0} = .9070237$, and $v_{pt} = v_{1.0} = .9579978$, then $p = .5$ and

$$v_{1.5} = v_{1.0}^{(1-.5)} \times v_{2.0}^{.5} \qquad (20\text{--}8b)$$

and $v_d = v_{1.5} = .9321624$.

By incorporating bootstrapping using exponential interpolation, bootstrapping then tries to find a midyear discount factor and full-year discount factor subject to the condition that exponential interpolation of discount factors is met.

$$c_t = \frac{y_t}{2}$$

where:

c_t = Semiannual par coupon cash flow

y = Par swap yield

For example, to obtain the 2-year and 1.5-year discount factors, we iterate on the 2-year discount factor ($v_{2.0}$) until the following relationship is satisfied:

Chapter 20 Deriving a Zero Coupon Curve for Pricing Interest Rate Swaps

3.5(1,278.5)	4.0(1,461)	4.5(1,643.5)	5.0(1,826)	5.5(2,008.5)	6.0(2,191)	6.5(2,373.5)	7.0(2,556)

Factors Recursive Semiannual Bootstrap

	6.02%		6.41%				6.84%
0.8161319	0.786176	0.7549118	0.7248909	0.6962688	0.6687768	0.6423703	0.6170065
5.805122%	6.014364%	6.247875%	6.434683%	6.582173%	6.705082%	6.809081%	6.898224%
5.821899%	6.021000%	6.238311%	6.411000%	6.546864%	6.659456%	6.754213%	6.835000%
7.479054%	8.115960%	8.115960%	8.057076%	8.057076%	8.057076%	8.057076%	8.326237%
1.2252921	1.2719798	1.3246581	1.379518	1.436227	1.4952672	1.5567344	1.6207284

Exponential Curve

3.010500	3.010500
3.810327	3.810327
−0.652765	−0.628805
0.628805	−8.67E-19

$$c_{2.0} \times (v_{.5} + v_{1.0}) + (c_{2.0} \times v_{1.5}) + (1 + c_{2.0})v_t = 1 \quad (20\text{--}9)$$

subject to the following constraints:

$$v_{1.5} = v_{1.0}^{.5} \times v_{2.0}^{.5} \quad (20\text{--}9a)$$

Table 20–3 illustrates the exponentially smoothed curve out to seven years. In Table 20–3, the .5-year and the 1-year discount factors remain the same as in Table 20–2. The 2-year and the 1.5-year discount factors are derived as follows:

$$c_{2.0} = .04924/2$$
$$v_{.5} = .9792687$$
$$v_{1.0} = .9579978$$

where the discount factors are derived from Equation (20–4b). A computer program could make iterative guesses at the two-year discount factor ($v_{2.0}$) until it arrives at .9070237 so that equations (20–9) and (20–9a) are satisfied as follows:

.02462 (.9792687 + .9579978) + (.02462 × .9321624)
$$+ (1 + .02462) \times .9070237 = 1$$

where

$$v_{1.5} = .9321624 = .9579978^{.5} \times .9070237^{.5}$$

As shown in Table 20–3, the resulting six-month forward rates beginning at 1 year and beginning at 1.5 years are exactly the same

(5.467685 percent) because the 1.5-year discount factor is consistent with the 1-year forward rate for 1 year between 1 year and 2 years.[7] An interim continuous compounding spot rate (δ_d) can likewise be calculated using the forward rate (*ptft*) as follows:

$$\delta_d = \frac{\ln(e^{\delta_{pt} \times pt} \times e^{\delta_{ptft} \times (d-pt)})}{d} \quad (20\text{--}9b)$$

where δ_{ptft} is derived using Equation (20–7b) and d = Target interim rate that requires interpolation.

Using the law of exponents, (20–5) simplifies (20–9b) to:

$$\delta_d = \frac{(\delta_{pt} \times pt) + (\delta_{ptft} \times (d - pt))}{d} \quad (20\text{--}9c)$$

Using our example in Table 20–3 and the Table 20–1 market rates, we obtain the following:

$$\delta_{1.5} = \frac{(.04290981 \times 1) + [.05467685 \times (1.5 - 1)]}{1.5} = 4.6832156\%$$

$$(20\text{--}9d)$$

where the one year forward continuously compounded one-year rate is:

$$\delta_1 f_2 = \frac{.04879333 \times 2 - .04290981 \times 1}{1} = 5.467685\%$$

Forward Rate Interpolation

The interpolation of forward rates is the same as exponential interpolation of discount factors. The above 1.5-year spot rate generates the same discount factor as the exponential interpolation of the discount factor equation in (20–9a) as follows from Equation (20–3a):

$$v_{1.5} = e^{-.0468321567 \times 1.5} = .9321624$$

The above discussion illustrates the solution for the 1.5- and 2.0-year discount factors. The generic bootstrap formula for the other years

$$\left[c_T \times \sum_{t=.5}^{T-T_{LC}} v_t \right] + \left[c_T \times \sum_{t=T_{LC}+.5}^{T-.5} v_t \right] + (1 + c_T)v_T = 1 \quad (20\text{--}9e)$$

subject to the following constraint:

$$\sum_{t=T_{LC}+.5}^{T-.5} v_t = v_{T_{LC}}^{(1-p)} \times v_t^{p} \qquad (20\text{-}9f)$$

T_{LC} is the last available par coupon rate, subject to exponential interpolation of missing yield curve dates.

Equation (20-9) is an example formula for bootstrapping with the exponential interpolation of discount factors lying at half-year points on the yield curve. But in the case where a year point, such as the six-year rate, is missing in the market rates, the formula given in (20-9e) will generate a smooth spot curve allowing for any gaps in the observed par swap market rates.

Equation (20-9e) can be used to find the 5.5-, 6.0-, 6.5-, and 7.0-year discount factors when only 5-year and 7-year par yield rates are available. Equation (20-9e) says that all the discount factors known so far multiplied by the par coupon rate plus the par coupon rate multiplied by all of the discount factors (spanning any skip in the par coupon rates) plus the final principal and coupon multiplied by the final discount factor must equal 1. A trial-and-error method is used to find the solution while skipped period discount factors are exponentially interpolated. A computer program would iterate until a solution is found. The solution in our example is shown in Table 20-3.

Forward Rate Interpolation of Missing Yearly Points

This would occur as follows;

Define:

t = Year of the next available observed par coupon yield in the yield curve (e.g., 7 year)

pt = Year of the previous available observed par coupon rate (e.g., 5-year rate)

$ft = t - pt$ = Time period of the forward between t and pt spanning the gap

i = Number of half-yearly intervals between t and pt

Also note that $pt = t - ft$.

The half-yearly semiannual coupon dates for the bootstrap method are then:

$$pt + .5, pt + 1, \ldots, t - .5, t$$

Iterate on guesses for v_t and associated δ_t and δ_{ptft}, where

$$\delta_{ptft} = \frac{\delta_t - \delta_{pt}}{ft}$$

Derive all half-year spot rates between t and pt in increments of half-years (i) such that the half-year forward $i = .5, 1.0,$ and 1.5 years forward from $pt = i, 2i, 3i$, respectively, where like (20–9c)

$$\delta_{pt + .5i} = \frac{\delta_{pt} \times pt + \delta_{ptft} \times .5i}{pt + .5i} \qquad (20\text{–}9g)$$

Method III: Creating a Spot Curve from Eurodollar Futures

Another method for creating spot rates is by using the Eurodollar futures derived curve. Eurodollar futures, despite their limitations in representing the LIBOR curve (see Chapter 21 by Hogan and Weintraub), are an attractive source for liquid market rates. Cash LIBOR are not readily available and are thinly traded beyond six months. Eurodollar futures are a contract for delivery of three-month LIBOR on the expiration date of the contract. They are essentially LIBOR forwards except for the fact that they are marked to market daily and therefore generate cash flows prior to the expiration date. The stochastic path that rates take prior to the expiration date of the contract can create a rate of return that differs from a true forward contract.[8] With these anomalies aside, or after making some adjustment for them,[9] the series of Eurodollar futures can be linked together to create an interest rate swap curve that can be compared to the actual swap rates. If one were to invest in the Eurodollar futures strip (that is, in the series of futures contract expirations), what would the value of the investment be at the horizon date? By investing at the cash LIBOR up to the expiration date of the first futures contract, then at the rate of the first futures contract, then at the rate of the second futures contract, and so on until the last contract, one should have a future value that can be used to define a spot curve. By "stringing" together the futures rates as if they were forward rates linked together to generate a future value, a spot curve can be derived. Each forward picks up where the previous one leaves off. In actual fact, there are gaps and overlaps in the expiration dates of the series of futures contracts,[10] but the effect is minimal when calculating the Eurodollar futures strip rates.[11] In this analysis, we assume the futures overlap precisely as explained below.

Eurodollar Futures Strip Calculation
Define:

Stub Rate = LIBOR from the valuation date up to the expiration of the first nearby Eurodollar futures contract

This rate could be calculated using the exponential interpolation of discount factors methodology, namely, Equations (20–8) and (20–8a).

$F1$ = First Eurodollar futures contract (IMM 90-day) rate
$F2$ = Second Eurodollar futures contract rate
$F3$ = Third Eurodollar futures contract rate
$F1D$ = Expiration date of the first futures contract
$F2D$ = Expiration date of the second futures contract

Assuming no overlaps or gaps between futures periods (3 months) and that the term of each contract is for a period between its expiration date and the expiration date of the next contract, then the Eurodollar futures future value curve is as follows:

$$\left[1 + \text{Stub rate} \times \frac{F1D - \text{Valuation date}}{360}\right]$$
$$\times \left[1 + F1 \times \frac{F2D - F1D}{360}\right] \times \ldots = FV \quad (20\text{–}10)$$

The future value (FV) can be calculated to the expiration date of each Eurodollar futures contract. Table 20–4 shows the series of futures expirations dates, the rate, the number of days between expiration dates, the horizon future values up to the maturity of each futures contract, the continuous compounding spot rate, the discount factor, and the semiannually compounded spot rate. From Equation (20–3b), the discount factor at the futures expiration dates can be obtained:

$$\frac{1}{FV_{Fn}} = V_{Fn} \quad (20\text{–}10a)$$

TABLE 20-4
Eurodollar Futures Strip Calculations

	Valuation Date 12/31/91	Rate	Number of Days	Future Value	Continuous Compounded Spot Rate	Discount Factor	Semiannual Spot Rate
LIBOR stub	Stub	4.25%	76	1.0089722	4.289812%	0.9911076	4.336149%
First futures	03/16/92	4.05%	91	1.0193016	4.178411%	0.9810639	4.222365%
	06/15/92	4.14%	91	1.0299686	4.177451%	0.9709034	4.221384%
	09/14/92	4.36%	91	1.0413200	4.234534%	0.9603196	4.279680%
	12/14/92	4.84%	91	1.0540599	4.367500%	0.9487127	4.415537%
	03/15/93	5.09%	91	1.0676219	4.497792%	0.9366612	4.548749%
	06/14/93	5.55%	91	1.0825997	4.657289%	0.9237024	4.711938%
	09/13/93	5.98%	91	1.0989644	4.830916%	0.9099476	4.889733%
	12/13/93	6.51%	91	1.1170488	5.025115%	0.8952160	5.088777%
	03/14/94	6.59%	91	1.1356567	5.187936%	0.8805478	5.255809%
	06/13/94	6.84%	98	1.1568026	5.354061%	0.8644517	5.426370%
	09/19/94	7.05%	91	1.1774178	5.499369%	0.8493162	5.575674%
	12/19/94	7.39%	84	1.1977204	5.638127%	0.8349194	5.718350%
	03/13/95	7.39%	98	1.2218152	5.775926%	0.8184544	5.860138%
	06/19/95	7.53%	91	1.2450714	5.895756%	0.8031668	5.983516%
	09/18/95	7.67%	91	1.2692109	6.009276%	0.7878911	6.100466%
	12/18/95	7.86%	91	1.2944280	6.120543%	0.7725420	6.215159%
The drop →	03/18/96	8.22%	288				
The drop →	12/31/96	0.36%					
Theoretical LIBOR drop		8.24%					

434

	Year	Continuous Compounded Spot Rate	Discount Factor	Semiannual Spot Rate	Hypothetical Coupon	Continuous Six-Month Forwards	4-Year Swap Cash Flow Present Value	Sum of Present Values
Strip rates Six-month rate	0.5	4.178180%	0.9793258	4.222129%	4.2221%	4.3473%	0.880841	0.880841
1-year rate	1.0	4.262716%	0.9582686	4.308468%	4.3075%	5.0665%	0.779147	1.659988
1.5-year swap rate	1.5	4.530647%	0.9342981	4.582354%	4.5755%	5.8915%	0.415656	2.075644
2-year swap rate	2.0	4.870873%	0.9071772	4.930670%	4.9125%	6.6176%	0.018968	2.094612
2.5-year swap rate	2.5	5.220218%	0.8776517	5.288942%	5.2547%	7.0114%	−0.310382	1.784230
3-year swap rate	3.0	5.518751%	0.8474169	5.595597%	5.5443%	7.4316%	−0.472333	1.311896
3.5-year swap rate	3.5	5.792012%	0.8165065	5.876696%	5.8062%	7.6539%	−0.632947	0.678950
4-year swap rate	4.0	6.024743%	0.7858497	6.116405%	6.0269%	n.a.*	−0.699877	−0.020927

* n.a. = Not available.

From the futures derived future value (FV_{Fn}), the continuous compounding spot rates at those dates can be obtained using Equation (20–2a):

$$\delta_{Fn} = \frac{\ln(FV_{Fn})}{\text{Number of days}/365} \qquad (20\text{–}10b)$$

Likewise, the semiannually compounded spot rates (also known as the *strip rate*) can be obtained using Equation (20–10c):

$$i^2 = 2[e^{\delta_{Fn/2}} - 1] \qquad (20\text{–}10c)$$

The Eurodollar futures derived future value curve extends out to over four years. In the example in Table 20–4, the last contract on 12/18/95 carries the future value to 1,539 days, or approximately 4.21 years. In Table 20–4, a rate is shown of 8.22 percent with a day count of 288 days, where 288 is the number of days from the last futures contract up to exactly five years. The "drop" rate is the implied forward rate that carries the future value from the Eurodollar strip up to the cash five-year swap rate, such that:

$$FV_{\text{Flast}} \times (1 + r \times 288/360) = FV_5 \qquad (20\text{–}10d)$$

The FV_5 is derived from the exponentially derived cash spot curve of Method II. The futures curve provides more points for deriving spot rates. The exponential interpolation of discount factors can again be used for valuing cash flows on any date. Through the exponential interpolation of discount factors, a theoretical discount factor for the .5-, 1.0-, 1.5-, 2.0-, 2.5-, 3.0-, 3.5-, and 4.0-year points can be derived. Given these half-year and full-year discount factors using Equation (20–6e) for the hypothetical semiannual par coupon yield, the strip curve can be derived as shown in Table 20–4. The futures derived swap rates can then be compared to the par swap rates as follows:

Year	Swap Rate	Futures Derived Par Yield
2	4.924	4.9125
3	5.555	5.5443
4	6.02	6.0269

Chapter 20 Deriving a Zero Coupon Curve for Pricing Interest Rate Swaps **437**

TABLE 20-5
Eurodollar Futures Richness/Cheapness

Eurodollar Futures Expiration Date	Futures Price	Exponential Curve Exponential Interpolation Theoretical Price	Linear Curve Linear Interpretation Theoretical Price	Start of Period Year t	Exponential Rich/ Cheapness	Linear Interpretation of Continuous Spot Rate Richness/ Cheapness
03/16/92	95.95					
06/15/92	95.86					
09/14/92	95.64	95.68	95.61	0.71	−0.04	0.03
12/14/92	95.16	94.78	95.13	0.96	0.38	0.03
03/15/93	94.91	94.57	94.77	1.21	0.34	0.14
06/14/93	94.45	94.57	94.47	1.45	−0.12	−0.02
09/13/93	94.02	94.57	94.18	1.70	−0.55	−0.16
12/13/93	93.49	93.48	93.79	1.95	0.01	−0.30
03/14/94	93.41	93.22	93.45	2.20	0.19	−0.04
06/13/94	93.16	93.21	93.09	2.45	−0.05	0.07
09/19/94	92.95	93.22	92.75	2.72	−0.27	0.20
12/19/94	92.61	92.65	92.90	2.97	−0.04	−0.29
03/13/95	92.61	92.55	92.72	3.20	0.06	−0.11
06/19/95	92.47	92.55	92.45	3.47	−0.08	0.02
09/18/95	92.33	92.55	92.20	3.72	−0.22	0.13
12/18/95	92.14	92.01	92.23	3.97	0.13	−0.09
Drop rate	91.78	91.76				
The drop	0.36	0.24				

On the other hand, the futures rates can be compared to the theoretical forward rates from the Cash LIBOR + Swap rates to calculate the richness/cheapness of futures as shown in Table 20–5.

If a discount factor is interpolated from the LIBOR + Swap curve for the Eurodollar futures expiration dates, then a theoretical forward rate (f), which uses the actual/360 day-count basis can be calculated as follows:

$$FV_{F\ start} \times (1 + f \times \text{Actual days}/360) = FV_{end} \quad (20\text{-}10e)$$

By making an adjustment for the actual/360 day count to Equation (20–7c), we obtain the theoretical futures forward (f_{F1}) as follows:

$$f_{F1} = \left[\frac{V_{F1D\ \text{from cash}}}{V_{F2D\ \text{from cash}}} - 1\right] \times \frac{360}{F2D - F1D} \quad (20\text{-}10f)$$

Also shown in Table 20–5 is a futures richness/cheapness measure, which is derived from linear interpolation of the continuous compounding spot rates as provided by the Method I linearly interpolated curve. Linear interpolation is commonly used for deriving a futures richness/cheapness indicator. Some insight into the factors affecting the futures richness/cheapness may be obtained by studying the differences in the three spot curves.

Table 20–6 compares the results of the three term structure methods. This shows the continuous compounded spot rates, the six-month forward for six months continuous compounded forward rates, the hypothetical semiannually compounded par coupon yields from the three curves as well as the differences between the three curves in basis points. There are notable differences in the half-year spot rates between the linear interpolated curve and the exponential interpolated curve. The linearly interpolated curve has lower midyear spot rates because of its lack of curvature. This difference is amplified by its effect on the resulting forward rates between these points. The linear curve forward rates have lower forward rates between the year points and the half-year points because of the lower midyear spot rates. Also, the linear curve forward rates between the midyear points and the next-year point is higher, due to "catching up" for lost ground from the previous low forward rate. The strip curve shows properties resembling the linear curve as of 12/31/91.

The richness/cheapness differences can be better understood in light of Table 20–6. For example, the 3/15/93 futures contract begins at time 1.21 spanning to time 1.45. The exponential curve expects a higher forward rate leading to richness in the futures price. For the 9/13/93 contract, the exponential curve expects a lower forward rate and, therefore, a higher theoretical price, resulting in cheapness relative to the actual futures price. Arbitrage opportunities may exist if one wishes to sell contracts spanning periods just after whole-year points, while buying contracts occuring between midyear and the whole-year points and while selling the next "just-after-the-year" point contract. This is like a butterfly trade to exploit linearly priced futures. As time passes, this trade could drift into profitability, by waiting six months for the futures to drift into the inverse interpolation mispricing. Rolling down the yield curve is typically more of an exponential process than a linear one. The exponential curve is more in line with nature.[12]

SWAP PRICING

A wide variety of interest rate swaps can be priced using the zero coupon curve pricing method as demonstrated in the following examples.

With the discount factors determined, the only task remaining is specifying the swap cash flows. On the fixed side of the swap, the cash flow is a straightforward interest calculation where the semiannual fixed rate is divided by 2 (assuming 30/360, no weekends), and then multiplied by the notional principal amount (NPA). The floating-rate side of the swap is predetermined for the first floating cash flows at the onset of the swap or at previous resets. Future floating-rate reset cash flows can be determined by the forward-rate floating-side forecast method, which estimates the future floating-rate reset cash flows as equal to the NPA times the forward rate for the period. Using Equation (20–7c), the forward rates can be directly determined from the discount factors. The present values of the floating-rate-side future reset cash flows would be:

$$NPA \times \left[\frac{V_{t-.5}}{V_t} - 1\right] \times v_t = PV_0 \text{ of the floating flow} \quad (20\text{–}11)$$

which simplifies to:

$$NPA \times (v_{t-.5} - v_t) = PV_0 \text{ of the floating cash flow} \quad (20\text{–}11\text{a})$$

Thus the net cash flow of a semiannual fixed-rate swap versus six-month reset floating-rate swap would be:

$$(F/2 \times NPA) - \left(NPA \times \left[\frac{v_{t-.5}}{V_t} - 1\right]\right) = \text{Net cash flow} \quad (20\text{–}11\text{b})$$

where F is the fixed rate of the swap.

The net present value of the net cash flow is:

$$(F/2 \times NPA \times v_t) - (NPA \times [v_{t-.5} - v_t])$$
$$= PV_0 \text{ of the net cash flow} \quad (20\text{–}11\text{c})$$

TABLE 20-6
Comparison of Curves from Bootstrap Approaches

	\multicolumn{8}{c}{Year}
	0.5	1.0	1.5	2.0	2.5	3.0	3.5

Continuous Compounding Spot Rates

Linear coupon	4.189833%	4.290981%	4.584824%	4.881157%	5.203026%	5.529064%	5.771357%
Exponential bootstrap	4.189833%	4.290981%	4.683216%	4.879333%	5.267413%	5.526134%	5,805122%
From EDS strip	4.178180%	4.262716%	4.530647%	4.870873%	5.220218%	5.518751%	5.792012%

Differences in the Continuous Compounding Spot Rates from the Exponential Bootstrap Approach (in basis points)

Linear coupon	0.000000	0.00000	− 9.8391	0.18237	− 6.43879	0.29303	− 3.37653
Exponential bootstrap	0.000000	0.00000	0.00000	0.00000	0.00000	0.00000	0.00000
From EDS strip	−1.6529	− 2.82650	−15.25688	− 0.84605	− 4.71950	− 0.73831	− 1.31104

Six-Month Forwards: Continuous Compounding

Linear coupon	4.392130%	5.172511%	5.770153%	6.490501%	7.159257%	7.225116%	7.742524%
Exponential bootstrap	4.392130%	5.467685%	5.467685%	6.819735%	6.819735%	7.479054%	7.479054%
From EDS strip	4.347253%	5.066508%	5.891549%	6.617602%	7.011412%	7.431580%	7.653857%

Differences in Six-Month Continuous Compounding Forward Rates from the Exponential Bootstrap Approach (in basis points)

Linear coupon	−0.0000	− 29.5174	30.2469	−32.9234	33.9522	− 25.3939	26.3469
Exponential bootstrap	0.0000	0.0000	0.0000	0.0000	0.0000	0.0000	0.0000
From EDS strip	−4.4877	−40.1176	42.3864	−20.2133	19.1677	− 4.7474	17.4803

Hypothetical SemiAnnual Coupon

Linear coupon	4.2340%	4.3362%	4.6301%	4.9240%	5.2395%	5.5550%	5.7880%
Exponential bootstrap	4.2340%	4.3362%	4.7283%	4.9240%	5.3033%	5.5550%	5.8219%
From EDS strip	4.2221%	4.3075%	4.5755%	4.9125%	5.2547%	5.5443%	5.8062%

Differences in Hypothetical Semiannual Coupon from the Exponential Bootstrap Approach (in basis points)

Linear coupon	0.0000	0.0000	− 9.8183	0.0000	− 6.3804	0.0000	− 3.3899
Exponential bootstrap	0.0000	0.0000	0.0000	0.0000	0.0000	0.0000	0.0000
From EDS strip	−1.1899	− 2.8688	−15.2789	− 1.1533	− 4.8607	− 1.0695	− 1.5734

* n.a. = Not available.

Chapter 20 Deriving a Zero Coupon Curve for Pricing Interest Rate Swaps

4.0	4.5	5.0	5.5	6.0	6.5	7.0
6.017753%	6.226002%	6.438354%	6.550582%	6.665672%	6.783584%	6.904354%
6.014364%	6.247875%	6.434683%	6.582173%	6.705082%	6.809081%	6.898224%
6.024743%						
0.33891	− 2.18727	0.36709	− 3.15910	− 3.94104	− 2.54975	0.61298
0.00000	0.00000	0.00000	0.00000	0.00000	0.00000	0.00000
1.03788						
7.891994%	8.349523%	7.672866%	7.931652%	8.198534%	8.474360%	7.908106%
8.115960%	8.115960%	8.057076%	8.057076%	8.057076%	8.057076%	8.326237%
n.a.*						
−22.3967	23.3563	−38.4209	−12.5424	14.1458	41.7284	−41.8131
0.0000	0.0000	0.0000	0.0000	0.0000	0.0000	0.0000
6.0210%	6.2160%	6.4110%	6.5170%	6.6230%	6.7290%	6.8350%
6.0210%	6.2383%	6.4110%	6.5469%	6.6595%	6.7542%	6.8350%
6.0269%						
0.0000	− 2.2311	− 0.0000	− 2.9864	− 3.6456	− 2.5213	− 0.0000
0.0000	0.0000	0.0000	0.0000	0.0000	0.0000	0.0000
0.5889						

Equation (20–11c) further reduces to:

$$NPA \times \left[\left(\frac{F}{2} \times v_t\right) - (v_{t-.5} - v_t)\right]$$

$$= PV_0 \text{ of the net cash flow} \quad (20\text{–}11d)$$

The price of the swap is equal to the difference between the present values of the two sides of the swap.

Pricing a Four-Year Plain-Vanilla Swap

Tables 20–2, 20–3, and 20–4 show the cash flow pricing of a plain-vanilla four-year swap with a fixed rate of 6.021 percent and an NPA of 100. The present value for the exponential and linear curve should be zero because the fixed rate is at the current four-year swap rate. The present value from the strip curve is a negative −20,927 because the strip curve is implying a slightly higher four-year swap rate (6.026889 percent versus 6.021 percent on the cash curve). A fixed rate of 6.026889 percent would generate a swap present value of zero using the strip curve. There is little difference in the pricing of the four-year swap, but the curves diverge greatly for the pricing of a 1.5-year plain-vanilla swap. For example, using an exponentially derived fixed rate of 4.7283 percent for all curves, the prices are as follows:

1.5-Year Swap at 4.7283%

	Present Value	Zero Present Value Fixed Rate
Linear curve	$140,932	4.630118%
Exponential curve	0.0	4.7283%
Strip curve	219,397	4.575511%

The linear curve is suggesting that an 18-month coupon rate of 4.630118 percent would generate a price of zero. The strip curve is suggesting that an 18-month coupon rate of 4.575511 percent would generate a price of zero.

Pricing a Forward Swap

The zero coupon curve pricing method can be used to price a forward swap. For example, a swap starting in one year and ending in four years (a 4/1 structure) would have the cash flows in Table 20-7 under the three curves using the fixed rate of 6.652873 per-

TABLE 20-7
Pricing of a 4/1 Forward Swap—Fixed-Side Coupon: 6.652873 percent

	\multicolumn{8}{c}{Year}
	0.5	1.0	1.5	2.0	2.5	3.0	3.5	4.0

Pricing with Linear Curve

Discount factors	0.9792687	0.9579978	0.9335392	0.9069907	0.878029	0.8471547	0.817097	0.7860695
Fixed side	0.000000	0.000000	3.326436	3.326436	3.326436	3.326436	3.326436	3.326436
Float side	0.000000	0.000000	2.619989	2.927098	3.298483	3.644468	3.678604	3.947172
Net cash flow present value	0.000000	0.000000	0.659496	0.362196	0.024544	−0.269422	−0.287755	−0.487941
Sum of present values	0.000000	0.000000	0.659496	1.021692	1.046236	0.776814	0.489059	0.001118

Pricing with Exponential Curve

Discount factor	0.9792687	0.9579978	0.9321624	0.9070237	0.8766168	0.8472292	0.8161319	0.786176
Fixed side	0.000000	0.000000	3.326436	3.326436	3.326436	3.326436	3.326436	3.326436
Float side	0.000000	0.000000	2.771555	2.771555	3.468670	3.468670	3.810327	3.810327
Cash flow present value	0.000000	0.000000	0.517240	0.503291	−0.124684	−0.120504	−0.394919	−0.380423
Sum of present value	0.000000	0.000000	0.517240	1.020531	0.895847	0.775342	0.3804233	0.000000

Eurodollar Strip Price

Strip discount factor	0.9793258	0.9582686	0.9342981	0.9071772	0.8776517	0.8474169	0.8165065	0.7858497
Cash flow present value	0	0	0.710835	0.305578	−0.033100	−0.204603	−0.374982	−0.451598
Sum of present values	0.000000	0.000000	0.710835	1.016413	0.983313	0.778710	0.403727	−0.047871

cent, which generates a zero present value under the exponential curve. The exponential curve gives a price of zero because a fixed rate was used, which would result in a zero present value. The prices from the three curves are as follows:

Forward Swap (4/1) at 6.652873 percent

	Present Value	Coupon Forward	Semiannual Spot Forward
Linear curve	$ 1,118	6.65244%	6.703228%
Exponential curve	0	6.65287%	6.698558%
Strip curve	−47,871	6.67139%	6.722599%

Show above are also the coupon-paying forward fixed rates that will generate a zero *PV* for each curve. Also shown are semiannually compounded forward rates for the period beginning in one year and ending in four years. It should be noted that the coupon-paying forward rate is not the same as a semiannual forward spot rate. The coupon-paying forward is like a hypothetical coupon par rate that is derived using Equation (20–6c). Using the semiannual spot forward as if it were the forward swap coupon rate is a common source of error for swap users. The pricing error for this mistake would be:

	Price	Semiannual Forward
Linear curve	$131,258	6.703228%
Exponential curve	117,989	6.698558%
Strip curve	132,331	6.722599%

Since the coupon-paying hypothetical forwards produce a price of zero, then the above table shows prices at the semiannual spot forwards. With this much pricing error, it would only require a few trades to justify hiring a good swap analyst.

Pricing a Forward Amortizing Swap

Table 20–8 shows the pricing of a forward amortizing swap that begins in one year with an *NPA* of 100, and then the *NPA* declines by 10 per six-month period to 50 in four years. A fixed-rate coupon

TABLE 20–8
Pricing of a 4/1 Forward Amortizing Swap—Fixed-Side Coupon: 6.470003 percent

	\multicolumn{8}{c}{Year}
	0.5	1.0	1.5	2.0	2.5	3.0	3.5	4.0
\multicolumn{9}{c}{*Pricing with Linear Curve*}
NPA	0	0	100	90	80	70	60	50
Discount factors	0.9792687	0.9579978	0.9335392	0.9069907	0.878029	0.8471547	0.817097	0.7860695
Fixed side	0.000000	0.000000	3.235001	2.911501	2.588001	2.264501	1.941001	1.617501
Float side	0.000000	0.000000	2.619989	2.634388	2.638786	2.551128	2.207162	1.973586
Net cash flow present value	0.000000	0.000000	0.574138	0.251339	−0.044591	−0.242817	−0.217480	−0.279908
Sum of present values	0.000000	0.000000	0.574138	0.825477	0.780886	0.538068	0.320589	0.040681
\multicolumn{9}{c}{*Pricing with Exponential Curve*}
NPA	0	0	100	90	80	70	60	50
Discount factor	0.9792687	0.9579978	0.9321624	0.9070237	0.8766168	0.8472292	0.8161319	0.786176
Fixed side	0.000000	0.000000	3.235001	2.911501	2.588001	2.264501	1.941001	1.617501
Float side	0.000000	0.000000	2.771555	2.494399	2.774936	2.428069	2,286196	1.905164
Cash flow present value	0.000000	0.000000	0.432008	0.378321	−0.163870	−0.138580	−0.281725	−0.226154
Sum of present value	0.000000	0.000000	0.432008	0.810329	0.646459	0.507879	0.2261537	−0.000000
\multicolumn{9}{c}{*Eurodollar Strip Price*}
Strip discount factor	0.9793258	0.9582686	0.9342981	0.9071772	0.8776517	0.8474169	0.8165065	0.7858497
Cash flow present value	0	0	0.625408	0.200367	−0.090679	−0.197461	−0.269784	−0.261726
Sum of present values	0.000000	0.000000	0.625408	0.825775	0.735096	0.537635	0.267851	0.006125

of 6.470003 percent would generate an exponential curve price of 0. The prices for the other curves are as follows:

Forward Amortizing Swap at 6.470003%

	Present Value	Fixed-Rate Coupon for Zero Present Value
Linear curve	$40,681	6.4449292%
Exponential curve	–0–	6.470003 %
Strip curve	6,125	6.466885 %

Solving for Unknowns

In order to find the fixed-rate coupon that generates a zero NPV, one could just make guesses at the fixed-rate coupon rate until the model produces a zero price. But there is also a closed-form solution for this problem. We know that the fixed-rate coupon is a par yield that is a blended average rate or internal rate of return number. We know that in theory this rate is equal to the present value–weighted blend of the periodic six-month semiannually compounded forward rates. In other words, a par bond yield is equal to the average of the periodic six-month semiannually compounded forward rates weighted by the discount factors. Similarly, when the NPA of a swap is varying, the weighting is the NPA times the discount factor.

The solution to finding the unknown average NPA times the discount factor–weighted semiannually compounded forward rate is shown in Table 20–9. The first rows show the six-month periodic semiannually compounded forward rates. The six-month forward rates can be derived from the six-month continuous compounded forward rates using equation (20–1c). Also shown are the cumulative at-the-money cash flow present values, which are the NPA times the periodic semiannually compounded forward rates times the discount factor plus the previous period present value. Also shown is the cumulative sum of the $NPAs$ times the discount fac-

TABLE 20-9
Solving for the Unknown Fixed-Rate Coupon on the 4/1 Forward Amortizing Swap

	\multicolumn{8}{c}{Year}
	0.5	1.0	1.5	2.0	2.5	3.0	3.5	4.0

Six-Month Semiannual Forward Rates

	0.5	1.0	1.5	2.0	2.5	3.0	3.5	4.0
Linear coupon	4.440712%	5.239978%	5.854196%	6.596966%	7.288937%	7.357207%	7.894343%	8.049771%
Exponential bootstrap	4.440712%	5.543109%	5.543109%	6.937340%	6.937340%	7.620655%	7.620655%	8.282882%
From EDS strip	4.394843%	5.131227%	5.979183%	6.728302%	7.135760%	7.571377%	7.802197%	n.a.*

Cumulative Fixed-Rate Present Values

	0.5	1.0	1.5	2.0	2.5	3.0	3.5	4.0
Linear coupon	0	0	2.445862	4.835228	7.152159	9.313359	11.116825	12.668200
Exponential bootstrap	0	0	2.583539	4.846018	7.278574	9.335705	11.201543	12.699337
From EDS strip	0	0	2.397048	4.837929	7.199971	9.316408	11.171032	12.703870

Cumulative Sum of (NPA × Discount factors)

	0.5	1.0	1.5	2.0	2.5	3.0	3.5	4.0
Linear coupon	0	0	93.35392	174.98307	245.22540	304.52623	353.55205	392.85552
Exponential bootstrap	0	0	93.21624	174.84838	244.97772	304.28376	353.25168	392.56048
From EDS strip	0	0	93.42981	175.07576	245.28790	304.60708	353.59747	392.88995

* n.a. = Not available.

tors. At the four-year point, if we divide the cumulative cash flow present value by the cumulative discounted *NPA*, then multiply by 2, we obtain the average semiannual fixed-rate coupon [(12.699336/392.56047) × 2 = 6.470003%] for the exponential curve.

CONCLUSION

This analysis shows the possibilities of zero coupon curve swap pricing and reviews the impact of interpolation methods. The automation of this process would create the capabilities to price any imaginable swap structure.

APPENDIX: COMPUTER EXAMPLE

In order to verify the accuracy of Method II, the bootstrap method with the exponential interpolation of discount factors, the following software program. In this example, an old three-year swap was marked to market. The swap had an effective date of 3/31/91 with a maturity of 3/31/94, as shown below. The swap is being valued on 12/31/91 using the same yield curve rates as shown in Table 20–1. The floating-side reset rate on 12/31/91 would be 4.25 because the swap resets quarterly as shown in the subsequent computer screen:

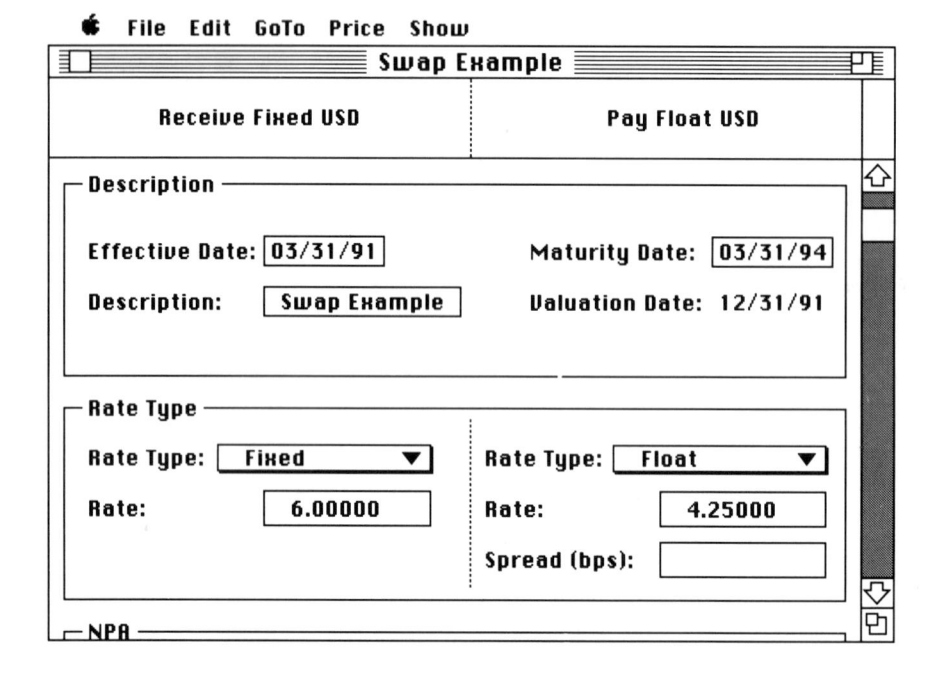

```
 File   Edit   GoTo   Price   Show
┌─────────────────── Swap Example ───────────────────┐
│        Receive Fixed USD    │    Pay Float USD     │
│ ┌─ Description ──────────────────────────────────┐ │
│ │                                                │ │
│ │  Effective Date: [03/31/91]   Maturity Date: [03/31/94] │
│ │                                                │ │
│ │  Description:  [ Swap Example ]  Valuation Date: 12/31/91 │
│ │                                                │ │
│ └────────────────────────────────────────────────┘ │
│ ┌─ Rate Type ────────────────────────────────────┐ │
│ │                                                │ │
│ │  Rate Type: [ Fixed    ▼ ]   Rate Type: [ Float    ▼ ] │
│ │  Rate:      [  6.00000  ]    Rate:      [  4.25000  ] │
│ │                              Spread (bps): [       ] │
│ └────────────────────────────────────────────────┘ │
│ ┌─ NPA ────────────────────────────────────────── │
```

A swap that resets quarterly to three-month LIBOR is tested to show the exponential interpolation of discount factors. The price of the swap is shown below. The full price of a swap would include the accrued interest as well.

Chapter 20 Deriving a Zero Coupon Curve for Pricing Interest Rate Swaps 449

Swap Example

Receive Fixed USD | Pay Float USD

Payments

	Receive Fixed USD		Pay Float USD
Pmt Freq:	Semiannual	Pmt Freq:	Quarterly
Day Count:	30/360	Day Count:	Act/360
Date Adjust:	Standard	Date Adjust:	Standard
Date Avoid:	Forwards	Date Avoid:	Forwards

Resets

	Reset Freq:	Quarterly
	Compound:	None

Swap Example

Receive Fixed USD | Pay Float USD

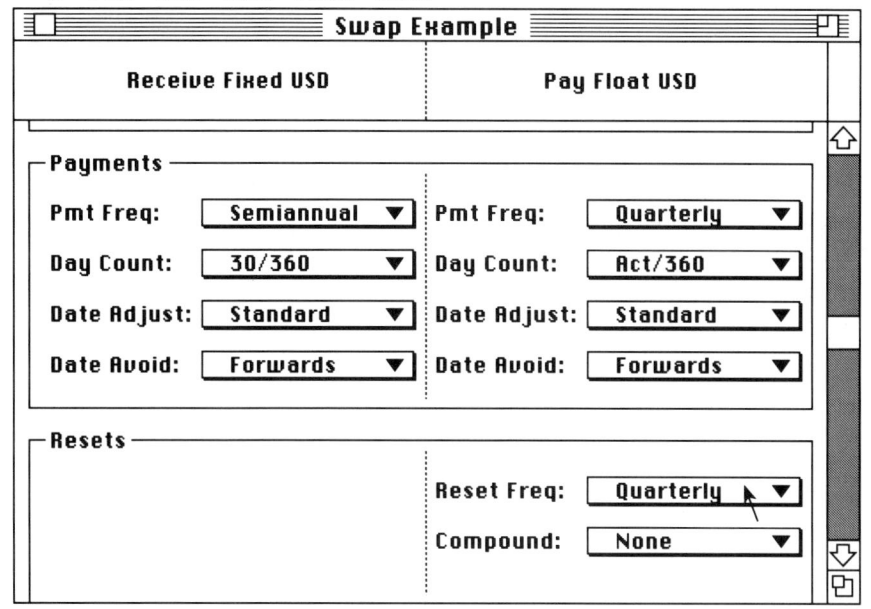

Price

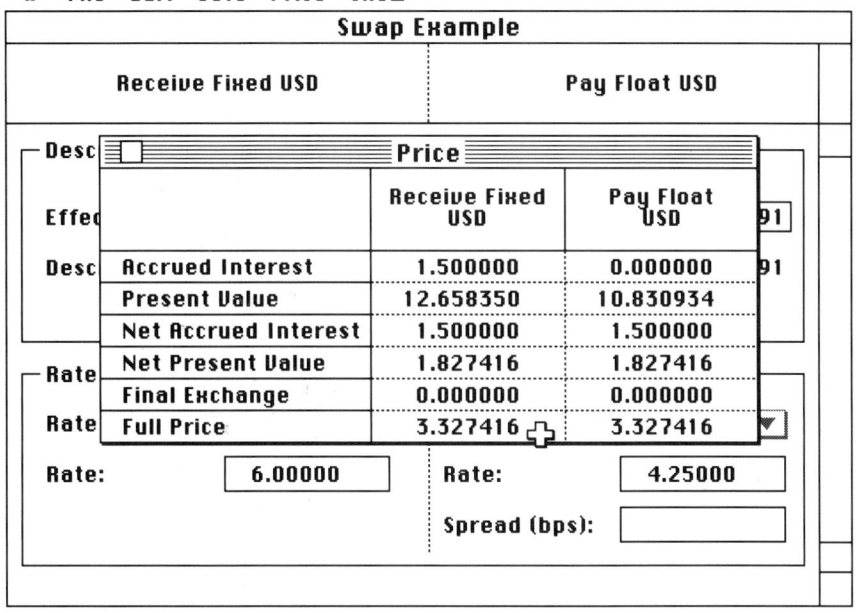

	Receive Fixed USD	Pay Float USD
Accrued Interest	1.500000	0.000000
Present Value	12.658350	10.830934
Net Accrued Interest	1.500000	1.500000
Net Present Value	1.827416	1.827416
Final Exchange	0.000000	0.000000
Full Price	3.327416	3.327416

Rate: 6.00000 | Rate: 4.25000

Spread (bps):

Provided by the MFE Group, Inc., New York, NY 10019, (212) 399-0076.

TABLE 20-10
Zero Coupon Curve Cash Flow Pricing

Date	NPA	Days	Cash Flow	Present Value	Spot Rate	Discount Factor
			Receive Fixed			
12/31/91	100.000000	90	1.500000	1.500000	3.99978	1.00000
03/31/92	100.000000	90	1.500000	1.484057	4.27430	0.98937
06/30/92	0.000000	0	0.000000	0.000000	0.00000	0.00000
09/30/92	100.000000	180	3.000000	2.905725	4.25727	0.96857
12/31/92	0.000000	0	0.000000	0.000000	0.00000	0.00000
03/31/93	100.000000	180	3.000000	2.834975	4.52632	0.94499
06/30/93	0.000000	0	0.000000	0.000000	0.00000	0.00000
09/30/93	100.000000	180	3.000000	2.758521	4.79528	0.91951
12/31/93	0.000000	0	0.000000	0.000000	0.00000	0.00000
03/31/94	100.000000	180	3.000000	2.675072	5.09493	0.89169
			Pay Float			
	100.000000	0	0.000000	0.000000	3.99978	1.00000
	100.000000	91	1.074306	1.062887	4.27430	0.98937
	100.000000	91	1.031626	1.010239	4.18983	0.97927
	100.000000	92	1.104083	1.069387	4.25727	0.96857
	100.000000	92	1.104083	1.057709	4.29098	0.95800
	100.000000	90	1.376306	1.300598	4.52632	0.94499
	100.000000	91	1.376306	1.282941	4.68322	0.93216
	100.000000	92	1.376306	1.265523	4.79528	0.91951
	100.000000	92	1.376306	1.248342	4.87933	0.90702
	100.000000	90	1.719551	1.533307	5.09493	0.89169

Table 20-10 shows the zero coupon curve cash flow pricing of this swap example.

NOTES

1. John Macfarlane, Daniel R. Ross, and Janet Showers, "The Interest Rate Swap Market: Yield Mathematics, Terminology, and Conventions," Salomon Brothers, New York City.
2. "By the Bootstraps," *Risk* 3, no. 6 (June 1990).
3. Mark Buono, Russell B. Gregory-Allen, and Uzi Yaari, "The Efficacy of Term Structure Estimation Techniques: A Monte Carlo Study," *The Journal of Fixed Income,* March 1992, p. 52-63.
4. David R. Smith, "By the Bootstraps," *Risk* 3, no. 6 (June 1990), pp. 40-42, discusses the bootstrap method using semiannual spot rates.

5. There is also an 18-month LIBOR that can be used to define the 1.5-year point. This rate is not readily available and is not a liquid rate. It is also an annual coupon rate and would not be a spot rate.
6. An 18 × 12 FRA is a forward rate agreement that begins in 12 months and ends in 18 months. FRAs are the topic of Chapter 10.
7. A term structure that is consistent with the forward rates between points is consistent with arbitrage pricing theory, which states that a swap price should be equal to its arbitrage equivalents, such as forward rate agreements (FRAs).
8. See Chapter 21 by Michael Hogan and Keith Weintraub, "The Swap Yield Curve."
9. One author has measured the effect of stochastic marking to the market and has suggested how the strip rates need to be adjusted to equal the swap curve. Daniel Nadler, "Eurodollar Futures/Interest Rate Swap Arbitrage," *The Handbook of Fixed Income Securities*, 3rd ed., ed. Frank J. Fabozzi, Richard D. Irwin, Inc., Homewood Ill. 1991, pp. 1218–42. For the one-year swap, the option premium is 0 to 1 basis points; for the two-year swap, 1 to 3 basis points; for the three-year swap; 3 to 6 basis points.
10. See Ira G. Kawaller, "Interest Rate Swaps versus Eurodollar Strips," *Financial Analysts Journal*, September–October 1989.
11. The effects of gaps and overlaps become more of an issue when one is replicating swaps with futures and arbitraging between the two markets.
12. Eugene P. Wigner, "The Unreasonable Effectiveness of Mathematics in the Natural Sciences," *Communications on Pure and Applied Mathematics* 13 (1960), pp. 1–14.

CHAPTER 21

THE SWAP YIELD CURVE

Michael Hogan
Citicorp, New York
Keith S. Weintraub
Citicorp, New York

INTRODUCTION

All swap curves are divided into three parts (see Figure 21-1). The first part consists of the cash LIBOR curve, which gives the rate that an investor can earn over some term on a dollar invested today. The second part consists of the Eurodollar futures contracts (futures, hereafter), which are supposed to give the investor some form of information about what he or she will earn on a dollar invested for 90 days at some time in the future. The third part is the swap rates themselves.

The cash curve covers the period up to the expiration of the first futures contract, which is guaranteed to occur within about three months (within 84 to 98 days, to be specific). The futures contracts pick up with the expiration of the first futures contract. There are 16 contracts going out four years. They expire four times a year in March, June, September, and December, and are "color coded," so the nearest contract expiring in December is called the *red DEC* and the most distant is called the *blue DEC*. The consensus is that there is not enough liquidity in the most distant contracts to trust the rate, so most people ignore the last four to eight contracts in constructing the yield curve. Because futures contracts differ from forward contracts, the distant contracts must be treated with care. Futures are traded at the Chicago Mercantile Exchange on a price basis and settle to 90-day LIBOR at expiration. For example, if 90-day LIBOR is 7 percent at the futures expiration, then the futures price would be 100% − 7% = 93%.

The swap curve picks up where the futures stop. The swap market is a dealer market. Swaps are not quoted on a public exchange, but swap quotes are available on many broker screens. This is how the market presents its information to potential transactors.

The goal of this chapter is to take the rate information presented to the investor by the market and put it into a form that allows him or her to calculate the fixed payment or the value of a swap with unusual features. There are two closely related forms that it is useful to have the information in, the discounting factors

FIGURE 21–1
How the Swaps Yield Curve Is Defined

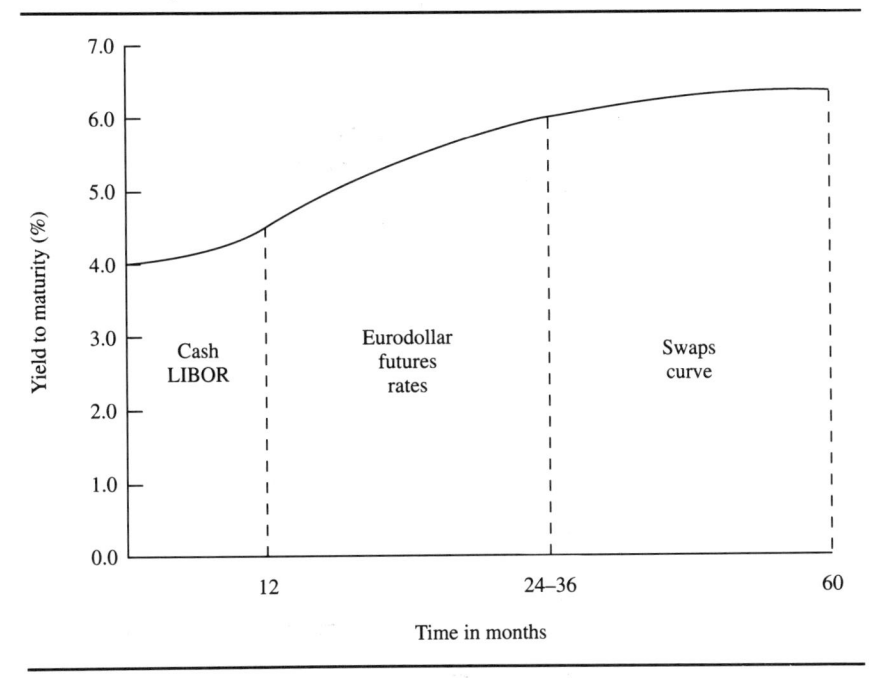

(or zero coupon bond prices) implicit in the curve, and the forward rates. These latter two curves can be algebraically derived from the swaps yield curve after it is constructed.

WHAT THE FUTURES CURVE IS SUPPOSED TO BE TELLING INVESTORS

Futures rates of the futures contracts that expire at Time t in the future are supposed to be telling investors how to discount cash flows over the period from t days to $t + 90$ days. Equivalently, they are supposed to be implying the rate for forward purchase of a zero coupon bond. Given the prices of zeros of all maturities, that rate is determined by simple arbitrage arguments involving only static long and short bond positions.

We illustrate this by example. Suppose that today is April 3, 1992 (11:08 A.M., to be precise). The next futures contract expires June 17, 1992. Suppose that the cash market's yield curve and futures rates are given in Table 21–1 and Table 21–2, respectively.

We want to value a contract that settles in two days, and pays $1 on September 16, 1992, which is 90 days after the expiration of

TABLE 21–1
Cash Market Interest Rates on April 3, 1992

Expiration	Rate (%)
1 month	4.2500%
3 months	4.3125%
6 months	4.4047%
1 year	4.8411%
2 years	5.7164%
3 years	6.3903%
4 years	6.8490%
5 years	7.2020%
7 years	7.5610%
10 years	7.8820%
30 years	8.3570%

TABLE 21–2
Futures Price Quotations and Expirations on April 3, 1992

Expiration	Price (%)
06/17/92	95.63%
09/16/92	95.31%
12/16/92	94.64%
03/17/93	94.39%
06/16/93	93.86%
09/15/93	93.36%
12/15/93	92.77%
03/16/94	92.67%
06/15/94	92.44%
09/21/94	92.24%
12/21/94	91.94%
03/15/95	91.99%

the futures contract. This is nothing other than a zero coupon bond that matures on September 16, 1992. We value it by first discounting the $1 over the period June 17 to September 16 at the futures rate of 4.37 (from Table 21–2 we take 95.63 and compute 100 − 95.63) applied for the 91 days between June 17 and September 16, and then discounting back to the present by using a rate obtained from the cash curve in Table 21–1. This rate applies over 75 days and is calculated as a linear interpolation between the one-month and three-month rates in Table 21–1. The one-month rate (4.25) applies for 30 days, and the three-month rate (4.3125) applies for 91 days. Since we want a rate that would apply for 75 days, we get a rate of:

$$4.27 = 4.25 \frac{46}{61} + 4.3125 \frac{15}{61}$$

We would then price the contract at:

$$\frac{1}{1 + .01 \times 4.27 \times 75/360} \times \frac{1}{1 + .01 \times 4.37 \times 91/360}$$
$$= (.9912)(.9891) \qquad (21\text{–}1)$$
$$= 0.9804$$

Now, the price of a zero coupon bond maturing on June 17, 1992, is $.9912 = 1/(1 + .01 \times 4.27 \times 75/360)$. It follows that the ratio of the price of the zero that matures on June 17 to the zero that matures on September 16 is $(1 + .01 \times 4.37 \times 91/360) = .9891$.

This zero coupon bond matures the settlement day of the second futures contract. Let's push this example one step further and price a zero coupon bond that matures on the settlement day of the third futures contract, December 16, 1992. Call this bond Z1216 (the notation Z1216 refers to the fact that the zero matures on 12/16). We discount over the 91 days between September 16 and December 16 at the futures rate of $100 - 95.31 = 4.69$ for the contract maturing September 16, and then we discount back to today (at 11:08 A.M.) using the zero coupon bond price from Equation (21-1). We get a price of:

$$\frac{1}{1 + .01 \times 4.27 \times 75/360} \times \frac{1}{1 + .01 \times 4.37 \times 91/360} \times \frac{1}{1 + .01 \times 4.69 \times 91/360} = \quad (21\text{-}2)$$
$$(.9912)(.9891)(.9883) = .9689$$

Again, the futures rate is related to the ratio of zero coupon bond prices. Specifically,

$$Z0916/Z1216 = 1 + .01 \times 4.69 \times 91/360$$
$$= 1.0119$$

We can push this argument as far out as we have futures rates we can rely on. Let d_i be the number of days between the settlement day of the ith and $i + 1$ futures contract. Let rf_i be the ith futures rate (that is, 100 minus the value in the ith row of Table 21-2). Then the price of a zero coupon bond that matures on the settlement day of the $n + 1$ futures contract is:

$$Z = 1/[(1 + .01 \times 4.3 \times 75/360) \times (1 + .01 \times rf_1 \times d_1/360) \times \ldots \times (1 + .01 \times rf_n \times d_n/360)] \quad (21\text{-}3)$$

Table 21-3 shows the discount factors to the dates of the maturities of underlying bonds for the futures in Table 21-2.

TABLE 21-3
Discount Factors to Futures Expirations on April 3, 1992

Expiration	Discount Factor
06/17/92	.9912
09/16/92	.9804
12/16/92	.9689
03/17/93	.9559
06/16/93	.9425
09/15/93	.9281
12/15/93	.9128
03/16/94	.8964
06/15/94	.8801
09/21/94	.8636
12/21/94	.8470
03/15/95	.8301
06/14/95	.8136

Now the price of a zero coupon bond that matures on the settlement day of one of the futures contracts can be calculated. Discounting a cash flow that is not receive on one of these dates, but is received before the last one, can be done in several ways. Here are two ways to proceed:

- Calculate discounting rates that apply to each settlement date. This yields a discount term structure that can be used to perform some form of interpolation on the rates to produce a discounting rate that applies to the desired date.
- Perform an interpolation on the cash and futures rates to obtain cash and futures rates, where one of the futures settle on the desired date; then proceed as above to derive a discounting rate from the cash and futures curve.

Here is an example of the first method. Suppose we wanted to find the discount factor to April 1, 1993. From Table 21-3 we know that the discount factor to March 17, 1993, is .9559. From Table 21-2 we see that the futures price for March 17, 1993, is 94.39. This implies that the rate we can use for the period March 17, 1993, to

June 16, 1993, is 5.61 (100 − 94.39). We want to use this rate from March 17, 1993, to April 1, 1993, a period of 15 days. This implies that the discount factor to April 1, 1993, is:

$$(.9559) \frac{1}{1 + .01 \times 5.61 \times 15/360} = (.9559)(.9977)$$
$$= 0.9537$$

WHAT THE FUTURES CURVE IS REALLY TELLING INVESTORS

Due to the day-to-day settlement of futures contracts, a Eurodollar futures price should be lower than the forward price on the same underlying. To see this, note that when Eurodollar futures prices go up, interest rates go down. An investor long the Eurodollar futures contract will receive money when the futures price goes up. He or she can now invest this money at a lower-than-average interest rate. Conversely, when the futures price goes down, the investor must finance the position at a higher-than-average rate of interest. An investor in a forward contract does not have to worry about intermediate cash flows since there is only one settlement (at maturity) on a forward contract. This shows that relative to a forward contract, the futures contract should be less desirable and, hence, the futures price should be lower than the forward price.

This argument[1] also shows that *the actual value of a futures contract depends on mathematical assumptions about the underlying interest rate process*. Some rate process assumptions give ridiculous futures values. The difference between the futures price and the forward price is larger the longer the maturity of the contract. The contracts are highly sensitive to the "tail" behavior of the interest rate processes. The (dauntless) reader is referred to Cox, Ingersoll, and Ross (1981) for the futures versus forwards issue, and to Hogan and Weintraub (1992) for the particular problems with the Eurodollar futures contract.

The fact that Eurodollar futures prices and forward prices differ is important because this implies that the information that the market gives the investor (in terms of futures prices) must be "distilled." The investor should at least be aware that the rates that are obtained by subtracting the futures price from 100 are not exactly the correct rates to use for discounting cash flows.

One well-known interest rate model that is capable of giving reasonable Eurodollar futures prices is the square-root or CIR model, presented in Cox, Ingersoll, and Ross (1985). We adopt their notation. The short-rate process is assumed to evolve according to this stochastic differential equation:

$$dr = [-(\kappa + \lambda)r + \kappa\theta]dt + \sigma\sqrt{r}dB(t) \quad (21\text{-}4)$$

where $B(t)$ is a standard Brownian motion. Set:

$$\gamma = \sqrt{(\kappa + \lambda)^2 + 2\sigma^2}$$

$$A(s,t) = \left\{\frac{2\gamma e^{(\gamma+\kappa+\lambda)(t-s)/2}}{(\kappa + \lambda + \gamma)[e^{\gamma(t-s)} - 1] + 2\gamma}\right\}^{2\kappa\theta/\sigma^2}$$

$$B(s,t) = \frac{2[e^{\gamma(t-s)} - 1]}{(\kappa + \lambda + \gamma)[e^{\gamma(t-s)} - 1] + 2\gamma}$$

$$c = \frac{2(\kappa + \lambda)}{\sigma^2[1 - e^{-(\kappa+\lambda)t_1}]}$$

$$u = cr(0)e^{-(\kappa+\lambda)t}$$

Then the *forward rate* from Time t to Time $t + .25$ is given by:

$$400\,(A(0,t)/A(0,t + .25)\,\exp\{r[B(0,t) - B(0,t + .25)]\} - 1) \quad (21\text{-}5)$$

The *futures rate* for the same time period is given by Equation (21-6):

$$400\,\{[1 - B(0,.25)/c]^{-2\kappa\theta/\sigma^2}\exp\left[\frac{uB(0,.25)/c}{1 - B(0,.25)/c}\right]/A(0,.25) - 1\}$$

$$(21\text{-}6)$$

Although it is not apparent from the above formulae, the difference between forward and futures rates is quadratic in the important variables, so it grows fast with time. The difference can be on the order of 10 basis points for futures expiring three years from the present at a volatility of 20 percent. Naturally, further out futures are even worse.

GETTING SWAP RATES FROM DISCOUNTING RATES

The swap rates for swaps that mature before the end of the futures curve can be calculated by using the fundamental fact of swap pricing: Swaps are just like bonds. On the face of it, a swap is a complicated series of partially offsetting cash flows: One side pays a fixed coupon and the other pays a floating rate (usually LIBOR based) that was set one period earlier. Two observations simplify it considerably. First, we might as well consider that there is an exchange of principal at the end. The floating payer pays the fixed payer the notional principal, and vice versa. Clearly this does not change the value of the swap. Secondly, on a swap's reset date, the present value of the floating payments plus repayment of principal is par. This follows from the following simple arbitrage argument.

If an investor wants to receive floating LIBOR every three months plus his or her principal back at some time in the future, this can be done by taking, for example, $100 and buying a three-month LIBOR note. Three months later, the note pays interest based on LIBOR, and repays its principal. The investor reinvests the principal in another three-month note, and continues until he or she wants the principal back. Since the strategy cost $100 to implement, the stream of payments is worth $100. This is the basis for swaps pricing.

Now one can figure out the fixed payments by figuring out the coupon that makes a bond with the same payments have a market price that equals its par value. Similarly, if the fixed-rate payer in a swap wants to "buy down" (or pay in order to obtain a reduction in) his or her coupon, the swap can be priced by considering that par less the value of the up-front payment made to the floating-rate payer should be the value of a bond with the same below-market coupon.

Any method that the investor is comfortable with for bond pricing can be used for swap pricing with very little risk. Obtaining the zero coupon bond curve is the theoretically soundest method both for swaps and bonds, but it is no more necessary for one than for another. In reasonable cases, reasonable methods will give reasonable results.

Now we illustrate the above with an example. We will derive a formula for the fixed rate on a two-year quarterly reset swap. Let

Z_i be the price of a zero coupon bond maturing in $3 \times i$ months (or i quarters). Our candidate for the two-year swap rate is assumed to have a coupon rate of c percent. For the par coupon, the value of the fixed-side payments is:

$$100 = (c/4)Z_1 + (c/4)Z_2 + \cdots + (c/4)Z_8 + 100Z_8$$

This equation is easily solved for c:

$$c = 4 \times 100 \times (1 - Z_8)/(Z_1 + \cdots + Z_8) \qquad (21\text{-}7)$$

Note that if we had a semiannual swap, the above equation would have four discount factors (Z_2, Z_4, Z_6, and Z_8) and we would multiply on the right side of the equation by 2 instead of 4.

There is another formula for the swap coupon that is too intuitive to pass up. The forward rate rf_i is given by $rf_i = 400(1 - Z_{i+1}/Z_i)$, so Equation (21-7) is the same as Equation (21-8).

$$c = (rf_0 Z_1 + rf_1 Z_2 + \cdots + rf_7 Z_8)/(Z_1 + \cdots + Z_8) \qquad (21\text{-}8)$$

Equation (21-8) shows that the *swap coupon is the weighted-average forward rate*. The extension of Equations (21-7) and (21-8) to different periodicities or maturities is straightforward, and, incidentally, they hold, *mutatis mutandis*, for forward swaps as well. In Equation (21-7), replace the zero coupon bonds with the zeros that mature on the swap's payment dates. In Equation (21-8), make the same changes to the zeros, and also replace the forward rates with those that apply from the day on which the rate is set till the swap's payment date.

A calculation of the two-year semiannual swap coupon using the data in Tables 21-1, 21-2, and 21-3 and the method for calculating discount factors to nonsettlement dates (discussed at the end of the "What the Futures Curve Is Supposed to Be Telling Investors" section) follows. Equation (21-7) shows that we need the discount factors every six months for two years. We need discount factors to October 3, 1992, April 3, 1993, October 3, 1993, and April 3, 1994—using the notation introduced above, these will be denoted by Z_2, Z_4, Z_6, and Z_8, respectively. The first of these is calculated (as done previously) as follows.

First, find the discount factor to the nearest date from Table 21-3, which is the discount factor to September 16, 1992–.9804. Next, find the Eurodollar futures rate that applies over the time from September 16, 1992, to December 16, 1992, from Table 21-2. This rate is $100 - 95.31 = 4.69$. We want to use this rate from September 16, 1992, to October 3, 1992—a period of 17 days. The discount factor from April 3, 1992, to October 3, 1992, is calculated as:

$$Z_2 = (.9804) \frac{1}{1 + .01 \times 4.69 \times 17/360} = .9782$$

Similarly, we can compute:

$$Z_4 = (.9559) \frac{1}{1 + .01 \times 5.61 \times 16/360} = .9535$$

$$Z_6 = (.9281) \frac{1}{1 + .01 \times 6.64 \times 18/360} = .9250$$

$$Z_8 = (.8964) \frac{1}{1 + .01 \times 7.33 \times 17/360} = .8933$$

Plugging these results into (the appropriate modification of) Equation (21-7) gives the two-year semiannual swap coupon:

$$\begin{aligned} c &= 2 \times 100 \times (1 - Z_8)/(Z_2 + Z_4 + Z_6 + Z_8) \\ &= 2 \times 100 \times (1 - .8933)/(.9782 + .9535 + .9250 + .8933) \\ &= 2 \times 100 \times .1067/3.75 \\ &= 5.691 \end{aligned}$$

Cash-Settled Swaps

Forward start swaps are characterized by the fact that the counterparties agree to delay the start of the swap for some period of time. Cash-settled swaps are a relatively new product in which a forward start swap is settled for its cash value on the forward date. There are three major advantages to the cash-settled swap. First, the settlement price for cash settlement may be calculated on a standard calculator. Second, it is easier for the parties engaged in the swap to agree upon the rates used for cash settlement. Third, as opposed to the generic (or plain-vanilla) swaps described above—where each party assumes the credit risk of the other until the maturity of the swap—the credit risk of the cash-settled swap ends on the forward date.

The structure of the cash-settled swap is that of a forward start swap with a coupon rate of c percent. The cash settlement is done on the forward date based on the present value of cash flows, which are the difference between c and the then par swap coupon rate of p percent times the notional principal amount. The cash settlement value is the present value of these cash flows discounted at a yield of p percent.

This price is exactly the difference between the price of a par bond that is priced at par, and the price of a bond with a coupon rate of c and a yield to maturity of p. So if a party to the swap is comfortable with pricing bonds of a given maturity at the same yield, regardless of whether they are at a slight premium or discount, he or she should be equally comfortable with cash-settled swaps.

Swaps settled for cash in this manner are easier to agree upon because the parties involved only have to agree on one reference rate p, which is readily available in the market. To cash-settle swaps according to the methodology laid out in the previous section, the parties would have to agree on an entire yield curve, forward rate construction, and swap valuation methodology.

An Example of a Cash-Settled Swap Settlement Computation

Suppose that A and B enter into a cash-settled swap where A agrees to pay a fixed semiannual coupon of 7 percent to B on a $1 notional amount for five years starting in three months. Suppose also that in three months the five-year par swap rate is 6.5 percent. Since the par swap rate is less than the agreed-upon coupon, A will have to pay B a semiannual coupon of .5 percent for five years. The present value of this stream of cash flows at a semiannual yield of 6.5 percent is:

$$\frac{.005/2}{(1 + .065/2)^1} + \frac{.005/2}{(1 + .065/2)^2} + \cdots + \frac{.005/2}{(1 + .065/2)^{10}}$$
$$= (.005/2) \times \frac{1 - 1/(1 + .065/2)^{10}}{.065/2}$$

which is approximately 2.10 cents per dollar of notional amount.

Notice that this method does not give a significantly different value from the swap calculations shown in Equation (21-7) and

TABLE 21–4
The May 28, 1992, LIBOR Yield Curve

Tenor	Rate
1 month	4.0000
3 months	4.0625
6 months	4.1995
1 year	4.6791
2 years	5.5132
3 years	6.1465
4 years	6.4000
5 years	6.5000

Equation (21–8) above. For example, according to the LIBOR yield curve of May 28, 1992 (see Table 21–4 and Figure 21–2), the value of a five-year swap with a semiannual coupon of 7 percent is 2.12 cents per dollar.

INFORMATION FROM THE SWAPS CURVE

Swaps are not traded on a public exchange. However, the swaps market is very liquid and swap rates are quoted on the screens of several competing swaps brokers. Swap rates at certain standard maturities are well determined, and we can start with the assumption that we know what the 3-, 4-, 5-, 7-, and 10-year swap rates are. The swaps market beyond 10 years in the dollar market, and even sooner in many foreign markets, is not very liquid, and, as a result, the prices are not firm and dependable.

At this point, there is more than one way to proceed. We will pursue the swaps' equivalent of the par bond method. We can use the method described at the end of the last section to calculate semiannual implied swap rates maturing at half-year intervals through the end of the futures curve. These rates plus the current swap rates at selected maturities can be interpolated to give the

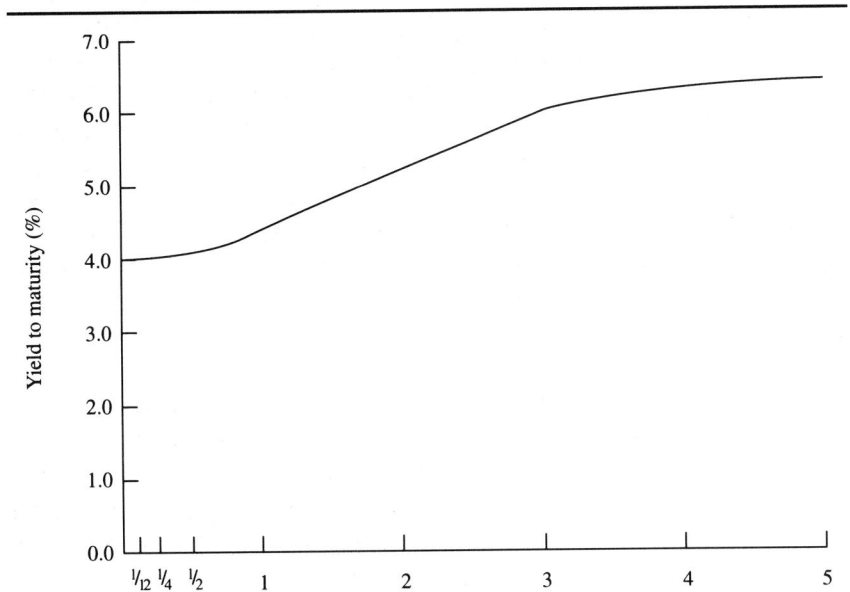

FIGURE 21–2
Graph of the May 28, 1992, LIBOR Yield Curve

fixed pay rate for swaps maturing at half-yearly intervals for 10 years. Using the fact that the swap rates can be treated as the coupon rates of par bonds means the bonds can be priced explicitly by discounting their cash flows. This leads to the following *par bond equations*:

$$100 = Z_1(100 + c_1/2)$$
$$100 = Z_1 c_2/2 + Z_2(100 + c_2/2)$$
$$100 = Z_1 c_3/2 + Z_2 c_3/2 + Z_3(100 + c_3/2)$$
$$\vdots$$
$$100 = Z_1 c_{20}/2 + \cdots + Z_{20}(100 + c_{20}/2)$$

The first few zeros can be treated as known, which they are, or as unknown; it makes no difference. The c_i rates are known, and these relations constitute a set of equations for the Z_i, and, in fact, they are a particularly easy set of equations to solve. The first equation can be solved by inspection to yield $Z_1 = 100/(100 + c_1/2)$. Now Z_1 is known and Z_2 is the only unknown quantity in the second equation, so it can be solved for Z_2. We can turn the crank again to solve the third equation for Z_3, and so on. Once we have obtained this standard set of zeros, we can proceed as in the previous section. This procedure is easy and efficient. Equations (21–7) and (21–8), and others like them, can be used in place of the par bond equations.

There is an alternative method that we mention for the sake of completeness. It depends on the perfectly reasonable assumption that bonds will be priced based on the yield of the current coupon bond of the same maturity. Suppose we have an N period ($N/2$ years) semiannual bond and an $N + 1$ period semiannual bond with the same coupon and price. Then the bond's coupon is the half-year forward rate that applies between the Nth and the $N + 1$ period. Let y_N be the N period current coupon yield, and y_{N+1} be the $N + 1$ period current coupon yield. With the bond's yields fixed, its price is a linear function of its coupon, and we can easily solve for the coupon that equates the prices of the two bonds, thereby getting an explicit expression for the forward rate. Let $Z(y, N) = 1/(1 + y/2)^N$. Then the forward is:

$$\frac{(-1)[Z(y_N, N) - Z(y_{N+1}, N + 1)]}{[1 - Z(y_N, N)]/y_N - [1 - Z(y_{N+1}, N + 1)]/y_{N+1}}$$

Once we have the forward rates, we can construct zeros or whatever is needed as in the previous section. This method is as good as the assumption that nonpar bonds should have the same yield as par bonds of the same maturity, which is a reasonable assumption.

As an example of just how close the approximate answers are, using the data in Table 21–1 gives a linearly interpolated 10.5-year yield of 7.894 percent. Using the previous methodology gives a forward rate from 10 to 10.5 years of 8.27 percent. Similarly, the 29.5-year yield would be 8.345 percent, giving a forward rate from 29.5 to 30 years of 12.5 percent. Using the par bond equations, we obtain the exact answers of 8.27 percent for the forward rate from 10 to 10.5 years and 12.31 percent for the forward rate from 29.5 to 30 years.

INTERPOLATION

We have shown that to calculate rates for dates that are not the maturities of cash securities, futures, or par swaps, some interpolation must be done. For interpolating between the futures or cash rates in the short end of the yield curve, the interpolation method does not matter much as long as one interpolates between rates and not discount factors. For interpolating between the par swap coupons, a reasonable method is essential if we want to get intermediate discount and forward rates that make sense. In this section, we will give some suggestions and references for choosing the proper interpolation method.

One commonly used method is simple linear interpolation to half-yearly intervals between the 4-, 5-, 7-, 10-, and 30-year par coupons. One problem with this method is that the fit is generally not pleasing to the eye with "corners" at the maturities of the on-the-run (or recently issued) bonds. Choosing higher-order polynomials between the maturities will alleviate the unpleasant look of the linear interpolation scheme. Curves that fit to data in this manner are called *splines*. Linear interpolation is a special case called a *1-spline* because the polynomial chosen between the points has degree 1. Fitting second-degree polynomials would yield a quadratic or 2-spline. The quadratic fit and its properties have been investigated by J. Huston McCulloch (1971, 1975).

Cubic splines, which fit polynomials of degree 3 between the data points, have some advantages over both the linear and quadratic fits. They possess some extra smoothness (more continuity of another derivative) yet do not require much more data to compute. The extra parameters needed to fit cubic splines allow for more shapes to fit a specific problem. Cubic spline fits can be computed quickly, and calculation/evaluation routines are available from commercial vendors and in the public domain. Several different spline routines are available in the IMSL (1989) math library. We recommend the method of Akima (available in the IMSL math library), which has constraints that produce fits that seem more natural and without the extraneous "wiggles" that other cubic spline methods suffer from.[2] Two good references on splines are Lancaster and Šalkauskas (1986) and de Boor (1978).

NOTES

1. A similar argument is found in John Hull, *Options, Futures, and Other Derivative Securities* (Englewood Cliffs, N.J.: Prentice Hall, 1989), Section 2.9.
2. If one has more data or needs more smoothness or other properties, B-splines (basis splines) may be used. B-splines are a generalization of the cubic spline methodology. A discussion of these splines is beyond the scope of this exposition.

REFERENCES

Cox, J. C.; J. E. Ingersoll, Jr.; and S. A. Ross. "The Relation between Forward Prices and Futures Prices." *Journal of Financial Economics* 9 (1981), pp. 321–46.

———. "A Theory of the Term Structure of Interest Rates." *Econometrica* 53, no. 2 (1985), pp. 385–407.

de Boor C. *A Practical Guide to Splines*. New York: Springer Verlag, 1978.

Hogan, M., and K. Weintraub. "The Lognormal Interest Rate Model and Eurodollar Futures." Citibank, New York City, 1992.

Hull John. *Options, Futures, and Other Derivative Securities*. Englewood Cliffs, N.J.: Prentice Hall, 1989.

IMSL Math/Library. Houston, Texas. 1989.

Lancaster, Peter, and Kęstutis Šalkauskas. *Curve and Surface Fitting: An Introduction*. London: Academic Press, 1986.

McCulloch, J. Huston. "Measuring the Term Structure of Interest Rates." *Journal of Business,* January 1971, pp. 19–31.

———. "The Tax Adjusted Yield Curve." *Journal of Finance,* June 1975, pp. 811–30.

CHAPTER 22

ACCOUNTING IMPLICATIONS OF INTEREST RATE SWAPS

Harold Bierman, Jr.
Cornell University

Although the accounting for swaps has not yet been defined by the Financial Accounting Standards Board (FASB), Wishon and Chevalier (1985) give a comprehensive survey of swaps and the accounting issues. More recently, the FASB published *Hedge Accounting: An Exploratory Study of the Underlying Issues,* a research report on hedge accounting that has implications for swap accounting. Financial Accounting Standards No. 105 gives guidance relative to financial statement disclosure for swaps.

There are several economic motivations for using interest rate swaps. One is to speculate on interest rate changes. For example, a firm that has borrowed at a 10 percent fixed rate can swap into a 9 percent floating rate because the management thinks the floating rate will stay below 10 percent. Second, a firm may swap to hedge risk. For example, an insurance company buying bonds at a 10 percent fixed rate might welcome the opportunity to swap its floating-rate debt into 9 percent fixed-rate debt, thus locking in a 1 percent profit spread. But the basic economic motivation giving rise to interest rate swaps is that they facilitate the raising of funds at the lowest cost in the international money markets.

The accounting for interest rate swaps is an important issue because any swap changes the economic position of the parties involved. Either journal entries or explanatory footnotes to financial statements are needed to make the economic consequences of a swap clear. There is general agreement that economic transactions engaged in by a firm give rise to accounting entries. Some transactions (e.g., swaps) do not require an immediate outlay and do not necessarily change the value of an asset or a liability, but may, nevertheless, change the financial situation of the firm and, thus, should be reported. Since the normal debit-credit process does not record a change in risk, it may be desirable to describe the changes in footnotes rather than on the financial statements.

In order to understand the accounting for interest rate swaps, it is necessary to understand the basic nature of an interest rate swap and the relationships of the several parties. There may be five basic parties with direct economic interest in the cash flows of a matched swap or the underlying debt:

1. Two counterparties who swap interest payment obligations.
2. A principal who is in the middle of the swap transaction and has legal obligations to pay both counterparties. (Instead of a principal, there can be an intermediary who arranges the swap and is not legally obligated to pay).
3. Two lenders to the two counterparties.

This chapter considers selected financial accounting issues (external reporting) for the counterparties and the principal of a swap transaction. Although swap terminology is not well defined, the term *principal* is used here to describe the party who contracts with the counterparties to swap interest payments. The counterparties are responsible for paying interest and the face amount of the debt to the basic lenders.

Although the FASB has taken a position on the accounting for foreign currency forward contracts that are intended to hedge an identified foreign currency commitment,[1] forward contracts and swap contracts are sufficiently different so that we cannot assume that the accounting for swaps has been implicitly defined by the FASB. Smithson defines these differences.[2] Swap contracts require their own set of accounting recommendations.

A BASIC INTEREST RATE SWAP

Figure 22-1 shows the structure of a basic interest rate swap. The point of the arrow indicates the party receiving payment. The tail indicates where the payment originates. With the transaction as shown, both counterparties contract with the principal, not with each other.

Firms AA and BB are the swap counterparties. AA wants to borrow at a floating rate but borrows at 10.15 percent fixed [it could have borrowed floating in its market at LIBOR plus 20 basis points (bp)]. (LIBOR refers to the London Interbank Offered Rate; 1 basis points equals one 100 of a percentage point in annual interest.) BB wants to pay a fixed rate (it could borrow in its market at a fixed rate of 11.65 percent), but it borrows at LIBOR plus 50 basis points.

FIGURE 22-1
Basic Interest Rate Swap

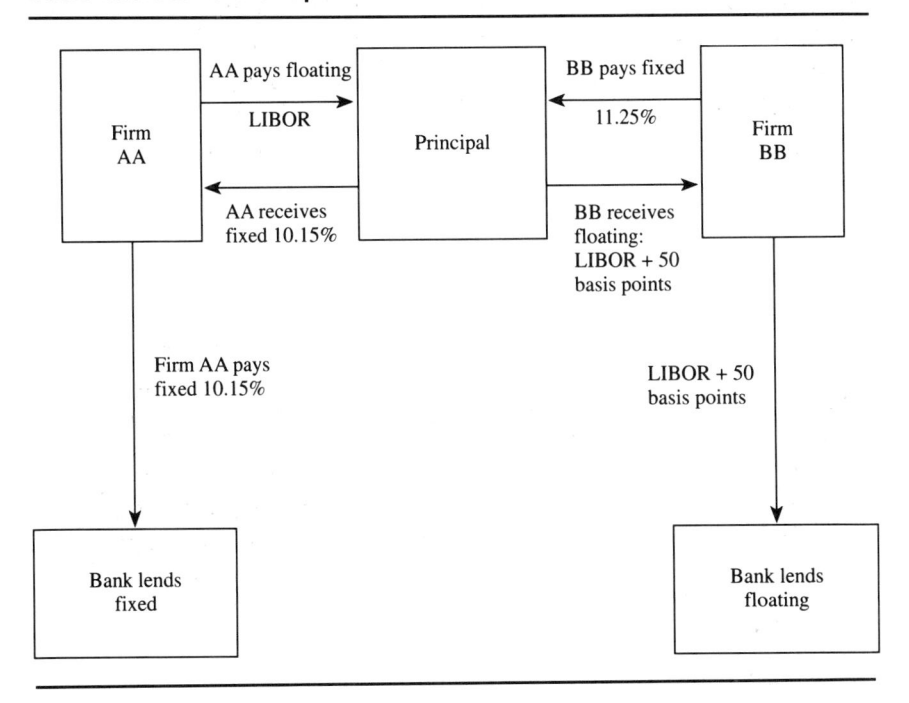

Principal receives 11.25 percent fixed and pays 10.15 percent fixed. It receives LIBOR and pays LIBOR plus 50 basis points. It has the following spreads:

Fixed rate	.1125 − .1015 =	.0110
Floating	LIBOR − (LIBOR + 50 bp) =	−.0050
	Net spread	.0060

On net, Counterparty AA pays LIBOR, and if it had borrowed directly, it would have paid LIBOR plus 20 basis points. It is better off by 20 basis points. On net, Counterparty BB pays 11.25 percent fixed. If it had borrowed directly at a fixed rate, it would have paid 11.65 percent; thus, it saved .40 percent, or 40 basis points.

The swap is profitable for both counterparties if we compare the swap with AA borrowing at a floating rate directly and BB borrowing at a fixed rate directly. The swap is profitable for principal (if both counterparties meet their contractual agreements). If LIBOR goes down, BB might regret that it wanted to pay a fixed rate, but it has achieved the original goal of paying a fixed rate. If LIBOR goes up, AA might regret that it swapped into a floating rate, but the swap was cheaper than borrowing floating directly.

The above example illustrates an advantage of swaps to the counterparties. By making use of world markets for capital, it is possible that a counterparty can raise money on a less costly basis by borrowing in one market and swapping into a second market.

Smith, Smithson, and Wakeman (1986) describe the reasons that swap profit opportunities exist as being financial arbitrage (see the above example) and tax and regulatory arbitrage (there have been tax motivations especially in Japan). Bicksler and Chen, however, focus on market imperfections only and "the presence of comparative advantages among different borrowers in these markets."[3]

As can be seen in the above example, an interest rate swap does not, in itself, raise new capital (but a swap may be part of new financing). It does change the nature of the debt contracts that are outstanding or are being formulated.

The primary accounting issue for a counterparty is whether or not an accounting entry is required when a swap contract, similar to that described above, is signed. If an accounting entry is not required, are other disclosures desirable? The economic impact of the swap on each of the counterparties must be considered. Reporting the details of a swap is desirable if the swap changes the total amount of liabilities or if it changes the firm's financial risk.

EXTERNAL REPORTING FOR A COUNTERPARTY

In some situations, a firm can only borrow at a floating rate even though it actually desires fixed-rate debt; thus, it swaps into fixed rates.

Consider the following swap entered into by Firm BB: Assume BB borrows $100 million from a creditor (bank) for 10 years and agrees to pay LIBOR plus 50 basis points. This is a conventional borrowing and is recorded as a liability by BB.

In a separate contract, BB agrees to pay a fixed rate of 11.25 percent to principal and in return will receive a floating rate (say, LIBOR plus 50 basis points) from principal. BB has to pay LIBOR plus 50 basis points to Bank. The swap is for 10 years and has a notional amount of $100 million. These arrangements are illustrated in Figure 22–2.

One of four things can happen with the swap: (1) payment and receipt occur over the life of the swap as contracted; (2) the swap is terminated by the counterparty (with suitable payment to the principal) or by the principal (with suitable payment to the counterparty); (3) neither payments to or from the principal are made, so a net amount is lost or gained; and (4) one party makes a payment, but the second party (or principal) does not pay. (This failure to receive payment after payment has been made is called *clean risk*.)

Assume LIBOR equals 10 percent at the date the interest rate is set. Both the $10.5 million interest owed the bank and the $11.25 million interest owed the principal are liabilities. With some swap contracts, BB would pay the net of the $11.25 million fixed to be paid and the $10.5 million floating rate to be received from the principal. Thus, only $750,000 would be a liability arising from the swap. The $10.5 million receivable cannot be offset against the $11.25 million liability if the latter is paid prior to receiving the $10.5 million from the principal.

FIGURE 22-2
A Counterparty Receiving Floating Rate

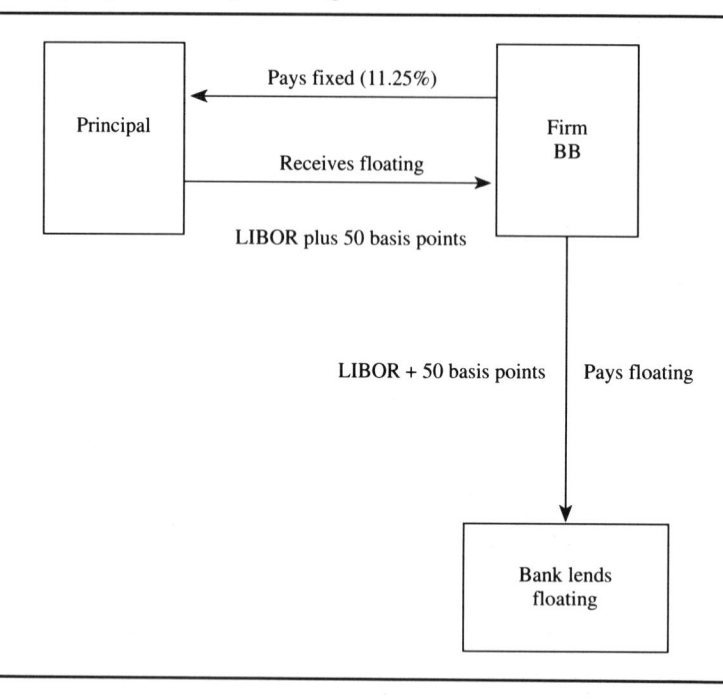

```
                    Pays fixed (11.25%)
    ┌───────────┐ ◄──────────────────── ┌─────────┐
    │ Principal │                        │  Firm   │
    │           │ ────────────────────►  │   BB    │
    └───────────┘    Receives floating   └─────────┘
                                              │
                  LIBOR plus 50 basis points  │
                                              │
                                              │ Pays floating
                     LIBOR + 50 basis points  │
                                              ▼
                                         ┌──────────┐
                                         │Bank lends│
                                         │ floating │
                                         └──────────┘
```

BB could have entered into the swap because it has fixed-rate assets (say, fixed-rate mortgages) and wants to reduce interest rate risk by paying fixed-rate interest. Although the swap offers imperfect protection against loss if interest rates decrease (the mortgages can be prepaid), the swap into fixed rates offers reasonable protection if interest rates go up. Or, alternatively, BB could have entered into the swap because its financial officer forecasts increased interest rates and wants to lock in a 11.25 percent cost of debt.

Consider a second counterparty (AA) who borrows $100 million for 10 years at a fixed rate of 10.15 percent from a bank and swaps into a floating-rate payment of LIBOR (currently at 10 percent). The swap is for 10 years. After one year, AA has an asset of $10.15 million, representing the one-period fixed interest it is scheduled to receive from principal. The fact that the fixed interest has been swapped into floating should be revealed. Also, AA owes the bank $10.15 million of current interest and owes the principal

$10 million. Figure 22–3 shows the structure of this swap. The fact that AA changed a fixed-rate debt into an obligation to pay floating by the use of an interest rate swap should be disclosed.

Wishon and Chevalier agree that disclosures by note of material swap agreements are needed "so that the description of the terms of the company's debt wouldn't be misleading."[4] Swaps are financial instruments that highlight the importance of notes to financial accounting statements. The parties to a swap contract should reveal in notes to their financial statements the effect of the swap on the firm's risk. Any swap changes the firm's financial risk, and, thus, a swap is an economic transaction worthy of being reported in the firm's financial statements. Footnotes could be of the following general nature:

1. BB has engaged in a $100 million interest rate swap. It has effectively exchanged its floating-rate debt for a fixed-rate

FIGURE 22–3
A Counterparty Receiving Fixed Rate

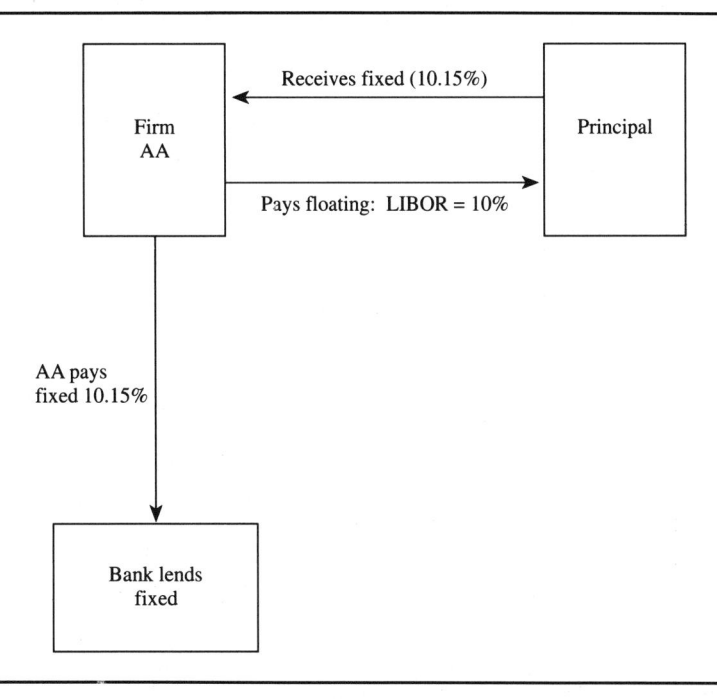

debt. Given the nature of $100 million of BB's assets (fixed-rate investments), this transaction will tend to be risk reducing.

2. AA has engaged in a $100 million interest rate swap. It has effectively exchanged its fixed-rate debt for a floating-rate debt. Given the nature of $100 million of AA's assets (fixed-rate investments), this transaction will tend to be risk increasing if interest rates increase but will be beneficial if interest rates decrease.

Changing interest rates can cause a counterparty to have the expectation of future gains or losses. For example, if the floating rates go up above 10.15 percent, AA will pay the principal larger sums than it is receiving (a fixed rate of 10.15 percent). A note to the financial statements to describe the situation is desirable. AA effectively has floating-rate debt. Assume AA has fixed-rate non-callable 10-year bonds as assets. It expects interest rates to go down and, thus, swaps fixed-rate debt into floating-rate debt. If it has guessed wrong (interest rates go up), it loses because it has fixed-rate assets and floating-rate debt. The swap gives rise to the necessity of a verbal description of AA's actions.

ACCOUNTING FOR TERMINATION

When a swap agreement is terminated before the end of the contract, there is likely to be a gain or loss on termination. The FASB's emerging issues task force concluded that termination of a matched swap position should not result in immediate gain or loss.[5] If Counterparty AA terminates a swap contract by buying out of it (paying a penalty) to avoid future net outlays, then the net termination costs should be amortized by AA over the remaining life of the swap. It is assumed that the costs are being incurred to benefit the future periods. This recommendation is similar to that of the FASB in Statement No. 80 for futures contracts that act as a hedge against price or interest rate risk.[6] The gains or losses are deferred until the hedged item itself is written off. The futures contracts are tied to the hedged item. If the swap is a risk-reducing device, then the analogy to a futures contract is appropriate. If the swap is speculative, then Accounting Principles Board (APB) Opinion No.

26 should be considered. Accounting Principles Board (APB) Opinion No. 26 states, "A difference between the reacquisition price and the net carrying amount of the extinguished debt should be recognized in income of the period of extinguishment."[7] FASB Statement No. 4 requires that the gain or loss, if material, be "classified as an extraordinary item, net of related income tax effect."[8]

ACCOUNTING FOR PRINCIPALS

Every swap changes the principal's assets and liabilities in complex ways. The principal performs a service for the counterparty by supplying credit enhancement. The principal with a high credit rating is more likely to pay the interest being swapped than the average counterparty. The principal accepts risk and may implicitly lend money because of the way the swap transactions are structured. For example, it might receive $10 million of floating-rate interest and pay $12 million of fixed-rate interest with one counterparty without receiving anything from the second counterparty. In return, it earns a spread and possibly a fee.

The effect of a swap agreement on a principal's periodic income is an interesting problem. It must be determined when the fees and spread revenues associated with a swap should be recognized as income. Accounting income recognition should be consistent with reasonable expectations of profit being realized. Premature recognition of profit is not desirable. Generally accepted accounting principles require stringent objective measures before income is recorded, but, in practice, judgment is necessary to determine the degree of uncertainty.

The accounting for up-front fees and spreads should be consistent. If it is appropriate to defer recognition of the income arising from the spread, it is also appropriate to defer the income effects of the fees that are collected. Fees and spreads are interchangeable amounts. A large amount of uncertainty associated with swaps would tend to restrict severely the amount of income that should be recognized up front and would lead to income recognition through time for either fees or spreads after the income has been realized.

Due to the existence of uncertainty, revenue recognition by

the accountant is an art, not a science. Because the revenue recognition policy of the principal drastically affects a period's income, it is a very important accounting choice. A nonrecourse cash sale with all the service performed immediately gives rise to revenue equal to the cash sale (and thus to income or loss). If cash has not been received at the end of the accounting period, the net revenue recognized should not be equal to the nominal sales price. The sales price must be adjusted for time value and for uncertainty. In the case of a swap where some of the service by the principal is to be performed in the future, even if a fee is received immediately, the revenue and income should be recognized over the life of the transaction. If the swap term is not yet completed, there is some probability that the fee will not result in income.

THE TIMING OF SWAP INCOME

Wishon and Chevalier state that "a payment that is essentially a yield adjustment should be deferred by both the payer and the recipient over the stated period of the agreement."[9] This implies that an up-front payment may be defined to be something other than a yield adjustment. They modify this position by quoting John Stewart's position that "there should be no up-front income recognition"[10] Given the impossibility of distinguishing between yield-adjustment fees and other fees, one must classify all fees as one type. In addition, given the difficulty of deciding whether a payment is made for up-front services or for the use of funds, all payments should be looked at as adjusting the interest cost through time. This is consistent with FASB Statement No. 91, which deals with the accounting for nonrefundable fees and costs associated with originating and acquiring loans. The FASB's position is that "loan origination fees should be deferred and recognized over the life of the loan as an adjustment of yield (interest income)."[11]

The problems associated with early income recognition are:

1. The payments may never be received (termination or default); the credit risk does not enter the net present value calculation.
2. There may be "clean risk at settlement"; that is, the principal may make an interest payment but not receive interest.

Although this type of loss has been very rare, it can happen.
3. Interest rates may change and a counterparty defaults. For example, if fixed rates fall to 6 percent and if BB defaults, then the counterparty that replaces BB will pay 6 percent and not 11.25 percent, but the principal will still pay 10.15 percent to AA. The principal will lose 415 basis points each year remaining on the swap contract. This is an effective liability after the default and the interest rate change.

A unilateral termination of a swap by a counterparty, given an interest rate change, can give rise to a significant loss for the principal (it is paying a large fixed interest rate but receiving a small floating rate), just as a unilateral termination of a swap by a principal can give rise to a large loss for the counterparty. Although there are legal steps that can be taken, a loss may be suffered if there are no resources.

The conclusions for measuring the income of the principal are:
1. With significant risk and a small interest rate spread, very little or none of the present value of swap interest differential should be recognized as income at Time zero.
2. With modest risk, some small percentage of the income can be recognized at Time zero for arranging the swap.
3. Under real-world circumstances, the income is not equal to the undiscounted sum of the interest differentials at Time zero.

Consider a $100,000 fee associated with a five-year swap that has significant risk. One reasonable solution is to allocate 20 percent of the $100,000 as income to each of the five years.

THE RISKS OF MATCHED SWAPS

With a matched swap there are four basic types of risks:
1. Trading risk.
2. Clean risk at settlement.
3. Termination risk.
4. Reset risk.

We can have asset swaps or liability swaps. The following example will illustrate liability swaps, but the same principles can be used for asset swaps. There are many different variations of the swaps that are illustrated. Remember that a principal has a legal obligation to pay counterparties but an intermediary does not.

Trading Risk

Trading risk occurs when a counterparty defaults and can be replaced only at a loss to principal because of an unfavorable change in interest rates. This risk arises when a counterparty defaults and can be replaced by the principal only at a loss because fixed interest rates have changed. The magnitude of the trading risk exposure depends on the size of the swap portfolio, the average maturity of the swaps, and the size of the change in fixed interest rates that has taken place since the swaps were negotiated. The losses that may actually be incurred are controllable to some extent by collateral, credit analysis before the swap, limiting the duration of the swaps, and selecting counterparties who are diversified in terms of the industries and geographic areas in which they operate. Trading risk is fundamentally a credit risk, with a significant difference from conventional loans since the size of the risk exposure is not fully determined at the time the agreement is negotiated but depends on subsequent changes in fixed interest rates. Also, with an interest rate swap the principal does not have to pay the notional amount at maturity.

The example assumes that payments are synchronized so that on each payment date only the net amount due is paid from one party to the other. The additional risk that occurs when payments are not synchronized is considered in the next section.

Consider the relationship between principal and Counterparty AA as shown in Figure 22-4. If floating interest rates have risen so that LIBOR exceeds the fixed rate in the swap contract, a default by AA is unlikely. If AA defaulted and the fixed rate for the remaining term of the swap were greater than 12 percent, there is no trading risk with AA.

If the fixed rate is below 12 percent, then AA might find it beneficial to default. If fixed rates for the remaining term of the contract are below 12 percent, AA could be replaced only at a loss

FIGURE 22-4
An Interest Rate Swap

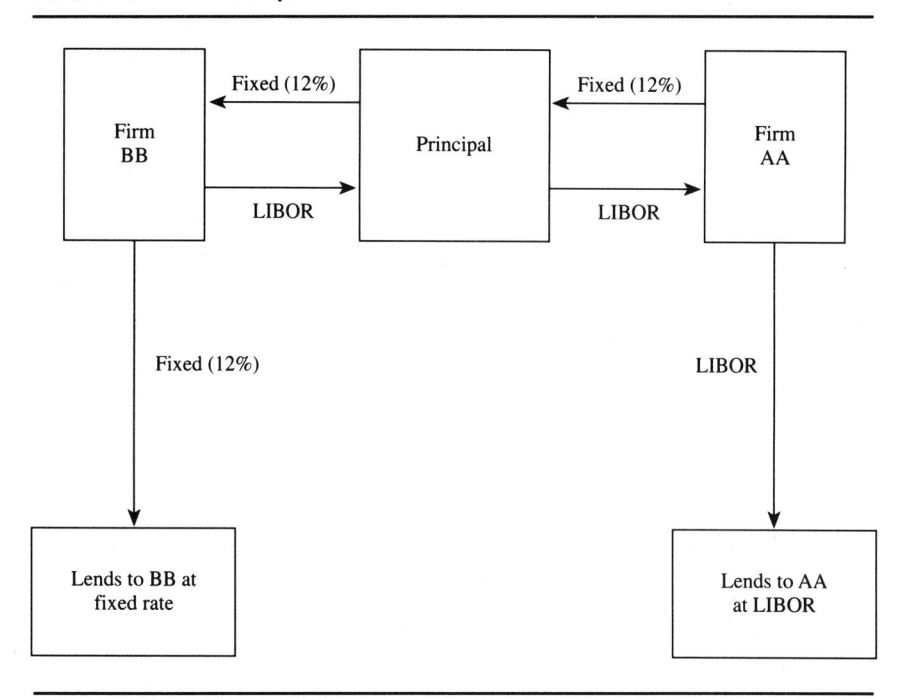

```
                  Fixed (12%)              Fixed (12%)
   ┌────────┐ ◄──────────── ┌──────────┐ ◄──────────── ┌────────┐
   │  Firm  │                │          │                │  Firm  │
   │   BB   │                │ Principal│                │   AA   │
   │        │ ────────────►  │          │ ────────────►  │        │
   └────────┘     LIBOR      └──────────┘     LIBOR      └────────┘
        │                                                     │
        │ Fixed (12%)                                    LIBOR│
        ▼                                                     ▼
   ┌──────────────┐                                   ┌──────────────┐
   │ Lends to BB at│                                   │ Lends to AA  │
   │  fixed rate  │                                   │   at LIBOR   │
   └──────────────┘                                   └──────────────┘
```

to the principal, so there is a trading risk. For example, if fixed rates for the remaining term of the swap decrease to 8 percent and AA defaulted, the replacement for AA will pay 8 percent. With a notional amount of $100 million the loss to principal is:

Original contract − Replacement = Loss
    amount   amount
    $12,000,000 −   8,000,000 = $4,000,000
                            per year

Now assume fixed rates have increased to 14 percent and BB defaults. While principal continues to receive 12 percent from AA, it will have to pay more than 12 percent to BB's replacement. Assume BBB replaces BB and principal has to pay 14 percent to BBB. The loss is now:

Replacement − Original contract = Loss
amount   amount
$14,000,000 − 12,000,000 = $2,000,000 per year

If default has occurred, the two different situations shown below can occur:

	Interest Rate Up	Interest Rate Down
Receives fixed from defaulted firm	No loss	Loss
Pays fixed to defaulted firm	Loss	No loss

There can also be trading risk with the floating-rate transactions, but this risk is smaller than with fixed rates.

Party paying LIBOR defaults	If this party is replaced by a firm paying less than LIBOR, there is a loss.
Party receiving LIBOR defaults	If this party is replaced by a firm receiving more than LIBOR, there is a loss.

The amount of credit risk is a function of:

1. Notional amount.
2. Years of contract remaining.
3. Probability that fixed interest rates will change the amounts of change.
4. Terms (including payment dates) of floating-rate contracts.
5. Creditworthiness of counterparties.
6. The degree of industry and geographical diversification among counterparties.
7. Amount of collateral.

A rule-of-thumb measure of risk used by swap professionals for a swap compared to a loan to the same firm is .03 × Years to maturity × Notional amount. This measure does not address the issue of the creditworthiness of the specific counterparty, or the degree of diversification among counterparties.

The profitability of a swap will not be known until all payments associated with the swap contract are fulfilled.

There will be situations where principal will be entering multiple transactions with the same counterparty. Some of the transactions may be offsetting or nearly offsetting. Offsetting transactions will tend to reduce risk (some risk might remain because of the change in interest rates between the times of the two transactions or different times of payment).

Counterparty risk is controllable, to some extent, by collateral and credit analysis before the swap, and by having well-diversified counterparties. However, the protection of collateral should not be assumed given the very small number of transactions covered by collateral.

Three events have to happen for principal to incur losses (we are assuming that the clean risk is equal to zero) when there is a default.

1. There have to be changes in the fixed interest rates.
2. Some counterparties must default.
3. There has to be an imbalance in the long and short fixed-rate counterparties who default.

Table 22-1 shows the losses (not discounted) that will occur for different lives and different interest rate changes for $10 million of defaults. The losses in the table can be multiplied by a factor to reflect a notional amount other than $10 million (the factor can be smaller or larger than one). Also, time discounting would reduce the amounts shown as losses.

Clean Risk at Settlement[12]

Clean risk at settlement occurs when the principal's disbursement for interest is due before its receipt of interest from the counterparty. It also arises with currency swaps even if the payments are

TABLE 22-1
Losses Assuming $10 Million of Notional Defaults (Zero Discount Rate)

Change in Interest Rate*	Contract Years Remaining					
	1	2	3	4	5	6
.00	–0–	–0–	–0–	–0–	–0–	–0–
.01	$100,000	$200,000	$ 300,000	$ 400,000	$ 500,000	$ 600,000
.02	200,000	400,000	600,000	800,000	1,000,000	1,200,000
.03	300,000	600,000	900,000	1,200,000	1,500,000	1,800,000
.04	400,000	800,000	1,200,000	1,600,000	2,000,000	2,400,000

* Principal loses if the counterparty is paying fixed and rates fall. Principal loses if the counterparty is receiving fixed and rates rise.

on the same date, and with zero coupon (or low coupon) debt where the principal is receiving the zero coupon or the low coupon. Clean risk is a credit risk. Without default there is no clean risk.

Clean risk at settlement is eliminated if the swap is written so that only the net amount is actually paid or received. To illustrate clean risk, assume that Firm AA is to pay LIBOR to principal on June 30 and principal is to pay a fixed 6 percent on May 30 (the semiannual payment on a 12 percent fixed rate) for a notional amount of $100 million. On May 30, principal pays $6 million, and on June 30, AA defaults on the $5.5 million payment it owes principal. Principal has a loss of $6 million.

When a swap with clean risk is entered into, principal is acting as a banker and offering the counterparty a series of forward loan commitments, one on each future payment date. At each such payment date, principal is making a short-term loan until the interest due is received.

If clean risk is included in the swap, the spread that is bid should compensate principal both for the interest cost of the loan and the credit risk. If the counterparty is the fixed-rate payer in the swap, the amounts of the forward loans are known in advance. If the counterparty is a floating-rate payer, the amounts of the forward loans on each payment date will depend on the unknown future level of the floating rate.

In the above example, suppose principal owes a $6 million fixed payment to the counterparty and the counterparty owes principal a LIBOR payment of $5 million. If only the net amounts were transmitted, there is no risk of default from nonpayment, since the counterparty has no payment to make. (A default could occur for some other reason such as bankruptcy.) If principal must make its payment a month before the counterparty, then there is a possibility of default from nonpayment. Unlike trading risks, which exist only if interest rates have changed and which affect only one side of the swap at any given time, clean risk exists each time a set of swap payments is to be exchanged, and can affect both sides of the swap. While the amount at risk is one year's interest or less, with large notional amounts the loss can be large.

Termination Loss

A loss can also arise because of early contract termination. Termination terms are part of each swap contract. The early termination agreement requires a legal interpretation. However, the conventional contractual statement, "a reasonable pre-estimate of loss," applied to the payments to be made implies that future profits are not guaranteed. If one neglects the existence of the termination agreements, profits that will never be realized will be recognized at Time zero. The contract clause does not say that the terminating firm has to pay the same level of profit to the principal as would be earned if the contract were not terminated. Clarification is needed as to how the courts are likely to interpret the above contractual statement.

Reset Risk

Reset risk arises when the rates of two matched floating-rate contracts are reset on different dates. Since the two rates may differ, the principal might win or lose unless it follows a hedging strategy.

The level of LIBOR is important if the rate has changed since the last rate setting and a firm defaults. If the three-month LIBOR has been set at 10 percent and if BB defaults when the rate is 8 percent, there is a one-shot loss of $2,000,000 (¼) = $500,000. This can be called the *reset risk* of trading.

Given the importance of the several types of risk that have been described, the FASB has recognized the need for disclosure regarding outstanding swaps.

STATEMENT OF FINANCIAL ACCOUNTING STANDARDS NO. 105

FAS No. 105, *Disclosure of Information about Financial Instruments with Off-Balance-Sheet Risk and Financial Instruments with Concentrations of Credit Risk,* was published in March 1990, and is relevant to the disclosure of information regarding interest rate swaps.

The statement requires disclosure of the notional amount of a swap as well as the nature and terms of the contracts.[13] In addition, it requires the disclosure in the body of the financial statement or in the accompanying notes the following information:

> The amount of accounting loss the entity would incur if any party to the financial instrument failed completely to perform according to the terms of the contract and the collateral or other security, if any, for the amount due proved to be of no value to the entity.[14]

The amount of accounting loss for a swap can be very large for a counterparty or a principal. For example, assume a principal is paying 9 percent fixed and receiving 10 percent. It is receiving and paying LIBOR from two counterparties. Assume the arrangement is not profitable for one counterparty and it defaults. Because of the increase in LIBOR and a change in fixed rate to 30 percent, the new counterparty will pay LIBOR only if it receives 30 percent fixed. Instead of 30 percent, the fixed rate can be any large percentage. With changing interest rates and defaults, the potential loss with a large notional amount can be extremely large. Satisfying paragraph 18 can require a large estimate of possible loss given that there is no cap on how high interest rates can go.

FAS No. 105 offers illustrative notes that can be used:

> The Corporation is an intermediary in the interest rate swap market. It also enters into interest rate swap agreements both as trading instruments and as a means of managing its interest rate exposure.
>
> As an intermediary, the Corporation maintains a portfolio of generally matched offsetting swap agreements. These swaps are carried at market value, with changes in value reflected in noninterest income. At inception of the swap agreements, the portion of the compensation related to credit risk and ongoing servicing is deferred and taken into income over the term of the swap agreements.

Interest rate swap agreements used in trading activities are valued at market. Realized and unrealized gains and losses are included in trading account profits. Unrealized gains are reported as assets and unrealized losses are reported as liabilities.

The differential to be paid or received on interest rate swap agreements entered into to reduce the impact of changes in interest rates is recognized over the life of the agreements.[15]

FAS No. 105 is not explicit in how the possible loss should be estimated.

MATERIALITY

Without a hedge, the potential risk of even a relatively small swap can be very large (there are no limits on the possible interest rate increases). Thus, it is very difficult to define materiality limits for swaps. All swaps should receive the same accounting and disclosure treatment so that effort is not wasted trying to distinguish between a material swap and a swap that is not material.

ACCOUNTING ON A CASH BASIS

If no accounting entries are made by a firm on the signing of a swap contract and the only entries are made on the receipt and disbursement of the interest, then the swap participant (principal or counterparty) is on a cash basis. This is current practice. This firm would then have to conform to FAS No. 105 and disclose the risk implications of the swap.

ACCOUNTING ON A MARKET-TO-MARKET BASIS

If the market value of the swap is recorded at the initiation of the swap and the swap is adjusted to market value periodically, this would be a market-to-market basis. Determining the market value of swaps is much more complex (many swaps are unique) than determining the market value of other securities and liabilities that are currently recorded at historical cost. Thus, universal market (or fair) value accounting for swaps is not likely to be implemented in the immediate future.

Matched swaps are somewhat easier to value than individual swaps (as when the firm has a portfolio of swaps). Consider a principal who has arranged a 10-year swap with one counterparty with whom it is paying LIBOR and receiving 12 percent fixed. With a second counterparty, the principal is receiving LIBOR and paying 11 percent fixed. The principal has a net spread of 1 percent for the two swaps. With a $10 million notional amount, this is a spread of $100,000 per year. Define $B(10, 11)$ to be the present value of an annuity for 10 years and 11 percent interest rate. The present value is:

$$PV = 100,000 \, B(10, 11) = \$588,923$$

A different present value would be obtained with a different discount rate, but the contractual cash flows are easily determined. Unfortunately, the cash flows are uncertain, and unique to this specific swap; thus, we cannot claim that $588,923 is a reliable fair value estimate.

The valuation of an individual interest rate swap (or a portfolio of swaps) is even more difficult then the evaluation of matched swaps, but the following section illustrates one effective method.

There are two unique problems with valuing a swap. One is that there is no principal payment. The second is that there are two cash flow streams—one fixed rate and one floating rate.

The first step to value a swap is to convert the actual swap into a LIBOR flat swap. For example, assume a counterparty is receiving floating (LIBOR − 1 percent) and is paying fixed (Treasury + 2 percent). This is converted to receiving LIBOR flat and paying Treasury + 3 percent) (receiving 1 percent more and paying 1 percent more).

If the Treasury rate for the period of the swap is 6 percent, the "all-in cost" for the firm's swap is 9 percent or 4.5 percent bond equivalent semiannual yield. The semiannual cost can also be defined as 1.5 percent over Treasuries and the annual cost as 3 percent over Treasuries or 300 bps over Treasuries.

Assume that given the above facts an all-in cost for the market is defined to be 7 percent per year or 3.5 percent per six months. The swap spread for the specific firm compared to the fixed-rate market is 9 percent − 7 percent or 2 percent per year (1 percent per six months assuming payments twice a year). With a notional amount of $20 million, there is a net outlay (compared to the market rate) of $200,000 per six months, with a present value of:

$200,000 B(10, 3.5) = $200,000(8.3166) = $1,663,000

The swap has a negative value of $1,663,000 to the counterparty, and a positive present value to the principal of $1,663,000, compared to the all-in cost for the market.

A second calculation, economically equivalent to the above, is to compute the present value of the two streams (fixed and floating) as if both streams had principal payments. The floating-rate stream is valued as of the reset date, so the present value of the floating-rate stream is equal to the notional amount of $20 million. The present value of the fixed-rate stream is $21,663,000 computed as follows:

$20,000,000 (1.035)$^{-10}$	$14,178,000
½($1,800,000) B(10, 3.5)	7,485,000
Present value of fixed-rate stream	21,663,000
Present value of floating-rate stream	20,000,000
Net value of swap	$ 1,663,000

The two values obtained from the two calculations must be equal.

In the above example, a six-month rate of 3.5 percent (7 percent bond equivalent annual rate) was used. Since only bid-offered rates are observed, the 7 percent of the above example can be assumed to be the midpoint of the bid-offered spread. To value a swap after the initiation period, there are several choices for the discount rate:

1. Current Treasury rate for same maturity plus the initial midpoint spread over the treasury rate.
2. Current all-in-cost market swap rate (using the midpoint).
3. A set of zero coupon rates (based on current midpoint rates).

FIGURE 22–5
Swap with 57-62 Bid-Offered Spread over Treasuries

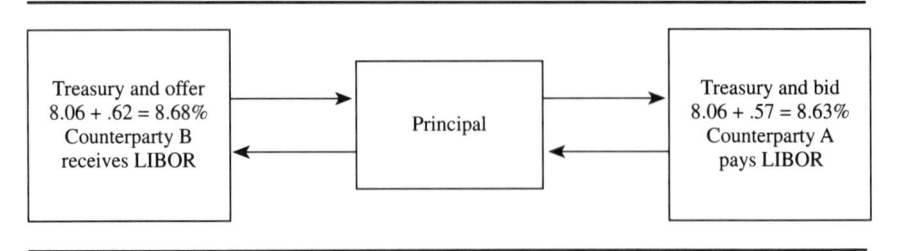

```
┌─────────────────────┐                          ┌─────────────────────┐
│ Treasury and offer  │ ──────────►              │ Treasury and bid    │
│ 8.06 + .62 = 8.68%  │            ┌──────────┐  │ 8.06 + .57 = 8.63%  │
│ Counterparty B      │            │ Principal│  │ Counterparty A      │
│ receives LIBOR      │ ◄──────────└──────────┘◄─│ pays LIBOR          │
└─────────────────────┘                          └─────────────────────┘
```

Interest rate swaps are quoted in spreads over U.S. Treasuries. Assume the spread is 57-62 for two-year swaps. The 57 is the bid spread over Treasuries and the 62 is the offered spread. Assume U.S. Treasuries maturing in two years are yielding 8.06 percent. With these facts, we have the swap shown in Figure 22–5.

The principal has a net spread of 8.68 percent minus 8.63 percent or .05 percent. It receives 8.68 percent from one counterparty and pays the other 8.63 percent.

Assume the notational amount is $1 million and the all-in cost for paying fixed for a market swap goes to 9 percent (9 percent is a market rate).

The present value of the two-year swap to B then becomes (with two years to maturity) $5,629.

$$PV = \frac{\$86,800}{1.09} - \frac{\$1,086,800}{(1.09)^2} + \$1,000,000 = \$5,629$$

Equivalently, the present value is:

$$PV = \$1,000,000(.0900 - .0868) \, B(2, 9) = \$5,629$$

B is paying fixed 8.68 percent but the discount rate is 9 percent; thus, there is a net value of $5,629. If the creditworthiness of the counterparty paying fixed is better than that of the average counterparty making up the market, this calculation would tend to lead to a positive present value.

We can also consider the swap from Counterparty A's viewpoint. A pays LIBOR and receives 57 basis points more than Treasuries (A receives 8.63 percent). On $1 million of notional amount this is a present value of:

$$PV = \frac{\$86,300}{1.09} + \frac{\$1,086,300}{(1.09)^2} - \$1,000,000 = -\$6,509$$

or equivalently:

$$PV = \$1,000,000(.0863 - .0900)\, B(2, .09) = -\$6,509$$

The firm's creditworthiness is not included in the discount rate calculation if the market rate of 9 percent is used.

HEDGE ACCOUNTING ISSUES

Except for foreign exchange hedges (see FAS No. 52) and futures (see FAS No. 80), the FASB has not yet taken a definitive position on the accounting for hedges.

Swaps are sometimes used as hedges, but they are also used to speculate and they are also used to reduce risk where there is not a hedge. They are also used for purposes unrelated to risk management or speculation purposes. Thus, even when definitive pronouncements regarding hedge accounting are accepted, they will be difficult to implement for swaps.

CONCLUSIONS

It is useful to remember that the principal of a swap earns its spread by performing the following economic functions:

1. Seeks a lower cost of money for the counterparty by using the world markets. This facilitates other aspects of the investment banking business (it is a selling point).
2. Acts as a lender (when there is clean risk at settlement).
3. Enhances the credit of less than AAA-rated entities by guaranteeing payment of interest.
4. Absorbs interest rate risk in unmatched swap transactions.

The principal has several different types of risk with matched swaps. These risks are trading risk, clean risk, termination risk, and reset risk. A portfolio or warehouse swap approach would add several types of interest rate risk. With matched swaps, the primary risks are credit types of risks. Thus, analysis of a swap from the viewpoint of a principal is very close to the credit analysis performed by a lender.

A counterparty of a swap has a different distribution of outcomes with the swap than before the swap. As well as having the possibility of reducing the cost of borrowing, a swap either reduces or increases a firm's risk. A swap can be a hedge against outstanding debt or assets, or it can be a speculation regarding future interest rate changes. Accounting statements should include notes that describe the economic consequences of the swap. Is the swap risk reducing or risk intensifying? By its nature, an interest rate swap must change the risk profile of a counterparty firm.

If interest rates change and if one of the counterparties defaults, a principal then has a liability. The status of swap contracts for a principal, including the fixed rates that are to be paid and to be received, should be revealed. It is important information for a person doing a risk analysis for the principal. It is necessary for the accountant to explain in footnotes the changes in risk that arise because of entering into swaps either as a principal or as a counterparty.

NOTES

1. FASB Statement No. 52, *Foreign Currency Translation* (Stamford, Conn.: FASB, 1981), paragraphs 15–19.
2. C. W. Smithson, "A Lego® Approach to Financial Engineering: An Introduction to Forwards, Futures, Swaps, and Options," *Midland Corporate Financial Journal,* Winter 1987, pp. 19–21.
3. J. Bicksler and A. H. Chen, "An Economic Analysis of Interest Rate Swaps," *The Journal of Finance,* July 1986, p. 646.
4. K. Wishon and L. S. Chevalier, "Interest Rate Swaps—Your Rate or Mine?" *Journal of Accountancy,* September 1985, p. 76.
5. Ibid., p. 78; and FASB Emerging Issues Task Force, Norwalk Conn., 1989.
6. FASB Statement No. 80, *Accounting for Futures Contracts* (Stamford, Conn.: FASB, 1984), paragraph 5.

7. APB Opinion No. 26, *Early Extinguishment of Debt* (New York: AICPA, 1972), paragraph 20.
8. FASB Statement No. 4, *Reporting Gains and Losses from Extinguishment of Debt* (Stamford, Conn.: FASB, 1975), paragraph 8.
9. Wishon and Chevalier, "Interest Rate Swaps," p. 78.
10. Ibid.
11. FASB Statement No. 91, *Accounting for Nonrefundable Fees and Costs Associated with Originating or Acquiring Loans and Initial Direct Costs of Lease* (Stamford, Conn.: FASB, 1986), paragraph 5.
12. *Clean risk at settlement* is conventional terminology.
13. FASB Statement No. 105, *Disclosure of Information about Financial Instruments with Off-Balance-Sheet Risk and Financial Instruments with Concentrations of Credit Risk* (Norwalk, Conn.: FASB, 1990), paragraph 17.
14. Ibid., paragraph 18.
15. Ibid., paragraph 97.

REFERENCES

APB Opinion No. 26. *Early Extinguishment of Debt*. New York: AICPA, 1972.

Bicksler, J., and A. H. Chen. "An Economic Analysis of Interest Rate Swaps." *The Journal of Finance*, July 1986, pp. 645–55.

Bierman, H., L. T. Johnson, and D. S. Peterson. *Hedge Accounting: An Exploratory Study of the Underlying Issues*. Norwalk, Conn.: FASB, 1991.

FASB Statement No. 4. *Reporting Gains and Losses from Extinguishment of Debt*. Stamford, Conn.: FASB, 1975.

FASB Statement No. 52. *Foreign Currency Translation*. Stamford, Conn.: FASB, 1981.

FASB Statement No. 80. *Accounting for Futures Contracts*. Stamford, Conn.: FASB, 1984.

FASB Statement No. 91. *Accounting for Nonrefundable Fees and Costs Associated with Originating or Acquiring Loans and Initial Direct Costs of Lease*. Stamford, Conn.: FASB, 1986.

FASB Statement No. 105. *Disclosure of Information about Financial Instruments with Off-Balance-Sheet Risk and Financial Instruments with Concentrations of Credit Risk*. Norwalk, Conn.: FASB, 1990.

Smith, C. W., Jr., C. W. Smithson, and L. M. Wakeman. "The Evolving Market for Swaps." *Midland Corporate Financial Journal,* Winter 1986, pp. 20–32.

Smithson, C. W. "A Lego® Approach to Financial Engineering: An Introduction to Forwards, Futures, Swaps, and Options." *Midland Corporate Financial Journal,* Winter 1987, pp. 16–28.

Wishon, K., and L. S. Chevalier. "Interest Rate Swaps—Your Rate or Mine?" *Journal of Accountancy,* September 1985, pp. 63–84.

CHAPTER 23

SWAPS: A LEGAL PERSPECTIVE*

*Albert S. Pergam**
Cleary, Gottlieb, Steen & Hamilton, New York

A *swap agreement* is a risk management device commonly used in world financial markets. In a basic interest rate swap, one party agrees to make periodic payments based on a fixed rate of interest to a counterparty who agrees to make reciprocal payments based on a floating rate. Such payments are calculated on the basis of a hypothetical principal, or notional, amount, which typically is not transferred. Because of the magnitude of the sums involved and the complexity of the terms of the agreement, it is imperative that the swap agreement accurately embody the parties' intent and be legally enforceable in case of any default or misunderstanding.

CREATION AND DOCUMENTATION OF SWAP AGREEMENTS

If a party to a swap defaults on its agreement (whether written or oral), the legal system will consider various factors in determining whether and how to enforce the agreement.

---

*This chapter is adapted from Anthony C. Gooch and Albert S. Pergam, "Legal Aspects of Swap Agreements: An Introduction" and "United States and New York Law," in *The Handbook of Currency and Interest Rate Risk Management*, ed. R. J. Schwartz and C. W. Smith, Jr. (New York: New York Institute of Finance, 1990). The assistance of Lech Kalembka and Luc Saucier of Cleary, Gottlieb, Steen & Hamilton is gratefully acknowledged. The author is also indebted to Linda B. Klein, a partner of Whitman & Ransom, New York.

Enforceability Issues

Financial executives have developed shortcuts and conventions designed to expedite and simplify swap transactions. The legal system has responded accordingly, and recognizes and respects these common business practices.

Enforceability of Oral Agreements
Swap agreements are almost always made on the telephone. Some swaps are between dealers and end users, that is, businesses or governmental agencies using the swap to reduce risk on some other asset or liability or packaging the swap with another asset or liability to change the interest rate or currency characteristics of the package. Other swaps are between dealers, who usually seek to maintain balanced portfolios of swaps, together with other positions and hedges.

Once the oral agreement is reached, the parties assume they have a binding agreement. An end user will rely on the assumption that it has successfully hedged a risk or changed the characteristics of an asset or liability at a particular market level; dealers will normally enter into another transaction immediately to hedge the swap position. Market practice is to confirm the oral agreement, often by an exchange of telexes or faxes.

Questions arise, however, as to whether such an oral agreement (with or without a confirmation) is enforceable. In many jurisdictions, the enforceability of oral agreements is limited by statute. In New York, Section 5-701 of the General Obligations Law (GOL) states the generally applicable statute of frauds. In addition, Section 2-201 of the New York Uniform Commercial Code (UCC), which states the statute of frauds for sales of goods, may apply to currency swaps.

Section 5-701 of the GOL. The New York Statute of Frauds, GOL S 5-701(a)(1), provides:

> a. Every agreement, promise or undertaking is void, unless it or some note or memorandum thereof be in writing, and subscribed by the party to be charged therewith, or by his lawful agent, if such agreement, promise or undertaking:

1. By its terms is not to be performed within one year from the making thereof.

Accordingly, if a swap agreed to by telephone has a term longer than one year and there is no writing that confirms the telephone agreement, the agreement is unenforceable. The adequacy of a facsimile or telex confirmation under the GOL statute of frauds should be considered in light of some important principals developed in interpreting this statute:

1. A telex can be a "writing" for the statute of frauds, and a typed signature at the end of the telex can suffice.
2. The note or memorandum required by the statute can be assembled from more than one document.
3. Documents that are not "subscribed" (that is, signed at the end of the document) may be considered together with documents that are subscribed, if the documents that are subscribed are sufficient to demonstrate the existence of the contractual relationship, and if the unsubscribed documents show on their face that they relate to the same transaction.
4. All the essential terms must appear in the documents; that is, none may be supplied by testimony. What terms are essential turns on the facts of the case.
5. The New York courts have shown greater willingness to admit unsubscribed documents if they have been prepared by the defendant rather than the plaintiff. The New York Court of Appeals (the state's highest court) has held that the statute of frauds does not prohibit the use of unsubscribed documents prepared by the defendant to establish the existence of an enforceable contract.

These principles suggest that if only one party sends a confirming telex, the agreement recorded in the telex will be enforceable against the party that sent the confirmation if the telex (together with all other related documents) contains all the material terms and is subscribed. However, the sender of the telex may be unable to enforce the agreement against the recipient, assuming there is no other written documentation. These principles also suggest that if both parties send confirming telexes, but the telexes disagree as to a material term, there is no binding contract as a matter of contract law.

Provisions sometimes found in master swap agreements to the effect that one party, by failing to respond, is deemed to have agreed to the other party's telex may be subject to challenge, as invalid appointments of one party as the other's agent under the statute of frauds.

Even if an interest rate swap agreement made over the telephone is held to be unenforceable by application of the GOL statute of frauds, in certain circumstances a party may be able to recover damages by showing that it reasonably relied on the other party's promise and suffered injury.[1] In one breach of contract action involving two swaps for which final documentation was never completed, the correspondence exchanged between the parties was found by a jury to be sufficient to constitute a binding agreement.[2]

Section 2-201 of the UCC. Because a currency swap may be thought of as involving the use of money as a commodity rather than a medium of payment, UCC Section 2-201, applicable to the sale of goods, may govern. Indeed, three recent cases applying New York law have applied Section 2-201 to foreign currency transactions.[3] UCC Section 2-201 provides that a contract for the sale of goods for the price of $500 or more is enforceable only if there is a signed writing indicating the existence of such contract, regardless of the duration of the agreement. The application of this statute of frauds involves the following additional considerations:

1. The document need not contain all the material terms. Only the quantity term must be stated.
2. The signature may appear anywhere on the document, unlike the GOL statute of frauds, which requires that the signature appear at the end of the document.[4]
3. If swap dealers and experienced end users are "merchants" under UCC Section 2-104(1), as would appear to be the case, the exception to the statute of frauds set forth in UCC Section 2-201(2) will apply. Under this exception, an oral agreement will be enforceable if a written confirmation (which may be a telex) is sent within a reasonable time,

and the recipient has reason to known of its contents and fails to object within 10 days.

A proposed amendment to GOL Section 5-701, if enacted, would create exceptions to that statute of frauds for "qualifying financial contracts," such as swaps and other derivative products, in certain circumstances, if sufficient evidence of the parties' intent could be established by an electronic recording (or if a confirmation were not objected to within a prescribed time period). The proposal was submitted to the legislature in 1993.[5]

Gaming Laws and Foreign Exchange Controls
Interest rate and currency swap transactions and, in particular, innovative arrangements such as swaps involving indexes or commodity prices may present other enforceability problems. For example, the gaming laws of some jurisdictions void agreements under which money is staked on the outcome of a future contingent event not within a party's control.[6] Such an agreement may be enforceable, however, if it is entered into for a valid business purpose. The gaming law analysis may turn on the motivation of the parties in entering into a swap; a swap entered into to hedge business risks may be treated differently from one entered into for purely speculative purposes.

The enforceability of a swap agreement must also be considered in the light of foreign exchange controls. Such controls may limit the ability of residents to enter into obligations to make payments in currencies other than the local currency, or may limit their ability to purchase foreign exchange with local currency for the purpose of honoring such commitments.

The effects of securities laws, commodities regulation, and insurance regulation in the United States on swap agreements should also be considered. See the section "Regulatory Considerations" later in this chapter.

Master Agreements

As the swaps market developed, many dealers began entering into repetitive transactions with each other. To facilitate documenting these transactions, market participants developed "master" agreements that made it possible to document swaps with a wide variety of characteristics under a single master. These master agreements present a variety of interesting legal issues.

In the early days of the swaps market, each swap was accounted for separately, usually as a percentage of its notional principal amount, and was treated as an exposure to the counterparty for purposes of internal lending limits, regardless of whether it was in the money or out of the money at the time of calculation.

Dealers soon found that this method of measuring risk produced unacceptably high levels of exposure. This led to the "one-big-agreement" approach under which the parties to a master swap agreement treat all their transactions as a single agreement that is supplemented each time they add a new set of cash flows (that is, a new swap) to the existing flows agreed to in earlier transactions.

The single-agreement approach also responds to the central concern of market participants: their ability to set off mutual payment obligations and entitlements under several swap transactions with a particular counterparty, particularly in the event of the counterparty's insolvency. (See the section on "Termination, Damages, and Insolvency," and the section on "The Netting Provisions of the Federal Deposit Insurance Corporation Improvement Act of 1991" later in the chapter.)

The single-agreement approach also can be important for banks and other financial institutions that have internal or regulatory limits on the amount of credit exposure they may assume vis-à-vis a given counterparty, or that are subject to other kinds of regulation based on such exposure. If the master agreement entitles the bank to net out amounts owing under the various rate swaps under the master, and entitles the bank to terminate all the swaps if the counterparty defaults under any one of the swaps, the bank may determine that only its net exposure is relevant for credit limit purposes. Since the net exposure is far less than the gross exposure, banks prefer this approach.

The enforceability of the single-agreement approach is discussed in the Section "Termination, Damages, and Insolvency." The status of swap agreements for capital adequacy purposes is discussed in the section on regulatory considerations.

Standardization Efforts

Through 1984, most major participants in the swaps market had their own forms of swap agreements. As a result, many dealers developed significant documentation backlogs, and the costs of the documentation process became unacceptably high. Moreover, the terminology used for transactions varied from dealer to dealer, resulting in misunderstandings and occasional broken trades.

A group of major participants and their counsel began meeting in New York City in 1984 to develop a common approach to these problems. Their work led to the formation of the International Swap Dealers Association (ISDA) and the publication, in 1985, of the first edition of the ISDA's *Code of Standard Wording, Assumptions and Provisions for Swaps* (known as the *swaps code*). The swaps code was basically a compendium of terms reflecting mechanisms widely used by market participants in U.S. dollar interest rate swap agreements. The terms included definitions of rates used to compute swap payments and conventions for netting and rounding, for the treatment of payments scheduled to be made on holidays, and for measuring loss of bargain on early termination of a swap. The 1986 edition built on that start by adding new terms to the vocabulary and, in some cases, by revising terms previously included.

The swaps code was not designed to deal with swaps involving currencies other than U.S. dollars, however. Accordingly, a similar lexicon was required to facilitate communication regarding currency swaps and rate swaps involving currencies other than U.S. dollars. This was supplied by the 1987 *Interest Rate and Currency Exchange Definitions* (referred to as the *1987 definitions*), published by ISDA as a companion to the ISDA's standard *Interest Rate and Currency Exchange Agreement*. The 1987 definitions created a basis for a common language for documenting swaps involving 15 currencies.

Recently, the ISDA issued the 1991 ISDA definitions, which update and expand the 1987 definitions. The 1991 ISDA definitions cover 18 currencies and include floating interest rates and other options. The 1991 ISDA definitions can be used to document new confirmations under an existing agreement without affecting confirmations documented under the 1987 definitions.

The ISDA took further steps toward standardization with the publication in 1987 of two forms of master agreements: first, a form of *Interest Rate Swap Agreement* for U.S. dollar rate swaps (called the *interest rate agreement*); and, second, a form of *Interest Rate and Currency Exchange Agreement* (together with the interest rate agreement known as the *1987 agreements*) that also accommodates currency swaps and rate swaps in other currencies. A current version of the *Interest Rate Swap Agreement* is included in the appendix at the end of this chapter. Each of the forms consists of two main parts: the text of the basic provisions and a schedule designed to permit completion or modification of those provisions. Apart from provisions included in the *Interest Rate and Currency Exchange Agreement* designed to accommodate swaps involving currencies other than U.S. dollars, the substance of the provisions of the two forms is almost identical. The language is, however, different, since many provisions in the *Interest Rate Swap Agreement* operate through the incorporation, by reference, of terms from the swaps code; the swaps code assumes that the parties will choose New York law to govern their agreement. The *Interest Rate and Currency Exchange Agreement,* on the other hand, spells out terms that are sometimes slightly modified so that the agreement may be made subject either to English law or New York law.

In 1992, the ISDA published a *Local Currency-Single Jurisdiction Master Agreement* (called the *local agreement*) and a *Multicurrency-Cross Border Master Agreement* (known as, together with the local agreement, the *1992 agreements*), intended to update the 1987 agreements. The 1992 agreements may be used to document a wider range of products under a single master, including equity and commodity swaps and options. This, in turn, is intended to permit expanded cross-product netting.

The ISDA has also published printed forms of confirmation to be used with the standard forms of agreement. Each includes variants designed to enable the parties to exchange confirmations by telex or on printed documents. The ISDA recently issued supplements to these forms that make it possible to adapt the forms for other rate protection transactions, such as interest rate caps, floors, collars, and options. In connection with publication of the 1992 agreements, the ISDA also issued a form of confirmation for cash-settled equity options, definitions and forms of confirmation for foreign exchange and currency transactions, definitions, and forms of confirmation for transactions involving U.S. municipalities, and an appendix containing a schedule for such counterparties. At some future date ISDA may publish definitions for commodities and additional definitions for equities, in addition to a user's guide to the new documentation. A sample ISDA confirmation is included in the appendix to this chapter.

Another standardization effort is reflected in the British Bankers' Association Interest Rate Swaps (BBAIRS) terms, developed by the Interest Rate Swaps Working Party of the British Bankers' Association, which sets forth recommended terms and conditions for short-term London interbank interest rate and currency swaps. Standardized terms have also been published for domestic swaps in other countries. In addition, in 1990, the *International Currency Options Market Master Agreement* was published. This agreement reflects the general practices followed in the interbank and professional currency options market.

Authorization Issues

A swap agreement (or any other contract for that matter) is not legally binding if executed by parties who were not authorized to do so. Accordingly, the authority of the counterparties' agents (e.g., a vice president) must be established.

Dealers and End Users Generally

For swaps between dealers, corporate power and due authorization issues ordinarily are not particularly important, although a prudent party will always satisfy itself that its counterparty has requisite power and authority. When end users are involved, however, power and authorization must be considered with greater care.

The power of a corporation to enter into a transaction generally flows from its charter and bylaws. In the case of a swap with a partnership or a trust, the partnership agreement or deed of trust must be reviewed. For these reasons, in the case of swaps involving end users, it is advisable to require the submission of certified resolutions and, in most cases, opinions of counsel as "closing documents" (i.e., those backup documents, such as certificates and opinions, furnished in connection with the swap agreement to permit the transaction to "close" or be completed).

Swaps with Counterparties in Regulated Industries

Special attention must also be paid to issues of authorization in swaps involving entities that operate in regulated industries. In addition to questions of the types discussed below in the section "Regulatory Considerations," careful consideration must be given to the possibility that an end user in a regulated industry (such as a public utility) may require special governmental approval to enter into a swap transaction.

Swaps with Public Sector Entities

Swaps with public sector entities, including nations, international organizations, states, and municipalities, present special legal issues. The constitution, charter, treaty, or other organizational document of the entity will usually be the point of departure in determining whether the public sector entity is authorized to enter into swaps and, if so, what the proper procedure is for the authorization of the transaction and the execution of the relevant documentation.[7] A legal opinion from counsel for the public sector entity is normally an appropriate condition precedent, except, perhaps, for entities that are regular, established participants in the market, such as the World Bank and the Student Loan Marketing Association.

TERMINATION, DAMAGES, AND INSOLVENCY

Most swaps are fully and punctually performed. Where a party fails to perform in some manner, however, the law provides certain remedies.

Termination

The rights of a party to terminate a swap transaction before the end of its stated term, and the proper measure of damages in the event of early termination, have provoked lively discussions among lawyers and others interested in swaps documentation.

Swap agreements now typically provide a right to terminate for specified events of default, which generally include (1) failure to perform obligations under the agreement, (2) bankruptcy or insolvency, and (3) certain credit-related events short of insolvency (such as a cross-default). Swap agreements also permit termination for certain no-fault "termination events," such as the imposition of exchange controls or the requirement to make payments pursuant to an obligation to "gross-up" or indemnify for taxes withheld from a party's basic swap payments in certain circumstances.

Measures of Damages

Swap agreements almost universally provide for measuring a party's damages (if any) on premature termination by looking to the amount that the party would have to pay another market participant to replace the economic benefits of the terminated swap. Swap participants agree that if a swap agreement is terminated because of a default, the defaulting party should pay the nondefaulting party damages sufficient to compensate for any loss (including loss of bargain) it suffers as a result of termination. The obligation of the nondefaulting party to compensate the defaulting party for any of its losses, however, is a controversial issue. According to one view, the nondefaulting party should never have to make a termination payment to the defaulting party.[8] The other view is that the nondefaulting party should not be allowed to reap a windfall from the default.[9] It is generally agreed, however, that on the occurrence of a no-fault termination event, the party that realizes a benefit from termination is required to share the benefit with the other party.

In case of early termination of a rate swap, several elements of damages, in addition to loss of bargain, may be suffered by one or both of the parties:

Unpaid amounts. These are swap payments that have become due and remain unpaid (or would have become due but for a contractual provision entitling a party to withhold payment).

Elapsed period amounts. A second element of damages is the portion of the next scheduled swap payment that is allocable to the period between the last payment date and the early termination date. This amount is now generally covered by provisions relating to compensation for loss of bargain.

The most complicated and interesting element of damages is loss of bargain. In most cases of early termination, one party will be damaged by losing what it bargained for, and the other will receive a benefit roughly equal to the first party's loss. There are three main approaches to measuring the value of the lost bargain:

1. *Indemnification.* Many rate swap agreements simply provide that if one party defaults, the defaulting party is required to indemnify the nondefaulting party for its damages, and that those damages will include the value (if any) of the loss of the bargain to the nondefaulting party. This approach is known as *indemnification* in the swaps code and as *loss* in the 1992 agreements.

2. *Liquidated damages.* The variants of this approach all involve formulas designed to estimate in advance the nondefaulting party's loss of bargain. Under New York law, the parties to a contract may liquidate (that is, fix in advance) the damages that might flow from breach as long as the actual amount of those damages is impossible or difficult to determine precisely at the time they enter into the agreement, and the liquidated amount bears a reasonable relationship to the probable loss in light of the circumstances existing at the time of contracting. However, a liquidated damages formula may be unenforceable as a penalty if it produces a result that bears no ascertainable relationship to the probable loss or is plainly or grossly disproportionate to it.

3. *Agreement value.* Described as *agreement value* in the swaps code and as *market quotation* in the 1992 agreements, this approach measures loss of bargain on early termination of a swap by looking at the cost of entering into a replacement swap. Under this approach, the nondefaulting party attempts to obtain quotations for entering into a new swap under which the provider of the quotation (referred to in the swaps code as a *reference market-maker*) would have payment obligations identical to those of the defaulting party for the remaining life of the swap. The cost (if any) to the nondefaulting party of its lost bargain would be equal to the front-end fee that would be charged by the reference market-maker to enter into the new rate swap. If the quotations are given at a time when the agreement has value to the defaulting party, the reference market-maker may be willing to pay a fee to enter into the new swap. However, as discussed above, under one approach in the market, a nondefaulting party would not be required to turn over to the defaulting party an amount equal to that fee, thus enabling the nondefaulting party to receive a windfall.[10]

The agreement value concept is intended to establish a method for determining actual, rather than liquidated, damages. The enforceability of each agreement value provision must be examined in the light of the duty (if any) of the injured party to mitigate its damages. At least theoretically, the identity of the reference market-makers might affect the amounts of the quotations received. It can be argued that the common law duty to mitigate damages imposes an obligation to make a reasonable effort to obtain quotations from market participants that are likely to provide low quotations. However, it can also be argued that the nondefaulting party should be permitted to obtain the quotations from market participants of the highest credit standing, with whom that party would be willing to do business under normal circumstances, even if the resulting quotations may be somewhat higher than those quotations that could be obtained from market makers of lesser credit standing.

The agreement value approach incorporated in the swaps code calls for obtaining a number of quotations and averaging them, often after dropping the highest and lowest quotations. In addition, a common approach (reflected in the swaps code) provides that if fewer than three quotations can be obtained, the agreement value method for determining damages is not to be used, and damages must instead be determined using an alternative method agreed to by the parties.

Although unsettled, the case law appears generally to recognize the parties' termination rights and the market-based approach to measuring damages. Still to be passed on by a court is the practice, described above, of permitting the nondefaulting party to retain a windfall in the event of termination. The enforceability of this practice has been the subject of litigation relating to the bankruptcy of Drexel Burnham Lambert. Although most of these cases appear to have been settled, a recent judicial decision by a New York federal court upheld the enforceability of this practice.[11] Walk-away provisions, however, can be expected to continue to come under attack, particularly in cases where the default was triggered by insolvency or a cross-default rather than a material performance failure.

Bankruptcy and Insolvency

When a corporation or other entity becomes insolvent and is unable to perform its obligations, either the insolvent party itself, its creditors, or its regulators may commence a judicial proceeding under the U.S. bankruptcy laws.

Bankruptcy Code Debtors
Bankruptcy and other insolvency laws typically impose a number of limitations on the exercise of contractual and other rights of creditors and counterparties of the debtor, in order to protect the debtor and its estate and permit an orderly and equitable disposition of claims against it. For example, under the U.S. Bankruptcy Code, once a petition for relief has been filed by or against the debtor, certain kinds of actions against the debtor's property, such as the exercise of setoff rights and the liquidation of collateral, will be prohibited unless judicially approved. Similarly, a provision in an "executory" contract (that is, one in which performance remains due on both sides) of the debtor to the effect that a party may terminate or modify the contract based on the bankruptcy or financial condition of the debtor typically is not enforceable in a bankruptcy proceeding. Indeed, the trustee generally has the power to assume, assign, or reject executory contracts, notwithstanding any bankruptcy default provisions. Also, the trustee can recover payments and other transfers made within 90 days (or, in certain circumstances, one year) prior to the bankruptcy filing.

Swap agreements characteristically provide that the agreement will terminate after written notice of the occurrence of an insolvency-related event of default has been furnished (and that the parties may elect instead to provide in the agreement that it will terminate automatically in such event). In the alternative, they may provide that termination will occur unless the nondefaulting party elects otherwise. Because of the bankruptcy code provisions described above, the enforceability of these provisions in bankruptcy was uncertain until June 1990. At that time, Congress amended the Bankruptcy Code to provide special protections for swaps (the 1990 amendments).

The 1990 amendments make it clear that the contractual right of a "swap participant" to terminate a "swap agreement" upon the bankruptcy of its counterparty may not be stayed, limited, or avoided by any provision of the Bankruptcy Code. *Swap agreement* is defined broadly and includes the master agreement and all supplements to it. By affording protection to the counterparty's right to terminate, these provisions eliminate the possibility that the exercise by the trustee of its power to assume or reject executory contracts could enable it to "cherry pick" (that is, assume transactions in the money to the debtor while rejecting those out of the money), which otherwise could effectively destroy the counterparty's netting rights.

Moreover, the 1990 amendments expressly protect the right of the counterparty to net out or offset any termination or payment amounts owed under a swap agreement in the event of bankruptcy of the debtor, notwithstanding any other provision of the Bankruptcy Code. The FDICIA will, in certain circumstances, reinforce the Bankruptcy Code's protection of netting rights under swaps.

Finally, except in unusual circumstances, the 1990 amendments protect transfers made under swap agreements, such as mark-to-market payments, from the exercise of a trustee's power to avoid "preferences" and "fraudulent conveyances." Because of a technical drafting point in the Bankruptcy Code, however, some recommend incorporating any security provisions into the swap agreement itself to ensure that these protections are available.

Financial Institutions

Banks and savings and loan institutions (thrifts) chartered under the laws of the United States or a state may not be debtors in proceedings under the Bankruptcy Code. FDIC-insured banks and thrifts in most cases are subject, instead, to the conservatorship and receivership provisions of the Federal Deposit Insurance Act (FDIA). The FDIA provides the Federal Deposit Insurance Corporation (FDIC) and the Resolution Trust Corporation (RTC) with powers roughly similar to those of the Bankruptcy Code trustees described earlier.

The status of swap transactions entered into by financial institutions that become subject to conservatorship or receivership proceedings was clarified by the enactment of the Financial Institutions Reform, Recovery, and Enforcement Act of 1989 (FIRREA). Although FIRREA grants broad powers to the FDIC and the RTC to deal with failed or failing financial institutions, it also includes important protections for counterparties to "qualified financial contracts" (QFCs), including swap agreements, with such institutions.[12]

Powers of Conservator or Receiver in General. The FDIC or RTC as conservator or receiver may enforce or assign contracts of the failed institution, notwithstanding insolvency-triggered contractual termination provisions. The FDIC or RTC may also repudiate contracts and may in certain cases have the power to avoid certain transfers made by the institution. In addition, the conservator or receiver is empowered to merge the institution with another depository institution, and to transfer its assets or liabilities selectively, without any approval.[13] The FIRREA does not include a Bankruptcy Code–like automatic stay, although the conservator or receiver may request, and a court is required to grant, a 45-day stay (in the case of a conservator) and a 90-day stay (in the case of a receiver) or any "judicial" action to which the institution, conservator, or receiver is a party.

Specific Protections for QFCs. The FDIC or RTC as *conservator* for a financial institution may enforce a "swap agreement"[14] notwithstanding insolvency-triggered default provisions in the agreement. If, however, there is a performance-related default, such as a payment default or a failure to honor a contractual obligation to mark collateral to market, the counterparty would be able to exercise its contractual rights to terminate the agreement, to proceed against collateral in its possession or control, and to offset termination values and payment amounts.

A contractual right to terminate based on the appointment of a receiver, however, *will* be enforceable unless the receiver carries out a "full" assumption transaction, in which all QFCs between the failed institution and the counterparty and its affiliates are assumed by a single bank or thrift, and the counterparty and its affiliates are notified of the assumption by the close of business on the business day following the receiver's appointment.[15] This provision is designed to protect the counterparty's (and its affiliates') netting and setoff rights.

The FDIC or RTC as conservator is empowered to repudiate a swap.[16] To date, neither the FDIC nor the RTC as conservator have not, to our knowledge, exercised repudiation powers in connection with swap agreements. If a swap were repudiated, the counterparty would have a claim for its damages (if any) measured as of the date of repudiation, which would include "normal and reasonable costs of cover or other reasonable measures of damages utilized in the industries for such contract and agreement claims."

Finally, transfers made in connection with a swap are generally protected from any avoidance powers the receiver or conservator may have, unless the FDIC or RTC determines that the transferee had actual intent to hinder, delay, or defraud the institution, its conservator or receiver, or its creditors.

Written Agreement Requirements. Certain written agreement and related requirements of the FDIA must be satisfied to permit enforcement of a claim against an FDIC-insured bank or thrift in conservatorship or receivership. These statutory requirements have been relaxed as to QFCs by the FDIC and RTC policy statements. Under the policy statements, a claim under a swap agreement is enforceable against the FDIC or RTC if evidenced by a writing (including a confirmation sent by or to the financial institution) sent "reasonably contemporaneously" with the agreement to enter into the swap. The writing need not be signed unless otherwise required by applicable law.

Under the policy statements, an institution's corporate authority to enter into a transaction will be presumed where the counterparty has relied in good faith on a resolution evidencing that authority, certified by the institution's corporate secretary or assistant secretary, or on a written representation as to such authority signed by an officer having at least the rank of vice president. Finally, the counterparty may establish the existence of a writing by appropriate evidence.[17]

THE NETTING PROVISIONS OF THE FEDERAL DEPOSIT INSURANCE CORPORATION IMPROVEMENT ACT OF 1991

The bilateral netting provisions of the FDICIA protect the enforceability of contractual provisions providing for the netting of *all* contractual obligations and entitlements between two or more financial institutions. *Financial institution* is defined to include banks located in the United States (including U.S. branches of foreign banks), thrifts, registered broker-dealers, and futures commission merchants, but not insurance companies and affiliates of such financial institutions. The FDICIA authorizes the Federal Reserve Board (the Fed) to expand the list of protected entities. We understand that the Fed is currently considering the advisability of doing so. The FDICIA by its terms supersedes any conflicting state or federal law.

The FDICIA protects the enforceability of netting contracts between financial institutions under which present or future payment obligations and entitlements are to be netted, even in the event of the bankruptcy or insolvency of one of the parties. Moreover, unlike the Bankruptcy Code and the FIRREA, the FDICIA protects the netting of obligations and entitlements under all types of contracts. Accordingly, the contractual right of a financial institution to net out payment amounts and termination values under a transaction with another financial institution should be protected even if the transaction does not qualify as a swap agreement under the Bankruptcy Code or the FIRREA.

REGULATORY CONSIDERATIONS[18]

Swap participants, such as commercial banks, investment banks, merchant banks, and insurance companies, are subject to various regulatory schemes.[19]

Bank Capital Adequacy Guidelines

In the United States, the principal regulation of swaps arises from bank and thrift capital adequacy regulations.

The risk-based capital guidelines promulgated by federal banking and thrift regulators to implement the Basle Accord have been in effect since 1989. These guidelines apply a risk-weighting scale (from 0 percent to 100 percent, depending upon perceived, relative credit risk) to different categories of on– and off–balance sheet items, including swaps. Once fully effective at year-end 1992, an institution must maintain total "qualifying" capital equal to at least 8 percent of its total risk-weighted assets, which include the on–balance sheet equivalents of off–balance sheet items. Under a separate leverage ratio requirement, "core" capital generally must equal or exceed between 3 percent and 5 percent of total assets, depending on an institution's financial condition. The pledge of certain types of collateral or the support of certain types of guarantees result in an asset or on–balance sheet equivalent amount being placed in a lower risk-weight category than would otherwise be appropriate.

For swaps, like all other off–balance sheet items, the applicable risk-weight factor is applied to an on–balance sheet "credit equivalent amount." The credit equivalent amount, generally calculated as the sum of current (i.e., mark-to-market) exposure and potential future exposure, attempts to measure a swap's replacement cost to the institution in the event of a counterparty default. For certain purposes, the capital guidelines distinguish between "interest-rate contracts" and "exchange-rate contracts" (e.g., the potential future exposure of rate swaps is generally lower than that of currency contracts). Once calculated, the credit equivalent amount is multiplied by the appropriate risk-weight factor, depending on the type of counterparty and the presence of qualifying collateral or guarantees, up to a maximum risk weight of 50 percent.

Currently, the only form of netting recognized for purposes of the capital guidelines is a limited form of "netting by novation" in respect to certain same-currency swaps. *Netting by novation* is defined, for these purposes, as "a written bilateral contract between two counterparties under which any obligation to each other to deliver a given currency on a given date is automatically amalgamated with all other obligations for the same currency and value date, *legally* substituting one single net amount for the previous gross obligations." Banking regulators from the G-10 countries, working under the auspices of the Bank for International Settlements, continue to exhibit a cautious approach to broader netting rules for swaps for capital adequacy purposes, although this issue is the subject of ongoing study.

Securities Regulation

Most investment banking firms today do not conduct interest rate and currency swap "dealer" operations through a registered broker-dealer. Since such swaps are not viewed as securities, principally because of their nontransferability and their two-way structure, swap dealers generally have not registered as broker-dealers under the Securities Exchange Act of 1934 (the Exchange Act).

In the wake of the Drexel Burnham Lambert bankruptcy, however, Congress became concerned about the lack of information available to the SEC concerning the indirect financial exposure of broker-dealers arising from the activities of their unregulated holding companies and affiliates. Accordingly, Congress amended the exchange act to provide the SEC with authority to require broker-dealers to report to the SEC certain information concerning affiliates whose business activities are reasonably likely to have a material impact on their financial or operational condition.

In 1992, the SEC issued temporary risk assessment rules. These rules will require a registered broker-dealer (or a municipal securities dealer for which the SEC is the appropriate regulatory authority) to make and to preserve records and to file quarterly reports with the SEC concerning the financial and securities activities of the holding companies, affiliates, or subsidiaries of the broker-dealer that are reasonably likely to have a material impact on its financial or operational condition (material associated persons).

The rules will require a broker-dealer to maintain and report, among other things, information reflecting the aggregate notional amounts and gross payments owed under interest rate, foreign exchange, and other swaps entered into by material associated persons of the broker-dealer that incur principal risk or operate a trading book. Specific information will be required for swaps where the notional or contractual amount exceeds a specified threshold. The risk assessment rules became fully effective on December 31, 1992.

Commodities Regulation

The interest rate swap industry did not give serious consideration to the possible application of the Commodity Exchange Act (CEA) until the Commodity Futures Trading Commission (CFTC) in 1987 published for comment its advance notice of a proposed rulemaking regarding the regulation of certain hybrid and related instruments.

CFTC jurisdiction was opposed on the ground that swaps are commercial transactions (as opposed to speculative investments), privately negotiated between sophisticated parties, and, therefore, are not susceptible to the abuses the CEA was designed to address.

In response to the concerns raised by the possible assertion of CFTC jurisdiction, the CFTC in 1989 issued a policy statement establishing a nonexclusive safe harbor for certain types of swap transactions not "appropriately regulated" as futures under the CEA and not subject to CFTC regulation. A swap will be safe-harbored if the following conditions are satisfied:

1. The swap transaction must result from individual credit determinations and private negotiation as to its material terms (although the documentation may be based on a standard form).
2. The swap transaction must create obligations that are terminable, absent default, only with the consent of the counterparty.
3. The swap transaction may not be supported by the credit of a clearing organization, and may not be "primarily or routinely supported by a mark-to-market margin and variation settlement system designed to eliminate individualized credit risk."
4. The swap transaction must be undertaken in connection with the parties' ordinary line of business, including financial intermediation services and the financing of its business.
5. The swap transaction must not be marketed to the general public (although "tombstone"-type advertising in the financial press should not cause disqualification).

If swap agreements were to be characterized as futures contracts, they would be unlawful unless traded on an organized exchange. An amendment to the CEA that would expressly exempt certain swaps from regulation under the CEA under certain conditions has been proposed. The House of Representatives and the Senate have passed different versions of the legislation but have not reached a compromise agreement at the time this chapter was written.

SECONDARY MARKET ISSUES

Participants in the swap market have long discussed the development of a secondary market in swaps that would provide liquidity to swap counterparties that wished to realize the inherent value in a swap at a particular time by selling their position (that is, their rights and obligations) to a third party. So far, however, this liquid market has not developed, though a counterparty always has the ability to close out a swap for something similar to its inherent value by negotiating a termination of the swap or an assignment of its position to a third party with the consent of its counterparty to the swap transaction.

Because of credit risk concerns raised by their two-party structure, swaps are inherently less tradable than one-party obligations such as stocks and bonds. The participants in the swap market have generally placed limitations on assignment in their standard swap documentation. For these reasons, the long-awaited secondary market in swaps has been slow to develop. Although beyond the scope of this chapter, significant development in the secondary market in swaps could, of course, raise numerous regulatory concerns, including the continued applicability of the CFTC safe harbor discussed in the preceding section.

CONCLUSION

Legislation and regulations are developing and changing to keep pace with the rapidly growing swaps market. Traditional commercial contracts law is being amended to provide for the enforcement of the (typically oral) agreements that create swaps contracts. Developments in New York State law will be particularly important because most swap agreements provide that they will be enforced in New York.

The International Swap Dealers Association (ISDA) is also developing and refining increasingly comprehensive formats for swap contracts that will expedite and clarify swap activities. In addition, new laws are being passed at the federal level that sanction the netting provisions found in most swaps transactions. The SEC, CFTC, and other federal authorities are establishing guidelines that address self-regulation of the transactions between counterparties and dealers who generate swap agreements. Only those contracts that involve disagreements or defaults, or swaps that may be traded like transferable securities (something that has not yet evolved), need come before the courts.

Old laws will doubtlessly continue to be amended and more legislation will certainly emerge. Regulatory concerns, such as those reflected in the new SEC capital rules, may continue to emerge. However, if we extrapolate the direction of past legislation and regulation into the future, the new legislation will continue to provide an environment within which the swaps industry should function effectively.

APPENDIX: ISDA MASTER AGREEMENT AND SCHEDULE TO THE MASTER AGREEMENT

(Local Currency—Single Jurisdiction)

ISDA®
International Swap Dealers Association, Inc.

MASTER AGREEMENT

dated as of ....

.... and ....

have entered and/or anticipate entering into one or more transactions (each a "Transaction") that are or will be governed by this Master Agreement, which includes the schedule (the "Schedule"), and the documents and other confirming evidence (each a "Confirmation") exchanged between the parties confirming those Transactions.

Accordingly, the parties agree as follows:—

1. **Interpretation**

(a) *Definitions*. The terms defined in Section 12 and in the Schedule will have the meanings therein specified for the purpose of this Master Agreement.

(b) *Inconsistency*. In the event of any inconsistency between the provisions of the Schedule and the other provisions of this Master Agreement, the Schedule will prevail. In the event of any inconsistency between the provisions of any Confirmation and this Master Agreement (including the Schedule), such Confirmation will prevail for the purpose of the relevant Transaction.

(c) *Single Agreement*. All Transactions are entered into in reliance on the fact that this Master Agreement and all Confirmations form a single agreement between the parties (collectively referred to as this "Agreement"), and the parties would not otherwise enter into any Transactions.

2. **Obligations**

(a) *General Conditions*.

(i) Each party will make each payment or delivery specified in each Confirmation to be made by it, subject to the other provisions of this Agreement.

(ii) Payments under this Agreement will be made on the due date for value on that date in the place of the account specified in the relevant Confirmation or otherwise pursuant to this Agreement, in freely transferable funds and in the manner customary for payments in the required currency. Where settlement is by delivery (that is, other than by payment), such delivery will be made for receipt on the due date in the manner customary for the relevant obligation unless otherwise specified in the relevant Confirmation or elsewhere in this Agreement.

(iii) Each obligation of each party under Section 2(a)(i) is subject to (1) the condition precedent that no Event of Default or Potential Event of Default with respect to the other party has occurred and is continuing, (2) the condition precedent that no Early Termination Date in respect of the relevant Transaction has occurred or been effectively designated and (3) each other applicable condition precedent specified in this Agreement.

Copyright ©1992 by International Swap Dealers Association, Inc.

(b) *Change of Account.* Either party may change its account for receiving a payment or delivery by giving notice to the other party at least five Local Business Days prior to the scheduled date for the payment or delivery to which such change applies unless such other party gives timely notice of a reasonable objection to such change.

(c) *Netting.* If on any date amounts would otherwise be payable:—

   (i) in the same currency; and

   (ii) in respect of the same Transaction,

by each party to the other, then, on such date, each party's obligation to make payment of any such amount will be automatically satisfied and discharged and, if the aggregate amount that would otherwise have been payable by one party exceeds the aggregate amount that would otherwise have been payable by the other party, replaced by an obligation upon the party by whom the larger aggregate amount would have been payable to pay to the other party the excess of the larger aggregate amount over the smaller aggregate amount.

The parties may elect in respect of two or more Transactions that a net amount will be determined in respect of all amounts payable on the same date in the same currency in respect of such Transactions, regardless of whether such amounts are payable in respect of the same Transaction. The election may be made in the Schedule or a Confirmation by specifying that subparagraph (ii) above will not apply to the Transactions identified as being subject to the election, together with the starting date (in which case subparagraph (ii) above will not, or will cease to, apply to such Transactions from such date). This election may be made separately for different groups of Transactions and will apply separately to each pairing of branches or offices through which the parties make and receive payments or deliveries.

(d) *Default Interest; Other Amounts.* Prior to the occurrence or effective designation of an Early Termination Date in respect of the relevant Transaction, a party that defaults in the performance of any payment obligation will, to the extent permitted by law and subject to Section 6(c), be required to pay interest (before as well as after judgment) on the overdue amount to the other party on demand in the same currency as such overdue amount, for the period from (and including) the original due date for payment to (but excluding) the date of actual payment, at the Default Rate. Such interest will be calculated on the basis of daily compounding and the actual number of days elapsed. If, prior to the occurrence or effective designation of an Early Termination Date in respect of the relevant Transaction, a party defaults in the performance of any obligation required to be settled by delivery, it will compensate the other party on demand if and to the extent provided for in the relevant Confirmation or elsewhere in this Agreement.

3. Representations

Each party represents to the other party (which representations will be deemed to be repeated by each party on each date on which a Transaction is entered into) that:—

(a) *Basic Representations.*

   (i) *Status.* It is duly organised and validly existing under the laws of the jurisdiction of its organisation or incorporation and, if relevant under such laws, in good standing;

   (ii) *Powers.* It has the power to execute this Agreement and any other documentation relating to this Agreement to which it is a party, to deliver this Agreement and any other documentation relating to this Agreement that it is required by this Agreement to deliver and to perform its obligations under this Agreement and any obligations it has under any Credit Support Document to which it is a party and has taken all necessary action to authorise such execution, delivery and performance;

   (iii) *No Violation or Conflict.* Such execution, delivery and performance do not violate or conflict with any law applicable to it, any provision of its constitutional documents, any order or judgment of any court or other agency of government applicable to it or any of its assets or any contractual restriction binding on or affecting it or any of its assets;

(iv) **Consents.** All governmental and other consents that are required to have been obtained by it with respect to this Agreement or any Credit Support Document to which it is a party have been obtained and are in full force and effect and all conditions of any such consents have been complied with; and

(v) **Obligations Binding.** Its obligations under this Agreement and any Credit Support Document to which it is a party constitute its legal, valid and binding obligations, enforceable in accordance with their respective terms (subject to applicable bankruptcy, reorganisation, insolvency, moratorium or similar laws affecting creditors' rights generally and subject, as to enforceability, to equitable principles of general application (regardless of whether enforcement is sought in a proceeding in equity or at law)).

(b) **Absence of Certain Events.** No Event of Default or Potential Event of Default or, to its knowledge, Termination Event with respect to it has occurred and is continuing and no such event or circumstance would occur as a result of its entering into or performing its obligations under this Agreement or any Credit Support Document to which it is a party.

(c) **Absence of Litigation.** There is not pending or, to its knowledge, threatened against it or any of its Affiliates any action, suit or proceeding at law or in equity or before any court, tribunal, governmental body, agency or official or any arbitrator that is likely to affect the legality, validity or enforceability against it of this Agreement or any Credit Support Document to which it is a party or its ability to perform its obligations under this Agreement or such Credit Support Document.

(d) **Accuracy of Specified Information.** All applicable information that is furnished in writing by or on behalf of it to the other party and is identified for the purpose of this Section 3(d) in the Schedule is, as of the date of the information, true, accurate and complete in every material respect.

4. Agreements

Each party agrees with the other that, so long as either party has or may have any obligation under this Agreement or under any Credit Support Document to which it is a party:—

(a) **Furnish Specified Information.** It will deliver to the other party any forms, documents or certificates specified in the Schedule or any Confirmation by the date specified in the Schedule or such Confirmation or, if none is specified, as soon as reasonably practicable.

(b) **Maintain Authorisations.** It will use all reasonable efforts to maintain in full force and effect all consents of any governmental or other authority that are required to be obtained by it with respect to this Agreement or any Credit Support Document to which it is a party and will use all reasonable efforts to obtain any that may become necessary in the future.

(c) **Comply with Laws.** It will comply in all material respects with all applicable laws and orders to which it may be subject if failure so to comply would materially impair its ability to perform its obligations under this Agreement or any Credit Support Document to which it is a party.

5. Events of Default and Termination Events

(a) **Events of Default.** The occurrence at any time with respect to a party or, if applicable, any Credit Support Provider of such party or any Specified Entity of such party of any of the following events constitutes an event of default (an "Event of Default") with respect to such party:—

(i) **Failure to Pay or Deliver.** Failure by the party to make, when due, any payment under this Agreement or delivery under Section 2(a)(i) or 2(d) required to be made by it if such failure is not remedied on or before the third Local Business Day after notice of such failure is given to the party;

(ii) **Breach of Agreement.** Failure by the party to comply with or perform any agreement or obligation (other than an obligation to make any payment under this Agreement or delivery under Section 2(a)(i) or 2(d) or to give notice of a Termination Event or any agreement or obligation under Section 4(a)) to be complied with or performed by the party in accordance with this Agreement if such failure is not remedied on or before the thirtieth day after notice of such failure is given to the party;

(iii) *Credit Support Default.*

(1) Failure by the party or any Credit Support Provider of such party to comply with or perform any agreement or obligation to be complied with or performed by it in accordance with any Credit Support Document if such failure is continuing after any applicable grace period has elapsed;

(2) the expiration or termination of such Credit Support Document or the failing or ceasing of such Credit Support Document to be in full force and effect for the purpose of this Agreement (in either case other than in accordance with its terms) prior to the satisfaction of all obligations of such party under each Transaction to which such Credit Support Document relates without the written consent of the other party; or

(3) the party or such Credit Support Provider disaffirms, disclaims, repudiates or rejects, in whole or in part, or challenges the validity of, such Credit Support Document;

(iv) *Misrepresentation.* A representation made or repeated or deemed to have been made or repeated by the party or any Credit Support Provider of such party in this Agreement or any Credit Support Document proves to have been incorrect or misleading in any material respect when made or repeated or deemed to have been made or repeated;

(v) *Default under Specified Transaction.* The party, any Credit Support Provider of such party or any applicable Specified Entity of such party (1) defaults under a Specified Transaction and, after giving effect to any applicable notice requirement or grace period, there occurs a liquidation of, an acceleration of obligations under, or an early termination of, that Specified Transaction, (2) defaults, after giving effect to any applicable notice requirement or grace period, in making any payment or delivery due on the last payment, delivery or exchange date of, or any payment on early termination of, a Specified Transaction (or such default continues for at least three Local Business Days if there is no applicable notice requirement or grace period) or (3) disaffirms, disclaims, repudiates or rejects, in whole or in part, a Specified Transaction (or such action is taken by any person or entity appointed or empowered to operate it or act on its behalf);

(vi) *Cross Default.* If "Cross Default" is specified in the Schedule as applying to the party, the occurrence or existence of (1) a default, event of default or other similar condition or event (however described) in respect of such party, any Credit Support Provider of such party or any applicable Specified Entity of such party under one or more agreements or instruments relating to Specified Indebtedness of any of them (individually or collectively) in an aggregate amount of not less than the applicable Threshold Amount (as specified in the Schedule) which has resulted in such Specified Indebtedness becoming, or becoming capable at such time of being declared, due and payable under such agreements or instruments, before it would otherwise have been due and payable or (2) a default by such party, such Credit Support Provider or such Specified Entity (individually or collectively) in making one or more payments on the due date thereof in an aggregate amount of not less than the applicable Threshold Amount under such agreements or instruments (after giving effect to any applicable notice requirement or grace period);

(vii) *Bankruptcy.* The party, any Credit Support Provider of such party or any applicable Specified Entity of such party:—

(1) is dissolved (other than pursuant to a consolidation, amalgamation or merger); (2) becomes insolvent or is unable to pay its debts or fails or admits in writing its inability generally to pay its debts as they become due; (3) makes a general assignment, arrangement or composition with or for the benefit of its creditors; (4) institutes or has instituted against it a proceeding seeking a judgment of insolvency or bankruptcy or any other relief under any bankruptcy or insolvency law or other similar law affecting creditors' rights, or a petition is presented for its

winding-up or liquidation, and, in the case of any such proceeding or petition instituted or presented against it, such proceeding or petition (A) results in a judgment of insolvency or bankruptcy or the entry of an order for relief or the making of an order for its winding-up or liquidation or (B) is not dismissed, discharged, stayed or restrained in each case within 30 days of the institution or presentation thereof; (5) has a resolution passed for its winding-up, official management or liquidation (other than pursuant to a consolidation, amalgamation or merger); (6) seeks or becomes subject to the appointment of an administrator, provisional liquidator, conservator, receiver, trustee, custodian or other similar official for it or for all or substantially all its assets; (7) has a secured party take possession of all or substantially all its assets or has a distress, execution, attachment, sequestration or other legal process levied, enforced or sued on or against all or substantially all its assets and such secured party maintains possession, or any such process is not dismissed, discharged, stayed or restrained, in each case within 30 days thereafter; (8) causes or is subject to any event with respect to it which, under the applicable laws of any jurisdiction, has an analogous effect to any of the events specified in clauses (1) to (7) (inclusive); or (9) takes any action in furtherance of, or indicating its consent to, approval of, or acquiescence in, any of the foregoing acts; or

(viii) *Merger Without Assumption.* The party or any Credit Support Provider of such party consolidates or amalgamates with, or merges with or into, or transfers all or substantially all its assets to, another entity and, at the time of such consolidation, amalgamation, merger or transfer:—

(1) the resulting, surviving or transferee entity fails to assume all the obligations of such party or such Credit Support Provider under this Agreement or any Credit Support Document to which it or its predecessor was a party by operation of law or pursuant to an agreement reasonably satisfactory to the other party to this Agreement; or

(2) the benefits of any Credit Support Document fail to extend (without the consent of the other party) to the performance by such resulting, surviving or transferee entity of its obligations under this Agreement.

(b) *Termination Events.* The occurrence at any time with respect to a party or, if applicable, any Credit Support Provider of such party or any Specified Entity of such party of any event specified below constitutes an Illegality if the event is specified in (i) below, and, if specified to be applicable, a Credit Event Upon Merger if the event is specified pursuant to (ii) below or an Additional Termination Event if the event is specified pursuant to (iii) below:—

(i) *Illegality.* Due to the adoption of, or any change in, any applicable law after the date on which a Transaction is entered into, or due to the promulgation of, or any change in, the interpretation by any court, tribunal or regulatory authority with competent jurisdiction of any applicable law after such date, it becomes unlawful (other than as a result of a breach by the party of Section 4(b)) for such party (which will be the Affected Party):—

(1) to perform any absolute or contingent obligation to make a payment or delivery or to receive a payment or delivery in respect of such Transaction or to comply with any other material provision of this Agreement relating to such Transaction; or

(2) to perform, or for any Credit Support Provider of such party to perform, any contingent or other obligation which the party (or such Credit Support Provider) has under any Credit Support Document relating to such Transaction;

(ii) *Credit Event Upon Merger.* If "Credit Event Upon Merger" is specified in the Schedule as applying to the party, such party ("X"), any Credit Support Provider of X or any applicable Specified Entity of X consolidates or amalgamates with, or merges with or into, or transfers all or substantially all its assets to, another entity and such action does not constitute an event described in Section 5(a)(viii) but the creditworthiness of the resulting, surviving or transferee entity is materially weaker than that of X, such Credit Support Provider or such Specified Entity, as the case may be, immediately prior to such action (and, in such event, X or its successor or transferee, as appropriate, will be the Affected Party); or

ISDA® 1992

(iii) *Additional Termination Event.* If any "Additional Termination Event" is specified in the Schedule or any Confirmation as applying, the occurrence of such event (and, in such event, the Affected Party or Affected Parties shall be as specified for such Additional Termination Event in the Schedule or such Confirmation).

(c) *Event of Default and Illegality.* If an event or circumstance which would otherwise constitute or give rise to an Event of Default also constitutes an Illegality, it will be treated as an Illegality and will not constitute an Event of Default.

6. Early Termination

(a) *Right to Terminate Following Event of Default.* If at any time an Event of Default with respect to a party (the "Defaulting Party") has occurred and is then continuing, the other party (the "Non-defaulting Party") may, by not more than 20 days notice to the Defaulting Party specifying the relevant Event of Default, designate a day not earlier than the day such notice is effective as an Early Termination Date in respect of all outstanding Transactions. If, however, "Automatic Early Termination" is specified in the Schedule as applying to a party, then an Early Termination Date in respect of all outstanding Transactions will occur immediately upon the occurrence with respect to such party of an Event of Default specified in Section 5(a)(vii)(1), (3), (5), (6) or, to the extent analogous thereto, (8), and as of the time immediately preceding the institution of the relevant proceeding or the presentation of the relevant petition upon the occurrence with respect to such party of an Event of Default specified in Section 5(a)(vii)(4) or, to the extent analogous thereto, (8).

(b) *Right to Terminate Following Termination Event.*

(i) *Notice.* If a Termination Event occurs, an Affected Party will, promptly upon becoming aware of it, notify the other party, specifying the nature of that Termination Event and each Affected Transaction and will also give such other information about that Termination Event as the other party may reasonably require.

(ii) *Two Affected Parties.* If an Illegality under Section 5(b)(1) occurs and there are two Affected Parties, each party will use all reasonable efforts to reach agreement within 30 days after notice thereof is given under Section 6(b)(i) on action to avoid that Termination Event.

(iii) *Right to Terminate.* If:—

(1) an agreement under Section 6(b)(ii) has not been effected with respect to all Affected Transactions within 30 days after an Affected Party gives notice under Section 6(b)(i); or

(2) an Illegality other than that referred to in Section 6(b)(ii), a Credit Event Upon Merger or an Additional Termination Event occurs,

either party in the case of an Illegality, any Affected Party in the case of an Additional Termination Event if there is more than one Affected Party, or the party which is not the Affected Party in the case of a Credit Event Upon Merger or an Additional Termination Event if there is only one Affected Party may, by not more than 20 days notice to the other party and provided that the relevant Termination Event is then continuing, designate a day not earlier than the day such notice is effective as an Early Termination Date in respect of all Affected Transactions.

(c) *Effect of Designation.*

(i) If notice designating an Early Termination Date is given under Section 6(a) or (b), the Early Termination Date will occur on the date so designated, whether or not the relevant Event of Default or Termination Event is then continuing.

(ii) Upon the occurrence or effective designation of an Early Termination Date, no further payments or deliveries under Section 2(a)(i) or 2(d) in respect of the Terminated Transactions will be required to be made, but without prejudice to the other provisions of this Agreement. The amount, if any, payable in respect of an Early Termination Date shall be determined pursuant to Section 6(e).

(d) *Calculations.*

(i) *Statement.* On or as soon as reasonably practicable following the occurrence of an Early Termination Date, each party will make the calculations on its part, if any, contemplated by Section 6(e) and will provide to the other party a statement (1) showing, in reasonable detail, such calculations (including all relevant quotations and specifying any amount payable under Section 6(e)) and (2) giving details of the relevant account to which any amount payable to it is to be paid. In the absence of written confirmation from the source of a quotation obtained in determining a Market Quotation, the records of the party obtaining such quotation will be conclusive evidence of the existence and accuracy of such quotation.

(ii) *Payment Date.* An amount calculated as being due in respect of any Early Termination Date under Section 6(e) will be payable on the day that notice of the amount payable is effective (in the case of an Early Termination Date which is designated or occurs as a result of an Event of Default) and on the day which is two Local Business Days after the day on which notice of the amount payable is effective (in the case of an Early Termination Date which is designated as a result of a Termination Event). Such amount will be paid together with (to the extent permitted under applicable law) interest thereon (before as well as after judgment), from (and including) the relevant Early Termination Date to (but excluding) the date such amount is paid, at the Applicable Rate. Such interest will be calculated on the basis of daily compounding and the actual number of days elapsed.

(e) *Payments on Early Termination.* If an Early Termination Date occurs, the following provisions shall apply based on the parties' election in the Schedule of a payment measure, either "Market Quotation" or "Loss", and a payment method, either the "First Method" or the "Second Method". If the parties fail to designate a payment measure or payment method in the Schedule, it will be deemed that "Market Quotation" or the "Second Method", as the case may be, shall apply. The amount, if any, payable in respect of an Early Termination Date and determined pursuant to this Section will be subject to any Set-off.

(i) *Events of Default.* If the Early Termination Date results from an Event of Default:—

(1) *First Method and Market Quotation.* If the First Method and Market Quotation apply, the Defaulting Party will pay to the Non-defaulting Party the excess, if a positive number, of (A) the sum of the Settlement Amount (determined by the Non-defaulting Party) in respect of the Terminated Transactions and the Unpaid Amounts owing to the Non-defaulting Party over (B) the Unpaid Amounts owing to the Defaulting Party.

(2) *First Method and Loss.* If the First Method and Loss apply, the Defaulting Party will pay to the Non-defaulting Party, if a positive number, the Non-defaulting Party's Loss in respect of this Agreement.

(3) *Second Method and Market Quotation.* If the Second Method and Market Quotation apply, an amount will be payable equal to (A) the sum of the Settlement Amount (determined by the Non-defaulting Party) in respect of the Terminated Transactions and the Unpaid Amounts owing to the Non-defaulting Party less (B) the Unpaid Amounts owing to the Defaulting Party. If that amount is a positive number, the Defaulting Party will pay it to the Non-defaulting Party; if it is a negative number, the Non-defaulting Party will pay the absolute value of that amount to the Defaulting Party.

(4) *Second Method and Loss.* If the Second Method and Loss apply, an amount will be payable equal to the Non-defaulting Party's Loss in respect of this Agreement. If that amount is a positive number, the Defaulting Party will pay it to the Non-defaulting Party; if it is a negative

number, the Non-defaulting Party will pay the absolute value of that amount to the Defaulting Party.

(ii) *Termination Events.* If the Early Termination Date results from a Termination Event:—

(1) *One Affected Party.* If there is one Affected Party, the amount payable will be determined in accordance with Section 6(e)(i)(3), if Market Quotation applies, or Section 6(e)(i)(4), if Loss applies, except that, in either case, references to the Defaulting Party and to the Non-defaulting Party will be deemed to be references to the Affected Party and the party which is not the Affected Party, respectively, and, if Loss applies and fewer than all the Transactions are being terminated, Loss shall be calculated in respect of all Terminated Transactions.

(2) *Two Affected Parties.* If there are two Affected Parties:—

(A) if Market Quotation applies, each party will determine a Settlement Amount in respect of the Terminated Transactions, and an amount will be payable equal to (I) the sum of (a) one-half of the difference between the Settlement Amount of the party with the higher Settlement Amount ("X") and the Settlement Amount of the party with the lower Settlement Amount ("Y") and (b) the Unpaid Amounts owing to X less (II) the Unpaid Amounts owing to Y; and

(B) if Loss applies, each party will determine its Loss in respect of this Agreement (or, if fewer than all the Transactions are being terminated, in respect of all Terminated Transactions) and an amount will be payable equal to one-half of the difference between the Loss of the party with the higher Loss ("X") and the Loss of the party with the lower Loss ("Y").

If the amount payable is a positive number, Y will pay it to X; if it is a negative number, X will pay the absolute value of that amount to Y.

(iii) *Adjustment for Bankruptcy.* In circumstances where an Early Termination Date occurs because "Automatic Early Termination" applies in respect of a party, the amount determined under this Section 6(e) will be subject to such adjustments as are appropriate and permitted by law to reflect any payments or deliveries made by one party to the other under this Agreement (and retained by such other party) during the period from the relevant Early Termination Date to the date for payment determined under Section 6(d)(ii).

(iv) *Pre-Estimate.* The parties agree that if Market Quotation applies an amount recoverable under this Section 6(e) is a reasonable pre-estimate of loss and not a penalty. Such amount is payable for the loss of bargain and the loss of protection against future risks and except as otherwise provided in this Agreement neither party will be entitled to recover any additional damages as a consequence of such losses.

7. **Transfer**

Neither this Agreement nor any interest or obligation in or under this Agreement may be transferred (whether by way of security or otherwise) by either party without the prior written consent of the other party, except that:—

(a) a party may make such a transfer of this Agreement pursuant to a consolidation or amalgamation with, or merger with or into, or transfer of all or substantially all its assets to, another entity (but without prejudice to any other right or remedy under this Agreement); and

(b) a party may make such a transfer of all or any part of its interest in any amount payable to it from a Defaulting Party under Section 6(e).

Any purported transfer that is not in compliance with this Section will be void.

8. Miscellaneous

(a) *Entire Agreement.* This Agreement constitutes the entire agreement and understanding of the parties with respect to its subject matter and supersedes all oral communication and prior writings with respect thereto.

(b) *Amendments.* No amendment, modification or waiver in respect of this Agreement will be effective unless in writing (including a writing evidenced by a facsimile transmission) and executed by each of the parties or confirmed by an exchange of telexes or electronic messages on an electronic messaging system.

(c) *Survival of Obligations.* Without prejudice to Sections 2(a)(iii) and 6(c)(ii), the obligations of the parties under this Agreement will survive the termination of any Transaction.

(d) *Remedies Cumulative.* Except as provided in this Agreement, the rights, powers, remedies and privileges provided in this Agreement are cumulative and not exclusive of any rights, powers, remedies and privileges provided by law.

(e) *Counterparts and Confirmations.*

    (i) This Agreement (and each amendment, modification and waiver in respect of it) may be executed and delivered in counterparts (including by facsimile transmission), each of which will be deemed an original.

    (ii) The parties intend that they are legally bound by the terms of each Transaction from the moment they agree to those terms (whether orally or otherwise). A Confirmation shall be entered into as soon as practicable and may be executed and delivered in counterparts (including by facsimile transmission) or be created by an exchange of telexes or by an exchange of electronic messages on an electronic messaging system, which in each case will be sufficient for all purposes to evidence a binding supplement to this Agreement. The parties will specify therein or through another effective means that any such counterpart, telex or electronic message constitutes a Confirmation.

(f) *No Waiver of Rights.* A failure or delay in exercising any right, power or privilege in respect of this Agreement will not be presumed to operate as a waiver, and a single or partial exercise of any right, power or privilege will not be presumed to preclude any subsequent or further exercise, of that right, power or privilege or the exercise of any other right, power or privilege.

(g) *Headings.* The headings used in this Agreement are for convenience of reference only and are not to affect the construction of or to be taken into consideration in interpreting this Agreement.

9. Expenses

A Defaulting Party will, on demand, indemnify and hold harmless the other party for and against all reasonable out-of-pocket expenses, including legal fees, incurred by such other party by reason of the enforcement and protection of its rights under this Agreement or any Credit Support Document to which the Defaulting Party is a party or by reason of the early termination of any Transaction, including, but not limited to, costs of collection.

10. Notices

(a) *Effectiveness.* Any notice or other communication in respect of this Agreement may be given in any manner set forth below (except that a notice or other communication under Section 5 or 6 may not be given by facsimile transmission or electronic messaging system) to the address or number or in accordance with the electronic messaging system details provided (see the Schedule) and will be deemed effective as indicated:—

    (i) if in writing and delivered in person or by courier, on the date it is delivered;

    (ii) if sent by telex, on the date the recipient's answerback is received;

(iii) if sent by facsimile transmission, on the date that transmission is received by a responsible employee of the recipient in legible form (it being agreed that the burden of proving receipt will be on the sender and will not be met by a transmission report generated by the sender's facsimile machine);

(iv) if sent by certified or registered mail (airmail, if overseas) or the equivalent (return receipt requested), on the date that mail is delivered or its delivery is attempted; or

(v) if sent by electronic messaging system, on the date that electronic message is received,

unless the date of that delivery (or attempted delivery) or that receipt, as applicable, is not a Local Business Day or that communication is delivered (or attempted) or received, as applicable, after the close of business on a Local Business Day, in which case that communication shall be deemed given and effective on the first following day that is a Local Business Day.

(b) *Change of Addresses.* Either party may by notice to the other change the address, telex or facsimile number or electronic messaging system details at which notices or other communications are to be given to it.

11. Governing Law and Jurisdiction

(a) *Governing Law.* This Agreement will be governed by and construed in accordance with the law specified in the Schedule.

(b) *Jurisdiction.* With respect to any suit, action or proceedings relating to this Agreement ("Proceedings"), each party irrevocably:—

(i) submits to the jurisdiction of the English courts, if this Agreement is expressed to be governed by English law, or to the non-exclusive jurisdiction of the courts of the State of New York and the United States District Court located in the Borough of Manhattan in New York City, if this Agreement is expressed to be governed by the laws of the State of New York; and

(ii) waives any objection which it may have at any time to the laying of venue of any Proceedings brought in any such court, waives any claim that such Proceedings have been brought in an inconvenient forum and further waives the right to object, with respect to such Proceedings, that such court does not have any jurisdiction over such party.

Nothing in this Agreement precludes either party from bringing Proceedings in any other jurisdiction (outside, if this Agreement is expressed to be governed by English law, the Contracting States, as defined in Section 1(3) of the Civil Jurisdiction and Judgments Act 1982 or any modification, extension or re-enactment thereof for the time being in force) nor will the bringing of Proceedings in any one or more jurisdictions preclude the bringing of Proceedings in any other jurisdiction.

(c) *Waiver of Immunities.* Each party irrevocably waives, to the fullest extent permitted by applicable law, with respect to itself and its revenues and assets (irrespective of their use or intended use), all immunity on the grounds of sovereignty or other similar grounds from (i) suit, (ii) jurisdiction of any court, (iii) relief by way of injunction, order for specific performance or for recovery of property, (iv) attachment of its assets (whether before or after judgment) and (v) execution or enforcement of any judgment to which it or its revenues or assets might otherwise be entitled in any Proceedings in the courts of any jurisdiction and irrevocably agrees, to the extent permitted by applicable law, that it will not claim any such immunity in any Proceedings.

12. Definitions

As used in this Agreement:—

"Additional Termination Event" has the meaning specified in Section 5(b).

"Affected Party" has the meaning specified in Section 5(b).

"*Affected Transactions*" means (a) with respect to any Termination Event consisting of an Illegality, all Transactions affected by the occurrence of such Termination Event and (b) with respect to any other Termination Event, all Transactions.

"*Affiliate*" means, subject to the Schedule, in relation to any person, any entity controlled, directly or indirectly, by the person, any entity that controls, directly or indirectly, the person or any entity directly or indirectly under common control with the person. For this purpose, "control" of any entity or person means ownership of a majority of the voting power of the entity or person.

"*Applicable Rate*" means:—

(a) in respect of obligations payable or deliverable (or which would have been but for Section 2(a)(iii)) by a Defaulting Party, the Default Rate;

(b) in respect of an obligation to pay an amount under Section 6(e) of either party from and after the date (determined in accordance with Section 6(d)(ii)) on which that amount is payable, the Default Rate;

(c) in respect of all other obligations payable or deliverable (or which would have been but for Section 2(a)(iii)) by a Non-defaulting Party, the Non-default Rate; and

(d) in all other cases, the Termination Rate.

"*consent*" includes a consent, approval, action, authorisation, exemption, notice, filing, registration or exchange control consent.

"*Credit Event Upon Merger*" has the meaning specified in Section 5(b).

"*Credit Support Document*" means any agreement or instrument that is specified as such in this Agreement.

"*Credit Support Provider*" has the meaning specified in the Schedule.

"*Default Rate*" means a rate per annum equal to the cost (without proof or evidence of any actual cost) to the relevant payee (as certified by it) if it were to fund or of funding the relevant amount plus 1% per annum.

"*Defaulting Party*" has the meaning specified in Section 6(a).

"*Early Termination Date*" means the date determined in accordance with Section 6(a) or 6(b)(iii).

"*Event of Default*" has the meaning specified in Section 5(a) and, if applicable, in the Schedule.

"*Illegality*" has the meaning specified in Section 5(b).

"*law*" includes any treaty, law, rule or regulation and "*lawful*" and "*unlawful*" will be construed accordingly.

"*Local Business Day*" means, subject to the Schedule, a day on which commercial banks are open for business (including dealings in foreign exchange and foreign currency deposits) (a) in relation to any obligation under Section 2(a)(i), in the place(s) specified in the relevant Confirmation or, if not so specified, as otherwise agreed by the parties in writing or determined pursuant to provisions contained, or incorporated by reference, in this Agreement, (b) in relation to any other payment, in the place where the relevant account is located, (c) in relation to any notice or other communication, including notice contemplated under Section 5(a)(i), in the city specified in the address for notice provided by the recipient and, in the case of a notice contemplated by Section 2(b), in the place where the relevant new account is to be located and (d) in relation to Section 5(a)(v)(2), in the relevant locations for performance with respect to such Specified Transaction.

"*Loss*" means, with respect to this Agreement or one or more Terminated Transactions, as the case may be, and a party, an amount that party reasonably determines in good faith to be its total losses and costs (or gain, in which case expressed as a negative number) in connection with this Agreement or that Terminated Transaction or group of Terminated Transactions, as the case may be, including any loss of bargain, cost of funding or, at the election of such party but without duplication, loss or cost incurred as a result of its terminating, liquidating, obtaining or reestablishing any hedge or related trading position (or any gain resulting from any of them). Loss includes losses and costs (or gains) in respect of any payment or delivery required to have been made (assuming satisfaction of each applicable condition precedent) on or before the relevant Early Termination Date and not made, except, so as to avoid duplication, if Section 6(e)(i)(1) or (3) or 6(e)(ii)(2)(A) applies. Loss does not include a party's legal fees and out-of-pocket expenses referred to under Section 9. A party will determine its Loss as of the relevant Early Termination Date, or, if that is not reasonably practicable, as of the earliest date thereafter as is reasonably practicable. A party may (but need not) determine its Loss by reference to quotations of relevant rates or prices from one or more leading dealers in the relevant markets.

"*Market Quotation*" means, with respect to one or more Terminated Transactions and a party making the determination, an amount determined on the basis of quotations from Reference Market-makers. Each quotation will be for an amount, if any, that would be paid to such party (expressed as a negative number) or by such party (expressed as a positive number) in consideration of an agreement between such party (taking into account any existing Credit Support Document with respect to the obligations of such party) and the quoting Reference Market-maker to enter into a transaction (the "Replacement Transaction") that would have the effect of preserving for such party the economic equivalent of any payment or delivery (whether the underlying obligation was absolute or contingent and assuming the satisfaction of each applicable condition precedent) by the parties under Section 2(a)(i) in respect of such Terminated Transaction or group of Terminated Transactions that would, but for the occurrence of the relevant Early Termination Date, have been required after that date. For this purpose, Unpaid Amounts in respect of the Terminated Transaction or group of Terminated Transactions are to be excluded but, without limitation, any payment or delivery that would, but for the relevant Early Termination Date, have been required (assuming satisfaction of each applicable condition precedent) after that Early Termination Date is to be included. The Replacement Transaction would be subject to such documentation as such party and the Reference Market-maker may, in good faith, agree. The party making the determination (or its agent) will request each Reference Market-maker to provide its quotation to the extent reasonably practicable as of the same day and time (without regard to different time zones) on or as soon as reasonably practicable after the relevant Early Termination Date. The day and time as of which those quotations are to be obtained will be selected in good faith by the party obliged to make a determination under Section 6(e), and, if each party is so obliged, after consultation with the other. If more than three quotations are provided, the Market Quotation will be the arithmetic mean of the quotations, without regard to the quotations having the highest and lowest values. If exactly three such quotations are provided, the Market Quotation will be the quotation remaining after disregarding the highest and lowest quotations. For this purpose, if more than one quotation has the same highest value or lowest value, then one of such quotations shall be disregarded. If fewer than three quotations are provided, it will be deemed that the Market Quotation in respect of such Terminated Transaction or group of Terminated Transactions cannot be determined.

"*Non-default Rate*" means a rate per annum equal to the cost (without proof or evidence of any actual cost) to the Non-defaulting Party (as certified by it) if it were to fund the relevant amount.

"*Non-defaulting Party*" has the meaning specified in Section 6(a).

"*Potential Event of Default*" means any event which, with the giving of notice or the lapse of time or both, would constitute an Event of Default.

"*Reference Market-makers*" means four leading dealers in the relevant market selected by the party determining a Market Quotation in good faith (a) from among dealers of the highest credit standing which satisfy all the criteria that such party applies generally at the time in deciding whether to offer or to make an extension of credit and (b) to the extent practicable, from among such dealers having an office in the same city.

"*Scheduled Payment Date*" means a date on which a payment or delivery is to be made under Section 2(a)(i) with respect to a Transaction.

"*Set-off*" means set-off, offset, combination of accounts, right of retention or withholding or similar right or requirement to which the payer of an amount under Section 6 is entitled or subject (whether arising under this Agreement, another contract, applicable law or otherwise) that is exercised by, or imposed on, such payer.

"*Settlement Amount*" means, with respect to a party and any Early Termination Date, the sum of:—

(a) the Market Quotations (whether positive or negative) for each Terminated Transaction or group of Terminated Transactions for which a Market Quotation is determined; and

(b) such party's Loss (whether positive or negative and without reference to any Unpaid Amounts) for each Terminated Transaction or group of Terminated Transactions for which a Market Quotation cannot be determined or would not (in the reasonable belief of the party making the determination) produce a commercially reasonable result.

"*Specified Entity*" has the meaning specified in the Schedule.

"*Specified Indebtedness*" means, subject to the Schedule, any obligation (whether present or future, contingent or otherwise, as principal or surety or otherwise) in respect of borrowed money.

"*Specified Transaction*" means, subject to the Schedule, (a) any transaction (including an agreement with respect thereto) now existing or hereafter entered into between one party to this Agreement (or any Credit Support Provider of such party or any applicable Specified Entity of such party) and the other party to this Agreement (or any Credit Support Provider of such other party or any applicable Specified Entity of such other party) which is a rate swap transaction, basis swap, forward rate transaction, commodity swap, commodity option, equity or equity index swap, equity or equity index option, bond option, interest rate option, foreign exchange transaction, cap transaction, floor transaction, collar transaction, currency swap transaction, cross-currency rate swap transaction, currency option or any other similar transaction (including any option with respect to any of these transactions), (b) any combination of these transactions and (c) any other transaction identified as a Specified Transaction in this Agreement or the relevant confirmation.

"*Terminated Transactions*" means with respect to any Early Termination Date (a) if resulting from a Termination Event, all Affected Transactions and (b) if resulting from an Event of Default, all Transactions (in either case) in effect immediately before the effectiveness of the notice designating that Early Termination Date (or, if "Automatic Early Termination" applies, immediately before that Early Termination Date).

"*Termination Event*" means an Illegality or, if specified to be applicable, a Credit Event Upon Merger or an Additional Termination Event.

"*Termination Rate*" means a rate per annum equal to the arithmetic mean of the cost (without proof or evidence of any actual cost) to each party (as certified by such party) if it were to fund or of funding such amounts.

"*Unpaid Amounts*" owing to any party means, with respect to an Early Termination Date, the aggregate of (a) in respect of all Terminated Transactions, the amounts that became payable (or that would have become payable but for Section 2(a)(iii)) to such party under Section 2(a)(i) on or prior to such Early Termination Date and which remain unpaid as at such Early Termination Date and (b) in respect of each Terminated Transaction, for each obligation under Section 2(a)(i) which was (or would have been but for Section 2(a)(iii)) required to be settled by delivery to such party on or prior to such Early Termination Date and which has not been so settled as at such Early Termination Date, an amount equal to the fair market value of that which was (or would have been) required to be delivered as of the originally scheduled date for delivery, in each case together with (to the extent permitted under applicable law) interest, in the currency of such amounts, from (and including) the date such amounts or obligations were or would have been required to have been paid or performed to (but excluding) such Early Termination Date, at the Applicable Rate. Such amounts of interest will be calculated on the basis of daily compounding and the actual number of days elapsed. The fair market value of any obligation referred to in clause (b) above shall be reasonably determined

ISDA® 1992

by the party obliged to make the determination under Section 6(e) or, if each party is so obliged, it shall be the average of the fair market values reasonably determined by both parties.

IN WITNESS WHEREOF the parties have executed this document on the respective dates specified below with effect from the date specified on the first page of this document.

....
          (Name of Party)   (Name of Party)

By: .... By: ....
   Name: Name:
   Title: Title:
   Date: Date:

(Local Currency—Single Jurisdiction)

ISDA®

International Swap Dealers Association, Inc.

SCHEDULE
to the
Master Agreement

dated as of ....

between .... and ....
                          ("Party A")   ("Party B")

Part 1. Termination Provisions.

(a) *"Specified Entity"* means in relation to Party A for the purpose of:—

    Section 5(a)(v), ...

    Section 5(a)(vi), ...

    Section 5(a)(vii), ...

    Section 5(b)(ii), ...

and in relation to Party B for the purpose of:—

    Section 5(a)(v), ...

    Section 5(a)(vi), ...

    Section 5(a)(vii), ...

    Section 5(b)(ii), ...

(b) *"Specified Transaction"* will have the meaning specified in Section 12 of this Agreement unless another meaning is specified here ....
....
....

(c) The *"Cross Default"* provisions of Section 5(a)(vi) will/will not * apply to Party A
                                              will/will not * apply to Party B

If such provisions apply:—

"Specified Indebtedness" will have the meaning specified in Section 12 of this Agreement unless another meaning is specified here ....
....

---

* Delete as applicable.

ISDA® 1992

"Threshold Amount" means ....
....

(d) The "*Credit Event Upon Merger*" provisions of Section 5(b)(ii) will/will not * apply to Party A
                                                                will/will not * apply to Party B

(e) The "*Automatic Early Termination*" provision of Section 6(a) will/will not * apply to Party A
                                                                will/will not * apply to Party B

(f) *Payments on Early Termination.* For the purpose of Section 6(e) of this Agreement:—

   (i) Market Quotation/Loss * will apply.

   (ii) The First Method/The Second Method * will apply.

(g) *Additional Termination Event* will/will not apply*. The following shall constitute an Additional Termination Event:— ....
....
....
....
....
....

For the purpose of the foregoing Termination Event, the Affected Party or Affected Parties shall be:— ..
....

Part 2. **Agreement to Deliver Documents.**

For the purpose of Section 4(a) of this Agreement, each party agrees to deliver the following documents, as applicable:—

Party required to deliver document	Form/Document/ Certificate	Date by which to be delivered	Covered by Section 3(d) Representation
....	....	....	Yes/No*
....	....	....	Yes/No*
....	....	....	Yes/No*
....	....	....	Yes/No*
....	....	....	Yes/No*

---
* Delete as applicable.

Part 3. Miscellaneous.

(a) *Addresses for Notices.* For the purpose of Section 10(a) of this Agreement:—

Address for notices or communications to Party A:—

Address: ....

Attention: ....

Telex No.: .... Answerback: ....

Facsimile No.: .... Telephone No.: ....

Electronic Messaging System Details: ....

Address for notices or communications to Party B:—

Address: ....

Attention: ....

Telex No.: .... Answerback: ....

Facsimile No.: .... Telephone No.: ....

Electronic Messaging System Details: ....

(b) *Calculation Agent.* The Calculation Agent is ...., unless otherwise specified in a Confirmation in relation to the relevant Transaction.

(c) *Credit Support Document.* Details of any Credit Support Document:— ....
....
....
....

(d) *Credit Support Provider.* Credit Support Provider means in relation to Party A, ...
....
....

Credit Support Provider means in relation to Party B, ...
....
....

(e) *Governing Law.* This Agreement will be governed by and construed in accordance with English law/the laws of the State of New York (without reference to choice of law doctrine)*.

(f) *Netting of Payments.* Subparagraph (ii) of Section 2(c) of this Agreement will not apply to the following Transactions or groups of Transactions (in each case starting from the date of this Agreement/in each case starting from ....*) ....
....
....

---

* Delete as applicable.

ISDA® 1992

(g) *"Affiliate"* will have the meaning specified in Section 12 of this Agreement unless another meaning is specified here ....
....

Part 4. Other Provisions.

NOTES

1. *Farash* v. *Sykes Datatronics, Inc.*, 59 N.Y.2d 500, 465 N.Y.S.2d 917, 452 N.E.2d 1245 (1983).
2. *Homestead Sav.* v. *Life Sav. & Loan Ass'n*, no. 86C20268, 1987 U.S. Dist. LEXIS 7706 (N.D. Ill. July 1, 1987) (reference to case history).
3. See *Intershoe, Inc.* v. *Bankers Trust Co.*, 77 N.Y.2d 517, 571 N.E.2d 641, 569 N.Y.S.2d 333 (1991); *see also In re Koreag, Controle et Revision S.A.*, 961 F.2d 341 (2d Cir. 1992); *Compania Sud-Americana de Vapores, S.A.* v. *IBJ Schroder*, 785 F. Supp. 411 (S.D.N.Y. 1992); *Saboundjian* v. *Bank Audi (USA)*, 157 A.D.2d 278, 556 N.Y.S.2d 258 (1st Dep't 1990).
4. See *Steinberg* v. *Universal Machinenfabrik GMBH*, 24 A.D.2d 886, 264 N.Y.S.2d 757 (2d Dep't 1965), *aff'd*, 18 N.Y.2d 943, 277 N.Y.S.2d 142, 223 N.E.2d 567 (1966).
5. The United Nations Convention on Contracts for the International Sale of Goods (the convention), which has no statute of frauds provisions, has been signed by a number of nations, including the United States (but excluding Great Britain). Parties who select New York law to govern their agreement (or, presumably, the local law of any jurisdiction) would appear effectively to have "opted out" of the convention in accordance with its provisions, although prudent parties may wish expressly to provide not only that New York law will govern but also that the convention will not apply. Because the Convention expressly excludes contracts for the sale of money, it would not appear to cover currency swaps.
6. *See*, for example, GOL Sections 5-401, 5-411, and 5-413 (1989).
7. An object lesson in the danger of ignoring these considerations was supplied by the English House of Lords when it held that the London Borough of Hammersmith and Fulham, and, therefore, other similarly situated entities, lacked authority to enter into swap agreements with notional amounts totaling millions of pounds. *Hazell* v. *Hammersmith & Fulham London Borough Council*, (1991) 2 W.L.R. 372, (1991) 1 All E.R. 545 (HL).
8. Any such "walk-away" provisions must be analyzed in light of applicable law or public policy against forfeitures. New York, for example, has a common law rule against forfeitures. Also, under the netting provisions of the Federal Deposit Insurance Corporation Improvement Act of 1991 (FDICIA), a defaulting financial institution would arguably have a right to receive its net entitlement, if any, despite any walk-away provisions. See the section "The Netting Pro-

visions of the Federal Deposit Insurance Corporation Improvement Act of 1991."
9. The 1992 agreements allow the parties to choose between limited and full two-way payments. If the parties fail to select an alternative, full two-way payments will be required.
10. As noted above, however, the enforceability of such walk-away provisions in agreements between financial institutions has been rendered uncertain by the netting provisions of FDICIA. See "The Netting Provisions of the Federal Deposit Insurance Corporation Improvement Act of 1991."
11. *Drexel Burnham Lambert Products Corp. v. Midland Bank PLE*, 1992 U.S. Dist. LEXIS 21223 (S.D.N.Y. Nov. 9, 1992). In some circumstances, the solvent party may not terminate the contract or may lack the "contractual right" (which under the Bankruptcy Code includes a right arising under common law or normal business practice) to do so. In that case, if the contract is rejected by the trustee, the solvent counterparty should be entitled to damages. In addition, it appears highly unlikely under these circumstances that the trustee could "cherry pick" because, as noted above, the definitional provisions of the 1990 amendments make it clear that transactions effectuated under a master swap agreement will be considered a single agreement.
12. The treatment of QFCs under the FDIA is discussed in detail in Walter Eccard and Seth Grosshandler, "Qualified Financial Contracts with FDIC-Insured Banks and Thrifts," *The Review of Banking and Financial Services,* April 10, 1991.
13. This would appear to render contractual nonassignment provisions generally unenforceable against the FDIC or RTC as conservator or receiver.
14. The definitions of *swap agreement* in the Bankruptcy Code and in the FDIA are not identical; for example, the FDIA includes interest rate futures and currency futures.
15. Similarly, if the conservator elects to transfer QFCs between the failed institution and a particular counterparty and its affiliates, the conservator must transfer all such QFCs to a single institution.
16. While there is some concern in the case of QFCs generally that the conservator would be able to repudiate transactions selectively, it would seem in the case of swaps that the definitional provisions treating a master swap agreement as a single agreement would prevent this result.
17. Neither the FDIA nor the policy statements address requirements under other applicable law relating to the authority of an institution to enter into swap agreements or the authority of an employee of a

financial institution to bind the institution. Nor do they address the remedial rights of a swap counterparty that has obtained only a confirmation documenting the economic terms of a swap transaction, but has not entered a master or other agreement providing for the exercise of remedies on default.

18. Regulatory considerations are more fully canvassed in William P. Rogers, Jr., "Regulation of Swaps in the United States," in *The Handbook of Currency and Interest Rate Risk Management,* ed. R. J. Schwartz and C. W. Smith, Jr. (New York: New York Institute of Finance, 1990).

    Accounting and tax considerations are beyond the scope of this chapter. A discussion of accounting issues may be found in Chapter 22, and of taxation issues in Chapter 24.

    In addition, on tax, for the regime subsequent to the issuance of proposed regulations on July 8, 1991, see Erika W. Nijenhuis, "*Arkansas Best* and the Taxation of Notional Principal Contracts and Other Derivatives," *Futures International Law Letter,* June 1992; Willard B. Taylor and Esta E. Stecher, "Interest Rate, Equity and Commodity Swaps and Other Notional Principal Contracts," in *Tax Strategies for Corporate Acquisitions, Dispositions, Financings, Joint Ventures, Reorganizations and Restructurings 1991* (PLI, 1991); for earlier, and still useful, articles, see Edward D. Kleinbard, "Equity Derivative Products: Financial Innovation's Newest Challenge to the Tax System," *Texas Law Review* 69 (1991), p. 1319; Frank V. Battle, Jr., Michael L. Schultz, and Gerard A. Mangieri, "Tax Considerations in the United States," in *The Handbook of Currency,* ed. Schwartz and Smith; and Note, "Tax Treatment of Notional Principal Contracts," *Harvard Law Review* 103 (1990), p. 1951.

    On accounting, see also Evan M. Bush, "Accounting for Currency and Interest Rate Risk in the United States," in *The Handbook of Currency,* ed. Schwartz and Smith. FASB Interpretation No. 39, No. 113-A, March 1992, sets forth the circumstances when a swap party can offset amounts under different swaps with the same party and recognize a net loss or gain.

19. Insurance companies are exempt from most forms of federal regulation and, in addition, are not covered by the provisions of the Bankruptcy Code, the FDIA, or, as noted above, the FDICIA.

CHAPTER 24

TAXATION OF INTEREST RATE SWAPS

Diane D. Fuller*
KPMG Peat Marwick

As with many new financial products, the tax laws have had a difficult time keeping up with the rapid development of the swaps markets. As a result, there has been uncertainty with respect to the proper tax treatment of interest rate swaps, and it has been necessary to look to analogies to other financial instruments in order to draw any conclusions. This chapter will review the current state of the art with respect to the basic tax issues of timing, character, and source as they relate to interest rate swaps and other related financial instruments.

As you look for possible analogies for interest rate swaps, the following types of transactions may come to mind:

1. A series of forward or futures contracts.
2. A forward contract with interim margin payments.
3. Back-to-back loans.
4. For swaps used as hedges, an offset to the type of income or expense that is being hedged.

The timing of recognition of income and expense would be different under each of the analogies:

---

*The author gratefully acknowledges the assistance of James Hunt, Patrick Murphy, Richard Solway, and Richard Turnure of KPMG Peat Marwick in preparing this chapter.

Series of forwards	Recognize interim payments when paid or received
Single forward	Recognize interim payments at the end of the swap
Back-to-back loan	Follow the rules for recognition of interest income and expense
Offset	Adjust the interest on the hedged obligation

In the absence of specific rules for interest rate swaps, each of these analogies has been considered, and aspects of several appear in the guidance that has been developing for swaps and other financial instruments. The direction the Treasury Department is likely to take with respect to swaps, however, has become clearer since the issuance of proposed regulations in July of 1991. These proposed regulations will be discussed in detail later in the chapter.

For tax purposes, interest rate swaps are considered to be part of a larger class of financial instruments known as *notional principal contracts* (NPCs). An NPC is a financial instrument that provides for the payment of amounts by one party to another at specified intervals calculated by reference to a specified index upon a notional principal amount in exchange for specified consideration or a promise to pay similar amounts. A contract under which neither party's obligations are determined by reference to a variable specified index is not an NPC. An option or forward contract that entitles or obligates a person to enter into, extend, cancel, or change the terms of a notional principal contract (e.g., a swaption) is not a notional principal contract, but payments made under such an option or forward contract may be governed by the rules below for nonperiodic payments. NPCs include interest rate swaps, basis swaps, interest rate caps, interest rate floors, commodity swaps, equity swaps, total return swaps, equity index swaps, and similar agreements.

As was common in the later 1980s, the first guidance issued that dealt specifically with swaps was issued in the form of a notice, Notice 89-21, aimed at what the Internal Revenue Service perceived to be abusive transactions involving swaps with lump-sum payments. For example, taxpayers were entering into swaps with up-front payments in order to utilize net operating loss carryovers or foreign tax credit carryovers that might otherwise expire unutilized. A long line of cases, including *Schlude* v. *Commissioner,* 372 U.S. 128 (1963), had generally held that advance payments of income must be recognized for tax purposes on receipt.

In Notice 89-21, the Internal Revenue Service concluded that the method of accounting prescribed in *Schlude* did not clearly reflect income in the case of NPCs. Consequently, the notice provided that in the case of a payment received during one taxable year with respect to a notional principal contract where such payment relates to the obligation to make a payment or payments in other taxable years under the contract, the taxpayer's method of accounting will only be considered to clearly reflect income if it takes such payments into account over the life of the contract using a reasonable method of amortization. Pending issuance of regulations, no particular method of amortization was required.

In July 1991, proposed regulations were issued regarding the tax treatment of NPCs. Although, in general, these proposed regulations are technically effective only for NPCs entered into after the regulations are finalized, the regulations represent the primary guidance dealing specifically with such contracts. In large part, these regulations adopt a loan analogy, and many of the concepts used are adapted from the rules for interest and original-issue discount. The most extensive regulation deals with the timing of recognition of income and expense. The regulations start by dividing payments received under notional principal contracts into three categories: periodic payments, termination payments, and nonperiodic payments.

PERIODIC PAYMENTS

Periodic payments are payments made or received pursuant to a notional principal contract that are payable at fixed periodic intervals of one year or less during the entire term of the contract. The payment amounts must be based on a single specified index. Special rules permit short or long first periods with certain limitations. All taxpayers, regardless of their method of accounting, must recognize the ratable daily portion (RDP) of a periodic payment for the taxable year to which that portion relates. The following example illustrates the recognition of periodic payments. This example and the remaining examples in this chapter are adapted from examples in the proposed regulations.

Example 1

On April 1, 1992, A enters into a contract with unrelated counterparty B under which, for a term of five years, A is obligated to make a payment to B each April 1, beginning on April 1, 1993, in an amount equal to LIBOR, as determined on the immediately preceding April 1, multiplied by a notional amount of $100 million. Under the contract, B is obligated to make a payment of A each April 1, beginning April 1, 1993, in an amount equal to 8 percent multiplied by the same notional principal amount. A and B are calendar-year taxpayers that use the accrual method of accounting. On April 1, 1992, LIBOR is 7.8 percent.

1. All payments under the contract are periodic payments since they are based on single specified indexes (i.e., 8 percent and LIBOR) and payable at fixed intervals of one year or less (i.e., each April 1) during the term of the swap contract.

2. Under the terms of the swap contract, on April 1, 1993, B is obligated to make a payment to A of $8 million (8% × $100 million) and A is obligated to make a payment to B of $7.8 million (7.8% × $100 million). The ratable daily portions for 1992 are the amounts of these periodic payments that are attributable to A's and B's taxable year ending December 31, 1992. The ratable daily portion of the 8 percent fixed leg is $6,027,397 (275 days/365 days × $8,000,000), and the ratable daily portion of the floating leg is $5,876,712 (275/365 × $7,800,000). The net amount for the taxable year is the difference between the ratable daily portions of the two periodic payments, or $150,685 ($6,027,397 − $5,876,712). Accordingly, A has net income of $150,685 from this swap for 1992, and B has a corresponding net deduction of $150,685.

3. The $49,315 unrecognized balance of the $200,000 net periodic payments that are made on April 1, 1993, will be included in A's and B's net income or deduction from the contract for 1993.

The periodic payments on at least one leg of the swap contract are tied to a variable index (e.g., a floating rate such as LIBOR). If the value of this index will not be determined until after the close of the tax year, the index value at year-end is used in calculating the floating-rate periodic payment deemed due. The floating-rate payor then calculates the year's ratable daily portion of this payment in determining the swap income or loss for the year. Often the value of this index will change between year-end and the determination date in the following year. In this case, an adjustment to swap income is made in the following year to correct for this change. Another example illustrates this rule.

Example 2
The facts are the same as in Example 1, except that A's obligation to make payments based upon LIBOR is determined by reference to LIBOR on the day each payment is due. LIBOR is 8.25 percent on December 31, 1992, and 8.16 percent on April 1, 1993.

1. On December 31, 1992, the amount that A is obligated to pay B is not known because it will not become fixed until April 1, 1993. The ratable daily portion of the periodic payment from A to B for 1992 is based on the value of LIBOR on December 31, 1992. Thus, the ratable daily portion of the floating leg is $6,215,753 (275 days/365 days × 8.25% × $100,000,000) while the ratable daily portion of the fixed leg is $6,027,397 (275 days/365 days × $8,000,000). The net amount for 1992 on this swap is $188,356 ($6,215,753 − $6,027,397). Accordingly, B has $188,356 of net income from the swap in 1992, and A has a net deduction of $188,356.

2. On April 1, 1993, A makes a net payment to B of $160,000 ($8,160,000 payment on the floating leg, $8,000,000 payment on the fixed leg). During 1993, A will have income and B will have a loss with respect to the April 1, 1993 payment of $28,356, which represents the difference between the actual income/loss for the period ($160,000) and the amount recognized in 1992 ($188,356).

TERMINATION PAYMENTS

A termination payment is a payment that extinguishes or assigns all or a proportionate part of the rights and obligations of any party under an NPC. The general rule is that parties to an NPC recognize a termination payment in the year of extinguishment or assignment. Any payments made or received pursuant to an NPC that have not previously been recognized (i.e., unamortized nonperiodic payments) are also recognized in the year of extinguishment or assignment. If only part of a party's rights and obligations is extinguished or assigned, the rule applies only to a proportionate part of such unrecognized payment.

If an NPC is terminated by assignment, these rules somewhat surprisingly require recognition of the termination payment by both of the original parties to the NPC, including the nonassigning party. The nonassigning counterparty would have offsetting amortization over the remaining term of the NPC. The assignee will treat the termination payment in accordance with the rules for nonperiodic payments described below.

The following example may clarify the application of these rules.

Example 3

On January 1, 1992, P enters into an interest rate swap agreement with unrelated counterparty O under which, for a term of seven years, P is obligated to make annual payments based on 10 percent and O is obligated to make semiannual payments based on LIBOR, both computed on a notional principal amount of $100 million. P and O are both calendar-year taxpayers. On January 1, 1994, when the fixed rate on a comparable LIBOR swap has fallen to 9.5 percent, P pays unrelated party R $1,895,393 to assume all of P's rights and obligations under the swap with O. In return for this payment, R agrees to pay 10 percent of $100 million annually to O and to receive LIBOR payments from O for the remaining five years of the swap.

1. The payment from P to R terminates P's interest in the swap contract with O and is a termination payment. P recognizes a loss of $1,895,393 in 1994. O recognizes $1,895,393 of income or gain in 1994 and is permitted to amortize its resulting $1,895,393 of basis in the interest rate swap over the remaining five-year term of the swap agreement, using the rules for nonperiodic payments.

2. The assignment payment that R receives from P is a nonperiodic payment for an interest rate swap. Because the assignment payment is not a significant nonperiodic payment, R amortizes the $1,895,393 over the five-year term of the swap agreement in accordance with the rules for nonperiodic payments.

NONPERIODIC PAYMENTS

Any payment pursuant to a notional principal contract that is neither a periodic payment nor a termination payment is treated as a nonperiodic payment. A nonperiodic payment must be recognized over the term of a notional principal contract in a manner that reflects the economic substance of the contract. This reference to economic substance is an example of an apparent move by the Treasury Department away from drafting detailed rules to cover specific transactions to broad general principles that might be applied to financial instruments yet to be developed.

The regulations further state that most notional principal contracts resemble other financial instruments, and the amount of a nonperiodic payment made pursuant to the notional principal contract corresponds to the value of those instruments, adjusted to reflect a discount for early payment or late payment. For example, a nonperiodic payment that relates to an interest rate swap must be recognized over the term of the contract by allocating it in accordance with the values of a series of cash-settled forward contracts that reflect the specified index and the notional principal amount. Similarly, a nonperiodic payment relating to an interest rate cap or floor must be recognized over the term of the agreement by allocating it in accordance with the values of a series of cash-settled option contracts. For purposes of this allocation, the forward prices, interest rate, and compounding method used by the parties to determine the amount of the nonperiodic payment will be respected, if reasonable.

Nonperiodic payments with respect to interest rate swaps may also be allocated using a constant yield to maturity method, and the Internal Revenue Service plans to issue a revenue procedure that provides an alternative method for allocating the premium paid or received for interest rate caps and floors. These alternative methods may not be used if the taxpayer, either directly or through a related party, hedges the notional principal contract. The following example illustrates the general rule for interest rate caps.

Example 4
On January 1, 1992, when LIBOR is 8 percent, F pays unrelated party E $600,000 for a contract that obligates E to make a payment to F each quarter equal to one quarter of the excess, if any, of

three-month LIBOR over 9 percent with respect to a notional principal amount of $25 million. Both E and F are calendar-year taxpayers. E provides F with a schedule of allocable premium amounts that indicates the cap was priced according to a variation of the Black-Scholes option pricing formula and that the total premium is allocable to the following periods:

1992	$ 55,000
1993	225,000
1994	320,000
	$600,000

The $600,000 cap premium paid by F to E is a nonperiodic payment. Since the schedule generated by the modified Black-Scholes model is consistent with the economic substance of the cap, it may be used by both E and F in calculating their ratable daily portions of the cap premium. Thus, E and F account for the contract as follows:

	Ratable Daily Portion
1992	$ 55,000
1993	225,000
1994	320,000
	$600,000

Swaps that have significant nonperiodic payments and caps and floors that are significantly in the money are treated as including one or more loans, which must be accounted for by both parties to the contract independently of the swap. If on the date a cap or floor is entered into the current value of the specified index in a cap agreement exceeds the cap rate by more than 25 basis points or the floor rate exceeds the current value of the specified index in a floor agreement by a similar amount, the cap or floor will fall under these rules. What constitutes significant nonperiodic payments with respect to swaps is not specifically defined although there are several examples of transactions that will or will not qualify.

MARKET VALUE ACCOUNTING

The proposed regulations would also permit a dealer or trader in derivative financial instruments to elect to account for those instruments on a market value basis. Derivatives, for this purpose, include not only notional principal contracts but also options, forward contracts, futures contracts, short positions in securities and commodities, and any similar financial instrument. A provision that would prohibit dealers and traders from making the mark-to-market election if they used lower of cost or market for any securities or commodities undercuts the potential usefulness of this election. Currently, legislation pending before Congress would require securities dealers generally to use market value accounting. If this legislation is ultimately enacted, it is likely to impact the chances of this proposed regulation ever being finalized in its current form.

CHARACTER

The general consensus is that periodic and nonperiodic payments with respect to notional principal contracts should be treated as ordinary income and expense. The controversy has been in the area of termination payments. The Internal Revenue Service has been recharacterizing termination payments as capital losses in its examinations of a number of taxpayers. Their principal line of argument is outlined in the proposed regulations. Under IRC Section 1234A, gain or loss attributable to the cancellation, lapse, expiration, or other termination or a right or obligation that is a capital asset in the hands of the taxpayer is treated as a capital gain or loss. As is not unusual in the tax law, personal property for purposes of this section does not have its everyday meaning but rather depends on a specific definition in IRC Section 1092. This section defines personal property as any personal property of a type that is actively traded. It was generally believed that notional principal contracts were not actively traded and therefore did not fall within this definition of personal property. In contrast, the proposed regulations state that a notional principal contract constitutes property of a type that is actively traded if similar contracts are actively traded, including trading on an interbank or interdealer market, and that the rights and obligations of a party to a notional contract constitute an interest in personal property. This would bring the termination payment under IRC Section 1234A and result in capital gain and loss treatment.

SOURCE

There was significant concern that a swap payment made by a U.S. counterparty to a foreign counterparty might be subject to a withholding tax. Withholding taxes apply to payments of certain U.S. source income to foreign persons. These concerns were allayed by adoption of sourcing based on the residence of the recipient. Thus, a payment to a foreign counterparty would be foreign source and not subject to withholding.

SECTION 5
OVER-THE-COUNTER OPTIONS

CHAPTER 25

INTRODUCTION TO OVER-THE-COUNTER (OTC) OPTIONS

Peter A. Abken
Federal Reserve Bank of Atlanta

Volatility in interest rates, asset prices, and exchange rates has spawned a variety of methods to mitigate the costs associated with these fluctuations. Risk management has become big business and a complicated activity. One facet of risk management involves the purchase and sale of so-called *derivative assets*, which can be used to offset or hedge changes in asset or liability values due to interest rate, stock price, or exchange rate fluctuations. As its name implies, a derivative asset depends on the value of another asset (or assets). Derivatives can be traded on organized exchanges, like the Chicago Mercantile Exchange, or bought and sold over the counter through commercial and investment banks. This introductory chapter concentrates on over-the-counter options. Because they are effectively tailor-made instruments, over-the-counter options come in many varieties compared to their exchange-traded relatives.

This chapter considers several types of over-the-counter options. The first are the option counterparts of interest rate swap agreements, namely, caps, floors, and collars. These are medium- to long-term agreements that have proved to be highly useful for hedging against interest rate uncertainties. Like interest rate swaps, caps, collars, and floors are designed to hedge cash flows over time rather than a cash flow at a single date. Insofar as they are used for hedging, caps, collars, and floors may be regarded as different kinds of insurance policies against adverse movements in interest rates. The discussion below will show how caps, collars, and floors are related to each other, as well as how they may be constructed from the most basic derivative asset, the option. It also covers the ways in which caps, collars, and floors are created in practice, along with the different kinds of financial intermediaries involved in the caps market.[1] The chapter examines caps in detail because they are prototypical over-the-counter options-based instruments.

Options on swaps are the next type of over-the-counter instrument reviewed in this introduction. They bear a superficial resemblance to caps, but in fact are quite different, not only in terms of their cash flows, but also in terms of the credit risk they pose to the counterparties involved.

The next section considers synthetic equity, which comprises a number of over-the-counter equity options as well as forwards and swaps. Currency options, including average rate options, break forwards, and range forwards, are then introduced.

Swaptions, average rate options, and break forwards are just a few examples of so-called exotic options, which offer a wide array of contractual features beyond those of standard options. All of the instruments will be defined as the exposition proceeds; no prior knowledge of derivative assets is assumed.

INTEREST RATE CAPS

An *interest rate cap,* sometimes also called a *ceiling,* is a financial instrument that effectively places a maximum amount on the interest payment made on floating-rate debt. Many businesses borrow funds through loans or bonds on which a periodic interest payment varies according to a widely quoted short-term interest rate. The most important such rate is the London Interbank Offered Rate, or LIBOR, which is the rate offered on Eurodollar deposits of one international bank held at another. A typical example of floating-rate borrowing would be a firm taking out a $20 million bank loan on which the interest would be paid every three months at 50 basis points (hundreths of a percent) over LIBOR prevailing at each payment date. Other short-term rates that are used in conjunction with caps include commercial bank certificate of deposit (CD) rates, the prime interest rate, Treasury bill rates, commercial paper rates, and even certain tax-exempt interest rates. Most common by far, however, are LIBOR-based caps (which is also true of interest rate swaps).

Most discussions of caps concern cap agreements offered by commercial or investment banks to borrowers seeking interest rate protection. These are often tailored to a client's needs, and, particularly in the case of caps, may be marketable (or negotiable). Caps, collars, and floors can also be manufactured out of more-basic derivative assets: options or futures contracts, or a combination of these. The discussion for now will proceed at a general level, without introducing further institutional detail, in order to highlight the concepts underlying these instruments. Caps, collars, and floors will be defined in terms of option contracts, which are the most basic or "primitive" derivative asset.

CAPS, FLOORS, AND COLLARS IN TERMS OF CALL AND PUT OPTIONS

An *option* is a financial contract with a fixed expiration date that offers either a positive return (payoff) or nothing at maturity, depending on the value of an underlying asset. At expiration, a call option gives the purchaser the right, but not the obligation, to buy a fixed number of units of the underlying asset if that asset's price exceeds a level specified in the option contract. The seller or "writer" of a call has the obligation to sell the underlying asset at the specified exercise or strike price if the call expires "in the money." The payoff on a call need not actually involve delivery of the underlying asset to the call buyer, but rather can be settled by a cash payment. (For example, the caps market uses cash settlement.) If the asset price finishes below the exercise price, the call is said to expire "out of the money."

Put options are analogous to calls. The purchaser has the right to sell a fixed number of units of the underlying asset if the asset price is below the exercise price. The options discussed in this article will all be European options, which can only be exercised on the expiration date, as opposed to American options, which can be exercised any time before or at expiration. As will be seen, caps, floors, and collars are European-style option-based instruments.

Options on debt instruments can be confusing if it is not clear just what the option "price" represents. Recall that the price of a debt instrument, such as a Treasury bill or CD, moves inversely with its corresponding interest rate. Thus, a call on a Treasury bill rate is like a put on its price. To keep the expostion clear, all discussion will be in terms of options on interest rates. The strike price will be referred to as the *strike level*.

It is easy to see that a call with a strike level of 8 percent (on an annual basis) on some notional amount of principal is effectively a cap on a floating-rate loan payment coinciding with the expiration of this option.[2] Assume the payment date (usually called the *reset date*) falls semiannually. If the interest rate is less than 8 percent, the call expires worthless on the reset date. If the interest rate is greater than 8 percent, the call pays off the difference between the actual interest rate and the strike level times the notional principal, in turn multiplied by the fraction of a year that has elapsed. For example, for an actual rate of 10 percent and $1 million notional principal, the payment received from the call writer would be 2% × $1,000,000 × 180/360 = $10,000 for the half- (180/360) year. The European interest rate call option is the basic building block for the interest rate cap.

A put option on an interest payment works in a similar way, and is the foundation for the interest rate floor. The holder of a floating-rate loan could protect against a loss in interest income from the loan by buying an interest rate put. A fall in the interest rate below the strike level of the put would result in a payoff from the option, offsetting the loss in income due to a lower interest payment on the loan.

An option writer is in effect an insurer and receives a *premium* payment from the option buyer when an option is created (sold initially). In fact, the option price is also called the *option premium*. The same party can simultaneously write and buy options, and this kind of position creates an interest rate collar. Before exploring this strategy further, option pricing needs to be briefly considered.

Option pricing theory is a complex subject. The price or premium for an option before expiration depends on several variables. They include the value of the underlying asset on which the option is written, the risk-free rate of interest (usually a Treasury bill that matures at the same time as the option), the time remaining before expiration, the exercise or strike price, and the variability or "volatility" of the underlying asset price. A detailed discussion of option pricing is beyond the scope of this article. A basic overview can be found in Cox and Rubinstein (1985) or Jarrow and Rudd (1983).

For later reference, it will be useful to review how an option price changes in response to a change in an underlying variable, all other variables remaining constant. A call price rises (falls) when the underlying asset price, volatility, or time to expiration increases (decreases). It falls (rises) with an increase (decrease) in the exercise price. A put price rises (falls) with an increase (decrease) in the strike price or volatility. It falls (rises) with an increase (decrease) in the underlying asset price or interest rate. Unlike a call price, an increase in the time to expiration does not have a clear-cut effect on the put price, but depends at any point in time on how far in or out of the money a put is.

For an interest rate call option, the higher the strike compared to the current interest rate, the lower the option value. Choosing a high strike level (out-of-the-money) call is cheaper than buying an at-the-money or in-the-money call. Similarly, selecting a low strike level (out-of-money) put is cheaper than one with a higher strike level. The amount the option is out of the money is analogous to selecting an insurance policy with a large deductible. The policy is less likely to pay off and is therefore less costly. The cost of interest rate "insurance" can be reduced by taking a large deductible and thereby protecting against only very large, adverse interest rate movements.

Creation of an *interest rate collar* is another method for reducing the cost of interest rate insurance. The call option premium for an interest rate cap may be partially or completely offset by selling a put option that sets in place an interest rate floor. The effect of an interest rate collar for a floating-rate debt holder is to protect against rate movements above the cap level, but simultaneously to give up potential interest savings from rate drops below the floor level.

To conclude this discussion of interest rate put and call options, it is instructive to observe that if the cap and floor level of a collar are narrowed to the point that they coincide at the current floating interest rate, the resulting collar is so tight that it is identical to a forward contract. Both put and call options are at the money. A *forward contract* on an interest rate is a derivative asset that locks in the current rate. At expiration of the contract, whatever increase or decrease in interest rates has occurred since the inception of the contract, the change in the contract's value exactly offsets the change in the interest payment due. A rise in the floating-rate payment is matched by an equal gain on the forward contract; a fall in the floating-rate payment, by an equal loss on the forward. The floating-rate payment is converted to a fixed-rate payment via a forward contract.

Extending the above discussion to include actual cap, collar, and floor agreements is now straightforward. Everything said thus far has been about a single payment. As mentioned above, actual cap, collar, or floor agreements are designed to hedge a series of cash flows, not just a single one. Thus, a *cap* is a series of interest rate call options for successively more distant reset dates, and a *floor* is a series of put options. For example, a cap sets the maximum interest payment on floating-rate debt. The interest payment on that debt would fall due at the next reset date, for example, in three months, and is said to be "paid in arrears." Payment in arrears is the typical convention for caps and swaps, though other timing arrangements are possible. If the interest rate exceeds the strike level, the cap writer would make a payment to the cap buyer three months after the reset date. This payment on the cap would coincide with the cap buyer's own payment date on the underlying floating-rate debt.

It is instructive to note that a collar that consists of a series of at-the-money call and put options is equivalent to an interest rate swap. Buying the cap and selling the floor transforms floating-rate debt to fixed-rate debt, whereas selling the cap and buying the floor switches fixed-rate debt into floating-rate. A swap that is constructed out of cap and floor agreements is called a *synthetic swap*. Caps brokers and dealers will sometimes determine rates on floors by deriving the rate from swap and cap rates, which come from instruments that are more actively traded than floors and therefore more readily reflect current market values. The "collaring" of a swap suggests that a floating-rate payer could completely offset a swap by buying a cap and selling a floor that both have strike rates equal to the swap rate. Similarly, a fixed-rate payer could nullify a swap by selling a cap and buying a floor with strike rates equal to the swap rate. In these cases, in effect, the floating-rate payer would be buying a "synthetic" swap and the fixed-rate payer would be selling one. However, this is not how swaps are usually unwound since it is generally cheaper simply to buy or sell the corresponding swap. Caps and floors may not be sufficiently liquid at the desired strike rates to execute these transactions at reasonable prices. (That is, an illiquid—infrequently traded—cap or floor would be quoted with large price spreads.) Nevertheless, arbitrage between the swap and cap/floor markets is possible and does occur if rates for these instruments get too far out of line.

A hybrid version of the fixed-rate swap and interest rate cap allows a counterparty to benefit partially from declining rates, while not requiring any up-front payment as with a cap. Consider an example using LIBOR. The counterparty would receive LIBOR to pay the interest on its floating-rate debt. In turn, instead of paying a fixed interest rate as for a plain-vanilla swap, a higher fixed rate is established (above the swap rate), which is the maximum rate the counterparty would have to pay if LIBOR rises above that level. However, if LIBOR falls below this maximum rate, the counterparty's payment would decline less than one for one with the LIBOR. For example, the swap terms could stipulate that a 1 percentage point drop in LIBOR would reduce the swap payment by half a percentage point. The so-called *participation rate* in this case is 50 percent. In other words, the counterparty would "participate" in 50 percent of any decline in LIBOR below the maximum rate. The maximum rate and the participation rate are set to price the swap at zero cost upon initiation. The price of the option feature contained in this swap is effectively paid by giving up part of the gains from falling rates.

The participating swap can also be structured to have the counterparty pay LIBOR and receive payments indexed to a fixed schedule. That is, a minimum rate would be specified in the swap, with payments above that minimum determined by the product of the prevailing LIBOR multiplied by the participation rate. A counterparty might want to use such a swap in conjunction with its floating-rate assets. Participation swaps can be structured for any interest rates and are also used for currencies and commodities.

SOME EXAMPLES OF CAPS, FLOORS, AND COLLARS

To help make the discussion more concrete, several examples of caps, collars, and floors will be given. Creating caps, floors, and collars amounts to an exercise in option pricing. One widely used option pricing model, the Black (1976) futures option model, will be used in the examples. The Black model is among those used by caps market participants. Tompkins (1989) explains caps pricing in terms of the Black model, and the examples that follow are loosely patterned on his approach.

The Black model's chief virtue is its simplicity and ease of use. However, the model has a serious internal inconsistency in its application to valuing debt options; namely, it is assumed that the short-term interest rate (i.e., Treasury bill rate) is constant. However, options on short-term interest rates have value only if those rates are stochastic, that is, less than perfectly predictable. Thanks to continuing research by financial economists, there is a burgeoning, competing supply of stochastic interest rate models that can be used to price interest rate derivatives of all kinds. For example, the Cox-Ingersol-Ross (1985), Black-Derman-Toy (1990), and Heath-Jarrow-Morton (1992) term structure models are readily used to price interest rate options. (Chapter 14 of this book considers various models and explores the Black-Derman-Toy model in depth.)

In order to give realistic yet simple examples of caps, collars, and floors, it will be assumed that the reset dates coincide with the expiration dates of Eurodollar futures contracts, which are traded at the Chicago Mercantile Exchange (CME) and also at the London International Financial Futures Exchange (LIFFE). Purchase of a Eurodollar futures contract locks in the interest payment on a $1 million three-month time deposit to be created upon expiration of the futures contract. The interest rate on the deposit is three-month LIBOR. Conversely, the seller of a Eurodollar futures contract is obligated to pay the specified LIBOR-based interest payment at expiration.[3]

Eurodollar futures expire in a quarterly cycle two London business days prior to the third Wednesday of March, June, September, and December. The CME currently offers contract expiration months extending out four years, with March and September contracts in the fourth year. The interest rate implied by a Eurodollar futures price may be regarded as a forward interest rate, that is, the three-month LIBOR expected by the market to prevail at the expiration date for each contract.[4]

The Black model takes the futures price at a particular contract expiration month as an input to determine the value of a European call and put option on that contract. In the case of Eurodollars futures contracts, it is the add-on yield (100 − Futures price) that gets plugged into Black's formula. Another crucial variable is the volatility, which is either estimated from the historical volatility of the Eurodollar futures yield or obtained as an implied volatility from traded Eurodollar futures options. Again, the higher the volatility, the higher will be the cost of call and put options, and, hence, caps and floors.

Table 25-1 gives two-year cap, floor, and collar prices on three-month LIBOR for two arbitrarily chosen dates, June 19, 1989, and December 14, 1987, which illustrate different slopes of the term structure of interest rates. The first date illustrates pricing during a relatively low volatility period when the term structure of LIBOR rates, as given by the "strip" of futures prices, that is, prices on successively more distant contracts, was just about flat. The market was predicting virtually no change in short-term interest rates over this two-year horizon. In panel A, the contract expiration months are given along with the add-on yields for each futures contract immediately below. The row labeled *days to expiration* is the number of days from the creation of the cap, floor, or collar to the expiration date for each option and futures contract. Another input into Black's option pricing formula, the risk-free rate, is taken to be the Treasury bill or zero coupon bond yield, for which the expiration falls nearest to the futures expiration date.

The first instrument to be priced is a two-year 10 percent cap (see Panel A, Scenario One), which consists of the sum of seven call options. This cap is clearly out of the money. The computed

TABLE 25–1
Examples of Two-Year Cap, Floor, and Collar Prices on Three-Month LIBOR

Panel A: June 19, 1989; Volatility, 18 percent

	September 1988	December 1988	March 1989	June 1989	September 1989	December 1989	March 1990
Days to expiration	91	182	273	364	455	546	637
Forward rate	9.02	8.84	8.64	8.71	8.77	8.87	8.86
Risk-free rate	8.46	8.47	8.54	8.56	8.59	8.59	8.56

Scenario One

Call prices (10.0% strike)	5.3	10.3	12.9	19.9	26.5	34.1	38.1
Put prices (7.5% strike)	.6	4.7	11.8	15.4	18.6	20.6	24.2
10% cap							
Cost in basis points: 147							
Cost in dollars: $3,677.60							
7.5% floor							
Cost in basis points: 96							
Cost in dollars: $2,396.61							
Zero-cost collar							
10% cap implies 7.85% floor							

Scenario Two

Call prices (11% strike)	.4	2.2	3.8	7.6	11.8	16.9	20.3
Put prices (7% strike)	.1	1.3	4.7	7.2	9.5	11.2	13.9
11% cap							
Cost in basis points: 63							
Cost in dollars: $1,575.84							
7% floor							
Cost in basis points: 48							
Cost in dollars: $1,198.08							
Zero-cost collar							
11% cap implies 7.19% floor							

Panel B: December 14, 1987; Volatility, 25 percent

	March 1988	June 1988	September 1988	December 1988	March 1989	June 1989	September 1989
Days to expiration	91	182	280	371	455	553	644
Forward rate	8.09	8.34	8.62	8.88	9.11	9.31	9.48
Risk-free rate	6.09	6.79	7.11	7.51	7.66	7.79	7.92
Call prices (10% strike)	2.1	12.5	28.9	45.9	62.0	78.0	91.6
Put prices (7.5% strike)	16.2	23.0	26.8	29.0	30.5	32.9	34.8
10% cap							
Cost in basis points: 321							
Cost in dollars: $8,025.53							
7.5% floor							
Cost in basis points: 193							
Cost in dollars: $4,829.68							
Zero-cost collar							
10% cap implies 8.05% floor							

Note: Dollar amount is for $1,000,000 in notional principal.
Sums may not add up due to rounding error. Cap rates are usually rounded to whole basis points. The dollar amounts shown are the exact amounts computed in constructing the table.

call option price is expressed in basis points (i.e., hundredths of a percent). The calls become progressively more expensive the farther out into the future they expire. This reflects the increasing time value of the calls. The shorter-maturity calls have little value because they are out of the money and, given the volatility, there is only a small probability that they might finish in the money. Although the more distant calls are also out of the money, there is more time (and more uncertainty) about what LIBOR will do. Thus, their value is greater because of the higher probability that they might expire in the money. The sum of these calls is the cap rate, which is 147 basis points. A basis point constitutes the smallest change in value of a Eurodollar futures (or traded options) contract. For a three-month contract, which has a nominal face value of $1 million, a 1-basis-point move is worth $25 ($1 million × .01 × 90/360). Translated into dollars, 147 basis points is $3,677.60 ($\cong$ 147 × $25), that is, the dollar cost of placing a cap for two years on a $1 million loan. This example was computed ignoring the risk of default on the cap. It also assumes that payments at reset dates, if owed, are made at the time of the reset date.

Next in Scenario One, a slightly out-of-the money 7.5 percent floor is shown. The total cost is about 96 basis points or $2,396.61. As mentioned above, the cost of interest rate protection can be reduced by creating a collar, which is also sometimes referred to as a *ceiling-floor agreement*. In this example, selling a 7.5 percent floor would substantially reduce the cost of a 10 percent cap. The combination would cost about 51 basis points or $1,281. By judiciously selecting the floor level, the price of the cap can be driven to zero! In fact, that floor turns out to be about 7.850 percent. Marketing people delight in explaining that downside interest rate protection (the cap) can be obtained at no cost: Just sell a floor. Of course, there is a cost. The holder of an interest rate collar has traded away potential savings on interest rate declines below the floor. This caveat notwithstanding, a collar for which the floor exactly matches the cap will be referred to as a *zero-cost collar*.

Scenario Two illustrates how the cost of caps and floors falls by selecting more out-of-the-money levels. Increasing the cap by 1 percentage point to 11 percent reduces the cap rate substantially to about 63 basis points or $1,575.84. Decreasing the floor by half a percentage point to 7 percent more than halves the cost to 48 basis points or $1,198.08. The effect on a zero-cost collar with an 11 percent cap is to lower the floor to 7.189 percent.

The final example, in panel B, shows prices for caps, collars, and floors during a relatively high volatility period following the October 1987 stock market crash. The date is December 14, 1987. Eurodollar futures volatility surged during and after the October 21 crash, and had abated greatly by late January, though had not completely returned to precrash levels. The implied volatility was 25 percent on December 14, 1987, as compared to 18 percent on June 19, 1989, used in the other two examples. The 10 percent cap in Panel B is substantially more costly than the one in Panel A, Scenario One. The cost is 321 basis points or $8,025.53. Another important factor contributing to the higher cost is the rising structure of LIBOR forward rates. Although the nearest futures to expire indicates a forward rate of 8.09 percent as compared to 9.02 percent in the June 19, 1989, example, the distant futures for December 14, 1987, have forward rates that are well above those for June 19, 1989. The upward-sloping term structure of interest rates for December 14 reinforces the effect of higher volatility on rising cap and floor rates. The floor is more expensive as well at 193 basis points or $4,829.68. Interestingly, the zero-cost collar with a 10 percent cap is only slightly more constraining with a floor of 8.050 percent as compared to 7.850 in the previous example with low volatility and flat term structure.

CAPS, COLLARS, AND FLOORS IN PRACTICE

At first sight, creating caps, collars, and floors would appear to be a simple matter because options are traded on the Eurodollar futures contract. Selecting the appropriate strike levels and expiration dates would appear to be all that is necessary to manufacture a cap, collar, or floor. However, as mentioned above, Eurodollar contracts extend into the future at most four years (which is an unusually large number of contract months for a futures contract). CME Eurodollar futures options currently have expiration dates ranging out two years, in a quarterly cycle that matches the Eurodollar futures contracts. Another limitation of the Eurodollar futures options is that only contracts expiring within the three months or so from the current date are liquid, that is, they are the only ones that are actively traded so their prices at any time are dependable if you want to execute a large transaction quickly. The options are also limited to strike levels in increments of 25 basis points, whereas the futures have increments of 1 basis point. Unlike Eurodollar futures and Eurodollar options, caps, collars, and floors have been created with maturities of as much as 10 years. Furthermore, actual caps, collars, and floors can be created on any day, not just on those that coincide with futures and options expiration dates. The actual use of futures and options to fashion caps, collars, floors, or any other over-the-counter option is not a straightforward nor riskless matter.

Existing futures and options contracts are used to *synthetically* create the desired contracts. Synthesizing an options position using options contracts, futures contracts, or a combination of both, requires taking appropriate positions in the existing liquid contracts *and* altering that position over time so that the value of the actual position tracks or "replicates" the desired position. This process is known as *dynamic hedging*. Theoretically, the replicating portfolio of actual futures and options contracts can exactly match the value of, say, a cap sold to a counterparty.[5] In actuality, managing a replicating portfolio is a risky and costly activity. Tracking errors cumulate because costly trading cannot be conducted continuously as is theoretically required and because of mismatches in the expiration dates, and possibly also the interest rates involved (e.g., using Eurodollar futures to hedge a cap based on the commercial paper rate).[6]

THE OVER-THE-COUNTER MARKET

In view of the complexities and risks of dynamic hedging strategies, most end users prefer over-the-counter instruments. That is, commercial and investment banks create the instruments themselves, possibly by manufacturing them by dynamic hedging. The nonfinancial users tend to rely on the expertise of these financial institutions and are willing to pay more for the convenience of interest rate risk management products issued by an intermediary. The intermediaries may also be more willing to bear the risks associated with hedging because of the scale of their operations. In fact, Brown and Smith (1988) describe the increasing involvement of banks in offering interest rate risk management instruments as the reintermediation of commercial banking. Since the 1970s, commercial banks have played less of a role in channeling funds from lender to borrower. But with the growth of interest rate risk management their intermediary role is being restored, though in a different form.

Commercial and investment banks, predominantly the largest institutions in the OTC market, are better able to absorb and manage the hedging risks associated with managing an options portfolio, and they are better able to evaluate the credit risks inherent in instruments that they buy from other parties. Credit risk arises because any counterparty selling a cap, for example, is obligated to make payments if the cap moves in the money on a reset date. That counterparty could go bankrupt at some point during the course of the cap agreement and would default on its obligation. By taking positions in caps or other derivative instruments, commercial banks and, to a lesser extent, investment banks act as dealers by buying and selling to any different counterparties. Within their portfolio or "book," individual positions partially net out, leaving a residual exposure that the banks then hedge in the options and futures markets. Much trading of marketable over-the-counter options, like caps, consists of purchases and sales of these instruments to adjust positions and risk exposures, so that much of the volume in the caps market is generated by interdealer transactions. In addition to the large commercial and investment banks in New York and London that dominate the over-the-counter market, there are a number of specialized brokers, such as in the caps market, who do not take positions themselves, but match buyer and seller.

Caps, collars, and floors are usually sold in multiples of $5 million dollars, but owing to the customized nature of the over-the-counter market, other amounts can be arranged. Most caps have terms that range from one to five years and have reset dates or frequencies that are usually monthly, quarterly, or semiannual. Caps based on three-month LIBOR are the most common and the most liquid. From the purchasers' point of view, it might seem best to buy a cap that matches the characteristics of the liability being hedged. Even strike levels and notional principal amounts can vary over the term of an agreement in a predetermined way. But good fit comes at a price. Transactions costs are higher, as reflected by the larger difference (or spread) between bid and offer rates on uncommon caps. The larger spread for uncommon caps also makes them more costly to sell before their term expires. Many users opt for a liquid cap and are willing to absorb the so-called basis risk (the risk due to mismatch of interest basis or other characteristics) in order to avoid the cost of a less liquid instrument.

Caps and floors are usually available at strike levels within several percentage points above and below the current interest rate basis. They are most commonly written out of the money. Settlement (payment) dates usually occur after reset dates upon maturity of the underlying instrument. For example, interest on a three-month Eurodollar deposit is credited upon maturity of the deposit. A cap on three-month LIBOR would have a three-month lag between a reset date and actual settlement. Most payments for caps are made up front, although they can also be amortized. In cases where a cap and a floating-rate loan come from the same institution, the loan and the cap are usually treated as a single instrument, so that payment when the floating rate exceeds the strike level is limited to the strike level and the cap does not pay off directly.

End Users

End users of caps, collars, and floors typically include firms seeking to limit exposure to adverse movements in short-term interest rates, such as a firm that sells commercial paper to fund its purchases of inventory and so on. Specific end users are depository institutions, particularly savings and loan associations (S&Ls); corporations going through leveraged buyouts (LBOs) or taking on debt to fend off hostile takeovers; and real estate developers, who are often highly leveraged with floating-rate debt. Unfortunately, the only information about these end users is anecdotal. Also, compared to the potential market, the actual market is probably very small. Many potential users are unaware of or are wary of interest rate risk management instruments. Promoters of these instruments, such as commercial and investment banks, regularly stage marketing campaigns to enlist new clients.

S&L Example

The interest rate risk borne by S&Ls (and depository institutions generally) may be considered in terms of their net interest margins, that is, the difference between the rates at which an institution lends and borrows. S&Ls are particularly vulnerable to changes in interest rates because the maturities (or, alternatively, the durations) of their assets, predominately long-term mortgages, greatly exceed the maturities of their liabilities, most often short-term time and savings deposits. Thus, a rise in rates increases the interest expense on an S&L's short-term liabilities with possibly little increase in interest earnings on its mortgages. The net interest margin narrows and could very well become negative. One solution is to convert the floating-rate interest expense on the liabilities into fixed-rate payments via an interest rate swap. The net interest margin would then become much more stable. However, a weak credit standing could make such a swap too expensive or unobtainable. A cap on the floating-rate liabilities could be an effective alternative. An S&L's credit rating would be irrelevant to a cap writer, who bears no credit exposure.[7]

Bank Example

Consider a portfolio manager at a commercial bank, who is responsible for overseeing the bank's portfolio of floating-rate notes. Suppose the manager is concerned about a large drop in short-term interest rates, currently at about 8 percent, that he believes is about to occur. He wants to protect the portfolio's earnings and therefore buys an out-of-the-money 7 percent interest rate floor. Concerned about the cost of this protection and reasonably convinced that rates will not rise substantially, he also decides to sell a 9 percent interest rate cap to create a collar on the portfolio. This example also highlights the discretion involved in selecting a hedge. A floor could have been in place all along, but this reduces a portfolio's return due to the premium expense. Only when the manager has strong concerns about a drop in rates is the floor purchased.

LBO Example

The corporate treasurer of a consumer products firm is worried about the prospects of a rise in interest rates because her firm has recently undergone a leveraged buyout. The financing strategy for the LBO included heavy reliance on floating-rate debt secured from a syndicate of commercial banks. The firm's debt-to-equity ratio has increased manyfold, and even a modest rise in rates could bankrupt the company. After the LBO, the firm's credit rating was downgraded by the rating services; consequently, access to the swap market is effectively foreclosed. Buying a two-year interest rate cap to cover the firm's floating-rate exposure seems to be a prudent action. The protection gained for a relatively short term horizon makes sense because this would be the period during which the firm would be downsizing and reorganizing its operations. The treasurer expects earnings will be more robust after a two-year interval.

SIZE OF THE MARKET

Data on the size of the caps market come from periodic surveys by the International Swap Dealers Association (ISDA) of its members. As of year-end 1991, the total outstanding U.S. dollar and non–U.S. dollar notional principal for caps, collars, and floors was $468 billion. Growth has been flat in these instruments since 1989; the annually compounded growth rate was only .8 percent over this period. U.S. dollar notional principal of $311 billion for 1991 was almost twice the dollar value of non–U.S. dollar caps, collars, and floors, although the number of contracts outstanding in each of these categories was about the same. There were 6,166 U.S. dollar contracts as of year-end 1991 as compared to 6,416 non–U.S. dollar contracts. While U.S. dollar contracts outstanding were down about 14 percent from the previous year, non–U.S. dollar contracts outstanding jumped 47 percent. For both categories, positions in caps dominated those in floors by a wide margin. Collars, participations, and other specialized combinations, including options on caps, made up less than 5 percent of the total contracts outstanding in the caps market overall. Though clearly a large and important market, the caps market is greatly overshadowed by the interest rate and currency swaps market, which as of year-end 1991 had combined U.S. and non–U.S. dollar notional principal of about $3.9 trillion.

SWAPTIONS

Option contracts can be written on any kind of financial instrument. In view of the continued growth in the swaps market, it is not surprising that a market has developed for options on swaps, known as *swaptions*. (There is also a market for options on caps and floors, which, as one might guess, are called *captions* and *floortions*!)

Like any option, swaptions entail a right and not an obligation on the part of the buyer. Unfortunately, the nomenclature for swaptions is confusing, so the details are often simply spelled out in talking about them. A *call swaption* (a call option on a swap or payer swaption) is the right to buy a swap—pay a fixed rate of interest and receive floating; a *put swaption* (put option on a swap or receiver swaption) is the right to sell a swap—pay floating and receive fixed. The swaption on the plain-vanilla swap is the most common, although swaptions can be written on more complicated swaps. Both the maturity of the swaption and the maturity or "tenor" of the underlying swap, which commences at a stipulated future date, must be specified. Also, like options, swaptions come in both American and European varieties. The European swaption, which accounts for about 90 percent of the market, may be exercised only upon its maturity date, whereas the American swaption may also be exercised at any time before maturity. Only European swaptions will be considered, unless otherwise noted.

A call swaption would be exercised at maturity if the swaption strike rate, the fixed rate specified in the contract, is lower than the prevailing market fixed rate for swaps of the same tenor. The swaption could be closed out by selling the low-fixed-rate swap obtained through the swaption for a gain, rather than entering into that swap. Similar reasoning applies to the decision to exercise a put swaption. Swaptions are quite different from caps and floors, although these instruments are frequently used in similar situations. A swaption involves one option on a swap, whereas a cap (or floor) represents a series of options expiring at different dates on a floating interest rate. In addition, cap prices partly depend on the volatility of near-term forward rates, whereas swaption prices reflect the volatility of future swap rates, which in turn are averages of more-distant, less-volatile forward rates. Consequently, swaptions tend to be much cheaper than caps or floors. American swaptions would be slightly more costly than European swaptions because of the additional right to exercise the instrument before maturity.

Swaptions bundled together with plain-vanilla swaps create a variety of more flexible swap structures. Callable, puttable, reversible, and extendible swaps are a few variations on a standard interest rate swap. For hedging applications, perhaps the most basic use of a swaption is to give a swap counterparty the option to cancel a swap, at no further cost beyond the initial swaption premium. A fixed-for-floating swap bundled together with a put swaption is known as a *callable swap*. The swap can be cancelled upon the maturity of the embedded swaption, for example, if interest rates have fallen. Exercising the swaption creates an offsetting floating-for-fixed swap. A floating-for-fixed swap combined with a call swaption is called a *puttable swap*. The swap can be terminated if interest rates have risen; that is, a higher fixed rate could be received from a new swap.

A *reversible swap* is one that allows a counterparty to change status from being a floating-rate payer to fixed-rate payer or vice versa at some point during the life of the instrument. It can be synthesized by combining a fixed-for-floating plain-vanilla swap with put swaptions for twice the notional principal of the underlying swap. Assuming a swaption has the same notional principal amount as the swap, the first swaption cancels the existing swap and the second creates a floating-for-fixed swap upon maturity, running for the remaining term of the original swap.

An *extendible swap* contains the option to lengthen its term at the original swap rate. Such a swap simply amounts to an ordinary swap with a swaption expiring at the end of the swap's tenor.

Another application of swaptions has been in leveraged buyouts, in which a firm's management takes on large amounts of debt to "take a firm private." Lenders, such as commercial banks, often require the firm to hedge its debt, which typically is floating rate. A call swaption with a strike rate at a level the firm could safely meet would accomplish this end. Should the floating rate rise sharply, the swaption would be exercised, converting the remaining floating-rate payments to manageable fixed-rate payments. However, caps are often preferred by lenders involved in LBO financing because the swaption, if exercised, makes the swaption writer a counterparty to a highly leveraged (and often low-rated) firm. A cap writer faces no credit risk from the cap buyer.

A final example of swaption usage is in stripping callable debt. This has been a popular strategy in the brief history of the swaption market. Corporate bonds are frequently issued with embedded options that allow the issuer to refinance the debt issue at lower coupon if interest rates fall before the bond's maturity. The embedded call usually cannot be exercised by the issuer until after some prespecified date. The buyer of the callable debt has effectively written (sold) a call option on the price of the bond to the issuer, the firm. If bond prices rise above the strike price of the calls (implying interest rates fall sufficiently), the issuer has the right to call the bonds away after paying the strike price.

Many participants in these markets have believed that the calls attached to these bonds have been undervalued. This mispricing led to an arbitrage opportunity that involved the following strategy: Firms wanting fixed-rate debt issued callable bonds and "stripped" the embedded call options by selling call swaptions. The net result was to create synthetic noncallable or "straight" bonds at a lower yield than that prevailing on comparable fixed-rate bonds. The yield reduction stemmed from selling the undervalued bond market calls at a profit in the swap market.

As an illustration of the basic strategy, assume the bond is callable at par. That is, if at the call date the relevant interest rate is at or below the original coupon rate, the bond will be called. To strip the call option, the issuer writes a put swaption, which, if exercised, obligates the firm to pay fixed and receive floating on a swap commencing on the bond's first call date and ending at the bond's maturity date. The swaption strike would, in this example, be set to the bond's coupon rate. If interest rates fall, the put swaption is exercised. In turn, the firm would call its debt and simultaneously issue floating-rate debt, whose coupon payments would be met by the floating-rate payments coming from the swap counterparty. Thus, the swaption undoes the embedded call, leaving the firm with the premium payment from the swaption, which effectively represents the proceeds from the "sale" of the embedded option. There are many variations on this strategy. Also, embedded put options can be stripped from bonds in a similar way.

Size of the Swaption Market

As of year-end 1991, there were $109.0 billion of U.S. dollar and non–U.S. dollar swaptions outstanding, as measured by the value of the underlying notional principal reported by the ISDA. The market grew at a compound annual rate of 11 percent from year-end 1989 to year-end 1991. The size of the caps, collars, and floors market is considerably larger, but as noted earlier, that market is experiencing only very slow growth. The relative growth pattern for swaptions was similar to that for caps, collars, and floors. U.S. dollar notional principal for swaptions dropped 9.5 percent from year-end 1990 to year-end 1991, while non–U.S. dollar notional principal surged 68 percent.

EQUITY-INDEX OPTIONS

Besides interest rates, over-the-counter options are written on equity indexes, foreign exchange rates, and commodity prices. Equity indexes have been particularly popular in the late 1980s and early 1990s, particularly the Japanese Nikkei 225. Japanese companies have sold equity-linked Eurobonds. These yen-denominated bonds carry Nikkei call options or warrants. Such warrants are sometimes referred to as *synthetic equity* because exposure to a foreign or domestic equity market is obtained without the costs (or privileges such as voting rights) that actual stock ownership entails. Transactions costs outside of U.S. equity markets can be a deterrent to international diversification. The synthetic equity market is estimated to have grown to $125 billion, as measured by notional principal, as of year-end 1991.[8]

As is often the case in financial markets, government regulation is often the impetus behind financial innovation (see Merton Miller 1986). The Japanese equity warrants are such an instance because, until 1990, Japanese insurance companies would not report appreciation on equity holdings as income. In the interest of producing additional income for policyholders, many insurance companies sold put and call options covered by their equity portfolios to foreign investors and speculators. Through 1990, before the collapse of the Japanese equity markets, Japanese equity warrants made up about 60 percent of all synthetic equity trading.[9] European pension funds and insurance companies have also turned to synthetic equity to circumvent accounting rules that limit their direct participation in equity markets. These rules prevent them from registering unrealized capital gains as income. However, buying a bond with an embedded equity call option allows these institutions to claim equity appreciation as fixed-interest income.[10]

Another form of over-the-counter synthetic equity is *asset allocation options*. Call options of this type allow portfolio managers to receive the greater of the return on two (or more) equity indexes, for example, the S&P 500 or the Nikkei 225. The asset allocation could also include choices between the performance of bond return and equity indexes.

The greatest problem with synthetic equity is the credit risk that a position in an equity-index option (or equity swap) entails. Instead of actually holding a diversified portfolio of stocks that generates a cumulative return by some future date, a derivative contract is held that mimics that return payoff. Receiving that return depends entirely on the solvency of the counterparty replicating the index return. Still, the principal of the underlying investment is not at risk, since it is not invested with the counterparty.

CURRENCY OPTIONS

There are standard European options on all major currencies available over the counter. Innovation influences options trading in the currencies markets as well. *Average-rate* (or *price*) *options* have become popular alternatives to standard options for many users in the foreign exchange market. These options are sometimes called *Asian options* because the investment bank that originated them did so out of its Tokyo office.[11] The most common type has a payoff that is determined by the difference between the exchange rate at maturity and the average exchange rate from a set earlier date to maturity. All terms are negotiable, and the options are cash settled. The option usually involves an arithmetic, rather than a geometric, average, although this formulation requires numerical approximations methods to price such options. Less common are floating-strike options, which compare the spot exchange rate at expiration to an average over past realized rates to set the strike price. Both types are examples of so-called path-dependent options because their payoffs depend on the particular history of underlying prices, not just the value at one point in time.

The Asian option is most useful for hedging a flow of purchases or sales over time in a foreign currency. In this respect, their use bears some resemblance to caps discussed above. In fact, there are no foreign currency caps per se, and a liquid market for strips of currency options does not exist. Asian options fill this niche. Caps or strips of options typically have payoffs that depend on the realized values of rates at reset dates, which may not coincide with the spot market transactions being hedged. For example, average-rate options would be preferred by importers who want to hedge their foreign exchange exposure from frequent purchases of foreign goods at prevailing exchange rates. An advantage of Asian options relative to caps or floors is that payoffs based on averages have lower volatility and hence will require a lower upfront premium payment.

Hybrid option constructions are just as feasible in foreign exchange as they are for the interest rate instruments discussed above. A long forward contract locks in a foreign exchange rate at a fixed rate. A forward can be modified to have a payoff similar to a standard call option, but without an upfront payment. Such an instrument is called a *break forward* because it allows the forward contract to be unwound or broken if the spot rate declines below a floor level. The break forward limits the loss to a long position when the spot rate falls below the break forward's rate at maturity. However, the trade-off on the upside is that the break-forward rate is higher than the corresponding standard forward rate, reflecting the cost of the protection (the call premium) and thereby reducing the payoff on the break forward relative to a standard forward.

A forward contract can be "collared" with the sale of a foreign exchange put option with strike above the forward rate and purchase of a call with strike below the forward rate. This combination of equal-value long low-strike call and short high-strike put has a payoff that looks like a forward contract with a cap set by a short put and a floor set by a long call. This over-the-counter instrument has been marketed with the name *range forward*. It has limited exposure on the upside and on the downside compared to a standard forward foreign exchange contract.

EXOTIC OPTIONS

Nonstandard option contracts are often referred to as *exotic options*. What is exotic today frequently becomes commonplace tomorrow. Caps and swaptions were once exotic. While hardly commonplace, instruments like break forwards and average-rate options have become less mysterious. Some exotic over-the-counter instruments eventually trade on organized exchanges. For example, in November 1991, the Chicago Board Options Exchange introduced capped call and put options (CAPS) on the S&P 100 and S&P 500, offering limited exposure to option writers.

Financial engineering techniques, using basic option building blocks, can structure contingent claims with all sorts of payoffs. Rubinstein (1991) and Conze and Viswanathan (1991) discuss a wide range of exotic option constructions and their valuation. The question is whether these over-the-counter options will find a niche in the marketplace. Will end users be willing to pay the price associated with customized instruments arising from the intermediary's costs of hedging the instruments and possibly from (temporary) monopoly profits that accrue to a novel product? Many types of over-the-counter options have become standard risk management tools. It seems safe to predict that innovation in option design and usage will continue.

NOTES

1. For brevity, the market for caps, collars, and floors will be simply referred to as the *caps market*.
2. The notional amount of principal is a sum used as the basis for the option payoff computation. Cap, collar, and floor agreements do not involve any exchange of principal.

3. Because the CME and most LIFFE Eurodollar futures are "cash settled," a $1 million deposit is rarely made, but instead only the difference between the current, or spot, LIBOR less the contracted LIBOR times the notional principal actually changes hands.
4. A Eurodollar futures price is actually an index value that equals 100 minus the "add-on" yield (three-month LIBOR). Thus, the futures price and add-on yield move inversely with each other. Both the add-on yield and the futures price are usually quoted in the financial press. For more detail on Eurodollar futures and short-term interest rate futures generally, see Kuprianov (1986).
5. The term *counterparty* is standard terminology for the other party in a swap, cap, floor, or collar agreement.
6. Another complication in using futures in a replicating portfolio is that futures contracts are marked to market daily. This may create cash flow problems since futures positions that lose value may be subject to frequent margin calls. Even though the replicating portfolio is used to hedge a cap, which matches it in value, the cash flows from the cap only come when it is sold and on interest payment dates.
7. The example given was described in terms of a "flow concept" of interest rate risk, that is, the impact of a change in interest rates on the net interest margin. Another way to view interest rate risk is in terms of a "stock concept," the change in the net worth of the firm. A parallel shift in the term structure of interest rates would reduce the value of an S&L's long-term mortgages more than it would reduce the value of its short-term liabilities. Net worth would be reduced or possibly turn negative. Purchasing a cap, an asset on the balance sheet, would offset loss of net worth (to some extent) because it would gain value as interest rates rise. For an exposition of this application of caps and how they hedge interest rate risk, see Spahr, Luytjes, and Edwards (1988).
8. Claire Makin, "Hedging Your Derivatives Doubts," *Institutional Investor,* December 1991, p. 114.
9. Saul Hansell, "Is the World Ready for Synthetic Equity?" *Institutional Investor,* August 1990, p. 58.
10. Makin, "Hedging," p. 116.
11. Krystyna Krzyzak, "Asian Elegance," *Risk* 3 (December 1989/January 1990), p. 30.

REFERENCES

Black, Fischer. "The Pricing of Commodity Contracts." *Journal of Financial Economics* 3 (January/March 1976), pp. 167–79.

Black, Fischer; Emanuel Derman; and William Toy. "A One-Factor Model of Interest Rates and Its Application to Treasury Bond Options." *Financial Analysts Journal,* January/February 1990, pp. 33–39.

Brown, Keith C., and Donald J. Smith. "Recent Innovations in Interest Rate Risk Management and the Reintermediation of Commercial Banking." *Financial Management* 17 (Winter 1988), pp. 45–58.

Conze, Antoine, and Viswanathan. "Path Dependent Options: The Case of Lookback Options." *Journal of Finance* 46 (December 1991), pp. 1893–907.

Cox, John C.; Jonathan E. Ingersoll; and Stephen A. Ross. "A Theory of the Term Structure of Interest Rates." *Econometrica* 53 (March 1985), pp. 385–407.

Cox, John C., and Mark Rubinstein. *Options Markets.* Englewood Cliffs, N.J.: Prentice Hall, 1985.

Hansell, Saul. "Is the World Ready for Synthetic Equity?" *Institutional Investor,* August 1990, pp. 55–61.

Heath, David; Robert Jarrow; and Andrew Morton. "Bond Pricing and the Term Structure of Interest Rates: A New Methodology for Contingent Claims Valuation." *Econometrica* 60 (January 1992), pp. 77–105.

Jarrow, Robert A., and Andrew Rudd. *Option Pricing.* Homewood, Ill.: Richard D. Irwin, 1983.

Krzyzak, Krystyna. "Asian Elegance." *Risk* 3 (December 1989/January 1990), p. 30ff.

Kuprianov, Anatoli. "Short-Term Interest Rate Futures." *Economic Review* (Federal Reserve Bank of Richmond), September/October 1986, pp. 12–26.

Makin, Claire. "Hedging Your Derivatives Doubts." *Institutional Investor,* December 1991, pp. 113–20.

Miller, Merton H. "Financial Innovation: The Last Twenty Years and the Next." *Journal of Financial and Quantitative Analysis* 21 (December 1986), pp. 459–71.

Rubinstein, Mark. "Exotic Options." Finance Working Paper No. 220, Walter A. Haas School of Business, University of California at Berkeley, 1991.

Spahr, Ronald W.; Jan E. Luytjes; and Donald G. Edwards. "The Impact of the Uses of Caps as Deposit Hedges for Financial Institutions." *Issues in Bank Regulation,* Summer 1988, pp. 17–23.

Tompkins, Robert. "The A–Z of Caps." *Risk* 2 (March 1989), pp. 21–23, 41.

CHAPTER 26

CHARACTERISTICS OF OTC OPTIONS

Kosrow Dehnad
Chase Securities, Inc.

Interest rate options are among the most important instruments for efficient management of interest rate risk. If selected and combined judiciously, they can provide vehicles for achieving diverse objectives such as hedging, speculating, or unbundling financial risk into various components. The latter is particularly important because it enables various market participants to assume the type of risk for which they have an appetite, thus making the market deeper and more efficient by increasing the number of participants.

As a brief illustration and a prelude to the applications we will discuss later, consider an investor who intends to buy a *LIBOR floater*. These are notes that pay a variable interest rate, namely LIBOR (London Interbank Offered Rate) plus a fixed spread, and the rate is reset, say, every three months. Should the investor have the view that LIBOR will most probably not exceed 8 percent over the next two years, he can use interest rate options to monetize this view and increase his yield. The investor will sell a cap on three-month LIBOR with a strike of 8 percent or more and use the cap premium to enhance the yield that he will receive on the floater. (See Figure 26–1.) Note that there is no "free lunch" in an efficient market; in this case, the investor is merely being compensated for assuming the risk of LIBOR rising above the cap strike and being stuck with a piece of paper that pays a below-market rate.

The example above was a simple use of interest rate options.

FIGURE 26–1
Capped Floater

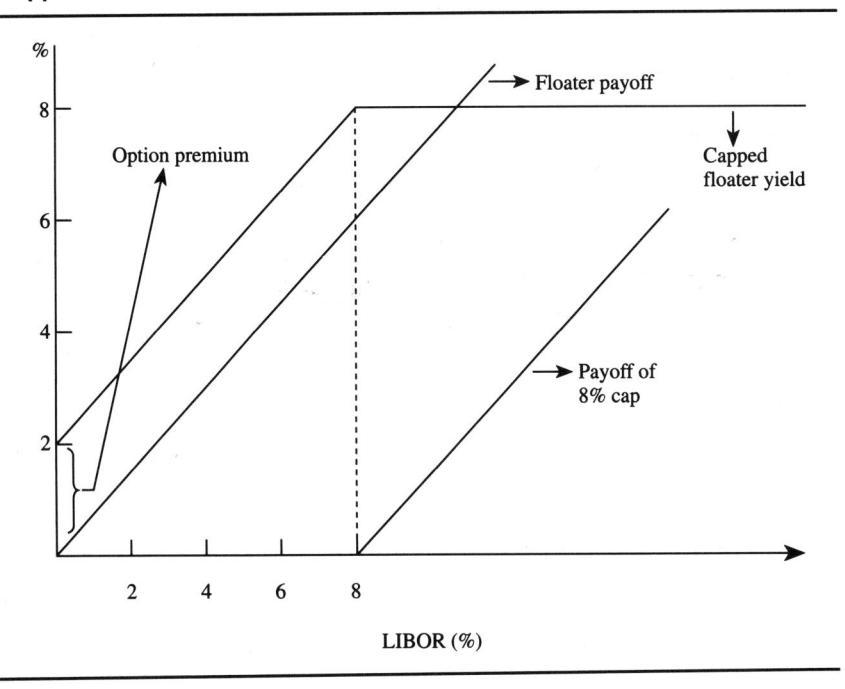

%
8
Option premium
6
4
2

Floater payoff
Capped floater yield
Payoff of 8% cap

2 4 6 8
LIBOR (%)

There are a large number of such products and structures in the market, and new ones are being introduced every day. This chapter deals with the salient points of interest rate caps and floors and some of their variations and applications. The chapter starts with a description and pricing mechanism of the standard "plain-vanilla" caps and floors. Next, it discusses the relationship between caps, floors, and swaps. The final section of the chapter discusses more complex products and structures like barrier options, cumulative caps, or options on the shape of the yield curve.

INTEREST RATE CAPS AND FLOORS

A standard plain-vanilla *cap* is a strip of (or series of sequentially maturing) European call options (or caplets) on an interest rate index, say, LIBOR. For example, a 9 percent two-year cap on

**FIGURE 26-2
Cap Payoff**

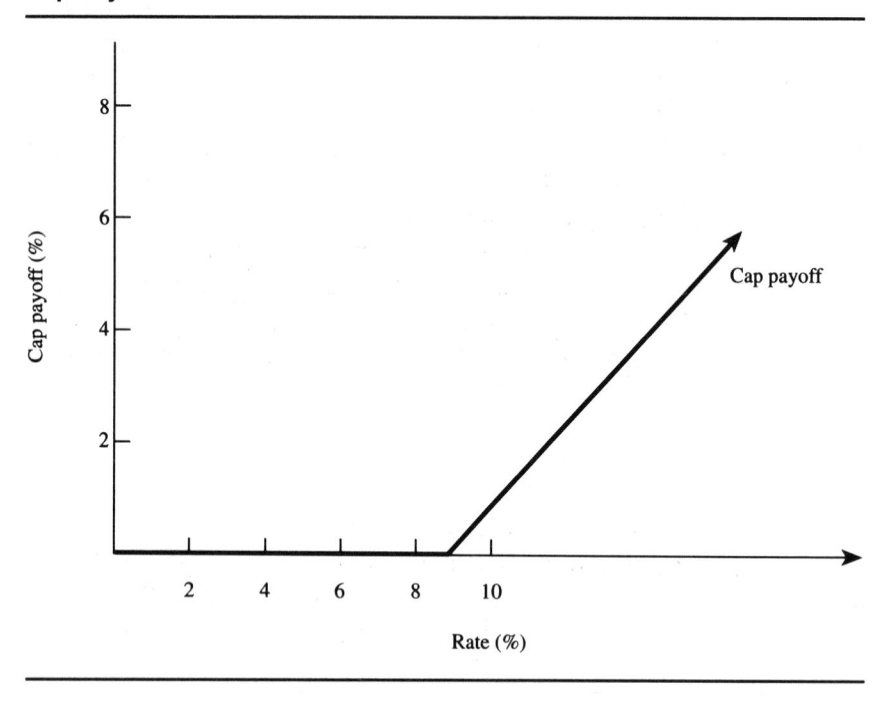

(figure: Cap payoff vs Rate (%), showing zero payoff until ~9% then linear increase labeled "Cap payoff")

three-month LIBOR, denoted by $L(3)$, on a notional amount of $100 million will have the following payoffs. For the next two years, every three months the $L(3)$ setting is compared with the strike of 9 percent. Should the setting exceed the strike, the buyer receives the difference in terms of the interest on the notional amount for the period corresponding to that LIBOR setting.

($100 million) (Number of days in the three months/360)
$$\{\text{Max } [0, L(3) - 9\%]\} = \text{Difference}$$

Figure 26–2 shows the payoff profile of a 9 percent caplet.

Similarly, a standard plain-vanilla *floor* is a strip of European put options (floorlets) on an interest rate index. For example, a 7 percent two-year floor on $L(3)$ for a notional amount of $100 million will have a specified payoff. At each resetting, for the next two years, $L(3)$ is compared with the floor strike of 7 percent. Should the setting be smaller than 7 percent, the buyer will receive the following difference:

($100 million) (Number of days in the three months/360)
$\{\text{Max } [0, 7\% - L(3)]\} = \text{Difference}$

Figure 26–3 illustrates the payoff profile of a 7 percent floorlet.

The above payoffs are usually made at the end of the period when the caplet or the floorlet is in the money. The buyer and the seller of the option, however, can agree on a discount rate and settle at the start of the period.

The interest rate index for caps and floors is not limited to LIBOR. Some of the other indexes are the commercial paper rate (CP), fed funds rate, Constant Maturity Treasury rate (CMT), and the prime rate. The important point to remember is that some of these indexes are the averages of daily rates. For example, in the case of a CP cap, the value that is compared with the cap strike is

FIGURE 26–3
Floor Payoff

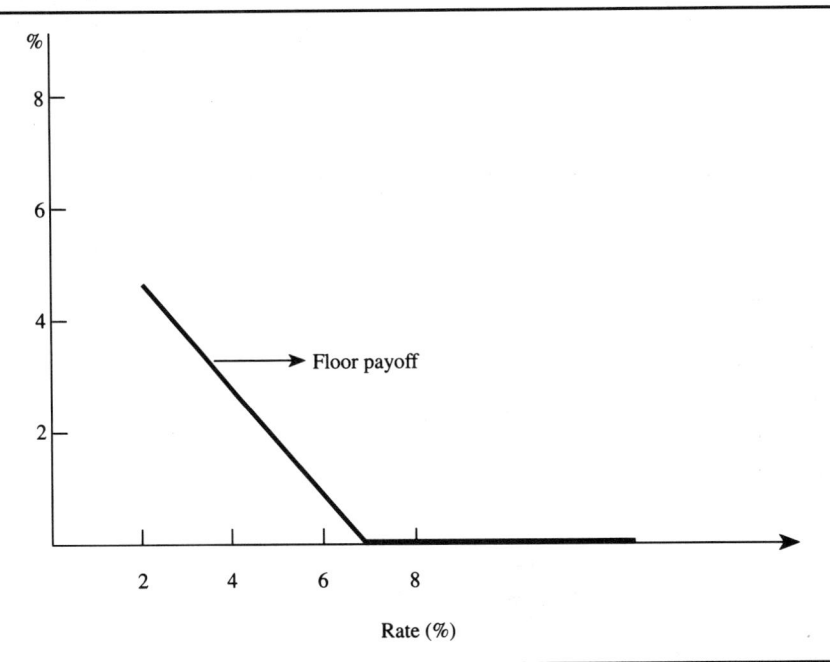

the average of daily CP rates over a caplet period. In this case, if Saturday and Sunday rates are included in the averaging process and are taken to be that of Friday's rates, then the average gives more weight to the Friday rates than other days. Consequently, it is imperative at the time of a trade to spell out explicitly the treatment of weekends, holidays, end of months, settlement procedure, sources of data for the index (such as Telerate or Reuter screens), and any other "loose ends."

PRICING OF CAPS AND FLOORS

Since a standard cap is a series of European options (or caplets), its price is simply the sum of the prices of these caplets. Therefore, the pricing of a cap reduces to calculating the price of its caplets. Current pricing methodologies are based on the Black-Scholes approach to pricing of options with the caveat that in their model the interest rate used for discounting is assumed to be constant. In this case, however, the discounting rate and the underlying index (that is, the interest rate) are highly correlated. And for long-dated or deep out-of-the money options, this point should be taken into consideration. There are also a number of approaches to modeling of the term structure of interest rates that are used in the pricing of interest rate options. In practice, trading houses modify these models and add bells and whistles to them based on their trading experience, risk appetite, and type of trades.

The basic idea behind the pricing is as follows. Consider a two-year 7 percent cap on $L(6)$. Given the current price of various financial instruments (such as Eurodollar futures, LIBOR, Treasuries, and swap rates), we compute the forward $L(6)$ rates for the reset days. These rates are viewed as unbiased estimates of the six-month LIBOR on reset days. If we assume that the difference of the logarithm of the rates is normally distributed (lognormality assumptions), then a future reset rate will have a distribution with a mean equal to the corresponding forward rate and a standard deviation that depends on the volatility of the $L(6)$. This standard deviation reflects the uncertainty concerning future rates and increases with the time to maturity of a caplet. (See Figure 26–4.)

The "fair value" of a caplet is the present value of its expected

FIGURE 26-4
Cap Pricing

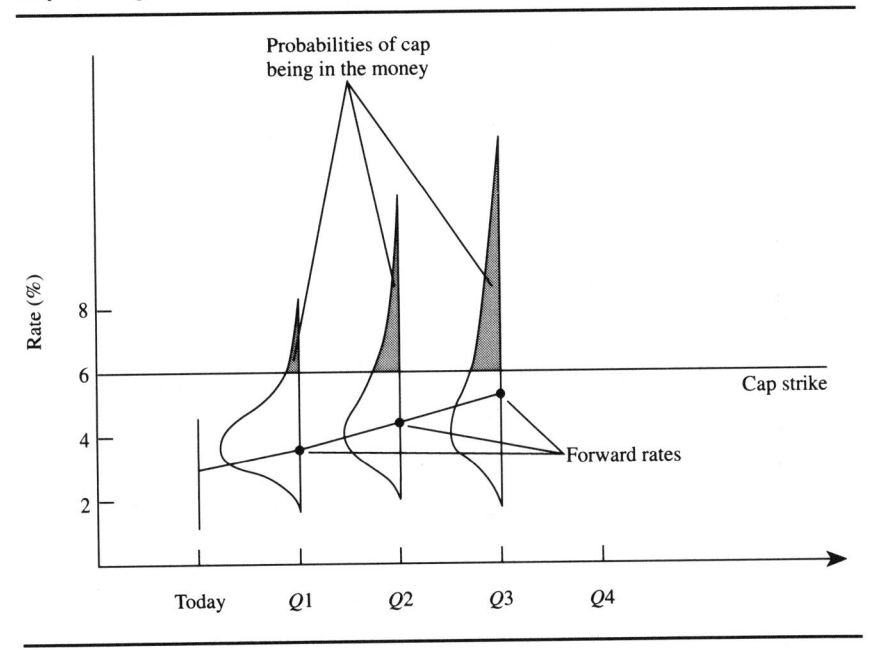

payoff. (The shaded areas in Figure 26-4 show the rates that would put the caplets in the money.) Formally, the expected payoff of each caplet at maturity can be written as shown below, where dF represents the expected changes in the forward rate.

$$\text{Expected payoff} = \int_{\text{strike}}^{\infty} (\text{Rate} - \text{Strike}) dF(\text{Rate})$$

And the fair value of a caplet is the present value of its expected payoff. Having calculated the fair value of each caplet, the value of a cap is the sum of these present values.

It follows from the above discussion that the higher the strike, the lower the price of the cap because there is a lower probability that the caplets will be in the money. (See Figure 26-4.) Conversely, the steeper the yield curve, the higher the cap price because a steeper yield curve makes it more probable that the caplets will be in the money (see Figure 26-4). Similarly, the cap price increases with the tenor because a longer tenor includes more

FIGURE 26–5
Impact of Volatility on Cap Prices

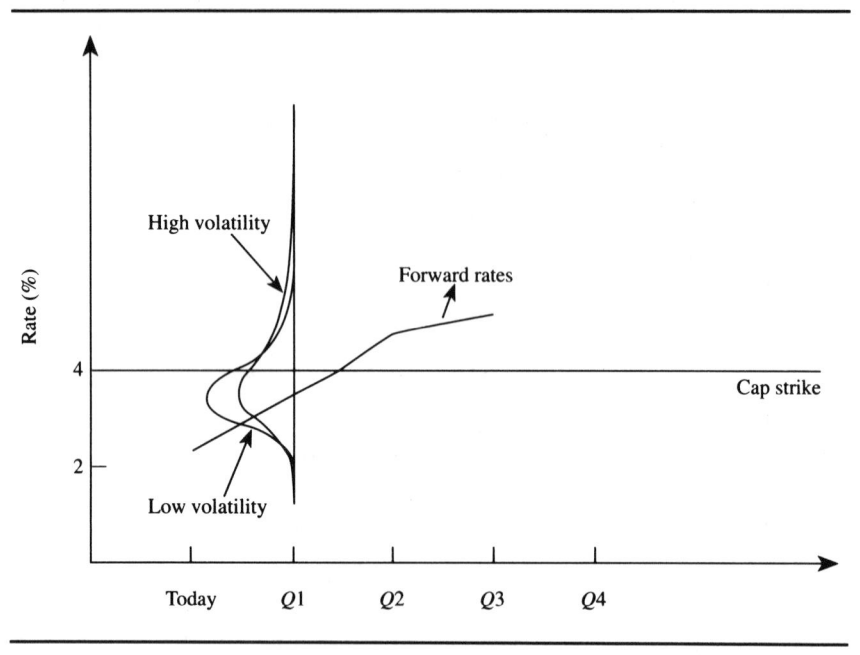

caplets. Finally, the price of a cap and volatility move in the same direction. Higher volatility flattens the probability distribution of interest rates, thus increasing the probability that a caplet will be in the money, which, in turn, increases the cap price (see Figure 26–5).

In fact, in the market, the cap bid-ask spread reflects the *volatility* that traders use to price their interest rate options. When buying a cap, they use a low volatility in their model to price that cap, and, conversely, when selling an option, they use a high volatility. And they talk about being short or long volatility when they are short or long options, respectively.

Similar analysis applies to interest rate floors with the obvious adjustments. For example, the price of a floor increases when the yield curve flattens or inverts. Finally, all the definitions and concepts of option pricing like delta, gamma, kappa (vega), and theta (time decay) apply to interest rate options (see Cox and Rubinstein 1985).

SOME APPLICATIONS

The typical application of caps is to provide protection against interest rate increases. Suppose a company has a two-year floating interest rate obligation that is reset quarterly at the prime rate. Clearly, a significant rise in the prime rate will greatly increase the company's interest payments, and might even put it in distress. As a preventive measure, the company can buy a two-year 9 percent prime cap, thus limiting its interest payments to 9 percent. Figure 26–6 compares the company's interest rate exposure in the presence and absence of the cap.

Caps with Varying Notational Amount

The interest rate risk exposure of an entity can vary over time. A typical example is a construction project financed with a line of

FIGURE 26–6
Prime Cap

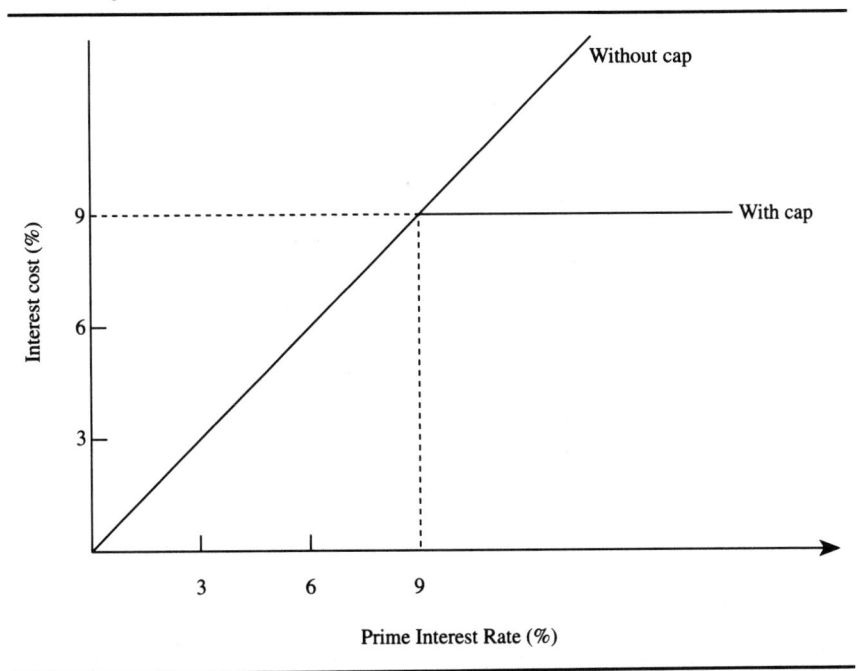

credit. In this case, the outstanding balance on which the interest is paid increases as the construction project progresses. After the completion of the project, the balance due is amortized during the payoff period that follows. Consequently, the cap that provides protection against rises in interest rates in this case will have a variable notional amount according to the dollar amount of the debt's draw down and the payoff schedule.

Step-Up Caps

Step-up caps are structures that are particularly attractive in a steep yield curve environment. In such an environment, the implied forward rate is generally much higher than the current spot rate. Since the price of a cap is the sum of the price of its caplets, and the underlying asset in pricing a caplet is the forward interest rate for that period, it could happen that for a given strike certain caplets are deep in the money and thus very expensive (see Figure 26–7).

A step-up cap remedies the above problem by raising the

FIGURE 26–7
Step-Up Cap

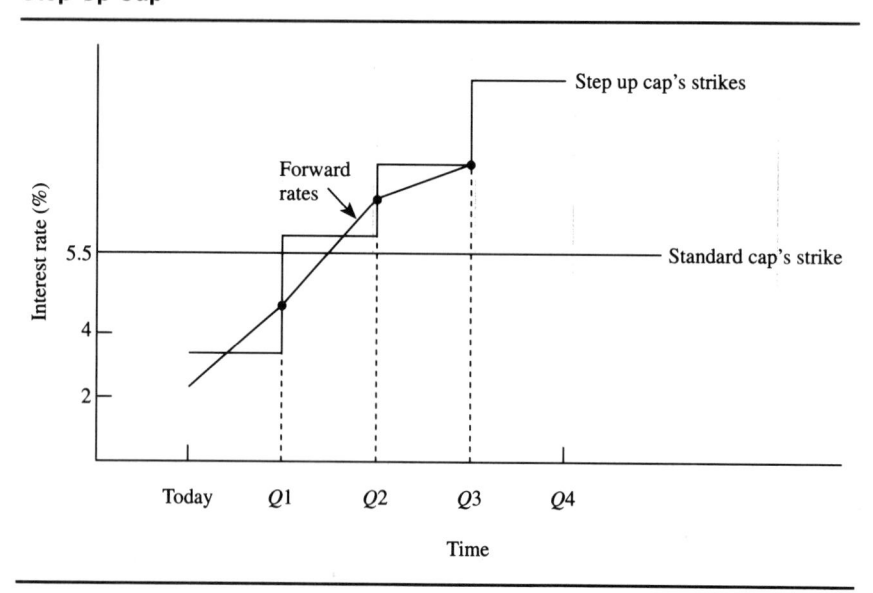

strike of those caplets that correspond to high forward rates. For illustration, consider the following table that gives the forward rates for $L(3)$ and the prices of a standard cap and a step-up cap. The standard cap has the fixed strike of 5.5 percent, and the strikes for the step-up cap are given under the column headed "Cap Strike."

	Standard Caps		Step-up Caps	
Forward Rate	Cap Strike	Caplet's Price	Cap Strike	Caplet's Price
4.563	5.5	0.0	4.6	0.0
4.913	5.5	0.7	5.1	2.7
4.697	5.5	1.0	5.2	2.1
4.830	5.5	2.5	5.3	3.6
5.119	5.5	5.7	5.5	5.7
5.619	5.5	12.5	5.7	10.3
5.883	5.5	17.1	6.0	11.4
6.302	5.5	24.5	6.5	12.4
		Total 64.0		48.2
	Standard cap price = 64.0 bps		Step-up cap price = 48.2 bps	

The step-up cap is 25 percent cheaper than the 5.5 percent standard cap because its last three caplets with strikes of 5.7, 6.0, and 6.5 percent are out of the money in view of the forward rates of 5.619, 5.883, and 6.302 percent, respectively. For the 5.5 percent standard cap, the same caplets are in the money and thus more expensive.

Reducing Swap Rate

Caps are used to reduce the swap rate in a floating-to-fixed-rate swap. Suppose a company has a three-year LIBOR (floating rate) liability and is concerned about rising short-term rates. It can either buy a cap or enter into a floating-to-fixed-rate swap (see Fig. 26–8).

**FIGURE 26–8
Swap**

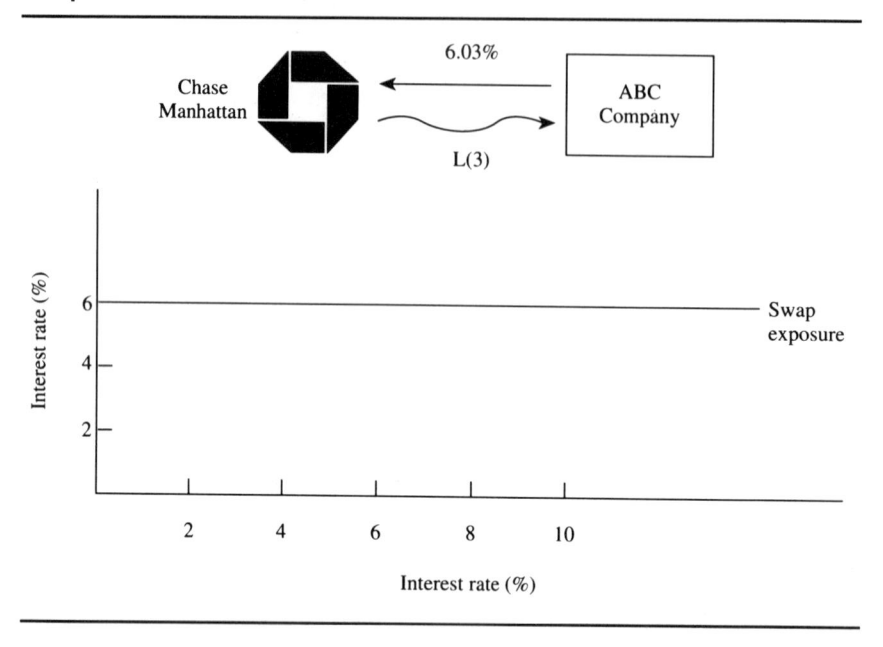

```
                    6.03%
    Chase    ←──────────────    ABC
  Manhattan  ──────────────→   Company
                     L(3)
```

Interest rate (%) — Swap exposure

Interest rate (%)

If the yield curve is very steep, then at the start of the swap, the company will have a large negative carry. Stated differently, in the beginning months, the company will be paying a fixed rate that is much higher than the floating rate. For example, the fixed rate might be a 6.03 percent annual money market rate versus a LIBOR of 4 percent (these are actual market conditions on June 6, 1992). If the company has the view that the rates will rise but not to the extent implied by the yield curve, then it can sell, say, an 8 percent cap and use its premium to reduce the swap rate. The company, in this case, is bearing the risk that the rates will rise above the cap strike of 8 percent and its liability will become floating again (see Figure 26–9).

The notional amount of the cap in the above example was assumed to be the same as that of the swap. This notional amount can, however, be a multiple of the swap's if the company desires to further reduce the fixed rate that it will be paying in the swap.

FIGURE 26–9
Capped Swap

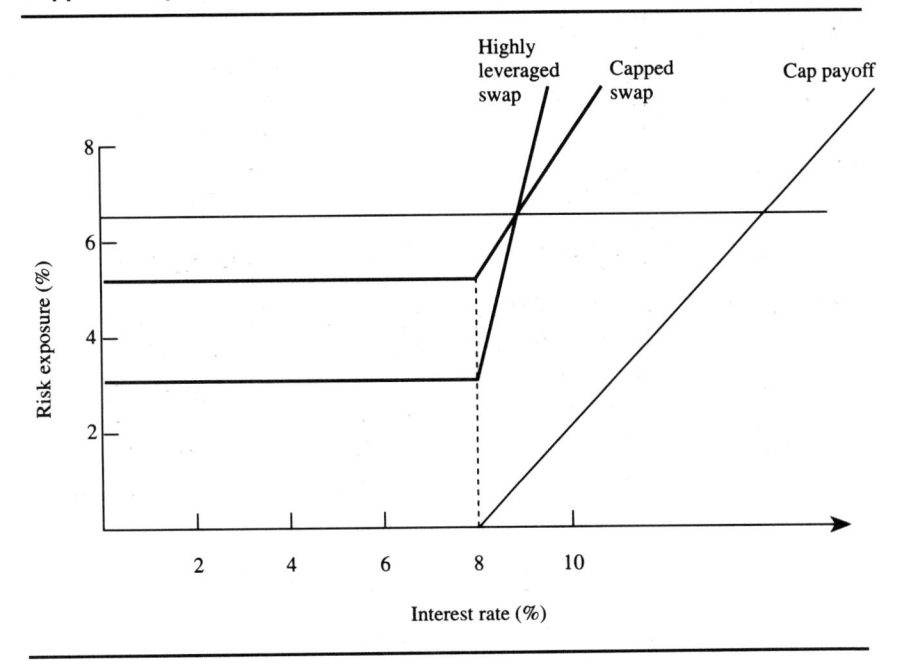

Figure shows risk exposure (%) vs interest rate (%), with lines labeled "Highly leveraged swap," "Capped swap," and "Cap payoff."

Clearly, this additional savings is achieved at the risk of having a greater interest rate exposure for rates above 8 percent (see Figure 26–9).

Corridors

Corridors are financial structures in which the cost of purchasing a cap is partially offset through the sale of another cap at a higher strike. For example, a floating-rate borrower who purchases an 8 percent cap to protect itself against rises in the interest rate can at the same time sell a 10 percent cap to reduce its cost. The caveat is that the borrower is not protected against rises in the interest rate above 10 percent (see Figure 26–10). The borrower can even offset all her cost if she is prepared to take additional risk and increase the notional amount of the 10 percent cap so the price of the two caps are equal.

**FIGURE 26–10
Corridor**

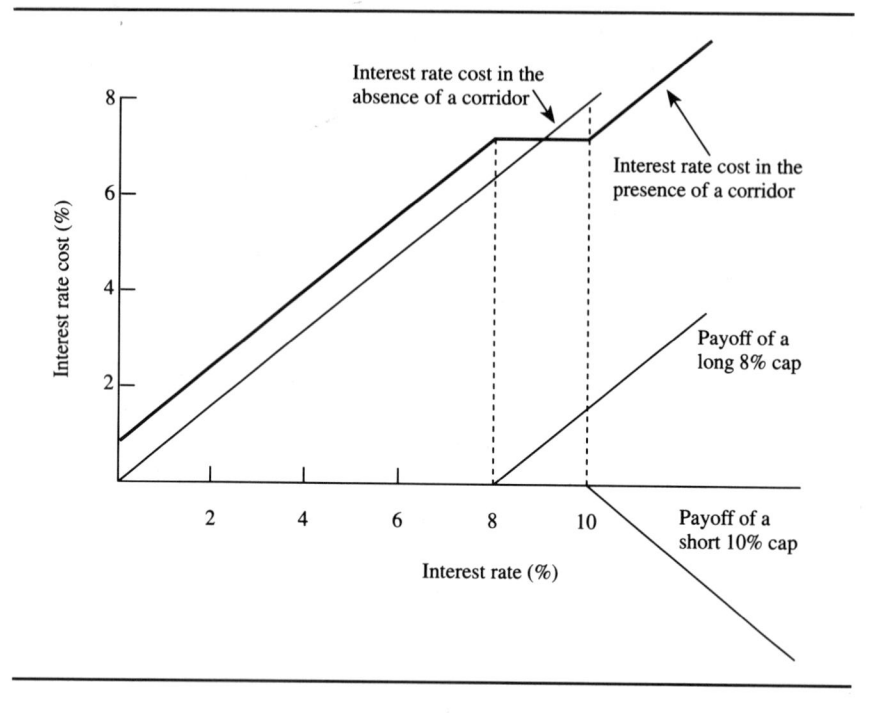

[Graph: Interest rate cost (%) on y-axis vs Interest rate (%) on x-axis. Shows interest rate cost in the absence of a corridor (diagonal line), interest rate cost in the presence of a corridor (flat between 8% and 10%), payoff of a long 8% cap, and payoff of a short 10% cap.]

Floors

A typical application of interest rate floors is to guarantee a minimum rate of return on an asset. For example, a finance company with assets earning the prime rate will experience a drop in the return from these assets should the prime rate fall. To protect itself, the company can buy a floor to ensure that the return will not fall below the floor's strike level. Figure 26–11 shows the return on the asset in the presence and absence of a floor with 5.5 percent strike.

Lowering Cost of Fund

Assets with returns that are inversely related to short-term rates are particularly attractive to investors in a falling-rate environment. Suppose $L(3)$ is 8 percent and a company can issue a two-year floating-rate note at LIBOR + 50 bps. In a falling-rate envi-

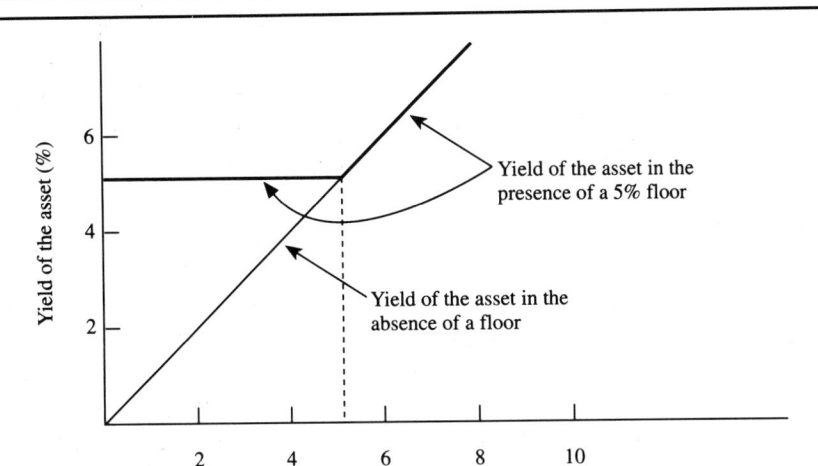

FIGURE 26-11
Asset Return in the Presence of a Floor

ronment, the investors might be wary of a drop in LIBOR that causes a fall in the return on their investment. The company can use this concern to lower its borrowing cost by selling to the investors, say, a 6 percent floor with twice the notional amount of the borrowing. The premium will be used to lower the company's borrowing cost. In return, the investors will receive a return of 12.5 − LIBOR = [2 × (6 − LIBOR) + LIBOR + .5] = (12.5 − LIBOR) on their investment should LIBOR fall below 6 percent (see Figure 26–12).

Collars and Zero-Cost Collars

Collars are similar to corridors where the cost of purchasing a cap is offset through the sale of another option, namely, a floor. If the cap and the floor have the same price, the structure is called a *zero-cost collar*. The downside of this structure is that should the rates fall below the floor strike level, the purchaser of the cap will have to pay the buyer of the floor the difference. See Figure 26–13 for the payoff of a collar with a cap of 8 percent and a floor of 5 percent. Collars are more frequently used than corridors because

**FIGURE 26-12
Floored Floater**

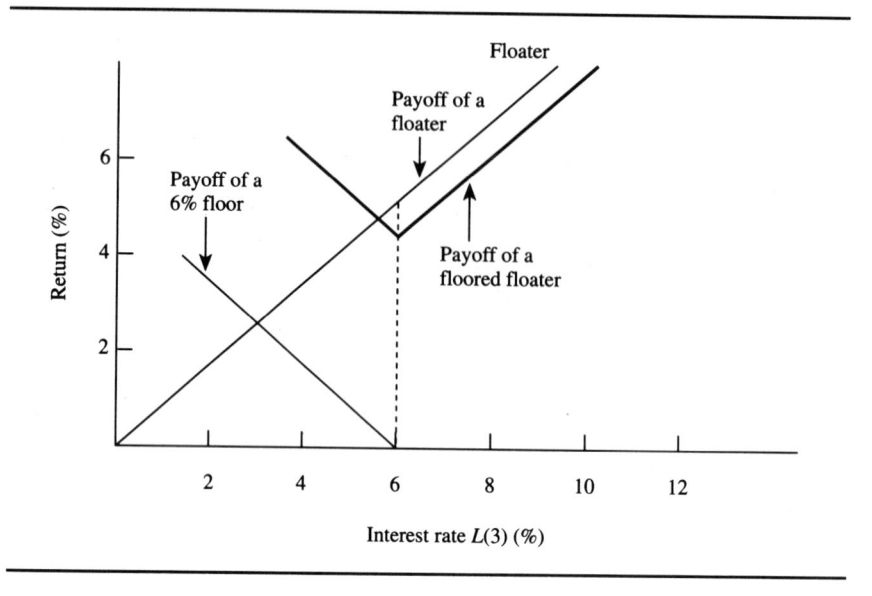

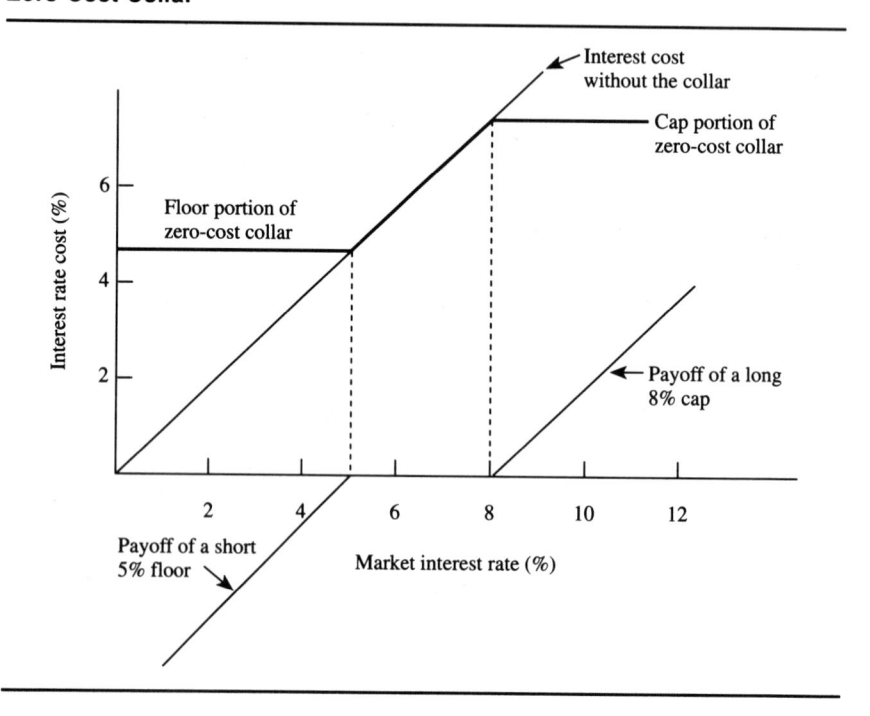

**FIGURE 26-13
Zero-Cost Collar**

FIGURE 26–14
Reverse Zero-Cost Collar

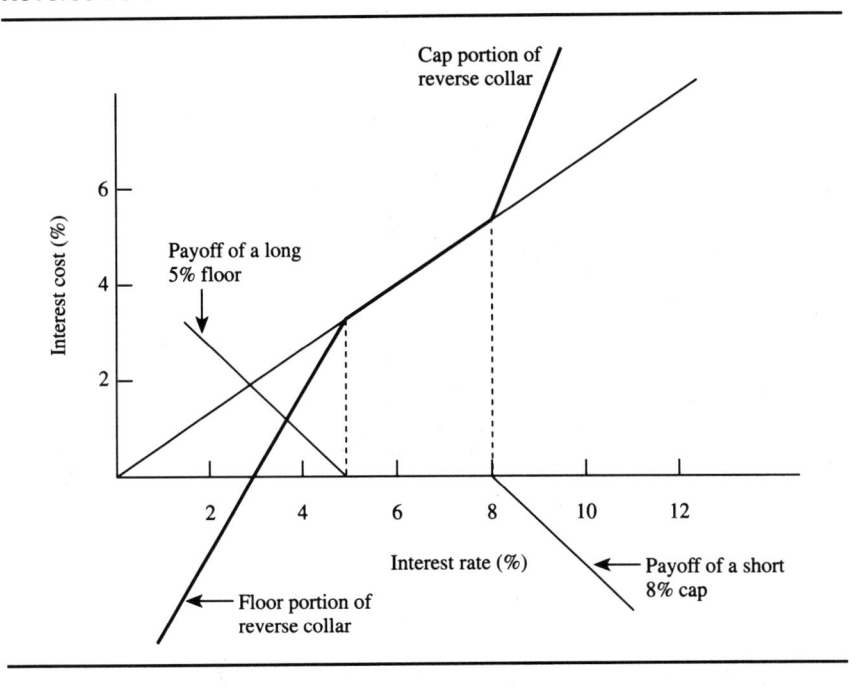

the purchaser of a cap is of the opinion that the rates will rise and is thus more disposed to sell a floor than a cap.

Similarly, a *reverse collar* consists of selling a cap and buying a floor. This structure is usually attractive in a falling-rate environment. The payoff of such a structure is illustrated in Figure 26–14.

Center Lock

Center lock is similar to a reverse collar with the difference that the cap and floor cover different periods of time. A typical application of this structure is when a company issues, say, 10-year fixed-rate debt and wants to benefit from a possible fall in the interest rates in the first two years. The company buys a two-year floor and pays for it through the sale of a two-year deferred cap that goes into effect at the start of Year 9.

FIGURE 26–15
Relationship of a Zero-Cost Collar and a Swap

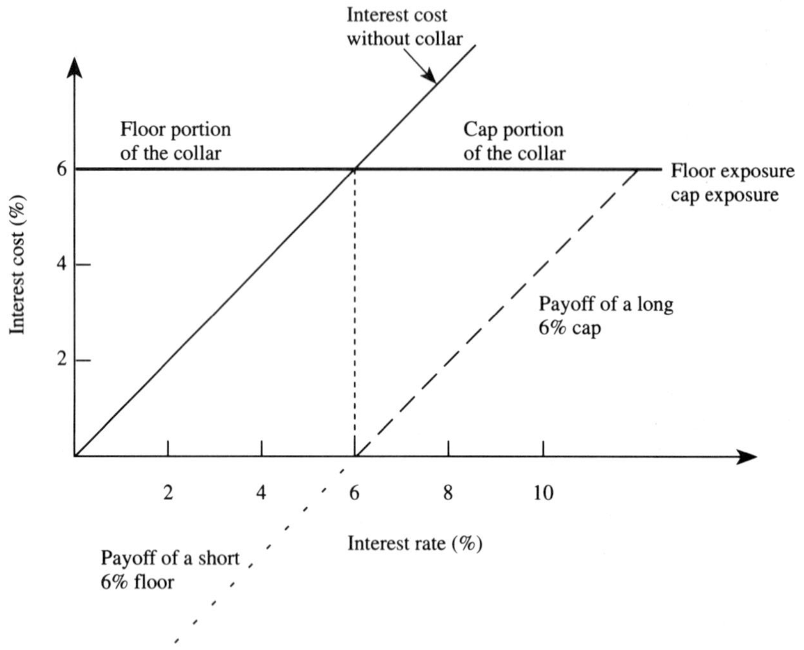

COLLARS AND SWAPS

As Figure 26–15 shows, a floating-rate borrower that buys a cap and a floor with the same strike is essentially fixing the interest rate that must be paid. If the rates go above the strike level, the cap will be in the money and the borrower's interest rate becomes the strike level. On the other hand, if the rates fall below the strike level, the floor will be in the money and the borrower has to compensate the buyer of the floor for the difference. This will increase the borrower's cost to that of the strike level. In other words, no matter where the floating rate is, the borrower's cost will always equal the strike level. This transaction is very much like a floating-to-fixed-rate swap. In fact, a swap is nothing but a zero-cost collar with the cap and the floor having the same strike as the swap rate. Similarly, a fixed-to-floating-rate swap is a zero-cost reverse collar with the cap and floor having the same strike as the swap rate.

FIGURE 26–16
An Interest Rate Cap as a Low-Pass Filter

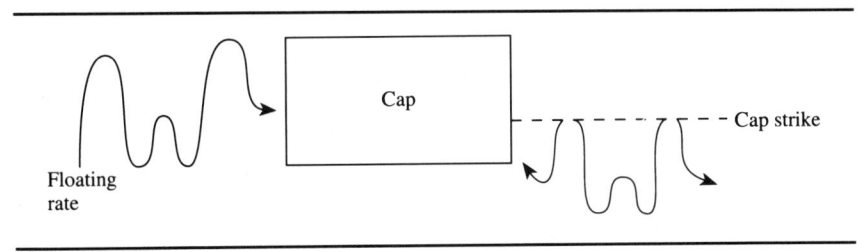

In fact, caps and floors can be schematically represented as "filters." A cap is a *low-pass filter* that lets rates lower than its strike pass unaltered while truncating rates higher than its strike to the strike level (see Figure 26–16). On the other hand, a floor is a *high-pass filter* that passes the rates above its strike level and reconfigures the lower rates to that of its strike (see Figure 26–17).

Increasing or decreasing the notional amount of the caps and floors only accentuates the dollar impact of the filter. A great number of interest rate structures are essentially combinations of various filters. For illustration, consider a *participating cap*—simply a swap together with a floor. In this structure, the fixed-rate payer also purchases a floor with a strike lower than the swap rate and a notional amount that reflects the degree of participation. Consequently, if the rates fall below the floor strike level, the fixed-rate payer will benefit from this fall with the size of the benefit depending on the notional amount of the floor (see Figure 26–18).

FIGURE 26–17
An Interest Floor as a High-Pass Filter

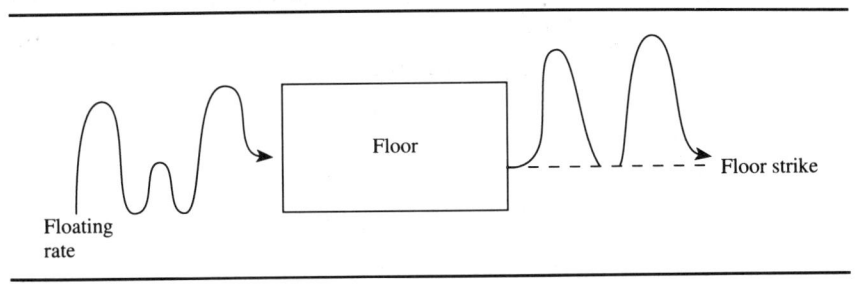

**FIGURE 26–18
Participating Cap**

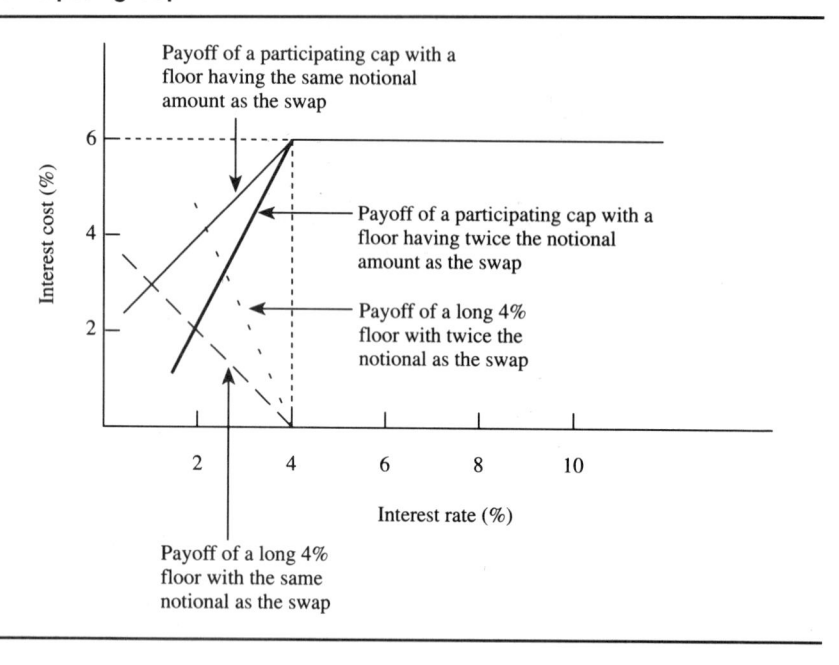

Payoff of a participating cap with a floor having the same notional amount as the swap

Payoff of a participating cap with a floor having twice the notional amount as the swap

Payoff of a long 4% floor with twice the notional as the swap

Payoff of a long 4% floor with the same notional as the swap

CAPTIONS, FLOORTIONS, SPREADTIONS, AND YIELD CURVE OPTIONS

Captions and *floortions* are options on caps and floors (that is, they are compound options, or an option on another option). They have a relatively small market, and their pricing and hedging are rather complicated.

Spreadtions are options on swap spreads. For example, a three-month option on a bid spread of 42 basis points for a two-year swap gives its buyer the right to enter into a swap in three months. Should the buyer decide to exercise the option, the buyer will receive the floating index, say, $L(3)$, and pay a fixed rate, which will be 42 bps plus the yield of the two-year on-the-run Treasury security at that time.

Options on the difference between the two points on a yield curve are called *yield curve options*. The most commonly used yield curve is that of the Treasuries. For example, a yield curve call option with a strike of 250 bps on the difference between the yields of the 2-year, $T(2)$, and 10-year, $T(10)$, Treasuries will have the following payoff at the time of exercise:

$$\text{Max}\{0, [T(10) - T(2)] - 250\} \times \text{Notional amount} = \text{Payoff}$$

SWAPTIONS

Swaptions are options on swap rates. For example, a six-month into a three-year payer swaption at the strike of 6.28 percent annual money market rate against $L(3)$ gives the buyer the right to enter into a three-year swap in six months in which the buyer will receive a fixed rate of 6.28 percent and will be paying the three-month LIBOR. Combining a swap with a swaption results in a *cancelable* or *extendable* swap.

A typical application of swaptions is in the "monetization" of a call. Suppose a company issues a 10-year bond callable in 5 years with a coupon of 10 percent. After three years, suppose the company finds itself in a very attractive low-rate environment and wishes to call the bonds and issue new ones with lower coupons. The call date, however, is two years away and there is a chance that by then the rates might no longer be attractive. The company can still take advantage of the low-rate environment by selling a two-year-into-five-year *receiver swaption* of, say, 9 percent (semi-annual bond). Since the option would be in the money, the seller would receive a substantial premium. On the expiration of the swaption, which is the same as the call date, if the rates are high, the swaption would not be exercised and the issuer will keep the premium whether the bonds are called or not. If the rates are low and the swaption is exercised, the bond will also be called and new ones issued at a lower coupon, then swapped into floating resulting in a floating rate of, say, LIBOR + 50 bps. The effective funding rate would then be 9.5 percent minus the option premium. In either case, the issuer would be better off to take advantage of the current low-rate environment and monetize the call through selling a swaption and thereby avoiding the risk of high rates on the call date. The important question for the issuer is to strike a balance between the swaption rate and the premium received based on forecasted future rates and the company's risk appetite.

PATH-DEPENDENT OPTIONS

A good way to discuss *path-dependent options* is through an example. Consider a standard two-year cap on the interest rate $L(3)$. The question whether, say, the third caplet is in the money or not depends only on the LIBOR setting for the third period and does not depend on previous LIBOR settings. In other words, whether the third caplet is in the money or not depends only on the LIBOR setting of that period and is independent of the path that LIBOR has taken to reach that setting; this is called *path independence*.

On the other hand, consider the working of a one-year "average cap" on $L(3)$. The payoff of this cap is based on comparing the cap strike with the average of the LIBOR settings for each of the four caplets. If this average is above the strike level, then the four caplets will be viewed as being in the money with the appropriate payoff. Otherwise, the whole cap expires out of the money. For illustration, suppose the cap strike is 6.5 percent and the following are the LIBOR settings for the four caplets:

$$6.5\%, 6.75\%, 7.125\%, 6.625\%$$

The cap is in the money because the average of these settings

$$6.625 = (6.5 + 6.75 + 7.125 + 6.6.25)/4$$

is above the cap strike. Clearly, whether the cap is in the money or not depends on each LIBOR setting, that is, the path of the LIBOR. For example, if the third setting was 4.5, then the cap would be out of the money.

The *cumulative cap (Q-Cap)*[1] is another example of a path-dependent option. Consider the interest payment on a loan of $1 million for two years with the interest rate being set quarterly at $L(3)$. The borrower can limit this quarterly interest to 8 percent by purchasing a two-year standard cap with the strike of 8 percent. Suppose, however, the primary goal is to limit his annual interest payment to $80,000, that is, 8 percent. A standard cap meets the objective. In such a case, however, the buyer is paying for protection or a limit on each quarterly interest payment when, in fact, they should only be sensitive to the annual expense. Q-Caps provide the type of protection the borrower is seeking. In the case of an 8 percent Q-Cap, the quarterly interest expense during the protection period (namely, the four quarters) is accumulated. When this sum reaches the limit of $80,000, from then till the end of that period, the seller of the Q-Cap compensates the buyer for the excess interest expense that the buyer incurs. The workings of an 8 percent Q-Cap are illustrated in Table 26–1.

In this example, the seller of a Q-Cap compensates the buyer as soon as the cumulative interest in a protection period (that is, a year) exceeds the limit of $80,000. This occurs at the fourth quarter in the first period and the third quarter in the second period.

Note that the standard cap is a special case of a Q-Cap where

TABLE 26–1
Illustration of an 8 Percent Q-Cap on a $1 Million Loan

	Period I			
	Quarter 1 (Q1)	Quarter 2 (Q2)	Quarter 3 (Q3)	Quarter 4 (Q4)
Three-month LIBOR	7%	9%	9%	8%
	Period II			
	Q1	Q2	Q3	Q4
Three-month LIBOR	12%	13%	12%	10%
	Period I			
	Q1	Q2	Q3	Q4
Quarterly interest	$17,500	$22,500	$22,500	$20,000
Cumulative interest	17,500	40,000	62,500	82,500
Q-Cap payment	0	0	0	2,500
Quarterly expense	17,500	22,500	22,500	17,500
	Period II			
	(Q1)	(Q2)	(Q3)	(Q4)
Quarterly interest	$30,000	$32,500	$30,000	$25,000
Cumulative interest	30,000	62,500	92,500	117,500
Q-Cap payment	0	0	12,500	25,000
Quarterly expense	30,000	32,500	17,500	0

TABLE 26-2
Two-Year Cap Prices (bps)

Strike	Standard Cap	Q-Cap	Net Savings	Percent Savings
8.5	46	39	7	15%
9.0	26	21	5	19%
9.5	15	11	4	27%

the protection period coincides with that of the resetting of the interest rate for the standard cap. Clearly, a Q-Cap costs less than the standard cap, and the savings depend on the structure of interest rates, the tenor, the protection periods, the strike, and the volatility of interest rates. A sample of such savings, based upon the prevailing market conditions at the time of the preparation of this document, is in Table 26–2.

DOWN-AND-OUT AND UP-AND-IN CAPS

Up-and-in and *down-and-out* caps are two other examples of path-dependent barrier options. In the case of an up-and-in cap, the buyer will have a cap if the rates reach a certain limit. For example, a two-year 9 percent cap on $L(3)$ will become effective anytime $L(3)$ is set at or above a barrier, say, 12 percent. Similarly, for a down-and-out cap, the option ceases to exist as soon as the rates fall below a certain level. For example, the buyer of a 9 percent cap loses the option if anytime during the life of the cap, $L(3)$ is set below a barrier of, say, 5 percent. These barrier conditions are all attempts to reduce the option premium.

TRIGGER OPTIONS

Trigger options are generalizations of up-and-in and down-and-out options. In these structures, whether an option is in the money also depends on the value of another index. A typical example of a

FIGURE 26–19
Delta of a Barrier Option

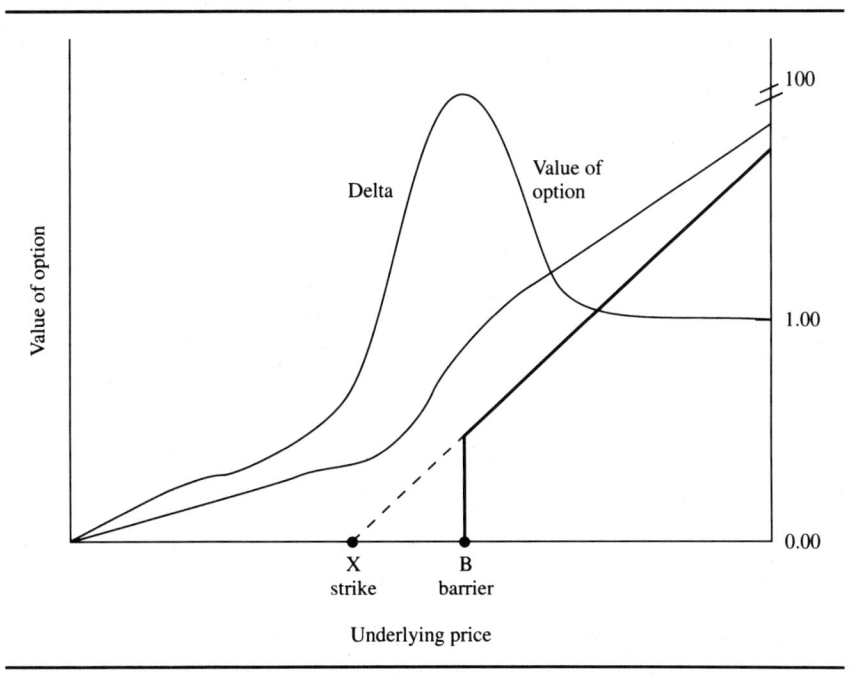

trigger option is the *barrier cap*. The working of a two-year 9 percent barrier cap on $L(3)$ with the barrier of 10 percent is analyzed next.

On a *reset date*, which is every quarter in this case, if $L(3)$ is less than the barrier, that is, 10 percent, the caplet is dead (or worthless) even though $L(3)$ could be, say, 9.75, which is greater than the strike of 9 percent. Should $L(3)$ be equal to or greater than the barrier, then the caplet is alive and the buyer will have a caplet of 9 percent. Figure 26–19 shows the payoff profile of this option. Clearly, the price of this option will be between those of 9 percent and 10 percent plain-vanilla caps.

Another example of the option is a cap with a trigger depending on the gold price. Namely, each caplet will be alive if the price of gold is above a certain level. This particular structure would be appealing to a gold mining company interested in selling interest rate options to generate income. By linking the cap to the price of gold, the company ensures that when the cap is in the money, the revenue of the company is also high, and it is thereby in a better financial position. These options are harder to hedge, particularly when they involve two or more assets, because they also involve the correlations between the prices of the assets. Estimation of these correlations can be quite complicated. Further, when the value of the index is close to the trigger, the value of the option can jump. If so, the jump causes very large delta hedge ratios.

To give a flavor of the type of difficulties that one might encounter in trying to hedge trigger options, consider the question of *delta hedging* of the barrier cap described above when LIBOR is close to the trigger level. For illustration, let us compute the option's delta one day before expiration when $L(3)$ is very close to the barrier of 10 percent, say, $L(3) = 9.99\%$. (For the sake of illustration, we are misusing the convention that LIBOR only moves in multiples of $1/16$.) The cap price in this case is almost zero; it contains no intrinsic value and very little time and option value. Let us increase $L(3)$ by 0.01, a very small amount, to 10 percent. The option value in this case is practically 100 bps. The delta in this case would be:

$$\text{Delta} = (1 - 0)/(10 - 9.99) = 100$$

In other words, to delta-hedge the position, one needs a large number of futures contracts (assuming that future prices move continuously). By the same argument, the option has a large gamma near the barrier. See Figure 26–19.

SUMMARY AND CONCLUDING REMARKS

Interest rate options are important instruments for managing interest rate risk. In this chapter, we considered the most common of such options: interest rate caps and floors and some of their variations and applications. This field is very active, and a stream of new products and structures are being introduced in the market every day. Of particular interest are correlation options that involve a number of assets and indexes. They are more flexible products and can be better tailored to a customer's needs. However, they are also more difficult to price and hedge.

NOTE

1. *Q-Cap* is a product developed by the author at Chase Securities, Inc.

REFERENCES

Bookstaber, Richard M. *Option Pricing and Investment Strategies.* 3rd ed. Chicago: Probus Publishing Company, 1991.

Cox, John C., and Mark Rubinstein. *Options Markets.* Englewood Cliffs, N.J.: Prentice Hall, 1985.

Figlewski, Stephen; William L. Silber; and Marti G. Subramanyan. *Financial Options: From Theory to Practice.* Homewood, Ill.: Business One Irwin, 1990.

CHAPTER 27

APPLICATIONS OF OTC OPTIONS

Anlong Li
Salomon Brothers
Paul Potocki
Lehman Brothers

INTRODUCTION

The over-the-counter, or OTC, market for options on interest rates has undergone radical changes over the past 10 years. Previously, the market has been characterized by a small number of dealers trading in short-dated options on specific government securities. Long-term deals on various interest rate indexes were privately negotiated between two parties. The market in these deals was characterized by illiquidity and a lack of pricing information. Following the acceptance of interest rate swaps by the financial community as a viable interest rate risk management tool, there evolved a market for longer-term options on various interest rate indexes. Currently, the base of users is increasingly broader in both profile and size, and the types of transactions have diversified. Tables 27–1 and 27–2 show the 1991 International Swap Dealers Association survey of the global volume of OTC options.

In this chapter, specific details of "standard" interest rate cap and floor transactions will be reviewed. These products fulfill the needs of hedgers and speculators alike. Examples of more complex instruments such as interest collars and range forwards will also be given.

TABLE 27-1
Volume of OTC Options Written during the Second Half of 1991

Currency	Instrument	Volume (millions)	Percent Change in Volume 6 months	12 months	2 years
U.S. dollars	Caps	$ 59,560	−6%	−8%	+47%
	Floors	17,487	−18%	+11%	+40%
	Collars, etc.	4,376	−9%	−8%	−12%
	Swaptions	20,980	+38%	+28%	+31%
	Total	102,403	−2%	+1%	+38%
Other currencies	Caps	35,866	+28%	+81%	+62%
	Floors	18,638	−27%	+31%	+106%
	Collars, etc.	3,383	−76%	+33%	+274%
	Swaptions	23,559	−12%	+46%	+116%
	Total	81,466	−14%	+55%	+90%
All currencies	Caps	95,446	+5%	+13%	+53%
	Floors	36,123	−23%	+21%	+66%
	Collars, etc.	7,758	−59%	+6%	+32%
	Swaptions	44,539	+6%	+37%	+65%
	Total	183,867	−8%	+55%	+57%

TABLE 27-2
Volume of OTC Options Outstanding at End of 1991

Currency	Instrument	Volume (millions)	Percent Change in Outstanding 1 year	2 years
U.S. dollars	Caps	$ 59,560	−10%	−23%
	Floors	17,487	−4%	+38%
	Collars, etc.	4,376	−62%	−18%
	Swaptions	20,980	−10%	+21%
	Total	102,403	−13%	+23%
Other currencies	Caps	35,866	+35%	+26%
	Floors	18,638	+64%	+103%
	Collars, etc.	3,383	+93%	+187%
	Swaptions	23,559	+68%	+155%
	Total	81,466	+51%	+69%
All currencies	Caps	95,446	−1%	+25%
	Floors	36,123	+17%	+60%
	Collars, etc.	7,758	−41%	+15%
	Swaptions	44,539	+16%	+62%
	Total	183,867	+3%	+37%

INTEREST RATE CAPS AND FLOORS

The largest and most successful OTC options market is that for interest rate caps and floors on the U.S. dollar LIBOR, or London Interbank Offered Rate. Quotes on "standard" interest rate caps and floors are now available from a multitude of brokers and dealers as well as the major financial news services.

As often-traded options, interest rate caps and floors are actually portfolios of individual call and put options. As bundles of options, however, these instruments possess many attributes common to more familiar exchange-traded options. First, the valuation of interest rate caps and floors relies heavily on option pricing theory. This means that the price or premium of the instrument is a function of the underlying interest rate indexes and the expected volatility. The strength of the relationship is well known to professional cap and floor traders, who typically express prices in terms of the volatility level implied for the underlying interest rate indexes.

Second, payoffs associated with interest rate caps and floors resemble those of exchange-traded call and put options. In the case of an interest rate cap, payments occur if the underlying interest rate index exceeds the strike rate on the rate calculation date. For an interest rate floor, payments occur if the interest rate index lags the strike rate on the rate calculation date. Typically, both the underlying interest rate index and the strike rate are the same across all options comprising the interest rate cap and floor. It should be remembered, however, that interest rate caps and floors are customized agreements, the terms of which may differ widely depending on the needs of the parties involved.

Two attributes that always differ across options composing any interest rate cap or floor are the rate calculation date and the payment date, also known as the *reset date*. The first rate calculation date usually occurs two business days before the effective date (or start date) of the agreement. The subsequent rate calculation dates are typically two business days before the proceeding payment date. The payment dates determine when the payoff, if any, will take place. In most interest rate cap and floor agreements, the month in which the payment date falls is calculated by adding the number of months specified by the payment frequency to the month containing the preceding payment date, or, in the case of the first payment date, the effective date. Typically, the effective date and the payment date fall on the same day of the month; however, should this day coincide with a bank holiday or be beyond the last day of the month, a convention known as the modified-following-business-day rule is usually applied. The example below illustrates the technical aspects of the business-day convention as well as the calculation of both rate calculation dates and payment dates.

On Thursday, August 27, Praise Lake Bancorp, a Midwest bank holding company, purchases an interest rate cap from Silverman Brothers, a prominent investment bank. The terms of the agreement resemble those of most deals found in the domestic market for interest rate caps and floors. The underlying interest rate index is the 90-day U.S. dollar LIBOR; the payment frequency is quarterly, and the payments are to be determined using the modified-following-business-day convention. Immediately following the transaction, on the same day, the treasurer of the Praise Lake Bancorp asked one of his analysts to determine the first two payment dates and their corresponding rate calculation dates.

Since the contract is a standard cap on the U.S. dollar LIBOR, the analyst knows the effective date is Monday, August 31, two business days after the initiation of the contract. Using the payment frequency, the analyst determines the first payment date will occur in November. Since November only has 30 days, the first payment date will fall on Monday, November 30—the last day of the month. The first rate calculation date is two business days prior to the effective date and coincides with the current date, Thursday, August 27. To obtain the second payment date, the analyst must apply the modified-following-business-day convention since the last day of the payment month, February 28, falls on a Sunday. Typically, this would require advancing to the nearest business day (Monday, March 1); however, this is beyond the last day of the payment month. In this case, the first preceding business day is used, making the second payment date Friday, February 26. The second rate calculation date is Wednesday, November 25—two business days prior to the first payment date. (Thursday, November 26 is Thanksgiving Day—a New York banking holiday.)

In the event a payment is to occur on the payment date, its exact value is computed by multiplying the positive differential between the underlying interest rate index and the strike rate by the product of the notional amount and the day-count fraction. The notional amount represents the underlying monetary value to which the payoff percentage is applied. It is usually held constant across all options of a particular interest rate cap or floor; however, accruing and amortizing notional amounts are occasionally formed. The day-count fraction adjusts the payoff rate, which is expressed as an annual percentage, for the payment frequency. Using the standard yield convention, actual/360, the day-count fraction is calculated by dividing the number of days between payment dates by 360 days. In the case of the first payment date, the number of days between the effective date and the first payment date is used. A continuation of the above example will help clarify the computation of the payment disbursed on the payment date.

Upon review of his analyst's findings, the treasurer of Praise Lake Bancorp realizes the first rate calculation date coincides with the contract's initiation date. Given this fact, the treasurer asks his analyst to determine the amount, if any, the bank's holding company will receive from Silverman Brothers on the payment date. The analyst gleans the following information from the confirmation notice:

$$\begin{array}{ll} \text{Notional amount} & \$100 \text{ million} \\ \text{Strike rate} & 7.00\% \end{array}$$

Since the U.S. dollar LIBOR on August 27 (the rate calculation date) was 7.64 percent, the first call option of the interest rate cap has expired in the money. The positive differential between the underlying interest rate and the strike rate is 64 basis points, and there are 91 days between the effective date and the first payment date. Using this information and the formula:

$$\text{Payoff} = (\text{Notional amount}) \times (\text{Day-count fraction}) \times (\text{Payoff differential})$$

the analyst computes the payoff as follows:

$$\$100,000,000 \times \frac{91}{360} \times 0.0064 = \$161,777.78$$

This sum will be distributed to Praise Lake Bancorp on November 30—the first payment date.

HEDGING INTEREST RATE RISK USING CAPS

As mentioned earlier, the standard interest rate cap is actually a portfolio of European options written on the future level of short-term interest rates. Each individual option, usually termed *caplet*, has a different maturity date while the strike price and underlying amount is held constant across the entire portfolio. The following example shows how caps can be used to hedge an unexpected interest rate increase in a floating-rate note.

The treasurer of Jay-Lee Corporation has been requested by the board of directors to submit a financing recommendation for the $500 million pending acquisition of Asil, Inc. After conversations with the firm's investment bankers, he decides to advocate the issuance of debt over any equity-linked funding alternative for three reasons. First, although the equity markets appear to be at high levels, stocks of lower-capitalized companies, such as Jay-Lee, have dramatically underperformed the major market indexes. Second, recent equity offerings by firms in the company's "peer group" have been received unfavorably by market participants. Finally, since interest rates across the term structure are at their lowest levels in recent history, the company should be able to obtain an attractive financing rate through a conventional debt issuance. Upon deciding to propose debt financing, the treasurer turns his attention to the type of coupon to be offered.

Given the anemic condition of the economy and the upward-sloping yield curve, the treasurer prefers the issuance of a floating-rate note over a more traditional fixed-rate debenture. In his opinion, the central bank must lower short-term interest rates much further to stimulate economic growth. Since the yield curve is positively sloped, the implied forward rates are higher than the treasurer's expectations of future short-term interest rates. With respect to the tenor of the debt, the treasurer suggests the debt be floating rate, which is tied to LIBOR plus a spread. This option is viewed as superior to the fixed-rate option for two reasons. First, the yield curve is very steep. The initial coupon of a 10-year bond is about 400 basis points over the floating-rate note. Second, the treasurer has the opinion that implied forward rates are high relative to future spot rates. If he is right, the cost of a floating-rate note will be less than that of the fixed rate even if the spot rate rises slightly (as long as it, on average, stays below the implied forward rates). If the treasurer is wrong, however, the cost of the floating-rate note could become substantially higher than that of the fixed-rate note. For this reason, the treasurer advises the board that the prudent thing to do is to purchase an interest rate cap, which would limit the company's exposure to increases in the floating rate.

The treasurer feels confident the firm can issue the debt at the 10-year Treasury rate plus 300 basis points. Given a current 10-year Treasury rate of 7 percent, the 10-year fixed rate would be 10 percent. The firm plans to enter a 10-year interest rate swap paying LIBOR and receiving a fixed rate of 7.5 percent, or equivalently, Treasury plus 50 basis points. As demonstrated below, this series of transactions transforms the company's 10 percent fixed-rate liability into a floating-rate one with a cost of LIBOR plus 250 basis points.

Fixed-rate financing (coupon on debenture)	10.00%
Receipt of fixed swap coupon	7.50%
Payment of floating-rate (swap coupon)	LIBOR
Total floating-rate cost	LIBOR + 2.50%

Jay-Lee Corporation feels comfortable that it can service debt payments to a maximum of 12 percent. Because of this, the company wants to strike the cap at 9.50 percent. This is 12 percent minus 2.50 percent, which is the cost above the LIBOR of the coupon on the floating-rate note.

SELLING CAPS AS YIELD ENHANCEMENT

The manager of a money market fund is reviewing yield enhancement strategies in an attempt to reduce the number of share redemptions that usually occur when short-term interest rates reach low levels. From past experience, the fund manager has found investors are more sensitive to yield differentials as the general level of interest rates declines. This problem is acerbated when the yield curve is steeply sloped and investors are rewarded for extending the duration of their portfolios. However, the fund is constrained in its prospectus to invest in assets with a duration of less than one year; therefore, it cannot invest in the higher-yielding, longer-dated, fixed-income assets. On the other hand, when interest rates are at high levels, investors appear relatively indifferent to yield differentials.

Given these observations, the fund manager believes the optimal yield enhancement strategy should produce higher returns in the current low interest rate environment at the expense of some income potential when rates rise. Also, this strategy should be consistent with her view on future interest rates. Currently, short-term interest rates are low and the yield curve is very steep. The fund manager believes the economy is heating up and the central bank will eventually be forced to tighten the money supply; this means a rise in short-term rates. This view on interest rates is the same as that of the corporate treasurer in the previous example. Each, however, has a different risk profile. The treasurer is extremely risk adverse and is willing to pay for the protection afforded by an interest rate cap. The money manager, on the other hand, feels that any increase in rates will give her a better performance in her portfolio of money market instruments. She is willing to forgo some of this upside potential to enhance the returns of her portfolio in the present.

ANOTHER INTEREST RATE CAP EXAMPLE

A company has purchased an inverse floating-rate note that has a typical payoff of 15 percent minus the prevailing LIBOR. The company does not have to pay if rates on the note become negative (or the LIBOR is above 15 percent); it is effectively long a cap with a strike price of 15 percent. Company officials feel this protection is unnecessary and would like to sell this component of the package. To do this, they merely need to sell a cap with the same maturity and frequency as that of the note with a strike of 15 percent. In this way, the company can strip the unwanted portion of the security with little added expense. (Similarly, an issuer of capped floating-rate notes may not feel the need for the cap if he can sell an offsetting cap and reap the premium up front.)

BUYING FLOORS TO HEDGE DOWNSIDE RISK

The manager of a pension fund has long-term liabilities that are presently valued at $300 million. Given the current interest rate market environment, the manager feels that longer-term rates will be increasing. If this scenario materializes, the manager can purchase the offsetting assets at a much cheaper level, thereby saving his company a tremendous amount of money. If he is terribly wrong, however, the manager stands to lose his company a great deal of money due to the maturity mismatch. To ensure that the mismatch of duration does not present a severe strain on the company, the manager decides it would be prudent to purchase an interest rate floor. The floor will protect him from an unrecoverable loss. The manager feels that he can risk a 200-basis-point drop in yields; therefore, he purchases a cap about 200 basis points below the current five-year yield.

SELLING FLOORS TO REDUCE FINANCING COST

The financing subsidiary of a large industrial company typically issues a 90-day commercial paper to fund its parent's accounts receivable. Since the age of the accounts receivable is estimated to be approximately that of the commercial paper issued, the subsidiary has no inherent asset-liability mismatch. The treasurer of the financing subsidiary, however, feels commercial paper funding rates are unlikely to drop any further. Given this view, the treasurer can either swap his floating-rate cash flows for fixed-rate flows, purchase interest rate caps, or sell interest rate floors.

Since the current environment exhibits a steep yield curve, the treasurer finds swapping out of a floating-rate debt into fixed rate to be highly unattractive. During the first part of the swap, his funding costs are likely to be much higher than the corresponding floating-rate costs. This is because a steep yield curve implies forward rates that are rapidly increasing. Since the fixed yield is the aggregate of implied forward rates, the fixed rate will begin much higher than the floating rate with the expectation that the floating rate will at some point in the future surpass the fixed rate.

If rates fall, the company will be able to borrow at substantially lower rates. Since the financing company passes the increases onto its customers, it is not worried about increases in the interest rates. Also, since a reduction in interest rates would probably spur additional business that would insulate the company from any losses on financing, it decides that selling an interest rate floor will help reduce present funding costs without substantially decreasing overall earnings should interest rates continue to fall.

INTEREST RATE COLLAR

An interest rate collar is a series of straddles on some interest rate index. It has the same payoff as that of buying a cap and selling a floor simultaneously. Usually, as shown in Figure 27–1, the strike price, X_1, for the floor components of the collar is smaller than the strike price, X_2, of the cap components. As shown in the following example, an interest rate collar often provides a relatively inexpensive vehicle to hedge interest rate risk.

FIGURE 27–1
Payoff of an Interest Rate Collar

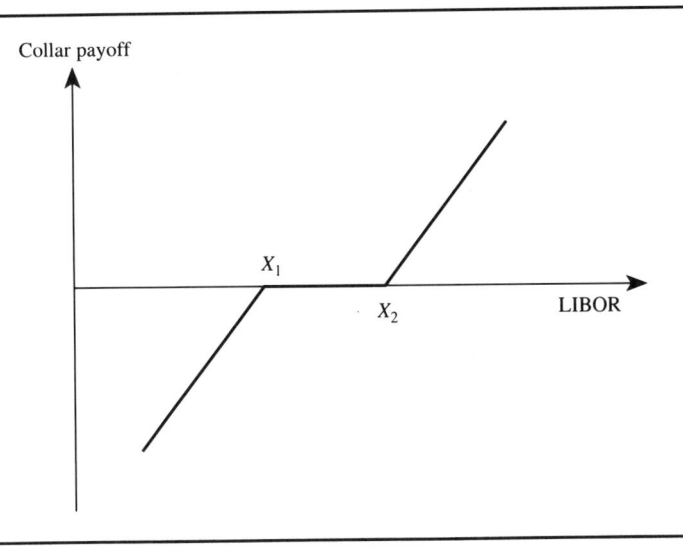

BCD Corporation borrows short term to finance its receivables. The cost structure of the company makes it only mildly exposed to interest rate risk. To a certain extent, the cost due to high interest rates can be passed on to the company's customers unless interest rates rise dramatically in the future. On the other hand, if rates are dropping, the company will pick up more business. Since the company feels that rates are moving lower in general, which is favorable, it is looking to hedging against dramatic rate increases.

The financing rate of the company is at the U.S. dollar LIBOR plus 150 basis points. Currently, the LIBOR stands at 4.25 percent, while the yield curve is steeply upward sloped. It seems that an out-of-the-money five-year interest rate cap striking at 9 percent will provide adequate protection in case rates swing up. However, the steepness of the yield curve makes such an interest rate cap quite expensive. (The cap is quoted at 120 basis points of the notional amount.) Upon reviewing this situation, the treasurer suggests the company use an interest rate collar instead, with call strike at 9 percent and floor strike at 3 percent.

Recall that the effect of buying into an interest rate collar is the same as buying a cap and simultaneously selling a floor, with possible savings in transaction costs because a collar is a single transaction. The proceeds from selling the floor are used to reduce the cost of the expensive cap. Actually, a five-year floor striking at 3 percent can be sold at 63 basis points. It effectively brings down the hedging cost from 120 basis points of a straight cap to 57 basis points of a collar. It should be realized that when the interest rate is below 3 percent, the floor portion of the collar may prevent the company from taking advantage of the low rates. The treasurer argues that such a loss may be more than offset by the increase in business as a result of lower interest rates.

RANGE FORWARDS

A range forward is a variation of the standard forward contract. The two counterparties who enter this contract agree on a range of the underlying variable S from X_{min} to X_{max}. At the maturity date, if the underlying S is greater than X_{max}, the party in the long position

FIGURE 27-2
Effective Financing Rate Using Range Forward

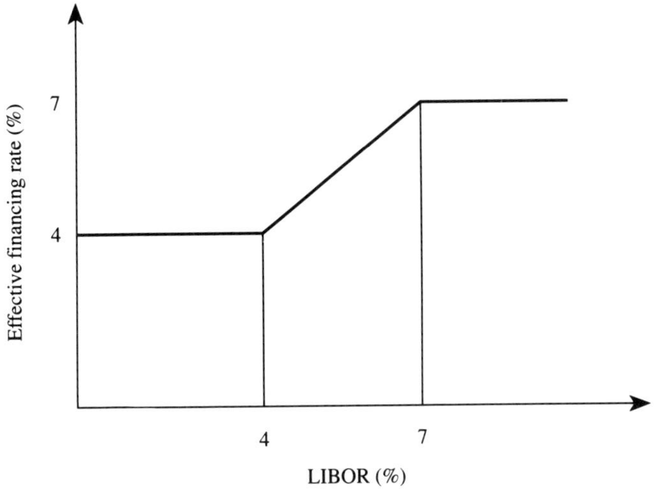

receives payment from the party in the short position in the amount of the difference, $S - X_{max}$. On the other hand, if S is less than X_{min}, cash flow is reversed with payment of X_{min} minus S. Such a payoff has the same pattern as a collar that involves simultaneously buying a call and selling a put. Because range forwards are structured as forward contracts, no cash changes hands at the initiation or during the life of the deal. This concept applies to any forward contract.

In the case of an interest rate swap range forward, the contract is actually made up of a sequence of interest rate range forwards on the same range. A swap range forward can also be viewed as a zero-cost collar. A long position in a range forward is equivalent to buying a cap and selling a floor simultaneously. The zero initial cost feature is obtained by choosing the appropriate strike rates for the cap and floor. Sometimes, an interest rate swap range forward is referred to as a *free collar*. When the two strikes coincide ($X_{min} = X_{max}$), the interest rate swap range forward is simply an interest rate swap. Normally, the strike rate for the cap component is above the swap rate of an interest rate swap with the same maturity, while the strike rate for the floor component is below the swap rate.

Interest rate swap range forwards can help borrowers effectively lock their future financing rates into a predetermined range. For example, a corporation issues a five-year floating-rate note of $100 million at the U.S. dollar LIBOR plus 75 basis points. At the same time, it enters into a five-year range forward contact with a cap strike of 7 percent and a floor strike of 4 percent. The current LIBOR is at 4.5 percent. During the next five years, the company will not pay higher than 7 percent. However, as an implicit cost, the company will have to pay 4 percent when the LIBOR drops below 4 percent. (See Figure 27–2.)

CONCLUSIONS

The recent development of interest rate derivative securities has made financial engineering a new part of the job description of many corporations' financial managers. Investment bankers and the executives at large commercial banks must be ready to serve their needs.

This chapter suggested several interest rate risk management applications. Chapter 25 illustrated some of the related concepts. In addition, entire books written on the subject of interest rate risk management provide even more detail; interested readers should check the books in the reference list.

REFERENCES

Marshall, John F., and Vipul K. Bansal. *Financial Engineering*. Boston: Allyn & Bacon, 1992.

Pitts, Mark, and Frank Fabozzi, *Interest Rate Futures and Options*. Chicago: Probus Publishing, 1990.

Smith, Clifford W., Jr., and Charles W. Smithson. *The Handbook of Financial Engineering*. New York: Harper & Row, 1990.

CHAPTER 28

ACCOUNTING FOR TRADED OPTIONS

Harold Bierman, Jr.
Cornell University

The options discussed in this chapter offer the right to either buy or sell a security. The buyer pays a premium for the right. The option has an expiration date and a strike or exercise price (the price at which the security can be purchased or sold), and the options are traded. The value of a call option (option to buy) is conventionally divided into two parts if the market price is larger than the strike price (comparable definitions can be offered for puts, the option to sell at a given exercise price):

$$\text{Market price} - \text{Strike price} = \text{Intrinsic value}$$
$$\text{Option price} - \text{Intrinsic value} = \text{Time value}$$

Intrinsic value is the amount that can be realized by exercising the option immediately and selling the stock. *Time value* is the value placed by the market on the option for the downside protection it offers (if the price drops below the exercise price, the option will not be exercised and the buyer only loses the premium paid for the option) and for the upside potential.

Relevant considerations and accounting issues for options are:

For Investor (buyer)
1. Is the underlying security already owned?
2. Is the transaction a hedge or speculation?

3. What should be the accounting at initiation of the option?
4. What should be the subsequent accounting for the option?

For Issuer (writer)
1. Is the option covered or naked?
2. Is the transaction a hedge or speculation?
3. What should be the accounting at initiation of the option?
4. What should be the subsequent accounting for the option?

The 1986 AICPA issues paper *Accounting for Options* offers the conclusions of both the Task Force on Options of the American Institute of Certified Public Accountants (AICPA) and the Accounting Standards Executive Committee AcSEC, which offers advisory conclusions). The AICPA 1986 issues paper conclusions are discussed in the appendix to this chapter. The FASB has not yet issued a standard defining the accounting for traded options.

THE PREMIUM

The buyer of an option pays a premium for the option. The size of the premium defines the maximum cost or loss the buyer can incur. The value of the option at maturity can be either zero or positive; it cannot be negative for the option buyer.

There are three choices for the accounting for the premium:

1. Expense at initiation of the contract.
2. Amortize over time.
3. Expense at maturity.

There is another element to the issue. How should the accounting for the premium be affected by mark-to-market accounting for the option?

Marked to Market

If the option is initially recorded at an amount equal to its cost (the premium) and then marked to market, the writeoff of the premium to expense becomes part of the mark-to-market process.

For example, assume the spot rate for Canadian dollars is now $.80 and Company A buys an option to buy 75 million Canadian dollars at a strike price of $.80 for a premium of $3 million. The option is good for a year. The value of the option is initially $3 million, equal to its cost. Assume that in one year the spot rate is $.84 for a Canadian dollar and the value of the option is:

$$75 \text{ million } (.84 - .80) = \$3 \text{ million}$$

The buyer of the option has a gain of $3 million on the option but the premium was $3 million, with the result that the net gain was zero.

Obviously, an accounting system that reported a $3 million expense in one accounting period and a $3 million gain in a following period would be subject to valid criticism for supplying misleading information in both periods.

Let us assume that the end of the accounting period is immediately before the option matures and that the option is marked to market. The market value is $3 million. What entry should be made? One reasonable possibility is:

Market Value: Option. 3,000,000
    Premium. 3,000,000

This entry is equivalent to making no entry if the premium account was already viewed as an asset.

Thus, if we combine mark-to-market accounting with the problem of accounting for the premium, we adjust the option to market value. One possibility is that there would be no gain recorded until the premium was exceeded by the market gain. A second possibility would be to prorate the premium over the life of the option. However, there would be a problem in having the sum of the unamortized premium and market value exceed the value of the option. The advisory conclusion of the AICPA 1986 issues paper is to mark to market the option.

Cost-Based Accounting

Cost-based accounting would lead to recording the option premium as an asset and either amortizing it through time or leaving it unamortized. Since with cost-based accounting there is no entry for recording the value additions through time, the amortization of the premium would result in a disappearing asset even though the option can be expected to have value at maturity. Leaving the premium unamortized would implicitly assume the value addition is exactly equal to the amortization of the premium at every moment in time until maturity.

Cost-based accounting has the advantage of requiring no fair value estimates where fair values are unavailable or unreliable. This is a large advantage if the calculations of fair value are not easily accomplished or are complex.

Investor: Speculation

Assume an investor buys a call or a put for speculation and the underlying security is not owned. At acquisition, the premiums of the call and the put are assets and are recorded at their cost. As time passes, the accounting choices are:

1. Cost.
2. Amortized cost (amortize the time-value component).
3. Mark to market.
4. LOCOM (lower of cost or market).
5. Formula.

These same choices are available for all other securities, and there is no reason why options as an asset should receive special treatment. If reliable fair values are available, they supply the most useful information. This is the recommendation of the 1986 AICPA issues paper.

If the underlying security is owned and, in addition, a call option is purchased, this is merely a speculative investment (somewhat more risky than if the option on a different security were purchased). If a put option is purchased on a security that is owned, a different interpretation is feasible. The purchase is insurance guaranteeing the investor that at least the put's strike price can be obtained on sale within the period of the put. The purchase of the put is a type of hedge (its value goes up as the stock price goes down) and will be discussed again in the hedging section.

INTRINSIC VALUE AND TIME VALUE

A primary problem with options is accounting for the time value component of value through time. The basic issues are:

1. Should the value of a purchased option be split between intrinsic and time value
   a. If speculation?
   b. If a hedge?
2. The same as (1) for a written option.
3. If there is a split, what should be the accounting for the two components?
4. Should the income or expense of the time-value component be immediately recognized or deferred in closing out an option qualified for hedge accounting?

For simplicity of presentation, the discussion will be in terms of stock options. Intrinsic value is equal to the difference between the market price of the stock and the exercise price if the market price is larger than the exercise price. It is the amount of value that can be realized immediately by exercising the option and selling the stock (excluding the transaction cost of selling the stock). Time value is equal to the difference between the option market value and the intrinsic value.

Since options are not normally exercised prior to maturity, the intrinsic value is an artificial construct that has the advantage of simplicity of calculation. At any moment in time, the value of an option is a function of:

1. The exercise price.
2. The present stock price.
3. The risk-free interest rate.
4. The time until maturity.
5. The standard deviation of the security's rate of return (return includes dividends and price changes).

At maturity, the value of the option is equal to the larger of zero or the intrinsic value, and the time-value component is equal to zero. Thus, the time-value component starts at one value and goes to zero at maturity. This implies that the time-value component should be systematically amortized through time. But a change in the risk-free rate, the present stock price, or the standard deviation can also cause a change in the value of the time-value component. Also, as the time-value component changes in value, the intrinsic value component is also likely to be changing in value.

At any moment in time, the option has a value. There is a value to the time-value component since the option provides insurance against stock price declines below the exercise price (if the stock price is below the exercise price, the loss is avoided by not exercising the option) as well as the opportunity for further stock price increases. In the next time period, the values of both the intrinsic value and the time value will change.

If the option is not marked to market, then the option has a cost and the time-value component of that cost will decrease through time. But the expectation is that the intrinsic value component will increase in value more than the time value will decrease. It is not obvious that the split accounting for the components of the option accomplishes a useful objective. From the viewpoint of both the investor and writer, and fair value of the option is relevant.

Investor: Hedge

Options are extensively used for hedging. Assume a situation in which a purchased option qualifies for hedge accounting, and the item being hedged is recorded at cost. What should be the disposition of the option's time-value component? The choices are:

1. Do not amortize.
2. Amortize and charge to expense (the option premium is a cost of insurance).
3. Amortize and debit the hedged item.
4. Amortize and debit the intrinsic value component.

The intrinsic value is expected to increase as the time value decreases; thus, based on expected value, there is no need to change the total value of the option. There is no obvious need to amortize the time-value component and charge an expense (the first alternative). It is possible that the intrinsic value stays constant or decreases and the time-value component and the value of the option both decrease in value through time. This situation would justify expensing the time-value component through time (the second alternative), but with an efficient option market this is not the expected outcome when the option is purchased. If the option is marked down to market, the item being hedged should also be marked to market if the transaction qualifies for hedge accounting.

Assume the hedge is effective and the option decreases in value. The value of the hedged item increases in value (or if the hedged item is a liability, it decreases in value). This leads to the third alternative of debiting the hedged item (assuming the hedged item has changed in value at least as much).

The fourth alternative is to debit the intrinsic value as the time-value component is amortized. This assumes the intrinsic value is increasing in value through time as the time-value component decreases in value. Thus, all of the four alternatives can be right or wrong, depending on the actual option value.

If the transaction qualifies for hedge accounting, any gain or loss on the option would be either accelerated or deferred (the hedge and the item hedged should be accounted for in a consistent manner). The same criteria as used for other securities should be used for options to determine if hedge accounting is appropriate.

If the underlying security is owned and a put on the security is purchased, that is a form of hedge (reduces downside risk). If eligible for hedge accounting, the security and the put should be accounted for in a consistent manner.

If an option is purchased as a hedge and the option is greatly out of the money, the price of the underlying security can change a large amount with the value for the option changing a relatively small amount. Thus, out-of-the-money options are not effective hedges for protecting the amount of value if only an equal number of options are purchased for a given number of shares of the underlying stock. To protect value, the hedge ratio would be affected by the amount the options are out of the money.

If the value of the option is initially C and it will be C_1 after one time period, and the stock price changes from S to S_1, the number of options that are needed to hedge the value of the stock (n) from an economic point of view are:

or

$$n(C_1 - C) = S_1 - S$$

$$n = \frac{S_1 - S}{C_1 - C}$$

Issuer: Speculation

Assume the writer of an uncovered call (the underlying security is not owned) is speculating. The possible losses are unlimited if the price of the underlying security has no upward bound. The written call is a liability to the writer. The best information is fair value.

Issuer: Hedge

Now assume the writer of a call option owns the underlying security. The writer is essentially selling the right tail of the price probability distribution for a given period of time. A written covered option changes (reduces) the risk characteristics of the underlying security. It might qualify for hedge accounting. However, the value of the underlying security may not be fully hedged by the writing of one call. This is likely to be the situation if the option is out of the money. The one call is fully hedged by the owning of the stock, but the underlying stock is not fully hedged (the investor can still lose with a price decline). The writer of the covered call receives cash (a debit) and credits either a liability or the underlying asset. Part of the underlying asset (the upside or the right tail of the probability distribution of outcomes) has been sold.

Can a company have a hedge if the hedge is only good for part of the range of outcomes? For example, assume a covered call option is written on stock that is owned. The stock price is $150 and the exercise price is $100. Assume the option value is $60. The $60 the company receives will cover the first $60 of stock price decrease. Beyond that magnitude of price drop, the company is not protected. If the stock price goes from $150 to $149, we would expect the value of the option that has been sold to go to about $59 (a gain for the seller of the option).

The hedge is this situation could logically qualify for hedge accounting. The possible deficiency in the hedge (not protecting the firm from large losses with large stock price decreases) is a managerial problem as well as an accounting problem. The limitation in risk protection could and should be described in footnotes.

The writer of an uncovered call option has a large amount of risk with no upside limit to the stock price. As the stock increases in value above the exercise price (and the option becomes deep in the money), the loss on the option is approximately equal to the stock price increase. The writer of a covered option has a somewhat different situation. The loss on the issued option caused by the stock price increase is approximately matched by the gain on the stock price. The nature of the risk is different with a covered option than with an uncovered option.

The writing of an uncovered option increases risk. The writing of a covered option reduces risk because the investment in the stock is reduced by the cash received for the option, but does not eliminate the downside risk. The hedge is imperfect.

RECOGNITION OF PROFIT

Assume a firm buys a call option in a financial market. At the time of purchase, there is not an immediate profit for the buyer. An asset is acquired (the option) with a market value equal to its cost. The buyer hopes the purchase has a value in excess of this cost, but this hope does not translate into an immediate gain.

Does the writer of the option have a gain at the initiation of the option contract? Again, there is no reason to conclude that the writer has a gain at the time of option issuance if there is a market transaction. Gains and losses are recognized through time with marked-to-market accounting, or at the option's maturity with a speculative position not marked to market, or at the maturity of a hedged position if the option has been the hedge item.

A SYNTHETIC FUTURE

If we combine the transactions of buying a call and selling a put with the same strike prices, we obtain results that are the same economically as buying futures (or forwards), except for transaction cost and credit differences. If there are interim cash inflows and cash outflows, then the buying of a call and selling a put are more like futures than forwards. If the call and put have different strike prices, it is more difficult to generalize.

To create a sale of futures, one would sell a call and buy a put. Buying a call gives rise to a cash outlay and the obtaining of an asset. Selling a put gives rise to cash and a liability. Since buying forwards (or futures) is equivalent to buying a call and selling a put, the accounting for the two transactions should be as similar as possible.

BUYING OPTIONS TO HEDGE STOCK ISSUE COMMITMENTS

Assume a corporation has firm (or conditional) obligations to issue common stock in the future to its managers. To lock in the maximum cost of the stock issue, the company buys call options. Is this an economic hedge? Does it qualify for hedge accounting?

Assume the exercise price of the option is $100 and the stock price is currently $90. The total cost to the corporation of the awarding of a share cannot be higher than the sum of the cost of the call option plus the $100 exercise price.

A complexity arises because the stock is the corporation's own stock. If the stock price is less than $100, the company will not exercise the option but will issue a new share of stock or alternatively buy a share in the market at a price less than $100. If the stock price is higher than $100, the company will exercise the option and earn the difference between the stock price and the exercise price.

Thus, the purchase of the stock option can affect the amount of the corporation's cash outlay. However, if the corporation were to issue a share of stock to satisfy the commitment, independent of the price, then with or without the option there would be dilution of one share because of the stock issue. There would also be a gain or loss on the option.

From the viewpoint of the corporate entity, stock equity transactions do not conventionally give rise to an accounting gain or loss. Even though the entity's cash flows can be affected by the transactions, it is generally accepted accounting that the income not be affected by stock equity transactions (for example, the purchase and issue of a corporation's own stock).

If the option on the corporation's own stock is treated in a manner analogous to Treasury stock, no gain or loss on the option would be recognized. Hence, there is no need to determine if the gain or loss should be deferred as with hedge accounting.

A corporation can buy its own stock for $100 and reissue (sell) it for $60. The remaining shareholders who did not sell will regret that the two transactions took place (they are $40 poorer). But following generally accepted accounting principles, the company did not have an accounting loss. The transactions with an option in its own stock are analogous.

Historically, the primary basis of the accounting system has been the reporting of the financial affairs of the corporate entity rather than the changes in the financial affairs of a specific group of stockholders. Consistent with this practice, gains and losses of calls and puts arising from transactions in a corporation's stock would not affect that entity's income. However, the gains and losses should be reported separately and explained.

The hedge accounting issue of "buying options to hedge stock issue commitments" is more appropriately an issue of accounting for transactions with owners.

OPTIONS AND DEBT

Some debts have contingent payments that are linked to the price of a specific commodity (oil, gold, silver, and so forth) to a specific index (a stock index), or to the value of a specific price of real estate. Refer to Emerging Issues Task Force (EITF) Abstract, Issue No. 86-28, *Accounting Implications of Indexed Debt Instruments,* for a discussion of the accounting issues of indexed debt.

Is the issuance of a security eligible for hedge accounting if the asset that is the basis of the contingent payments is owned by the firm? The transaction satisfies reasonable definitions and requirements of hedging as long as there is not a large "conversion" premium (the conversion value of the security is approximately equal to its market value). With no conversion premium, there is a transaction that could qualify as a hedge. The larger the conversion premium, the more difficult it is for the security to qualify as a hedge, since the prices of the debt and the underlying asset are less highly correlated.

If the asset that is tied to the debt is not owned or if the option aspect of the debt is far out of the money, the transaction involving the security has less strong hedge characteristics. Also, some indexed debt securities guarantee the investor the par value; thus, they are less like a hedge and less eligible for hedge accounting.

Assume a situation where Company A owns stock in Company X and issues a debt security:

1. With detachable warrants that can be exchanged for Company X's stock owned by Company A using the debt component as payment for the exercise price.
2. That is convertible into the common stock of Company X that is owned by Company A.

The two types of debt securities are close to being identical (they are different since the warrants can be detached and sold separately). If with the issue of the warrants the exercise price can only be paid with the debt, the two debt securities are economic equivalents, if we include the warrants with the first alternative. They should be accounted for in the same manner.

EITF Abstract, Issue No. 85-9, *Revenue Recognition on Options to Purchase Stock of Another Equity,* invokes APB Opinion No. 14, *Accounting for Convertible Debt and Debt Issued with Stock Purchase Warrants,* and does not conclude that the convertible could be accounted for using the same accounting as the debt with warrants.

Since there are elements of a hedge here, if the conversion premium is small, the stock that is owned and the debt that is used could be considered to be a hedge eligible for hedge accounting. This would mean extending the definition of hedge accounting to include securities that provide options to acquire other securities or real assets.

EITF Abstract: Issue No. 87-31

This abstract deals with the sale of put options on the issuer's stock.

Assume a company sells puts on its stock for cash, and the puts are publicly traded. The puts have a finite life. How should the proceeds (the credit) from the sale of the puts be recognized? The EITF concludes that the firm "should record the proceeds of the sale of the options in permanent equity."[1]

When a put is sold by the firm, it receives cash and it accepts an obligation to buy a share of stock at a given price. Assume the put is sold for $30 and it has an exercise price of $90. If the common stock price is $50 when the put expires, the firm will have to pay out $90 in exchange for the put and one share. It can issue one share for $50. In summary,

Cash outlay		$90
Cash proceeds		
From put	$30	
From stock	50	80
Net loss		$10

In practice, following Issue No. 87-31, the three transactions would be treated as capital transactions with no recognition of gain or loss. The liability (obligation) for the put would not be recognized.

FOREIGN CURRENCY OPTIONS

Foreign currency options are used to hedge foreign currency exposure for both firm commitments and more uncertain anticipatory transactions. There are accounting issues:

1. When should the premium be expensed?
2. When should the gains (if any) be recognized? Should the options be marked to market?

3. Should the options be eligible for hedge accounting if the options are bought or sold to hedge an anticipated position?

The three issues are tied together (how is future income to be affected?).

Hedge Accounting: A Foreign Currency Option

Assume a firm is importing products from Canada that cost 75 million Canadian dollars, which, in U.S. dollars, is 75 million (.80) = $60 million. while the spot rate is now $.80 (the cost of a Canadian dollar), it is feared the spot rate will increase. The company buys options to buy 75 million Canadian dollars in the next year at an exercise price of $.80 per dollar. The cost of the option is $2 million.

If the spot rate after a year is $.84, the option at maturity will have a value of 75 million (.84 − .80) = $3 million. The net cost of buying 75 million Canadian dollars' worth of Canadian goods is 75 million (.84) = $63 million, and with the $3 million gain on the option, the net cost is $60 million. The net product cost is unchanged from the cost of the previous year. But, since the option premium was $2 million, the total cost is $62 million. Without the option, the cost would have been 75 million (.84) = $63 million.

By deferring both the gain on the option and the option premium, the firm reports a cost of $62 million. If the premium had been expensed at the initiation of the option (rather than over the life of the option or at the expiration of the option), the cost in the next period would have been $60 million.

Deferring both the premium cost and the option gain are consistent with hedge accounting's objective. Assume all the previous facts except the spot rate after one year is $.90 so that the value of the option at maturity is $7.5 million. The cost of the 75 million Canadian dollars is now .90(75 million) = $67.5 million. The cost, net of the option value, again is $60 million. The value of the option balances the increased product cost. Adding the $2 million premium, we again have a total cost of $62 million.

But, we have assumed the same 75 million Canadian dollars for each example. Suppose the product costs only 66,666,667 Canadian dollars when the exchange rate is $.90, so that the cost in dollars remains $60,000,000. The net product cost is $52.5 million (equal to $60 million minus the $7.5 million gain on the option) without the premium of the option and $54.5 million with the premium. The projected cost in terms of Canadian dollars is a major uncertainty as is the exchange rate. The option purchase solves the exchange rate uncertainty (at a cost), but the projected cost remains uncertain.

There are two other hedge accounting issues for options used for anticipated transactions if the premium is expensed:

1. Is it appropriate to allow the deferring of gains on the option (consistent with cost-based accounting)?
2. Is the hedge accounting for options consistent with the hedge accounting of other securities?

If it is decided to allow the deferral of gains on the option, it is still necessary to make sure the hedge accounting for options is consistent with the hedge accounting for other securities.

While the above example used one year to illustrate the hedging situation, multiple-year options are used for the same types of situations; thus, the deferral of losses and gains can be for several years if hedge accounting is allowed.

Hedging Risks with a Put

Competitive risks can be hedged with options. Assume a Japanese firm is the major competitor with parts being imported from Japan. The spot rate for yen is now $.08 (1 yen costs $.08). Imports of 1 billion yen now cost $80 million. If the value of the yen were to weaken to $.06, to earn 1 billion yen the firm only needs $60 million, and the Japanese firm could lower its prices since it no longer needs $80 million.

Assume the U.S. firm wants to hedge the above contingency. It buys a put option to sell 1 billion yen at an exercise price of $.08. If the spot price drops to $.06, the put option makes 1 billion (.08 − .06) = $20 million. While the Japanese firm can now import the parts at $60 million rather than $80 million and can lower its prices, the U.S. firm can also use the $20 million gain on the option to lower its prices.

Should the transaction be treated as a hedge eligible for hedge accounting? Currently, hedge accounting cannot be used for this situation. There are two primary issues: Can the gains be deferred and is the accounting consistent with that of other transactions? If it is decided that hedge accounting could be used, there is the remaining issue of how long into the future risks of this nature can be hedged (and thus the gains and losses be deferred).

CONCLUSIONS

There are mathematical models that allow the valuation of options through time. It is also possible, for many options, to obtain market value estimates. There is no reason to expect that options will decrease in value through time. Unfortunately, some accounting models are built on the faulty assumption that a component of option value should be expensed through time, independent of market value information or theoretically correct value estimate calculations.

The appendix to this chapter summarizes the 1986 AICPA issues paper, *Accounting for Options*. This is the most authoritative statement on accounting practice for options.

APPENDIX: AICPA ISSUES PAPER, *ACCOUNTING FOR OPTIONS* (March 6, 1986)

Pages 79–83 list 16 issues and the advisory conclusions of AcSEC. The issues and advisory conclusions are listed here with comments.

	Issues	Advisory Conclusion
1	Should hedge accounting be permitted for options?	Hedge accounting should be permitted for options (paragraph 148).
1A	Should hedge accounting be permitted for options that hedge an asset stated at cost or a liability stated at proceeds?	Hedge accounting should not be permitted for options used to hedge an asset stated at cost or a liability stated at proceeds (paragraph 161).

Comments

Why not allow hedge accounting with Issue 1A? AcSEC voted no to allowing hedge accounting. The task force voted no to the above advisory conclusion (pp. 90 and 91).

	Issue	Advisory Conclusion
2	How should options that do not qualify for hedge accounting be accounted for?	Such options should be marked to market (paragraph 180).

Comments

Marked to market may be desirable, if there are reliable market measures. However, the use of mark to market for options raises the issue: Why not for other securities not currently marked to market?

	Issue	Advisory Conclusion
3	What should the criteria be for purchased options to qualify for hedge accounting?	Use criteria similar to that in paragraph 4(b) of FASB Statement No. 80 (paragraph 195).

Comments

Statements 52 and 80 should be reconciled. Options should be part of a broader solution.

	Issue	Advisory Conclusion
3A	Should hedge accounting be permitted for purchased out-of-the-money options?	Hedge accounting should be permitted for out-of-the-money purchased options (paragraph 202).

Comments

No comment.

	Issue	Advisory Conclusion
4	Should the time and intrinsic values of purchased options qualifying for hedge accounting be split?	In accounting for purchased options qualifying for hedge accounting, time and intrinsic value:

	Issue	Advisory Conclusion
4		• Should be split if the item to be hedged is carried at other than market, or is carried at market and changes in the intrinsic value of the option are included in a separate component of shareholders' or policyholders' equity. • Should not be split if the item to be hedged is carried at market and changes in the intrinsic value of the option are included in income (paragraph 218).

Comments

"They view the time value as an insurance premium whose cost should be charged to income over the exercise period of the option" (p. 108). This captures the disagreement. The insurance may not result in an expense. The expected value of the option is equal to the premium.

	Issue	Advisory Conclusion
5	Should hedge accounting be permitted for written options?	Hedge accounting should be permitted for written options only to the extent of the amount of premium received (paragraph 242).

Comments

No comment.

	Issue	Advisory Conclusion
6	What criteria should be met for written options to qualify for hedge accounting?	Written options should meet the same criteria that purchased options should meet to qualify for hedge accounting (paragraph 253).

Comments

The criteria should be standard and comparable to that of other securities.

Chapter 28 Accounting for Traded Options

	Issue	Advisory Conclusion
7	Should the time and intrinsic values of written options qualify for hedge accounting be split?	Time and intrinsic values of written options qualifying for hedge accounting should not be split (paragraph 267).

Comments

Refer to Issue 4. Consistency would be nice.

	Issue	Advisory Conclusion
8	How should the time value be accounted for if the time and intrinsic values are split in accounting for options that qualify for hedge accounting?	If the item being hedged is carried at other than market or at market and changes in the intrinsic value of the option are included in a separate component of shareholders' or policyholders' equity, the time value should be amortized by a systematic and rational method. If the item being hedged is carried at market and changes in the intrinsic value are included in income, the time-value component should be stated at market value.
8A	In closing out an option qualified for hedge accounting, should recognition in income of the net time value be immediate or deferred?	The net time value should be recognized immediately in income (paragraph 283).

Comments

Refer to Issue 4. There is a need for consistency and theory.

	Issue	Advisory Conclusion
9	Should use of hedge accounting be contingent on continuing high correlation?	Use of hedge accounting should be contingent on continuing high correlation (paragraph 290).

638 Section 5 Over-the-Counter Options

	Issue	Advisory Conclusion
9	Should hedge accounting have a fair value limitation?	Hedge accounting should have a fair value limitation (paragraph 291).

Comments

A good hedge may not have a high correlation. The fair value limitation should be considered.

	Issue	Advisory Conclusion
10	Should hedge accounting be applied to anticipated transactions that meet specified criteria?	Hedge accounting should be applied to anticipated transactions meeting specified criteria (paragraph 297).
10A	How should the cumulative gain or loss on an option closed out before the anticipated transaction occurs whose recognition in income has been deferred be subsequently accounted for?	The cumulative gain or loss should be included in the measurement of the related transaction (paragraph 301).
10B	What accounting method should be used if the amount of the hedged item required for the anticipated transaction is less than that originally hedged by options?	A pro rata portion of the cumulative gain or loss whose recognition in income has been deferred should be recognized in income immediately (paragraph 304).
10C	Should changes in time value that occur before the commitment or anticipated transaction occurs be included in the measurement of the transaction?	Changes that occur before the commitment or transaction occur may be included in the measurement of the transaction (paragraph 308).

Comments

10B   Probably "is less than" means, "The actual transaction is less than the amount that had been anticipated."

10C   Changes in time value cannot be considered in isolation.

	Issue	Advisory Conclusion
11	Should amortization or changes in market value of time value be included directly in a separate component of equity if changes in intrinsic value are so included?	Amortization or changes in the market value of time value should be included in income (paragraph 314).

Comments

Time value plus intrinsic value equals option value. It is one problem. While the time-value component decreases through time, there is no reason to conclude that total option value decreases.

	Issue	Advisory Conclusion
12	Should hedge accounting be permitted to be applied to an option hedging a possible transaction?	Hedge accounting should not be permitted to be applied to an option hedging a possible transaction (paragraph 326).

Comments

This should be part of a broader solution.

	Issue	Advisory Conclusion
13	Should the method of accounting for a futures contract be used to account for a synthetic future that qualifies for hedge accounting as a unit?	The method of accounting for a futures contract should be used to account for a synthetic future (paragraph 337).

Comments

No comment.

	Issue	Advisory Conclusion
14A	If hedge accounting should be applied to a call bull spread or a put bear spread, should it be applied as a unit?	The spread should be accounted for as a unit following guidance for purchased options (paragraph 344).

Comments

No comment.

Section 5 Over-the-Counter Options

	Issue	Advisory Conclusion
14B	Can a call bear spread or a put bull spread qualify for hedge accounting?	The spread can qualify for hedge accounting only to the extent of the amount of the net premium received (paragraph 350).

Comments

No comment.

	Issue	Advisory Conclusion
14C	Should hedge accounting be applied to a combination option as a unit?	Hedge accounting should be applied to a combination option as a unit if appropriate criteria are met (paragraph 358).

Comments

No comment.

	Issue	Advisory Conclusion
15	Should hedge accounting be applied to an option position that provides a hedge on an after-tax basis?	Hedge accounting should be applied to an option qualifying for hedge accounting that provides a hedge on an after-tax basis (paragraph 361).

Comments

   Reasonable.

	Issue	Advisory Conclusion
16	Should accounting for options not traded on exchanges be the same as that for options traded on exchanges?	The method of accounting for options traded on exchanges and options not traded on exchanges should be the same (paragraph 373).

Comments

The issue becomes one of determining how value is to be determined and should the value estimate be used.

NOTE

1. EITF abstract, Issue No. 87-31, (Norwalk, Conn.: Financial Accounting Standards Board, 1989), p. 391.

CHAPTER 29

THE LEGAL STRUCTURE OF OTC OPTIONS

Richard A. Miller
Katten Muchin & Zavis, New York
David T. Novick
Katten Muchin & Zavis, Chicago

There are a number of over-the-counter interest rate option structures, and their particular legal ramifications vary. The following analysis is a general overview of some of the legal issues encountered when entering into OTC options. This chapter should be read in conjunction with Chapter 20, which discusses the legal structure of swaps transactions in considerably more depth.

OTC interest rate options are individually negotiated agreements between commercial counterparties. In contrast to swaps, which are continuing two-way payment agreements with continuous bilateral credit exposure, options have noncontinuous payment and credit exposures. The option purchaser (or holder) generally pays a single premium to the option seller (or writer), who is obliged to fulfill the option in the future in the event of exercise. Thus, once the option is fully paid for, the holder is thereafter exposed to the seller's creditworthiness and ability to perform. Obviously, the longer the option's time to maturity, the greater the risk of adverse events affecting the option seller's financial strength and ability to perform. Another, perhaps more subtle, credit risk arises in the case of straight options on swaps when, as discussed below, the option *holder's* future creditworthiness will be relevant to the option writer.

As the following sections describe, participants in the OTC options markets have developed methods for factoring their credit exposures into the deal structures. As this growing market matured, it has adopted relatively standard documentation that was originally designed by the International Swap Dealers Association (ISDA). In 1989, the ISDA published the "Addendum to Schedule to Interest Rate and Currency Exchange Agreement" (known as the *cap addendum*), which covered interest rate caps, collars, and floors, and in 1990, it published the "Addendum to Schedule to Interest Rate and Currency Exchange Agreement" (referred to as the *options addendum*) covering options. In 1991, the ISDA incorporated most, but not all, of the cap and options addenda's provisions into the "1991 ISDA Definitions."

The most common OTC financial options fall into two general classes: options on swaps and the group of transactions that include caps, collars, and floors. Another less widely used OTC option involves trade options offered under the rules of the Commodity Futures Trading Commission (CFTC). We will consider each class of option in the following sections and conclude by discussing a few of the special concerns that have been expressed concerning the OTC options market.

SWAPTIONS

Options on swaps, commonly known as *swaptions,* are literally options to enter into, extend, modify, or cancel underlying or related swap agreements. Swaptions may be settled by one of two means: physical delivery or cash settlement.

Physical Delivery

In the case of physical delivery, the option *holder* possesses the right to require the option *writer* to effect the underlying swap transaction. However, circumstances may change between the time that the option is granted and the time that it is exercised. To protect the option holder's rights versus the writer, the deal documentation may provide for acceleration and cash settlement (see below) in the event that the writer suffers an "event of default."

On the other hand, the option *holder*, who paid a premium for the option to enter into a two-way swap later, may suffer such financial reversals that it would not qualify as an appropriate swap counterparty. To provide for this contingency, the parties may specify in the option contract that the holder's right to exercise physical delivery will be subject to the condition precedent that no "event of default," as defined in the underlying swap agreement or original option agreement, shall have occurred and be continuing in respect of the holder at the time of exercise.

One method for dealing with the possibility of an intervening event of default is to provide that, instead of physical delivery, the swaption will be settled upon exercise by the second method—cash settlement.

Cash Settlement

The ISDA's standard option agreement documentation provides for the alternative of cash settlement of a swaption. However, the documents do not specify the means of calculating the cash settlement amount. Consequently, the parties must come to some agreement and reduce it to writing. There are three common means of calculating cash settlement values, as follows:

Average Reference Pricing
The parties agree, at the time the option is written, that upon exercise they will obtain bid and offered rates for the fixed and/or floating side of the underlying swap transaction from a number of financial institutions, which the ISDA terms *reference banks* or *reference dealers*. The bid and offered rates of each reference institution are averaged, and the group of averages are also averaged, generally with the high and low average disregarded. Based upon the calculation of the mean of the average bid and offered rates, it is determined whether any sums are due from the option seller to the option buyer.

Discounting the Payment Streams
The cash settlement amount is calculated by discounting to present value the fixed-rate and floating-rate payment streams of the underlying swap transaction. Again, reference banks or reference deal-

ers may be consulted to determine the appropriate interest rate to calculate present values.

By Reference to the Standard Agreement
The cash settlement value of the option is calculated as though the underlying swap transaction were terminated. The standard swap agreement is consulted, and the provisions of paragraph 6(e), "Payments on Early Termination," are applied.

CAPS, FLOORS, AND COLLARS

Interest rate caps, floors, and collars are variants on the standard swap agreement. In a cap, the buyer purchases protection against increasing rates, thus locking in the buyer's maximum borrowing expense. Conversely, a floor guarantees a party against declining interest rates, while its counterparty agrees to pay the difference between prevailing rates at a future date and the specified floor rate at the time. In a collar, a party buys a cap and sells a floor, or buys a floor and sells the cap. The financial details of these transactions are discussed elsewhere in this book.

As mentioned above, the legal terms for these OTC options are, for the most part, provided by standard ISDA documentation. In the case of interest rate and currency exchange agreements, the 1991 ISDA definitions incorporate terms that were previously included in the 1989 caps addendum. However, users of the ISDA documentation should note that not all of the cap addendum's terms were carried into the "1991 ISDA Definitions." The omitted paragraphs 3 and 4, as well as optional paragraph 5, concern the fact that the buyer of a cap or floor has fully paid for the transaction and only the seller has any further obligation.[1]

Where, for example, the parties conduct "one-way" business, so that one party is always the cap or floor buyer and the other the seller, the buyer would be prejudiced if the seller were able to designate an "early termination date." This is because, for instance, the buyer goes bankrupt, as would be permitted under standard ISDA documentation. To remedy this potential problem, the ISDA has suggested amendments to its standard agreements. These, in effect, recognize that where an option buyer has fully paid and the only remaining obligation is the seller's, the option, cap, or floor should be treated as an asset that should not be adversely affected by changes in the buyer's financial condition. Another suggested amendment results in the paid-for option, cap, or floor surviving a challenge of a trustee or receiver in the event that the seller is bankrupt or in receivership.

It should be noted, however, that these amending provisions remain controversial. They depart from the usual two-way payment schemes that generally apply to swap transactions. Whether they are appropriate to a particular transaction will depend upon the nature of the parties' transactions with each other and particularly whether they are counterparties to each other in standard swap agreements and tend to always be on one side of the options, caps, and floors. Finally, the parties also need to consider whether to link their swap agreements and option, cap, and floor agreements in one master agreement or two separate master agreements, one for their swaps and one for their options.

COMMODITY TRADE OPTIONS

Trade options issued pursuant to regulations promulgated by the Commodity Futures Trading Commission (CFTC) represent another OTC options product. The trade option is an exception to the general rule that all commodity options must be traded on a licensed board of trade, for example, the Chicago Board of Trade. Under the trade option rule, an offeror may enter into an option agreement as either the seller/writer or buyer/holder, provided it "has a reasonable basis to believe that the option is offered to a producer, processor, or commercial user of, or a merchant handling, the commodity that is the subject of the commodity option transaction, or the products or byproducts thereof, and that such producer, processor, commercial user, or merchant is offered or enters into the commodity option transaction solely for purposes related to its business as such."[2]

The CFTC recently interpreted the trade option rule to permit such transactions if the qualifying commercial offeree is entering into the transaction solely for nonspeculative purposes demonstrably related to its commercial business in the commodity that is the subject of the option.[3] However, whether an offeree is a qualifying offeree, because it is a producer, processor, commercial user, or merchant handling a commodity, may become problematic when financial securities or intangibles (e.g., interest rates) are the subject of the option. The CFTC has not formally stated that banks, broker-dealers, and other financial intermediaries are appropriate offerees for these kinds of trade options. Nonetheless, some have argued that such trade options are consistent with the purpose of the exemption and the meaning of the regulation.[4] The futures industry and its regulators at the CFTC are currently considering expanding the trade option exemptions.

SPECIAL CONCERNS

The astonishingly rapid growth of the volume and dollar-weighted size of off-exchange transactions has, of course, caught the attention of financial market regulators in Washington, D.C., and elsewhere. They are concerned with the credit and systemic risks posed by these customized and generally unregulated instruments. In recent months, these regulators have taken concrete steps to learn more about the off-exchange market. Indeed, as this is written, Congress is enacting the Futures Trading Practices Act of 1992, which includes in its legislative history a specific direction that the Commodity Futures Trading Commission—with the cooperation of and in consultation with the Securities and Exchange Commission and the Federal Reserve—conduct a comprehensive study of swaps and off-exchange derivative financial products.[5] The study should be completed by October 1993 and will include recommendations regarding the future regulation of swaps and derivatives and whether a single U.S. agency should have authority over all exchange-traded and off-exchange financial products. As this important new study progresses, it is likely to focus upon the size of the products, their market and their illiquidity.

Unknown Size of the Market

Mary Schapiro, commissioner of the Securities and Exchange Commission (SEC), in an address to the National Options and

Futures Society in late 1991 stated that a key problem with the OTC index options market is that no one can get a handle on its size. She said:

> A recent [Chicago Board of Options Exchange] survey estimated—conservatively, in their view—a range of $10 [billion] to $50 billion, measured in underlying contract value. . . . Other players in the market have pegged the combined international/domestic market of between $60 billion and $70 [billion]. But at this point, no one, including the regulators, knows for sure and therein lies a problem.[6]

The SEC and other regulatory authorities are concerned because OTC products are not governed by the SEC or exchange regulations and are treated as privately negotiated transactions falling outside the securities laws. With no easy way of determining the size of the OTC market, any judgment concerning the necessity of further regulation by the SEC or banking authorities is difficult to reach.

Responding in part to the need to understand the breadth of the OTC market, either firm by firm or industrywide, Congress enacted the Market Reform Act of 1990.[7] This act gives the SEC expanded authority to review the businesses of the parents and affiliates of registered broker-dealers and requires broker-dealers to obtain and make available information concerning the financial activities of their "material associated persons" whose activities are reasonably likely to have a material impact on the financial and operational condition of the broker-dealer.[8] The statute requires a broker-dealer to make and keep available such records as the SEC may require concerning the broker-dealer's policies, procedures, and systems for monitoring and controlling financial and operational risks that may result from its affiliate company activities. Furthermore, the holding company risk assessment rule provides the SEC with greater access to the books and records of every broker-dealer's parent and affiliates. This expanded oversight ability was believed to be necessary because the SEC's preexisting authority under the net capital and broker-dealer reporting rules failed to provide access to the books of the broker-dealer's swap dealer affiliates.

The SEC's proposed temporary risk assessment rules may further close the information gap. Proposed Rule 17(h)-(1)(T) will require broker-dealers to maintain records that reflect the aggregate notional amounts and gross payments owed pursuant to all financial instruments with off–balance sheet risk where the firm incurs principal risk.[9] This rule should encompass OTC options, equity index swaps, and interest rate and currency exchange swaps.

Illiquidity

A second special concern respecting the customized OTC market is the near-complete absence of secondary trading or an interdealer market. While the OTC market allows institutional customers to more accurately hedge their portfolios, the broker-dealers and banks that create and sell the product are forced to utilize the conventional exchange-traded markets to lay off their portfolio risk. From the customer's perspective, the absence of secondary market liquidity means that it will have to rely upon its counterparty to "take it out" of the trade, which may lead to wider price spreads. Alternatively, the customer will have to do business with a third party and risk having two counterparties in transactions thar are not legally nettable.

CONCLUSION

Once swaps and swaptions gain even wider acceptance, and their place in the regulatory scheme becomes clearer, these transactions will probably become so common that they will be perceived like everyday debt, security, and commodity trades. For the moment, however, that day lies in the future and the off-exchange market remains somewhat mysterious and intimidating. First-time users of derivatives will want to proceed cautiously until they grasp the particular nuances that affect this market.

NOTES

1. In 1993 ISDA published the *Users Guide to the 1992 ISDA Master Agreements* (International Swap Dealers Association, December 1993), which should be consulted in connection with these transac-

tions. Also, in the 1992 ISDA Master Agreement, the previously omitted paragraph 3 of the cap addendum was made part of the master agreement. Therefore, parties need to consider inclusion of paragraph 4 of the caps addendum (and paragraph 5 of the options addendum) when the 1992 documentation is employed.
2. Commodity Futures Trading Commission Regulations, Section 32.4(a)
3. CFTC Statement of Policy, 54 F.R. 30694, July 21, 1989.
4. J. Medero, "Hybrid Instruments and the Commodity Exchange Act—A Practical Guide," in *Advanced Strategies in Financial Risk Management,* eds. R. J. Schwartz and C. W. Smith (New York Institute of Finance, 1993).
5. H. Rept. 978, 102nd Cong., 2 sess., October 4, 1992, p. 83.
6. Mary Schapiro, "The Growth of the Synthetic Derivative Market: Risks and Benefits," before the National Option & Futures Society, November 13, 1991.
7. Market Reform Act of 1990, Pub. L. 101-432, October 16, 1990.
8. Securities Exchange Act of 1934 (15 U.S.C. 78l(c)), Section 12(k).
9. Securities Exchange Act of 1934, Regulation Section 240.17(h)-(1)(T).

SECTION 6

ASSET-LIABILITY MANAGEMENT

CHAPTER 30

HEDGING AN ANTICIPATED DEBT OFFERING

Laurie S. Goodman
Merrill Lynch
Eileen Baecher
Goldman, Sachs & Co.

INTRODUCTION

What is the best way to hedge the interest rate exposure of our proposed debt offering? Because corporations issue debt for a variety of reasons and under a range of circumstances, there is no single correct answer. A variety of hedging considerations and techniques may be appropriate. The choice of a particular hedge instrument will depend on the size, timing, and nature of the interest rate exposure, the firm's risk tolerance, its interest rate expectations, and the costs of different techniques.

This chapter will address these issues in several segments. In the first section, we present a framework for identifying the precise exposure to be hedged, discuss the objectives of the hedge, and consider issues of hedge design. In the next two sections, we present the various techniques and instruments that corporations are currently using to hedge interest rate exposure. In these sections, we examine costs, liquidity, and other important considerations bearing on the choice of a hedging strategy.

PRELIMINARY CONSIDERATIONS

Risk Identification

In the case of a planned debt issuance, the fundamental risk is that the firm will be hurt by an increase in interest rates before the issue goes to market. This involves two separate but related risks. In the United States primary and secondary markets, corporate yields are often expressed as a spread over the yield of the Treasury security of a corresponding maturity. An increase in the issuance yield can result from either a rise in Treasury yields or a widening of the spread of corporate yields off Treasury yields, or both.

The first possibility is called *base rate risk*; the second is called *spread risk*. For most firms, base rate risk will be more significant than spread risk, as the general level of interest rates tends to be much more volatile than spreads for highly rated companies. The two risks can be hedged separately or collectively, as we illustrate in the following examples.

Example 1
A firm plans to issue debt in three months to cover the cost of retiring existing debt and is concerned that interest rates will rise in the interim. The firm has a high credit rating and its debt has a fairly stable yield spread over Treasuries.

The primary risk for this firm is an increase in the general level of rates; it should design the hedge to cover only changes in Treasury yield levels. There are several techniques that will accomplish this, and they will generally be among the least expensive approaches because they involve instruments for which a ready market exists, rather than customized instruments.

Example 2
A firm plans to issue debt in two months but expects the general level of interest rates to decline. Its current credit spread is highly attractive and probably would not improve in a declining rate environment.

In this instance, the firm would want to hedge only its credit spread. There are a limited number of techniques that can do this, but they may be worth pursuing if a firm is confident of its rate-forecasting ability and fears only the possibility that market conditions may cause the currently attractive credit spread to widen.

Example 3
A rapid decline in interest rates provides a firm with an opportunity to issue debt at a threshold level. Although it doesn't need the funds for three months, the firm wants to ensure its ability to issue at current yield levels or lower.

In this situation, the firm needs to hedge the combined level of the base rate and the yield spread. It might hedge by issuing debt immediately and investing the proceeds in a short-term instrument. An alternative would be to sell interest rate futures and/or purchase a put option on corporate yields.

Defining the Environment

Once the firm has identified the risks that are to be hedged, the next step is to consider its environment—specifically, the degree of funding uncertainty and the outlook for changes in interest rates. To quantify its hedge requirements accurately, a firm must be able to identify the exact amount, term, and timing of the issuance. If there is uncertainty concerning any of these, or if the funding need is contingent upon some event or decision, then the firm should consider certain hedging techniques that are appropriate mainly under uncertain conditions.

Example 4
A firm will need to issue debt in the next three to six months if it receives a particular contract. But a rate rise in the interim would cut into the profitability of the project.

In this case, the firm faces both funding uncertainty and interest rate risk. Although the interest rate risk—that the firm will suffer from a rate increase—is the same as in Example 1, the funding uncertainty makes the situation in Example 4 much more difficult to hedge. The firm cannot decide how much of the interest rate risk to hedge without simultaneously choosing how much of the funding uncertainty it wants to cover.

Even if the firm can identify all the risks, it may want to allow its expectations for the course of interest rates to point it toward a hedging strategy. The hedge strategy can take three directions. One alternative is to "lock in" or "fix" rates, which would be desirable if the firm expected rates to rise either before the issuance or over the life of the issue. This choice might also be desirable if the firm found current rates acceptable but had no idea of the direction of interest rates. Another alternative is to set a maximum yield and let the borrowing rate float under that "cap." The third alternative is to not hedge at all. The firm would select a no-hedge strategy if it had a strong prior view that rates would remain constant or fall before the bond was to be issued. It might also select a no-hedge strategy if its funding needs were uncertain and if it had no idea of the direction of interest rates.

Over the course of the hedge period, the uncertainties concerning the issuance will be resolved, the firm's outlook on rates will change, or both. As the environment changes, the initial choice of hedge instruments may no longer be appropriate, and the firm may want to adjust its hedge design. For example, it may replace option strategies with techniques that fix the base rate or the spread rate of the issuance. Figure 30–1 illustrates how the firm may combine hedge techniques and how the mix may change as the funding date approaches.

Balancing Hedge Objectives

Although the identification of the risks to be hedged and an analysis of the environment will suggest the most appropriate hedge techniques, the final choice of a hedge vehicle depends upon the priorities the firm sets for the various hedge criteria.

We have identified seven objectives that most borrowers will wish to consider in choosing a hedge design:

- Minimize basis risk (the risk that changes in the price of the hedge instrument will not offset the changes in issuance cost).
- Maximize liquidity so that the hedge can be unwound prior to expiration.
- Keep hedging costs as low as possible.
- Avoid unfavorable tax treatment.
- Avoid unfavorable accounting treatment.

FIGURE 30-1
Blended Hedge Strategy

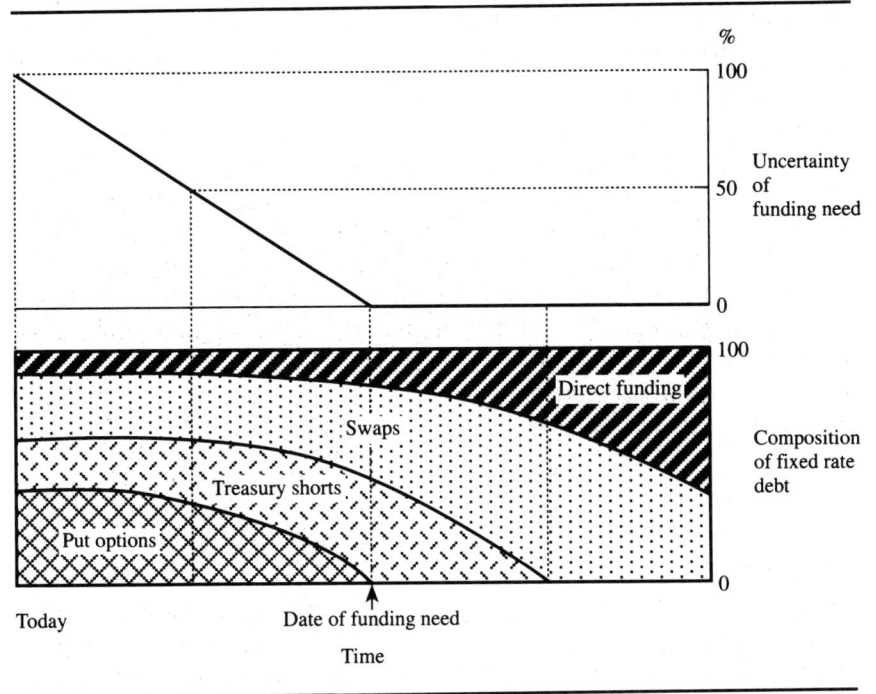

- Preserve the ability to benefit from a decline in rates.
- Keep execution and maintenance of the hedge simple.

Each of these objectives is desirable in itself. The problem is that no single hedge meets all seven criteria better than another hedge. For example, a hedge that minimizes basis risk is often a customized, over-the-counter hedge, but these hedges are usually more costly to unwind prior to maturity than a simple cash or exchange-traded instrument. If the firm wants to preserve its ability to issue at lower rates, it must cap rather than fix its borrowing rate. This requires the purchase of a put option or a series of options. Because the option preserves the opportunity to benefit from lower rates, the firm's cap rate must be higher than the fixed rate it could have locked in.

How a firm ranks these objectives will depend to a large extent on its risk tolerance, its capacity to handle operational details, and differences in tax and accounting treatment. Some firms will prefer to pay an "insurance premium" to preserve the upside potential. Others will be more willing to fix a rate. One firm will try instruments that are less commonly used, if they best suit the company's needs. Another firm may be less inclined to establish the legal, accounting, and margin systems to deal with certain hedging vehicles. For example, a hedge using futures contracts requires daily repricing of the position and cash margin flows. For some firms, this may be a burden that outweighs the benefits of the liquidity and efficiency of the futures markets. The impact of differences in the accounting and tax treatment of hedge instruments may also influence the firm's choices. For example, a corporation must treat the returns on some hedge vehicles as capital gains or losses rather than ordinary income. For some firms, this may be a strong deterrent to using a particular hedge instrument.

Table 30-1 summarizes the advantages and disadvantages of each of the hedging alternatives, including the tax and accounting treatment. Since, however, the tax and accounting implications are discussed in detail elsewhere in this book, they will not be covered in this chapter. As the table indicates, we break the specific hedging techniques into two principal types: methods that fix the issuance rate, which we will treat in the next major section of the chapter, and strategies that cap interest rates, to be discussed in the final section.

Hedge Design

The underlying principle of hedging is to match the interest rate sensitivity of a liability (or asset) with an offsetting position of the same interest rate sensitivity. One way to determine an appropriate hedge ratio for a debt issuance begins with calculating the change in the present value of cash flows of the liability for a 1-basis-point (1 bp) change in interest rates. One may then follow the same procedure for the hedge instrument and multiply the ratio of these price sensitivities (the "hedge ratio") by the face value of the issuance to determine the required face value of the hedge vehicle.

For previously issued securities, duration, in its various expressions, is the most commonly used measure of price sensitiv-

TABLE 30–1
Comparison of Hedging Strategies

	(1) Prefund	(2) Forward Sale of Treasuries	(3) Short Sale of Treasuries	(4) Sale of Futures	(5) Forward Interest Rate Swap	(6) Rate Hedge Agreement	(7) Purchase Put Option	(8) Purchase Cap Option
Type	Fix (Absolute)	Fix (Treasury)	Fix (Treasury)	Fix (Treasury)	Fix (Treasury)	Fix (Treasury)	Cap (Treasury)	Cap (LIBOR)
Avoid spread risk	Yes	No	No	No	No	No	No	No
Preserve upside potential	No	No	No	No	No	No	Yes	Yes
Hedge costs	Medium	Low	Low	Low	Medium	Low	High	High
Unwind spread (bp)	n.a.*	2–4	2–4	2–4	5–10	2–4	4–6	5–10
Avoid repo risk	Yes	Yes	No	Yes	Yes	Yes	Yes	Yes
Accounting:								
Mark to market	n.a.	Yes	Yes	No	No	No	No	No
Gain/loss at termination	n.a.	Amortized	Current	Amortized	Amortized	Amortized	Amortized	Amortized
Tax:								
Mark to market	n.a.	No	No	Yes	No	No if OTC; Yes if exchange traded	No	No
Gain/loss at termination	n.a.	Capital	Capital	Capital	Ordinary	Ordinary	Capital	Ordinary (IRS guidance expected soon)
Maximum time period for hedge	n.a.	6 months	6 months	18 months	3 years	6 months	9 months	10 years
Credit exposure	No	Yes	Minimal	Minimal	Yes	Yes	If OTC, yes; if exchange traded, minimal	Yes

*n.a. = Not applicable.

ity.[1] In determining hedge ratios, we use "dollar duration," which quantifies the amount that a security's price changes for a given change in its yield and is simply the modified duration multiplied by the price. Dollar duration depends upon the security's coupon and maturity. In the case of a planned issue, one cannot accurately make duration estimates because the coupon rate will not be determined until the issue date. Therefore, one must determine the interest cost sensitivity of the issuance by calculating the present value of a 1 bp change in the coupon rate. That is, the coupon is generally set such that the bond will initially sell at par, and thus the coupon yield and the yield to maturity are equivalent. The coupon is determined when the issue is priced.

If there were not tax considerations, the use of these techniques to quantify the price sensitivities of the hedge instrument and the issuance would be straightforward. The simple ratio of the sensitivities would determine the required notional amount of the hedge instrument. Tax considerations can, however, make hedge design more difficult. The increase or decrease in coupon payments receives ordinary income treatment, while the price gain or loss on many hedge vehicles is treated as capital gain or loss. A precise hedge would then be one in which the aftertax value of the change in the hedge instrument's price was equal to the aftertax present value of the additional coupon payments. Note that the actual aftertax cost can be determined only if the capital loss carry forwards and other tax attributes of the firm are known.

FIXING A RATE

We are now ready to describe the various hedging techniques that may be selected to fix a cap or a rate. As we have discussed, one should make the selection only after defining the risks and environment. The flow chart in Figure 30–2 illustrates the decision process and the likely choices. Our discussion of techniques begins with fixed-rate hedges; in the next section, we will move on to option strategies that serve to cap, rather than fix, the borrowing rate.

The borrower will usually decide to fix an issuance rate if there is little uncertainty surrounding the need or amount of the funding and if the current level of interest rates is attractive. If it leaves the issuance unhedged, the firm will benefit from a decline in interest

FIGURE 30–2
Choosing a Hedge Vehicle

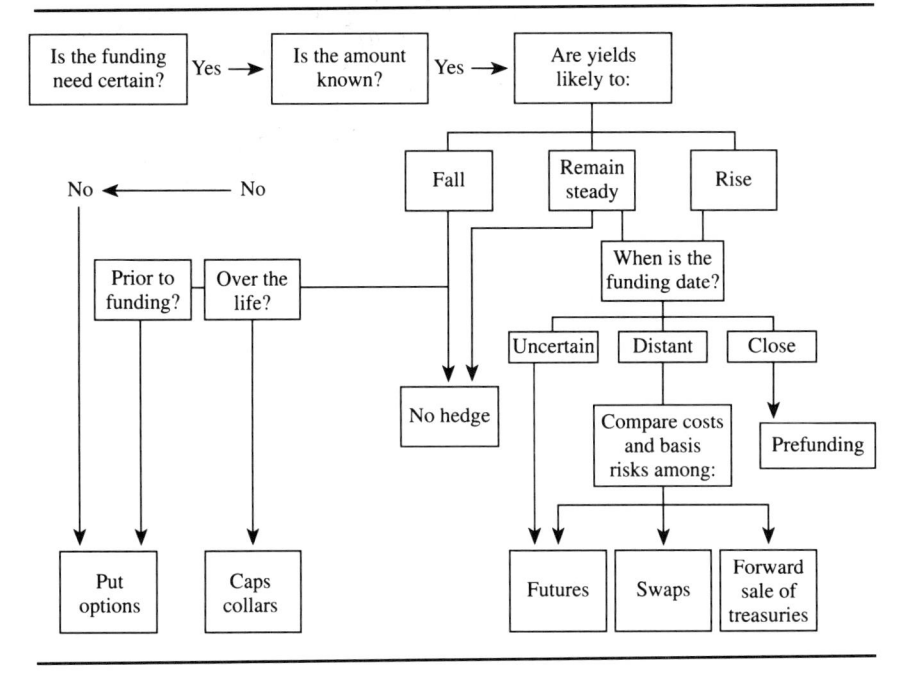

rates and will be hurt by an increase in rates before the issue date. This exposure is similar to that of a long position in a bond. By selling a bond with the same price sensitivity to changes in interest rates as that of the initial long position, the firm's exposure to changes in interest rates will be eliminated, effectively locking the rate at which debt will be issued.

As we pointed out earlier, there are two components of a corporate bond's yield: the base Treasury rate and the corporate spread. These components can be hedged jointly or separately. We will first describe techniques that fix the combined rate and then look individually at base rate-fixing and spread-fixing techniques.

Full Rate Fix

If a firm wants to fix not only the current rates of interest in the Treasury market but also the current spread of corporate issues off Treasury rates, it will generally opt to prefund. In a prefunding, the borrower brings the issue to market immediately, investing the proceeds at a short-term rate until they are needed. This technique can work very well if the details of the funding, the amount, and the maturity have been established. The cost of a prefunding is the difference between the debt's coupon rate and the short-term rate over the hedge period. If the yield curve is steep, or if the hedge period is lengthy, this technique may become expensive. Thus, if the yield curve is such that the coupon rate is 10 percent and the short-term rate is 8 percent, the cost of the hedge is 200 bp during the hedge period. For a three-month hedge period, this is $0.50 per $100 par, or 8 bp per year for 10 years.

Fixing the Base Rate

As Table 30–1 indicates, there are five techniques (columns 2 through 6) available for fixing the base Treasury rate of an issuance: (1) forward sales of Treasury securities, (2) short sales of Treasury securities, (3) futures contracts, (4) forward interest rate swaps, and (5) rate hedge agreements.

The most direct method of fixing a base rate is through the sale of Treasury securities of a similar maturity and price sensitivity to the funding. This can be done as either a forward sale or a short sale. The forward sale is an agreement between two parties to sell a security at a date in the future at a price agreed upon today. A short sale requires that the security be delivered immediately, which means that it must be borrowed through the repurchase market. Forward and short sales will have similar net costs. They differ in their execution and credit concerns.

Forward Sales
Forward sale prices are based on the net value of interest income—not simply the coupon rate—that a buyer would receive between the current date and the forward settlement date. Consider an investor who has $1 million and wants to purchase a 10-year, 9 percent coupon Treasury note. He can buy the note for spot settlement at a price of 100. For settlement 90 days forward, the price would be approximately 99.5. Is one alternative better than another? To answer this, we compare the returns of the alternatives. If the investor purchased the note for current delivery, he would

earn the coupon income over the 90 days, an annualized rate of return of approximately 9.0 percent. If he purchased the note in 90 days, the investor would have to leave the $1 million in a short-term investment, which might provide a rate of return of only 7.0 percent. Even though the investor has not actually received the note, he bears all the price risk of ownership and therefore should earn the full 9.0 percent. By using a 90-day forward price 50 cents lower than the spot price, he can increase the 7.0 percent return to the 9.0 percent level.

The difference between the short-term and long-term rates is called the *cost of carry*, and can be expressed as a rate, for example, 2.0 percent (9.0 percent less 7.0 percent). The difference between the spot price and the forward price is commonly called the *drop* (see Appendix A at the end of this chapter for details on the carry calculations).

A firm that is hedging a debt issuance is effectively taking the other side of our investor's position, selling the security for forward settlement. If security prices have declined by the end of the forward settlement period (rates have risen), the firm will be able to buy the bonds more cheaply in the market. Thus, the issuer will have a gain on the forward contract to offset losses resulting from the higher coupon rate on the new issue. Similarly, if security prices have risen by the end of the forward period (rates have fallen), the firm will have a loss on the forward contract, which will be offset by gains on the bond resulting from a lower coupon.

As we explained, the selling prices are based on the difference between short- and long-term rates. The firm that sells notes forward will be giving up the carry of 2.0 percent if interest rates remain unchanged. Since a hedging firm does not own the security it is selling, the carry will be an outright cost as opposed to forgone income. The firm is essentially locking in forward interest rates in this transaction.

A forward sale is fairly simple to execute. The firm just asks for a forward bid from a Treasury dealer. No securities or money will change hands until the forward settlement date, even though the ownership of the securities has been exchanged. The dealer (buyer) takes on the security's price risk over the forward period and in return receives only the firm's promise to deliver at the end of the period. Essentially, the forward sale is an uncollateralized credit agreement between the dealer and the firm.

The forward settlement date generally is set on or just after the planned issuance date.[2] On the settlement date, the hedger has two alternatives for closing the hedge. One way is to issue debt and use the proceeds to purchase Treasury securities for delivery against the forward settlement. The hedger will then use the funds received on the forward sale just as he would have used the debt proceeds in an unhedged situation. A much simpler way to remove the hedge is to enter into an offsetting forward purchase. To eliminate the need to actually make or take delivery, the hedger could make this forward purchase with the original counterparty for the same settlement date as the original contract.

Short Sales

The alternative to the forward sale is a short sale in which the issuer hedges by selling Treasury securities at the beginning of the hedge period. The hedging firm must borrow the notes in the repurchase (repo) market. In a repurchase agreement, a government securities dealer borrows money from the hedging firm and pledges as collateral the securities the hedging firm will need to short. The dealer will pay the hedging firm a short-term rate of interest for the use of its cash.

To execute a short sale, the hedging firm will generally borrow the Treasury security that will determine the base rate of the issuance, such as the current 10-year Treasury for a 10-year issuance.[3] The firm simultaneously sells the security into the market at the best available price and hands over the proceeds of the sale to the counterparty in the repurchase agreement. (The buyer of securities lends money.) At the end of the hedging period, the hedging firm buys notes to replace the original collateral and returns the securities, closing the repurchase agreement. The firm uses the money received from returning the collateral to buy the notes in the marketplace. To reduce the credit risk, the parties must make the exchange of securities and funds simultaneously. The dealer that "counterparts" the repo often handles the open market sale and purchases the Treasury securities, as this saves the hedging firm the effort of taking delivery of the borrowed securities and redelivering them for the short sale.

If the yield curve slopes upward and interest rates do not change, the hedging firm will incur a loss on the short sale equal to the difference between the yield on the Treasury rate and the repurchase interest rate. If the price of the security rises, the loss on the short sale will be largely offset by the lower coupon on the bond issuance. If the price of the security falls, the gain on the short sale will be slightly more than offset by the higher coupon on the bond issuance. Thus, the results from a short sale will be very close to those of a forward sale.

Hedgers should be aware that the repurchase rate can either be fixed or be allowed to float during the hedge period. If the rate is fixed, the arrangement is called a *term repo*. A floating-rate agreement is called an *open repo*. Most hedgers will prefer to use a term rate because it removes uncertainty about the cost of the hedge. An open repo may be simpler to use if the end of the hedge period is uncertain. An open repo is reestablished daily and net interest payments are made daily. The term repo usually has no interim payments.

Futures Sales

Futures on many types of government securities are actively traded on several exchanges around the world. The Chicago Board of Trade has the largest grouping of Treasury futures: 15- to 30-year bonds, 7- to 10-year notes, and 5-year notes. The bond future is by far the most active of the contracts, trading an average of $30 to 40 billion par value daily.

Futures contracts are standardized forward agreements, where the buyer and seller agree to exchange a type of (but not a specific) Treasury security during a future period at a price agreed upon today. Through either the actual delivery of a security or a cash settlement procedure, futures prices are inextricably linked to the underlying cash market prices. Consequently, the sale or purchase of a futures contract can be considered a substitute for the sale or purchase of the underlying security.

When the firm is choosing between futures and forward sales as hedge techniques, there are two primary considerations: (1) the strong liquidity and efficiency of the futures versus the ability to customize the specifics of a forward sale, and (2) the need to establish daily operations for managing futures margining versus the ability to establish a credit arrangement of the necessary size with a dealer. The following section on the valuation and nuances of futures contracts will be useful to most firms hedging a debt issuance. Some firms, for whom the additional attention and operational requirements of futures have been a deterrent in the past, may wish to reconsider in light of point one above.

Pricing and Valuation of Futures Contracts. The price of a futures contract is determined in roughly the same way as that of any forward contract. The difference between the spot and future (or forward) prices reflects the amount of carry available over the contract period. In the cash market, the difference is called the *drop*. In the futures market, the difference, which is calculated by subtracting the security's current price from the price used in the delivery process, is called the *basis*.[4] At the time of delivery, a future and its underlying security must have the same price, since they are interchangeable at that time. The basis spread must therefore "converge" to zero as delivery approaches.

The convergence of spot and futures prices does not proceed according to a fixed pattern. In an upward-sloping yield curve environment, spot prices are initially higher than futures prices. During the period after the initial hedge is put on until the contract expires, futures prices may remain constant, in which case spot prices must decline by the delivery date. Conversely, spot prices may remain constant and futures prices may increase to the spot price levels. In either case, the hedger has locked in forward prices. If futures do not move, there will be no gain or loss on the futures contract, and the debt will be issued at the then-current spot rate (the old forward rate). If futures prices increase, these will be a loss on the short futures position, which will affect an issuance at the spot rate. Note that with an inverted yield curve, the forward rate will be lower than the spot rate, and futures prices will be higher than spot prices.

Even though futures and cash prices will converge at the time of delivery, this does not imply that their prices are always in line during the contract's life. The calculation of carry will determine much of the appropriate value of the basis. For contracts that include delivery options favoring the party with the short futures position, there will be an additional discount of the futures price.[5]

The borrower must take these considerations into account when determining the relative value of futures versus cash—and, consequently, the attractiveness of futures as a hedge vehicle.

The most common technique for tracking the richness or cheapness of futures versus cash is to compare short-term investment rates with the return from buying a bond and selling it for future delivery. Consider an investor who can purchase a 30-year U.S. Treasury bond and lock in a sale price by selling futures. Ignoring for a moment the delivery options, we know that the bondholder will receive the coupon income between the purchase date and the delivery date. The delivery price, however, is lower than the purchase price, so the total return of this "cash-and-carry" trade should have a net return equal to a money market instrument because it has the same amount of price risk.

The holding period return from the cash-and-carry trade is called the *implied repo rate*; it is on this rate that arbitrageurs focus. If money could be borrowed in the dealer repurchase market at an interest rate below the holding period return of the cash and carry, then there would be an opportunity to arbitrage the two markets. In fact, this opportunity almost never appears, and the implied repo rate—the financing rate at or below which the arbitrageur would have to borrow—averages 1 to 3 percent below normal lending rates. This suggests that futures are always cheap versus cash prices (remember that futures are the selling price in the cash-and-carry trade) and that arbitrageurs should sell cash bonds and buy futures. This trade, however, is not really an arbitrage; it carries the risk that the cash bond sold will not be the one received in delivery. Any one of a number of bonds that meet the specified maturity requirements can be delivered at the discretion of the seller of the future. In addition, the seller has a variety of options regarding the date the bond is to be delivered during the expiration month. To compensate the buyer for these risks, the price of the future is reduced and the implied repo rate will be lower than the rates on other short-term investments.

When contemplating the use of futures as a hedge vehicle, a firm must take into account whether futures prices are rich or cheap. A firm would determine this by considering where the future should trade without delivery options, less the value of the delivery options. If futures are rich, one is more likely to want to short them than if they are cheap. In addition, futures contracts that have relatively low volumes, or are in markets where arbitrage between cash and futures is difficult to implement, will have wider swings in their value relative to cash securities. Thus, relative richness or cheapness is more of an issue in these markets than in the bond futures market.

Futures Hedge Ratios. The price sensitivity of a futures contract is based upon the duration of the deliverable securities (or of the securities that make up the index on cash settlement contracts). For contracts that require physical delivery of securities, there will generally be one or two securities in the pool of deliverable issues that will be the most attractive for sellers of the contract to use to meet the delivery requirement. The reason for their attractiveness usually has less to do with their actual cash yields than with the peculiarities of the delivery process.[6] A hedger should be aware of which securities are the "cheapest to deliver" when the hedge is established and should monitor any changes in deliverability. The future's price sensitivity is usually calculated as the dollar duration of the cheapest-to-deliver security divided by its delivery conversion factor. Appendix B at the end of the chapter illustrates the calculation of a futures hedge ratio.

Simple duration hedging, as commonly applied, will reduce the exposure to changes in the level of interest rates, but there are two other exposures that it cannot remove: the risk of a nonparallel yield curve shift ("yield curve risk") and the risk that yields on corporate bonds will not move by the same amount as Treasury bond yields ("systematic corporate spread risk").[7] The latter risk is present whenever just the base rate is hedged, whether the hedge vehicle is a futures contract or a sale of Treasury securities. The risk of a nonparallel shift is usually greater for futures hedges than for cash hedges, because there are active futures contracts in a limited range of maturity sectors. In U.S. markets, the most active is the long bond sector, including maturities between 15 and 30 years, with the next largest the intermediate 7- to 10-year notes. The five-year Treasury note contracts are generally not liquid enough for hedges of more than $50 million. Clearly, an issue with a different maturity from that of the futures will be less than perfectly hedged with a futures position. For example, if 10-year note futures are used to duration hedge a 7-year issuance, most of the interest exposure is eliminated. But the hedge will not be precise if 7-year yields increase more than 10-year yields do.

It is worth noting that futures contracts are available on indexes of corporate bonds: the Bond Buyer Index future traded on the Chicago Board of Trade and the Moody's Corporate Bond Index traded on the Financial Instruments Exchange in New York. Both of these contracts, which were introduced in the fall of 1987, were designed to remove much of the sector mismatching problem that occurs when Treasury futures are used to hedge corporate debt issuance. Neither of these contracts, however, is currently trading, as neither has attracted enough interest to make it efficient or suitable for executing hedges of any size.

Despite the limitations created by standardization, futures contracts have been used extensively for hedging because of their advantages in liquidity, cost, and capital requirements. Moreover, their use involves minimal credit considerations, and the performance of the hedge is easy to track.

Mechanics of the Futures Market. Futures trade on exchanges, and the clearinghouse associated with each exchange becomes the counterparty to all trades. By acting as the counterparty, the clearinghouse eliminates the need for individual credit arrangements between buyers and sellers. The exchange values all open positions at the closing price of each day's trading session, and members settle accounts with one another each evening. In this way, futures positions are marked to market daily. Under these arrangements, the holder of the position must make (or receive) a cash payment equal to the difference of the current day's closing price and that of the previous day. For example, if the closing prices of the future were 99.0 on Day 1 and 98.0 on Day 2, the holder of a long (buyer) position would have to make a cash payment to the exchange equal to $1,000 per contract. The short (seller) position would receive a $1,000 cash payment from the exchange.

In addition to the daily margin call, every account must maintain an "initial" or "good faith" margin. This requires a pledge of securities or cash, equivalent to approximately 3 percent of the face value of the futures position held, or $3,000 per contract. This margin remains in the firm's segregated futures account at the brokerage and earns interest (on the cash deposits) or coupon payments (on the securities).

The liquidity of the futures markets allows hedge design and maintenance to be more flexible and generally more cost-efficient than physical Treasury transactions. The bid-offered spreads in futures are usually only $1/32$ of a point as opposed to $1/8$ of a point for less liquid Treasuries, making it simple and efficient to adjust the hedge size and close the hedge.

Most contracts are settled on a quarterly cycle, for example, March, June, September, and December for the U.S. Treasury contracts. The greatest liquidity is found in the "front" contract, the next contract to be delivered against. For long-term hedges, this may require that the hedge be initiated with the front contract and then "rolled" into the next contract just prior to the delivery period. The cost of rolling is usually $1/32$.

Forward Swaps

Another technique for fixing a base rate is a forward interest rate swap transaction. An interest rate swap is a contractual agreement between two parties to exchange payments, expressed as a percentage of a notional principal value, on a periodic basis for a number of years. There is no exchange of principal. The volume of U.S. dollar interest rate swaps totaled $677 billion in 1990, up from $100 billion in 1985 and $5 billion in 1982. Outstanding swaps are estimated at $1.273 trillion as of year-end 1990. Both commercial and investment banks position and trade interest rate swaps, and an active market provides reasonable liquidity. The most liquid swaps are those based on exchanging three- or six-month LIBOR for the yield on a current Treasury note plus a spread. The majority of swaps have terms of 3 to 7 years, but swaps are available to 10 years. There is also a short-dated swap market for terms of less than three years. Pricing of short-dated swaps is closely tied to the three-month Eurodollar futures.[8] The futures are based on three-month LIBOR and therefore provide an efficient hedging mechanism for the swap dealers.

Generally, swaps that begin immediately are used to adjust the character of interest payments on existing assets or liabilities. Hedges of anticipated issuances or receipt of assets can be more effectively done with a forward swap. A forward swap is just a normal interest rate swap transaction, except that the swap begins on a forward date—normally, the date of the bond issuance. A forward swap hedge proceeds as follows:

1. A firm enters a three-month forward swap in a notional amount equal to the planned debt issuance, agreeing to pay the current five-year Treasury yield plus 75 basis points. In return, the firm will receive six-month LIBOR.
2. In three months, the firm issues floating-rate debt. Six months after issuance, the first payments are exchanged. The firm pays the fixed rate available at the time the swap was entered and receives six-month LIBOR. The LIBOR payment is used to pay the interest on the floating-rate debt.
3. The net cost of the issuance will be the swap's fixed-rate level plus the difference between six-month LIBOR and the floating-rate index at which the firm issues. For example, if the firm issues floating-rate debt at six-month LIBOR + 25 bp, its all-in cost of funds is the five-year Treasury yield plus the 75 bp swap spread plus the 25 bp margin on the floating-rate debt. If the firm instead issues floating-rate debt at the commercial paper rate, the cost of funds to the firm will be less than the five-year Treasury yield plus 75 bp, reflecting the fact that the commercial paper rate is below LIBOR. In lieu of issuing floating-rate debt, the firm may terminate or assign the swap, recognizing any gain or loss, and issue fixed-rate debt.

The rates on a forward swap are higher as the swap is priced off forward interest rates further into the future. For example, the rate for a five-year swap beginning in six months is 10 basis points higher than for a five-year swap beginning immediately.

The swap market developed as a result of differences in the borrowing capabilities of various institutions—banks, insurance companies, and corporations in general. Swaps are frequently used to manage the structures of assets and liabilities, since they can be customized to meet specific needs and, if they meet settlement accounting criteria, they have no balance sheet implications. For hedging purposes, however, the more customized a swap becomes, the more difficult it will be to reverse if the hedging need is changed or eliminated. Entering into a swap costs nothing in the way of fees or commission payments. The cost of any odd payment dates or fluctuation of paramounts will initially be reflected in an increase in the spread over the fixed rate that the firm is obligated to pay. Additionally, a wider-than-normal bid-offered spread will be an added cost if the swap is reversed. Depending on the circumstances, this spread will generally be in the range of 5–8 bp. Swaps based on floating-rate indexes other than LIBOR are also available, but they tend to be much less liquid than LIBOR-based swaps.

One way of eliminating the uncertainty over the cost of closing a swap is to add a call provision to the swap. In a callable swap, the firm paying a fixed rate of interest and receiving a floating rate has the option to terminate the transaction. It will choose to do so if rates have declined. It pays for the option through an increase in the fixed rate, which is quoted on the swap. As in a forward swap, the firm will issue floating-rate debt to achieve fixed financing. Callability may be attractive enough to warrant its added expense if the firm wants the option to shift entirely to floating debt, or if it wants the flexibility to retire debt early (in which case, it should add a call option to the floating-rate debt).

In a swap, the issuer will be exposed to the credit risk of the counterparty. This is usually a financial institution that acts as the intermediary between one final user who wants to pay fixed and receive floating, and another final user who wishes to receive fixed and pay floating. This risk initially appears smaller than that of a forward sale of Treasury securities, in that there is no notional exchange of principal. The credit risk on a swap, however, extends throughout the swap's life.

Rate Hedge Agreements
A final alternative for fixing the base rate is a rate hedge agreement (RHA). An RHA is a customized contract in which a dealer hedges the yield on a Treasury security on behalf of a prospective issuer. The term of the contract is generally limited to six months. Economically, a rate hedge agreement is no different from a Treasury short sale, but it receives far more favorable tax and accounting treatment because there is no formal sale of securities. For short

hedge periods, an RHA is generally less costly than a forward swap.

An RHA specifies a base price for a particular Treasury security or other instrument. This base price is derived from the current price, net of carry. When a prospective issuer enters into an RHA with a dealer, the client may terminate the agreement at any time during its life by asking the dealer to quote a "takedown price" on the underlying Treasury security. An excess of the takedown price over the base price would be payable by the prospective issuer to the dealer; a shortfall would be payable by the dealer to the client. Under the RHA, there is no right or obligation to make or take delivery of the specified Treasury or any other property. Settlement is completed solely in cash.

Fixing a Spread

If a firm expects interest rates to stay steady or decline but expects credit spreads in general or its firm-specific spread to widen before funds are needed, the firm may wish to consider fixing a spread. It can accomplish this in either of two ways—by doing a spread lock to fix the generic spread, or by prefunding and investing the proceeds in Treasury securities of the same maturity to fix the firm-specific spread. Both of these techniques have been used, with a spread lock being the more common choice.

Fixing a Generic Credit Spread
Fixing a generic credit spread is most easily done through the swap market. The fixed rate on a swap of a given maturity is generally quoted as the current Treasury of the same maturity plus a spread. This so-called swap spread tends to narrow and widen in tandem with general corporate spreads. A spread lock allows a firm to fix the credit spread without fixing the base rate. Thus, a spread lock can be viewed as a tool for hedging the general level of corporate spreads. A spread lock is most effective when a firm knows it will have to come to market within a relatively short time—two or three months.

In a spread lock, the firm agrees to enter into a swap deal at a particular spread to Treasuries, but has a period ranging up to three months to fix the absolute rate. That is, the firm must fix the absolute rate by the end of the period, but may choose when within that period to fix the rate. When the base rate is fixed, the prespecified spread is added to give the fixed rate payable on the swap. The spread lock is typically offered at a 2–4 bp premium over the straight swap.[9] If Treasury rates decline over the near term, the firm can take advantage of this.

To see how a spread lock would work, assume that a firm wants to fix the spread for the next two months. At the end of a two-month period, or earlier if Treasury rates looked attractive, the firm would issue floating-rate debt and take down the swap in which it receives fixed and pays floating. Assume the fixed swap spread was 80 bp and its issuing rate was LIBOR + 25 bp. The firm would, on net, pay the Treasury rate prevailing at the time the swap was taken down plus 105 bp (80 + 25).

Fixing a Firm-Specific Spread

If a firm wants to fix a spread on a specific issue, it can prefund the issue and invest the proceeds in a Treasury security of the same maturity until the funds are needed. Assume a firm is able to fund today for 10 years at $T_{10} + 80$ bp. If it invests the proceeds at T_{10}, the firm's cost is the 80 bp credit spread plus the bid-asked spread on the Treasury purchase and sale. If we neglect the transaction cost on the Treasury issue, paying the 10-year rate at the time of prefunding plus taking the loss or gain on the Treasury is equivalent to paying the 10-year rate at the time the funds are needed. If rates have risen, the firm's borrowing rate will be lower than the currently prevailing rate, but the Treasury investment will have experienced a loss. Similarly, if rates have fallen, the borrowing rate will be higher than the currently prevailing rate, but the Treasury investment will have experienced a gain. In our example, the 80 bp cost for three months is roughly equivalent to an extra 2.2 bp over the life of the 10-year issue. The purchase and subsequent sale of Treasury securities could be done through a rate hedge agreement as well as through the physical purchase and sale of securities.

This technique differs from a prefunding to fix the entire rate in that the proceeds are invested differently. The firm invests the proceeds of a prefunding in a short-term money market instrument.

In fixing a firm-specific spread, it invests the proceeds of the prefunding in longer-term notes, the price movements of which will offset changes in the interest rate on the bond issuance.

CAPPING A RATE

As Figure 30-2 indicates, circumstances may arise in which it will be advantageous for the issuer to put a ceiling on its borrowing rate through the purchase of options. There may be uncertainty as to the details of the issuance, or the firm may feel that interest rates are likely to decline either before the issuance date or over the life of the issue. An option hedge allows the issuer to take advantage of a rate decline while protecting itself from an increase in rates above a specific level. If the borrower is not sure of its funding needs, options can guarantee a maximum all-in funding cost. If it turns out that the funding is needed, the protection is helpful. If the funding is not needed and there is a gain on the option, the firm can exercise the option and liquidate. In any event, the maximum loss is limited to the option premium.

The benefits of options must, however, be balanced against their costs, which can seem relatively higher when compared with the costs of fixed-rate hedges. The costs are higher because an option has an asymmetric risk profile. That is, the price gain from a decline in interest rates is not mirrored by an equal price loss from a rise in interest rates. Figure 30-3 illustrates the difference in the risk profiles of (1) an issuance hedged with the purchase of a put option and (2) an unhedged issuance.

The two most common option hedges are individual Treasury put options and option packages called *caps* or *collars*. A less well-known alternative is the *caput*. We will discuss each of these in turn.

Buying Put Options

The purchase of a put option can cap the level of the base rate or the base rate plus a spread, depending on whether the option is written on a Treasury or a corporate bond. The latter is a custom-

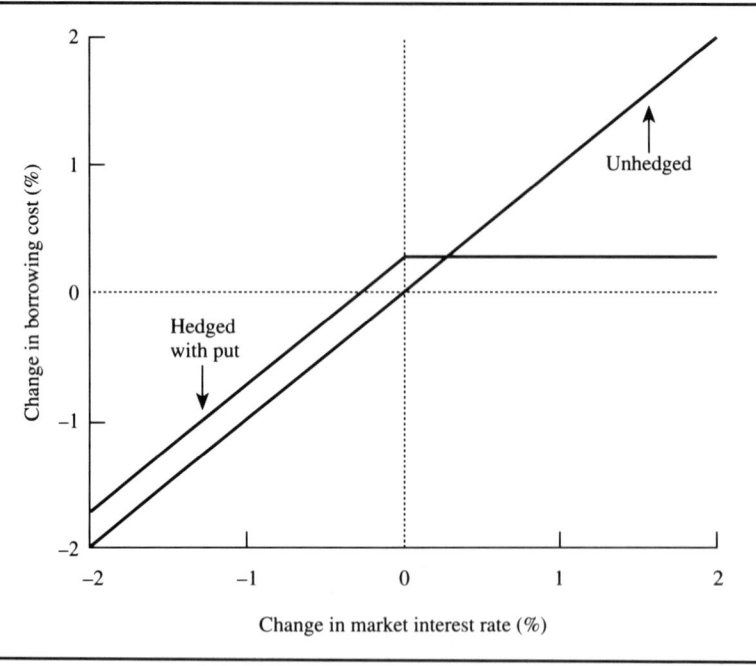

FIGURE 30–3
Borrowing Costs: Unhedged and Hedged with Put

ized product that generally entails a wider bid-asked spread. A put buyer purchases the right, but not the obligation, to sell a bond at a specified price (or yield) at some point during a stated time period. The cost of this protection from rate increases is the option premium, which the buyer must pay when purchasing the option at the beginning of the hedge period.

One of the advantages of option products is their flexibility. The firm can choose to cap the cost of the issue at a price level that corresponds to its needs rather than simply using the current price level in the market. The selected price level is called the *strike price*. A put that is struck at a price below the market is an out-of-the-money option. It will cost less but will provide less protection than an option that is struck at current price levels, an at-the-money option. That is, if the current price is 98 and a firm purchases an option with a strike price of 95, the option will be less expensive than a 98 strike, but the firm will have to absorb the three points of price decline before the option will begin to pay off. Options are frequently compared to insurance policies, where the amount that the option is out of the money is the policy deductible. Distant strikes can be used to provide "disaster insurance."

The flexibility of strike levels and the known cost (premium) of options are particularly important in the presence of funding uncertainty. Borrowers may be reluctant to buy at-the-money options because of cost considerations, but some level of insurance may be desirable.

Issuers can use either exchange-traded or over-the-counter (OTC) options. Exchange-traded options are available on almost all the major futures contracts. The open interest of options on bond futures traded on the Chicago Board of Trade (CBOT) is higher than the open interest on the futures themselves, although the daily volume of options is lower. The advantages and disadvantages of exchange-traded options on futures are the same as those of the futures themselves. One must balance liquidity and lower transaction costs against the limitations of standardization.

OTC options are traded by securities dealers. These dealers stand ready to make markets in options at a bid-asked spread. The more customized the product, the wider the spread. On-the-run Treasuries have narrower bid-asked spreads than off-the-run Treasuries, which in turn have narrower spreads than options on corporates.

An exchange-traded option will hedge movements in particular Treasury rates but cannot hedge the specific characteristics of the corporation's debt. OTC options can be customized to cap borrowing costs at the desired level and eliminate any mismatch between the option term and the borrower's hedging period. A firm that wishes to use an OTC option has three choices: (1) purchasing an option on a Treasury security of the same maturity as the anticipated issue, (2) purchasing an option on one of its own outstanding bonds, or (3) purchasing an option on the anticipated issue. Options on Treasury securities would entail a lower bid-asked spread than either of the other two choices. These options, however, require the firm to assume the risk that its credit spread may widen. With options on an outstanding corporate bond or an anticipated issuance, a firm can cap both the base rate and the credit spread for the desired period. The disadvantage to a corporate client of buying an option on the anticipated issuance is that if the issue does not come to market, the firm cannot exercise the option. Before pursuing this alternative, a company should be absolutely sure of its need for funding. If a firm is unsure of the need for funding, buying an option on one of its outstanding issues may be preferred.

The disadvantage of OTC options is the frequently high cost of unwinding them before expiration. Although this applies to both options on Treasuries and options on corporates, it is a more serious problem for options on corporates. If a firm is unsure of exactly when funding may be needed, an exchange-trade option will be preferable. Since most issuers have some degree of funding uncertainty, exchange-traded options are used far more commonly than OTC options. If a firm's credit spread fluctuations are small, it may well prefer to use an exchange-traded option, since it is important to hedge only the base rate. It is unnecessary to pay for a customized product.

Setting Up a Hedge

When OTC options are used, it is fairly straightforward to hedge a given par amount of new issuance. The par value of the options is equal to that of the issuance, and the expiration date is set for the exact funding date. If the funding date is not set specifically, the option should be purchased for as long a period as one is likely to need it. If the funding occurs early, the issuer can sell the option back or exercise it early. The latter is permissible on OTC options that are generally American style (the option can be exercised at any point prior to the expiration date).[10]

An exchange-traded option hedge can be established with the same technique used for an outright futures hedge. This requires the price sensitivity of the futures position to match the price sensitivity of the issuance. Once the correct number of futures contracts is determined, one purchases options on that number of contracts. Appendix B at the end of this chapter illustrates the calculation of futures hedge ratios.

Option market participants should be aware that the liquidity of the exchange is concentrated in the first two contracts with the nearest maturity dates.[11] The most effective hedges will generally be those where the expiration date of the option is close to the funding date. If the option expires before the funding date, the hedge will be prematurely removed. If the option expires more than a couple of weeks after the funding, the price movement of the option will be unlikely to have fully hedged the change in the issuance price. Because of the importance of expiration timing and the complexities of option pricing, exchange-traded options should be used to hedge large market movements; they cannot be used to lock in a maximum issuance rate. Moreover, they are best suited for relatively short hedge periods—five months or less.

If a firm wants to use an exchange-traded product but the desired option expiration date does not match the expiration dates of exchange options, a synthetic option can be created. This has a price performance much more satisfactory than, for example, a combination of September and December options used to replicate an October expiration date. The September contract will expire before the option is to mature; the December contract will expire after the option is needed. Moreover, in October, the December option will be worth more than its intrinsic value (the amount that the option is in the money); it will also have some time value remaining. Thus, to accurately tailor the expiration date, one must construct a synthetic option. To do so, the firm would buy and sell futures in amounts such that their price performance matches that of the target option. This technique is discussed in detail in Rubinstein and Leland (1981) and Asay and Edelsburg (1986). Synthetic options can be particularly useful for long hedge periods—that is, hedge periods longer than the liquid option contracts.

If the desired strike price does not match the strike price on existing exchange-traded options, a firm can either create a synthetic option with the desired strike price or use a combination of the nearest two strike prices. Thus, if the borrower wanted a strike of 101 on December 1991 options on bond futures, it could create a similar—but not identical—risk/return profile by using December put options with strike prices of 100 and 102.

If the firm wanted to cap only the spread, it could do so by purchasing a put option on the spread. This would work as follows: If the firm would currently come to market at $T_{10} + 50$ bp, the exercise price on the put option might be 50 bp. On the funding date, if spreads had widened to 70 bp, the firm would exercise its option and the counterparty would pay the firm—in cash—the present value of 20 bp per year over the life of the issue. The option could be written on the spread of an outstanding bond or on the spread of the anticipated issuance.

One should be aware that the market for spread options is illiquid, and not every dealer participates. Moreover, these options tend to be relatively expensive because they are difficult to hedge.

In sum, a borrower can use either OTC, exchange-traded, or synthetic put options to cap the rate on a new debt issuance. OTC options provide more protection (at a greater cost), but they are expensive to resell prior to maturity. Exchange-traded options have greater liquidity, but their strikes and maturities are less flexible. If the characteristics of the options desired by the issuer do not match those of an option traded on the exchange, the borrower can create a synthetic option using futures. Synthetic option positions require close monitoring and trading of futures, but they do allow the borrower to have a customized option with lower costs than a typical OTC option.

Caps and Collars

Occasionally, a firm may have determined a funding need, but either does not find the prevailing level of interest rates to be attractive or expects interest rates to move lower prior to the issuance date or over the life of the issue. In these circumstances, caps and collars are suitable hedge vehicles. Borrowers use them in conjunction with a floating- rather than a fixed-rate issuance. Caps and collars are negotiated transactions between the firm and a commercial or investment bank, where the firm pays an initial premium to the bank and in return receives interest payments if the underlying rate moves above an agreed-upon level. For example, if the firm purchases a LIBOR-based cap at 11 percent, the bank agrees that if LIBOR rises above 11 percent, the bank will pay the firm for that reset period at a rate equal to the difference between the prevailing rate and 11 percent.

Thus, if a firm purchased an 11 percent cap that reset semiannually on $100 million, and LIBOR rose to 13 percent, the firm would receive $.02 \times \frac{1}{2} \times \$100$ million, or $1 million. Its net borrowing costs for that period would be:

Interest cost	.13 × ½ × $100,000,000 =	$6,500,000
Less receipt from cap	.02 × ½ × $100,000,000 =	−1,000,000
		$5,500,000

Note that the net cost corresponds to an interest rate of 11 percent (.11 × ½ × $100 million = $5.5 million). If LIBOR were 10 percent, the firm would receive no cap payments, and its floating-rate debt would be set at 10 percent for the period. To compute the maximum all-in borrowing cost with a cap, one must add the amortization of the initial cap premium to the maximum borrowing rate. The up-front cost of the cap is dependent on the level of interest rates, interest rate volatility, and the shape of the yield curve.

Caps are available based on a wide range of money market indexes, including Treasury bills, commercial paper, LIBOR, the prime rate, and the rate on certificates of deposit. LIBOR caps are, by far, the most common. Caps based on other indexes may be arranged but will be slightly more expensive. The firm would select the floating-rate index, as well as the maturity of the cap (up to 10 years, but most commonly in the 3- to 7-year range), the ceiling rate, the start date, and the payment frequency (three or six months). An unofficial estimate of the size of the cap market is $300 to $400 billion of outstanding caps.

A cap is actually a series of options. Consider a three-year cap that pays every six months. It is a series of five options: a 6-month option, a 12-month option, an 18-month option, a 2-year option, and a 2 ½-year option. There are five rather than six options because payments are determined by the LIBOR rate at the beginning of the period and paid at the end. Thus, the rate for the first six months is determined immediately and hence has no option component. The payment for the period from 6 to 12 months is determined by LIBOR at the end of month 6, and this option would be exercised if LIBOR exceeds the cap level.

If an issuer buys a cap and, at the end of three months, decides not to issue the security, it can sell the cap back to the dealer. However, the bid-asked spreads on caps are wider than those on put options; a 25- to 50-cent bid-asked spread would be typical. This translates into 5 to 10 bp per year on a five-year issue. If the bond is to be issued and rates have declined, the buyer can either resell the cap and issue a fixed-rate bond, or keep the cap and issue at the lower floating rate. If rates have risen, the issuer can issue floating and keep the now more valuable cap. Alternatively, the issuer can resell the cap at a gain and issue at the then-higher fixed rate.

A variation on the cap is the floating-rate collar. The collar market was created for issuers who prefer capped floating-rate liabilities but consider caps too expensive. With a collar, a borrower buys a cap and sells a "floor" at the same time. If rates fall below the floor level, the firm is obligated to pay the difference between the floor level and the floating-rate index. The income from selling the floor offsets some of the cost of the cap. For example, if the issuer purchased a cap 260 bp above current rates and sold a floor 100 bp below current rates for three years, the cost of the collared position would reduce the up-front fee by close to 50 percent.

Figure 30-4 shows the risk/return profile of a collared position vis-à-vis a capped position and an unhedged position. As one can see, when rates are low, both the unhedged position and the capped position are preferable to the collar. As rates rise, the collar looks quite attractive—it is more favorable than either capped debt or unhedged debt.

Another cap product is the forward cap. A firm may use a forward cap if it expects to issue debt in the future and believes that rates will go up by more than the expectations implied by the existing yield curve. If an issuer decides not to issue the debt, it can sell back the cap. This type of transaction requires that a counterparty write one cap (the longer cap) and buy another cap (the shorter cap). Thus, the transaction costs on this type of hedge are greater than on a normal cap.

Caputs

Caps and puts are the two most common devices used to place an upper limit on borrowing costs. Less common but often useful is a *caput*—a call on a put. This gives an issuer the right to purchase a specific put at a given strike price at a particular date in the future. If interest rates rise, the put will increase in value. Thus, the caput, which conveys the right to purchase the put at a preset price, also

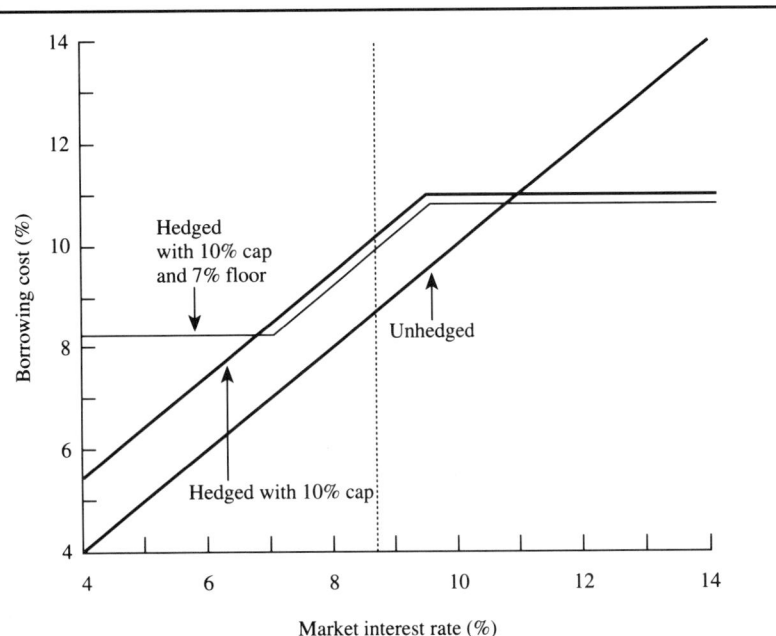

FIGURE 30-4
Borrowing Costs: Unhedged and Hedged with Caps and Floors

becomes more valuable. If interest rates decline, the caput will not be exercised.

The caput gives the purchaser the right to purchase another option at a fixed price. Thus, there are two separate fees—one fee for each of the options. This is often referred to as a *split-fee option* or a *compound option*. A caput is useful if there is a period of uncertainty before the financing need can be verified and another period between the verification and the actual issuance. The first fee is payable up front; the second fee is not payable until after the financing uncertainty has been resolved.

For example, assume that a caput contains the right to buy a three-month put option in three months at a strike yield of 9 percent for a cost of 3 points. If the cost of the caput is $2.50, the cost of initially purchasing a six-month put option may be $4.50. Thus, a caput requires a smaller up-front payment than an option with a time to expiration equal to that of the caput plus the put. If the caput is not exercised, it is because rates have declined. If the caput is exercised, the total payment is higher than on the six-month put. If the financing is not going to occur, the put can be purchased and resold at a profit. When there is a great deal of uncertainty about the financing, the caput should be considered as an alternative to a cap or a put, as the up-front fee is lower. However, caputs are highly customized products and therefore are hard to resell prior to expiration.

SUMMARY

In this chapter, we have described a variety of ways to hedge an anticipated bond issuance, by fixing and/or capping a rate. The appropriate hedging solution will depend on the firm's desired risk profile and the relative importance to the firm of the various hedging criteria.

Table 30–1 summarizes the ways to hedge an anticipated debt issuance. Clearly, no single technique dominates in all circumstances. Hedge design will depend on the firm's goals and priorities. For example, if an issuer wants a low-cost, liquid hedge of the base Treasury rate, and preservation of the upside potential is relatively unimportant, interest rate futures may be the hedging method of choice. If the issuer wants to preserve the upside potential and is willing to spend the money to do so, a put option or a cap is a more appropriate hedge.

Figure 30–2 identifies critical questions that arise in the choice of a hedge. An issuer may well use one hedge technique for one issue and a different hedge technique for another issue at a different time. That is, an issuer may want to fix the base rate for one issue and purchase a cap for another. A firm may even want to change the hedge technique during the course of a single issue. For example, if the issuer believes interest rates will rise for a short while, but are uncertain thereafter, it may want to initially fix a rate and think about the possibility of capping a rate later. If there is funding uncertainty, fixing a rate may be less desirable than alternatives that preserve upside potential. Once the uncertainty is resolved, fixing a rate may be preferable.

In short, there is no magic key to choosing the best hedge. The appropriate vehicle will vary among issuers, and the decision will be different for a single issuer at different times. The decision may even change for a single issue during the anticipation period. In general, the best hedge in any given situation is the one that largely offsets the price risk of the issuance and most closely meets the firm's own hedge criteria.

APPENDIXES TO CHAPTER 30

APPENDIX A: FORWARD SALE OF COUPON BOND

Spot Market on August 1, 1988

U.S. Treasury	9s of 5/15/98
Yield	9.07%
Price	99 17/32
Short-term rate	7.0%

To buy the U.S. Treasury note for forward settlement on September 1, 1988:

$$\text{Forward price} = \text{Spot price} + \text{Carry}$$
$$\text{Carry} = (P_o + A_o)(rt/360) - A_s + A_o - C(1 + rd/360)$$

where

P_o = Spot price

A_o = Spot accrued

A_s = Accrued on forward settlement

r = Short-term rate

t = Days from spot to settlement

d = Days from coupon payment to settlement

C = Coupon payment if there is a coupon drop; 0 otherwise

To express the carry in price terms: Divide the dollar value of the carry by the dollar value of a 32nd ($312.50 per million dollars face).

$$\text{Carry} = \frac{(\$1{,}014{,}389)(.06 \times 31/360) - \$26{,}657 + \$19{,}076 - 0}{312.50}$$

$$= -2{,}340/312.50$$

$$= -7.5 \text{ 32nds}$$

$$\text{Forward price} = 99\ 17/32 - 7.5/32$$
$$= 99\ 9.5/32$$

APPENDIX B: DETERMINING THE FUTURES HEDGE RATIO

To determine the appropriate number of futures contracts to use when hedging a proposed $100 million, 10-year debt issuance:

1. Determine the price sensitivity of the issuance to a change in its yield by averaging the change in prices for a 1 bp increase in yield and a 1 bp decrease in yield.

Price at forward yield of 9.5%	100.000
Price of 9.5% coupon at yield of 9.51%	99.935
Price of 9.5% coupon at yield of 9.49%	100.065

$$\text{Issuance price sensitivity} = [(100.00 - 99.935) + (100.065 - 100.00)]/2 = .065$$

2. Determine which security is the cheapest to deliver (CTD) and calculate its price sensitivity. CTD note is the 8.125 percent of 2/15/98.

Price at 9.0% yield (on issuance date)	94.393
Price of 9.01% yield	94.332
Price of 8.99% yield	94.455

$$\text{CTD price sensitivity} = .067$$

Then divide this sensitivity by the delivery factor of the bond for the contract period being used, the September U.S. Treasury note contract.

$$\text{Futures price sensitivity} = .067/1.0079 = .0665$$

3. Hedge ratio equals the price sensitivity of the issuance divided by the price sensitivity of the future.

Hedge ratio = .065/.0665 = .98 futures per $100,000 face value of issue

NOTES

1. Modified duration quantifies the percentage price change for a given change in bond yield, and Macaulay duration measures the weighted-average time to receipt of a security's cash flows.
2. If the forward settlement fell prior to the funding date, that would leave a period in which a change in the issuance yield would not be covered by a change in the value of the hedge instrument. If, for

whatever reason, the forward date does come before the issuance date, the forward sale must be offset with a purchase for that date, and a new forward sale must be established.
3. More precisely, the firm will attempt to borrow a security with a maturity equal to the time to maturity of the anticipated bond plus the time to issuance. In practice, it will select the on-the-run Treasury with a maturity most closely matching the anticipated issue.
4. Delivery prices for contracts that require the physical delivery of coupon-bearing bonds are equal to the futures price multiplied by a conversion factor. Factors provide the mechanism for invoicing each of the deliverable securities.
5. Delivery options exist for contracts that are completed by the physical delivery of any one of a variety of securities. These include the popular U.S. Treasury bond and U.S. Treasury note contracts, both traded on the Chicago Board of Trade.
6. For details on this point, see Marcelle Arak, Laurie S. Goodman, and Susan Ross, "The Cheapest to Deliver Bond on the Treasury Bond Futures Contract," in *Advances in Futures and Options Research,* vol. 1 (Greenwich, Conn.: JAI Press, 1987), Part B; James F. Meisner and John W. Labuszewski, "Treasury Bond Futures Deliver Bids," *The Journal of Futures Markets* 4 (1984), pp. 569–73; and Alex Kane and Alan J. Marcus, "The Quality Opinion in the Treasury Bond Futures Market: An Empirical Assessment," *The Journal of Futures Markets* 6 (1986), pp. 230–48.
7. Actually, there are duration measures that do not depend on parallel shifts of the yield curve. See Chulsoon Khang, "Bond Immunization When Short-Term Interest Rates Fluctuate More Than Long-Term Rates," *Journal of Financial and Quantitative Analysis* 14, no. 2 (December 1979); and G. O. Bierwag, George G. Kaufman, and Cynthia M. Latta, "Duration Models: A Taxonomy," *The Journal of Portfolio Management,* Fall 1988.
8. Eurodollar futures are traded on the Chicago Mercantile Exchange, the Singapore International Monetary Exchange, and the London International Financial Future Exchange.
9. The premium is present because the swap counterparty will short Treasury securities and invest the proceeds in short-term instruments until the swap is taken down. The negative carry during the hedge period is figured into the quoted spread. Thus, 150 bp of negative carry for two months is $0.25 per $100 par, or 2.5 bp for a seven-year issue.
10. The alternative is a "European style" option, which can be exercised only on its expiration date.

11. Contracts expire quarterly in February, May, August, and November. Liquidity is satisfactory when the options have remaining lives of approximately five months or less.

REFERENCES

Arak, Marcelle; Laurie S. Goodman; and Susan Ross. "The Cheapest to Deliver Bond on the Treasury Bond Futures Contract." In *Advances in Futures and Options Research*, Vol. 1. Greenwich, Conn.: JAI Press, 1987, Part B.

Asay Michael, and Charles Edelsburg. "Can a Dynamic Strategy Replicate the Returns of an Option." *The Journal of Futures Markets* 6 (1986), pp. 63–71.

Bierwag, G. O.; George G. Kaufman; and Cynthia M. Latta. "Duration Models: A Taxonomy." *The Journal of Portfolio Management*, Fall 1988.

Kane, Alex, and Alan J. Marcus. "The Quality Opinion in the Treasury Bond Futures Market: An Empirical Assessment." *The Journal of Futures Markets* 6 (1986), pp. 230–48.

Khang, Chulsoon. "Bond Immunization When Short-Term Interest Rates Fluctuate More Than Long-Term Rates." *Journal of Financial and Quantitative Analysis* 14, no. 2 (December 1979).

Meisner, James F., and John W. Labuszewski. "Treasury Bond Futures Deliver Bids." *The Journal of Futures Markets* 4 (1984), pp. 569–73.

Rubinstein, Mark, and Hayne E. Leland. "Replicating Options with Positions in Stock and Cash." *Financial Analysts Journal*, July–August 1981, pp. 3–12.

CHAPTER 31

FIXED-INCOME RISK MANAGEMENT: DESIGN AND PRACTICE

Joseph Langsam
Morgan Stanley & Co.
Leon Tatevossian
Salomon Brothers Inc.

OVERVIEW

In the absence of arbitrage, excess return is earned by assuming risk. At the same time, there exists risk that does not make a positive contribution to expected return. The task confronting the fixed-income portfolio manager is to structure a portfolio to obtain the desired risk/reward profile. The risk manager has at his disposal the financial engineer's toolbox of derivative securities—an arsenal that includes futures, forwards, options, swaps, swap options, and other customized products. In this chapter, we introduce a framework for the effective use of these risk management devices.

Building the analytical framework requires a number of steps. Our first task is to identify an unambiguous working definition of risk. This is accomplished in the first section with a few examples. The second section is a primer on fixed-income valuation models. The quantification and management of risk is invariably linked to a valuation model. In the third section, we discuss the standard methodologies for quantifying risk. The fundamentals of hedging are introduced in the fourth section and elaborated with straightforward examples. This section also contrasts the pros and cons of naive and sophisticated risk management strategies. The next section is an informal survey of the principal types of interest rate hedging vehicles and a brief discussion of their applicability. A summary and concluding remarks are contained in the final section.

This chapter will occasionally sacrifice theoretical accuracy to obtain greater clarity of exposition. It should be clear where this sacrifice is being made. We will make every attempt to ensure that these simplifications do not compromise the correctness of our conclusions.

DEFINING RISK

While risk is one of those concepts that most investors feel they can recognize, it defies easy definition. We need a working definition of risk to measure and, ultimately, manage it. We will take the circuitous path of first looking at some hypothetical examples and then attempting a more formal definition.

Example 1
Consider an insurance company CFO who is examining an asset portfolio assigned to finance a pension annuity. The annuity represents a long-duration interest rate–sensitive liability for the company. The CFO recognizes that his company would absorb a capital loss if the present value of the asset portfolio failed to grow as fast as the present value of the liability. Accordingly, he instructs the portfolio manager to set the duration of the assets equal to the duration of the annuity. Nonetheless, the assets may underperform the liability if the yield curve reshapes or the asset portfolio suffers a disproportionate credit deterioration. In this example, *risk is uncertainty in the prospective value of the total portfolio (assets minus liabilities); it is an implication of indeterminate changes in interest rates and credit spreads.*

Example 2
A mutual fund entrusts the management of a large fixed-income portfolio to a money manager. The money manager does not see

the liabilities of the fund. From the manager's perspective, there are no explicit liabilities attached to the portfolio. Suppose that the fund requires the manager to match the duration of a specific bond index and indicates that the manager's performance will be measured relative to that index. In this case, the implicit liability is a portfolio that replicates the performance of the index. The money manager might attempt to outperform the index using a duration-matched barbell of short and long maturity bonds. *The risk of this strategy is that yield curve changes (most notably, reshapings) can trigger underperformance of the barbell relative to the implicit liability.*

Example 3

We now investigate the risks that are native to the trading of interest rate options. An interest rate options trader typically manages a highly leveraged book of bonds, futures, options, swaps, and, possibly, more exotic derivatives. Her portfolio may reveal no explicit or implicit distinction between assets and liabilities. We assume that this trader does not have an opinion on market direction but anticipates an increase in volatility; in this case, she positions her book so that its net mark-to-market value increases with an uptick in volatility. At the same time, she seeks to make the portfolio insensitive to interest rate changes. Specifically, suppose the trader purchases longer-dated options against selling short-dated options and hedges the interest rate risk with positions in the underlying assets (bonds, futures, swaps, and so on).

What are the sources of risk for this trader? Since the trader has a long volatility position, she would experience a loss if volatility declines over the holding period. Even if the expected volatility environment is realized, the portfolio may decline in value if the volatility time curve substantially reshapes—that is, shorter-dated volatility increases more than longer-dated volatility. In both outcomes, *risk is introduced by uncertainty in interest rates and volatility—these are the variables that determine portfolio revaluation.* This category of risk might be called *fundamental risk*.

Further scrutiny suggests that this trader is exposed to another origin of risk. To identify the portfolio that optimally achieves her desired risk/reward profile, the trader uses an *option valuation model*—this model gives the theoretical price of the option as a function of underlying interest rates, volatility, and the option's characteristics. It also determines the composition of the hedge portfolio. Imperfections in this model can have undesirable and unexpected consequences. For example, our options trader believes that she has hedged the net effect of interest rate changes. If, in fact, the model is deficient and the trader has mistakenly taken a net long bond position, an increase in interest rates would generate an unanticipated loss in the book. This type of uncertainty—derived from shortcomings of the model—might be called *model-related risk*.

Motivated by these examples, we now propose our working definition. *Risk is a measure of a portfolio's potential to suffer (anticipated or unanticipated) loss*; it is an inherent by-product of uncertainty in forecasting the fundamental determinants of value. But as we have seen, risk is also generated by model inadequacies through the accompanying misestimation of how changes in the determinants affect value.

One might think of fundamental risk as the risk that the trader consciously undertakes to earn excess returns. For example, a trader who anticipates a decline in interest rates might restructure an asset portfolio in order to extend duration. This action magnifies his fundamental risk. On the other hand, model-related risk arises because the trader has an imperfect model of how the value of an instrument relates to market fundamentals. Figure 31–1 suggests how this trader might (ex post) attribute the portfolio's performance to the existence of fundamental and model-related risk.

FIGURE 31–1
The Relationship between Portfolio Performance and Risk

	Interest rates increase	Interest rates decrease
Portfolio generates profit	Model risk	Fundamental risk
Portfolio generates loss	Fundamental risk	Model risk

VALUATION MODELS

Models are abstractions of reality. They are based upon assumptions that are known to be false and imply mathematical relationships that are known to be inaccurate. For these reasons, we accept that models are themselves a source of risk. Nevertheless, *modeling is required to estimate the fundamental risk embodied in all but the most simple portfolios.*

Valuation models begin with the explicit identification of the underlying determinants of security prices. The choice of determinants depends on the characteristics of the option and the modeler's understanding of market fundamentals. For our discussion, the determinants will be the yields (or prices) of the *on-the-run* U.S. Treasury bonds and the anticipated volatilities of these yields. (Fixed-income models that incorporate these variables are called *yield curve–based* models.) The next step is to specify those determinants that are parameters in the model and those that change by virtue of some random process.[1] For the latter, we need to designate the *dynamics*—the probabilistic engine that drives the evolution.[2] For instance, the dynamics formulate (in a mathematically precise way) how the yields of the on-the-run U.S. Treasury bonds change. (Depending on the modeler's market view, she could decide to impose dynamic assumptions on the volatilities as well.) The distinct sources of uncertainty are said to be the model's *factors*. A model in which price changes for all securities are driven by changes in a single random variable (frequently modeled as the short-term default-free interest rate) would be called a *one-factor model*.[3]

The valuation function is derived from these assumptions and relates the price of securities to the levels of the determinants. For some default-free securities, the valuation function can be given in *closed form*—the price can be expressed as a weighted sum of the prices of the on-the-run U.S. Treasury bonds.[4] In other instances, valuation requires a numerical procedure. Such would be the case for the price of an American put option on a default-free zero coupon bond[5] and for more complicated securities such as callable and putable bonds, interest rate futures (notably those with embedded *delivery options*), and mortgage-backed securities. Nevertheless, our choice of determinants means that the idealized (or theoretical) price of a default-free security can be completely determined from its cash flow, knowledge of the yield curve, and knowledge of volatility.

A crucial ingredient in the use of any model is an accurate and contemporaneous estimation of the levels of the inputs. For some of the determinants, this is straightforward—prices of exchange-traded or highly liquid over-the-counter (OTC) instruments are readily available. Determinants like volatility pose a different problem—they must be estimated based on the trader's market view. Identifying the inputs for the current generation of multifactor yield curve–based models is a nontrivial problem requiring substantial computational power and excellent access to real-time market data.

MEASURING RISK

Risk is measured by estimating the price sensitivity of the portfolio to changes in the determinants. There are fundamentally two measures of this sensitivity; each method contributes to the evaluation and effective management of risk. To compute the *instantaneous sensitivity*, a small change is made in a determinant and the model is used to calculate the expected change in the portfolio's present value. The instantaneous sensitivity is the change in portfolio value divided by the change in the determinant. (The mathematically inclined reader will recognize this as the *partial derivative* of the valuation function with respect to the determinant.) The *scenario sensitivity* reports the hypothetical value of the portfolio in one or more terminal states. In this approach, levels for the determinants are revised and the valuation function is used to present-value the portfolio at the specified workout date. The instantaneous methodology has appeal for actively traded portfolios, while the scenario methodology is more appropriate for analyzing risk/reward tradeoffs and for less actively managed portfolios.

If the valuation formula is a closed-form function, the instantaneous calculation is straightforward. If, however, valuation requires a complicated numerical routine such as induction over a lattice or Monte Carlo simulations, the numerical computation of the sensitivities can impose extensive demands on computer capacity. Moreover, the instantaneous approach must be employed with the recognition that risk routinely changes over time. For instance, the duration of a coupon bond decreases as the bond ages and increases as its yield falls. The phenomenon of time-dependent sensitivities is even more prevalent for options and instruments with embedded options (such as callable bonds and mortgage-backed securities).

At this point, we can introduce the basic concepts of risk measurement. For conventional models, instantaneous interest rate risk is conveyed in terms of *equivalent exposure* in the underlying securities. The seminal example is that of a bond option. The *delta* of the option is the instantaneous change in option premium per unit price change of the underlying bond. If delta is 0.5, for example, a $0.01 increase in bond price would imply a $0.005 increase in theoretical option price. Accordingly, if the face value of the option were $1 million, the equivalent interest rate exposure would be a $500,000 face value position in the underlying bond—this bond position and the option position have commensurate (instantaneous) interest rate sensitivities. The second-order interest rate risk measure for a bond option is *gamma*—the sensitivity of delta to changes in the underlying bond price. Gamma is a measure of the rate of change of the option's price sensitivity. Instantaneous volatility risk is reported via *kappa*—the change in option value for a 1 percent change in volatility.

If the other determinants are held constant, the value of an option declines as we move closer to expiration. Because of this phenomenon, options are sometimes classified as *wasting assets*. The *time decay* is measured by *theta*—the rate of change of option price as a function of the time to expiration.

Readers familiar with the Black-Scholes formula may notice that we have overlooked one of the formula's variables—the short-term interest rate. If an option model assumes a *constant financing rate* for the underlying asset, we can straightforwardly define a corresponding sensitivity. For these models, *rho* is the rate of change of option price as a function of the short-term financing rate. Yield curve–based models, on the other hand, typically propagate the short-term rate and, in some cases, link changes in the rate to changes in bond prices or volatilities. As a result, defining rho in the context of yield curve–based models is not a transparent task.

Extending these notions to a diverse portfolio of bonds and derivatives requires some elaboration. At first appearance, the equivalent exposure technique appears unworkable because there may be multiple underlying securities in the portfolio. However, under appropriate assumptions, instantaneous sensitivities can be reported in terms of a *benchmark bond*. For example, if the valuation model relates price changes in the benchmark to price changes in the various underlyings, the net effect of a small price change in the benchmark can be calculated. In this way, the portfolio's delta and gamma can be computed. Analogous model-based relationships for volatilities are necessary to define the kappa of a portfolio. The best way to crystallize these ideas is by example.

Example 4

A financial institution needs to fund a five-year bullet liability with a face value of $10 million and an 8 percent annual coupon (paid on a semiannual basis). Suppose that the obligation is issued at a (bond equivalent) yield of 8 percent. The company decides to buy $10 million face value of a new issue five-year 8 percent coupon corporate bond at a dollar price of 96.043 (this price corresponds to a yield of 9 percent) and invests the excess proceeds ($395,700) in 5 percent 90-day commercial paper.

Analysis. What is the fundamental risk of the net position? The first observation is that the supporting asset achieves an exact matching of the cash flow streams. In addition, interest rate changes will have only a marginal impact on the market value of a short-term investment such as 90-day commercial paper. Does this mean that the instantaneous interest rate risk is zero? In fact, the dollar price and duration disparities between the corporate bond and the liability imply that interest rate changes will not have identical effects on present values. An immediate 1-basis-point increase in each of the applicable interest rates would actually generate a gain of $290. The calculation is given below.

Assets
Five-year 8 percent coupon corporate bond (Notional amount = $10 million). Initial yield = 9%, Initial price = 96.043%, Initial market value = $9,604,300

90-day 5 percent commercial paper (Face amount = $400,709) Initial market value = $395,700

Liabilities
Five-year 8 percent coupon bond (Notional amount = $10 million)
Initial yield = 8%, Initial price = 100%, Initial market value = $10 million

If Rates Increase by 1 Basis Point

Price of corporate bond = 96.005%, Market value = $9,600,500
Market value of commercial paper = $395,690
Price of liability = 99.959%, Market value = $9,995,900
Profit/Loss = +$290

This portfolio's *equivalent interest rate exposure* would probably be stated in terms of the five-year U.S. Treasury note, which we take to have a 7.50 percent coupon and a current dollar price of par. If rates move up 1 basis point, a $690,476 face value *short* position in the five-year Treasury note will undergo the same price change as the portfolio, as shown below.

Five-year 7.50% U.S. Treasury note; Initial price = 100%

A 1-basis-point increase in yield results in a 0.042 percent decline in price. This amount is the bond's *dollar value of an 01 (DV01)*.

The notional amount of five-year U.S. Treasury notes that matches the market exposure of the portfolio is given by:

$$(290 \div -0.042) \times \$100 = -\$690,476$$

Implicit in this assertion is the *modeling assumption* that the liability reprices *at the same spread* to the five-year Treasury. Thus, we see a straightforward incarnation of our earlier remark—the assessment of fundamental risk generally requires invocation of a model and the acceptance of model risk.

What kinds of risk information do we obtain from the scenario sensitivity procedure? As before, the duration difference means that interest rate changes will exert a disproportionate effect on the market values. To apply the scenario method, the company would identify hypothetical paths for the relevant interest rates as they change over the holding period. Terminal interest rate levels are then used to revalue the portfolio. In actuality, the profit or loss in a given scenario would depend on the complete path of interest rates and not just on the terminal values. For instance, the company is exposed to market rates when it finances intermediate cash flow shortfalls (resulting from timing mismatches on the coupons) and reinvests periodic income.

Example 5
Suppose the company from Example 4 decides instead to fund the obligation by purchasing a $10 million face value position in 10-year 8.50 percent U.S. Treasury notes that are trading at par.

Analysis. With this alternate strategy, the company acquires a positive net coupon margin but assumes additional interest rate risk since the portfolio is exposed to a sizable duration mismatch as well as to the possibility of yield curve reshaping. In this case, a uniform 1-basis-point increase in yields will generate a loss of $2,600. To evaluate the risk of a reshaping, we'll use the scenario sensitivity approach.

The initial yield spread between the 10-year and 5-year U.S. Treasury notes is 100 basis points. Assuming that the liability is marked to market at the initial spread to the five-year U.S. Treasury, what is the sensitivity of the portfolio's one-year performance to a change in the spread between the Treasury notes? A revealing way to answer this question is to construct a matrix that displays the terminal profit or loss as a function of interest rates. This matrix is shown in Table 31–1; the numbers are calculated assuming a reinvestment rate of 4 percent.

Due to the positive aggregate duration, the profit and loss numbers in Table 30–1 are dependent on the absolute yields and not just on the shift in the yield spread. In an acutely steep yield

TABLE 31–1
Net Profit/Loss with a One-Year Horizon ($ thousands)

		\multicolumn{5}{c}{Yield at Workout (%) (5-Year Treasury)}
		7.00	7.25	7.50	7.75	8.00
Yield at Workout (%) (10-Year Treasury)	8.00	+197	+282	+367	+451	+534
	8.25	+37	+123	+207	+291	+374
	8.50	−120	−34	+51	+134	+217
	8.75	−273	−188	−103	−19	+64
	9.00	−424	−338	−254	−170	−87

curve environment, scenario analysis of this type can compactly illustrate the interaction between yield curve reshaping and the price appreciation attributable to *rolling down the curve.*

A variety of other funding strategies are conceivable. The company could achieve a wider cash flow margin by using (more risky) corporate debt. Interest rate swaps and bond futures can also be incorporated as a means of managing duration mismatches.

Example 6

The financial institution decides to fund the obligation with a $10 million face value position in 10-year 8.50 percent U.S. Treasury notes. Anticipating an increase in interest rates, the portfolio manager writes a six-month European at-the-money call on the 10-year Treasury position and places the option premium in 2-year 7 percent U.S. Treasury notes that are priced at par.

Analysis. Using a conventional option model and a yield volatility of 9 percent, the theoretical premium for the call is $51,700. The call option erodes the price appreciation potential of the portfolio because the 10-year Treasury bond will be called away if the market rallies. As we would suspect, the option also reduces the expected aggregate loss from a rate increase. We indicated that without the call and the two-year Treasury position, a 1-basis-point increase in rates lowers the value of the portfolio by $2,600. After the option and the two-year notes are incorporated, the same change generates a loss of only $1,010, as shown below.

Assets
10-year 8.50 percent U.S. Treasury notes (Notional amount = $10 million), Initial yield = 8.50%, Initial price = 100%, Initial market value = $10 million

2-year 7 percent U.S. Treasury notes (Notional amount = $51,700), Initial yield = 7%, Initial price = 100%, Initial market value = $51,700

Liabilities
Five-year 8 percent coupon bond (Notional amount = $10 million), Initial yield = 8%, Initial price = 100%, Initial market value = $10 million

Six-month at-the-money call option; Underlying position = $10 million 10-year U.S. Treasury notes, Strike price = 100%, Initial price = $0.517 (per $100 face of underlying), Total premium = $51,700

If Rates Increase by 1 Basis Point
Price of 10-year note   = 99.933%, Market value = $9,993,300
Price of 2-year note   = 99.981%, Market value = $51,690
Price of corporate bond = 99.959%, Market value = $9,995,900
Price of call option   = $0.501, Market value = $50,100
$$\text{Profit/Loss} = -\$1{,}010$$

When evaluating the rationale for writing the option, the portfolio manager must judge the benefit of attenuating interest rate exposure against the volatility risk that she is unequivocally assuming. The kappa of the option is $0.1207 per $100 face value of underlying bond. This means that for small changes in volatility, the impact on the (normalized) option price is approximately $0.1207 multiplied by the (percent) change in volatility. For our $10 million face value position, a 1 percent increase in volatility generates a theoretical loss of $12,400.

Example 7

Savings plan sponsors typically use *guaranteed investment contracts* (GICs) to fund the fixed-income portions of the savings plan. This component of the plan enables the participants to earn a predetermined rate of interest on their contributions. The GIC is an obligation (usually issued by an insurance company) to credit a constant interest rate to deposits received over a specified window period. The contract contains a final maturity date, although early redemption (at book value) of a portion of the contract is possible, often with the imposition of a penalty. Since the realized sequence of contributions and withdrawals is sensitive to future interest rates, the pricing of GICs (i.e., the determination of the credited rate that is high enough to win the business and still permits the writer to derive an adequate profit) is a complicated exercise.

Analysis. Consider an insurance company bidding for five-year GIC business. If the deposits and payments on the contract were known with certainty, the company would compute the duration of the liability stream and examine the yields that could be earned by assets (such as investment-grade corporate bonds) matching this duration target.

Suppose that the best available yield is 10 percent—in this case, the company might offer 9.50 percent in order to build in compensation for credit risk and a sufficient profit margin. If the bid is accepted, the company establishes a position in the supporting asset.[6] This must be done with borrowed funds since the GIC deposits (or *takedowns*) will be made in the window period. To achieve an accurate asset-liability match, the firm endeavors to make this borrowing correspond to the expected accumulation of GIC contributions. In reality, neither the deposit nor the withdrawal schedule is known with certainty and this indeterminacy exacerbates the risks to the carrier. For instance, deposits would be expected to increase if rates decline and the locked-in rate becomes more attractive. In this case, the assets allocated to hedge the GIC may not be adequate for satisfying the cash flow obligation. On the other hand, an increase in rates would probably lessen the deposit stream and generate a capital loss on the excess assets.

Antiselection risk is the term for the risk engendered by these tendencies. Although it may be moderated by contractual penalties, there may also be antiselection risk in the withdrawals from the GIC. If rates decline, withdrawals would decrease since the credited rate would presumably exceed the available market return. In a rising-rate environment, an increase in withdrawals would force the carrier to liquidate (at a loss) portions of the asset portfolio.

Techniques have been developed to manage the implications of antiselection risk in GICs. These methodologies begin with a mechanism for generating future interest rate scenarios. A model is then superimposed that expresses the dependence of deposits and redemptions on the interest rate environment. These approaches identify by what degree the firm should reduce the credited rate as compensation for the antiselection phenomenon. By-products of this analysis are the sensitivities of the GIC liability (such as gamma and kappa)—this information can be used to refine the hedging strategy. In particular, the theory can indicate how risk management tools (such as OTC options) can be employed to *explicitly* hedge the antiselection risk. In practice, the marginal liquidity of customized option products would probably limit this undertaking.

The risk management process for GICs is another demonstration that fundamental and model-related risk are invariably intertwined. Suppose that the company expected a rise in rates and intentionally set up a market-directional position via its GIC business. The most natural way of achieving this is to set up an asset portfolio of equal initial market value but lower duration. The firm's assessment of its fundamental market risk (and, thus, the anticipated profit in the event of an increase in rates) is based on the antiselection model. The actual performance may differ to the extent that parameters (such as volatility) can be misspecified. Moreover, the model's overall implications may not be an exact reflection of market behavior.[7]

HEDGING

The intent of hedging is to reduce the portfolio's exposure to risk. Typically, the hedger identifies a target risk profile and modifies the portfolio so that the net risk position approximates the target. In theory, a dynamically adjusted portfolio of derivatives and underlyings can be constructed to precisely reflect each risk factor. These unit risk portfolios could be blended to build, at a cost, any risk profile. Not surprisingly, this approach would be exceedingly model-sensitive and would demand continuous monitoring and frequent rebalancing. In practice, one targets risk bands and incrementally adjusts the position to bring the portfolio into these bands.

Example 8

An options trader writes a six-month European at-the-money call option on his position in 10-year 8.50 percent coupon U.S. Treasury notes. The bond is currently trading at par and the notional amount is $1 million. The option premium of $5,170 is invested at 4 percent in a six-month instrument.[8]

Current Risk Profile

The trader is obviously vulnerable to interest rate and volatility risk. The option delta is 0.234; thus, the option's equivalent exposure is a $234,000 face value position in the underlying 10-year Treasury notes. The option kappa is $0.1207 per $100 face value of bond; an instantaneous 0.01 percent increase in volatility would generate an immediate loss of approximately $12.07.

The scenario approach plainly illustrates the risk of this position. Figure 31–2 graphs the six-month total return of the portfolio as a function of terminal bond *yield*. Since workout is at option expiration, the workout option price is just its *intrinsic value*. The figure is the mirror image of the familiar profit and loss diagram for a covered call (because it is stated in terms of terminal yield and yield moves inversely to price).[9]

Modifying the Risk Profile

The trader's original motivation may have been a belief that interest rates would be stable or increase over the next few months and then decline significantly. Suppose his opinion changes due to market events and his revised objective is to be neutral to interest rate changes. How does the trader modify his risk parameters? Since the call option's underlying exposure has a face value of $234,000

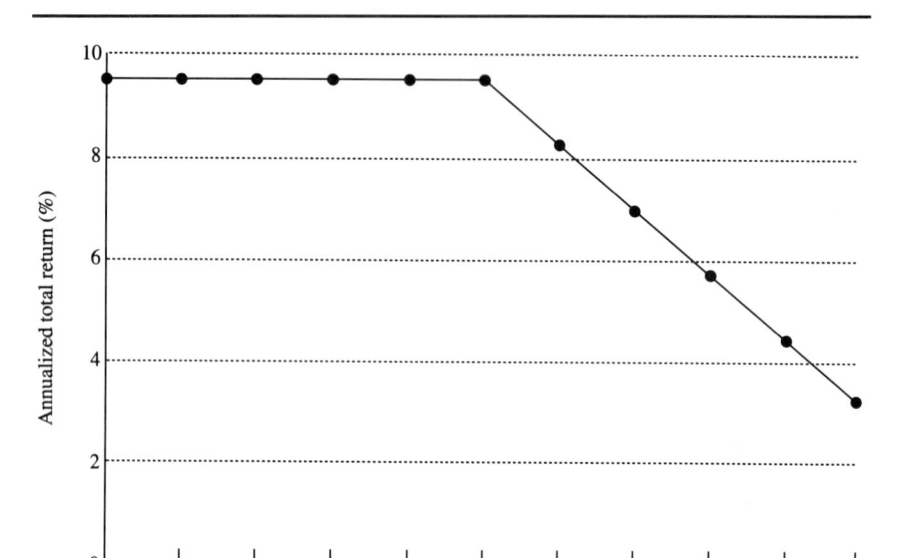

FIGURE 31–2
Total Return on a Six-Month Horizon

[Graph: Annualized total return (%) vs Yield at workout—10-year Treasury (%). Return is flat near 9.5% from 8.00 to 8.50, then declines to about 3% at 9.00.]

and the trader has *sold* the option, his *net bond market exposure* is initially $766,000 (notional) of the 10-year notes. Accordingly, he *sells* $766,000 of his bond position and places the cash in a short-term vehicle.

With this modification, the instantaneous interest rate sensitivity (delta) of the net portfolio is zero. What remains is a residual risk to interest rate shocks due to *non-zero gamma*. In Figure 31–3, the net value of the portfolio is graphed as a function of shifts in the yield of the underlying bond. To understand the effect, recall that for both positive and negative changes in bond price, the net delta will migrate away from zero and portfolio value declines because short option positions have negative gamma. This means that *the hedge underperforms the option* in case of a market move.

Furthermore, the delta-neutral portfolio is exposed to *volatility risk*. To evaluate this risk, we'll use the scenario sensitivity technique over a one-month holding period. The trader marks the option at a higher (or lower) volatility because he believes that the volatility over the remaining time to expiration will be higher (or lower) than his original estimate. Since he has written the option, he absorbs a loss when volatility increases. Figure 31–4 displays the one-month total return as a function of volatility. Note that the best performance occurs when the bond reprices at the initial yield to maturity (corresponding to a $0.01 decline in the bond price.) This is due to the fact that negative gamma has no impact if the underlying price does not change. The inferior performance in a rallying market can also be attributed to gamma risk. As the market trades up, delta increases and the size of the bond hedge becomes insufficient to offset gains in option value.

It is apparent that for this trader, a position in the underlying asset provides only partial protection against adverse market or volatility changes. To achieve enhanced risk control, the trader can use options as hedge vehicles. For example, he could buy back some gamma and kappa by purchasing options at trade origination. Of course, the choice of option length, strike price, and underlying

FIGURE 31–3
Portfolio Sensitivity to Interest Rate Shocks

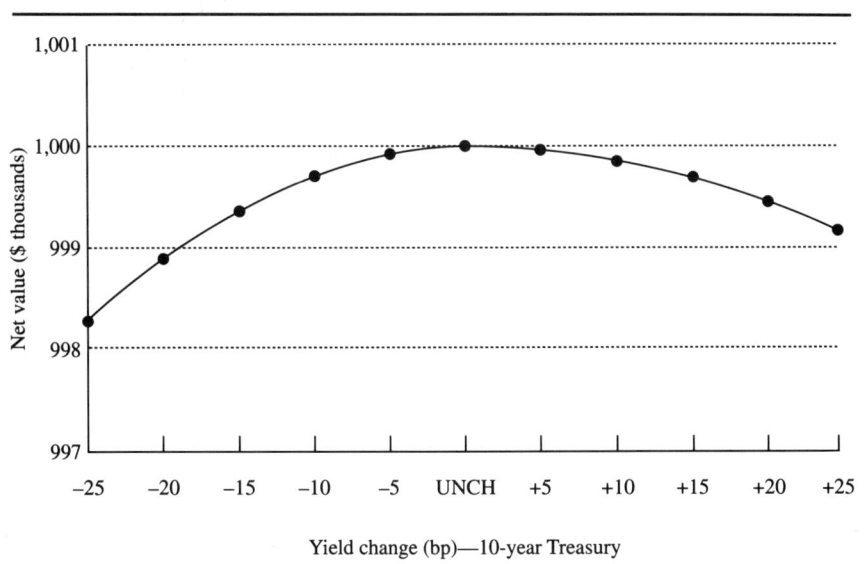

FIGURE 31-4
Total Return on a One-Month Horizon

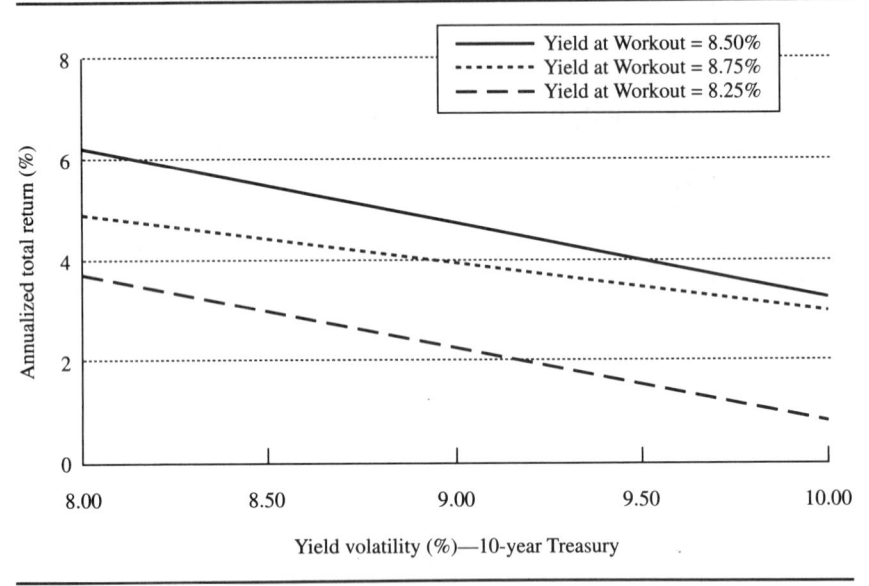

[Figure: Line chart showing annualized total return (%) vs. yield volatility (%)—10-year Treasury. Three lines: Yield at Workout = 8.50% (solid), Yield at Workout = 8.75% (dotted), Yield at Workout = 8.25% (dashed). All lines decline from left to right as yield volatility increases from 8.00 to 10.00.]

asset would be highly model-dependent. For example, the model could suggest that calls on two-year U.S. Treasury notes are undervalued. The trader might accept the risk of yield curve flattening (and the concomitant outperformance of the 10-year over the 2-year) and gamma hedge using calls on the 2-year Treasury.

By adding option and bond positions, we can obtain a delta-, gamma-, and kappa-neutral portfolio.[10] We can even create a portfolio that is kappa-neutral (at current volatility) and is approximately delta-neutral at a range of prices for the underlying bond. However, we cannot synthesize a portfolio that remains delta- and kappa-neutral over time for all possible changes in interest rates and volatility. This is due to the complexity of yield curve dynamics and to the fact that individual bonds will, in general, trade at nonconstant spreads to the theoretical yield curve. Idiosyncratic forces pertaining to a particular bond may be hard to observe and extremely difficult to model. For these reasons, hedging and risk management remain art forms for which skilled judgment and market savvy are as important as mathematical discipline.

In practice, options traders adopt a dynamic approach and regularly adjust the composition of the hedge in response to changing market conditions. Highly dynamic rebalancing strategies are potentially very effective but require accurate yield curve models and real-time market data. Less sophisticated schemes may stipulate rebalancing on a daily, weekly, or even monthly basis. When choosing the preferred technique, the investment manager must take into account the access to real-time market data as well as the willingness to research and support sophisticated yield curve models.

Restructuring the risk/reward profile of a portfolio is, in general, not without cost. How and why this expense is incurred depends on the designated hedging methodology. Strategies that utilize customized OTC products entail significant transaction costs (commissions, and so on) and are subject to burdensome bid-asked spreads. Interest rate futures require the deposit of initial margin and additional capital commitments if a mark-to-market loss causes the existing margin to fall below the maintenance level. The presence of the mark-to-market adjustment means that the risk manager who uses futures must be prepared to absorb transient losses. In theory, these losses would be recouped when gains from other positions are monetized at the end of the holding period.

Hedging via the outright purchase of derivatives entails paying the premium at initiation of the strategy. In other cases, the hedger pays nothing up front but surrenders some upside potential. For example, a trader who is long the market could, at zero net premium, buy puts and sell calls to mitigate her interest rate exposure (and, of course, reduce her potential to benefit from a market rally).[11] Still other techniques result in the amortization of the expense (possibly unpredictably) over the hedging horizon. Evaluating the conceivable costs of a strategy is an important responsibility of the risk manager.

HEDGING INSTRUMENTS

We have alluded to the multitude of interest rate derivatives and explained why the astute portfolio manager should gain a working familiarity with each of them. In this section, we briefly describe the structural attributes and risk management qualities for the major classes of fixed-income hedging instruments.

On-the-Run Bonds

For each maturity, the most recently auctioned U.S. Treasury issue is known as the *on-the-run* bond for that maturity. These bonds are the most liquid securities in the fixed-income market with the average daily trading volume in the on-the-runs exceeding $75 billion. The *U.S. Treasury yield curve* is determined by the yields to maturity of the on-the-runs; other outstanding U.S. Treasury securities (the *off-the-runs*) and instruments in the other sectors of the fixed-income market (such as corporates and swaps) are normally priced relative to the yield curve. For example, corporate bonds are quoted via a yield spread to the on-the-run of comparable maturity. This process decomposes the bond's price risk into two components: the risk of changes in Treasury yields and the risk of changes in the spread. In cases in which the yield spread is fairly stable, the preponderance of the risk should be hedgable using the on-the-runs.

The *U.S. Treasury strip (or zero) curve* plots the yield to maturity of zero coupon Treasury securities. The Treasury grants dealers the authority to create these instruments; dealers separate the coupon and principal (or *corpus*) portions of Treasury bonds and notes and act as market makers for these engineered products. As a representation of the prevailing default-free discount function, the strip curve serves as the benchmark for the pricing of other zero coupon claims. Since any fixed cash flow stream is a sum of single-payment bonds, zero coupon Treasuries can, in principle, be used to hedge the price risk of any fixed payment obligation. For instance, insurance companies regularly use Treasury zeros to defease their long-duration liabilities. As is the case in hedging with the on-the-runs, the primary source of hedge slippage in this strategy are transaction costs and unforeseen shifts in yield spreads.

Many factors can cause variability in yield spreads. For corporate bonds, changes in the perceived credit quality of the issuer dominate the other determinants. For U.S. Treasury securities, shifts in the shape of the yield curve can trigger systematic changes in the spreads of the off-the-runs to the on-the-runs.

Interest Rate Futures

Interest rate futures are the most liquid hedging vehicles in the fixed-income market. Futures provide a mechanism for dealers and end users to efficiently manage the large market exposures that they regularly assume in their business activity. For example, an aggressive mortgage banker that has locked in a large portfolio of fixed-rate lending needs protection against an increase in interest rates before the mortgages close. By selling bond futures, the banker can transfer most of the interest rate risk of the position. As another example, consider a major swaps dealer that has written a large portfolio of LIBOR interest rate caps. The market risk of this position can be hedged by selling a *delta-weighted* amount of Eurodollar futures. (This strategy does not transfer the dealer's exposure to LIBOR volatility.)

The past several years have witnessed a dramatic globalization of interest rate futures markets. Contracts on short- and long-term interest rates in the major currencies are now traded worldwide. Standardization of contract structures and the continuing integration of interest rate and exchange rate risk management strategies has contributed to the development of these instruments.

There are two principal types of futures contracts: *physical delivery* and *cash settled*. Physical delivery, in which the contract seller delivers the physical commodity in exchange for cash, is employed in the U.S. Treasury bond and 10-, 5-, and 2-year U.S. Treasury note futures contracts at the Chicago Board of Trade. These contracts are distinguished by the delivery month and the basket of U.S. Treasury securities that are eligible for delivery. The choice of deliverable bond and delivery date resides with the seller (short side). For each eligible bond, the corresponding invoice price is a contractually determined function of the futures price; this conversion process accounts for differences in coupon, maturity, and call provisions. The existence of a deliverable basket attenuates pricing anomalies and prevents the creation of short squeezes in the days immediately preceding delivery. These effects enhance the efficiency of the contract.

Naturally, the primary price sensitivity of bond futures is to the interest rates of the underlying cash bonds. In conjunction with the contracts' strong liquidity and low transaction costs, this relationship has installed these derivatives as the primary apparatus for major hedging adjustments of bond positions. (Typically, the greatest liquidity is found in the *near contract*—the one that is closest to delivery. For this reason, hedgers with a longer horizon usually establish positions in the near contract and roll the trades as the contract expires.) Any futures contract, by definition, involves the exchange of the asset (or the cash-settled equivalent) at a future date; consequently, the bond's net cost of carry (and, thus, short-term interest rates) also affects the futures price. In addition, the *delivery option* renders a sensitivity to market volatility since, all other things being equal, greater volatility implies a greater likelihood that the short side can benefit by delivering a cheaper bond. Due to these complications, fine tuning a bond portfolio is more effectively accomplished via transactions in the cash market than by the use of bond futures.

Interest rate futures that use cash settlement include the three-month Eurodollar futures contract at the International Monetary Market of the Chicago Mercantile Exchange (CME).[12] For the Eurodollar contract, the value at delivery is determined by polling 16 London banks for their rates on three-month Eurodollar time deposits. Since several contracts enjoy strong liquidity at any given time, Eurodollar futures provide a good means for hedging forward rates. The contracts do not settle on an arrears basis; this feature and the mark-to-market condition that is characteristic of all futures contracts imply that a static hedge using Eurodollar contracts cannot perfectly neutralize future movements in short-term interest rates. They are, however, the best available hedges against changes in these rates.

Interest Rate Options

Interest rate options have emerged as valuable constituents of the risk management toolbox. Their development has been fueled in part by the realization that options (and, thus, option risk) are structural components of a variety of fixed-income products. For example, an investor in a capped floating-rate note earns a higher effective margin (over the floating-rate index) as compensation for the call option she is writing to the issuer. If the interest rate is near the exercise rate (the cap *strike*), an increase in volatility can cause significant price erosion of the floating-rate note. This investor's negative kappa exposure can be mitigated via the purchase of options. Fixed-income investors with specific speculative mandates have also contributed to the expansion of the options market. They have recognized that the leverage afforded by options can be exploited when placing risky directional trades. On the liability side, financial engineers have proposed advantageous capital-raising strategies that incorporate (explicitly or implicitly) the buying (or selling) of interest rate options.

Several major dealers make markets for OTC options on U.S. Treasury notes and bonds. They typically engage in both European- and American-style options and are willing to transact in a wide variety of strikes and times to expiration, although most of the market is in options of one year or less in length. As counterparty risk is a major concern, the OTC market tends to be most accessible to the major institutional accounts and less so to the individual investor. In the exchange-traded arena, most of the listed interest rate futures have accompanying options contracts.

As we have indicated, options provide simultaneous exposure to several factors including the price of the underlying security, short-term rates, and, most importantly, volatility. The asymmetric return pattern of an option means that they can be used to customize the investor's risk/reward profile. For instance, an investor who purchases a put option on his bond portfolio gives up a known amount but establishes a floor to the value at expiration of the covered position. More simply stated, he pays the premium, retains all upside potential, and truncates potential losses. The investor's risk management objective and the cost of the option are the necessary ingredients for evaluating this option strategy.

Frequently, the only way to hedge embedded options is with other options. It is unlikely that the listed markets will provide the risk manager with the identical option structure. Customized transactions are generally available from the OTC dealers, but the costs to the risk manager can be prohibitive. Accordingly, it is often necessary to hedge embedded options by dynamically adjusting the risk-related factors. The manager measures the portfolio's interest rate and volatility exposures and replicates them via the acquisition or sale of standardized options. This procedure can be complicated by the fact that the valuation of unusual embedded options is a nontrivial exercise. Detailed information regarding the applicability of interest rate options can be obtained from the other chapters of this book.

Swaps and Swaptions

A *swap* is a contractual agreement to exchange one set of future cash flows for another. The most common swap structure is the exchange of a regular sequence of fixed- and floating-rate cash flows (typically based on LIBOR). In this basic contract, the rates are applied to a notional amount that remains fixed for the life of the agreement. A *swaption* is an option (European or American) on an underlying swap. Swap and swaptions provide exceptional flexibility and, therefore, equip the risk manager with the ability to accurately tune interest rate and volatility sensitivities. As a result, swaps are frequently the instruments of choice of corporate treasurers who seek to restructure the liability portfolio of the company. For example, a treasurer who anticipates a decline in interest rates would endeavor to convert fixed-rate liabilities to floating-rate debt. This conversion can be achieved with a swap in which the corporation receives fixed and pays floating.

In theory, an investor could enter into a contract (possibly with an up-front positive or negative payment) to trade total returns on a pair of portfolios. These portfolios can even reside in different asset classes—*equity swaps*, for instance, exchange a floating-rate index with the total return on an equity index. *Currency swaps*, agreements that link interest rate and exchange rate exposure, are an important risk management device for corporations that generate revenue and raise capital in multiple currencies.

The flexibility of swaps as a fixed-income hedging instrument comes at an expense, that of introducing additional credit risk. Swap contracts are frequently long-term (three years or longer) off–balance sheet contingent liabilities with a single counterparty. Occasionally, this credit exposure is hedged through the passing of collateral on a market-to-market basis, but frequently it is left unhedged or partially hedged through diversification of counterparties. Due to this sensitivity to counterparty risk, swaps are not accessible to most individual investors. Chapters 16 through 24 examine swaps in greater detail.

CONCLUDING REMARKS AND SUMMARY

Successful risk management requires a mixture of science, art, and luck. The investor must establish her risk tolerance and contrast it with the risk/reward trade-off that she perceives in the portfolio. The quantification of the trade-off and, consequently, the acceptability of the portfolio's current composition depend upon the investor's market view. She then formulates a hedging program to mold the risk profile into that which is consistent with the investment objectives. All of these judgments are, by their very nature, dynamic. As the market moves, the risks (as well as the value) of a portfolio change.

As was seen in previous chapters and mentioned in this chapter, there are a multitude of financial instruments available for modifying the risk/reward characteristics of a portfolio. How does the successful investor choose among them? Unfortunately, there is no magic recipe; there are, however, guideposts to help the investor in this formidable task.

Myriad combinations of options, futures, swaps, swaptions, and cash positions can be added to a portfolio to realize a target duration, convexity, kappa, gamma, rho, and theta. In general, we would expect these hedge portfolios to differ in cost. Furthermore, subtle (and not so subtle!) differences will exist in the extent of model risk and credit exposure that is associated with the hedge. Dynamically adjusted portfolios can also differ in their dependence on frequent rebalancing; a strategy whose effectiveness is sharply degraded by less frequent adjustment should be used with caution.

Some of these distinctions arise because the market is not perfectly efficient. It may, in fact, be possible for two strategies to promise comparable hedging performance (with tantamount levels of risk as outlined above) at two different costs. All other considerations being equal, the investor should scan the range of hedging instruments to take advantage of these temporary mispricings. This must be done with care since (as we have already seen in the section on hedging) the cost of a hedging instrument can be manifested in several ways. Selling an interest rate futures contract, for example, has very little initial cost outside of the initial margin. Over the hedging horizon, however, the futures position could accumulate costs due to the mark-to-market condition and the investor's susceptibility to variation in the cash/futures basis.

The rationale for adopting a dynamic hedging program merits additional discussion. A variety of factors determine to what extent hedge effectiveness depends on the frequency of rebalancing. Most prominent is the choice of hedge vehicles. For example, skillful and timely readjustment is essential when hedging with synthetic positions, such as when bonds and cash are used to replicate an option position. If specialized products are used over a fairly certain investment horizon, intraday valuations become less important and a more static approach is probably acceptable. As we have already pointed out, the access to timely market data and computational capabilities are also considerations when embarking on a dynamic hedging strategy.

While effectively mitigating interest rate and volatility exposure, risk management strategies can exacerbate the risks of other events. There are two classes of risk that can inadvertently be added: model risk and credit risk. The preponderance of hedging instruments are derivative securities—this means that they can be synthesized at a known price. In other words, their prices are determined less by supply and demand and more by the prices of their underlying securities. How one estimates their intertemporal risk characteristics is a function of the model used to price them. If the assumptions underlying the model are inconsistent with market reality, then these instruments might behave very differently from expectations.

Many hedging instruments introduce counterparty risk. While we have chosen not to emphasize counterparty risk in this chapter, it remains an important consideration. As we indicated in the section on hedging instruments, interest rate swaps and options on physical bonds are OTC transactions between credit-sensitive counterparties. Theoretically, prices for these instruments would adjust to compensate the investor for the intrinsic credit risk of the chosen counterparty. In practice, most derivatives markets (such as interest rate swaps) have forged minimum credit standards above which pricing differences are negligible. Dealers that fail to meet these criteria are priced out of the business. The general rule is that participants in any OTC market should practice careful monitoring of credit lines.[13]

In this chapter, we have endeavored to show that the risk management decision process, from modeling to implementation, demands as much attention as the selection of portfolio composition. Indeed, we would submit that the seasoned practitioner comes to regard these disciplines as two sides of the same coin.

NOTES

1. In general, some of the parameters can appear as constants while others as deterministic functions of time.
2. In the conventional models, the overall form of the engine is fixed and the engine's parameters are among the model determinants. In the Black-Scholes valuation of stock options, for example, the volatility input is a parameter of the stock price's *lognormal* dynamics.
3. One-factor models imply that instantaneous interest rate changes along the yield curve are perfectly correlated. Some model builders reject the one-factor approach on the grounds that actual yield curve behavior is not compatible with the condition of perfect correlation. Moreover, the one-factor framework is probably inadequate if the universe of securities includes credit-sensitive instruments (such as corporate bonds or LIBOR-based products) and the modeler believes that credit spreads will undergo indeterminate changes.
4. The prices of zero coupon and off-the-run U.S. Treasury bonds seldom agree with their yield curve–based theoretical prices. Differentials (typically called the *basis*) are variable and often due to liquidity distinctions and supply and demand constraints. The modeler can decide to incorporate the basis as an additional determinant in the valuation model.
5. In theory, early exercise should never occur for an American call option on a zero coupon bond. In contrast, certain circumstances will trigger early exercise of an American put on a zero coupon bond.
6. If corporate bonds are deemed temporarily rich, a short-term position in an equal-duration U.S. Treasury bond may be established.
7. For a detailed discussion of antiselection risk, see the Morgan Stanley publication, Mark Griffin, "Measuring and Managing Cash Flow Antiselection Risk in Window GICs," May 1989.
8. In this example and in Example 6, the option valuation is derived from a standard *yield-based* option model. The *random variable* in this *single-factor* method is the yield of the underlying bond. For

short-dated bond options, this model and a *price-based* model (such as Black-Scholes) will produce similar results. Neither of these approaches satisfies the conditions for a *yield curve–based* model. For a discussion of this concept and its implications, see the Morgan Stanley publication, "A Practitioner's Guide to Fixed Income Options Models," Lawrence J. Dyer and David P. Jacob, August 1988.

9. The call option will be exercised if, at option expiration, the bond is trading at a yield below 8.50 percent. In this case, the trader's return is composed of the strike ($1 million), one coupon payment on the bond ($42,500), and the maturing short-term investment ($5,273), realizing an annualized total return of 9.55 percent.

10. See the Morgan Stanley publication, "Understanding Option Replication Technology," Richard M. Bookstaber, May 1989.

11. As well as modifying the portfolio's market risk, buying puts and selling calls will, in general, alter the volatility exposure. (All other things being equal, at-the-money (forward) options have higher kappas than in-the-money or out-of-the-money options.) Accordingly, the trader could simultaneously manage her market and volatility risk by the judicious use of this technique.

12. Similar Eurodollar contracts trade on the London International Financial Futures Exchange (LIFFE) and on the Singapore Exchange (SIMEX). SIMEX contracts can be used to offset positions established at the CME.

13. For example, a financial institution seeking to limit the interest expense of a sizable floating-rate liability could purchase interest rate caps. To minimize nonperformance risk, the institution could acquire the interest rate caps in smaller face amounts from a number of dealers.

CHAPTER 32

MANAGING A PORTFOLIO OF POSITIONS

Henry Green
FTSD Consultants Ltd.
Robert Mark
Chemical Bank

INTRODUCTION

The increasing complexity and variety of today's financial instruments in a volatile environment have made the need to measure and control financial risk an important task. At present, however, risk is mostly managed on a product- or instrument-specific basis. Few generalized methods for managing the risk of a portfolio of instruments have been advanced. In this chapter, a risk management model is presented with the objective of measuring and controlling risk. Mark (1988), has created, refined, and implemented in 1989 a portfolio risk measurement approach called *risk measurement units* (RMUs) at Manufacturers Hanover Trust (MHT). The RMU method discussed in this chapter focuses on problems involving interest rate risk. Green has catalogued an overview of mathematical tools and techniques used to analyze risk. In this overview, the use of a diverse set of quantitative methods was considered in relation to an overall portfolio approach for risk measurement and detection.

The purpose of this chapter is to show how the RMU method can be applied as a practical risk management methodology. The underlying principle of the RMU method is that it should be possible to consider for any portfolio the degree of risk that all trades have relative to each other and to the portfolio as a whole. RMUs allow one to quantify risk through the use of analytical tools that are robust and objective. The RMU method does not provide predictions or forecasts of market trends. The method is built on a number of principles, and this chapter documents these.

FRAMEWORK

Financial institutions need to accelerate their efforts toward establishing a uniform and meaningful risk control infrastructure for a number of reasons. The most important reason is due to increasing competition, shortened time horizons for development and distribution of financial products, and the overall need to maintain a rational and consistent approach to market risk management, independent of the traded instruments or markets. Failing to have accurate measures of risk can seriously threaten a financial institution. A business unit's obligation to seek profit while assuming market, credit, and operational risk should be predicted solely on the unit's capability to compute and manage the amount at risk. Unfortunately, most financial institutions only pay lip service to investing in the necessary infrastructure and management information systems. This lip service often leads to a flawed framework that fails to reflect actual risk. There is also the additional problem of working with an established methodology on a firmwide basis.

It's startling, with all the well-publicized risk-related problems, that there has not been a more concentrated effort to develop a uniform set of generally accepted risk principles (GARP). Mark argued that GARP should be developed with the same rigor as found in generally accepted accounting principles (GAAP), which guide accounting standards.[1] From a risk perspective, GARP moves us beyond the accounting focus of GAAP toward a more relevant economic and financial market reality. Risk-literate organizations recognize the danger of flying blind without the necessary risk radar. Because RMUs embody the concept of diversification, certain aspects of credit and liquidity risk can utilize RMU analysis. The scope of this chapter, however, is limited to the application of RMUs to market risk problems.

FIGURE 32-1
Risk Categories

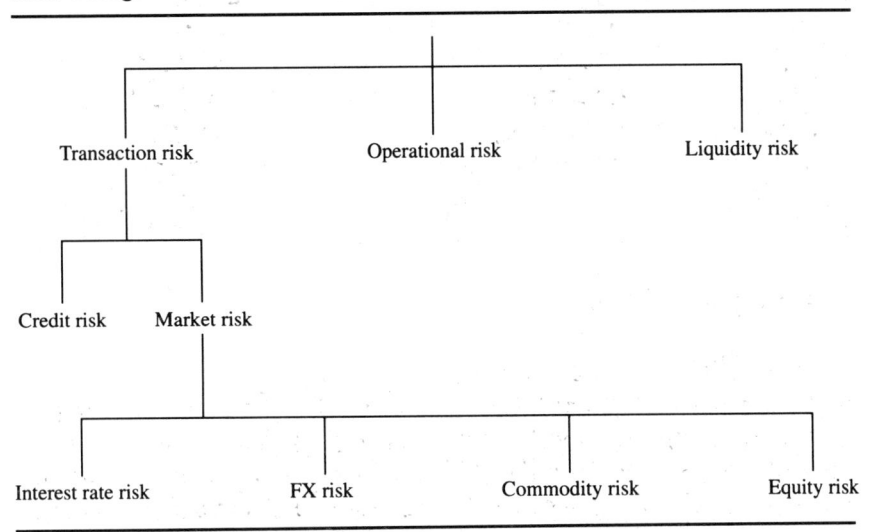

```
                              |
         ┌────────────────────┼────────────────────┐
   Transaction risk      Operational risk      Liquidity risk
         │
   ┌─────┴─────┐
Credit risk  Market risk
                  │
       ┌──────────┼──────────┬──────────┐
  Interest rate   FX risk  Commodity   Equity risk
      risk                    risk
```

Categories of Risk

The basic categories of risk for a financial institution are schematically diagrammed in Figure 32-1. Trading and Treasury operations are mainly concerned with price (or market) and credit risk. RMUs do not measure liquidity or operational risk. The credit risk of certain financial assets is driven by market risk. Credit risk driven by market risk, such as a swap, is a fraction of the total credit risk and is sometimes referred to as an *asset equivalent* or *fractional exposure* (FE).

Risk Management Strategies

A well-designed, clearly articulated strategic plan calls for the implementation of increasingly sophisticated systems and analytical tools (see Figure 32-2). The plan should be designed to recognize that most of the major risks can be handled in the first 20 percent of the effort. Further, the plan should be an evolutionary one. If a fixed-income risk control system is based solely on limiting the nominal amount traded, then the next higher level of risk control is

FIGURE 32-2
Market Risk—Evolutionary Steps

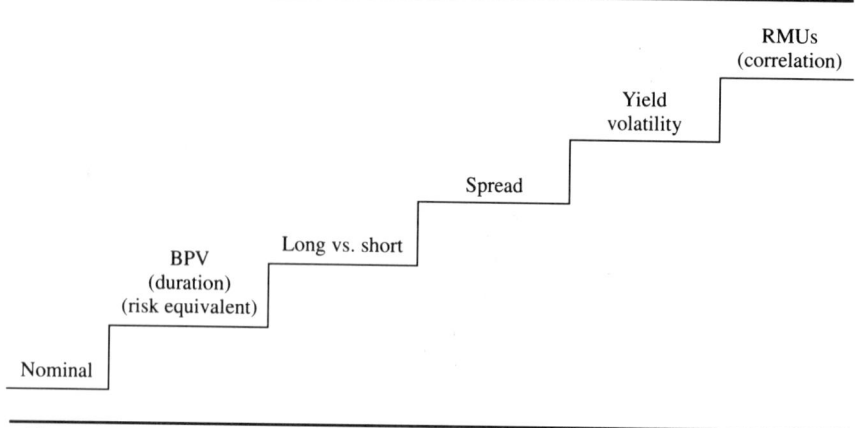

```
                                            RMUs
                                            (correlation)
                                  Yield
                                  volatility
                       Spread
             Long vs. short
   BPV
   (duration)
   (risk equivalent)
Nominal
```

Figure adapted from Robert Mark, "Units of Management," *Risk*, June 1991, pp. 3–7.

based on a basis-point value (BPV) approach. A BPV approach can facilitate the risk detection in certain traded instruments arguably. This approach calculates the change in price arising from a 1-basis-point (bp) change in the yield of some benchmark security (e.g., the four-year T-note) and then compares other securities to the benchmark security's change in price. The next higher level of sophistication combines BPV with volatility, which is achieved using the concept of a risk measurement unit method.

An instrument-level risk measurement unit (IRMU) is determined by multiplying the instrument's BPV by a multiple of its overnight volatility (set at, say, two standard deviations) to arrive at a desired confidence level. For example, one RMU (set at, say, $1,000) is a basic measure of risk such that actual losses will exceed the number of RMUs on only 1 day in 40. If a four-year T-note has a BPV of $312 on a $1 million position and the change in yield volatility is 9 bps, then the overnight dollars at risk (DAR) equals 5.6 RMUs. Observe that ($312 per $1 million) × (9 bps) × (2 standard deviations) = 5.6 RMUs per $1 million. We note that the selection of dollars is arbitrary; any currency can be denominated in terms of RMUs.

Measuring the price volatility of financial instruments is central to the RMU method. This is best approached by analyzing the underlying volatility of interest and exchange rates because this allows one to build a general risk management model that can accommodate a broad variety of financial instruments. As reported by Schiller (1990), there is yet to be found a single adequate measure of volatility that can be applied to hedge complex portfolios. Determining the correct approach or best practice in the calculation of volatility remains an empirical process, and each instrument, market, and portfolio requires individual tuning. Numerous authors have compiled results of different volatility calculation techniques applied to different instruments and markets. Because of the mixture that can result in a portfolio of different instruments and transactions involving multiple markets, it remains a challenge to define a universally accepted single measure of volatility for a portfolio.

A still higher level of sophistication combines volatility with correlations across key points on the yield curve to produce a portfolio RMU. Because correlation measurements as a statistic are independent of the underlying pricing or rate distributions, correlation measurements provide an invariant method to detect and quantify risk. This approach enables the DAR measure to capture nonparallel yield curve shifts. Similarly, a well-formulated approach for a foreign currency portfolio would incorporate volatility and correlation parameters into the DAR computation. For example, the risk associated with simultaneously buying and selling two highly correlated currencies (e.g., DM and CHF) is less than the risk associated with simultaneously buying and selling two negligibly correlated currencies (e.g., DM and AUD). The choice of currency pairs in this discussion is based on recently quantified measures, which we note may not hold indefinitely. Furthermore, options risk can be calculated utilizing RMU matrix techniques. In the case of options risk, RMUs have been developed with reference to option risk sensitivity parameters such as delta, gamma, vega, and theta risk.[2]

The price risks of holding two or more instruments in a portfolio is not necessarily the sum of the individual price risks or volatilities. As discussed by Markowitz (1952), if assets are combined in a portfolio, then the riskiness of the resulting portfolio should be less than the sum of the individual risks of the constituent assets. Simply stated, diversification reduces risk. Miller (1991) expands on the concept of market structures through the proposition of a model that is particular in its discussion of liquidity and how pricing and, thus, price risk can be rationalized in real-world terms for purposes of trading and risk management decisions. The discussions in Miller are general and broad, but they do serve to suggest guidelines in understanding the interrelationships between market, liquidity, and credit risk. To measure the price risk of a portfolio, one therefore needs to measure the degree to which the prices of different instruments move together (i.e., are correlated). A portfolio RMU must take into account the correlations and covariances between the prices of different instruments. Hence, measuring the correlation between instruments is central to the RMU portfolio analysis method.

A key property of an RMU-based risk system is that total risk can be aggregated across different business units to provide one overall DAR measure. Ultimately, a system can be designed where risk limits for lower-level organizational units can be dynamically shared within one overall limit. Further, the same tools used to measure risk can be used to construct optimal hedges to reduce risk. Under an RMU-based system, risk can be added both horizontally and vertically across an organization to produce meaningful measures of total risk. The RMU approach can be used to measure risk and make money; it is a proposition that has been well established in practice. Portfolios that are managed using full immunization techniques offer no upside return opportunities. Riskless strategies employing duration or financial futures hedging can also offer no income opportunities. The RMU method considers these shortcomings by being sensitive to the different volatilities of different instruments.

Similarly, loan credit risk at Chemical Bank is measured according to a credit risk measurement unit (CRMU) philosophy. For example, a loan to a AAA company has a very different loan loss expectation than a loan to a BBB company. Credit spreads observed in the financial markets for public companies can be used to construct loan loss distributions. The distribution can then be entered into a CRMU algorithm to compute the "unexpected" dollar value of loan losses, which, in turn, can be used to determine required managerial capital. Standard credit grading techniques can be utilized to convert public spreads into private-company spreads so as to apply the CRMU approach to both public and private companies.

In the real world, financial risk management is a necessity. For the firm involved in numerous financial markets, involving numerous financial instruments, subject to variable time horizons for such investments and subject to regulatory control, risk management must be expected to return a measure of its achievement through a positive contribution to the firm's net cash flow.

OBJECTIVES

Before launching into the technical details of RMUs, however, it is important to establish clear market risk program objectives. We recommend four primary objectives for any market risk program:

1. Control market risk.
2. Relate market risk measures to the level of capital consumed.
3. Provide a consistent methodology for looking at and aggregating market risk.
4. Introduce a standard way of incorporating market risk into the credit risk evaluation process and where possible, liquidity risk.

As pointed out, the evolution of market risk measurement as shown in Figure 32-2 normally proceeds from the lowest level, where risk is controlled based on the nominal amount traded, to higher levels where risk is controlled based on an RMU such as dollars at risk (DAR) approach. In Figure 32-2, for example, we can see that the next evolution beyond nominal is a system based on BPVs. This is also sometimes referred to as a *duration-based* or *risk-equivalent system*. As pointed out above, the essential idea of a BPV approach is to measure the risk arising from a 1-basis-point change in yield. Given coupon, maturity and market price (or yield to maturity), we can compute the BPV for an individual security.

These observations allow us to establish risk equivalents to some benchmark (say, the four-year T-note). For example, if the trader were given a $2.1 million 4-year T-note risk-equivalent limit, then the trader has a choice of trading $2.1 million 4-year T-notes or $1 million 10-year T-notes. These two positions are said to be risk equivalent.

In order to appreciate the strength and weakness of risk equivalents, we need to review BPV basics. BPV basics start with recognizing that modified duration (D') can be related to Macaulay's duration (D). For example, if we look at a U.S. Treasury bond, then $D' = D/[1 + (i/2)]$, where i equals the bond's yield to maturity. D' can be viewed as the percentage change in price (P) for a 1 percent change in yield. Accordingly, the change in price equals $-D'$ times P times change in yield (di). Expressed in terms of BPV, the change in price equals $-$BPV (equals D' times P) times the change in yield.

Duration-based confidence bands on change in price can be constructed. For example, a one-day risk confidence band on the change in price equals ABS (D') [ABS (di) + (K standard deviations) (di)], where di is the one-day change in yield, standard (s) deviation (di) is the standard deviation of di, and ABS is the absolute value of the item shown. A two-day risk confidence band equals ABS (D') [2 ABS (di) + 1.414 K × Standard deviation (di)], where K is the confidence interval factor. For example, a 95 percent confidence band ($K = 2$) is equal to {2 ABS (D') [ABS (di) + 1.414 × Standard deviation (di)]}.

The basic approach beyond BPV is to express product risk in terms of risk measurement units and add up RMUs across a portfolio of products to compute the dollars at risk (DAR). The rationale behind a DAR system is straightforward. Risk for an individual financial instrument is measured by its overnight volatility. Long and short positions net out according to their degree of correlation.

A notional system (sometimes referred to as a *cumulative total dollar system*) is deficient in that it simply adds that notional value, does not differentiate between a long and short position, and ignores actual volatility as well as correlations. The key is to incorporate volatility and correlation. For example, if a trader's limit equals $100 notional or if portfolio limit equals $200 notional, then one does not explicitly know how much one can risk over a given time period. The RMU system only needs to know two quantities (volatility and correlation) to characterize relative risk. Because markets reflect these quantities in their behavior, volatility and correlation measures can be combined for determining the risk of positions so as to result in minimizing capital allocation requirements.

Consider some examples from Mark (March 1991) associated with a portfolio of three assets. Example 1 (see Table 32–1) deals with a portfolio of $5 million long A, $10 million short B, and $5 million long C. Example 2 (see Table 32–2) deals with the same portfolio of A and C as Example 1 without the B position. Example 3 (see Table 32–3) deals with a $10 million short B and $10 million long C. In Example 1, assume the measurement of twice the one-day rate change volatility (two standard deviations) of A to be equal to 1.87 percent. Similarly, twice the volatility of B and C equals 1.56 percent and 1.54 percent, respectively. Assume also that the correlation between B and C equals .97. Similarly, the correlation between C and A equals .08, and between A and B equals .06.

The item RMUs for the A position in Example 1 is computed

TABLE 32–1
RMU Example 1

Item in Portfolio	Dollar Position	Item RMUs	Overnight Volatility (Two Standard Deviations)
A	5,000,000	93.5	1.87%
B	−10,000,000	156.0	1.56%
C	5,000,000	77.0	1.54%
Gross Position	20,000,000	326.5	
Net position	0	122.9	

	Correlations		
	A	B	C
C	0.08	0.97	1.00
B	0.06	1.00	
A	1.00		

TABLE 32-2
RMU Example 2

Item in Portfolio	Dollar Position	Portfolio Composition	RMU	Overnight Volatility (Two Standard Deviations)
A	5,000,000	0.500	93.5	1.87%
C	5,000,000	0.500	77.0	1.54%
Gross position	10,000,000	1.00	170.5	
Net position	10,000,000		125.8	

by multiplying 1.87 percent times $5 million, which equals $93,500 or 93.5 RMUs. Similarly, the item RMUs for B and C are, respectively, 1.56 percent × $10 million and 1.54 percent × $5 million. The gross position item RMUs of 326.5 is simply the sum of the item RMUs (326.5 = 93.5 + 156 + 77.0). The net position of 122.9 RMUs is computed based on an RMU portfolio volatility algorithm that allows offsets between positions based on their correlation. The algorithm to compute RMUs for a portfolio is described in a later section. It indicates that the one-day DAR in this portfolio is $122,900. This latter amount is much lower than the gross position and largely results in this case from the high correlation between the short B and long C positions.

Assume the $10 million short B position in Example 1 has been closed. One can observe that the gross position in Example 2 ($10

TABLE 32-3
RMU Example 3

Item in Portfolio	Dollar Position	Portfolio Composition	RMU	Overnight Volatility (Two Standard Deviations)
B	-10,000,000	0.500	156.0	1.56%
C	10,000,000	0.500	154.0	1.54%
Gross position	20,000,000	1.00	310.0	
Net position	0		38.0	

million) is less than that in Example 1 ($20 million), yet the DAR in Example 2 (125.8 RMUs) is higher than that in Example 1 (122.9 RMUs).

Consider next the positions in Example 3. The gross position in Example 3 ($20 million) is higher than that in Example 2 ($10 million), yet the DAR in Example 3 (38 RMUs) is lower. The DAR in Example 2 (125.8 RMUs) is about the same if we were long A and short C or were short both A and C. Observe that neither gross or net notional amount by itself is a good indicator of market risk.

VOLATILITY AND CORRELATION

At the heart of the RMU method lies the calculation of volatility and correlation. There are two main considerations: the form of the data and the statistical methodology.

Time Series Data

Data can be collected using daily rates. Two commonly used transformations of the "raw" data to establish a time series $[x(t)]$ used in statistical studies are:

$$X(t) = \ln [P(t)/P(t-1)]$$

which is the natural logarithm of the relative prices. Its close approximation is:

$$X(t) = [P(t) - P[t-1)]/P(t-1)]$$

which is the percent price change. Expressed another way,

$$X(t) = [P(t)/P(t-1)] - 1$$

An interesting property of these two transformations is that the resulting time series are "dimensionless." Since dollars at risk (measured in dollar units) are calculated by multiplying the dollar position (also in dollar units) by the overnight volatility, it is important that the volatility measurement be dimensionless. The transformed time series of original rate or price data $P(t)$ into a new series $X(t)$ is then used to compute the volatility (or statistical variance) needed for RMU analysis.

Statistical Methods

Variance of the $X(t)$ time series data can be calculated without any assumption concerning the transformations of the underlying generation process; but to allow for probability statements and parameter tests, the probability function must be known. The assumption frequently made is that the percentage change distribution is normally distributed (e.g., Gaussian) and results in the familiar bell-shaped distribution.

Empirical studies, however, suggest that market rates and price volatility are characterized by alternating periods of stability and instability, suggesting the variance of exchange rates is time-dependent. Mark (1989) and Green (1992) have pointed out where systems and analytic technology can substantially facilitate the manipulation of real-time market data. Hence, analytical models such as GARCH[3] may provide better estimates of overnight volatility than the classic variance of an assumed normal distribution. Further, the length of the "time window" used to calculate the variance is a consideration in the RMU method. For example, should overnight volatility be based on data from several weeks, months, or years? If based on, say, five years of data, should the most recent data be weighted differently than prior years' data?

In practice, "rolling" time windows are needed. For example, each week (or month) a new standard deviation can be computed by adding time series data from the current week (or month) and removing the earliest data from the series. This is necessary because the variance itself varies with time (i.e., rates are more volatile in some periods than others), and determining when such transitions occur still remains an unsolved problem. The longer the window, the smaller are the day-to-day or week-to-week fluctuations of the rolling standard deviation. However, the window should not be so long that current market volatility is dampened out. Otherwise, the measure of overnight volatility (and hence RMUs) will not adequately reflect the current risk in the market. Our calculations suggest that windows of 180 days may be appropriate in most cases. In other cases, longer historical data periods involving weighting of the data using exponential or time-weighted techniques are necessary. The right answer results when the choice of averaging and length of historical data result in realistic sensitivity of the RMU values to the observed market movements.

Correlations between prices can be calculated using a standard correlation algorithm. As discussed above, the size of the window (days) over which the correlation calculations are carried out is an important consideration. Again, there has to be a trade-off between minimizing large fluctuations of the correlation coefficient and maximizing the responsiveness of the coefficient to recent market trends. Covariance and correlation calculations are sensitive to the choice of rolling window. Although the overall large-scale trends appear preserved independent of rolling window size, the short-term statistics are greatly influenced. Selecting the appropriate rolling window is based on trial and error.

RMU OF A PORTFOLIO

The RMU measurement of a single instrument (called an *instrument-level RMU*) was defined earlier as twice the overnight price volatility (standard deviation) of the instrument times the dollar position in that instrument. Thus, the RMU of a single instrument is the market value of the instrument times 2 standard deviations of overnight price movements. [$RMU = 2 \times$ (Standard deviation) $\times$ (Dollar market value)].

The RMU of a two-instrument portfolio (RMU_p) is the sum of the position-weighted variances and covariances of the two instruments:

$$RMU_p = SQRT\ (RMU_1^2 + RMU_2^2 + 2\rho_{12}RMU_1 RMU_2)$$

where ρ_{12} is the correlation between the two instruments.

The RMU calculations for the portfolios in Examples 2 and 3 are below.

Sample RMU Calculations for a Two-Instrument Portfolio

Since one RMU represents 1,000 dollars at risk, to calculate the RMU of the portfolio for Example 2:

$$\begin{aligned}RMU_p &= SQRT(RMU_A^2 + RMU_C^2 + 2 \times \rho_{AC} \times RMU_C \times RMU_A) \\ &= SQRT[(93.5)^2 + (77.0)^2 + 2(.08)(93.5)(77.0)] \\ &= 125.8\end{aligned}$$

Sample RMU Calculations for a Two-Instrument Portfolio

Similarly, the RMU for the portfolio in Example 3 is:

$RMU_\rho = SQRT(RMU^2_B + RMU^2_C + 2 \times \rho_{AB} \times RMU_B \times RMU_C)$
$= SQRT[(156.0)^2 + (154.0)^2 + 2(-0.97)(156)(154)]$
$= 38.0$

Since B and C are positively correlated, *the short B and long C positions are negatively correlated.* This means that the cross-terms in the equation are negative, which reduces the total variance of the portfolio. Hence, the RMU of the net position is also reduced.

HEDGING AND TRADING

RMU Hedging Approach

One of the benefits of installing an RMU system is that one can utilize the RMU-based volatilities and correlations, not only to measure the DAR, but also to help determine the best hedge. In other words one can compute the minimum DAR.

If one wanted to hedge a single asset (A) using a single liability (L), then the best hedge ratio, which by definition equals the dollar amount of A($A) divided by the dollar amount of L ($L), would equal minus their correlation times the volatility of A (Standard deviation A) divided by the volatility of L (Standard deviation L). We also have a precise formula to compute the residual systematic risk that cannot be hedged away. The residual risk using this hedge ratio would equal Standard deviation (A) × Square root (1 − Correlation × Correlation). Conversely, if we wanted to hedge L using A, then the hedge ratio would equal $L/$A = − Correlation × Standard deviation L/Standard deviation A. The residual risk would equal Standard deviation (L) × [Square root (1 − Correlation × Correlation)]. Looking at only volatility ratios and ignoring correlation minimizes risk only when the correlation equals 1. Using volatility ratios causes one to overhedge and possibly create more risk then you would have without the hedge.

Let us return to basic hedging techniques where the requirement is to compute the number of liability instruments needed to hedge an asset (N). Let P_A and P_L equal the price of the asset and liability, respectively. Let D_A and D_L equal modified duration of the asset and liability, respectively. Let dP_A and dP_L equal change in price of the asset and liability, respectively; di_A and di_L equal the change in the yield of the asset and the change in the yield of the liability, respectively; and, N equals dP_A/dP_L. As mentioned previously, the general formula is dP equals $-D' \times P \times di$. Accordingly, since dP_A equals $-D'_A \times P_A \times di_A$, and dP_L equals $-D'_L \times P_L \times di_L$, then N equals $(D'_A \times P_A \times di_A)/(D'_L \times P_L \times di_L)$.

BPV matching assumes parallel yield curve shifts ($di_A = di_L$) so that $N = (D'_A P_A)/(D'_L P_L) = BPV_A/BPV_B$. Modified duration matching assumes that if $di_A = di_L$ and $P_A = P_L$, then $N = D'_A/D'_L$. Macaulay duration matching assumes that if $di_A = di_L$, $P_A = P_L$, and $i_A = i_L$, then $N = D'_A/D'_L$. The key point to observe is that each of these approaches requires strong assumptions, which if violated greatly weakens their applicability. The RMU hedging approach does not require strong assumptions.

To see why the BPV approach is not as good as the RMU hedging approach, we use an example. Assume we used the BPV matching technique to hedge a $100 million 30-year T-bond long position. According to the BPV approach, one would short $536 million of the two-year T-note, as computed below.

$$\text{Hedge ratio} = \frac{BPV\ (30\text{-year})}{BPV(2\text{-year})} = \frac{\$949.8}{\$177.1} = 5.36$$

The resultant DAR is 889.7 RMU. Optimal matching via an RMU approach, which looks at volatility and correlation, would be to hedge $100 million long position in a 30-year bond through shorting $327 million of the 2-year T-note as shown below.

Optimal
Hedge ratio
$$= \frac{BPV(30\text{-year}) \times \text{Standard deviation (Change in 30-year yield)}}{BPV(2\text{-year}) \times \text{Standard deviation (Change in 2-year yield)}}$$
$$\times \text{Correlation (30Y, 2Y)}$$
$$= \frac{\$949.8 \times 5.64\ BP}{\$177.1 \times 7.12\ BP} \times 0.77$$
$$= 3.27$$

The resultant DAR is 760.8 RMUs, which shows that the optional hedge reduced the risk over the BPV hedge by 128.9 RMUs.

Trading

After establishing a hedge, further trading may be considered mainly for one of two reasons. The first reason is to take advantage of any new favorable position. The second reason for trading a hedged position is dynamic and tends to result when changes in a position size result in an increase or decrease in overall exposure. Trading a hedged position must include a net appraisal of costs such as commissions, fees, and other transaction costs. In addition, the frequency for conducting position revaluations needs to be systematically aligned with the ability to transact any new hedge or trading decision that may be established. The alignment of available market price data with mark-to-market valuations and execution requires an appraisal to best identify hedging and/or trading frequency, whether using traditional or RMU hedging techniques.

RMU APPLICABILITY TO TECHNICAL ALCO

To counteract structural pressures on net interest margin levels, volatility, and trends, banks have resorted to a number of conventional approaches to make money in today's competitive environment. These approaches are not enough. What is necessary for high earnings performance is a risk management process that can be consistently applied to the rapidly proliferating marketplace of new financial instruments and processes. This can be called *technical ALCO,* (Binder and Mark 1988).

Technical ALCO in the new marketplace consists of managing market strategies and instruments on a transaction and overall balance sheet level to profitably move along the efficient frontier. In contrast to the "gut feelings" point of view, the fundamental building block in technical ALCO is the ability to quantify reward/risk trade-offs. A gap RMU approach can help to quantify those trade-offs. The following is a simplified example of quantifying reward/risk trade-offs in terms of a bank's efficient frontier. A bank's efficient frontier is an optimal set of trade-offs between reward

**TABLE 32-4
Investment Opportunities**

	Investment	(1) Expected Return	(2) Low	(3) High	(4) Range (4 = 3 − 2)	(5) Variance around Expected Return (5 = 3 − 1 = 1 − 2)	(6) Sharpe Ratio (6 = 1/5)
On the efficient frontier	I	$10	$ 5	$15	$10	$ 5	2.0
	II	15	5	25	20	10	1.5
	III	20	0	40	40	20	1.0
Off the efficient frontier	IV	10	10	20	20	10	1.0
	V	15	−5	35	40	20	0.75
	VI	20	−20	60	80	40	0.50

(such as net interest income) and risk (such as net interest income volatility).

Consider choosing from among six investments that are presented in Table 32–4. The investments' expected net interest income is shown in column 1 of the table while their net interest income variability (as measured by their range) is shown in column 4. As shown in column 4, Investments I, II, and III have less net interest income variability than Investments IV, V, and VI. Note that Investment II, as shown in column 1, has an expected net interest income $5 million higher than Investment I, and expected net interest income $5 million lower than Investment III, and the same $15 million expected net interest income as Investment V. Risk is measured by range around expected return (column 5). As shown in column 5, Investment V has two times as much risk as Investment II for the same expected $15 million net interest income return.

Thus, given a choice between Investment II and Investment V, a bank would select Investment II as the more efficient investment. That is, it would reason that Investment V is riskier as measured by its range of outcome around the expected outcome. (A more formal determination can be established by applying the central limit theorem.) Furthermore, with no loss in expected return, the less risky Investment III is preferred over Investment VI.

FIGURE 32–3
The Efficient Banking Frontier

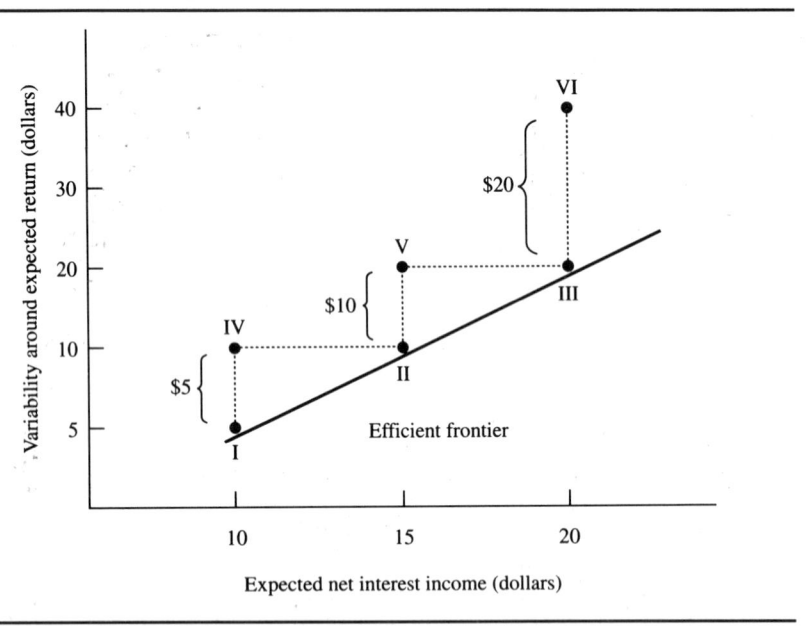

[Figure showing efficient frontier with points I, II, III on the frontier line, and points IV, V, VI above it. X-axis: Expected net interest income (dollars) from 10 to 20. Y-axis: Variability around expected return (dollars) from 5 to 40. Brackets show $5, $10, and $20 differences.]

The approximate Sharpe measure shown in column 6 (which is constructed by dividing return by range) indicates that the most efficient investments have the highest Sharpe ratio. (See Sharpe 1966.)

Investments I, II, and III are considered to be on the efficient frontier, as illustrated in Figure 32–3. Any point on the efficient frontier is efficient because any point above it has too much risk for that level of income, and any point below the curve is impossible to achieve. Having eliminated a set of nonefficient investments, the bank can then focus on efficient Investments I, II, and III.

CONCLUSION

The RMU system is easily understood at the trader level without the need for significant analytical insight or complex algorithms. RMUs cut across all levels of the organization and can be summarized vertically or horizontally to provide total portfolio risk. The RMU approach clearly measures the dollars at risk whereas other commonly used approaches, such as BPVs, fail to measure true risk. Finally, the RMU system can be used to construct optimal hedges.

NOTES

1. Robert Mark, "Risk According to Garp," *Wall Street Computer Review,* December 1991.
2. Delta, gamma, theta, and vega (or more formally, kappa, or sigma) are discussed in *Options Markets,* by John C. Cox and Mark Rubinstein (Englewood Cliffs, N.J.: Prentice Hall, 1985), pp. 215–35. Alternatively, see Hans R. Stoll and Robert E. Whaley, *Futures and Options* (Cincinnati: South-Western Publishing Company, 1993), pp. 219–30.
3. GARCH stands for generalized autoregressive conditional heteroscedasticity.

REFERENCES

Binder, B., and R. Mark. "Technical ALCO in the New Marketplace." *Bankers Treasury Handbook,* 1988.

Green, H. G. "Future Information Technology Strategies." *Creating a Business-Based IT Strategy,* ed. A. Brown. London: Chapman and Hall, 1993.

Mark, Robert. "Technology of Risk." *Proceedings of Amtech Conference* 1988.

———. *EDP Audit Journal* 4, no. 1 (November–December 1989).

———. "Risk Management." *International Derivative Review,* March 1991, pp. 12–14.

———. "Units of Management." *Risk,* June 1991, pp. 3–7.

———. "Risk According to Garp." *Wall Street Computer Review,* December 1991.

Markowitz, H. M. "Portfolio Selection." *Journal of Finance* 7 (March 1952), pp. 77–91.

Miller, M. H. *Financial Innovations and Market Volatility.* Cambridge, Mass.: Blackwell, 1991, pp. 24–31.

Rubinstein, Mark, and John C. Cox. *Options Markets.* Englewood Cliffs, N.J.: Prentice Hall, 1985.

Schiller, R. J. *Market Volatility.* Cambridge, Mass.: MIT Press, 1990.

Sharpe, William F. "Mutual Fund Performance." *Journal of Business,* Supplement on Security Prices, January 1966, pp. 119–38.

Stoll, Hans, and Robert Whaley. *Futures and Options.* Cincinnati: South-Western Publishing Company, 1993.

SECTION 7

FUTURE OF THE MARKETS

CHAPTER 33

INNOVATIONS: BELLS AND WHISTLES

Julian Walmsley
ISMA Center, Reading University

This chapter focuses on some of the current innovations in interest risk management that are taking place and also where the future direction of the marketplace is going. It may be helpful to define innovations into two categories: financial instruments and financial structures. For example, a collateralized mortgage obligation (CMO) is an innovation in financial instruments, but the trust entity that issues the bond is a financial structure created for the purpose of issuing the CMO. The reason for making this distinction is that the financial structures that provide risk intermediation, traditionally banks, are coming under increasing pressure for systemic reasons. Accordingly, the central contention of this chapter is that the focus of innovation will probably shift to financial structures for disintermediating interest risk transfer. However, we begin with the developments that have taken place in the instruments, starting with the money and foreign exchange markets and moving on to look at other exchange-traded and over-the-counter (OTC) derivatives markets.

FRA, SAFE, AND THE FRA CLEARINGHOUSE

In this category, there are two instruments, the forward rate agreement (FRA) and the synthetic agreement for forward exchange (SAFE), that are worth exploring. FRAs were developed in the mid-1980s, and perhaps deserve to be more widely known and used. Similarly, the SAFE is a useful method of reducing the capital required to trade a position involving relative interest rates in two currencies.

Forward Rate Agreement

The FRA can be thought of as a single-period interest rate swap or as the money market equivalent of forward foreign exchange contracts. The FRA is an agreement where a notional borrower agrees with a notional lender on the rate of interest that will be applied to a notional loan for some period in the future. As with an interest rate swap, there is no actual borrowing or lending involved. When the time comes to settle, all that happens is an exchange of cash equal to the difference between the actual rate on the day of expiry and the rate agreed to in the FRA. FRAs are dealt through an active market in London, New York, and other centers. For money market traders, the interesting thing about FRAs is that they are a simple and clean way to taking a view on a change in shape in the yield curve, as much as a change in the level of interest rates.

The settlement sum is the sum paid to settle the FRA. The custom in the FRA market is to pay the settlement sum on the settlement date. (The practical benefit is that this clears the deal off the books and cuts down the credit exposure that would arise if one had to wait until the notional maturity date to be paid.) Thus, the settlement sum has to be discounted back from that would be payable at maturity to its present value today.

As an example, suppose we buy a 3 × 6 FRA for a contract amount of $10 million. The rate is 10.5 percent. The contract period is 90 days. When the contract comes to settle, the settlement rate is 12.25 percent. Then the settlement value of the FRA is [(12.25 − 10.5) × 90/360 × 10,000,000/100]/[1 + (12.25 × 90/36,000)]. This gives us $43,750/1.030625 = $42,449.97.

It follows from the way in which an FRA is priced that the pricing of the FRA is affected if the yield curve changes shape, even if the general level of rates does not change. The size of the impact depends on the relative length of the period to settlement date compared with the contract period. (The effect is similar to the effect on an interest rate futures price of a change in carrying cost.) See Chapter 10 for more details about FRAs.

FRA Clearinghouse

An interesting development of the FRA occurred in Australia. It is called the *FRACH contract*. FRACH stands for FRA Clearinghouse. There are one-month and two-month contracts. Trading takes place in minimum amounts of 5 million Australian dollars (AUD) and multiples thereof. The contract is based on the average daily 11 A.M. cash rate of each contract month. The contract is traded up to the last business day of the previous month and the rate is set for the contract month in arrears. For example, if the contract month was May, trading would occur up to and including April 30th.

Bid and offer rates for the two traded contract months can be inserted by members on the Reuters computerized price display system, on the Reuters "page," YBCX; the best bid and offer is then displayed on page AFMZ. Each day a daily reference rate is set between the times of 10:30 A.M. and 11:00 A.M. by Reuters using the information from AFMZ. The rate is the continuous average of the second highest bid and the second lowest offer. The monthly settlement rate is then calculated from the average of the daily rates.

There are obvious merits in the clearinghouse approach, provided it is structured to minimize counterparty credit risk. An alternative approach would be to further extend the International Swap Dealers Association's efforts in swap netting (and the netting arrangements advocated in the foreign exchange market by the Angell Report produced for the Bank for International Settlements). In both these areas, the intent of the netting arrangements is to provide that, where a bank has multiple contracts with a single counterparty, the profits and losses on each contract could be totaled to provide a single net figure. This is, of course, exactly what a clearinghouse does on a multilateral basis.

SAFEs

SAFEs originated in proprietary products developed by certain commercial banks, and were developed into an instrument available to the London market as a whole under the aegis of the British Bankers' Association, which in April 1989 published the SAFEBBA Master Terms (analogous to the FRABBA terms for

FRAs). SAFEs come in two types: exchange rate agreement (ERA) or forward exchange agreement (FXA). The difference is that while the FXA is an agreement regarding changes in both forward spreads and spot rates, the ERA covers the forward spread only.

The SAFE is an instrument allowing a trader to trade forward foreign exchange swaps i.e., to take a position on relative interest rate movements in two currencies) without forcing the exchange of the principal amount customary in the traditional foreign exchange swap markets. By being structured in this manner, the capital requirements under the Bank for International Settlements (BIS) rules are treated as being those applied to interest rate risk (i.e., 1 percent per annum) rather than foreign exchange risk (5 percent per annum). In essence, the SAFE cuts down the settlement risk, and thus the credit exposure, on a forward foreign exchange contract.

SWAPTIONS

The market for swaptions (options granting the right to enter into a swap) has been available in sporadic form for a few years although not in large size. In the U.S. market, the traditional source of supply was the issuer of a callable corporate bond. The call option would be stripped out by the issuer and sold to banks. That is to say, the issuer would write an option to a bank under which the bank would have the option to receive a fixed rate of interest from the issuer for a certain period. If rates fell, the issuer would exercise the call option on the bonds, but the profit from this would be offset by the fact that the bank would, in turn, exercise the right to receive a fixed rate (which is now above current market levels since rates have fallen).

The market has been relatively limited, with most volume either in straight swaps or interest rate options. That said, the most recent figures from the International Swap Dealers Association, covering the first half of 1991, show a rise in swaptions volume of 27 percent over the corresponding period of a year earlier (compared with 29 percent for plain-vanilla U.S. dollar interest rate swaps) to an outstanding volume of $42 billion (compared with $923 billion in interest rate and currency swaps outstanding).

As with many other derivative products, the market flourishes when there is a noncommercial market participant supplying the product. An example was seen in the deutschemark market during 1990–91. Following the reunification of Germany and the consequent need to boost the German government's borrowing program, the government began a program of issuing Schuldschein debt with put options embedded in them. The Schuldschein embodying these puts were bought by banks who stripped out the options and sold them as swaptions to those wishing the option to pay fixed rates under the swap. Rising rates would trigger the exercise both of the swaption and the put.

Thus, supposing the Schuldschein yielded 8 percent on issue. The bank might write a swaption at 8 percent under which it commits to receive a fixed rate of 8 percent in exchange for a floating rate. Suppose now that rates rise by 2 percent. The right to put the Schuldschein would increase in value giving the bank a profit of say 200,000 deutschemarks (DM). But the bank's customer now exercises its swaption: It contracts to pay 8 percent to the bank (whereas it would have to pay 10 percent in the market). The bank's profit on the put would compensate it for the cost of having to receive a fixed rate of 2 percent below the market for the next several years.

Other examples of how the swaption market's activity tends to respond to economic pressures came during 1991–92 in the United States when interest rates fell to cyclical lows, leading to a rise in swaption purchases; and, conversely, in the United Kingdom, when a steeply inverted yield curve attracted some corporations to writing swaptions under which they offered to receive the fixed rate, essentially a bet that rates would fall, aimed at generating some immediate premium income.

EQUITY SWAPS

Perhaps the biggest area of expansion in the OTC markets in the early 1990s has been in swaps of LIBOR against equity indexes. Equity-index swaps have provided an alternative means for the fund manger to achieve exposure to an index. For example, a firm might enter into a swap under which it pays three-month LIBOR and is paid, every three months, the total return on the S&P 500 index. This technique has been particularly popular in Germany, where swaps have at times paid DAX + 70 basis points or more (that is, the counterparty promises to pay an amount equal to the percentage change in the DAX stock market index plus 0.7 percent). The reason is that the domestic German investor who owns the equities and is swapping the total DAX return for LIBOR receives a tax credit not available to the foreigner who wishes the DAX return—carving up the tax benefit between the parties can produce attractive spreads.

As an example, suppose a German bank wishes to earn a LIBOR-linked return. It can enhance this return by buying a portfolio of equities whose return is expected to match that of the DAX index and entering into an equity swap. Suppose this year the DAX rises 10 percent and the tax credit is 10 percent; then the bank's total return is 11 percent (10% + 10% of 10%). If the bank has entered into a swap with a foreign counterparty under which it pays DAX + ½ percent, it will pay out 10.5 percent to the foreigner, in exchange for LIBOR. It has earned 11 percent, paid out 10.5 percent, and received LIBOR, so its net return is LIBOR + ½%. The foreigner will deposit its cash with a bank, earning a rate close to LIBOR (say, LIBOR − ⅛%). It pays LIBOR to the German bank and receives DAX + ½% for a net return of DAX + ⅜%. Thus, the foreign investor is certain of beating the DAX index by ⅜% during the period of the swap.

The growth of equity derivatives raises deeper questions than the interest rate derivative market. Suppose in the example above that the German entity swapping out the DAX return were a bank. The bank would be funding at LIBOR, buying holdings of German equities, and swapping away the equity price risk. It is left with an interest rate spread, and the ownership of crucial voting rights. Equity swaps of this type provide the means of splitting the benefits of voting control conveyed by the ownership of equity from the equity risk that is traditionally associated with voting control. Alongside the growing popularity of equity-index funds, there are potentially profound implications for corporate governance. Corporations could find that large portions of their equity are controlled by index funds, which own the shares simply because of their membership of the selected index, with the free float controlled by institutions that have stripped out the equity risk. In the extreme, 100 percent of the corporation's voting equity could be controlled by parties who were indifferent to the firm's performance.

A factor that inhibits the growth of equity and other novel swaps in the United States is the ambiguity of the Internal Revenue Service's attitude. The IRS changes proposed in August 1991 on the tax treatment of interest rate and currency swaps have left open the risk that equity and commodity swaps will not benefit from the same tax treatment. In particular, the issue of "unrelated business taxable income" is unclear.

WARRANT ISSUES

Another interesting area of innovation during the early 1990s has been the warrant market. A number of banks and securities firms issued warrants on the spread between two interest rates. Issues have been done, for example, on the spread between Bunds and OATs (Obligations Assimilables du Tresor, French government bonds) or the spread between Danish and German government bonds. Similarly, issues have been done on the spread between U.S. Treasury bills and U.S. Treasury bonds. For investors capable of running short positions and managing their own hedge programs, such instruments probably have limited appeal. But for those with operational or tax difficulties in handling such an approach, the spread warrants have at times offered a simple means of backing a view on the relative performance of two markets.

NEW DIRECTIONS

In which directions are these derivative markets moving? One answer is that the techniques developed in the interest rate hedging market are now being applied in a range of markets around the world. The swap technique has been applied in energy markets, with banks becoming active in oil swaps, jet fuel, and related products. (The volatility at the time of the Iraqi invasion of Kuwait showed both the importance and the risk of this area.) In London, electricity prices are now the subject of an FRA market, and gold FRAs have been in existence for some time.

Another stimulus for development is the continuing pressure on the international financial system from capital shortages, caused by adaptation to the BIS capital adequacy requirements and the parallel arrangements introduced by the European Community (EC). These are discussed further below. In the context of new instruments, rather than new financial structures, it is worth noting that there is a systemic bias in the BIS rules. The buyer of an OTC option is considered to have a credit risk on the seller, since if the seller fails to perform, the buyer will be exposed. This does not apply to the seller, since as soon as the premium is paid, the seller has no further rights on the buyer. This is, of course, valid for any individual participant. But for the system as a whole, there is thus a net incentive for the system to be a net seller of options. Each firm will want to be a seller. Thus, the system as a whole will want to sell options, hedging the risk through dynamic hedging or other techniques rather than buying matching options. This will mean that the system will tend to be naturally short on volatility. The system will substitute volatility or market risk for credit risk. The reason is that, at present, market risk is not penalized under the BIS rules.

A possible solution to this could be the development of futures contracts on volatility. For example, one could envisage a futures contract whose settlement price was the implied volatility on the Chicago Mercantile Exchange Eurodollar option contract, and so on. Thus market makers could trade volatility direct. Another exposure that market makers cannot at the moment trade directly is convexity.[1] Perhaps there might be scope for an instrument allowing for convexity trading, although this would probably be much more difficult to design.

NEW FINANCIAL STRUCTURES

We come now to the question of innovation in financial structures. Traditionally (i.e., since 1981) a corporation wanting to hedge its interest rate liabilities for 5 to 10 years would enter into an interest rate swap with a bank. The bank would lay off the risk with another counterparty, or disaggregate the cash flows and integrate them with its own interest risk management activities. The bank would make a charge (excessive or negligible, depending which side of the fence you sit on) for interposing the quality of its credit.

Two things could destroy the smooth functioning of such a process: loss of credit quality of the bank, or a significant increase in the cost of intermediation caused by capital requirements. Both have begun to take place. In the United States, both seem highly likely to continue much further. Congress' failure to put in place an adequate reform of the banking system does not augur well for a rapid healing of the self-inflicted wounds sustained by U.S. banks in the 1980s. The continuing structural problems of the industry suggest that the interest risk intermediation function of the U.S. banking system will either have to be radically reorganized, or it will shrink considerably.

A second pressure on the system is the continuing adaptation of the markets to the explicit disciplines on capital usage that are being imposed—firstly by the BIS harmonization of capital adequacy for banks, and now by the agreement within the EC on capital adequacy requirements for securities firms. The clear implication must be that exchange-traded instruments, or other instruments that do not require the use of banks or securities firms as credit risk absorbers, will be favored over those instruments where a bank or securities firm intermediates between two sides.

Insofar as intermediation is required, the most probable result of the pressures on the U.S. financial system will be that much of the market will migrate to non-U.S. banks, operating out of London or other locations. An analogy from another market beset with the twin evils of U.S. lawyers and the U.S. Congress may be of interest.

Some years ago, the U.S. liability insurance market passed through a capacity crisis. The response that evolved was for so-called association captives to be formed in locations such as Bermuda, which helped to fill the gap. For example, JP Morgan organized two companies called ACE and XL to provide this type of capacity. In principle, there is no reason why interest risk should not be reinsured through such an entity. To circumvent the difficulty that capital ratios would be applied more onerously to a bank's interest rate swap contract with an insurance company than with another bank, perhaps the entity might be structured as an old-fashioned consortium banking operation. If sufficient banks became part of an entity whose whole rationale was to buy in existing interest rate swap positions, while maintaining a AAA balance sheet, its risks would be widely spread. (To continue the insurance analogy, the entity would function rather as the so-called monoline insurers, Financial Security Assurance (FSA) or Financial Guaranty Insurance Corporation (FGIC), currently do—a firm whose raison d'etre is a clean balance sheet.)

Be this as it may, the impact of the factors listed above will almost certainly be to increase the pressure on banks to find some means of providing risk-bearing capacity without consuming too much scarce capital. Other alternatives would be the revival of that hardy perennial, a clearinghouse for the swaps market; a relaunch of the interest rate swap futures contract; or a straightforward process of disintermediation whereby industrial corporations simply deal with one another direct, as in the commercial paper market.

NOTE

1. Convexity is defined in *Investments: Analysis and Management,* 5th ed., by Jack Clark Francis (New York: McGraw Hill, 1991).

CHAPTER 34

THE ELEMENTS OF INTEREST RATE DERIVATIVES

Jane Sachar Brauer
Merrill Lynch,
Vincent M. Matsui
Citibank

This chapter will attempt to synthesize all the material in the prior chapters. It will risk oversimplification so as to bring perspective to the vast amount of information contained in this book. The measurement of market risk and the valuation problem are two sides to the same coin, so what is discussed will have value to both hedgers and speculators. The chapter has four major sections:

- The first section advances five basic principles that underlie both the fixed-income cash and derivatives markets.
- The section on trading and hedging rules outlines some simple rules to prosper by.
- The Common Problems section identifies those areas all practitioners must confront sooner or later that make the cash, exchange-traded, and OTC markets less interchangeable and arguably less efficient.
- The final section discusses the types of applications different participants have adopted towards interest rate derivatives.

ELEMENTARY PRINCIPLES OF FIXED-INCOME DERIVATIVES

Exchange-Traded and OTC Derivatives Are Equivalent to Leveraged Cash Positions

There are no absolute differences when comparing exchange-traded derivatives, OTC derivatives, and their leveraged cash alternatives. They all perform the same economic function; each has a direct analogy in the other two markets. They differ, however, importantly in the details of their usage, details that impose costs and confer benefits that differ among different classes of users.

Exchange-traded and OTC derivatives share an overriding characteristic in the form of leverage. Broken apart, the bond futures contract consists of two positions, a bond position and an associated short-term loan or investment. The bond futures contract can be, and indeed is, replicated in the cash market with bonds financed through the repo market (ignoring the various delivery options embedded in futures, and the differing margining requirements in the repo and futures markets). The interest rate swap is the OTC analog to the bond futures contract because it provides the same economics of leveraged shorting or investing, and is itself commonly hedged by dealers using bonds or futures.

Once you understand the notion of *leverage*, you can clearly see how the valuation principles are the same for exchange-traded derivatives, OTC derivatives, and leveraged cash instruments: what academics refer to as the *law of one price*. The various instruments differ in their operational details, which can certainly be important; however, their raw economic behavior will be fundamentally identical.

For example, owning a bond on repo is economically equivalent to owning (being long) the futures contract on that bond, which is equivalent to receiving fixed and paying floating under an interest rate swap with the same tenor as the bond (ignoring spread risk). The differences among these three trades are smaller than their similarities, and these differences have varying costs and benefits for different users.

Large institutional traders that have few impediments to trade across markets will generally attempt to arbitrage among them.

This cross-market activity ensures the law of one price. OTC dealers lay off risk in the cash and exchange markets; basis traders trade cash and futures; institutional investors and corporations use the OTC and exchange markets to hedge and speculate against cash. The relentless arbitrage by floor traders, dealers, and consumers among these three markets results in similar pricing for similar risk versus return profiles.

One might take issue whether being short and being leveraged is moral. Leverage confers all the pleasure and pain of owning a security, without the need for cash (ignoring things like haircuts and margin). Leverage works both ways in that you can own something for which you have paid no cash (you have received financing), and you can sell something you do not currently own (benefiting from the interest earnings on the sales proceeds).[1]

The ability to leverage and short sell is intrinsic to modern capital markets theory and practice. If an efficient market is good, because each investor gets a fair shake, then the ability to leverage and sell short is inherently good, because all this leveraging and short selling, in conjunction with the traditional activity of trading, ensure users of these products liquidity and fair prices. An efficient market is one in which the law of one price applies, prices readily adjust to new information with more or less equivalent speed, and no participant has a systematic advantage over any other participant. Although any one market participant may only be a natural seller, and another only a natural buyer, there are those who can and will do either side whenever mispricing occurs, and thereby precipitate one price.

In the exchange versus OTC versus cash analysis, remember that in the beginning, there was cash. There is an old debate among practitioners about which leads a market move, cash or futures. There is the illusion that futures drive the market. Is this the tail wagging the dog? Futures simply appear to move more quickly due to the open outcry system, where cash moves through phone calls and brokers. Within a short period of time, the cash and futures end up in the same place. The role of the arbitrageur, who is indifferent between buying and selling, is to ensure this convergence.

Table 34-1 shows pairs of transactions that, in many situations, can be viewed as interchangeable hedges.

**TABLE 34-1
Common Analogs**

U.S. Treasury repo	Swaps
Swaps	Eurodollar futures
Eurodollar futures	U.S. Treasury repo
U.S. Treasury repo	Bond and note futures
Caps, floors, collars	Eurodollar futures options
OTC bond options	Bond futures options
Rate and spread locks	Bond and note futures
Forwards and FRAs	Eurodollar futures

You should know and understand the institutional details of the cash market, the OTC market, and the exchange-traded derivatives market to make an informed decision about relative value among the three markets. If you don't know, others will be there to arbitrage the price so that under most market conditions, the law of one price will operate, and you will be protected. However, large market moves can cause temporary disequilibrium among the three markets, and it is at such times that the knowledgeable participant gains an advantage. Table 34-2 identifies the major characteristics of the most common interest rate derivatives.

Outrights and Options Are Pieces of the Same Puzzle

Outrights are positions that confer the benefits and costs of outright ownership or the outright sale of a position. You earn one for one on the upside (however defined), and you lose one for one on the downside. The payoff profile is that of the familiar 45-degree line, positively sloped for long positions, and negatively sloped for short positions.

Think of options as discrete pieces of long or short outright positions: At the option's maturity, you earn or lose one for one beginning at a specified price or yield level. Below or above that specified level, there is no gain or loss attributable to the position, except for any option premiums paid or received.

The common arbitrage techniques of conversion and reversal

consist of assembling options positions that replicate cheaper/ richer outright long or short positions. For example, the combination of short calls and long puts creates a synthetic short of the underlying security; a long call position with a short put position creates a synthetic long in the underlying. Arbitrageurs look at these relationships constantly and will take advantage of short-term mispricings, and thereby preserve the linkage between options and their underlying security (also referred to as *put-call parity*).[2]

Under the sobriquets of "dynamic hedging" or "delta-neutral hedging," outright positions are used to hedge a short option position. One high-profile version of dynamic hedging is portfolio insurance, which is a strategy to replicate the payoff profile of a put option by selling the underlying security in proportion to a hypothetical option's delta.

In sum, options are intrinsically linked to their underlying security. They constitute the pieces of an outright position.

The Zero Coupon Yield Curve Is the Touchstone of Fixed-Income Cash and Derivative Markets

The zero coupon curve is the great invisible reality of the fixed-income markets. Without an understanding of this reality, the behavior of other market participants appears irrational. Why would someone pay more than the simple discounted spread for an above-market interest rate swap? Why should the deferred bond contract trade cheaper than the front contract, and when does it trade richer? Why do caps seem so expensive when the strike is above today's rate? Why do futures prices appear to converge to cash over time?

The zero coupon curve answers these questions and solves the bulk of the valuation problem in fixed-income markets (ignoring default risk). If you understand the notion of carry, then the concepts of the zero coupon yield and forward rates naturally follow.

Assume you can invest for one year at 10 percent simple interest, paid at maturity. Also assume you can invest for two years at 20 percent per annum, with interest paid annually. Out of this simple two-year term structure, you can derive two additional rates: the two-year zero coupon rate (21.1 percent per annum), and

TABLE 34-2
Characteristics of Major Interest Rate Derivatives

Interest Rate Derivatives	Available Maturities	Longest Term	Minimum Trade Size
Exchange-traded interest rate futures:			
Short term	3-month T-bill 3-month LIBOR 1-month LIBOR Fed funds (1 month average)	T-bill: 1 year (4 cts*) 3-month LIBOR: 4 years (16 cts) 1-month LIBOR: 6 months (6 cts) Fed funds: 9 months (9 cts)	T-bills and 3-month LIBOR: $1 million; 1-month LIBOR: $5 million; Fed funds: $5 million
Long term	2 year, 5 year, 10 year, 30 year	2 year: 6 months; 5 year: 9 months; 10 year: 15 months; 30 year: 2 ½ years (10 cts)	2 year: $200 million; 5 year, 10 year, 30 year: $100 million
Exchange-traded interest rate options:			
Short term	3-month T-bill 3-month LIBOR 1-month LIBOR	T-bill: 9 months (3 cts) 3-month LIBOR: 18 months (6 cts) 1-month LIBOR: 6 months (6 cts)	$1 million
Long term	2 year, 5 year, 10 year, 30 year	9 months	2 year: $200 million; 5 year, 10 year, 30 year: $100 million
OTC interest rate options	2 to 30 years	5 years +	$1 million
Interest rate swaps	1 to 10 years	10 years +	$5 million
Interest rate forwards	3 month to 30 years	1 year +	$10 million
Interest rate caps/floors	3/6-month T-bill 3/6 month LIBOR 3/6-month CP	10 years +	$5 million

*cts = contracts.

Bid-Ask Spread	Credit Exposure	Documentation	Other Characteristics
T-bill: 1 to 2 bp* front cts, 2 to 5 bp back cts; 3-month LIBOR: 1 bp front cts, 1 to 4 bp back cts; 1-month LIBOR: 1 to 2 bp front cts, 5 to 10 back cts; Fed funds: 1 to 2 bp front cts	Low; daily margin required	Exchange standard	March, June, September, December cycle; 1-month LIBOR: 6 months
2 year: 2/32; 5 year: 1/32, 10 year: 1/32; 30 year: 1/32	Low: daily margin required	Exchange standard	March, June, September, December cycle
T-Bill: 3–4 bp 3-month LIBOR: 1–2 bp 1-month LIBOR; 3–4 bp	Low: daily margin required	Exchange standard	March, June, September, December cycle; T-bills and 3-month LIBOR also have some serial months; 1-month *libor*: 6 months
2 year: 2–4/32; 5 year and 10 year: 2–3/32; 30 year: 1–2/32	Low; daily margin required	Exchange standard	March, June, September, December cycle and in first 3 months, serial on all 4 maturities
2/32 to 4/32	Medium; buyer exposed to writer; no clearinghouse	PSA standard for bonds and notes; ISDA standard for swaptions	Custom tailored; less liquid than ET options; not very liquid past one year
Up to 10 bp	High; exposure normally limited to net difference checks; no exchange of principal; no clearinghouse	ISDA standard with modifications made by each dealer	3/6-month LIBOR index is most liquid; 3-month T-bill and 1-month CP available
1/4 to 3/4 point	Medium; no clearinghouse	Not standardized	Available on most treasuries and MBS pass-throughs
1/4 to 3/4 point	Medium; no credit enhancement protection; no clearinghouse	ISDA standard	3-month LIBOR is the only liquid index

*bp = basis point.

the one-year forward rate (33.3 percent).[3] It is this invisible reality that drives the valuation of OTC and exchange-traded derivatives. Forward rates and strip rates are not simply exercises in theory; the hedger or speculator can lock in these rates and make them real. Forward rates are the basis for establishing cap values, futures prices, forward bond prices, and forward start swaps. Zero coupon rates are the basis for discounting future cash flows whether they occur in the cash, futures, or the OTC market.

A specific application for the zero coupon curve lies in the valuation of irregular future cash flows. Market convention of pricing any security with an irregular cash flow to the average life can be misleading. Pricing to the duration (however measured) of irregular cash flows addresses a part of the problem; however, this approach also has its weaknesses. When the yield curve is especially steep or especially inverted, the resulting mispricing of these approaches becomes ever more apparent. There is no substitute for a zero coupon valuation approach when you want to present-value irregular cash flows.

On a final note, remember that forward rates do not predict future yields. Research has yet to prove any significant predictive ability. Forward rates are real at any point in time because they can be realized and locked in at that point in time. However, forward rates do not tell you what the shape and levels will be of future yield curves. The corollary to this observation is that the shape of the yield curve is all important, since it is just as much the shape of the yield curve as the level of yields that determines forward rates.

Develop an Intuition about the Behavior of Option Prices and Sensitivities within a Portfolio of Options

An increasingly important percentage of the fixed-income valuation problem revolves around options, making it important to understand where option prices come from and how they behave with respect to the underlying securities. To be effective with option valuation, you should develop an intuitive understanding of the various price sensitivities—specifically, delta, gamma, theta, and vega (or, more formally, kappa, or sigma), and their behavior over the life of the option. Knowledge of these sensitivities will determine your success in using options.[4]

For example, a portfolio of options has sensitivity characteristics not achievable with any single option. A typical OTC bond option dealer's portfolio is one big calendar spread. The dealer generally owns one- and two-week American-style call options sold by fixed-income mutual funds. The funds sell OTC options to enhance their portfolio yield. To hedge volatility exposure, OTC dealers in turn sell their volatility on the futures exchanges in the form of note and bond futures options. Typically, the exchange-traded options sold are of longer maturity than the OTC options owned. The net result for the dealer is a long straddle position whereby the dealer loses money if the market does nothing, but will make money for a given market change in either direction; technically speaking, the dealer is long gamma and short volatility.

One option-pricing parameter that is generally overlooked but of great importance to valuation is the nature of the option's exercise: The European option allows the option holder to exercise only at maturity in contrast to an American option, which allows the option holder to exercise at any time. Holding all else constant, when the forward bond price is lower than today's price (implied by a positively sloped yield curve), early exercise has more value on calls than on puts. When the forward price is higher (slope negative) early exercise has more value on puts than on calls.[5]

Options introduce a risk dimension to a portfolio that is not available with outright positions, namely, volatility. The intuition behind volatility and its impact on option valuation has to do with the price behavior of the underlying asset—How much does it actually thrash around relative to the level assumed in an option price? In general, you want to buy options when you think the observed volatility of the outright will exceed the volatility implied in the option's price. Conversely, you would look to sell options when the volatility of the underlying is expected to exceed the volatility implied in the option's price.

The stock market crash of 1987 reminded option traders that dynamic hedging, portfolio insurance, and option replication strategies assume continuous price changes and cannot work in gapping or discontinuous price change markets. While stock prices were crashing, interest rates were plummeting. Behind the scenes, another form of dynamic hedging was failing—the hedging of interest rate cap portfolios where dealers needed to buy back Eurodollar futures contracts to rebalance portfolios to short the market. In the deep and liquid Eurodollar futures pit, there were plenty of bids, but few to no offers. The point of the story is that an option price and its underlying sensitivities are only as good as the assumptions made in deriving that price. At the time of the crash, the assumption of the availability of continuous prices did not hold, and there was no price for Eurodollar options; you could say that volatility had become infinite or zero, depending on which side of the trade you stood.

Finally, be aware that an implied volatility term structure exists. Like the interest rate term structure, it possesses a slope and an inherent volatility of its own. However, the volatility of one underlying is not interchangeable with that of another.

Measure Your Risks in Aggregate, Not Trade by Trade

Measure your risks and exposures in the aggregate. Unless you have a very simple portfolio, chances are you will have offsetting exposures, and what may appear to be the properly sized position will often be too much. You can minimize hedging costs by recognizing these offsetting exposures.

Measuring your risks in aggregate also brings to bear the benefits of cross-correlation among securities. Different instruments do not necessarily move lock-step with each other, and may indeed move in opposite directions for a given event. If two instruments are negatively correlated, the risk inherent in the combined instruments is less than either instrument taken alone. Negative correlation among instruments in a portfolio further reduces hedging needs; you cannot recognize this benefit looking at each instrument's risk in isolation.

Increasingly, practitioners measure risk in maturity buckets to capture the effect of independent changes to different parts of the yield curve. Use of the zero coupon (the *spot*) yield curve is essential to the measurement of risk under such an approach. You cannot manage risk if you do not know where your risks lie.

ELEMENTARY RULES OF TRADING AND HEDGING

Transact in the Market that Offers You the Lowest Cost per Unit of Benefit

One user has impediments that another does not. This means that on a number of dimensions not all costs are the same for all users. The user with the lowest costs is the dealer who has set up systems and staffing to reduce their cost for cash, OTC, and exchange-traded derivatives. At one end of the spectrum are dealers who made trading decisions on the basis of the economic value of the derivatives they trade. At the other end are end users who bear additional costs related to:

- Management fears.
- Operational problems.
- Counterparty credit risk.
- Risk controls.
- Regulatory restrictions.
- Accounting treatment.
- Tax issues.

These will be addressed in detail later on. Users will choose the cheapest alternative relative to their own costs. This makes some choices seem rational as viewed by end users, but they may seem to be the most expensive alternative from a dealer's perspective.

Your Broker/Dealer Is a Resource

Both futures brokers and OTC dealers are selling service, as well as price. Any derivatives user should expect to receive quality service. Broker/dealers typically have materials, analyses, and expertise in educating customers to use their products, and they are only too eager to share them with you. They will be able to do simulations, provide sample documentation, discuss credit issues, recommend risk control methods, and provide or recommend software. They will work closely with you to develop a "feel" for the market and let you know what other managers, similar to yourself, are doing. Plan on working with more than one broker/dealer, since each has a different expertise and approach to risk. You will find, in the case of futures, that brokers have different commissions, and, in the case of OTC derivatives, that each dealer may have a different price for the same risk because of where their individual portfolios are positioned.

You Must Be Able to Value What You Trade

This rule applies especially to the OTC sector where specialized (i.e., illiquid) structures abound and valuation technology and appetite for risk are unevenly spread among dealers. The market and the law of one price afford the user with a degree of protection; however, this protection fades as one moves beyond standardized products and structures into the domain of complex OTC products.

For futures, you must understand the security underlying the contract and how to derive the forward price of that security. The remaining 10 percent of the futures valuation problem relates to contract idiosyncracies such as good delivery requirements and mark-to-market and settlement procedures. These details can be assimilated rather quickly and exploited.

The ability to independently value and manage the risk of complex derivatives is an objective users must continuously struggle to maintain and improve. The corollary rule is: If the sum of the parts is less than the whole, buy the parts. Possessing the expertise to manufacture gives you the benefit of better pricing and the greater liquidity of the discrete parts.

Consciously Choose the Risks You Are Prepared to Live with in Exchange for the Risks You Cannot Afford to Assume

Derivatives cannot completely eliminate all risks. They can only substitute risks that you do not choose to take for one you are more comfortable assuming. Common risk-for-risk trade-offs include:

- Basis risk versus level of interest rate risk.
- Outright payoff versus option payoff.
- Customized OTC derivative versus standardized exchange-traded derivative.

- Volatility risk versus directional risk.
- Reshaping of the yield curve risk versus duration risk.
- Exchange margining versus counterparty credit risk.

There is no such thing as the perfect hedge because you cannot take T-bill risk and earn long bond returns.

The More Customized the Derivative, the Less Liquid, and the More Expensive

Typically, a customized derivative combines several different component derivatives. It is harder to price a package, and not all dealers will trade all components of a package. When the customized derivative contains many unusual features, such as conditions for early closeout, many dealers may not want to price it at all. Therefore, it should be no surprise that the more customized transactions will be less liquid. Remember that the liquidity and cost effectiveness of a customized OTC transaction depends critically on the liquidity and market risk a dealer must bear to create and hedge such a transaction. Fewer dealers to price a transaction means wider bid-ask spreads. There is a direct, inverse relationship between liquidity and cost—the less liquid, the higher the cost.

Know the Liquidity Associated with Your Name and That of Your Counterparty when Dealing in the OTC Market

OTC derivatives will always call for one or both parties to the trade to make one or more payments during the life of the transaction. It is this future performance requirement that distinguishes OTC derivatives from their exchange-traded counterparts. For this risk, the OTC user gets the flexibility to structure the derivative to his/her unique requirements. Because the subsequent performance and value of the derivative depends in large measure on the financial health of your counterparty, select your counterparties carefully. In addition, if you choose to later liquidate your position by assigning it to another party, that party's ability to make a price will depend on the creditworthiness of your existing counterparty. Know your counterparties, and manage your exposures to each.

Avoid Self-Critical 20-20 Hindsight

When you look at how your trades are performing, if you look back, do so to learn how you could have taken market information available at the time and made a different hedge decision. It is bad for the spirit to look back and say, "I shouldn't have hedged" or "I should have bought an option and not fixed the rate," and so on. There will always be cases where a different hedge would have performed better. The important thing to keep in mind is this: Were your objectives defined properly at the time of the hedge and did the hedge meet your objectives? If so, be happy.

COMMON PROBLEMS/EXTRA COSTS

A Management Comfortable with Derivatives Is Rare

Nothing strikes fear in a manager more than authorizing "risky commodity futures trading." It is something he/she does not have the time or patience to understand. For example, it is much easier to explain swaps than to explain futures hedges; swaps take the uncertainty out of the hedge.

Similarly, long puts or covered calls can be relatively straightforward to explain and have a limited downside. On the other hand, short uncovered options have an unlimited downside and would not be a good hedge choice for a conservative manager. Regulatory bodies try to protect the unknowing company by specifying the admissible types of hedge transactions. Often short options positions are not on the list of admissible hedges.

In many cases, OTC derivatives appear more management friendly:

- OTC derivatives are off balance sheet, and losses are not immediately apparent.
- Swap cash flows are known, subject only to the prevailing index rates. Cap, floor, and swaption cash flows can be shown relatively simply as well.
- They can help to eliminate the basis risk in many cases, and a swap, cap, floor, and swaption can be tailored to each situation.

- It is straightforward to match cash flows of a corporation's liability or an investor's asset. Some swap dealers are even prepared to take the uncertainty out of a swap against a variable amortizing security by allowing the notional amount of the swap to vary with the principal outstanding on the asset.

Exchange-traded futures and options appear more complex:

- The exchange margining process forces the immediate recognition of losses.
- You must conform to the standardized features of futures: expiration dates, indexes, and contract size.
- Basis risk can be large. Although you can estimate the yield level of a strip, the precise value is unknown. With Treasury futures, hedge performance is even more variable. Several factors contribute to the variability of performance, including:
  - Expiration date mismatch.
  - Notional amount mismatch.
  - Convergence.
  - Basis risk on closeout.
  - Cash-futures risk.
  - Repo on Treasury risk.
  - Curve risk.
  - Roll risk.
  - Reinvestment risk.
  - Compounding formula.
  - Proper adjustments for the margin account by tailing the hedge.

To demonstrate to management that you can competently use futures, you must:

- Demonstrate the business purpose of the hedge.
- Establish the appropriate approval process.
- Identify and quantify potential risks and establish risk limits.
- Develop adequate controls to assure that your margin payments and positions are correctly maintained by the back office.

You Have to Worry about Counterparty Defaults

With swaps and other OTC derivatives, you must be aware of counterparty risk. The challenge is to assess the exposure, set limits by counterparty, and monitor exposures. The risk in OTC derivatives is that of your counterparty's future ability to perform under the terms of the contract. Therefore, the longer the maturity, the greater the exposure. For example, credit quality is very important in a 15-year swap, and less of a concern for a two-week bond option. Similarly, the greater the volatility of expected payments because of market moves, the greater your potential exposure.

The difficulty of the task lies in assessing your maximum credit exposure. Since interest rate swaps are an exchange only of interest payments and not of principal, your exposure is effectively the mark-to-market value of the swap today and the maximum likely increase in value over the life of the trade. As time passes, future potential mark-to-market exposure decreases because the maturity of the swap decreases. There are several rules of thumb for estimating future mark-to-market exposure. One approach is to estimate the change in market value for a two–standard deviation move in interest rates against your counterparty. Remember that you can generally think of the cash analog of a derivatives position if this helps you better understand the nature of your counterparty exposure.

Ways in which counterparties minimize their credit exposure include either provisions for collateral calls if the mark-to-market value exceeds some threshold amount, or provisions for market value termination in the event of a credit rating downgrade.

With exchange-traded derivatives, exposure is limited to your margin on deposit with the broker. This margin is to cover daily mark-to-market settlement risk. However, customer margins are held in a segregated account, so even if your broker goes under, customer margins remain intact. If you determine that your broker's credit is deteriorating, you can transfer your positions, including your margins, to another broker. Unlike swaps, you are not locked in to the broker for the duration of the position. Even if your broker fails before you transfer the positions, because customer funds and positions are segregated, the futures clearinghouse can transfer your positions for you. Given the complexity of legal proceedings, in the event of a broker insolvency, you may lose access to your margin cash on deposit, although you will eventually get your margin back.

Do You Want to Pay for the Convenience of OTC Derivatives?

There is an implicit cost in having a passive OTC position using swaps or OTC options, compared with an active hedge position with futures or listed options. OTC derivatives are generally less liquid than exchange-traded derivatives because of the previously discussed credit dimension. For example, shorter-maturity swaps have wider bid-ask spreads (approximately 5 basis points) than the comparable futures positions with 2 to 3 basis point spreads (including commissions). Although longer-term swaps have even wider bid-ask spreads, you can only approximately replicate these positions with futures. Thus, it is impossible to even calculate the "spread" of a long maturity futures hedge. Any such hedge has quite a bit of basis risk, and there is no simple calculation of all-in yield using the futures contract. The more complex the OTC derivative, the harder it is to hedge, the wider the transactions costs, and the more difficult to calculate what the spread would be if you actively managed the comparable exchange-traded or cash alternative yourself.

There are, of course, many cases where it makes sense to use a passive OTC strategy, even if the initial costs are slightly higher.

Example: A treasurer thinks he can save 2 basis points (bps) on the next hedge by using futures instead of a swap. In dollar terms, he can save $4,000. Of course, he will have to spend two full weeks selling the concept to management and half an hour a day figuring out his position and any hedge adjustments. What would you do?

Example: An insurance company's margin moneys are deducted from its capital account when computing regulatory capital. OTC derivatives require no capital be set aside. In a capital-scarce environment, what would you do?

Example: A manager has just been told to downsize the risk management department, regardless of performance improvement using exchange-traded derivatives. She was planning to start a futures hedging program. What would you do?

The Back-Office Processing of All Derivatives Will Make or Break You

The daily mark to market of exchange-traded contracts gives users the security of knowing that their counterparty risk has been significantly reduced. For this peace of mind, users must review and reconcile their positions every business day.

OTC derivatives sometimes call for mutual margining. These margin calls can be made based on market moves or with a certain periodicity, resulting in monitoring and frequent calculations, as well. There are also varied haircuts depending on the price volatility of any margin securities. There are some derivative payments that require tedious calculations. Reconciling these cash flows and mark-to-market calculations will generally be less frequent than exchange-traded contracts, but more effort intensive.

Cash positions in the repo market require margin adjustments based upon market moves and reconciliation of prices and accrued interest.

Trade verification is critical for all securities markets trades; derivatives are no different. With exchange-traded contracts, the trades are easy to verify given the standardization of contract terms. With OTC derivatives, you must verify all the dates, amounts, and conditions under which payments are to be made.

Managing any derivatives position is not easy even if you are doing it properly. Although your broker/dealer can generally recommend the right going-in position that meets your objectives, nobody cares about your position quite like you would, so you must take responsibility. Risk management systems must be in place for you to do a good job.

You need the proper administrative controls in place to allow a trader to modify the position, but be assured that you are still properly hedged. You need the ability to account for gains and losses on the position. Although a futures hedge and an OTC hedge can be economically equivalent, the futures cash flows are much more visible.

After the trade is done, that is when the real work begins. Out-trades, a miscalculated position, and a failed delivery are all examples of a failed back office. They will cost you money and time if you let them happen.

Your Regulatory Environment Dictates Which Derivatives Market to Use

The myriad of regulatory authorities, many of whom are offering guarantees to depositors, policyholders, and investors, often specify under what circumstances you can use which derivatives and when. Some require evidence that the derivatives trades satisfy a legitimate business purpose. Their public policy objective is to limit speculation and imprudent behavior. OTC derivative applications will thrive in an environment where arbitrary regulatory restrictions conflict with the otherwise sound economic objectives of the regulated.

Accounting Treatment Will Define Success or Failure

Exchange-traded derivatives will be marked to market if you cannot get hedge accounting. Of course, most people prefer to have the flexibility to defer gains and losses. However, the standards for hedge accounting can be difficult to meet. For example, you must show a significant correlation between the derivative and an on–balance sheet item. The on–balance sheet item must be identified; you may not be able to trade the derivative and the balance sheet position separately.

OTC derivatives, through their ability to provide cash flows over time, can effectively provide deferral accounting. You can choose to mark to market, but no accounting rules are yet in force to require a particular accounting treatment. This latitude may make OTC derivatives more attractive than exchange-traded derivatives when the balance sheet asset or liability cannot be marked to market.

All derivatives are currently accorded off–balance sheet treatment with footnote disclosure, if material. With the active promotion of the SEC, mark-to-market accounting has taken the initiative in the world of generally accepted accounting principles (GAAP). The SEC believes that mark-to-market accounting exerts a salutary discipline on practitioners who are accustomed to postponing the day of reckoning in the freedom of accrual and investment accounting. If you are such a practitioner, you must begin preparing now for the inevitable day when your derivatives activities will flow immediately to the bottom line.

Using Derivatives' Tax Advantages Can Be a Profitable Enterprise

Tax motivations with derivatives are centered around two components, timing and character. Timing concerns when you take the gains or losses. Character concerns whether the gains or losses are treated as ordinary income or capital gains or losses.

Timing

Are the gains and losses taxed daily, on expiration of the hedge, or over time? Some derivatives are subject to mark-to-market treatment:

- Exchange-traded futures.
- Foreign exchange forwards, if there are futures traded in the United States on those currencies.
- Exchange-traded options, except for equity options on single stocks.

Swaps and other OTC options are not subject to mark-to-market rules. However, in the case of hedging, when the hedge is unwound, or the option expires or is exercised and then unwound, it is considered a taxable event. Thus, for transactions that straddle year-end, it is better to hedge in the OTC market than the exchange-traded markets.

Character

Are the gains and losses capital or ordinary income? Although the 1992 tax rates for corporate gains are the same as those for ordinary income, capital losses can only be used as an offset against capital gains, not against ordinary income. Therefore, corporations are concerned about hedges that would result in capital losses. Hedges are treated as independent transactions from a tax perspective, even though they may get hedge accounting; the gain or loss is considered capital. Thus, a corporation that hedges a forward issue with a derivative and reverses the hedge at the time of issue will have a capital gain or loss to deal with. The only way to defer gains and losses is by using swaps that are not unwound.

In the exchange-traded market, tax opportunities are limited. In the OTC market, there is more flexibility. Without creating assets, you can restructure cash flows, allowing interest income in years in which you have losses and interest expense in years in which you have profits. You can convert ordinary income into capital gains and losses or vice versa more easily than in the futures markets. In short, creative solutions to tax problems are still available with OTC derivatives; however, the rules are definitive with respect to exchange-traded derivatives.

SOME APPROACHES TO USAGE

Banks Are Active in Both OTC and Exchange-Traded Markets

Banks and thrifts historically have made money by borrowing at short-term rates and lending at long-term rates. In an era of low-interest rate volatility, this strategy successfully carried them for years. When short-term rates rose dramatically during the early 80s and the yield curve became inverted, these same banks and thrifts unhappily found themselves with negative carry. Various regulatory bodies stepped in to identify asset-liability mismatches, and the result was a conscious effort on the part of banks and thrifts to hedge their exposures. In the late 80s, there were further mandates to control interest rate exposure by demonstrating portfolio performance on a mark-to-market basis through simulations.

Current practice varies widely. The least sophisticated banks will not use any derivatives. They will create liabilities, such as deposit notes, to match their assets. Those a bit more daring will use swaps when a fixed-rate asset is created, allowing for no maturity or timing mismatches whatsoever.

The most sophisticated and active banks often use futures and options, as well. The funding desks at many of the money center and superregional banks are active users of derivatives. The more active the user, the more likely the derivative is futures and options. The use of futures and swaps for hedge purposes at times now includes various trading strategies to enhance yield, such as covered call writing, spread trading, and so on. Although banks do not actively speculate, the timing of a hedge can help enhance its yield. Those who want to manage their hedges closely and frequently find futures are a more cost-effective avenue.

Banks also have securities portfolios that may be hedged, at times, with derivatives. They must now distinguish between securities held in an investment portfolio and those held for trading. Covered call writing is often used as a yield enhancement strategy for bonds held. The type of securities held affects the selection of hedge. Portfolios consisting of long bonds and mortgage pass-throughs, for example, are rarely hedged with swaps.

The BIS capital adequacy guidelines require capital for swaps, but not for futures. This is due to the mark-to-market of futures, protecting against counterparty default risk. Although the requirements are not large, this tends to support futures activity more than swap activity. On the other hand, there is an accounting disadvantage to using futures. Bank call reports use regulatory accounting principles (RAP), rather than GAAP. RAP requires mark-to-market on futures regardless of whether it is a hedge or a speculative position. Therefore, banks who are managing their call reports will prefer hedging with swaps.

Mortgage swaps, a relatively recent development, have given banks an opportunity to have the performance of a leveraged mortgage position that is held off balance sheet. Structures that replicate any type of collateralized mortgage obligation (CMO) can be created to meet their needs.

Swaps based on tax-exempt rates (muni-swaps) have been a small but profitable specialty for some broker/dealers, with some of the risk offset using the municipal bond futures contract.

Foreign banks interested in buying high-yielding dollar assets turned to the swap market to create synthetic floating-rate assets with high yields by matching securities, such as asset-backed bonds, with swaps. They have not actively sought these same synthetic structures with futures due to the need to manage the hedge.

Many thrifts, it is well-known, followed a strategy called *risk-*

controlled arbitrage, which required putting on fixed-rate swaps against mortgage assets. When rates subsequently fell and the mortgage assets prepaid, thrifts were left holding the bag. In the bag was an obligation to pay fixed at a much higher rate than the current market. The thrifts who suffered from this overhedging forgot about the options they had implicitly sold to mortgagors in the form of rights to prepay.

Insurance Companies Are Becoming Increasingly Sophisticated

More life insurance companies use fixed-income derivatives than property/casualty companies. In the general account of a life insurance company, derivatives are primarily used for asset-liability management and for creating higher-yielding synthetic assets. In their separate account products, insurance company requirements are similar to those of an investment advisor or plan sponsor of pension funds (see the discussion on pension funds later on in this section), and derivative applications are directed to total return strategies. Asset-liability management solutions include monthly analyses of duration exposure with futures hedges to reduce the mismatch. In addition, insurance companies have started to realize that their balance sheets look like short straddles; they had sold calls in their mortgage and callable investments, and they sold puts on their liabilities in giving termination and redemption provisions to policyholders. They have identified the need to buy convexity and they have done so by buying caps, corporate bond warrants, and swaptions. Insurance companies have also become a lot smarter in their ability to use the derivatives markets to meet their needs. The synthetic assets that they have promoted include put bonds, synthetic callable bonds, synthetic floaters, and gap swaps (buying a long-maturity floater or perpetual and fixing the rate to a maturity shorter than that of the asset, being left with the market risk of security at the end of the swap). Insurance companies have been able to enhance yields when credit spreads on longer-maturity corporate bonds have been wider than swap spreads compared to the shorter maturity bonds. They have bought lower-grade long-term corporates and swapped to floating, and they have bought higher-grade floating-rate bonds and swapped to fixed.

Corporations Prefer the OTC Markets to the Exchange-Traded Markets

Corporations typically have a particular type of funding they are seeking. They are usually indifferent between obtaining that funding directly or synthetically using OTC derivatives. A dealer can monetize the corporation's indifference between a synthetic issue and an ordinary issue with various OTC derivatives. Ever since Citicorp intermediated the first swap between IBM and the World Bank, swaps have provided a tool to link disparate markets. This credit spread arbitrage is now commonplace. Since one of the corporate treasurer's main functions is to minimize the cost of funding, if an OTC derivative combined with some other type of issuance gives them the precise cash flows they require, they will fund synthetically. This allows them to explore a variety of sources of funds by tapping many market segments (short end, long end, callable, puttable, noncallable, and so on). Although swaps are often incorporated in new-issue underwriting, they have become secondary market hedge tools as well. They allow treasurers to restructure their debt via the swap market rather than through the more cumbersome new-issues market.

The swaption market evolved through its ability to monetize the embedded call in callable bonds. An institutional investor buying a callable bond is effectively buying a call-free bond and selling an embedded call option. The issuer is buying the call option. The swaption market was a response to the need to strip out the cheap call option within callable bonds. When Wall Street was willing to buy call swaptions at higher prices than the investors were implicitly demanding, issuers of fixed-rate debt chose to issue callable debt and sell the embedded call option to the dealer community. Issuers were effectively arbitraging the two option markets, providing them with significant interest savings. At this point, investors are getting smarter and are less willing to sell convexity for a small pickup in yield.

Most corporations have looked into the futures markets at one time or other as a substitute to the swap markets. However, very few have taken the leap into the world of futures—for good reason. A corporation who puts on a few swap hedges a year typically finds futures to be more of a management headache than it is worth.

Even the larger corporations' managers of intermediate-term debt have not found the futures markets to be a better alternative. Very few corporations issue debt frequently enough and with enough size to warrant setting up a futures operation. It seems that only a few corporations have found that they can actively and adequately manage a portfolio with futures.

Mutual Funds Have Been and Will Continue to Be More Active in Exchange-Traded Markets

A mutual fund must have the authority written in its prospectus to be able to trade any of the listed and OTC derivatives. Some of the funds have amended their existing prospectuses, and fund sponsors commonly include authority to trade derivatives in the prospectuses of their new funds. Many open-end mutual funds groups are very active in futures and options, primarily to hedge or to enhance yield. Although regulations have eliminated some of the misleading advertising by high-yielding funds, a fund can still buy a long-maturity bond with high coupon income and sell a futures contract to hedge itself. The interest income from the bond is reported as additional yield while the futures position generates a capital gain or loss. Another strategy among funds is covered call writing, with funds that practice this strategy referred to as *buy-write funds* (buy the asset, write the call). There have been some futures exchange rule impediments to using futures that have been overcome. For example, mutual funds are prohibited by the SEC from providing margin to futures exchanges. Therefore, the exchanges now permit them to put their margin funds in a third-party custodial account.

There is a disadvantage to using swaps or illiquid derivatives in a mutual fund; the funds need liquidity and a way to mark to market daily for purposes of calculating net asset value. This requirement is not as easily met with swaps, and certainly not with complex structures. A swap counterparty to an open-end fund that is authorized to trade swaps must be assured that redemptions will not dry up the fund—that collateral is pledged or some other mechanism is available to assure payment by the fund under the terms of the swap.

A number of mutual funds that do not have OTC derivatives

specified in their prospectuses have found another vehicle for achieving the return profiles they would have wanted with derivatives. Medium-term notes (MTNs) are structured by dealers that have derivatives embedded in the payoff of both the cash flows and the notional amount. By doing so, the mutual fund buys a security, instead of an explicit derivative, and the issuer monetizes the derivatives embedded in the MTNs by taking offsetting positions in the OTC market.

Closed-end mutual funds, marked to market, have been able to use futures and swaps more readily. Swap dealers can take the fund as a counterparty, since there is limited redemption risk. These funds can be found buying asset swaps, with the intention to buy and hold.

Pension Funds and Their Investment Advisors Are Moving beyond Exchange-Traded Derivatives into the OTC Market

Most of the large pension funds use futures and options indirectly for hedging and yield enhancement. The futures and options transactions by pension funds are primarily through their investment advisors. They choose investment advisors on the basis of their specialties, and it has become commonplace for a pension fund to select advisors who use derivatives, as well as cash instruments, in their money management strategies. Many of these money managers have since requested expanding their trading authorization to include most OTC derivatives.

Plan sponsors themselves may also use derivatives for various purposes. Rather than disrupt the money managers' assets under management, they may apply asset allocation strategies via overlay programs, for example, by selling bond futures and buying equity futures. Some have decided to manage a portion of plan assets passively by "investing" in total return index swaps.

Perhaps the most significant derivatives foray by pension funds is in the area of managed futures programs. A managed futures program can have long or short positions on any futures exchange worldwide, trading contracts on any of the available underlying commodities. Managed futures have been shown to have noncorrelated but high expected returns with the traditional equity and fixed-income investments. Those pension funds that have invested in managed futures have hired investment advisors to run the managed futures program.

SUMMARY

As this book goes to press, regulators around the world have become increasingly vocal about the need for increased oversight of derivatives markets. More-extensive disclosure and reporting requirements on the part of users is likely. These requirements could include the marking to market of OTC derivatives and some form of on-balance sheet recognition or capital charge. A recent article viewed this development as "shining a light on the shadowy world of derivatives." The short-term appeal of resisting disclosure and staying in the shadows lies in the greater profitability and freedom afforded users and dealers in these markets. However, derivative practitioners must view greater scrutiny of their markets as an important means of raising market confidence and broadening the base of informed participants, thereby assuring the long-term health of these important markets.

NOTES

1. In general, only large institutional investors can obtain the proceeds from the short sale of a security and use that money to invest elsewhere. As a result, this paragraph does not apply to individuals who sell short and must give margin money to their broker instead of receiving the proceeds from their short sale. To reemphasize the point, this discussion does not apply to personal finances or to investors who trade in small quantities infrequently because, even though there are such small investors, they have no substantial effect on market prices.
2. Jack Clark Francis, *Investments: Analysis and Management*, 5th ed. (New York: McGraw-Hill, 1991), pp. 701-2, explains put-call parity. Using options to create synthetic positions is the topic of pages 712-23 of Francis's textbook.
3. Question: What is the zero coupon yield for a two-year maturity?
    Question: What is the forward rate in one year for one year?

These two questions are related in that you need to know the answer to the first question to be able to answer the second. The second question can be rephrased as: What interest do you need to earn in one year, for one year, such that you are indifferent between owning the one-year security and reinvesting the proceeds for a second year, versus owning the two-year security.

You know that the one-year zero coupon rate is 10 percent (assumed in this example). To derive the two-year zero coupon rate, you also know you will receive in one year a coupon payment of 20 percent on the two-year security. Therefore, the present value of this first coupon is equal to 20 percent/(1.10), or $18.18 for each $100 invested. With this information, the present value of the two-year security, ignoring the first coupon, must be $100 − $18.18, or $81.82. The future value of the two-year security, again ignoring the first coupon, you know is $120.00. Therefore, the zero coupon return for a two-year investment must be an annualized rate that will compound $81.82 to $120.00 over a two-year period. This rate is $[(\$120.00/\$81.82)^{0.5}-1]$, or 21.10% per annum. Notice how this invisible zero coupon rate is higher than any observed rate in this example. This will generally be true if the observed yield curve is upward sloping; conversely, the zero coupon term structure slopes more negatively than any observed negatively sloped yield curve.

To derive the one-year forward rate, you will need to think in future value terms. You know the future value of the $100 one-year security is $110. You also know that the future value of a $100 zero coupon two-year security is $146.65 through the calculation $100 × $(1 + 21.10\%)^2$. Therefore, the forward rate is that rate that will compound $110 to $146.65, or $146.65/$110, which is equal to 33.32 percent.

4. Delta, gamma, theta, and vega (or, more formally, kappa, or sigma) are discussed in *Options Markets* by John C. Cox and Mark Rubinstein (Englewood Cliffs, N.J.: Prentice Hall, 1985), pp. 215–35. Alternatively, see Hans R. Stoll and Robert E. Whaley, *Futures and Options* (Cincinatti: South-Western Publishing Company, 1993), pp. 219–30.
5. American puts on stock or currencies that trade at a discount are generally more valuable than American calls for the same reason: Their forward prices, reflecting the negative carry of these low-yielding asset classes, will be higher than their spot prices.

APPENDIX

COMPUTER PROGRAMS FOR THE HEWLETT-PACKARD MODEL 12C HAND-HELD CALCULATOR

George A. Mangiero
Iona College, New Rochelle, New York

HP-12C PROGRAM TO CALCULATE THE RISK (STANDARD DEVIATION) OF A THREE-STOCK PORTFOLIO

Input Data

1. Stock returns variance-covariance matrix.
2. Portfolio weights.

Preexecution Initialization

1. $R_1 = W_1$. 4. $R_5 = Var_2$. 7. $R_8 = Cov_{13}$.
2. $R_2 = W_2$. 5. $R_6 = Var_3$. 8. $R_9 = Cov_{23}$.
3. $R_4 = Var_1$. 6. $R_7 = Cov_{12}$.

Program

1. RCL 1   4. 1   7. STO 3
2. RCL 2   5. $\boxed{-}$ 8. RCL 1
3. $\boxed{+}$ 6. CHS   9. 2

10. Y^x
11. RCL 4
12. $\times$
13. RCL 2
14. 2
15. Y^x
16. RCL 5
17. $\times$
18. $+$
19. RCL 3
20. 2
21. Y^x
22. RCL 6
23. $\times$
24. $+$
25. RCL 1
26. RCL 2
27. $\times$
28. 2
29. $\times$
30. RCL 7
31. $\times$
32. $+$
33. RCL 1
34. RCL 3
35. $\times$
36. 2
37. $\times$
38. RCL 8
39. $\times$
40. $+$
41. RCL 2
42. RCL 3
43. $\times$
44. 2
45. $\times$
46. RCL 9
47. $\times$
48. $+$
49. 2
50. $1/x$
51. Y^x
52. STO 0 (The answer is stored in R_0.)

Example

Calculate the risk (standard deviation) of a three-stock portfolio whose variance-covariance matrix is given as follows:

	1	2	3
1	.25	.15	.17
2		.21	.09
3			.28

If the portfolio in question is $W_1 = .06$, $W_2 = .58$, $W_3 = .36$.

Preexecution Initialization

.06
STO 1
.58
STO 2
.25
STO 4
.21
STO 5

Appendix Programs for Hewlett-Packard Model 12C Handheld Calculator 779

.28
STO 6
.15
STO 7
.17
STO 8
.09
STO 9

Executing[1] the program gives the result 0.403980198 = 40.398%.

HP-12C PROGRAM TO CALCULATE CONVEXITY FOR AN ANNUAL COUPON PAYING BOND (WITH ADDED INSTRUCTIONS TO CALCULATE MODIFIED CONVEXITY)

Input Data

1. Coupon interest rate.
2. Yield to maturity (YTM).
3. Two dates separated by *half* the number of years to maturity.
4. Counter initialization.

Preexecution Initialization

1. R_0 = Coupon interest rate percent (as an integer, i.e., 6 percent is entered as 6 not .06).
2. R_1 = YTM (as an integer, i.e., 10 percent is entered as 10 not .10).
3. $R_3 = (T - .5)$ (T = Number of years to maturity).
4. R_8 = Beginning date (M.DY).[2]
5. R_9 = A second date that is *half* the number of years to maturity later (M.DY).

Program

1. 1
2. CHS
3. STO 7
4. 1
5. STO 4
6. STO 5
7. 0
8. STO 6
9. f FIN
10. RCL 0
11. 2
12. ×

780 Appendix Programs for Hewlett-Packard Model 12C Handheld Calculator

13. STO 0
14. PMT
15. RCL 1
16. 2
17. ×
18. i
19. RCL 8
20. RCL 9
21. f PRICE
22. 1
23. 0
24. ×
25. STO 2
26. RCL 0
27. 5
28. ×
29. RCL 1
30. .
31. 0
32. 1
33. ×
34. 1

35. +
36. RCL 4
37. Y^X
38. ÷
39. RCL 2
40. ÷
41. RCL 5
42. ×
43. RCL 5
44. 1
45. +
46. ×
47. RCL 6
48. +
49. STO 6
50. RCL 5
51. 1
52. +
53. STO 5
54. RCL 4
55. 1
56. +

57. STO 4
58. RCL 3
59. RCL 4
60. g X≤Y
61. g GTO 26
62. RCL 7
63. 1
64. +
65. STO 7
66. g X=0
67. g GTO 69
68. g GTO 78
69. RCL 0
70. 5
71. ×
72. 1
73. 0
74. 0
75. 0
76. +
77. g GTO 29
78. RCL 6   (The answer is stored in R_6.)

Example

Calculate the convexity of a $1,000 face value bond that offers a 6 percent annual coupon *paid annually* and that has a *YTM* of 10 percent, given that the bond matures four years from today. (*Note*: This program is designed to be used for bonds with $1,000 face values that have maturities that are integer multiples of one year.)

Preexecution Initialization

6
STO 0
10
STO 1

3.5
STO 3
1.011980
STO 8
1.011982   (*Note: This date is 4/2 years later.*)
STO 9

(*Note*: Any two dates separated by exactly *two* years can be used.)

Executing the program gives the result 17.66760008 (years) for convexity.

Modified convexity can be calculated with the following keystrokes performed immediately after the above program terminates.

1. RCL 1   5. $\boxed{\div}$ 9. $\boxed{Y^X}$
2. 1   6. 1   10. $\boxed{\div}$
3. 0   7. $\boxed{+}$
4. 0   8. 2

Performing these keystrokes gives the result 14.60132238 (years) for modified convexity.

HP-12C PROGRAM TO CALCULATE MODIFIED DURATION FOR AN ANNUAL COUPON PAYING BOND

Input Data

1. Coupon interest rate.
2. Yield to maturity (*YTM*).
3. Two dates separated by *half* the number of years to maturity.
4. Counter initialization.

Preexecution Initialization

1. R_0 = Coupon interest rate percent (as an integer, i.e., 6 percent is entered as 6 not .06).
2. R_1 = *YTM* (as an integer, i.e., 10 percent is entered as 10 not .10).
3. $R_3 = (T - .5)$ (T = Number of years to maturity).
4. R_8 = Beginning date (M.DY).

5. R_9 = A second date that is *half* the number of years to maturity later (M.DY).

Program

1. 1	28. $\times$	55. STO 4
2. CHS	29. RCL 1	56. RCL 3
3. STO 7	30. .	57. RCL 4
4. 1	31. 0	58. g X≤Y
5. STO 4	32. 1	59. g GTO 26
6. STO 5	33. $\times$	60. RCL 7
7. 0	34. 1	61. 1
8. STO 6	35. +	62. +
9. f FIN	36. STO i	63. STO 7
10. RCL 0	37. RCL i	64. g X=0
11. 2	38. RCL 4	65. g GTO 67
12. $\times$	39. Y^x	66. g GTO 76
13. STO 0	40. $\div$	67. RCL 0
14. PMT	41. RCL 2	68. 5
15. RCL 1	42. $\div$	69. $\times$
16. 2	43. RCL 5	70. 1
17. $\times$	44. $\times$	71. 0
18. i	45. RCL 6	72. 0
19. RCL 8	46. +	73. 0
20. RCL 9	47. STO 6	74. +
21. f PRICE	48. RCL 5	75. g GTO 29
22. 1	49. 1	76. RCL 6
23. 0	50. +	77. RCL i
24. $\times$	51. STO 5	78. $\div$ (The answer appears in the display when the program stops.)
25. STO 2	52. RCL 4	
26. RCL 0	53. 1	
27. 5	54. +	

Appendix Programs for Hewlett-Packard Model 12C Handheld Calculator

Example

Calculate the modified duration of a $1,000 face value bond that offers a 6 percent coupon *paid annually* and that has a *YTM* of 10 percent, given that the bond matures four years from today. (*Note*: This program is designed to be used for bonds with $1,000 face values that have maturities that are integer multiples of one year.)

Preexecution Initialization

6
STO 0
10
STO 1
3.5
STO 3
1.011980
STO 8
1.011982   (*Note: This date is 4/2 years later.*)
STO 9

(*Note*: Any two dates separated by exactly *two* years can be used.)
Executing the program gives the result 3.315821735 (years).

HP-12C PROGRAM TO CALCULATE DURATION FOR AN ANNUAL COUPON PAYING BOND

Input Data:

1. Coupon interest rate.
2. Yield to maturity (*YTM*).
3. Two dates separated by *half* the number of years to maturity.
4. Counter initialization.

Preexecution Initialization

1. R_0 = Coupon interest rate percent (as an integer, i.e., 6 percent is entered as 6 not .06).
2. R_1 = *YTM* (as an integer, i.e., 10 percent is entered as 10 not .10).
3. $R_3 = (T - .5)$ (T = Number of years to maturity).

4. R_8 = Beginning date (M.DY).
5. R_9 = A second date that is *half* the number of years to maturity later (M.DY).

Program

1. 1
2. CHS
3. STO 7
4. 1
5. STO 4
6. STO 5
7. 0
8. STO 6
9. f FIN
10. RCL 0
11. 2
12. ×
13. STO 0
14. PMT
15. RCL 1
16. 2
17. ×
18. i
19. RCL 8
20. RCL 9
21. f PRICE
22. 1
23. 0
24. ×
25. STO 2
26. RCL 0
27. 5
28. ×
29. RCL 1
30. .
31. 0
32. 1
33. ×
34. 1
35. +
36. RCL 4
37. Y^x
38. ÷
39. RCL 2
40. ÷
41. RCL 5
42. ×
43. RCL 6
44. +
45. STO 6
46. RCL 5
47. 1
48. +
49. STO 5
50. RCL 4
51. 1
52. +
53. STO 4
54. RCL 3
55. RCL 4
56. g X≤Y
57. g GTO 26
58. RCL 7
59. 1
60. +
61. STO 7
62. g X=0
63. g GTO 65
64. g GTO 74
65. RCL 0
66. 5
67. ×
68. 1
69. 0
70. 0
71. 0
72. +
73. g GTO 29
74. RCL 6 (The answer is stored in R_6.)

Example

Calculate the duration of a $1,000 face value bond that offers a 6 percent annual coupon *paid annually* and that has a *YTM* of 10 percent, given that the bond matures four years from today. (*Note*: This program is designed to be used for bonds with $1,000 face values that have maturities that are integer multiples of one year.)

Preexecution Initialization

6
STO 0
10
STO 1
3.5
STO 3
1.011980
STO 8
1.011982 (*Note: This date is 4/2 years later.*)
STO 9

(*Note*: Any two dates separated by exactly *two* years can be used.)
 Executing the program gives the result 3.647403908 (years).

HP-12C PROGRAM TO CALCULATE DURATION FOR A SEMIANNUAL COUPON PAYING BOND

Input Data

1. Coupon interest rate.
2. Yield to maturity (*YTM*).
3. Beginning and ending dates (today's date and the bond maturity date).
4. Counter initialization.

Preexecution Initialization

1. R_0 = Coupon interest rate percent (as an integer, i.e., 6 percent is entered as 6 not .06).
2. R_1 = *YTM* (as an integer, i.e., 10 percent is entered as 10 not .10).
3. $R_3 = (2T - .5)$ (T = Number of years to maturity).
4. R_8 = Beginning date (M.DY).
5. R_9 = Ending date (M.DY).

Program

1. 1
2. [CHS]
3. STO 7
4. 1
5. STO 4
6. [.]
7. 5
8. STO 5
9. 0
10. STO 6
11. [f][FIN]
12. RCL 0
13. [PMT]
14. RCL 1
15. [i]
16. RCL 8
17. RCL 9
18. [f][PRICE]
19. 1
20. 0
21. [×]
22. STO 2
23. RCL 0
24. 5
25. [×]
26. RCL 1
27. [.]
28. 0
29. 0
30. 5
31. [×]
32. 1
33. [+]
34. RCL 4
35. [Y^X]
36. [÷]
37. RCL 2
38. [÷]
39. RCL 5
40. [×]
41. RCL 6
42. [+]
42. STO 6
44. RCL 5
45. [.]
46. 5
47. [+]
48. STO 5
49. RCL 4
50. 1
51. [+]
52. STO 4
53. RCL 3
54. RCL 4
55. [g][X≤Y]
56. [g][GTO] 23
57. RCL 7
58. 1
59. [+]
60. STO 7
61. [g][X=0]
62. [g][GTO] 64
63. [g][GTO] 73
64. RCL 0
65. 5
66. [×]
67. 1
68. 0
69. 0
70. 0
71. [+]
72. [g][GTO] 26
73. RCL 6   (The answer is stored in R_6.)

Example

Calculate the duration of a $1,000 face value bond that offers a 6 percent annual coupon *paid semiannually* and that has a *YTM* of 10 percent, given that the bond matures four years from today. (*Note*: This program is designed to be used for bonds with $1,000 face values that have maturities that are integer multiples of one half of one year.)

Preexecution Initialization

6
STO 0
10
STO 1
7.5
STO 3
1.011980
STO 8
1.011984
STO 9

(*Note*: Any two dates separated by exactly four years can be used.) Executing the program gives the result 3.581861680 (years).

HP-12C PROGRAM TO CALCULATE MODIFIED DURATION FOR A SEMIANNUAL COUPON PAYING BOND

Input Data

1. Coupon interest rate.
2. Yield to maturity (*YTM*).
3. Beginning and ending dates (today's date and the bond maturity date).
4. Counter initialization.

Preexecution Initialization

1. R_0 = Coupon interest rate percent (as an integer, i.e., 6 percent is entered as 6 not .06).
2. R_1 = *YTM* (as an integer, i.e., 10 percent is entered as 10 not .10).
3. R_3 = $(2T - .5)$ (T = Number of years to maturity).
4. R_8 = Beginning date (M.DY).
5. R_9 = Ending date (M.DY).

Appendix Programs for Hewlett-Packard Model 12C Handheld Calculator

Program

1. 1
2. [CHS]
3. STO 7
4. 1
5. STO 4
6. [.]
7. 5
8. STO 5
9. 0
10. STO 6
11. [f][FIN]
12. RCL 0
13. [PMT]
14. RCL 1
15. [i]
16. RCL 8
17. RCL 9
18. [f][PRICE]
19. 1
20. 0
21. [×]
22. STO 2
23. RCL 0
24. 5
25. [×]
26. RCL 1
27. [.]
28. 0
29. 0
30. 5
31. [×]
32. 1
33. [+]
34. STO [i]
35. RCL [i]
36. RCL 4
37. [Y^x]
38. [÷]
39. RCL 2
40. [÷]
41. RCL 5
42. [×]
43. RCL 6
44. [+]
45. STO 6
46. RCL 5
47. [.]
48. 5
49. [+]
50. STO 5
51. RCL 4
52. 1
53. [+]
54. STO 4
55. RCL 3
56. RCL 4
57. [g][X≤Y]
58. [g][GTO] 23
59. RCL 7
60. 1
61. [+]
62. STO 7
63. [g][X=0]
64. [g][GTO] 66
65. [g][GTO] 75
66. RCL 0
67. 5
68. [×]
69. 1
70. 0
71. 0
72. 0
73. [+]
74. [g][GTO] 26
75. RCL 6
76. RCL [i]
77. [÷]   (The answer appears in the display when the program stops.)

Example
Calculate the modified duration of a $1,000 face value bond that offers a 6 percent annual coupon *paid semiannually* and that has a *YTM* of 10 percent, given that the bond matures four years from today. (*Note*: This

program is designed to be used for bonds with $1,000 face values that have maturities that are integer multiples of one half of one year.)

Preexecution Initialization

6
STO 0
10
STO 1
7.5
STO 3
1.011980
STO 8
1.011984
STO 9

(*Note*: Any two dates separated by exactly four years can be used.) Executing the program gives the result 3.411296838 (years).

HP-12C PROGRAM TO CALCULATE CONVEXITY FOR A SEMIANNUAL COUPON PAYING BOND (WITH ADDED INSTRUCTIONS TO CALCULATE MODIFIED CONVEXITY)

Input Data

1. Coupon interest rate.
2. Yield to maturity (*YTM*).
3. Beginning and ending dates (today's date and the bond maturity date).
4. Counter initialization.

Preexecution Initialization

1. R_0 = Coupon interest rate percent (as an integer, i.e., 6 percent is entered as 6 not .06).
2. R_1 = *YTM* (as an integer, i.e., 10 percent is entered as 10 not .10).
3. $R_3 = (2T - .5)$ (T = Number of years to maturity).
4. R_8 = beginning date (M.DY).
5. R_9 = Ending date (M.DY).

Program

1. 1	27. $.$	53. STO 5
2. $\boxed{\text{CHS}}$	28. 0	54. RCL 4
3. STO 7	29. 0	55. 1
4. 1	30. 5	56. $\boxed{+}$
5. STO 4	31. $\boxed{\times}$	57. STO 4
6. $\boxed{.}$	32. 1	58. RCL 3
7. 5	33. $\boxed{+}$	59. RCL 4
8. STO 5	34. RCL 4	60. $\boxed{g}$ $\boxed{X \leq Y}$
9. 0	35. $\boxed{Y^X}$	61. $\boxed{g}$ $\boxed{\text{GTO}}$ 23
10. STO 6	36. $\boxed{\div}$	62. RCL 7
11. $\boxed{f}$ $\boxed{\text{FIN}}$	37. RCL 2	63. 1
12. RCL 0	38. $\boxed{\div}$	64. $\boxed{+}$
13. $\boxed{\text{PMT}}$	39. RCL 5	65. STO 7
14. RCL 1	40. $\boxed{\times}$	66. $\boxed{g}$ $\boxed{X=0}$
15. $\boxed{i}$	41. RCL 5	67. $\boxed{g}$ $\boxed{\text{GTO}}$ 69
16. RCL 8	42. $\boxed{.}$	68. $\boxed{g}$ $\boxed{\text{GTO}}$ 78
17. RCL 9	43. 5	69. RCL 0
18. $\boxed{f}$ $\boxed{\text{PRICE}}$	44. $\boxed{+}$	70. 5
19. 1	45. $\boxed{\times}$	71. $\boxed{\times}$
20. 0	46. RCL 6	72. 1
21. $\boxed{\times}$	47. $\boxed{+}$	73. 0
22. STO 2	48. STO 6	74. 0
23. RCL 0	49. RCL 5	75. 0
24. 5	50. $\boxed{.}$	76. $\boxed{+}$
25. $\boxed{\times}$	51. 5	77. $\boxed{g}$ $\boxed{\text{GTO}}$ 26
26. RCL 1	52. $\boxed{+}$	78. RCL 6 (The answer is stored in R_6.)

Example

Calculate the convexity of a $1,000 face value bond that offers a 6 percent annual coupon *paid semiannually* and that has a *YTM* of 10 percent, given that the bond matures four years from today. (*Note*: This program is designed to be used for bonds with $1,000 face values that have maturities that are integer multiples of one half of one year.)

Appendix Programs for Hewlett-Packard Model 12C Handheld Calculator

Preexecution Initialization

6
STO 0
10
STO 1
7.5
STO 3
1.011980
STO 8
1.011984
STO 9

(*Note*: Any two dates separated by exactly four years can be used.)

Executing the program gives the result 15.52100283 (years) for convexity.

Modified convexity can be calculated with the following keystrokes performed immediately after the above program terminates:

1. RCL 1   5. $\div$ 9. Y^X
2. 2   6. 1   10. $\div$
3. 0   7. $+$
4. 0   8. 2

Performing these keystrokes gives the result 14.07800710 (years) for modified convexity.

HP-12C PROGRAM TO CALCULATE HORIZON YIELD FOR A SEMIANNUAL COUPON PAYING BOND WHEN TIME TO HORIZON IS LESS THAN TIME TO MATURITY AND BOND YIELD TO MATURITY HAS CHANGED

Input Data

1. Coupon interest rate.
2. Original yield to maturity (YTM_O).
3. Yield to maturity at horizon (YTM_H).
4. Beginning and ending dates (today's date and the bond maturity date).

5. Horizon date.
6. Number of years to horizon.

Preexecution Initialization

1. R_0 = Coupon interest rate percent (as an integer, i.e., 10 percent is entered as 10 not .10)
2. $R_1 = YTM_O$ (as an integer, i.e., 8 percent is entered as 8 not .08).
3. $R_2 = YTM_H$ (as an integer, i.e., 12 percent is entered as 12 not .12).
4. R_3 = Beginning date (M.DY).
5. R_4 = Horizon date (M.DY).
6. R_5 = Ending date (M.DY).
7. R_6 = Number of years to horizon [(an integer multiple of one half of one year: (.5, 1. 1.5, and so on)].

Program

1. [f] [FIN]
2. RCL 0
3. [PMT]
4. RCL 1
5. [i]
6. RCL 3
7. RCL 5
8. [f] [PRICE]
9. 1
10. 0
11. [×]
12. STO 8
13. [f] [FIN]
14. RCL 0
15. [PMT]
16. RCL 2
17. [i]
18. RCL 4
19. RCL 5
20. [f] [PRICE]
21. 1
22. 0
23. [×]
24. STO 9
25. RCL 0
26. STO 7
27. [f] [FIN]
28. RCL 8
29. [CHS]
30. [g] [CF₀]
31. RCL 7
32. 5
33. [×]
34. [g] [CFⱼ]
35. RCL 6
36. 2
37. [×]
38. 1
39. [−]
40. [g] [Nⱼ]
41. RCL 7
42. 5
43. [×]
44. RCL 9
45. [+]
46. [g] [CFⱼ]
47. [f] [IRR]
48. 2
49. [×]
50. STO .0   (Answer appears in the display and is stored in $R_{.0}$.)

Appendix Programs for Hewlett-Packard Model 12C Handheld Calculator   793

Example
Calculate the yield to a two-year horizon of a $1,000 face value bond that offers a 10 percent annual coupon *paid semiannually* and that has a YTM_O of 8 percent, given that the bond matures five years from today and that the yield to maturity in two years (YTM_H) will have risen to 12 percent. (*Note*: This program is designed to be used for bonds with $1,000 face values that have maturities that are integer multiples of one half of one year.)

Preexecution Initialization

10
STO 0
8
STO 1
12
STO 2
1.011980
STO 3
1.011982
STO 4
1.011985
STO 5
2
STO 6

(*Note*: Any two dates exactly two and five years after the first date respectively can be used.)

Executing the program gives the result for Horizon yield = 3.374744984 percent per year.

HP-12C PROGRAM TO CALCULATE EUROPEAN CALL PRICE USING THE BLACK-SCHOLES OPTION PRICING FORMULA

Input Data

1. The option's exercise price (X).
2. The risk-free rate of interest (r).

3. The variance of the underlying stock's annual return (σ^2).
4. The time remaining to option expiration (T).
5. Four constants needed to calculate $N(d_1)$ and $N(d_1 - \sigma\sqrt{T})$.

Preexecution Initialization

1. $R_0 = X$.   5. $R_4 = 0.196854$.   9. $n = 0$.
2. $R_1 = r$.   6. $R_5 = 0.115194$.   10. $PMT = 0$.
3. $R_2 = \sigma^2$.   7. $PV = 0.000344$.
4. $R_3 = T$.   8. $i = 0.019527$.

(Note: Items 1–8 above are not altered by the program *but* 9 and 10 *must* be repeated before every execution of the program.)

Program

1. STO 6
2. RCL 0
3. $\div$
4. g LN
5. RCL 1
6. RCL 2
7. 2
8. $\div$
9. +
10. RCL 3
11. $\times$
12. +
13. RCL 2
14. RCL 3
15. $\times$
16. g $\sqrt{}$
17. $\div$
18. STO FV
19. ENTER
20. CLX
21. g X≤Y
22. g GTO 28
23. 1
24. STO PMT
25. R↓
26. CHS
27. g GTO 18
28. RCL FV
29. RCL 4
30. $\times$
31. RCL FV
32. 2
33. Y^x
34. RCL 5
35. $\times$
36. +
37. RCL FV
38. 3
39. Y^x
40. RCL PV
41. $\times$
42. +
43. RCL FV
44. 4
45. Y^x
46. RCL i
47. $\times$
48. +
49. 1
50. +
51. 4
52. CHS
53. Y^x
54. 2
55. $\div$
56. RCL PMT
57. g X=0
58. g GTO 65
59. CLX
60. STO PMT

Appendix Programs for Hewlett-Packard Model 12C Handheld Calculator   **795**

61. RCL [FV]
62. [CHS]
63. STO [FV]
64. g [GTO] 70
65. [R↓]
66. 1
67. [−]
68. [CHS]
69. g [GTO] 71
70. [R↓]
71. RCL [n]
72. g [X=0]
73. g [GTO] 75

74. g [GTO] 88
75. g [e^x]
76. STO [n]
77. [R↓]
78. RCL 6
79. [×]
80. STO 6
81. RCL [FV]
82. RCL 2
83. RCL 3
84. [×]
85. g [√]
86. [−]

87. g [GTO] 18
88. [R↓]
89. RCL 0
90. [×]
91. RCL 1
92. RCL 3
93. [×]
94. [CHS]
95. g [e^x]
96. [×]
97. RCL 6
98. [−]
99. [CHS]

Example

Calculate the price of a European call option where the price of the underlying stock, $S = \$17.50$, $X = \$17.00$, $r = .08$, $T = .25$ years, and $\sigma^2 = .10$.

Preexecution Initialization

17.00
STO 0

.08
STO 1

.10
STO 2

.25
STO 3

.196854
STO 4

.115194
STO 5

.000344
STO [PV]

.019527
STO [i]

0
STO [n]
0
STO [PMT]

Finally, key in the underlying stock's price and run the program as follows:

17.50
[R/S]

When the program stops running, the answer for $C^E = \$1.55$ appears in the display.

To calculate the price of a European put option, P^E, use the put-call parity program included herein.

HP-12C PROGRAM TO CALCULATE EUROPEAN CALL OR EUROPEAN PUT PRICE USING THE PUT-CALL PARITY EQUATION

Put-call parity is a condition developed by H. Stoll (1969) that relates corresponding *European* call and put prices.[3]

For zero-leakage assets (non-dividend paying stock), put-call parity is given by (I and II below are based on this premise):

$$C^E = P^E + S - Xe^{-rT}$$

I. To Calculate C^E when P^E Is Known

Input Data

1. The price of the underlying stock (S).
2. The option's exercise price (X).
3. The risk-free rate of interest (r).
4. The time remaining to option expiration (T).

Preexecution Initialization

1. $R_1 = S$. 3. $R_3 = r$.
2. $R_2 = X$. 4. $R_4 = T$.

Appendix Programs for Hewlett-Packard Model 12C Handheld Calculator   797

Program

1. ENTER   5. CHS   9. RCL 2
2. RCL 1   6. RCL 4 10. ×
3. +   7. ×   11. −
4. RCL 3   8. g e^x

Example

Given that $S = \$35$, $X = \$40$, $r = .10$, $T = .50$ years, and that P^E is known to be \$7, determine the price of the corresponding European call option, C^E.

Preexecution Initialization

35
STO 1
40
STO 2
.10
STO 3
.50
STO 4

Key in the value for P^E and run the program as follows:

7.00
R/S

When the program stops running, the answer for $C^E = \$3.95$ appears in the display.

II. To Calculate P^E when C^E Is Known

Input Data

1. The price of the underlying stock (S).
2. The option's exercise price (X).
3. The risk-free rate of interest (r).
4. The time remaining to option expiration (T).

Preexecution Initialization

1. $R_1 = S$.   3. $R_3 = r$.
2. $R_2 = X$.   4. $R_4 = T$.

Program

1. ENTER   5. CHS   9. RCL 2
2. RCL 1   6. RCL 4   10. ×
3. −   7. ×   11. +
4. RCL 3   8. g e^x

Example

Given that $S = \$35$, $X = \$40$, $r = .10$, $T = .50$ years, and that C^E is known to be $3.95, determine the price of the corresponding European put option, P^E.

Preexecution Initialization

35
STO 1
40
STO 2
.10
STO 3
.50
STO 4

Key in the value for C^E and run the program as follows:

3.95
R/S

When the program stops running, the answer for $P^E = \$7.00$ appears in the display.

When the underlying stock pays a known dividend, D_t, t years from now ($t < T$), put-call parity is given by (III and IV below are based on this premise):

$$C^E = P^E + (S - D_t e^{-rt}) - X e^{-rT}$$

III. To Calculate C^E when P^E Is Known

Input Data

1. The price of the underlying stock (S).
2. The option's exercise price (X).
3. The risk-free rate of interest (r).
4. The time remaining to option expiration (T).
5. The time remaining to dividend payment (t).
6. The dividend amount paid at time t (D_t).

Preexecution Initialization:

1. $R_1 = S$. 3. $R_3 = r$. 5. $R_5 = t$.
2. $R_2 = X$. 4. $R_4 = T$. 6. $R_6 = D_t$.

Program

1. ENTER
2. RCL 1
3. +
4. RCL 3
5. CHS
6. RLC 5
7. ×
8. g e^x
9. RCL 6
10. ×
11. −
12. RCL 3
13. CHS
14. RCL 4
15. ×
16. g e^x
17. RCL 2
18. ×
19. −

Example

Given that $S = \$35$, $X = \$40$, $r = .10$, $T = .50$ years, and that a dividend of $D_t = \$3.50$ will be paid in $t = .25$ years, if P^E is known to be \$7, determine the price of the corresponding European call option, C^E.

Preexecution Initialization

35
STO 1
40
STO 2
.10
STO 3

800 Appendix Programs for Hewlett-Packard Model 12C Handheld Calculator

.50
STO 4
.25
STO 5
3.50
STO 6

Key in the value for P^E and run the program as follows:

7.00
R/S

When the program stops running, the answer for $C^E = \$0.54$ appears in the display.

IV. To Calculate P^E when C^E Is Known

Input Data

1. The price of the underlying stock (S).
2. The option's exercise price (X).
3. The risk-free rate of interest (r).
4. The time remaining to option expiration (T).
5. The time remaining to dividend payment (t).
6. The dividend amount paid at time t (D_t).

Preexecution Initialization

1. $R_1 = S$. 3. $R_3 = r$. 5. $R_5 = t$.
2. $R_2 = X$. 4. $R_4 = T$. 6. $R_6 = D_t$.

Program

1. ENTER
2. RCL 1
3. −
4. RCL 3
5. CHS
6. RCL 5
7. ×
8. g e^x
9. RCL 6
10. ×
11. +
12. RCL 3
13. CHS
14. RCL 4
15. ×
16. g e^x
17. RCL 2
18. ×
19. +

Example

Given that $S = \$35$, $X = \$40$, $r = .10$, $T = .50$ years, and that a dividend of $D_t = \$3.50$ will be paid in $t = .25$ years, if C^E is known to be $\$0.54$, determine the price of the corresponding European put option, P^E.

Preexecution Initialization

35
STO 1
40
STO 2
.10
STO 3
.50
STO 4
.25
STO 5
3.50
STO 6

Key in the value for C^E and run the program as follows:

0.54
R/S

When the program stops running, the answer for $P^E = \$7.00$ appears in the display.

HP-12C PROGRAM TO CALCULATE PRICE SENSITIVITY HEDGE RATIOS

The price sensitivity hedge ratio, developed by R. Kolb and R. Chiang (1981), is designed exclusively to be used with interest rate futures contracts. It determines a position in the interest rate futures contract such that wealth is insulated from unanticipated changes in interest rates.

Input Data

1. The total face value of the spot asset being hedged (FV).
2. The current spot asset discount rate (DR).

3. The duration of the spot asset (D_S).
4. The futures contract size ($1,000,000).
5. The T-bill or Eurodollar IMM Index (IMM).
6. The duration (maturity) of the futures contract (D_F).

Preexecution Initialization

1. $R_1 = FV$.   3. $R_3 = D_S$.   5. $R_5 = IMM$.
2. $R_2 = DR$.   4. $R_4 = \$1,000,000$.   6. $R_6 = D_F$.

Program

1. RCL 2
2. RCL 3
3. $\boxed{\times}$
4. 3
5. 6
6. 0
7. $\boxed{\div}$
8. 1
9. 0
10. 0
11. $\boxed{-}$
12. $\boxed{CHS}$
13. STO 7
14. RCL 1
15. 1
16. 0
17. 0
18. $\boxed{\div}$
19. $\boxed{\times}$
20. RCL 5
21. 3
22. 0
23. 0
24. $\boxed{+}$
25. 4
26. $\boxed{\div}$
27. STO 8
28. RCL 4
29. 1
30. 0
31. 0
32. $\boxed{\div}$
33. $\boxed{\times}$
34. $\boxed{\div}$
35. RCL 8
36. $\boxed{1/x}$
37. 1
38. 0
39. 0
40. $\boxed{\times}$
41. 3
42. 6
43. 5
44. RCL 6
45. $\boxed{\div}$
46. $\boxed{Y^X}$
47. $\boxed{\times}$
48. RCL 7
49. $\boxed{1/x}$
50. 1
51. 0
52. 0
53. $\boxed{\times}$
54. 3
55. 6
56. 5
57. RCL 3
58. $\boxed{\div}$
59. $\boxed{Y^X}$
60. $\boxed{\div}$
61. RCL 3
62. $\boxed{\times}$
63. RCL 6
64. $\boxed{\div}$
65. $\boxed{CHS}$
66. $\boxed{ENTER}$

Example

Suppose that it is March 1 and that a corporate treasurer seeks to issue $8 million of 270-day commercial paper on June 1. If the current 270-day commercial paper rate is 4.00 percent and the June T-bill IMM Index = 91.00, use the price sensitivity hedge ratio to determine the number of June T-bill futures contracts the treasurer should short.

Preexecution Initialization

8,000,000
STO 1
4.00
STO 2
270
STO 3
1,000,000
STO 4
91.00
STO 5
90
STO 6

Executing the program results in the value −25.06 appearing in the display. Thus, the treasurer should short 25 contracts.

HP-12C PROGRAM TO CALCULATE CONVERSION FACTORS FOR T-BONDS ELIGIBLE FOR DELIVERY AGAINST T-BOND FUTURES CONTRACTS

"The CBOT allows the delivery of T-bonds exhibiting a wide variety of coupon payments and which have at least fifteen years remaining to maturity or first call date. Thus, there are often thirty or more deliverable bonds for any given contract.

Because there are many T-bonds eligible for delivery, officials at the CBOT have designed a system to price all bonds on an equivalent coupon basis for the purpose of delivery. Specifically, the T-bond contract is built on the assumption that the underlying bond coupon is 8 percent, and a conversion factor (CF) is used to adjust the price paid by the long party to the short party upon delivery. The conversion factor is the price of a bond with a $1.00 face value, a coupon and maturity equal to that of the delivered bond, and an 8 percent yield. For the purpose of computing the conversion factor, maturity is defined as the bond's maturity on the first day of the delivery month. If the T-bond is callable, the first call date is used to define maturity."[4]

Input Data

1. The date of the first day of the delivery month (M.DY).
2. The maturity date (M.DY) of the bond to be delivered.
3. The coupon interest rate offered by the bond to be delivered. (This rate is entered as a percent, *not* its decimal equivalent. Thus, a coupon interest rate of 12.5 percent is entered as 12.5 *not* .125.)

Preexecution Initialization

1. R_1 = First day of the delivery month (M.DY).
2. R_2 = Maturity date (M.DY) of the bond to be delivered.
3. R_3 = Coupon interest rate of the bond to be delivered. (12.5 percent is entered as 12.5 *not* .125.)

Program

1. RCL 1
2. RCL 2
3. g ΔDYS
4. 3
5. 6
6. 5
7. .
8. 2
9. 5
10. ÷
11. 2
12. ×
13. g INTG
14. f FIN
15. n
16. RCL 3
17. 5
18. ×
19. PMT
20. 4
21. i
22. 1
23. 0
24. 0
25. 0
26. FV
27. RCL n
28. 2
29. ÷
30. g FRAC
31. g X=0
32. g GTO 34
33. g GTO 37
34. PV
35. PV
36. g GTO 52
37. PV
38. PV
39. RCL PMT
40. −
41. 1
42. .

Appendix Programs for Hewlett-Packard Model 12C Handheld Calculator **805**

43. 0	49. $\div$	55. 0
44. 4	50. $+$	56. 0
45. g $\sqrt{}$	51. PV	57. 0
46. $\div$	52. RCL PV	58. $\div$
47. RCL PMT	53. CHS	59. STO 4
48. 2	54. 1	

Example

Find the conversion factor for a T-bond eligible for delivery against a T-bond futures contract with a September 1987 delivery month if the bond's coupon interest rate is 10.75 percent and the bond to be delivered matures on August 15, 2005.

Preexecution Initialization

9.011987
STO 1

8.152005
STO 2

10.75
STO 3

When the program stops running, the conversion factor $(CF) = 1.2581$ appears in the display.

ACKNOWLEDGMENTS

Several of the examples and explanations related to futures and options programs used to illustrate how the programs function are taken from A. L. Tucker. *Financial Futures, Options, and Swaps,* (New York: West Publishing Co, 1991).

NOTES

1. This and all programs to follow are executed by pressing the R/S key.
2. (M.DY) represents *Month. Day Year.* For example, July 1, 1993 is entered as 7.011993.
3. Hans R. Stoll, "The Relationship between Put and Call Option. Prices," *Journal of Finance* 24, no. 5 (1969), pp. 801–24.
4. From A. L. Tucker, *Financial Futures, Options, and Swaps* (New York: West Publishing, 1991). p. 222. See Chapter 10 for complete details.

Index

AA Corporate commercial paper rate, 400
Abrahamson, Allen, 300
Accounting
　cash basis, 487
　for derivative instruments, 767–68
　external reporting for a counterparty, 473–76
　FASB *Statement No. 105*, 469, 486–87
　for a forward contract for financial security, 217–21
　for a forward contract for foreign currency: a discount, 223–24
　for a forward contract for foreign currency: a premium, 222–23
　for hedging, 491
　for interest rate swaps, 469–92
　market-to-market basis, 487–91
　market value, 548
　for OTC options, 619–40
　for premium contract, 219–20
　for principals, 477–78
　separate, 224–25
　for termination, 476–77
Accounting for Convertible Debt and Debt Issued with Stock Purchase Warrants (APB), 630
Accounting for Futures Contracts (FASB), 214
Accounting for Options (AICPA), 643–40
Accounting Implications of Indexed Debt Instruments (EITF), 629

Accounting Principles Board
　Opinion 14, 630
　Opinion 26, 477
"Addendum to Schedule to Interest Rate and Currency Exchange Agreement" (ISDA), 643
Adjusted duration ratio, 109
Administration of forward rate agreements, 235
After-hours trading, 288
Agreement value concept, 506–8
AICPA; *see* American Institute of Certified Public Accountants
Allen, L., 42 n
American Institute of Certified Public Accountants, 621, 622
　issues paper contents, 634–40
American options, 269
American Stock Exchange, 274–75
Amsterdam Stock Exchange, 280
Anderson, Torbenjuul, 300
Angell Report (BIS), 741
Anticipated transactions, 102–3
Antiselection risk, 702
A-Pack: An Analytical Package for Business, 130
APB; *see* Accounting Principles Board
Arak, Marcelle, 687 n, 688
Arbitrage approach to interest rates, 354
Arbitrage-free distribution, 410
Arbitrage-free interest rate movements, 55

808 Index

Arbitrage opportunity, 7–8, 45 n
Arkansas Best case, 327–29
Asay, Michael, 679, 688
Asian options, 575–77
Asset allocation, synthetic, 139–40
Asset allocation options, 575
Asset equivalent, 719
Asset/liability management, 96–99
Asset values
   coupon effect, 76–78
   determinants, 73–75
   impact of interest rate changes, 73–80
   interest rate sensitivity, 75
   maturity effect, 78–80
At-market swap, 379
At the money, 251
Automated pit trading, 288
Automated trading systems, 165–66
Average-rate options, 575–76
Average reference pricing, 644
Avner, Wolf, 301

Balance sheet exposures, 97–99, 102
Bank for International Settlements, 770
   Angell Report, 741
   capital adequacy guidelines, 359–60, 373–74, 513–14, 742, 746, 747
Bank loan pricing, 359–63
Bankruptcy, and swap agreements, 508–10
Banks
   borrowing from Federal Reserve, 34–35
   capital structure, 360–63
   and derivative instruments, 769–71
   interest rate risk, 569
   regulatory framework, 373–74
Bansal, V. K., 130
Barrett, W. Brian, 49, 70
Barrier cap, 603
Barrter, Brit J., 303, 319 n, 381, 382, 384, 398

Baseline equivalent, of interest rate exposures, 116–17
Base rate fix, 662–73
Base rate risk, 654
Basic interest rate swap, 471–73
Basis, 666
Basis point, dollar value of, 114–17
Basis-point value approach, 724
Basis-point value risk control, 720
Basis risk, 119–20, 138, 141, 193
   forward rate agreements, 235
Basis swap, 335
Basis trades, 133
Basle Accord, 513
Bass, Arthur, 300
Battle, Frank V., Jr., 539 n
Belgian Futures and Options Exchange, 286
Benchmark; *see* Baseline equivalent
Benchmark bond, 696
Bicksler, J., 472, 492 n, 493
Bid-ask spreads, 295
Bierman, H., 493
Bierwag, G. O., 93, 687 n, 688
Binder, B., 732, 735
Binomial option valuation models, 303
BIS; *see* Bank for International Settlements
Black, Fischer, 40, 70, 318 n, 320 n, 382, 397, 410, 411, 416, 560, 579
Black-Derman-Toy model, 303–18, 396–97
Black model, 560–65
Black-Scholes model, 55, 63–64, 302, 584
Blue DEC contract, 452
Bond Buyer Index, 669
Bond equivalent yield, 346 n
Bond market
   default risk, 363–65
   new ways of viewing, 3–4
Bond option valuation models
   alternative, 317–19
   Black-Derman-Toy model, 303–17
   first, 303
   key features, 303–4

Index **809**

Bond provision pricing model, 55
Bonds
  consols, 39
  conversion factor, 143
  coupon effect, 76–78
  definition, 23
  maturity effect, 78–80
  perpetual maturity, 39
  prices and forward rates, 26–27
  prices and interest rates, 75
Bookstaber, Richard M., 605, 716
Bootstrapping
  definition, 417
  using exponential interpolation of discount factors, 427–32
  using linear interpolation of par coupon rates, 422–27
Borrowing cost, lowering, 592–93
BPV; *see* Basis-point value approach
Break forward option, 576
Brennan, Michael J., 41 n, 55, 71, 354, 375 n, 383, 397
Brennan-Schwartz model, 382
British Bankers' Association, 228–30, 337
  Interest Rate Swaps terms, 503
  SAFEBBA Master Terms, 741–42
Broken date contract periods, 231
Brokers, 326, 759–60
Bucketing orders, 169
Bulent, N., 130
Buono, Mark, 450 n
Bush, Evan M., 539 n
Buy-write funds, 773

Caks, J., 94
Calendar assumption, 337
Calendar spread, 203–4
Call, monetization of, 599
Callable swap, 335, 572
Callable Treasury bond prices, 54
Callable Treasury securities
  dummy variable approach, 51–52
  first call approach, 51
  noncall approach, 51
  option pricing approach, 52–53

Call-adjusted estimation technique
  abstract, 46
  callable Treasuries, 51–53
  diversity in call provision, 61–65
  embedded call option valuation, 55
  interactive procedure, 54–55
  significance of call provision, 57–60
  spot curve basics, 47–50
  summary, 65–66
  uniqueness and existence of spot curve, 55–56
Call option, 125
  definition, 251, 269
  expiration, 273
  prices, 252
  Treasury bonds, 312–14
  uses, 555
Call price, 557
Call provision
  diversity, 61–65
  significance, 57–60
Call swaption, 571–72
Cancelable swap, 59
Cap addendum, 643
Capital adequacy guidelines; *see* Bank for International Settlements
Capital assets, 325
Capital gains
  interest rate swaps, 540–49
  treatment of financial futures, 237–46
  treatment of options, 321–29
  wash sale rules, 244
Capital markets, inefficiencies, 405
Capital requirements, 175
Capital structure of banks, 3606–63
Caplet
  pricing, 583–86
  use, 611
Capped call and put options, 577
Cap position, 298
Cap rate, techniques for fixing, 660–75
Caps, 125, 554–55, 675–83
  characteristics, 581–84
  definition, 298, 558

810 Index

Caps—*Cont.*
 down-and-out, 602
 example of use, 613
 examples of, 560–65
 in hedging, 680–83
 hedging with, 611–12
 legal framework, 645–46
 market for, 608–10
 in practice, 565–66
 pricing, 584–86
 put and call options, 555–60
 selling of, 567–68
 up-and-in, 602
 uses, 587–97
 with varying notional amount, 587–88
 as yield enhancement, 612–13
Captions, 571, 598–99
Caputs, 683–84
Cash basis accounting, 487
Cash flow analysis, and hedging, 193–94
Cash flow mismatching, 90–91
Cash flow projections, 418
Cash flows
 dedicated portfolio, 98–99
 swap, 439–42
Cash LIBOR curve, 452–53
Cash position, 99, 115
Cash-settled futures, 124
 function, 187–89
Cash-settled options, 125
Cash-settled swaps, 462–64
Cash settlement, 709
 of swaptions, 644–45
CBOT; *see* Chicago Board of Trade
Ceiling; *see* Caps
Ceiling-floor agreement, 564
Center lock, 595
CFTC; *see* Commodity Futures Trading Commission
Cheapest-to-deliver bond, 143–44
Chemical Bank, 722
Chen, Andrew H., 71, 472, 492 n, 493
Chevalier, L. S., 469, 475, 478, 491 n, 493 n, 494

Chew, D. H., 130
Chicago Board of Trade, 133, 134–35, 141, 142–44, 161, 166, 169, 175, 182, 269, 273–74, 281, 287, 288, 292, 408, 646, 665, 669, 677
 interest rate options contracts, 277–78
Chicago Board Options Exchange, 249, 285, 286, 577, 648
Chicago Mercantile Exchange, 133, 134–35, 139, 144–45, 161, 163, 166, 169, 172, 174, 175–76, 181, 191, 274, 281, 288, 289, 453, 553, 560–61, 565, 710
 classes of membership, 163–64
 contracts, 276–77
 Eurodollar option contract, 746
 Standard Portfolio Analysis of Risk, 173–74
Citicorp, 772
Clean risk at settlement, 483–85
Clearinghouse, 167–69, 272
 default procedures, 175–76
 interest rate options, 289–90
 performance bonds, 171
 tools of, 170–72
Clearing members, 160, 169–70
Clearing process, 167–69
Clientele hypothesis, 38–39
Closed-end mutual funds, 774
Closed form valuation, 693
CME; *see* Chicago Mercantile Exchange
Code of Standard Wording, Assumptions, and Provisions for Swaps (ISDA), 501
Coefficient of determination, 119
Collar position, 298
Collars, 264
 examples of, 560–65
 in hedging, 680–83
 legal framework, 645–46
 in practice, 565–66
 put and call options, 555–60
 selling of, 567–68
 and swaps, 596–97

Collars—*Cont.*
 uses, 593–97
 uses of, 615–16
 zero-cost, 564
Collateralized mortgage obligation, 40, 739
Collective clearing members, 169–70
Commercial paper rate, 583–84
Commercial traders, 161
Commodities regulation, 515–16
Commodity Exchange Act, 179–80, 515–16
Commodity Exchange Authority, 179
Commodity Futures Trading Commission, 159, 175, 179–81, 239, 241, 275, 643, 646–47
 on swap agreements, 515
Commodity trade options, 646–47
Comparative advantage law, 403
Composite hedge, 122
Compounding, 194
Compounding conversion formulas, 419
Compound option, 683
Computerized reconstruction of trading, 165
Computerized trading cards, 166
Computer programs, 777–805
Conservators, 510–11
Consol bond values, 385–87
Consol rate mode, 383–93
Consol rate movements
 and coupon bond values, 385–87
 and short-rate movements, 387–88
Consols, 39
Constant financing rate, 695
Constant Maturity Treasury rate, 583
Consumer price index, 30
Convergence demand, 188
Conversion factor, 143
Conversion premium, 630
Convexity problem, 86–87
 and hedging, 107–17
Conze, Antoine, 577, 579
Cooper, Ian A., 93, 346 n

Copenhagen Stock Exchange and Guarantee Fund for Danish Futures and Options, 280, 285
Core business risk, 95
Core inflation, 31
Corn Products doctrine, 327–29
Corn Products Refining Company case, 327–29
Corporate spread, and long-term swap spreads, 406
Corporations, and derivative instruments, 772–73
Corridor position, 298
Corridors, 591
Cost-based accounting, 621–22
Cost of carry, 663
Counterparties, 125
Counterparty default, 406, 764–65
 probability of, 359–65
 risk, 345
 trading risk, 480
Coupon bonds
 forward sale, 685
 series of separate loans, 6–8
 yield curve, 11–13, 19–20
 yield to maturity, 5
Coupon effect, 17–18, 76–78
Coupon stripping, 67
Coupon swap, 333
Covered call, 272
Cox, John C., 40, 44 n, 45 n, 93, 303, 319 n, 354, 375 n, 381, 383, 384, 397, 458–59, 468, 557, 560, 579, 586, 605, 735 n, 736, 776 n
Cox-Ingersoll-Ross model, 319
Credit, OTC options, 296–97
Credit equivalent amount, 513
Credit guarantees, interest rate options trading, 289–93
Credit risk, 482, 719
 equity index option, 575
 forward rate agreements, 234
 OTC market, 567
Credit risk measurement unit, 722–23
CRMU; *see* Credit risk measurement unit

Cross-hedging, 118–19
Cross-trading, 284
CRSP government bond tape, 56
Cubic spline model, 70, 467
Cumulative cap, 600–602
Cumulative total dollar system, 724
Currency cycles, 349–50
Currency options, 575–77
  accounting issues, 631–34
Currency swaps, 712
Current market value, 373
Customer protection
  financial safeguards, 169–76
  futures commission merchants, 176–78
Cylinder position, 296
Cylinders, 264

DAR; see Dollars at risk computation
DAX stock market index, 744
Day count, 343–44
Days to expiration, 561
Dealer equity options, 240
Dealer market, 287–88
Dealers, 325–25, 759–60
De Boor, C., 467, 468
Debt
  offering, 653–85
  and options, 629–30
Dedicated portfolio, 82, 98
Default, 178
  calculations, 369
  clearinghouse procedures, 175–76
  commercial considerations, 371–72
  full two-way payments, 370
  history, 372
  limited two-way payments, 370
  mechanics for handling, 367–74
  reason for exposures, 348–50
  security, 370–71
  survey, 372–73
Default risk, of swaps, 345, 347–75
Deflation, 29–30
Delayed-rate set saps, 335

Delayed-reset interest rate swaps, 379
  valuation, 381, 393–96
Delivery contract, 186–89
Delivery options, 143–44, 710
Delta-based performance bonds, 173
Delta hedging, 604
Delta-neutral hedging, 252–56, 258
Delta of an option, 695
Deltas, 252
Delta-weighted Eurodollar futures, 709
Department of Agriculture, 179
Derivative instruments, 123–28, 237, 253
  accounting treatment, 767–68
  back-office processing, 766–67
  and banks, 769–71
  convenience, 765–66
  and corporations, 772–73
  counterparty default, 764–65
  default risk, 347–75
  exchange and off-exchange, 133
  fixed-income, 750–58
  future of market, 745–46
  and insurance companies, 771
  management fears, 762–63
  market value accounting, 548
  and pension funds, 774–75
  regulatory environment, 767
  tax advantages, 768–69
Derman, Emanuel, 319 n, 382, 397, 410, 411, 416, 560
Deutsche Terminboerse, 165, 280, 286, 287, 291
Direct futures trading, 160
Disciplinary Information Access Line (DIAL), 180–81
Discount factor, bootstrapping using linear interpolation of par coupon rates, 422–27
Discount factor formula, 419–20
Discount factors, bootstrapping using exponential interpolation of, 427–32
Discount function, 47–48
  initial, 54

Discounting to present value, 644–45
Discount rate, 14–15, 34, 35
　calculation, 11
　swap rates from, 460–64
Discount yield curve, 388
Dollars at risk computation, 720–24, 730
Dollar value of a basis point, 114–17
Dow Jones Industrial Average, 188
Down-and-out caps, 602
Downside risk, 106, 125
Drexel Burnham Lambert, 372, 507, 514
Drop, 663, 666
DTB; *see* Deutsche Terminboerse
Dual trading, 284–85
Dummy variable approach, 51–52, 61–65
Duration-based system, 723–24
Duration drift, 87–88
Duration hedging, 668–69
Duration measure, 84–85
　conclusions on, 90–91
　convexity problem, 86–87
　duration drift, 87–88
　generalized approach, 91–92
　and hedging, 107–17
　shortcomings, 85–91
　stochastic process risk, 88–89
Duration ratios, 108–9
Dyer, Lawrence J., 716 n
Dynamic hedging, 255, 566, 714, 753
Dynamic replication, zero coupon bond valuation, 388–93

Eccard, Walter, 538 n
Economic Recovery Tax Act of 1981, 237–39
Economies of scale, 129–30
Edelsburg, Charles, 679, 688
Edwards, Donald G., 578 n, 579
Efficient hedge, 121–22
Elapsed period amounts, 505–6
Electronic markets, 26–88
　clearing and margin calculations, 292

Embedded call option valuation, 55
Embedded option, 298–99
　and swaptions, 572–74
Embedded option bond, 298–99
Emerging Issues Task Force *Abstract Issue*
　No. 85–9, 630
　No. 86–28, 629
　No. 87–31, 631, 641 n
Enterprise risk, 216
Equilibrium approach to interest rates, 354
Equity index options, 574–75
Equity swaps, 712
　market for, 743–45
Equivalent interest rate exposure, 695
Eurodollar, origin of, 190
Eurodollar futures, 144–45, 157–58
　expiration date, 560–65
　origin of trading, 163
　three-month, 146–47, 152–53
Eurodollar futures contracts, 211, 408, 452
　availability, 231
　creating spot curve from, 432–39
　hedging with, 258–66
　prices and rates, 458–59
　strip calculation, 433–39
Eurodollar futures market, 250–51
　and short-term swap spreads, 401–2
Eurodollar futures options, limitations, 565–66
Eurodollar market, 145
Eurodollar rates, 190
Eurodollar Time Deposit, 135
Eurodollar time deposit market, 250–51
European Community, 374, 746
　common tax policies, 281–82
European option, 269
European Options Exchange, 280, 285, 291
Evans, Ellen, 416
Ex-cash flow value, 393
Exchange environment, 159–60
Exchange instruments, 133

Exchange rate agreement, 742
Exchanges
  clearinghouse, 272
  customer protection, 165
  financial safeguards, 169–76
  futures commission merchants, 176–78
  governance, 162
  international listing, 181–84
  market participants, 289
  membership restrictions, 163–64
  modes of trading, 162–67
  multilateral and offset clearing, 167–69
  regulation of, 179–81
  seats on, 160, 163–64
  structure, 160–62
  types of market participants, 325–26
Exchange-traded options, 677–78
Exercise of an option, 272–74
Exotic options, 577
Expectations hypothesis, 37, 400
  alternate statement of, 43–44
Expiration, of call option, 273
Exponential spline 49
  methodology, 409–10
Extendable swap, 334, 572, 599
External reporting, for a counterparty, 473–76

Fabozzi, Frank J., 68, 71, 300, 301, 346 n, 451 n
Fabozzi, T. Dessa, 68, 71, 340 n
Fair pricing, 285
Fama, E. F., 42 n, 93, 388, 397
FASB; *see* Financial Accounting Standards Board
FCM; *see* Futures commission merchants
Federal Deposit Insurance Act, 509
Federal Deposit Insurance Corporation, 509–11
Federal Deposit Insurance Corporation Improvement Act of 1992, 500, 509
  netting provisions, 512

Federal National Mortgage Association case, 328–29
Federal Reserve, 134, 141, 407, 647
  and credit markets, 34
  and short-term interest rates, 34–36
Federal Reserve Board, 512
Federal Reserve Commercial Paper Index, 335
Fed funds rate, 35, 189, 583
Fences, 264
Figlewski, Stephen, 300, 301, 605
Final settlement price, Eurodollar futures contract, 211
Financial Accounting Standards Board, 469, 470, 476, 485
  Statements of Financial Accounting Standards
    No. 52, 224–25, 491
    No. 80, 216, 216, 217, 224–25, 476, 491
    No. 91, 478
    No. 105, 469, 486–87
Financial futures, 186–89
  avoiding Internal Revenue rules, 244–46
  definition, 186–88
  and Economic Recovery Tax Act, 237–39
  and Internal Revenue Code Section 1256, 239–41
  offsetting positions, 242–43
  straddle, 241–44
Financial Guaranty Insurance Corporation, 748
Financial institutions
  conservatorship and receivership, 509–11
  risk control infrastructure, 718
  scope of definition, 512
Financial Institutions Reform, Recovery, and Enforcement Act, 510, 512
Financial instruments
  futures market, 134–35
  for hedging, 86–87, 99, 123–28
  interest rate futures, 146–58
Financial Instruments Exchange, 669

Financial markets
  Federal Reserve policy, 35–36
  price fluctuations and, 31
Financial risk, 95–96
Financial safeguards, 167–76
Financial Security Assurance, 748
Financial Times, 146
Firms, gains from hedging, 129–30
Firm-specific risks, 104–6
Firm-specific spread, 674–75
First call approach, 51
First method and market quotation, 370
  ambiguity in, 41
Fisher, Irving, 41 n
Fisher, Lawrence, 85, 92, 93
Fisher's Law, 28–31
Five-year Treasury note futures, 150
Fixed coupon bond, 380
Fixed-income derivatives, 750–58
Fixed-rate payers, 334–35, 337, 406–7
Fixed-rate payment period, 337
Flexibility, forward rate agreement, 235
Floating-rate borrowing, 554–55
Floating-rate borrowing environment, 138
Floating-rate collar, 683
Floating-rate definition, 336
Floating-rate note, 380
Floating-rate payor, 335, 336
Floating-rate reset frequency, 336
Floating short rates, 377–78
Floors, 125
  characteristics, 581–84
  definition, 557
  examples of, 560–65
  hedging with, 614–15
  legal framework, 645–46
  market for, 608–10
  in practice, 565–66
  pricing, 584–86
  put and call options, 555–60
  to reduce financing cost, 614–15
  selling of, 567–68
  uses, 592–93
Floortions, 571, 598–99

Floor traders, 160–61
Flow concept of interest rate risk, 578 n
Flow mismatching, 90–91
Fong, H. Gifford, 49, 51, 70, 72, 409, 415, 416
Foreign currency contracts, 240
Foreign currency options; *see* Currency options
Foreign exchange, in swap spreads, 407
Foreign exchange controls, and swap agreements, 499
Foreign securities options, 281
Form 6781 (IRS), 245
Forward amortizing swap, pricing, 445–46
Forward cap, 683
Forward contracts, 558
  accounting for, 217–25
  compared to futures contracts, 214–15
  financial futures, 186–88
  for foreign currency, 222–24
  paying interest, 220–21
Forward exchange agreement, 742
Forward forward contract, 226, 228, 236
Forward loan, 15
Forward price, and spot price, 37
Forward rate
  and bond prices, 26–27
  calculation, 426–27
  factors determining level of, 27–28
  impact of changes in, 16–17
  nature of, 9–10
  and T-bond prices, 10–11
  yield curve on one-period, 11–13
Forward rate agreements, 124, 226–35, 740
  availability and pricing, 230–32
  credit risk, 234
  definition, 227
  flexibility and basis risk, 235
  versus futures, 234–35
  liquidity, 235
  market, 227–30

Forward rate agreements—*Cont.*
  terms and conditions, 228–30
  uses, 232–34
Forward rate curve, 12–13
  constructing, 20–23
  interpreting, 13–18
Forward rate interpolation, 430–32
Forward sale
  of coupon bonds, 685
  of Treasury securities, 662–64
Forward start swaps, 462–64
Forward strip, 123
Forward swap, 334, 670–72
  pricing, 443–44
Forward term structure estimation, 410–13
FRABBA terms, 228–30
FRACH contract, 741
FRA Clearinghouse, 741
Fractional exposure, 719
France, OTC options market, 297
Francis, Jack Clark, 24, 41 n, 42 n, 299 n, 300, 400, 416, 748 n, 775 n
F rates; *see* Forward rate
Free collar, 617
French curve, 20
Fry, John, 236
Full rate fix, 661–62
Full two-way payments, 370
Fundamental risk, 691
Futures, options on, 276
Futures commission merchants, 160, 161
  functions, 176–78
Futures contracts, 124
  administration of, 235
  asset allocation, 139–40
  compared to forward contracts, 214–15
  credit risk, 234
  definition, 186
  delta-neutral hedging, 254–56
  Eurodollar, 250–51
  Eurodollar swaps, 136–39
  expanding array of products, 145–46

Futures contracts—*Cont.*
  expiration dates, 452–53
  FASB rules, 216
  forward rate agreement as substitute for, 227
  versus forward rate agreements, 234–35
  history of, 134–35
  inventory hedging of Treasury securities, 141–42
  and liquidity, 123
  marketing of, 215–16
  pricing and evaluation, 666–68
  pricing of, 142–45
  put option on, 269
  regulated, 239–40
  scenario analysis, 198–201
  settlement, 709
  short-term, 191
  specifications, 146–58
  synthetic, 127
  tail effect, 10–11
  trading uses, 135–42
Futures curve, information in, 454–59
Futures funds, 161–62
Futures hedge ratio, 686
Futures hedge ratios, 668–69
Futures Magazine, 300
Futures market
  environment, 159–60
  financial safeguards, 169–76
  futures commission merchants, 176–78
  growth of, 133
  international listing, 181–84
  liquidity, 235
  mechanics of, 669–70
  modes of trading, 162–67
  multilateral and offset clearing, 167–69
  new financial structures, 746–48
  regulation of, 179–81
  short-term hedging, 185–210
  structure and governance, 160–62
Futures rates, information in, 454–59

Futures richness/cheapness measure, 438
Futures sales, 665–70
Futures Trading Practices Act of 1992, 647
Future value, calculation, 421

GAAP; *see* Generally accepted accounting principles
Gaming laws, 499
Gamma-neutral hedging, 256–58
Gamma sensitivity, 695
Gantner v. Commissioner, 323
Garbade, K. D., 67, 71
GARCH analytical method, 728
Garlicki, T. D., 71
Geist, Charles R., 300
Generally accepted accounting principles, 767, 770
Generally accepted risk principles, 718
General Obligation Law, Section 5-701, 496–99
Generic credit spread, 673–74
Generic swaps; *see* Plain-vanilla swaps
German government bond futures, 156–57
GIC; *see* Guaranteed income contract
GLOBEX, 166, 288
GNMA; *see* Government National Mortgage Association
GNP deflator, 30
Gooch, Anthony C., 495 n
Goodman, Laurie S., 300, 687 n, 688
Government National Mortgage Association, 278
  contract, 134–35
Grain Futures Act, 179
Grain Futures Administration, 179
Grannan, Lawrence, 416
Granularity of prices, 22
Great Depression, 29–30
Green, H. G., 728, 735
Gregory, D. W., 69, 71

Gregory-Allen, Russell B., 450 n
Griffin, Mark, 715 n
Grosshandler, Seth, 538 n
Gross margining system, 172
Guaranteed income contract, 98
Guaranteed investment contracts, 701–2
Gultekin, N. B., 92, 130

Haircuts, 173
Hansell, Saul, 578 n, 579
Heath, David, 354, 579
Hedge
  issue of option, 626–27
  setting up, 678–80
Hedge Accounting (FASB), 469
Hedge accounting, 491, 632–33
Hedge design, 658–60
Hedge horizon, 122–23
Hedge ratio, 117–18, 658, 686
Hedgers, 326
Hedging; *see also* Options; Over-the-counter options; *and* Risk management
  anticipated debt instrument, 653–85
  applicable rate calculation, 201–3
  balancing objectives, 656–58
  capping a rate, 675–84
  cash flow analysis, 193–94
  choosing the index, 193
  collars, 264
  costs of swap dealers, 407–8
  critical factors, 103
  delta-neutral, 254–56
  determining direction of, 192
  dollar value of a basis point, 114–17
  duration and convexity, 107–17
  and duration measure, 90–91
  elementary rules, 759–62
  Eurodollar futures contract, 211
  financial and cash-settled futures, 196–89
  financial instruments for, 3–4, 96–97, 125–28
  with floors, 614–15

Hedging—*Cont.*
  with forward rate agreements, 232
  gamma-neutral, 256–58
  hedge horizon, 122–23
  hedge ratios, 117–18
  interest rate risk, 95–130
  inventory hedging of Treasury securities, 141–42
  LIBOR benchmark, 189–91
  and measures of interest rate sensitivity, 82–91
  measuring cost of, 120–22
  measuring effectiveness, 118–20
  methodology, 191–201
  miscellaneous considerations, 128–30
  options, 249, 258–66
  with OTC options, 624–25
  parallel shift assumption, 208–9
  purpose of, 185–86
  with put options, 633–34
  quantifying interest rate risk, 106
  rate-fixing techniques, 660–75
  rate hedge agreements, 672–73
  risk identification, 654–60
  risk profiles, 99–101
  RMU approach, 730–332
  rolling technique, 203–10
  scenario analysis, 198–201
  stock issue commitments, 628–29
  strip versus stack hedge, 205–8
  tail effect, 210–12
  tax factors, 326–29
  timing factor, 194–98
  translating market risk to firm-specific risk, 104–6
  Treasury bill futures contract, 212
  ultra vives contracts, 372
  using caps, 611–12
  vertical spread, 264–65
  yield value of 1/32
Hedging instruments, 707–8
  interest rate futures, 709–10
  interest rate options, 710–12
  on-the-run bonds, 708
  swaps and swaptions, 712

Hedging the portfolio, 140
Hegel, G. F. W., 44 n
Hewlett-Packard Model 12C hand calculator programs, 777–805
Hicks, John R., 85, 92, 93
High-pass filter, 597
Ho, Thomas S. Y., 55, 71, 300, 303, 319 n, 354, 375 n, 382 397
Hogan, Michael, 432, 451 n, 458, 468
Ho-Lee bond pricing model, 55, 64–65
Homer, Sidney, 44 n
Honeygold, Derek, 300
Hopewell, M., 93
Hull, John, 318, 320 n, 468
Hull and White model, 318
Hunt, James, 237 n, 321 n, 540 n
Hurdle rate, 30

Ibbotson Associates, 42 n
IBM, 772
Immunization concept, 99
Immunization models, 109–14
Implied repo rate, 667
Implied volatility of an option, 251
IMSL math library, 467, 468
In-arrears swaps; *see* Delayed-reset interest rate swaps
Indemnification, 506
Index, 139
  choosing, 192
  options linked to, 298–99
Index and Option Market, 163–64
Inflation
  and asset values, 73
  contrasted with price fluctuations, 31
  of early 1970s, 134
  and Fisher's Law, 30–31
  and interest rates, 28–31
  long-run determinants of rate, 33
  rate calculation, 29–30
  short-run determinants, 32–33
  and swap spreads, 407

Index 819

Ingersoll, Jonathan E., 40, 44 n, 93,
  319 n, 354, 375 n, 381, 397, 458–
  59, 468, 560, 579
Initial margin, 291
Initial performance bond level, 171
Insolvency, and swap agreements,
  508–11
Instantaneous interest rate risk, 695
Instantaneous sensitivity, 694
Instrument-level risk measurement
  unit, 720, 729
Insurable risk, 97
Insurance, as risk management, 96, 97
Insurance companies, and derivative
  instruments, 771
Interest payments, frequency of, 344
*Interest Rate and Currency Exchange
  Agreement* (ISDA), 501, 502
*Interest Rate and Currency Exchange
  Definitions* (ISDA), 501
Interest rate caps; *see* Caps, Collars,
  and Floors
Interest rate collar; *see* Collars
Interest rate cycles, 349–50
Interest rate exposure
  baseline, 116
  fully hedged position, 192
Interest rate futures, 124, 709–10
Interest rate indexes, 583–84
Interest rate options, 40, 125–27, 710–
  12; *see also* Over-the-counter
  options
  alternative valuation models, 317–
    19
  American and European, 269
  CBOT contracts, 277–78
  characteristics, 580–604
  CME contracts, 276–77
  credit guarantees, 289–93
  definition, 268–69
  electronic markets, 286–88
  exercise of, 272–74
  first listings, 275
  margin, 272
  markets outside U. S., 278–82
  nontradable, 298–99

Interest rate options—*Cont.*
  open outcry/specialist markets,
    285–86
  prices, 269–71
  purchase of, 271
  pure open outcry markets, 282–85
  puts and calls, 268–69
  United States markets, 274–78
  valuation models, 304–10
  valuation on Treasury bonds, 310–
    17
Interest rate risk
  basics of hedging, 103–30
  definition, 96
  financial institutions, 568–70
  flow concept, 578 n
  forward rate agreements, 231
  hedging, 95–130
  quantifying, 106
  sources of, 102–3
Interest rates; *see also* Forward rate;
  Long-term interest rates; *and*
  Short-term interest rates
  on coupon bonds as separate loans,
    6–8
  distribution of, 104–5
  and Eurodollar futures, 458–59
  hedging against changes in, 80–82
  historical observations, 352–53
  impact on asset values, 73–80
  and inflation, 28–31
  and LIBOR, 190–91
  long- and short-term, 189
  long-run determinants, 33
  modeling, 354–57
  rule-of-thumb approach, 357–58
  short-run determinants, 2–33
  term structure, 399–400
Interest rate-sensitive instruments, 40
  valuation models, 304–10
Interest rate sensitivity
  of asset values, 75
  duration measure, 84–85
  measures of, 82–91
  shortcoming of duration measure,
    85–91

Interest Rate Swap Agreement
(ISDA), 502
Interest rate swap date, 336
Interest rate swaps, 124–25, 376–77,
712; *see also* Swap agreements
  accounting implications, 469–92
  assessment of default probability,
    365–67
  basic, 471–73
  and collars, 596–97
  with counterparties in regulated
    industries, 504
  dealers and users, 503–4
  default probability, 359–65
  default risk, 347–75
  definition, 333
  definitions and terms, 335–37
  delayed rate set, 335
  delayed-reset swaps, 379
  economics of, 343–45
  execution of, 340–43
  floating short rates, 377–78
  forward transaction, 670–72
  guidelines, 373–74
  in- and out- of-the-money contracts,
    348–49
  market price expectations, 358–59
  market quotation, 368–69
  mark-to-market value, 350–59
  matched, 479–85
  no-arbitrage term structure models,
    381–93
  occurrence of default, 367–74
  plain-vanilla, 378
  pricing, 439–47
  with public sector entities, 504]
  reasons for exposure, 348–50
  risk, 345
  secondary market, 516
  and swaptions, 571–74
  taxation of, 540–49
  termination, 504–5
  terms structure, 399–405
  timing of income, 478–79
  types, 334–35
  types of transactions, 540

Interest rate swaps—*Cont.*
  uses, 337–40
  valuation of delayed-reset swaps,
    381, 383–96
  valuation of plain-vanilla swaps,
    380–81
  yield curve, 452–67
  zero coupon on curve for pricing,
    417–47
Interest rate volatility, 3, 406
Interest Settlement Rate (British
  Bankers' Association), 229
Internal Revenue Code
  avoiding Section 1092, 244–46
  avoiding Section 1256, 244–46
  Revised Rule 58–234, 324
  Revised Rule 77–185, 238
  Revised Rule 78–182, 323
  Section 63, 244
  Section 1091, 243, 323
  Section 1092, 29, 237–38, 241–44,
    327, 548–49
  Section 1234, 324–25, 326, 548–49
  Section 1256, 238–41, 321–22, 329
Internal Revenue Service, 242, 324
  Notice 89–21, 541–42
International banks, forward forward
  contracts, 226
"International Convergence of Capital
  Measurement and Capital Stan-
  dards" (BIS), 373
International Currency Options Mar-
  ket Master Agreement, 503
International Futures Exchange Ltd.,
  239–40
International interest rate futures
  contract specifications, 146–58
International Monetary Market, 134,
  710
  seat owners, 163–64
  short-term contracts, 191
International Swap Dealers Association, 517, 570, 574, 606, 643, 644,
  741, 741
  Agreement of 1992, 367–68, 370–72
  definitions, 645

International Swap Dealers Association—*Cont.*
definitions and terms, 335–36
Master Agreement text, 518–32
regulatory agreements, 501–3
Schedule to the master agreement, 533–36
Interpolation methods, 467
Intex, 165
Intrinsic value, 251, 271, 619, 623–27, 703
Inventory hedging of Treasury securities, 141–42
Investments: Analysis and Management (Francis), 24, 41 n, 42 n, 400
Investors, 325

Jacob, David P., 716 n
Jamshidian, Farshid, 319, 320 n
Japanese equity warrants, 574–75
Japanese government bond futures, 153–54
Japanese yen forward rate agreements, 227
Jarrow, Robert A., 354, 557, 579
Johnson, J. T., 493
Jordan, J. V., 68, 71

Kalembka, Lech, 495 n
Kane, Alex, 687 n, 688
Kappa of an option, 695
Karasinski, Piotr, 318, 320 n
Kaufman, George G., 93, 687 n, 688
Kawaller, Ira G., 267, 451 n
Keynes, John Maynard, 43 n
Khang, Chulsoon, 94, 687 n, 688
Khouri, Walid, 416
Klaffky, T. E., 67, 68, 69, 71
Klein, Linda B., 495 n
Kleinbard, Edward D., 539 n
Kochan, J. L., 67, 71
Kolb, Robert W., 299 n, 300
Krzyzak, Krystyna, 578 n, 579
Kuprianov, Anatoli, 578 n, 579

Labuszewski, John W., 687 n, 688
Lancaster, Peter, 467, 468
Lanstein, R., 94
Latta, Cynthia M., 687 n, 688
Lattice that recombines, 384
Law of exponents, 421
Law of one price, 750
Lee, Song-bin, 55, 71, 303, 319 n, 354, 375 n, 382, 397
Legging, 204
Lehman Brothers Government Corporate Bond Index, 139
Leland, Hayne E., 679, 688
Leveraged buyouts
  interest rate risk, 569–70
  and swaptions, 572–73
Li, Anlong, 319, 320 n
Liability insurance market, 747–48
Liability swaps, 480–85
LIBOR; *see* London Interbank Offered Rate
Liebowitz, M., 94
LIFFE; *see* London International Financial Futures Exchange
Limited two-way payments, 370
Linear interpolation, 467
Liquidated damages, 506
Liquidity
  forward rate agreements, 235
  futures contracts, 123
  of futures markets, 670
  knowledge of, 761
  performance bond collateral, 172–73
Liquidity premium hypothesis, 37–38, 399
Litzenberger, Robert H., 70, 71
Livingston, M., 69, 71, 94
Local Currency-Single Jurisdiction Master Agreement (ISDA), 502
Local traders, 161, 163
London Eurodollar Market, 227
London Interbank Offered Rate, 124, 229, 231, 232, 400, 401–2, 403–4, 408, 421, 432, 452, 460, 471–74, 485, 486, 490, 554–55, 559, 560–

London Interbank Offered Rate—*Cont.*
  65, 567–68, 584, 590, 599–600, 608–13, 670–72, 680–81, 709, 712, 743–44
  Eurodollar time deposits, 250
  determinants, 211
  floating line, 136–38
  and hedging, 189–91
  interest rate swaps, 333, 335, 350
  nature of, 190–91
London Interbank Offered Rate floater, 580–83
London International Financial Futures Exchange, 182, 281, 282, 288, 291, 560
Long futures, 162
Long gilt futures, 155
Long-term credit, 39
Long-term interest rate futures, 277–78
Long-term interest rates, 189
  influences on, 36–41
Long-term municipal bond index futures, 149
Long-term swap spreads, 402–8
  maturity, 400
Looping procedure, 54–55
Loss-deferral rule, 243
Low-pass filter, 597
Luytjes, Jan E., 578 n, 579

Macaulay, Frederick R., 84, 92, 94, 107, 130
Macaulay duration, 84, 88, 107–8
MacBeth, J., 93
Macfarlane, John, 450 n
Maintenance margin, 291
Maintenance performance bonds, 171
Makin, Claire, 578 n, 579
Malkiel, B., 94
Managed pools of funds, 161–62
Mangieri, Gerard B., 539 n
Manufacturers Hanover Trust, 717
Marche à Terme International de France, 183, 281, 282, 284, 288, 289, 292, 297

Marcus, Alan J., 687 n, 688
Margin, 171–75
  clearinghouse deposit, 290–92
  on option position, 272
Margin calls, 766
Margining system, OTC options, 297
Mark, Robert, 718, 720, 725, 728, 730, 732, 735
Marked to market, options, 620–21
Market interest rate, three-month deposits, 226–27
Market makers, 294
Market quotation, basic principles, 368–69
Market quotation clause, 506–8
Market Reform Act of 1990, 648
Market segmentation hypothesis, 38–39
Market surveillance, 169–76
Market-to-market basis accounting, 487–91
Market value accounting, 548
Markowitz, H. M., 721, 735
Mark-to-market, 174
  rule, 240–41
Mark-to-market value
  historic observations, 352–53
  predicting, 350–59
Marshall, J. V., 130
Marshall, John F., 618
Master agreements, 499–500
Matched swaps
  risks, 479–85
  valuation, 488
Materiality limits, 487
Mattoo, M., 92 n
Maturity, OTC options, 295–96
Maturity date, 122
Maturity effect, 78–80
McCulloch, J. Huston, 70, 71, 467, 468
McEnally, R. W., 68, 71
Medero, J., 649 n
Medium-term notes, 774
Medium-term swap spreads, 408
  maturity, 400
Meisner, James F., 687 n, 688

Mello, Antonio S., 346 n
Mercado de Opciones Financierias Espanol, 280–81, 287
Merrill Lynch 1–3 Year Government Index, 139
MFE Group, Inc., 448–50
Miller, Merton H., 574, 579, 721–22, 736
Mixed straddle, 244–45
Mixed straddle account election, 245
Model-related risk, 692
Models, interest rate, 354–57
Modified wash-sale rule, 243–44
Money supply, and open market operations, 35
Monte Carlo simulation, 345, 694–95
Montreal Exchange, 280
  Mercantile Division, 240
Moody's Corporate Bond Index, 669
Mooney, M., 67, 71
Mortgage-backed futures, 278
Mortgage-backed securities, 40
Mortgage swaps, 770
Morton, Andrew, 354, 579
MTIF; see Marcheà Terme International de France
Muffett, Mark, 346 n
Multicontract applicable rate calculation, 202–3
Multicurrency Cross-Border Master Agreement (ISDA), 502
Multilateral offset, 167–69
Multiperiod options, 125
Muni Bond Index Futures, 278
Murphy, Patrick, 237 n, 321 n, 540 n
Mutual funds, 161–62, 773–74
Mutual margining, 766

Nadler, Daniel, 451 n
National Association of Securities Dealers Automated Quote System, 288
National Futures Association, 179–81
  Disciplinary Information Access Line, 180–81
Near contract, 710

Nelson, D., 397
Net bond market exposure, 704
Net margining system, 172
Netting
  contracts, 512
  by novation, 513
New York Statute of Frauds, 496
New York Stock Exchange, 274, 285–86, 287
New York Uniform Commercial Code, 496
  Section 2–201, 498–99
Nijenhuis, Erika W., 539 n
Nikkei index, 574–75
No-arbitrage term structure models, 381–82
Nominal interest rate
  Fischer's law, 30–31
  fluctuations, 29–30
Noncall approach, 51
Nonequity options, 240
Nonfinancial corporations, users of forward rate agreements, 27–28
Nonperiodic payments, 546–48
Nonstandard contract periods, 231
Non-zero gamma, 704
Norway, OTC options market, 297
Notional principal amount, 333, 336, 439, 442, 445, 446–47
Notional principal contracts
  definition, 541
  nonperiodic payments, 546–48
  periodic payments, 542–44
  as property, 549
  and taxes, 541–42
  termination payments, 544–45
NPC; see Notional principal contracts

Off-exchange instruments, 133
Off-market swap, 379
Offsetting positions, taxation, 242–43
Off-the-run Treasury bonds, 708
One-factor model, 318, 693
One-month LIBOR futures, 148–49
One-period credit, 9
  expectations hypothesis, prices, 27

One-period forward rates, yield curve, 11–13
One-spline, 467
On-the-run securities, 19
On-the-run Treasury bonds, 693, 708
Open contest concept, 168
Open market operations, 34, 35
Open outcry markets
 compared to automated trading, 166
 environment, 162–63
 pure, 282–85
 rules, 179
 rules of trading, 164–65
 with specialist markets, 285–86
Open repo, 665
Opportunity risk, 345
Optimal hedge, 121–22
Option hedge ratios, 314–16
Option premiums, taxes, 321–23
Option pricing, 556, 557
 approach, 52–53
 models, 560–65
Options; *see also* Interest rate options *and* Over-the-counter options
 on actuals, 280
 at-the-money, 251
 character of income taxes, 323–26
 definition, 555
 deltas, 252
 on foreign securities, 281
 gamma, 256–58
 hedging with, 258–66
 implied volatility, 251
 interest rate, 710–12
 nature and function, 251–54
 nature of, 125–27
 nontradable, 298–99
 origin and use, 249
 out-of-the money, 251
 and outrights, 752–53
 prices and sensitivities, 756–58
 spreads, 173
 tax factors, 321–29
 trading and traders, 254–58
 Treasury bond valuation, 310–17
 types of, 251
 valuation, 54

Options addendum, 643
Options commission fee, 286
Option valuation models, 52, 691–92, 693–94
 binomial bond, 303
 early, 302
Option writer, 556
Oral swap agreements, 496–99
Order book official, 285–86
Order-driven market, 287
Order flow, 285
Ordinary forward contract, 236
Organization for Cooperation and Development, 361, 373
Original exposure method, 373
Original option position, 254
Out of the money, 251
Outrights, 752–53
Out-trades, 290
Over-the-counter derivatives market, 739–42
Over-the-counter financial futures, 227
Over-the-counter options
 accounting for, 619–40
 characteristics, 580–604
 combinations of, 297–98
 and debt, 629–30
 embedded options, 298–99
 end users, 568–70
 equity swaps, 743–45
 to hedge stock issue commitments, 628–29
 for hedging, 710–12
 interest rate caps, 554–55
 market microstructure, 294–96
 option maturity, 295–96
 premium, 620–22
 prices, 295
 pricing models, 560–65
 speculation in, 622
 swaptions, 742–43
 swaptions and, 571–74
 time/intrinsic values, 623–27
 types, 553–54
 uses, 606–18

Over-the-counter options market
  American and foreign, 293
  characteristics, 566–70
  credit arrangements, 296–97
  currency options, 575–77
  equity index options, 574–75
  exotic options, 577
  illiquidity, 649
  legal framework, 642–49
  market makers, 294
  market participants, 293–94
  pension funds in, 774–75
  size of, 570
  unknown size of, 647–49

Parallel shift assumptions, 208–9
Parallel yield curve shift, 44 n
Par bond equations, 465
Parente, Gloria M., 416
Participating cap, 597
Participation rate, 559
Par value, 116
  floating-rate note, 380
Par yields, calculation, 422–23
Path-dependent options, 600–602
Payoff profile, 100–101, 125–26
Pension funds, 774–75
Performance bonds, 171–75
Pergam, Albert S., 495 n
Periodic tax payments, 542–44
Perodicity, hedge horizon, 123
Perpetual maturity bonds, 39
Personal property, in straddles, 241
Peterson, D. S., 493
Philadelphia Board of Trade, 274–75
Physical delivery, 643–44, 709
PIBOR futures, 154
Pitts, Mark, 301, 618
Plain-vanilla cap, 581–82
Plain-vanilla floor, 582–83
Plain-vanilla swaps, 378
  pricing, 442
  and swaptions, 572
  valuation, 380–81
Pollack, I. M., 71
Polynomial splines, 70

Portfolio duration, 139–40
Portfolio immunization, 99
  strategies, 109–14
Portfolio management, risk measurement units method, 717–35
Premium, of options, 620–22
Premium account, 219–20
Present value
  of a basis point, 115
  calculation, 420
Price fluctuations, 31
Price Information Project Europe, 282
Price risk, 97–99
Prices
  granularity, 22
  interest rate options, 269–71
Price sensitivity, 694
Price value, of a basis point, 115
Price-yield relationships, 75, 77–78, 79–80
Pricing
  and delivery options, 143–44
  futures contracts, 142–45
  interest rate swaps, 417–47
Principals, accounting for, 477–78
Prisman, E. Z., 69, 71
Probability density function, 104–5
Profit recognition, 627
Profit volatility reduction, 129
Public customers, 162
Pure open outcry markets, 282–85
Put-call parity, 753
Put option, 268–69
  buying, 260
  collars, 264
  purchase, 675–78
  Treasury bonds, 312–14
  uses, 555–56
Put options, 125, 251
Put price, 557
Put swaption, 571
Puttable swap, 335, 572

Q-cap; *see* Cumulative cap
Qualified financial contracts, 510–11
Quality basis risk, 138
Quotation conventions, 343

Ramaswamy, K., 397
Range forward, 264, 296, 577
  use, 616–18
Ratable daily portion of periodic payment, 543
Rate-fixing techniques, 660–75
Rate hedge agreements, 672–73
Rawls, S. Waite, 301
Real estate mortgage investment conduits, 40
Real interest rate, 28–29, 189–90
Real rate of interest
  long-run determinants, 33
  short-run determinants, 32–33
Rebundling, 68–69
Receivers, 510–11
Receiver swaption, 599
Red DEC contract, 452
Redington, F. M., 94, 99, 114, 130
Reference banks/dealers, 644
Reference market-maker, 506–7
Reference rate, 124
Regulated futures contracts, 239–40
Regulation, 179–81
Regulatory accounting principles, 770
Rendleman, Richard J., 303, 319 n, 381, 382, 384, 398
Replacement value approach, 373
Repurchase agreement, 664–65
Required return on equity, 359–60
Reset date, 556, 603, 608
Reset risk, 485
Resolution Trust Corporation, 509–10, 511
Reuters, 166
Revenue recognition, 477–78
Revenue Recognition on Options to Purchase Stock of Another Equity (EITF), 630
Reverse collar, 595
Reversible swap, 572
Revised Rule; *see* Internal Revenue Service
Rho of an option, 695
Ricardo, David, 403
Richness/cheapness measure, 438

Risk
  basis risk, 138, 141, 193
  categories of, 719
  concepts of, 690–92
  downside risk, 125
  exposures in interest rate swaps, 348–50
  long-term exposure to, 205–10
  option valuation models, 693–9-4
  quality basis risk, 138
  swaps, 345
  translated to firm-specific risks, 104–6
Risk and return, quantifying, 413–14
Risk assessment rules, 514
Risk cash flow, 194
Risk-controlled arbitrage, 770–71
Risk equivalent, 116
  system, 723–24
Risk-free rate, 377
Risk identification, 654–60
Risk management
  asset/liability management, 97–99
  basis of hedging, 103–30
  by derivative assets, 553
  fixed-income, 689–715
  hedging, 99–103
  insurance as, 97
  program objectives, 723–27
  short-term hedge, 185–210
  strategies, 719–23
  swap agreements, 495
  types, 96–97
Risk managers, 258–66
Risk measurement, 694–702
  aggregate, 758
Risk measurement units method, 717–35
  volatility and correlation, 727–29
Risk profile, 99–101, 703–4
Risk-weighting scale, 513
RMSE; *see* Root of the mean squared error
RMU; *see* Risk measurement units method
Rogalski, Richard J., 92 n, 130

Rogers, William P., 539 n
Rolfo, Jacques, 70, 71
Rolling down the curve, 699
Rolling technique, 200, 203–10, 208–10
  definition, 204
  long-term expense to risk, 205–10
  strip versus stock hedge, 205–8
Root of the mean squared error, 55, 61, 63–64
  callable bonds, 57–60
Ross, Daniel R., 450 n
Ross, Derek, 236
Ross, Stephen A., 40, 44 n, 93, 303, 319 n, 354, 375 n 381, 383, 384, 397, 458–59, 468, 560, 579
Ross, Susan, 687 n, 688
Round trip commission, 271
Rubinstein, Mark, 303, 319 n, 383, 384, 397, 557, 577, 579, 586, 605, 679, 688, 735 n, 736, 776 n
Rudd, Andrew, 557, 579
Rule-of-thumb measure of risk, 483

SAFEBBA Master Terms, 741–42
Sales revenue effects, 103
Salkauskas, Kestutis, 467, 468
Same-day funds, 174
Samuelson, Paul A., 94
Santayana, George, 44 n
Saucier, Luc, 495 n
Saunders, A., 42 n
Savings and loans, interest rate risk, 569
Scalpers, 283–84
Scenario analysis, 198–201
Scenario sensitivity, 694
Schaefer, S. M., 130
Schapiro, Mary, 647–48, 650 n
Schiller, R. J., 42 n, 721, 736
Schlude v. Commissioner, 542
Scholes, Myron, 40, 70
Schuldschein debt, 743
Schultz, Michael L., 539 n
Schwartz, Eduardo S., 41 n, 55, 71, 354, 375 n, 383, 397
Schwartz, Robert J., 301, 495 n, 539 n

Schweitzer, R., 93
Schwert, G. W., 42 n
Seats, 160
  Chicago Mercantile Exchange, 163–64
  fixed number of, 163
  membership restrictions and prices, 164
Secondary market, in swaps, 516
Second method and market quotation, 370
Securities and Exchange Act of 1934, 241
Securities and Exchange Commission, 13, 119, 122–23, 239, 276, 647–48
  on mark-to-market accounting, 767–68
  Proposed Rule 17(h)-1(t), 648–49
  on swap agreements, 514
Securities Exchange Act of 1933, 514
Securities valuation, 304–10
Segmentation theory, 399–400
Segregated funds, 174–75
Separate accounting, 224–25
Settlement amount, 369
Sharp, W., 94
Sharpe, William F., 736
Shea, Gary S., 49, 72
Short-rate movements, 383–85
  and consol rate movements, 387–88
Short rates
  floating, 377–78
  from term structure, 306–10
Short sales, 664–65
Short swap position, 407–8
Short-term credit, 39
  interest rate influences, 28–36
Short-term hedging, 185–210
Short-term interest rates, 189
  determinants, 28–36
  and Federal Reserve policy, 34–36
Short-term swap spreads, 401–2
  maturity, 400
Siegel, J. J., 42 n
Silber, William L., 300, 301, 605
Simple hedges, 122

Singapore International Exchange, 183
Singapore Monetary Exchange, 281, 282, 284
Single-contract applicable rate, 201–2
Single-factor consol rate term structure model, 383–93
Skelton, J., 93
Smith, Clifford W., Jr., 236, 301, 379, 398, 472, 494, 495 n, 539 n, 618
Smith, David R., 450 n
Smithson, Charles W., 236, 301, 379, 398, 472, 492 n, 494, 618
SOFFEX, 165
Solway, Richard, 237 n, 321 n, 540 n
Spahr, Ronald W., 578 n, 579
SPAN; *see* Standard Portfolio Analysis of Risk
Specialist Markets, 285–86
Speculation, 622, 626
Speculators, 120
Spline
  functions, 49
  methodologies, 70
  routines, 467
Split-fee option, 683
Spot curve, from Eurodollar futures, 432–39
Spot interest rate, 9
Spot price, and forward price, 37
Spot rate, calculation, 423–25
Spot rate curve
  basics, 47–50
  theoretical and actual, 66–69
  by Treasury market, 48–49
  uniqueness and existence of, 55–56
Spread, fixing, 673–75
Spread risk, 654
Spreadtions, 598–99
Stack hedge, 205–8
Standard & Poor's 500, 164, 188, 284
Standard deviation, 104
Standard Portfolio Analysis of Risk, 173–74, 292
Stapleton, Richard C., 301
Statistical mean, 104

Stecher, Esta E., 539 n
Step-up caps, 588–89
Stern, J. M., 130
Stewart, John, 478
Stignum, Marcia, 236, 346 n
Stochastic process, 40
  risk, 88–89
Stockholm Options Market, 286, 287, 289
Stock indexes, 188
Stock market crash of 1987, 757–58
Stoll, Hans R., 301, 735 n, 736, 776 n
Straddle
  definition, 241
  offsetting positions, 242–43
  regulation of, 241–4
  rules applied to, 243–44
Strategic price risks, 95–96
Strike level, 556
Strike price, 125, 251, 676
Strip hedge, 205–8
Strip hedging, 138
Stripping callable debt, 573
Strip rate, 436
Strips, 10–11, 123
  Eurodollar, 136
  forward interest rate curve, 20–23
  yields on, 68
Subrahmanyan, Marti G., 300, 301, 605
Swap agreements
  agreement value, 506–8
  authorization issues, 503–4
  bank capital adequacy guidelines, 512–14
  bankruptcy and insolvency, 508–11
  and commodities regulation, 515–16
  creation and documentation, 495–504
  definition, 495
  enforceability issues, 496–99
  indemnification, 506
  liquidated damaged, 506
  master agreements, 499–500
  measure of damages, 505–8
  securities regulation, 514

Swap agreements—*Cont.*
  standardization efforts, 501–3
  and swaption settlement, 645
  termination rights, 504–5
Swap cash flows, 439–42
Swap documentation, 337
Swap Engineer Computer Program, 448–50
Swap option, 334–35
Swap rate
  from discounting rate, 460–64
  par yields, 422–23
  reduction, 589–91
Swaps, 123
  Eurodollar, 136–39
  types of, 124–25
Swaps code, 501–3
Swaps curve, 453
  information from, 464–66
Swap spread risk and return, 409–14
Swap spreads, 400
  boundary condition, 404–6
  factors, 400
  factors affecting, 406–8
  long-term, 402–8
  medium-term, 408
  quantitative strategy, 408–14
  short-term, 401–2
Swaptions, 298, 712
  characteristics, 571–74, 599
  market for, 742–43, 772
  settlement, 643–45
  size of market, 574
Swiss Options and Financial Futures Exchange, 287
Sydney Computerized Market, 288
Sydney Futures Exchange, 281, 282, 284–85, 288
Synthesizing an option position, 566
Synthetic agreement for forward exchange, 739, 741–42
Synthetic asset allocation, 139–40
Synthetic equity trading, 574–75
Synthetic futures, 127, 627–28
Synthetic option, 679–80
Synthetic swap, 558–59

Tail effect, 210–11
Takedowns, 701
Taxation
  capital assets, 325
  of derivatives, 768–69
  derivative securities, 237
  European Community policies, 281–82
  financial futures, 237–46
  hedge design, 660
  and hedging, 129
  hedging, 326–29
  interest rate swaps, 540–49
  and market participants, 325–26
  option premiums, 321–23
  periodic payments, 542–44
  straddles, 241–44
  strips, 68
  termination payments, 544–45
Tax Reform Act of 1986, 324
Tax shelters, 238
Taylor, William B., 539 n
Technical ALCO, 732–34
TED spread, 409
Tenor, 125
Ten-year Japanese government bond futures, 153–54
Ten-year Treasury note futures, 150
Termination loss, 485
Termination payments, 544–45
Term repo, 665
Term structure, 303–4
  finding short rates from, 306–10
  of interest rate swaps, 399–415
  no-arbitrage models, 381–82
  pricing theory, 388
  single-factor consol rate model, 383–93
  theories, 399–400
Term structure estimation
  deriving discount factors, 421–39
  methods of pricing swaps, 417–47
Term structure fitting, 409–10, 415
Theta of an option, 695
Three-month deposits, market interest rate, 226–27

Three-month Eurodollar futures, 146–47, 152–53
Three-month Eurodollar time deposit, 191
Three-month PIBOR futures, 154
Three-month sterling interest rate futures, 155–56
Three-month Treasury bill contract, 191
Three-month Treasury bill futures, 147–48
Tian, Yisong, 319, 320 n
Time decay, 695
Time series data, 727
  statistical methods, 728–29
Time table, 195–97
Time value, 251, 271, 619, 623–27
Time windows, 728
Timing, 194–98
  of swap income, 478–79
Timing rule, 240
Toevs, A., 93
Tokyo International Financial Futures Exchange, 184, 289
Tokyo Stock Exchange, 184, 281
Tompkins, Robert, 560, 579
Toronto Stock Exchange, 285
Total exposure table, 196
Toy, William, 319 n, 382, 397, 410, 411, 416, 560
Trade practice rules, 180
Traders
  definition, 325
  in options, 254–58
Trading
  credit guarantees, 289–93
  cross-trading, 284
  dual trading, 284–85
  electronic markets, 286–88
  elementary rules, 759–62
  after establishing a hedge, 732
  interest rate options, 274–78
  market participants and taxation, 325–26
  open outcry/specialist markets, 285–86

Trading—*Cont.*
  options, 249
  in options, 254–58
  OTC option market structure, 294–96
  pure open outcry, 282–85
  scalpers, 283–84
  swap spreads, 408–14
  twenty-four hour, 281
Trading ahead rule, 179
Trading control, 178
Trading risk, 480–83
Trading the spread, 204
Treasury bill futures, 134–35
  three-month, 147–48
Treasury bill
  futures contract, 212
  index, 400
  CME futures contract, 144–45
Treasury bond futures, 142–43, 151–52
Treasury bonds
  call-adjusted estimation technique, 46–49
  determining F rates from prices, 10–11
  interest rate calculation, 6–8
  option hedge ratios, 314–16
  puts and calls on, 312–14
  spot curve, 48–49
  valuing options on, 310–17
Treasury Department, 19–20, 541
Treasury note futures
  five-year, 150
  ten-year, 151
Treasury securities
  forward sales, 662–64
  inventory hedging of, 141–42
  short sales, 64–65
  yield curve, 4–5
Treasury yield curve, 708
Treasury zero yield curve, 67–68
Trigger option, 602–4
Tucker, A. L., 805
Turnure, Richard, 237 n, 321 n, 540 n
Two-instrument portfolio, 729–30

Underlying assets, 123–24
United Nations Convention of Contracts for the International Sale of Goods, 537 n
United States Bankruptcy Code, 508–10
United States Supreme Court, 328
United States Treasury strip curve, 708
Unpaid amounts, 369, 505
Up-and-in caps, 602

Vasicek, Oldrich A., 49, 51, 70, 72, 94, 354, 375, 381, 382, 383, 396, 398, 409, 415, 416
Vertical spread hedge, 264–65
Volatilities, 104
Volatility curve, 303
Volatility risk, 704–5
Volume concept, 168

Wakeman, L. M., 472, 494
Wallas, G. E., 94
Wall Street Journal, 4, 19, 20, 21, 68, 69 n, 146
Warrant issues, 745
Wash-sale rules, 243–44, 323
Wasting assets, 695
Weighted average forward rate, 461
Weighted average time to maturity, 107
Weil, Roman, 85, 92, 93
Weinberger, A., 94
Weiner, Lisabeth, 346 n
Weintraub, Keith, 432, 451 n, 458, 468
Whaley, Robert E., 735 n, 736, 776 n
White, Allen, 318, 320 n
Wigner, Eugene P., 451 n
Wilford, D. Sykes, 236, 379, 398
Wishon, K., 469, 475, 478, 491 n, 493 n, 494
Wong, M. Anthony, 301
Wood, J. H., 44 n

Wood, N. L., 44 n
World Bank, 772
Write-off, 224–25
Written agreement requirements, 511

Yaari, Uzi, 450 n
Yield beta assumption, 118
Yield beta coefficient, 114
Yield curve, 4–5
  coupon bonds and one-period forward rates, 11–13
  expectations hypothesis, 37
  forecasting models, 355–57
  impact of changes in forward rates, 16–17
  interest rate swaps, 452–67
  interpreting, 13–18
  liquidity premium hypothesis, 37–38
  market segmentation/clientele hypothesis, 38–39
  newer theories, 40–41
  short-term end, 276
  in single-factor consol rate model, 383–93
  and spot rate curve, 66–69
  traditional theories, 36–39
  Treasury, 708
  for Treasury coupon bonds, 19–20
Yield curve-based models, 693, 695–96
Yield curve options, 598–99
Yield to maturity, 4–5
  annual, 24
  coupon bonds, 5
  coupon effect, 17–18
  definition, 23–24
  loss of information, 6–8
Yield value of 1/32, 117
YTM; *see* Yield to maturity

Zero-cost collars, 564
  uses, 593–97
Zero coupon bonds, 10–11

Zero coupon bonds—*Cont.*
　discount yield curve, 388
　finding short rates from term structure, 306–10
　forward rate curve, 20–23
　price calculation, 454–59
　in single-factor consol rate model, 388–93

Zero coupon bonds—*Cont.*
　valuation, 305
　volatility, 67–68
Zero coupon curve, for pricing interest rate swaps, 417–47
Zero coupon yield curve, 753–56
Zero curve, 708
Zero yield curve, 67–68